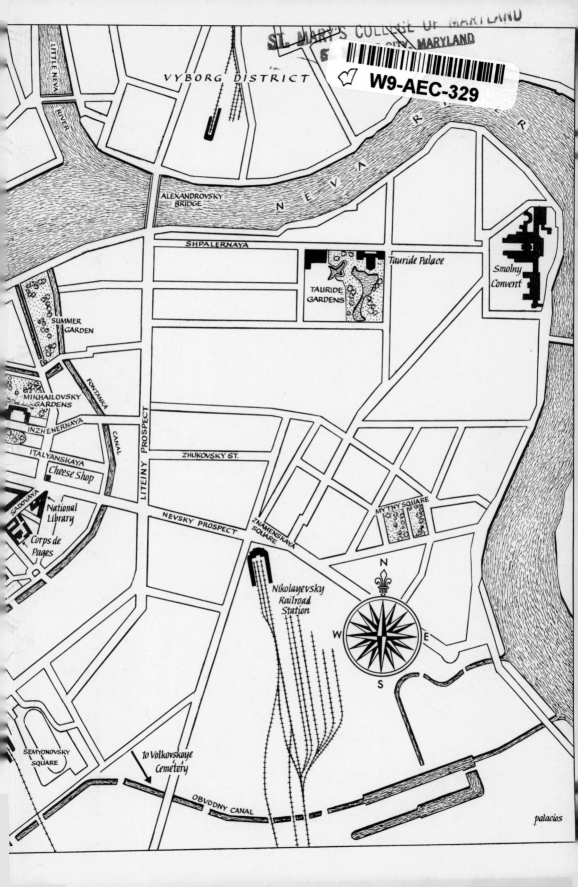

VYBORG DISTRICT

LITTLE NEVA RIVER

NEVA RIVER

ALEXANDROVSKY BRIDGE

SHPALERNAYA

TAURIDE GARDENS

Tauride Palace

Smolny Convent

SUMMER GARDEN

FONTANKA CANAL

MIKHAILOVSKY GARDENS

INZHENERNAYA

LITEINY PROSPECT

ZHUKOVSKY ST.

ITALYANSKAYA

Cheese Shop

SADOVAYA

National Library

NEVSKY PROSPECT

ZNAMENSKAYA SQUARE

MYTNY SQUARE

Corps de Pages

Nikolayevsky Railroad Station

N
W E
S

SEMYONOVSKY SQUARE

to Volkovskoye Cemetery

OBVODNY CANAL

palacios

THE
FORTRESS

BY ROBERT PAYNE

SIMON AND SCHUSTER · NEW YORK

LIBRARY OF CONGRESS CATALOG CARD NUMBER: 66-10522
DESIGNED BY EVE METZ
MANUFACTURED IN THE UNITED STATES OF AMERICA
BY H. WOLFF MFG. CO. INC., NEW YORK

For Janet and Nikita

CONTENTS

INTRODUCTION

THE RUSSIAN REVOLUTIONARIES have profoundly affected our age. For nearly a hundred years, from 1825 to 1917, they hammered at the gates of the autocracy, attempting to destroy the Tsar and all his works, employing their small weapons against the entrenched power of an absolute monarchy. Their punishment was to be thrown into the Peter and Paul Fortress in St. Petersburg, where they were tortured and sometimes beaten to death, or left to rot in the silence of their cells. It was the most dreaded of all Russian prisons.

This strange fortress, built on a small island off the northern shore of the Neva, has witnessed many of the great events of Russian history. Here the first stones of St. Petersburg were laid, here the Tsars were buried, and from here the Bolsheviks trained their guns in 1917 on the Winter Palace. All that is dreadful and sinister in Russian history seems in some way to be connected with the Fortress, but to the visitor who sees it for the first time lying low on the water, dominated by a slender golden spire and the cupola of a cathedral, it resembles a fortress in a fairytale. Serenely beautiful, it gives an impression of delicacy and impermanence. On the very tip of the spire a golden angel holds up a golden cross, and there is nothing at all menacing in those grayish-pink walls with their gunports, bastions and ravelins, which seem to have been arranged for no other purpose than to please the eye. Architecturally the Fortress is brilliantly conceived as the hub around which the whole city revolves. When the mists hover over the Neva, the Fortress is even more beautiful as it mysteriously vanishes and comes to life again.

9

St. Petersburg is now Leningrad, and no longer an imperial city. The Fortress is no longer a prison, and the last Tsar of Russia was not buried in the cathedral. It has become a museum, and children troop in to listen to the guides who dilate on the enormities committed by the Tsar, while forgetting the enormities committed by the Bolsheviks. When the guides speak about the revolutionaries who were once imprisoned there, the children sometimes give them an uncomprehending stare. The present-day rulers of Russia would prefer to forget the revolutionaries, and very little is said about them in the history books given to Soviet students.

These revolutionaries were brave and resourceful men and women who pitted themselves against a tyranny. They were idealists dedicated to the task of bringing about a state in which the welfare of all, not of the few, was the concern of the government. With one notable exception—the strange and terrifying Nechayev, whose motives are still obscure—they were determined to bring about a state where human liberties were prized, where the powers of the state police were severely limited, and where the people would rule through their elected parliament. They were not attempting to destroy an autocracy in order to replace it with another autocracy. They were young men in their teens and twenties and early thirties, with the dedication and generosity of the young. Acting in pathetically small groups, always in danger of arrest and execution, they fought a continuing battle against the Tsar, the bureaucracy, the army, the secret police, the informers and *agents provocateurs* who were always in their midst. Sometimes they seemed to be fighting blindfold with their arms tied behind their backs, for the odds were always against them.

A surprisingly large number of Russian revolutionaries came from the nobility, possessed landed estates, and regarded themselves as the inheritors of an aristocratic tradition. The Decembrist uprising which broke out on December 14, 1825, was led by aristocrats and noblemen who believed that the institution of absolute monarchy had outlived its usefulness; they had known the winds of change in their travels through Europe. They were young officers of the Guards regiments, some of them bearing resounding titles, and they brought their troops out onto the Senate Square in St. Petersburg only to see them mown down by the gunners loyal to the Tsar. This brief dramatic uprising is little known in the West, and I have accordingly described it at some length. The uprising was over in a single day, although there were a few minor clashes in the following weeks. The survivors were thrown into the Peter and Paul Fortress, and the Tsar, Nicholas I, himself examined the prisoners, assuming the roles of judge and prosecutor and chief witness for the prosecution. Those who proved to be members of a secret revolutionary organization, and many who were not, received savage punishment. Five of the ringleaders were hanged—the Tsar had originally ordered them to be drawn and quartered—while the rest were sentenced to lifelong exile in Siberia.

Although the Decembrist uprising is rarely mentioned in our history books, it was to have an incalculable influence on Russia and the world. On that day the Russian revolutionary age was ushered in.

The Decembrists were amateur revolutionaries; the professionals came later. While the Decembrists appeared openly in a public square, wearing their uniforms, acting as though they were on maneuvers and employing the conventional weapons of the time, their successors, remembering the five hanged men, accustomed themselves to wearing disguises, haunted the shadows and rarely used conventional weapons. Their weapons were terror and cunning, homemade bombs, secret printing presses. By the end of the century the revolutionaries were all "underground men" living out their conspiratorial lives. They lived in hiding, rarely knew where they would spend the next night, and spent as much energy covering their traces as in attempting to murder the Tsar and his chief ministers. They argued that terror was the only weapon left to them. Terror proved to be a two-edged weapon, almost as dangerous to the revolutionaries as to their enemies.

In the end terror proved to be their undoing. That instrument had been tempered so well, and sharpened to such a fine point, that the Bolsheviks were able to use it against the revolutionary parties which brought about the February Revolution of 1917. The techniques of terror worked out over nearly a century were used by Lenin to put an end to the Russian Revolution; and in the place of the absolute monarchy of the Tsars a new and more terrible autocracy was introduced. The dictatorship of the proletariat proved to be an absolute monarchy under another name.

In the following pages I have been chiefly concerned with the human qualities of the revolutionaries as they fought against appalling odds. They were large men and threw large shadows, and were aware of their human dignity. When the young Kaliayev saw the Grand Duke Sergey riding past in a carriage, he would have hurled the bomb if he had not observed the Grand Duchess and her two children sitting beside the Grand Duke; he put the bomb back in his pocket, and waited for a luckier day. When Nechayev was imprisoned in the Peter and Paul Fortress, shackled to the wall, all writing instruments forbidden to him, he wrote an attack on the prison warden with a nail dipped in his own blood. When Alexander Ulyanov, Lenin's brother, stood on trial for the attempted murder of the Tsar, he whispered urgently to the other defendants to throw the blame on him. Sazonov, the murderer of Plehve, killed himself in prison not because he did not want to live—he wanted very much to live—but because he hoped his suicide would attract attention to the horrors of the prison system in Siberia. Such men were the authentic heroes of a revolutionary age.

I have told the story as a continuing history, beginning with the Decembrist uprising and ending with the Bolshevik *coup d'état* in 1917. Not all the revolutionaries who achieved prominence have been included, for to do so would have involved a book four or five times as long as this, and I have preferred to keep mainly to the Russian scene, with the result that Herzen and Ogaryev who influenced the course of the Russian revolution from abroad have been introduced only in passing. I have quoted extensively from the writings of the revolutionaries, because they wrote passionately and with a fine feeling for the dramatic phrase, and because it seemed to me that their voices still deserve to be heard. They will be heard again when a new revolutionary age dawns in Russia.

So this is the story of the Russian revolutionaries over whom there fell the shadow of the Peter and Paul Fortress, who fought for a greater freedom and unwittingly opened the way for a greater tyranny.

THE
AND PAUL
FORTRESS

The seeds of madness will bring forth a harvest of slavery.

> —VLADIMIR PURISHKEVICH, on the walls of his cell in the Peter and Paul Fortress.

THE PETER AND PAUL FORTRESS

WITHIN THE WALLS of the Peter and Paul Fortress in St. Petersburg nearly all the Russian revolutionaries of the nineteenth century came to expiate their crimes. Here they were interrogated and tortured, murdered or permitted to live out their lives in solitary confinement. Some, like Dostoyevsky and Chernyshevsky, found a strange contentment in their prison cells, discovering at last the leisure which enabled them to write at their best, for paper and ink and sometimes books were given to them. Others went mad, and few ever recovered completely from the experience of being imprisoned within those ten foot thick walls.

Only the most important state prisoners were admitted into the Fortress. They were the men who assailed the autocracy where it was weakest—not only the murderers of the Tsar and of great officers of state, but

13

the men who thought dangerous thoughts and were prepared to defend their thoughts with their lives. For such men the severest punishment was necessary, and in the eyes of the Russians no punishment except execution was more to be dreaded than imprisonment in those small narrow cells lapped by the cold waters of the Neva. The Fortress was built on an island, and no one ever escaped from it. In all its long history only one man was able to subvert the guards and plan an escape which had some chance of succeeding, but the guards were arrested before the escape could take place. Well guarded and well designed, this formidable prison represented in miniature the vast, compact and terrifying powers of the autocracy.

It was not aways so. When Peter the Great first set eyes on that small low-lying island which went by the Finnish name of Enisary, meaning 'the island of hares', he decided to convert it into a fortress with no thought of transforming it into a state prison. It was intended as a bastion against the invading Swedes, with whom he was at war. The task of designing the Fortress was given to the Italian architect Domenico Trezzini, who was also invited to design the cathedral which stands in the middle of the island with its slender golden spire. The cathedral was not an afterthought. It was an essential part of the general design, for Peter had decided that he would be buried there and that all his successors would also be buried there. For two hundred years the members of the house of Romanov, the Tsars, the Tsarinas, the Grand Dukes and Grand Duchesses, were all buried in that small and ornate cathedral.

There was nothing unusual in building a church inside a fortress. What was unusual was that within two weeks of establishing himself in these marshes where St. Petersburg would later arise, Peter had already decided that this small island was the most hallowed spot in his kingdom. Some special beauty attached to it. He was building more than a cathedral: it was a sanctuary for the dead and for the living, a source of spiritual power, as the Fortress was the source of military power. Out of this white island there would come the power to dominate his kingdom.

On May 27, 1703, on the site of the future cathedral, Peter the Great laid the foundation stone of the whole city. The stone enclosed a golden reliquary containing some bones of Saint Andrew, the patron saint of Russia, and there was the inscription: "In the year of Our Lord 1703 the city of St. Petersburg was built by the Tsar and Grand Duke Peter Alexeyevich, Autocrat of All the Russias." But in fact the city rose very slowly, and the first houses on the north bank of the Neva were not built until the following year. For the moment the city of St. Petersburg consisted only of the Fortress.

While St. Petersburg was being built, Peter lived on the island, which he had dedicated to Saint Peter and Saint Paul, the foremost champions of the Christian faith. It was the hub around which the state revolved. It was his port, for his ships berthed beside the walls of the Fortress. Here he kept his treasury and the regalia. Here he held court and sat in judgment and formulated his vast plans of conquest. Here, too, were his prisons. One of the first of his prisoners was his own son, the Tsarevich Alexis.

The most clearheaded and intelligent of the Tsars was capable of ferocious acts of cruelty. He hated his son, bullied him unmercifully, and made his life so unendurable that he fled abroad and placed himself under the protection of the Holy Roman Emperor Charles VI, an act which Peter the Great regarded as treason. He summoned his son back to Russia, offering him a full pardon, promising "before the Almighty and the judgment seat of God" that no harm would come to him and that he would be received with the honors due to a Tsarevich. The solemn promise was made in order to be broken, and when the Tsarevich returned to Russia he was thrown into a dungeon of the Peter and Paul Fortress and placed on trial for his life. Because it was necessary to know the full extent of his crimes, he was tortured. Peter the Great hoped he would reveal the names of his accomplices and the exact nature of the rebellious ideas he had nurtured abroad. Under torture the Tsarevich confessed that he had hoped to dethrone his father with the aid of a popular uprising and the intervention of Charles VI, and that he planned to abandon St. Petersburg and make Moscow once more the capital. He was ailing, and scarcely knew what he was saying. On June 19, 1718, he was given twenty-five strokes of the knout, and survived. Five days later, before his wounds had healed, he was given another fifteen strokes, many of them administered by Peter the Great himself in a frenzy of murderous hatred. For two more days the Tsarevich lingered on. He died toward evening on June 26, and Peter the Great issued an imperial rescript in which he announced that after confessing his abominable crimes and seeking the pardon of all those he had harmed, the Tsarevich had succumbed to a stroke. The torture had been inflicted in the Trubetskoy Bastion, named after one of the princely families of Russia. Thereafter the most dangerous state prisoners were always held in the bastion, or in the Alexis Ravelin, named after the Tsarevich, which was built later.

Under torture the Tsarevich incriminated many members of the old nobility. His aunt, the Tsarevna Maria Alexeyevna, was thrown into the Trubetskoy Bastion. So, too, was Prince Semyon Shcherbatov, who was punished by having his nose cut off and his tongue pulled out by the roots. He survived to become a monk, but there were others who disappeared without a trace.

One might have thought the body of the Tsarevich Alexis would simply be thrown into a potter's field, so great was Peter the Great's hatred for his son, but at the last moment the Tsar seems to have had a change of heart. Alexis could not be buried within the church itself, for this honor was reserved for Peter and his imperial descendants, the Tsars of the future. Nor could he be buried outside the church, since he possessed royal blood. The solution was to bury him on the margin of the church, neither inside nor outside, and today the guards in the Peter and Paul Fortress point to his tomb under a staircase leading to the belfry. He lies far from his father, whose tomb lies at the left of the entrance to the cathedral, near the high altar.

Peter the Great supervised all the building of the Fortress, and named the eight bastions after his own favorites. One bastion was named after Vasily Zotov, who had been the tutor of the young Tsar, and later combined the offices of secretary of state and court jester. Another was named after Prince Alexander Menshikov, a swaggering bully who began life as a vendor of meat pies in the streets of Moscow and became the Tsar's confidant and the second most powerful man in Russia. It was Prince Menshikov who was charged with the task of draining the marshes so that St. Petersburg could be built, a task which he performed with a princely indifference to the number of Russians who perished during the long and bitter winters. Corrupt to the core, he ended his life in exile in Siberia. Another bastion was named after the noble family of Naryshkin, a family so proud that it refused the offer of a title however many times the offer was made. Peter the Great's mother had been a Naryshkin. Sometimes the bastions lost their original names. When it was thought necessary to obliterate the memory of Prince Menshikov, the bastion bearing his name became the Peter II Bastion, after Peter Alexeyevich, the son of the murdered Tsarevich. Peter II reigned briefly, dying of smallpox at the age of fifteen.

The Empress Anne, who succeeded Peter II, was a wily and luxury-loving woman who milked the wealth of Russia to pay for her pleasures. She had a bizarre taste in sadistic humor, and it would sometimes amuse her to send perfectly innocent people to the Peter and Paul Fortress for a few hours. From the Russian journals of Martha and Catherine Wilmot, who were visitors at her court, we learn that one day when she was in "a merry mood," she decided to send one of her ladies in waiting under guard to the Fortress. The wretched woman was taken to the secret apartment where justice was administered, given a gentle flogging, and then forced to sign a statement that she would never reveal what had happened to her on pain of death or banishment to Siberia. The next day the lady in waiting was permitted to return to the court. From time to time

Anne would ask her what had really happened when she visited the secret apartment and she would burst into gales of laughter at the sight of the woman's discomfiture. The lady in waiting was strong-willed and very wisely said nothing at all about her experiences.

In the reign of Catherine the Great there occurred the strange affair of Princess Tarakanova, who was abducted from Italy by Grigory Orlov, the lover of Catherine. The princess claimed to be the daughter of the Tsarina Elizabeth I, and Catherine regarded her as a dangerous pretender, to be silenced at all costs. She was thrown into a dungeon in the Alexis Ravelin immediately after her arrival in Russia in May 1775. An officer and two soldiers were ordered to keep watch on her all day and all night. Prince Golitsyn was placed in charge of the investigation. He reported that the princess had only one thought—to plead her cause before the Tsarina. Catherine replied in a letter to Golitsyn: "So this wanton liar dares to beg an audience with me. Let the harlot know I shall never receive her. If she continues to indulge in her lies, she will receive the strictest punishment of the law."

By being jailed in the Alexis Ravelin the princess was already receiving the strictest punishment of the law. She was abandoned to her fate. No one except her guards was allowed to approach her. Golitsyn reported that she was dying of consumption and spitting blood, but Catherine made no effort to make her life more tolerable. On December 4, 1775, the princess was found dead in her cell. She was buried in the courtyard of the Alexis Ravelin, leaving a legend and an insoluble mystery.

No one knows her real name; everything about her is enshrouded in a mist of romance. In the popular imagination she was a true princess, the rival of Catherine, who had no Russian blood in her veins and achieved supreme power by murdering her husband. It was said that the princess died during the inundation of the Fortress by the river Neva, when the waters rose in her cell. She screamed frantically for help, but no one heard her, and the rats clung to her as she drowned in her prison cell. Such was the legend, but in fact the river Neva did not rise that year.

The French Revolution brought about a fierce unrest in Russia. Catherine, who regarded herself as the personification of the Enlightenment, boldly encouraging education and a free press, suddenly discovered that the Russian intellectuals were studying the progress of the Revolution too closely for her comfort. Liberal schoolteachers and editors were arrested and flung into the Fortress. Anyone who suggested that there should be political changes in the regime found himself under suspicion. The most brilliant of her critics was Alexander Radishchev, a forty-year-old St. Petersburg custom-house official. In May 1790 he published *A Journey from Petersburg to Moscow* with the full approval of the censor. Under the guise of a travel book in imitation of Sterne's *Sentimental Journey* it contains a savage attack on the regime. There was scarcely an aspect of Russian life which was not cruelly described and violently derided. Catherine read the book, was enraged, and ordered the arrest of the author, who was evidently—for she saw revolutionaries everywhere—the leader of a vast revolutionary conspiracy aiming to topple her from her throne. Radishchev was examined and ordered to write down the names of his fellow conspirators. He was genuinely astonished, and muttered something about leading a rather friendless life, knowing scarcely anyone, and having not the least idea of what conspiracies were about. He was thrown into "the usual place" in the Peter and Paul Fortress, probably the Trubetskoy Bastion, charged with high treason and sentenced to death, but Catherine graciously commuted the sentence to ten years' exile in Siberia. Catherine herself died six years later, and he was permitted to return. He was luckier than Ivan Pososhkov, who wrote a treatise *On Poverty and Riches* during the reign of Peter the Great. He was a merchant interested in ideas, and he had the misfortune to inquire into the principles of political economy before such principles were openly discussed. He abhorred serfdom and believed all men should be equal in the eyes of the law. In his view the Tsar's image and superscription alone gave value to coins and therefore they could be minted on paper or leather. Peter the Great threw him into the Alexis Ravelin, where he died in 1726.

A hundred years later the young aristocratic revolutionaries who came to be known as the Decembrists were imprisoned in the Peter and Paul Fortress, and within the Fortress walls five of them met their deaths. Thereafter throughout the nineteenth century it became the prison of the revolutionaries, the place where they were consigned to oblivion. Chernyshevsky, Dostoyevsky, Petrashevsky, Bakunin, Nechayev, and hundreds of others were imprisoned there. Legends accumulated around the Fortress, and it was said and believed that no one ever left the cells unless he was dead, or unless he went mad and was transferred to an insane asylum.

For the Russians living in St. Petersburg the Fortress was a perpetual reminder of the power of the autocracy, all the more menacing because it was beautiful. It stood at the heart of the city, visible from all the embankments, the grayish-pink walls and the golden spire of the cathedral gleaming in the sun or dying into the mists floating over the Neva. It floated there in quiet majesty. Those who entered it saw it in its naked ugliness.

The prisoner usually came across the Troitsky Bridge, to confront the great barred gate with its flanking statues of Venus and Mars. No doubt Mars had some reason to be there, but the presence of Venus, always an ambiguous goddess, left unanswered questions. So, too, did the bas-relief which showed Simon Magus falling head foremost to the ground after being cursed by Saint Peter. A boy with an astonishingly long arm can be seen pointing in derision at the sorcerer as he tumbles out of the clouds, in danger of being impaled by the spire of the church which occupies the center of the relief, while on both sides boys and young men in the costumes of Roman legionaries gaze apprehensively at the prodigy or look languidly in the distance. Saint Paul is present, and so is Peter the Great, in the uniform of a Roman emperor. The relief was carved in 1708 by Conrad Osner, who also carved the pediment showing Christ carrying the orb of power, attended by angels. Below the relief there is a huge double-headed eagle symbolizing the power of the reigning dynasty. Surprisingly the Bolsheviks have made no effort to remove the relief or the pediment, and the double-headed eagle is still in place. Nothing has changed since the time when the prisoners of the Tsar were led through the Fortress gate.

When Saint Paul cursed Simon Magus, he said:

> Repent therefore of this thy wickedness, and pray God, if perhaps the thought of thine heart may be forgiven thee.
> For I perceive that thou art in the gall of bitterness, and in the bond of iniquity.
>
> (Acts 8, 22–23)

They were words which must have appealed strongly to Peter the Great.

Once inside this ornamental gateway the prisoner would have seen what appeared to be a small provincial town with streets and shops and guard posts. The shops served the officers and guards with cheese, milk, bread and the ordinary necessities of life. The main impression produced by the town was one of cultivated emptiness and desolation. Everything was drab, few people walked the streets, and a deep pervading silence seemed to cling to the walls.

In the center of the town there rose a remarkably elegant church, light and spacious, with a wildly decorative iconostasis of marble Corinthian columns and gold plating. The thrones of the Tsar and of the Metropolitan stood side by side. The pulpit was reached by a golden stairway. The tombs of the Tsars lay beneath slender columns adorned from top to bottom with silver funeral wreaths. The glinting of the wreaths in the northern light filled the church with a cold, barbaric magnificence.

The tombs, which were grouped in threes, were of gray frosty granite with two exceptions. These were the tombs of Alexander II, murdered by the revolutionaries in 1881, which was carved out of a block of red marble to symbolize his martyrdom, and of his wife, Maria Alexandrovna, which

for some reason was carved from a block of green porphyry. In the nineteenth century the tomb of Paul I, murdered at the instigation of his own
sons, was usually covered with flowers, with wreaths of daisies, cornflow-
ers and marigolds. He was half-mad, but the people loved him for his
eccentricities. Believing he was a saint, they worshiped at his tomb, and
prayed to be relieved of the burden of their sins and of their infirmities.
Prayers at the tomb of Paul I were thought to be especially efficacious in
cases of toothache.

Above the church rose the immense spire of gold surmounted with a
golden angel, reaching four hundred feet above the ground. It was shaped
with incredible delicacy and seemed to vanish in the heavens. Bells in the
spire chimed the liturgical response "Have mercy, O Lord" every quarter
of an hour and the canticle "How glorious is our Lord in Zion" every hour.
At midnight they chimed "God save the Tsar." Sometimes these bells and
the noon gun were the only sounds heard by the prisoners.

Beyond the church, which was known as the Cathedral of St. Peter and
St. Paul, stood the Imperial Mint with its doubly barred windows and
brown smokestacks. Here, too, in an open space, was the small building
sheltering a boat built by Peter the Great. The boat was the sacred em-
blem of the Romanov empire, and it was appropriately placed near the
church. Beyond the boat and the Mint, in the outermost corners of the
Fortress, stood the Trubetskoy Bastion, where the prisoners in their tomb-
like cells expiated their crimes, dying like sacrificial offerings within a
stone's throw of the dead emperors.

There was nothing at all menacing in the approach to the Trubetskoy
Bastion. There were clumps of trees in the broad grass-covered square between the church and the Mint, and there were more trees rising above
the walls surrounding the house of the Fortress commandant. The gate
leading to the bastion was crude and unimpressive, locked with three iron
bars, and made of wood. A visitor in 1917 speaks of the tumbledown carts,
rusty kettles and other quite prosaic objects at the foot of the wall, and
there seems to have been a deliberate attempt at all times to make this
wooden wall with the wooden gate appear as commonplace as possible,
like the garden wall of an old farmhouse. There was absolutely nothing to
suggest the terror which existed a few feet away.

Nor, having passed through the gate, would the prisoner feel that he
was entering a tomb. He would see the high red-brick walls of the bastion,
and if he tilted his head he would observe the ancient cannon thrusting
through the gun ports and an inscription proclaiming that the walls were
encased in stone during the reign of Catherine II. There had in fact been
stone walls during the reign of Peter the Great, but Catherine II built
them higher and stronger. Then he would be led through an iron gate,

which was always guarded by two gendarmes. Now at last he was entering the mysterious holy of holies.

Even here, if he was taken immediately into the little triangular garden, with its boarded walk laid along the walls of the triangle, he might be excused if he thought he had come to a small farmhouse. There were a few trees, the grass was thick, and under one of the trees stood a diminutive wooden bathhouse. The prison occupied two sides of the triangle and there were two more wings, forming a rough square. All together there were seventy cells arranged on two stories, and an uncounted number of underground cells, but even those who lived on the upper story remained in perpetual shadow, for the bastion wall was high enough to keep out the light of the sun. Here silence reigned, for the prisoners were not permitted to speak and the guards wore felt boots. Facing the cells was a vaulted corridor where the gendarmes paced silently.

While the Trubetskoy Bastion inspired terror, a still greater terror was inspired by the Alexis Ravelin, which stood at the extreme western end of the Fortress. It stood on an island, being separated from the rest of the Fortress by a moat. Once again the cells were arranged in the form of a triangle, and there was a small triangular garden with a boarded walk. Once again there was the eerie suggestion of a pastoral scene: that low-roofed triangular building might have been a cattle shed. There was only one story, and there were only nineteen cells. On the average there were no more than four or five prisoners in the Alexis Ravelin.

Those who penetrated so far expected to die in their cells. They had reached the antechamber of the tomb. The silent guards were strict and merciless. The cells were small and damp, the walls were gray, the triple-barred window looked out on a wall which was once white and a wilderness of dead trees; but the prisoner could not see the trees, for the high window was painted with lime or chalk so that even on bright sunlit days there was perpetual twilight in the cell. There was a judas in the door to permit the guards to watch the prisoner unobserved, and the outside of the door was covered with a curtain of dark green felt. As soon as a prisoner coughed or moved about the cell or knocked loudly on the wall, the guard would lift the felt curtain and peer at him from the shadowed corridor.

Everything about the cells in the Alexis Ravelin was dark, somber and menacing. The walls were curved, continuing the curve of the vaulted corridor. Over this vaulted archway hung a cloud of cobwebs; black beetles, spiders and centipedes, and strange creatures which only half appeared through the cracks, inhabited the walls. The slime of the Neva crept through the floors, and sometimes the water rats appeared from their mysterious holes in the stone floor.

The bed was bolted down to the floor; so was the table; and the oil lamp, which is a necessity of life during the long St. Petersburg winters, was half concealed in a wall niche and protected by iron bars out of reach of the prisoners. At all costs he must be protected from setting fire to himself. The iron stovepipe was either oppressively hot or completely cold.

The small triangular garden of the Alexis Ravelin was overgrown with bushes of lilac, elderberry and bird cherry, with dandelions growing in the wild grass. There were three or four birch trees with glistening, sticky leaves. A half-broken wooden bench stood among the birches. Near one of the walls there was a green mound with an age-worn cross which had fallen to one side; legend and rumor insisted that it was the grave of the unfortunate Princess Tarakanova. Only very rarely were prisoners permitted to walk in this garden set in the triangular walls with their yellowish-gray lichen.

The revolutionary Ekaterina Breshkovskaya, "the Grandmother of the Revolution," knew the Alexis Ravelin well, and she remembered that the most terrible part was the silence, the guards in their felt boots walking over felt mats. For an old person, she said, it was perhaps endurable, for such people could melt into the walls and quietly accept their fate. For the young it was a continual torture even when no torture was applied. The young drowned in the silence, and gave up hope, and paced the floor like caged beasts. "Many, many young lives have perished in this terrible place," she wrote. "They were the best souls and the best characters."

The Peter and Paul Fortress was a machine for generating madness out of silence. A strange unreality hovered over it, and stories were told which had no relation to anything that ever took place in it. We hear of prisoners confined in egg-shaped cells where it was impossible to sit or stand, their bodies so twisted that they came to resemble monsters. Stories were told of prisoners led out across the frozen river and made to dig their own graves in the ice, but such stories were invented. Perhaps it was inevitable that legends should have accumulated around the Fortress, which was so close to the people of St. Petersburg that it entered their dreams and became an intimate part of their lives; they could never remember a time when these walls did not fill them with horror. Not until the February Revolution, when the documents of the Tsarist secret police were opened up for inspection and people began to enter a little more freely into the prison, was the real horror known. The real horror lay in the essential barrenness and vulgarity of the place. Silence, after all, had always been the most formidable of the weapons in the hands of the Tsar.

In November 1917 Vladimir Mitrovanovich Purishkevich, the Monarchist member of the Duma who had taken part in the plot to kill Rasputin, was a prisoner of the Bolsheviks in one of the cells of the Alexis Ravelin.

To pass the time away he scratched a long poem on the walls of the cell, signing it ironically: "Vladimir Mitrovanovich, wretched Purishkevich, once the pride and glory of the revolution." The last line of the poem comprised his verdict on both the Russian revolutionaries and the autocracy. "The seeds of madness," he wrote, "will bring forth a harvest of slavery."

In 1922, when the harvest of slavery was being reaped, the Peter and Paul Fortress no longer served any useful purpose. It was, after all, a very small prison, never holding more than thirty or forty prisoners except after the Decembrist uprising, when perhaps two hundred were crowded within its walls. Under the Tsars it was the place of special detention for important state prisoners. The Bolsheviks needed vastly more space for their state prisoners, and accordingly they requisitioned the large building of a life insurance company in Moscow as the place of special detention. Here, in the early years, prisoners were killed in rooms where the walls were still decorated with tables of life expectancy. Meanwhile orders were given that the Peter and Paul Fortress should be transformed into a museum.

Today when the school children are taken on guided tours through the Fortress, the guides recite the names of the revolutionaries who were imprisoned there, but since most of the names are unknown to the children they are inclined to stay longer in the cell where Gorky was imprisoned briefly. A visit to the prison makes a pleasant outing. There are vendors of lemonade, and the trees provide a pleasant shade. The angel still holds the gold cross high above the slender spire of the cathedral, and although there are no longer flowers on the tomb of the mad Tsar Paul I, and no one any longer goes there to cure his toothache, there is a potted plant on the grave of Peter the Great.

The Peter and Paul Fortress has joined the ancient monuments of the past, and to those who visit it it seems as old as the prisons of the Doges in Venice. Nevertheless it has some importance in history: this is where the modern prison state began.

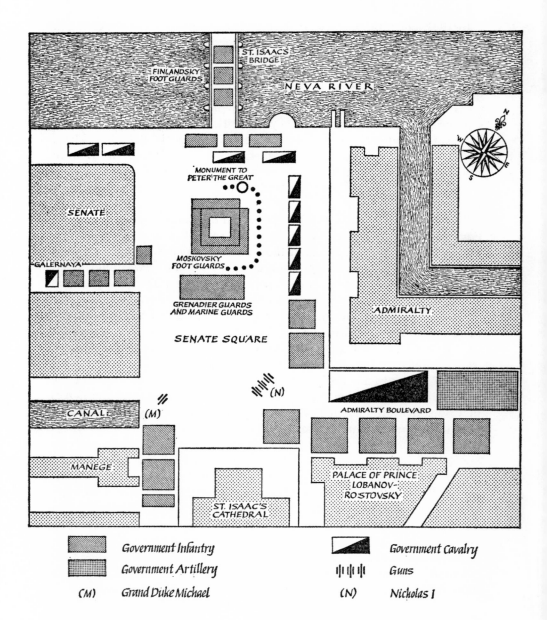

FINLANDSKY
FOOT GUARDS

ST. ISAAC'S
BRIDGE

NEVA RIVER

MONUMENT TO
PETER THE GREAT

SENATE

GALERNAYA

MOSKOVSKY
FOOT GUARDS

GRENADIER GUARDS
AND MARINE GUARDS

SENATE SQUARE

(N)

CANAL

(M)

MANEGE

ADMIRALTY

ADMIRALTY BOULEVARD

PALACE OF PRINCE
LOBANOV-
ROSTOVSKY

ST. ISAAC'S
CATHEDRAL

N
W   E
S

	Government Infantry		Government Cavalry
	Government Artillery		Guns
(M)	Grand Duke Michael	(N)	Nicholas I

THE

DECEMBRISTS

I foresee that we shall have no success, but an upheaval is necessary, for it will awaken Russia, and with our failure we shall teach others.

—KONDRATY RYLEYEV, on the night
of December 13, 1825.

THE BATTLE IN THE SQUARE

DURING THE NIGHT a light snow had fallen over the Senate Square, but when the sun came through the low clouds the snow melted; later the cobblestones gleamed with a coating of ice. As the morning advanced a chill north wind began to blow in gusts across the Neva, while the fog still clung to the islands and the river. In the distance all of St. Petersburg turned to whiteness and emptiness, but the buildings that could be seen glowed with a winter freshness. The city, which was still being built by its Italian architects, was wonderfully beautiful in winter. Yet on this particular day—December 14, 1825—the air was so raw and cold that many people preferred to stay at home. As usual, fires were burning at street corners, and the few carriages made a leaden sound as they drove through the streets. It was not a good day for starting a revolution.

The yellow-and-white Senate stood on one side of the Square facing the Admiralty, and St. Isaac's Cathedral, still unfinished, faced the Neva. The three buildings and the river boxed in the Square. Only the lower walls

25

of the Cathedral had been built, and this gave the Square a curiously impermanent lopsided appearance. The Cathedral did not dominate the scene as it does today. In those days the most impressive thing in the Square was the massive bronze statue of Peter the Great on a wildly rearing horse rising from a wave-shaped block of granite. A serpent glides along the rock beneath the horse's hind legs, but the symbolism of the serpent was perhaps less important than the fact that it helped to anchor the horse's heavy tail. Peter the Great wears the robes of a Roman emperor and a laurel crown, and with one hand he points imperiously to the west.

Dawn comes late in St. Petersburg in winter, and it was not until nine o'clock that the first ghostly rays of the sun probed through the thick mist. An hour later the sun had burned the mist away. Then gradually as the city awoke out of its stupor into the gray light of a winter morning, the shapes of people and carriages acquired outline and definition. A few people were wandering across the Square, and some carriages rolled leisurely over the cobblestones. During the following hour the north wind drove away the low-hanging clouds. It was a bright, cold, frosty morning, with the sun shining on the white city.

Although the Square was still very nearly empty, a good deal of activity was going on in the neighboring buildings, especially in the Winter Palace where rumors of an intended uprising had reached the Tsar, although as yet he had no information about where the uprising would take place. He gave orders that the Winter Palace should be placed in a state of defense and the generals were sent to the various army barracks in the city to ensure the loyalty of the soldiers. Nicholas I had only just come to the throne. He was the son of the mad Emperor Paul I, and the younger brother of Alexander I, who had died earlier in the month. He was twenty-seven, tall, slender, well-built, superbly corseted. German blood flowed in his veins, and with his finely carved features, deep-set eyes, straight nose, and strong chin he resembled both a Teutonic drill sergeant and a Greek god. Though he gave an impression of great calm, he was violently excitable and usually in pain. All his life he had been a blind partisan of autocracy.

As his generals fanned out across St. Petersburg, young army officers were already attempting to forestall them and bring the regiments out in open rebellion. The thought uppermost in their minds was to overthrow the autocracy before it was fully entrenched. The young staff captain, Alexander Bestuzhev, appeared at the barracks of the Moskovsky Regiment, made an impassioned speech to the soldiers, urged them to march on the Senate Square, and promised them that once they had seized power, there would be an end to serfdom and Russia would enter a golden age of freedom. The Moskovsky Regiment was a St. Petersburg regiment which had earned renown during the fighting around Moscow in 1812. Alexander Bestuzhev, who was the same age as the Tsar, was one of those men who inspire immediate confidence, and soon eight hundred soldiers of the regiment were vociferously applauding him and offering to follow him wherever he led them. Shaken by the experience, he marched the men out of the barracks square, shouting deliriously and holding his three-cornered hat on the point of his naked sword.

He had gone only a little way down the long Gorokhovaya when he realized that they had forgotten to bring with them the regimental colors. There was nothing to be done but to march the men back to the barracks, where officers loyal to the Tsar were waiting for them. Among them was a certain Colonel Baron Frederichs, who had only that day been appointed to command the Moskovsky Regiment. He was a man known for his stern sense of discipline, his courage, and his loyalty to the Tsar, and now it was his turn to make an impassioned speech to the soldiers, reminding them of their duty. Bestuzhev ran up to him and threatened him with the Circassian pistol he wore at his belt. The colonel had never paid any attention to threats and simply disregarded him. The young Prince Dmitry Shchepin-Rostovsky, a close friend of Bestuzhev, a timid man who had never previously showed any particular skill in fighting, suddenly advanced threateningly on the colonel and shouted to him to stop speaking to the soldiers. The colonel turned on him and snapped something to the effect that the Prince must have gone out of his mind. A moment later the colonel fell to the ground, his head split wide open by a tremendous blow from the Prince's sword. General Shenshin, the regimental commander, came running up, and he too was struck down by the Prince's sword. Colonel Khvoshchinsky jumped forward, only to meet the same fate. Frederichs and Shenshin were killed, Kvoshchinsky was lightly wounded. Later in the morning he was to make his way to the Winter Palace and inform the Tsar about the mutiny of the Moskovsky Regiment.

At about half past eleven the rebels started to march down the Gorokhovaya, drums rolling and regimental colors flying briskly in the wind. The sun was streaming down and the city was now fully awake. The people in the streets, seeing the soldiers marching with fixed bayonets and shouting themselves hoarse, applauded and joined the procession. At the end of the Gorokhovaya some twenty minutes later, the procession turned sharply left and entered the Senate Square. To the surprise of Bestuzhev, who had expected to see detachments from half the regiments in St. Petersburg taking up positions in the Senate Square, it was completely deserted except for a few passers-by. He marched his men up to the statue of Peter the Great, where they stood in formation facing the Admiralty.

Here, some fifteen minutes later, they were joined by a large contingent of Grenadiers who had marched across the frozen Neva from their barracks in the north of the city, and a much smaller contingent of Marine Guards. All together there were rather fewer than three thousand men standing in formation near the statue of Peter the Great. Although none of the soldiers had had the least intention of taking part in a revolution an hour before, they were in high spirits and eagerly awaited the order to attack. Soon the long years of autocracy would be over, and a new and more glorious Republic of Russia would come into existence.

From the moment when he saw the empty Square, Alexander Bestuzhev had the curious feeling that all the carefully laid plans of the secret society, of which he was a member, had gone awry. A hundred young officers had sworn an oath of loyalty to the society, and they were, or thought they were, in a position to bring out about half the troops in St. Petersburg. No doubt some troops would remain neutral in the conflict, while others, perhaps a quarter, would give their loyalty to the Tsar. He had only to look round the immense gleaming Square to see how small a part of it was occupied by the rebel troops. Unless more came, and came soon, the rebellion was doomed.

The rebellion, which had begun so cavalierly, had in fact been planned in great detail, with a chain of command, and political and military strategies cleverly coordinated. The rebels had their own spies in the Imperial Chancellery. They knew exactly what they intended to do. The Marine Guards and the Ismailovsky Regiment would seize the Winter Palace and arrest the Tsar and his entire family. The Finland Regiment and the Grenadiers were to seize the Peter and Paul Fortress. There would be little bloodshed, for it was assumed that Russian soldiers would refuse to shoot at one another. The ultimate fate of the Tsar and his family would be decided by the Grand Assembly, which would immediately draw up a constitution. For an interim period the country would be ruled by a dictator, who had already been chosen. Meanwhile the Senate would be ordered to approve and sign a Manifesto to the Russian Nation, promising an end to serfdom and a reduction from twenty to fifteen years of the term of military service. The dictator would rule for only a few days or weeks, and his place would be taken by the provisional government. This, in turn, would be replaced by the Grand Assembly, a representative body chosen or elected by all the people of Russia.

Something had gone wrong, and what had gone wrong most of all was that the chosen dictator, Prince Sergey Trubetskoy, a colonel of the Preobrazhensky Life Guards, had failed to appear. In the eyes of the young officers on the Square he was one of those men who inspire trust and affection, because he was naturally calm and well-mannered, behaved kindly toward his soldiers, and had an excellent reputation as a soldier.

He was tall, round-shouldered, and narrow-chested, with pleasantly ugly features. For a man who belonged to one of the most ancient families of Russia and who could claim descent from the royal house of Lithuania, he was astonishingly simple and direct. He had a winning smile, but men remembered most of all his large gray eyes, which were childishly simple, gentle and melancholy. He had the military skill to lead them to victory, and having no hankering for power he could be relied upon to lay down the burden of dictatorship at the earliest possible moment.

Prince Trubetskoy had been one of the most determined leaders of the secret society, and he had himself drawn up the Manifesto to be proclaimed by the Senate and outlined the strategy for attacking the Winter Palace. In the Manifesto he declared that all distinction between the classes was abolished, the Tsar had been dethroned, and the serfs no longer had to serve their masters. He spoke as an aristocratic liberal rather than as a convinced revolutionary, and early that morning he had panicked and decided not to lead the revolution but to make his peace with the Tsar.

With the defection of Prince Trubetskoy, the revolutionaries were left leaderless. For a while it was thought that he had fallen ill or was in some other way unavoidably detained, and they waited in the hope that he would appear, perhaps at the head of his troops. By one o'clock, when every effort to locate him had been exhausted, it was decided that a new dictator must be appointed, and the choice fell on Prince Evgeny Obolensky, a twenty-nine-year-old Guards officer who had been one of the original band of conspirators, but was notable neither for his forthrightness nor his courage. He had glassy blue eyes, a weak voice, a lisp, and he moved with an air of studied elegance. He was an unlikely candidate for the leadership of an insurrection.

Meanwhile crowds were gathered in front of St. Isaac's Cathedral, and in front of the Senate and the Admiralty. Some, foreseeing that there would be a battle, were beginning to tear down the railings round the Cathedral to be used as weapons or to shield off cavalry attacks. Old swords, knives, axes, even spades could be seen among the motley crowd of spectators, and there were some who began to arm themselves with logs and torn-up paving stones. Yet few of the spectators knew what was happening. They were in a pleasantly expectant mood, scenting danger. The rebels made no attempt to win these people over to their side. No proclamations or pamphlets were being distributed, no speeches were being made. Because the wind was rising and they had come without their greatcoats, the soldiers shivered and rubbed their hands and stamped their feet. A canteen appeared, and hot mead was distributed among them. Some of the spectators still thought it was a regimental parade.

From the nearby Winter Palace the Tsar gazed out of the windows at the crowds forming in the palace square, and from time to time he would saunter out to talk to the people. Drunken peasants embraced him and called him "Little Father," while he smiled and explained that nothing of importance was happening, that General Miloradovich, Governor General of St. Petersburg had personally assured him that there was no cause for alarm, and that everything would be put right. Since General Miloradovich was immensely popular among the people and an efficient administrator, the Tsar was prepared to let him deal with the situation. Unhappily the general had vanished, and like Prince Trubetskoy could not be found.

The general had in fact been spending the morning with the ballerina Katya Teleshova. He had known about the intended uprising, but it was not a matter to which he had given any concentrated thought, and he had forgotten all about it when, while he was lunching with the ballerina, a police officer drove up to say that he was wanted urgently by the Tsar. He drove at full speed to the Winter Palace, to find the Tsar talking to the crowd in the palace square. There was time for only a few words, and then Miloradovich was driving off in the sleigh toward the nearby barracks of the Horse Guards. He had to make a detour, for the crowds were thick, and so more time was lost. When at last he reached the barracks, he found the Horse Guards buckling on their breastplates and grooming their horses; they were in no hurry to follow the Governor General against the rebels. Alexey Orlov, who commanded the Horse Guards, seemed to be half in sympathy with the rebels, for he made no effort to order his troops out of their barracks. With a terrible oath, Miloradovich leaped onto a horse belonging to one of Orlov's officers and then, followed by his adjutant on foot, he rode toward Senate Square, intending to quell the rebellion singlehanded.

General Miloradovich was one of those bluff, heavy-set, choleric men who are always dangerous in battle, because they are capable of the utmost foolhardiness. Such men win victories, and during the Napoleonic Wars he had distinguished himself by incredible acts of bravery. He had his vanities—he never appeared in public without the broad blue ribbon of St. Andrew across his breast. He had good lungs and a fine presence, and he told himself that he had only to talk to the rebels and they would follow him wherever he wanted them to go.

In this he was mistaken, for the rebels knew him well and had no desire to listen to him. By riding up to them, he placed himself at their mercy.

At first they pretended to ignore him, for they were standing at ease and talking among themselves, and when he ordered them to come to attention, they simply looked the other way. But they listened more eagerly when he drew his sword from its scabbard, reminding them that the sword was a gift of the Tsarevich Constantine Pavlovich, and then spoke of the battles they had fought together against Napoleon. Surely they trusted him! Had they not been comrades in arms together? They had made their protest, and now it was time for them to go quietly back to their barracks. He was still talking when Prince Obolensky hurried up, seized the horse's bridle, and said: "Please ride away, Your Excellency, and leave the soldiers alone. It will be dangerous if you don't!" The general glared at him, and then resumed his speech. The Prince took a musket from one of the soldiers and pricked the croup of the general's horse with a bayonet, which slipped and cut into the general's side. There was a moment of confusion, as the horse shied, and then the general picked up the reins and began to edge the horse away. He seemed to realize that nothing further was to be gained by addressing the soldiers, and he was about to return to the Winter Palace when a tall, lean man with a protruding underlip, cavernous eyes and wispy mustache, wearing a coarse sheepskin coat tied with a scarlet sash round the waist, shot at him from point-blank range. As he fell from the horse, he was impaled on the bayonet of one of the soldiers standing near. The man who had fought through so many Napoleonic battles unscathed was to die of a Russian bullet in the chest and a Russian bayonet in the back.

As he lay in the snow it was obvious that his wounds were mortal. He was lifted into a passing sleigh and driven to the Horse Guards barracks, where he died later in the day.

Pyotr Kakhovsky, the man who shot at him, was one of those improbable figures who nearly always emerge in revolutionary times to act the role of the executioner. The son of a Smolensk landowner, he had lost his entire fortune at cards, served in the army, fought in many wars, taken part in at least five duels, and demonstrated a talent for memorizing thousands of lines of poetry. He knew and admired Pushkin, whose poems he recited to anyone who cared to listen. He had traveled across Russia, observing the lives of the oppressed peasants, and he had traveled across Europe for the same purpose. Returning to St. Petersburg in 1825, he had thought of joining the Greeks in their war of independence against Turkey, until a chance meeting with some Guards officers led him to join the conspiracy. On the night before the uprising he had promised to storm the Tsar's private apartments and assassinate him. He had failed in this, as he failed in many other things, but he was still determined to act the role of the executioner. He killed General Miloradovich in cold blood, calmly, methodically, without rancor.

More emissaries arrived from the Tsar, who still hoped against hope that the rebels could be talked into surrender. A certain Captain Sturler was sent to parley with them. He was told that he would only place himself in danger if he spoke to the soldiers, but he was a brave man and disregarded their advice. Kakhovsky whipped out his pistol and shot him dead before he was able to say more than a few words.

The third emissary was not a man who could be shot out of hand, if only because the soldiers would not have permitted it. He was no less a person than Serafim, the Metropolitan of St. Petersburg, who drove up in a sleigh accompanied by two deacons. The Metropolitan had just put on his sacerdotal robes in preparation for offering a *Te Deum* in the palace church to celebrate the Tsar's ascension to the throne, when an officer burst into the vestry and begged him to go out into the Square and plead with the rebels. He was wearing his purple vestments and a diamond-studded crown, the deacons wore their brocaded surplices. Near the square of soldiers the Metropolitan alighted, placed a jeweled cross on his crown, and then walked slowly up to the Marine Guards, who formed a detachment of their own a little to the south of the rest. In the name of the Church, of which he was the ruling primate, he begged them to take the oath to the new Tsar and to return to their barracks. He spoke well, and some of the soldiers were wavering. Kakhovsky was hovering near, and for a moment he entertained the thought that he might have to add the Metropolitan to his roster of victims. Some of the soldiers shouted: "Traitor!" Others came forward and kissed the Metropolitan's cross. There were cries and countercries until Lieutenant Wilhelm Kuchelbecker, a tall, thin, gangling man with round spectacles and an expression of intelligent bewilderment over the sins of the world, marched up to him and said quietly: "You must go now, Father. This is no place for you." Kuchelbecker was a Protestant, and could therefore speak as a neutral in the strange war which was being fought by the soldiers and the Primate of All the Russias.

By this time it was nearly two o'clock in the afternoon, and soon the sun would set. What the Tsar feared most of all was that the rebels would remain on the Senate Square after nightfall, to be joined in the darkness by the other regiments which were still undecided whether to remain loyal. It occurred to the Tsar to send his brother, the Grand Duke Mikhail Pavlovich, to attempt to bring them to their senses. Unlike Nicholas I, who looked like an actor in a romantic tragedy with his marble pallor and wide dreaming brow, the Grand Duke Mikhail was a rugged, weather-beaten man who resembled a hard-drinking soldier. He was Colonel in Chief of the Moskovsky Regiment and popular with his troops. His coming might be dangerous. Completely fearless, he rode across the square, and when he began to address them in his homely way, the words seemed to take effect. Suddenly the voice was drowned by a roll of drums. Someone whispered to the shortsighted Kuchelbecker: "What about knocking Mikhail off his horse?" Kuchelbecker replied: "I'd like to, but where is he?" and when at last he saw the Grand Duke, he aimed with his pistol and pulled the trigger. A Marine Guard standing near touched his elbow, and the shot went wide. Since he felt that he had inherited the role of executioner, he then aimed at General Voinov, who had accompanied the Grand Duke across the Square, but the pistol misfired. Earlier in the day Kuchelbecker had been thrown from his sleigh and the pistol had fallen in the snow. In this way the most studious and intelligent of the rebels was saved from becoming a murderer.

The Grand Duke and General Voinov rode back to Admiralty Boulevard, realizing at last that nothing was to be gained by parleying with the troops on the Square. At about the same time the Horse Guards, who had finally decided to remain loyal to the Tsar, rode from their barracks past St. Isaac's Cathedral and took up positions near the palace of Prince Lobanov-Rostovsky, opposite the Admiralty. Like the Cathedral the palace was only half built, thus adding to the air of desolation and improvisation which marked the southern end of the Square. Alexey Orlov, in command of the Horse Guards, ordered the first two columns of cavalry across the Square, hoping the rebels would flee in panic. The hope was not to be fulfilled, for the attack failed. There were shouts, glinting sabers, the shock and fury of a cavalry charge, but the horses slithered on the icy cobblestones and fled before the concentrated fire of muskets. The rebels were holding their ground, and like the spectators, who were now filling all the corners of the Square, they burst out laughing and shouting in mock applause. The long shadows were falling across the Square; soon it would be dark. The rebels were praying that darkness would come quickly, for they had received news that the Semyonovsky Regiment would join them after nightfall, that the Ismailovsky Regiment had refused to leave its barracks, and that there were still other regiments which might come over to them. The Finland Regiment, called out from their barracks north of the river, had marched across St. Isaac's bridge and then abruptly stopped, refusing to take any part in the battle.

In despair the Tsar sent one last emissary to parley with the rebels. He had ordered up four guns of the Foot Artillery Brigade, and he was prepared to blast the rebels off the Square by gunfire if everything else failed. His choice for emissary fell on General Sukhozanet, the commander of the Guards Artillery, a stern martinet uniformly unpopular with the soldiers, so that his arrival was greeted with derisive cheers and catcalls. He rode straight up to the Moskovsky Regiment and began to harangue them sternly, saying that he had not come to parley with them, but to offer them their lives if they surrendered. He spoke of the Tsar's infinite mercy and understanding, and for a while the troops listened eagerly, bemused by the presence of an officer so reckless that he was prepared to follow men who had been killed for haranguing them with less fervor. When some soldiers raised their muskets, the officers cried: "Let the swine alone, he isn't worth a bullet!" With that General Sukhozanet decided not to claim the crown of martyrdom and galloped back in the direction of the Cathedral, bending low over the horse's neck. Someone fired a joy-shot at the white plumes of his hat, and a few feathers went flying in the wind. There were more derisive cheers when the general reached up and broke off the tattered plumes to preserve them from further damage.

It was now dusk, and some bivouac fires were burning. For some time the Tsar with a suite of generals and aides-de-camp had been present in the Square or in the Admiralty Boulevard. He rode a white horse, and wore the uniform of the Preobrazhensky Regiment with the blue ribbon of St. Andrew across his chest, and there was something about his appearance which made him instantly recognizable. He knew he was not popular, and perhaps would never be popular, but he rode fearlessly through the crowds of spectators and sometimes he would sally out into the square to take a closer look at the rebels. He was still a prey to indecision, for although he had ordered up the artillery, he still hoped for a miracle.

The rebels, too, hoped for a miracle. The officers discussed endlessly among themselves what should be done, and came to no conclusions. Someone suggested that they should seize the guns and turn them against the forces loyal to the Tsar, but it was generally agreed that it was better to wait until nightfall; during the night more than half the troops of St. Petersburg would come over to them; it was enough to wait and snatch victory from the darkness.

As it grew darker more and more people entered the Square. People were hanging on trees, on lantern posts, on gutterings; they crowded the portico of the Senate and the galleries of the Admiralty tower; soon it became evident that if there was any fighting, the civilians were in as much danger as the soldiers. More and more loyal troops were converging on the Square. The entire length of the Admiralty was lined with loyal cavalry and infantry. To the north they blocked off the passage to St. Isaac's Bridge, and there were still more beside the Horse Guard's riding school. Altogether the Tsar had assembled on the Square or in the streets leading to it a force of twelve thousand men. Prince Trubetskoy had said he could capture St. Petersburg with six thousand, but the rebels still had no more than three thousand. Heavily outnumbered, still hoping that the loyal troops would come over on their side, they had waited patiently while the Tsar gradually formed a ring round them, spellbound by their own immobility.

As the Tsar began to realize that the time was soon coming when he would have to make a final decision—a decision which he had postponed less out of weakness than out of a genuine desire for peace—he began to ask his generals if there was any way left which would permit him to disperse the rebels without bloodshed. "Your Majesty," said General Vasilchikov, "you cannot lose a minute; there is nothing else you can do; only canister shot will save the situation." "So you wish me to celebrate the first day of my reign by shedding blood—the blood of my subjects?" the Tsar said. "Sire," replied the general, "it is the only way to save the Empire!" Vasilchikov was no Sukhozanet. He was a calm, high-minded man who had hoped all through the afternoon that the rebels would return quietly to their barracks. The Tsar turned away, remarking bitterly: "What a wonderful way to start my reign!"

Orders were given to man the guns which had stood so uselessly and pathetically on the Square for more than half an hour. For most of that time they presented no threat to the rebels, for the caissons contained only blank ammunition, and it was with some difficulty that the live shot was found. At first the officer in charge of the ammunition depot refused to deliver the shot without a written order, and when at last the written order came, he permitted only one round of shot for each gun to leave the depot. Later a new order was handed to him, and he was compelled to load the sleighs with massive amounts of ammunition, which moved slowly through the darkening streets in the direction of the Square.

At about a quarter past four the Tsar gave the first of several orders to the gun crews. There were three batteries under the Tsar's command just outside Admiralty Boulevard, and another battery on the opposite side of the Square under the command of Grand Duke Mikhail. Suddenly the Tsar said: "On the right flank fire in consecutive order, commencing with number one gun." The order was carried down the chain of command until at last it reached a certain Captain Bakunin, a junior gunnery officer. Immediately there came a countermanding order: "Hold the fire!" Some minutes passed, while the Tsar discussed the state of affairs with his generals and aides-de-camp and sent messengers over to the Grand Duke, and then the order was repeated, only to be countermanded again before it reached the gun crew. Some minutes passed, again there came the order, and again there came the countermanding order. And then at last, as though weary of this display of power and weakness, the Tsar permitted the order to reach the gun crews, and this time there was no countermanding order. "Fire!" shouted Captain Bakunin, but nothing happened. The captain was on horseback. He threw himself off his horse, ran up to the gun crew, and shouted: "Why don't you fire?" "They are our men, we can't shoot!" the master gunner answered, and it was left to the captain to fire the first shot singlehandedly. The gun crew had deliberately aimed the gun away from the rebels and the first shot struck the upper floor of the Senate, and some people sitting on the roof toppled to the ground. The second shot struck the cobblestones, sending up a cloud of smoke and snow, and did no harm. Captain Bakunin made sure that the third salvo would be aimed at the rebels, who seemed to be pleased that after long waiting the battle had begun, for they shouted "Hurrah!" as they fired back with their muskets. Then there was confusion, for all over the Square there was shooting. Some shots went wild, for we hear of broken windows in the Academy of Arts on Vasilyevsky Island. The rebels held for about ten minutes. Alexander Bestuzhev remembered how silent they were, and even the dying made no sound. Sometimes in the silence between the shots he heard the strange sound made by the blood melting the ice followed by a curious cracking sound as the blood froze.

On that bitterly cold night, in the near darkness, lit by the red glare of the shells and the yellow bursts from the muskets, the Square became a pandemonium of noise. People were running madly across the Square in all directions, screaming and calling to one another, and their screams could be heard above the roar of the guns and the rattle of musket fire. There was the sound of shattering glass, of falling bricks, of canister shot ricocheting off the cobblestones, and of the horses' pounding across the Square and slithering on the ice. Now everyone was shouting, and the only person who seemed to be completely calm and self-possessed was the young Tsar, who rode beside the broken railings of St. Isaac's Cathedral exactly as though he were on parade. Kakhovsky had slipped away from his post near the statue of Peter the Great and in the confusion he had no difficulty in reaching the railings which rose from a low wall. He climbed up on the wall, braced himself against the railing, and fired at the Tsar from a distance of twenty paces. He missed. Then he jumped down, vanished into the seething crowd, and the Tsar, who had not heard the shot, continued his stately progress, from time to time giving orders to one of his generals.

When the ranks of the rebels broke, some fled in the direction of the Neva and the Anglisky embankment, others made their way to Galernaya Street which was long and narrow, and could perhaps be defended. Alexander Bestuzhev, showing for the first time that day a resourcefulness and knowledge of strategy which had failed him during all those hours of waiting, decided to send a company of his men across the frozen Neva and capture the Peter and Paul Fortress, and then train its guns on the Winter Palace. The Tsar, however, had already thought of this possibility, and ordered his guns trained on the river, to break up the ice. A battery of guns was rushed across the Square, taking up positions along the bridge. The column was making its way over the ice when the grapeshot began to fall around them. The ice broke, drowning men struggled in the water, and the survivors, abandoning all hope of reaching the Fortress, set out for the Academy of Arts on Vasilyevsky Island, which was built like a fortress. When they reached the academy, they discovered that the gates were closed. A beam from a broken barge was being used as a battering ram and the gate was already giving way when a company of Chevalier Guards came racing out of the darkness.

Bestuzhev shouted: "Save yourselves as best you can!" and the rebels scattered, leaving only Bestuzhev and the standard-bearer behind.

They embraced, and then Bestuzhev told the standard-bearer to offer the banner in surrender to the officer in command of the cavalry. As he ran, he glanced over his shoulder and saw the standard-bearer surrendering the banner. When he turned again, he saw the glint of a sword flashing in the air and the standard-bearer falling at the horse's feet.

No mercy was shown that night. Many of the captured rebels were shot out of hand, and many of the wounded were killed where they lay. For a little while longer the fighting went on along Galernaya Street. The Tsar ordered guns to be brought up to the entrance of the street, to fire canister shot at the rebels who had hoped that this narrow lane could be defended against cavalry charges. Soon the whole length of the Galernaya was carpeted with the dead and dying.

An hour after the Tsar ordered the guns to fire, the Square was deserted except for the strange shapes lying on the cobblestones. The dead were everywhere—men, women, children, horses, rebels and loyal troops. No one ever counted the dead. Prince Eugene of Württemberg, a cousin of the Tsar, who at one time had been regarded as a claimant to the Russian throne, spoke of "several hundred dead." A high government official mentioned two hundred dead as a "reasonable figure"; others spoke of "three hundred dead and wounded." The official government figure was "two dead and thirty-three wounded, of whom two later died of their wounds," making a total of four. Official casualty lists are rarely reassuring, and it is probable that about four hundred died.

During the night the Horse Guards were given the task of rounding up the rebel troops now scattered all over St. Petersburg. By the Tsar's orders they were marched back to the Senate Square, where they were made to stand near the statue of Peter the Great before being marched off to prison. The names of the rebel leaders were known, and warrants were issued for their arrest. Most of them were arrested during the night.

All night orders were being issued by the Tsar, and the strangest of all was an order to cleanse the Senate Square of every sign of the battle. When the sun rose the next day, there were to be no bodies, no bloodstains, no broken windows, no marks of canister and grapeshot, no bullet holes. The task was given to Alexander Shulgin, the St. Petersburg Chief of Police. First, it was necessary to remove the bodies. The problem was solved ingeniously by throwing into the river all the bodies lying in the Square; some of the wounded were also thrown into the river. Then workmen with iron scrapers scraped off the congealed blood and laid a smooth carpet of fresh snow along the whole length of the Square. The frozen pools of blood on the Senate steps were washed away with boiling water, the glaziers put in new windowpanes, the plasterers concealed the bullet holes and bloodstains on the yellow walls and white columns of the Senate, and on the roof the metalsmiths mended the scales of Justice which had been smashed by a cannonball. So they went about the work of obliterating every trace of the battle, and a man might walk casually across the Square the next morning and reflect that nothing of importance had occurred, for except for a few broken windows which the workmen had forgotten to replace and some cornices chipped by cannonballs there was nothing to suggest there had been any uprising at all. The day had seen a battle; the night proclaimed that it did not take place. The principle had been established: a battle that reflected no credit on the autocracy must be wiped off the page of history.

In the spring the frozen bodies rose to the surface and were seen floating on the Neva. The police were given orders to pull them out of the water and to bury them secretly.

THE ARISTOCRATIC REVOLUTIONARIES

T HE BATTLE WHICH took place in the Senate Square on December 14, 1825, thirteen years after Napoleon's Grande Armée had been driven out of Russia, resembled one of those sudden clashes between the armies of the Tsar and the pretenders to the throne which broke out at intervals during the seventeenth century. In those clashes, too, we find princes and noblemen fighting on opposing sides, and mysterious secret societies ordering events for obscure purposes, while the people look on like spectators of a strange nightmarish dance. The uprising resembles a ballet, with the dancers moving in slow motion. Occasionally a madman runs screaming through the ranks of the assembled dancers, and when the madman has departed there is a roll of drums, a burst of gunfire, and blood spills over the stones. To the onlookers in the Senate Square the soldiers in their brilliant uniforms appeared to be performing a senseless dance and no longer remembered the roles they had been called upon to play.

But in fact something of vast and continuing importance was taking place. For the first time in the history of Russia a battle was being fought for an abstract idea. The rebels were engaged in a struggle for freedom against a deeply rooted autocracy, which was determined to remain in power and to rule with absolute authority. If the revolt was desperately amateurish, badly planned, and ill timed, it was all the more an expression of revolutionary fervor. These aristocratic officers knew what they were doing, they counted the risks, and they seem to have known from the beginning that they were doomed to failure.

The uprising was planned by a secret society composed of young officers. Within a few years the secret society changed its name several times, being known variously as the Union of Salvation, the Society of True and Faithful Sons of the Fatherland, the Society of Prosperity. Later it split into two separate but related parts known as the Northern and Southern Societies. The founders were a few close friends, most of whom had fought in the Napoleonic Wars. They included Prince Sergey Trubetskoy, Alexander Muraviev, his brother Mikhail Muraviev, who later became Governor General of Vilna where he acquired a reputation for ferocious misgovernment and the nickname "Muraviev the Hangman," and his cousin Sergey Muraviev-Apostol, whose father was tutor to the Grand Duke Alexander Pavlovich, the future Tsar Alexander I. Another member of the circle was Ivan Yakushkin, a subaltern of the elite Semyonovsky Guards, who related in his memoirs an incident which suggests some of the reasons why they turned their thoughts to revolution.

The incident occurred in St. Petersburg during a review of the troops who had returned from France. Tsar Alexander I had already welcomed the troops at Oranienbaum, where their safe return was celebrated with a solemn *Te Deum*. During the chanting of the prayers the returning soldiers saw the police beating the people who came too close to the parade ground, and this made an unfavorable impression on them. There was worse to come when the troops reached St. Petersburg, and in the shadow of a vast triumphal arch dominated by a bronze Victory riding in a chariot drawn by six alabaster horses—the arch was erected to honor the Tsar's triumphs in the Napoleonic Wars—there was another parade, attended by the Empress Dowager, who drove onto the parade ground in a gilded coach. The Tsar, riding a sorrel stallion, made the grand gesture of lowering his naked sword in a salute to his mother, and at that very moment he saw a peasant walking nonchalantly across the road almost under his horse. Incensed by the presence of the peasant on the parade ground, the

Tsar slashed at him with his sword, while the police came running up with clubs. "We turned our eyes away, because we were so ashamed of our beloved Tsar," Ivan Yakushkin wrote later. "That was the first time he disappointed me; and involuntarily I recalled the story of a cat transformed into a beautiful maiden, who never saw a mouse without leaping upon it."

Others besides Yakushkin were disappointed by the brutality of the Tsar, his essential shallowness and grotesque misunderstanding of the Russian character. An aura of legend surrounded him. Napoleon called him "the northern Sphinx," the Russians called him "Alexander the Blessed," for he had conquered Napoleon and was reputed to have liberal tendencies. In reality he cared little for anything except upholding the power of the autocracy. When he died in Taganrog in southern Russia on November 19, 1825, the legend died with him. He left no legitimate offspring. The crown therefore would pass to his brother Constantine, and in the normal course of events the army would swear an oath of loyalty to the new Tsar. Constantine was popular: he was by far the most gifted and tolerant of the sons of Paul I, and it was expected that he would impose few burdens on the Russian people.

The news of Alexander's death was strangely delayed, and reached St. Petersburg only on November 27. Constantine, who was in Warsaw, received the news two days earlier, and at once announced that he had renounced the throne in favor of his younger brother Nicholas. The Act of Renunciation had been signed the previous year and secretly deposited in the Uspensky Cathedral in Moscow. The Act was so secret that no one apart from Alexander, Constantine and Nicholas and perhaps two other people knew of its existence, and it was of doubtful validity. For reasons of his own Constantine refused to become the Tsar and insisted that the Act should take effect, even after he had been acclaimed the legitimate Tsar in St. Petersburg and his brother Nicholas had taken an oath of loyalty to him. For nearly three weeks therefore there was no Tsar, for Constantine refused to rule. Nearly every day letters passed between St. Petersburg and Warsaw, as Constantine and Nicholas disputed the succession, each demanding that the other should wear the crown. It was an intolerable situation calculated to make the Russians cynical about the intentions of their two self-denying Tsars, neither of whom appeared to want to rule. "We're just sheep," they said. "They'll sell us in the end!" But as the days passed, they began to wonder when the final bargain would be sealed.

This is how events stood on December 12, twenty-three days after the death of Alexander I. By this time it was becoming clear to Nicholas that his strong-willed brother refused to leave Warsaw and that any further delay would be fatal to the autocracy. He had also learned that the secret societies were prepared to lead an insurrection and take over the government. He must move quickly and decisively, if he was to preserve the autocracy from collapse. He announced that on December 14 he would convene the State Council in order to confirm his assumption of power and at the same time he would order the army to swear an oath of loyalty to him as the rightful Tsar. He had received an unusually coarse and violent letter from his brother, and this too had stung him into action. At long last he knew what was expected of him, and he said to one of his aides: "On the day after tomorrow I shall either be Tsar, or I shall be dead!"

While the Tsar was debating in the Winter Palace with his aides and with members of the imperial family, the conspirators were also debating among themselves. The most active of the conspirators was the poet Kondraty Ryleyev, a friend of Pushkin, formerly a second lieutenant in the Horse Artillery, now the secretary of the Russian-American Company engaged in developing Alaska. He was a slight, intense man with a dark skin, dark eyes, and thick black eyebrows. He wore his hair in a fashionable coxcomb with ringlets above his ears, but it was one of those strong narrow faces of great power which suggest immense reserves of energy and will power. He smiled easily, and charmed everyone he met. During the long discussions with the conspirators he was suffering from a high fever, and it was observed that his eyes were unusually bright and piercing. He was a close friend of Prince Trubetskoy.

Most of the meetings of the conspirators took place in Ryleyev's house, where the young Alexander Bestuzhev was also living. Together they edited a magazine called *The Pole Star*, which appeared annually. It purported to be a literary magazine, but was in fact the organ of the Northern Society.

The discussions which took place around the dinner table of Ryleyev's apartment near the Sini Bridge and just off Voznesensky Prospect were centered on three main topics. First, how many regiments stationed in St. Petersburg could be induced to come out in revolt? Second, the date of the uprising. Third, liaison with the Southern Society and especially with its brilliant organizer Pavel Pestel, a veteran of Borodino where he won a gold sword for bravery and the author of an elaborate treatise called *Russian Truth, or the Instruction to the Supreme Provisional Government*, in which he outlined a political program for the new Republic of Russia to be ruled from a new capital in Nizhny Novgorod. This inflammatory and very secret treatise was buried in a field just before he was arrested on December 13, 1824, on the eve of the uprising. He took no part in the decisions made by Ryleyev and the other conspirators in St. Petersburg, and he was condemned to death only when it became clear that he was the intellectual leader who would inevitably have assumed power if the uprising had been successful.

On the day Pestel was arrested, the conspirators had their last long meeting around the dinner table in Ryleyev's apartment. The table was heaped with loaves of black bread. Sometimes Ryleyev's wife would appear briefly and mysteriously, her beautiful face clouded with despair, for she knew enough about the conspiracy to be mortally afraid. The apartment was only two minutes' walk from the Senate Square. So it happened that the conspirators found themselves gazing out the window in the direction of the Square, where it sometimes seemed to them that the uprising had already taken place, for in their discussions words seemed to be more credible than deeds, and manifestos read out in a small ill-lit room were more potent than orders uttered by a sovereign power. They met in a mood of exaltation. When the morning came, they scarcely remembered what they had discussed.

Prince Trubetskoy's plan of action with some minor modifications was adopted. According to this plan the regiments would mass in the Senate Square, refuse to take the oath of allegiance to Nicholas, and demand that Constantine come immediately to St. Petersburg. Since they had already taken the oath of allegiance to Constantine, the appearance of legality was preserved. The next step was to offer a manifesto to the Senate demanding the election of new senators from a new electorate comprising all classes of society. Meanwhile the Senate would appoint a provisional government with supreme powers, and the regiments would be led out from their barracks to encampments around the city. In this way law and order would be preserved in the midst of a rebellion.

The political decisions at the meeting followed the instructions given by Pestel in *Russian Truth*. The capital would be transferred to Nizhny Novgorod, which would henceforth bear the name of Slavyansk, "the city of the Slavs." There would be freedom of the press and of religious cults, the censorship and serfdom would be abolished, all trials would be open to the public and the jury system would be introduced to Russia. Finally the standing army would be abolished. Pestel had read deeply in the works of the French philosopher Destutt de Tracy, and the state he envisioned was modeled on the blueprint prepared for a country which had little in common with Russia.

Early in the evening the conspirators returned to their homes to catch some sleep. In the morning they expected to seize power.

On the evening of December 14 most of the chief conspirators and some seven hundred soldiers were under arrest. Prince Trubetskoy, who had found refuge in the house of his brother-in-law, the Austrian ambassador, was arrested in bed. Ryleyev went home and calmly waited for the moment when there would be a knock on his door. Most of the conspirators were arrested just as easily.

When Prince Trubetskoy was led into the presence of the Tsar in the Winter Palace, he was already a broken man. He had deserted the conspirators and he had deserted the Tsar. He belonged nowhere; least of all did he belong to this ornate room with the chandeliers, the silk-covered sofas, the delicate inlaid writing tables. His hands tied with rope, four soldiers with naked swords guarding him, he was thrust into the room. Nicholas went straight up to him, tapped him on the forehead with the index finger of his right hand, and said: "Tell me, what was in that head of yours—with your name and your family traditions—that you got yourself mixed up in this affair? Prince Trubetskoy, Colonel of the Guards, eh? Aren't you ashamed of yourself? Aren't you ashamed of getting mixed up with that rabble?"

General Toll, one of the Tsar's aides-de-camp, began to read aloud a deposition made by one of the arrested men. According to the deposition Prince Trubetskoy knew a good deal about the secret society's members in St. Petersburg and in the Fourth Army Corps in Kiev.

As he listened to the deposition, the Prince's face lit up. To his certain knowledge there was no secret society in the Fourth Army Corps.

"Your Excellency is wholly mistaken," he said. "I answer for the fact that there is no secret society in that corps."

General Toll looked surprised; he had relied on the deposition to open up the inquiry into the Prince's activities. The Tsar had a simpler way of getting to the heart of the problem.

"Are you a member of the secret society?" he asked.

"Yes, Your Majesty."

"You were the dictator?"

"Yes, Your Majesty."

Nicholas motioned him to a sofa.

"Write down everything," he said, and then he murmured: "How could a Prince Trubetskoy, a colonel of the Guards, get mixed up in an affair like this? And what about your charming wife? So you have sacrificed your wife, too! Do you have any children?"

"No, Your Majesty."

"You're lucky to have no children! Your fate will be dreadful, *dreadful!*"

For a while Prince Trubetskoy was left alone to write his deposition. While he was writing, the Grand Duke Mikhail entered the room, went straight up to the Prince, peered at him for a long time in silence, and then departed. An hour later General Toll came to collect the deposition.

Soon Nicholas summoned him, complaining that the deposition was too short.

"Is that all you have to say for yourself?" he said. "Do you know I can have you shot this moment?"

"Yes, Your Majesty."

Nicholas sat down at a table and wrote an order that Prince Trubetskoy should be taken immediately to Cell No. 7 of the Alexis Ravelin. The order was addressed to General Alexander Sukin, the commandant of the Peter and Paul Fortress, an old gray-haired man with a wooden leg. But in fact Prince Trubetskoy was being entrusted to the care of someone far older, the legendary Lilien Ankern, the commandant of the Alexis Ravelin. Lilien Ankern was a Swede, who had taken service in the Russian army so long ago that no one remembered when he first wore Russian uniform. He wore a long-skirted green military coat with red collar and cuffs, and because he was so small and withered, it always seemed too big for him. He had spent fifty years in the Ravelin, and they said he was ninety years old. All over the Peter and Paul Fortress there were these veterans of another age.

Nicholas had very little sleep in the days following the uprising. He was continually examining prisoners, receiving reports, pondering the long confessions which the conspirators were ordered to write, and sending off letters to his brother Constantine; and these letters, always written in French, in the chiseled style appropriate when an emperor writes to a former emperor, sometimes break down into appeals for pity and sympathy.

Early in January came the news which he dreaded most of all. Another regiment had revolted, and there was the danger that this second uprising would produce a chain reaction throughout Russia. What particularly irked him, as he wrote to his brother Constantine, was that he was about to arrest the leader of the rebellion when he received news that the rebels were marching on Kiev.

News traveled very slowly in Russia, and many days passed before the full story became known. Like the battle in the Senate Square, the battles in the south were confused and strangely concluded, and although many accounts have come down to us, the exact sequence of events is still not clear. On both sides the soldiers seemed to be moving recklessly through a nightmare.

With Pestel under arrest, the leadership of the revolutionary arm of the Southern Society had fallen to Sergey Muraviev-Apostol, the son of a high official who owned 35,000 acres and 4,000 serfs in the Kursk *guberniya*, south of Moscow. His mother was a Serbian woman, the daughter of a

general. His parents had traveled abroad, and were remarkable for their
cultivation, their fine manners, and their liberal outlook. Like Pestel, Sergey Muraviev-Apostol was one of the heroes of the Napoleonic Wars, receiving the golden sword of honor for bravery on the battlefield. Yet he
had no particular feeling for army life, and after the defeat of Napoleon
he thought seriously of studying political science and government abroad.
With his Byronic profile, his gift for conversation, his fiercely held liberal
opinions and his deep religious feeling, he was in danger of being led by
his ideas, and his father sighed with relief when he finally decided to
continue his military career. There seemed to be not the slightest doubt
that in time he would become a general, an aide-de-camp of the Tsar, and
the governor of a province. He was now, at twenty-nine, the commander
of the second battalion of the Chernigov Regiment in winter quarters at
Vasilkov, a pleasant little provincial town near Kiev.

The news of the uprising in St. Petersburg and the arrest of the leaders
reached him on December 24, and he at once decided to bring out the
Chernigov Regiment in open rebellion. The regiment was honeycombed
with members of the Southern Society, although few of them were in
positions of authority. He addressed his troops so forcefully that they decided to throw in their lot with him, and the fifth battalion also joined
forces with him. Other battalions were quartered in neighboring villages,
and as he saw it, it was merely a question of parading his troops through
the villages to bring the remaining battalions out in mutiny. Progress was
slow; there was a constant coming and going of officers weighing up the
prospects of success; and to make matters worse there was a blizzard. It
was thought that many regiments—the Akhtirka, the Alexopol and Alexandrisky regiments among them—might be induced to march on Kiev, but
as more detailed news of the debacle in St. Petersburg reached the conspirators, the less anxious some of them became to take part in the uprising. News of the conspiracy reached Colonel Gustav Hebel, the commander of the regiment, and Sergey Muraviev-Apostol was promptly
placed under arrest, his own troops being ordered to guard him. This
was no arrest, and he marched off at the head of his troops. On the night
of December 30 he captured Vasilkov with the second and fifth companies of the Chernigov Regiment. A young sublieutenant of the Poltava Regiment, Mikhail Bestuzhev-Riumin, maintained contact with the other local
regiments, and it was hoped that by the next evening the revolutionary
army would have swelled to at least five thousand men.

Sergey Muraviev-Apostol spent part of the night composing a declaration of independence to be read to the troops in the Vasilkov square the
next day. Because this strange declaration took the form of a revolutionary
catechism with heavy religious overtones, he decided that it should be

read by the local priest, Father Daniel Keiser. The declaration was addressed to his peasant soldiers who would be more likely to fight if they believed that God was on their side. He wrote:

THE ORTHODOX CATECHISM

In the name of the Father, the Son and the Holy Ghost.

Q: Why did God create man?
A: That men might believe in Him and be free and happy.
Q: What does it mean to be free and happy?
A: There is no happiness without freedom. The apostle Paul declares: "We have redemption through His blood; be ye not slaves of others."
Q: Why are the Russian people and the Russian soldiers unhappy?
A: Because the Tsars have robbed them of their freedom.
Q: Do the Tsars act contrary to the will of God?
A: Indeed they do. The Lord has said: "Whosoever shall desire to be first, the same shall be the servant of all." But the Tsars only tyrannize over the people.
Q: Must the Tsars be obeyed when they act against the will of God?
A: No, for Christ said: "You cannot serve God and Mammon." That is why the Russian soldiers and the Russian people suffer by obeying the Tsar. . . .

There were altogether fourteen questions and answers in the "Orthodox Catechism" which Father Daniel Keiser read to the soldiers on the snowbound square of Vasilkov, and all of them sprang from the inflexible idea that the Tsar had usurped the powers of the common people and oppressed them unmercifully. He was the accursed tyrant who had been visited on Russia. Father Keiser was a very young and nervous priest, who had only recently taken holy orders and entered the service of the Chernigov Regiment, and he was understandably nervous as he read the catechism. He read it badly, without interest, in a thin voice.* Sergey Muraviev-Apostol had built high hopes on the catechism, and it puzzled him that the soldiers paid more attention to his rousing speeches than to the catechism which was intended to provide the theoretical basis for the revolt.

Many other things puzzled him: most of all he was puzzled by the fact that most of the couriers he had sent to the neighboring regiments had failed to return. There was a strange feeling of walking into a vacuum. Where was the enemy? Should he attack Kiev? And what about Belaya Tserkov, where the Seventeenth Jäger Regiment, which was honeycombed with members of the Southern Society, was stationed? If he could secure Belaya Tserkov, he believed he would have no very great difficulty in

---

* Father Daniel Keiser's subsequent fate was terrible. He was unfrocked by the Synod, court-martialed, disenfranchised, and sentenced to hard labor. Thirty-two years later he was given an amnesty. By this time his wife and children had died. He had been a reluctant Decembrist for perhaps twenty minutes.

taking Kiev. Accordingly he marched at the head of his army to Moto-vilovka, the next town on the way to Belaya Tserkov. He was heartened by the arrival of a company of musketeers under the command of a certain Lieutenant Bystritsky who, although not a member of the secret society, offered to place his troops under him. There were now a thousand troops, and every likelihood that there would soon be more.

At Motovilovka he made a mistake which was to have fatal consequences: he permitted his soldiers to rest. It was a Sunday, the first day of the year, a glorious clear day with blue skies like a sudden breath of spring in the midst of winter. The local peasants came out of church to see the rebel troops lined up on parade, bouquets were thrown, and there was some fraternizing, but no attempt was made to bring the people to the side of the rebels. In the eyes of Sergey Muraviev-Apostol a rebellion was a military affair, to be decided by force of arms.

While he was hesitating in Motovilovka, government agents were busy rounding up officers in the local regiments suspected of being members of the secret society. No mercy was to be shown to them. They were to be shot out of hand if they attempted to escape; and if they were captured, they were to be taken in chains to the fortress at Kiev. Sergey Muraviev-Apostol was still waiting for the couriers to bring him news of the regiments which had come out against the government. He did not know that they had all been arrested.

He decided to march on Belaya Tserkov early the next morning. Then, abruptly, he decided to march in the direction of Zhitomir, the headquarters of the Third Army Corps. He saw now that Belaya Tserkov might be a trap: the town was surrounded by regiments whose officers had never been members of the society. The truth was that he had no knowledge of what the government was doing, and all his lines of communication had broken down.

On January 3, toward two o'clock in the afternoon, he was marching with his troops in the Ustimovsky hills when he saw straight ahead of him a detachment of Mariupol Hussars with a battery of cannon. A feeling of wild exultation came over him, for the Hussars were known to be devoted to the secret society. Some of the officers were members, and they had pledged allegiance to the revolt. He did not know that on the previous day all the officers had been arrested and new officers loyal to the government had taken their place.

The rebels advanced at a quick pace, shouting and singing. Even when they heard the roar of the guns they were shouting with pleasure at the thought of the reinforcements that had come to their aid. The second burst of canister shot dispelled the illusion. Sergey Muraviev-Apostol was wounded by a shell splinter in the head, and blinded by his own blood.

The Hussars charged. Sergey's young brother Ippolit was killed. Within five minutes, the light going down on the hills, the rebellion was destroyed.

At least one of the captured officers succeeded in committing suicide. The rest were bound with ropes, and led off in chains.

The Decembrist uprising was over.

THE TRIAL OF THE DECEMBRISTS

THREE DAYS AFTER the uprising in St. Petersburg there came into existence the Secret Committee to Investigate the Members of the Criminal Society, and this small body, composed of men determined to demonstrate their loyalty to the Tsar, was given limitless powers to investigate all aspects of the uprising. The Secret Committee succeeded so well in its examination of the conspirators that we know day by day and sometimes hour by hour how they plotted and changed position and lost themselves in an unhappy maze of intrigue, until they scarcely knew what they were doing. They had entered the revolt like sleepwalkers, and they continued to behave like sleepwalkers when they were being cross-examined and forced to confess their crimes.

The ex-officio president of the Secret Committee was the Tsar, who assumed the role of chief prosecutor and examining magistrate and showed himself to be the most skillful and relentless of inquisitors. At various times he played the role of detective, policeman, *agent provocateur*, judge, jury, father-confessor, and champion of the oppressed. He played his roles so well that he sometimes appeared to be an actor in a play of which he alone knew the denouement. By turns savage, ironical, cleverly intimidating, and capriciously merciful, he dominated the inquiry by the sheer force of his passion to uproot the conspiracy and to see that none of the conspirators went unpunished. Just as he had interviewed some of the conspirators on the night of the uprising, so in the following months he continued to examine them and to read reports of the examinations in which he had himself listed the questions to be answered. It amused him to punish the prisoners by putting them on a diet of bread and water or ordering them to be shackled. He had a vast and instinctive knowledge of how to extract confessions, and he seems to have invented the psychological trick of bringing the prisoners blindfold into a room filled with junior officers jingling their spurs, joking and telling stories, behaving exactly as they behaved in their military clubs. At such moments the blindfold prisoners would feel that they had been suddenly transported into the carefree and innocent past. Then they would be led into a narrow anteroom, the handkerchief would be whipped away from their eyes, and they would find themselves standing at the end of a table covered with a red baize cloth, facing their accusers.

The accusers were all men of proved loyalty to the Tsar. At the other end of the long table, the prisoners would see General Alexander Tatishchev, the Minister of War, a small, fat, ungainly, bulletheaded man, who seemed to drowse through the long meetings of the Secret Committee, but was always wide-awake and far more dangerous than he looked. Prince Golitsyn, the sallow and elderly Minister of Education usually sat on his left, and took little part in the investigation. General Alexander Chernyshev assumed the role of chief prosecutor. He had a sharp, foxy face under his exquisitely curled thick black hair, and there was something about him which suggested both the fop and the executioner; and he did in fact superintend the execution of the conspirators who were condemned to death. He particularly enjoyed startling the prisoners with sudden tirades designed to reduce them to incoherence, and he liked to scream at the top of his voice. Among the others who regularly attended the sessions of the Secret Committee were the Grand Duke Mikhail, General Golenishchev-Kutuzov who had replaced Miloradovich as Governor General of St. Petersburg, and General Adlerberg, who acted as the personal representative of the Tsar with the right to see all documents and to approach the throne at all times. He had the bland good looks and the exact, disciplined mind which Nicholas I particularly admired in his officers. He was the one who would quietly inject specific and damning questions, and he was aware of his special responsibility as chief adviser to the Tsar.

Only two of the men who attended the meetings of the committee had even a remote sympathy for the prisoners who were brought before them. One was the committee secretary Alexander Borovkov, a colorless civil servant, who had pretensions as a littérateur, moved in the same literary and Masonic circles as some of the conspirators, and genuinely disliked the arbitrary manner in which the proceedings took place. The other was Count Alexander Benckendorf, who became the head of the Third Department, the Tsar's secret police, and who possessed a horror of hypocrisy. Like General Adlerberg he possessed the pleasant, bland features of a typical German aristocrat, with a curling mustache and wavy hair, but there the resemblance ended. He was well-read, intelligent, and humane, and consistently attempted to mitigate the fate of the prisoners. Borovkov, being merely a secretary, could have little influence on the other members of the board of inquiry, and Benckendorf was in no position to influence the final verdict.

The task confronting the members of the Secret Committee appeared to be a difficult one, but was in fact very simple. The Tsar wanted the abject confessions of all the conspirators, and in addition he wanted a complete and detailed picture of the conspiracy in its remotest ramifications. All the artifices of coercion were employed. Torture was used unsparingly. Psychological tortures were also used with striking effect. In the early stages false confessions were used, or a prisoner who refused to speak would find himself confronted with one who had spoken too much. Brought before the Secret Committee in the middle of the night after being hustled from his damp cell, a prisoner, after the blindfold was removed, would find himself dazzled by the bright lights and immediately he would be confronted with a barrage of shouted questions, and peremptorily ordered to say "Yes" or "No" in reply to abstruse or difficult questions. With his mind dulled by imprisonment and torture, he felt like someone who has been introduced into a cage of wild beasts. He would say "Yes" when he meant "No," hesitate, plead for time in which to formulate an answer, and he would be told that the only reason he was in such a state of panic was because he was guilty of crimes even more abominable than those for which he was accused. In the name of the Tsar he would be promised a full pardon if he confessed everything to the last detail, but in fact he never received a pardon. If he refused to confess, he was hurried back to his cell, heavy arm and leg fetters were attached to him, and the prison doctor was ordered to determine how much more torture he could endure. Priests in the pay of the government came to their cells and promised them the comforts of religion if they confessed in secret, and some time later these secret confessions would be read out to them by one of the members of the Secret Committee.

So the months passed, while the Tsar debated with himself what must be done with the conspirators. He was so immersed in the details of the conspiracy, and was so often in the company of the conspirators, that he seemed to know more about it than any of them. With some of the prisoners he had established a strange relationship, even a kind of affection. Kakhovsky intrigued him especially, for he had escaped death at Kakhovsky's hands only by a miracle; and they were often together. Once Kakhovsky described the miseries which had fallen upon Russia, and the Tsar wept.

At the end of May the Tsar still did not know in what direction to turn.

A judgment must be affirmed, the guilty must be punished, and the empire saved. But how? and where? and on what basis? He consulted his legal experts, who suggested that there should be a formal trial. It was decided that the formal trial should be held in secret. Accordingly a Special Supreme Tribunal under three princes known for their loyalty to the Tsar was called into session on June 3, nearly six months after the uprising, with orders to arrive at a satisfactory verdict. Eight days later it had completed its work and was ready to pronounce its final and irrevocable judgment on the accused.

The Supreme Tribunal was not in any real sense a tribunal. It was simply a body of men brought together under a grandiose title to satisfy the Tsar's longing for formality and legality. The tribunal was a fictitious body which never seriously investigated the uprising, never discussed the issues, and never met for more than a few minutes. It did however meet long enough to appoint two subcommittees, one to draw up a list of the defendants according to their varying degrees of guilt, the other to recommend the appropriate penalties and to draft the final report which would be submitted to the Tsar.

Since the three princes knew themselves to be incompetent, it was decided to entrust the working of the two subcommittees to Count Mikhail Mikhailovich Speransky, a legal scholar and devoted friend of the Tsar Alexander I, in whose reign he had set about instituting some wide-scale reforms, thus incurring the displeasure of the landed aristocracy and the more determined advocates of autocracy. The Tsar was sympathetic to the reforms until he found himself caught in a web of political intrigues. Overnight Count Speransky was banished to Nizhny Novgorod. A few years later he was appointed Governor General of Siberia, where under grave difficulties he was able to introduce some of the reforms he had hoped to introduce into Russia. The landed aristocracy congratulated themselves that he was a long way from St. Petersburg. He was a liberal of the old school, generous, well educated, and mild in temper. It was believed that in some remote way he was implicated in the Decembrist uprising, and it is certain that the Decembrists themselves held him in great veneration and planned to make him head of the provisional government after they had taken power. All this was known to the Tsar, who took a diabolical pleasure in forcing him into an untenable position. From being the favorite of the Decembrists he was compelled to become the advocate of their destruction; the liberal reformer became the chief pillar of the autocracy.

It was one of those cunningly contrived appointments for which Nicholas was later to become notorious, for few things pleased him more than to set men in simple moral quandaries. He delighted in intrigue, and the appointment was a calculated act of intrigue. Count Speransky dared not refuse the imperial command, for that would prove his sympathies with the Decembrists; nor did he dare to plead for leniency for the accused. He could shoot himself, and thus vanish from the scene, or he could carry out his duties with strict impartiality; he had no other alternatives. If he shot himself, his suicide would be regarded as a confession of guilt, and his family would suffer the same punishment as the conspirators. If he carried out his duties with strict impartiality, splitting every hair and introducing a massive Byzantine legalism into the apportionment of guilt and punishment, with elaborate definitions and vast addenda of aggravating and extenuating circumstances, he might succeed in confusing many issues, and at the very least he might be able to teach the Tsar respect for the intricacies of the law.

Weighed down by this terrible burden, he did the best he could. He produced a masterly brief full of infinite complexities. The conspirators were charged with regicide, mutiny and military sedition. He showed that none of these words were precise and could be interpreted in countless ways, and he offered a breath-taking list of interpretations, exceptions, and degrees of guilt. A man might be determined to kill the Tsar, with intent and malice aforethought, or he may simply have uttered some vague words which others interpreted as a desire to rid the country of the autocrat, and between these two extremes there were many possible variations of intent. Had he incited others to commit regicide, and then withdrawn his incitement? Had he known that others intended to commit regicide, and for his own reasons kept silent? If he had consented to the act of regicide, but taken no part at all in the conflict, was he as guilty as the man who deliberately set out on a course which would lead to regicide? Count Speransky knew that the Tsar was obsessed with the thought of a mathematically accurate assessment of guilt. It was as though guilt was something which could be weighed on a jeweler's scales.

The voluminous report which was presented to the Tsar divided the prisoners into five categories. In the first category were the "ring leaders," Pestel, Sergey Muraviev-Apostol, Mikhail Bestuzhev-Riumin, Ryleyev and Kakhovsky. In the second category were thirty-one Decembrists, including Prince Trubetskoy, Prince Obolensky and Prince Volkonsky, who were regarded as men who had taken a leading part in the conspiracy. The remaining eighty-five prisoners were divided among three categories, though the last was scarcely a category at all, for it contained the names of two men who had never had any sympathy with the uprising. The verdict of the Special Supreme Tribunal was that all the conspirators except those in the fifth category should be sentenced to death.

It was a grotesque verdict, and illegal according to Russian law, for the death penalty had been abolished in Russia during the reign of the Tsarina Elizabeth. It is just possible that Count Speransky deliberately devised the grotesque verdict in the hope of shocking the Tsar into some semblance of sanity. He had enjoyed the curious distinctions between the degrees of guilt; now these distinctions were cast on the rubbish heap as all except two were confronted with the death penalty. The secret trials, the endless interrogations and examinations, were now reduced to futility. The sweeping verdict of the tribunal permitted the Tsar to proclaim an act of clemency.

According to the tribunal the proper punishment for the five ringleaders was to be found under Article 19 of the Military Regulations of 1716, which provided that the condemned be drawn and quartered. This barbaric punishment, which had been commonplace in the time of Ivan the Terrible and Peter the Great, had long since been abandoned, and when Speransky announced that this was the proper and indeed inevitable punishment, it is possible that he deliberately chose the most barbaric punishment in order to shame the Tsar to mercy. When he dressed up the verdicts in a suitable legalistic panoply, he did not fail to add that "the abundant mercy flowing from the autocratic power has no limits whatsoever."

In fact, the Tsar's mercy was abundantly limited. His chilling, precise mind moved awkwardly in the realm of mercy. He decreed that the sentence of death by drawing and quartering, being repulsive to the present age, should be canceled, and instead they were to be hanged. Hanging was a suitable punishment for these bandits, and as they had lost their military rank, shooting was too good for them. As for the thirty-one Decembrists of the second category, he decreed that they should be exiled to Siberia for life; if their wives were so stupid as to follow them, any children would be born illegitimate. The remaining eighty-five prisoners were sentenced to various terms of exile or imprisonment. The Decembrists who perished in the uprising in the South were not forgotten, and the Tsar decreed that since they could not be hanged, "the death sentence was to be read over their graves, and instead of crosses there should be erected gallows and their names shall be nailed on the gallows to their everlasting disgrace."

As usual in Russia the processes of execution were prolonged and terrible, and they were all the more terrible because until the very last moment the hope of a pardon was held out to the prisoners. No one seemed to believe that the Tsar would sentence them to be hanged or to interminable exile in Siberia. It was generally believed that a singular act of clemency would be announced on the eve of the Coronation, which was now only a few weeks away.

While they waited to hear the verdict of the tribunal the prisoners were strangely jaunty. Nearly all of them were young—their average age was only twenty-seven—and in their cells they behaved with youthful assurance, joking and laughing and sending messages to one another by rapping on the walls or by employing the services of good-natured guards. Occasionally they would give way to hysterical outbursts or religious mania, but such moments were rare. There were only a few prisoners in the Peter and Paul Fortress whose spirits remained unbroken. Their lightheartedness, therefore, puzzled the guards and the prison officers, and the authorities were even more puzzled.

It is not difficult to explain their attitude. When the Decembrists themselves looked back on the uprising, they were perfectly aware that they had set in motion a chain of events which could only end with the overthrow of the Tsar, or their own downfall. They had entered upon the conspiracy with their eyes open; they had long ago counted the cost. They believed—wrongly—that it was only a question of time, a very short time, when the autocracy would give place to a liberal government, and the Age of Enlightenment would descend upon Russia. They regarded themselves as the representatives of the new age which would inevitably supplant an age of barbarism. They saw themselves as the instruments of change, and nothing more. They did not want to become officials in the new government; they were happy to bring about the end of a tyranny; they asked nothing for themselves.

When on July 9, 1826, the prisoners were summoned to an office in the Fortress to hear the verdict, they behaved in a manner which the Tsar found inexplicable. Many were smiling and laughing, and there were few who showed a proper respect for the solemnity of the occasion. Three tables, covered with red baize cloth, were arranged in the form of a U. On one side sat the judges, while the prisoners stood in the hollow formed by the tables. The judges included the four Metropolitans who for religious reasons had refused to sign the death sentences, and they wore their ceremonial costumes with diamond crosses on their snow-white hoods. The military officials were in full regalia, with the broad and heavy epaulettes customary at the time. The windows were closed, but the suffocating heat of the July sun filled the room. There was a glittering display of medals, sashes and brilliantly colored vestments, all the accouterments of power. The prisoners who wore the clothes they had been arrested in, or drab prison garb, looked like dirty interlopers at a wedding feast.

The prisoners were brought in by categories. It was expected that some would faint or suffer convulsions when the verdicts were read to them, and the Tsar had accordingly ordered a doctor and nurses to be located in a nearby room. They were never needed.

When the five ringleaders were brought in, they displayed such a happy and childish delight in each other's company that they missed the opening words of the verdict which was read to them by a young officer standing at a lectern. Only Kakhovsky, weighed down by the knowledge of the Tsar's treachery and by many sleepless nights, seemed ill at ease.

The young officer, reading the verdict in the name of the Tsar and the assembled judges, had been chosen for his powers of elocution, his pleasant manner, and the precise, almost mathematical way of displaying his disinterest in the proceedings. He resembled one of those automata which played chess games with Peter the Great, and the amused Decembrists found themselves wondering whether he was human.

"These five," said the automaton, "surpass all the rest in their evil intent, their ferocious malice, their savage tenacity of purpose and their cold-blooded readiness to commit regicide. The court has sentenced them to capital punishment by quartering."

The prisoners showed no emotion except puzzlement and a kind of childish relief. They moved closer together. There was a long pause, and then the automaton continued:

"In accordance with His Majesty's most merciful command, the decision mitigating this sentence is as follows: Pavel Pestel, Kondraty Ryleyev, Sergey Muraviev-Apostol, Mikhail Bestuzhev-Riumin and Pyotr Kakhovsky are sentenced to death by hanging."

The prisoners showed no more emotion than before. They were calm and self-possessed, and it was observed that Ryleyev gazed, not at the judges but at a picture on the wall. They were still outwardly unmoved when they were led back to their cells.

Then it was the turn of the second category, and to the surprise of the judges they showed no more emotion than the famous ringleaders. They embraced one another and whispered throughout the recital of their crimes. Only half-listening to the automaton, who seemed to be discussing crimes committed by other people in another age. They were sentenced to be beheaded. Some moments later they learned that the Tsar in his infinite mercy had commuted the punishment to penal servitude for life. When the automaton had completed listing their names, the young Nikolay Bestuzhev shouted defiantly: "What are the legal grounds for the verdict? We have not yet been committed to trial." The judges hissed in astonishment, and the guards quickly hustled the prisoners back to their cells.

They were on their way to their cells when an incident occurred which demonstrated the curiously carefree and adolescent attitude of the conspirators to the verdict. Mikhail Lunin, who had heard that he would be beheaded and then that he would be sentenced to penal servitude for life, shouted jubilantly to his companions: "*Messieurs, ce jugement mérite d'être arrosé!"* and then went to the wall and proceeded to carry out his own summary judgment on the verdict.

Many of the prisoners thought the sentences would not be carried out. Even the saintly Father Pyotr Myslovsky, the dean of the Cathedral of Kazan, who comforted them in their cells, believed there would be a last-minute pardon, and he would whisper to his charges that they should take heart, for the mercy of the Tsar, like God's, was illimitable. Long after it had become generally known that the Tsar would exact the last ounce of guilt and expiation from his victims, Father Myslovsky was still reassuring them. Of the ringleaders only Kakhovsky seems to have known from the beginning that there was no hope, and in the last days he became dour and bitter, nursing his grievances, convinced that he had been betrayed, and so despondent that he looked out on the world with the air of a man who is already dead to the world, beyond hope, as silent as the grave. On the rare occasions when he saw his companions in the corridor he looked away. He remained faithful to himself to the end, a lonely man taking refuge in his own loneliness, his only consolation being a copy of the *Divine Comedy*, which he read with difficulty, for though he had traveled in Italy he knew only a little Italian.

As might be expected, Ryleyev also remained faithful to himself in his own way, having more resources than Kakhovsky. Sometimes fear gripped him and he would shake convulsively, but these moments would soon pass and he was calm again. What sustained him was his affection for his wife Natasha and the knowledge that his poetry would outlive him. Pestel, a Protestant, was visited both by Father Myslovsky and by Pastor Reinbot, to whom he addressed a sermon on the advantages of the English parliamentary system, and sometimes they would engage in futile discussions on the nature of God; and the more Pestel saw of the pastor, the less he believed in God's mercy. He, too, was sustained by a deep affection for a woman—his sister Sophia. Mikhail Bestuzhev-Riumin sometimes fell into long fits of weeping, but afterward he became strangely serene, and he would read the Bible or listen while it was read to him with a look of intense excitement. He had grown very thin during his months of imprisonment, and the freckles stood out on his pale face. Sergey Muraviev-Apostol was perhaps the least affected by the knowledge that he would soon die, and during the last days he usually found some way to be close to Bestuzhev-Riumin, the youngest of the ringleaders and the one therefore who might be expected to show the greatest fear.

Fear, indeed, was exactly what the Tsar wanted to encourage among the prisoners. It was not enough that they should receive the punishment they deserved; they must come to know his dreadful powers. He sought eagerly for signs of contrition, and exacted from his prisoners the full weight of their shame. He spent his hours brooding over reports from the prison governor, and to the very last moment he was giving orders on how the prisoners should be punished. Finally he devised the ceremonies of degradation and death.

He had come to the conclusion that the early morning hours of July 13 were the proper time for the execution, for on the following day, exactly eight months since the uprising in the Senate Square, he intended to celebrate a solemn service of thanksgiving. The Metropolitan would sprinkle holy water on the cobblestones, hymns would be sung, and the city would be cleansed of its crimes.

The official ceremony of degradation had been worked out in great detail. In the darkness all the prisoners except the five condemned to death would be taken under an escort of guards to a place where they would be compelled to perform the final act of submission and symbolic annihilation which the Tsar regarded perhaps as even more important than the punishment. The military officers would be herded into a field where they would confront detachments from their own regiments; they would kneel, an officer would recite their crimes, swords would be broken over their heads, their insignia of rank and then their uniforms would be torn from them and hurled into the fire, and then they would be given the striped garb of convicts. At the same time the naval officers who had taken part in the uprising would be led out of their cells and brought to the island fortress of Kronstadt, which guarded the approaches to St. Petersburg. On the flagship *Prince Vladimir,* no longer flying the double-headed eagle but with a black flag at the masthead, they too would have swords broken over their heads as they knelt and their uniforms would be stripped off them and thrown into the sea. Fire and water, *ignis et aqua,* the old weapons of the Romans, would be employed to reduce their lives to insignificance. The Tsar believed that in this way he would bring home to the culprits the full ignominy of their punishment in the destruction of all their rights and the loss of all their hopes. They would become living corpses, separated forever from the world of men.

But if the Tsar expected to provide a spectacle of moral suffering and repentance with the condemned men stricken with shame and remorse, he failed to take the character of his young officers into account. Just as he thought they would faint or go out of their minds when they heard the verdict, and provided doctors and nurses to restore them to a full awareness of their errors, so now he arranged that a field ambulance should be in attendance on the parade ground where they would suffer the indignities which his fruitful imagination and relentless will had prepared for them. Some would scream for mercy; others would have to be cupped and bled by the barber attached to the ambulance; still others would need restoratives. The ambulance was an expression of his pity for them in their last extremities, but there were few other expressions of pity. A few days before the ceremony he wrote: "Since the prisoners are assassins, their punishment must take the form of an impressive warning to others. Nothing we do can be too grim for them."

Although the Tsar was later informed that everything had happened as he desired it to happen and that the prisoners showed an exemplary contrition, this was not the case. The carefully constructed timetable was abandoned, the high officials in charge of the ceremonies blundered and lost their heads, and none of the prisoners demonstrated any signs of contrition. The second group of prisoners were taken from their cells to the square outside the Mint at about two o'clock in the morning, and then there began the first of those inexplicable delays which were to continue until sunrise. For about half an hour they stood about the square, talking to one another, laughing and joking. They were relieved to be in the open after having been confined for so long. They thought the five condemned men would be led out and they would be forced to watch the execution. Meanwhile they formed small groups and embraced one another, behaving as though they were free men. They were then marched off through the deserted streets of the Fortress to the Petrovsky gate and escorted to the glacis of the Kronwerk curtain where they could see the scaffold, which was still being erected. At about the same time the naval officers were being huddled into two barges which would take them to Kronstadt.

The glacis had only recently been converted into a parade ground, and still looked very much what it had been in the past, a dumping ground for all the filth on the island. Heaps of refuse lay about, and even at night, in the light of bonfires, this strip of land looked empty and useless. Troops formed a semicircle around the prisoners, and one by one the prisoners were compelled to kneel, while a sword which had been partly filed through beforehand, was solemnly broken over their heads, and then their epaulettes, their decorations, and their uniforms were stripped from them and thrown into the bonfires. The Tsar ordered that the ceremony should take place in an atmosphere of grave solemnity, but the prisoners were still too busy greeting one another to pay much attention to the ceremony. General Chernyshev and Governor General Golenishchev-Kutuzov rode around the parade ground giving orders, but no one seemed to be paying much attention to them. Benckendorf, the Tsar's Chief of Police, was also present, and it was observed that this kindly man had no taste for the ceremony, said nothing, and seemed to have withdrawn into himself. General Chernyshev's saddle kept slipping and he was continually in danger of falling to the ground.

The sound of shrill commands and countercommands, the reading of the sentences, the snapping of swords, the muffled drums of the Pavlovsky Guards, and the hammering from the distant scaffold were drowned by the voices of the prisoners, who gave the impression of people attending a festive occasion. Few of them saw the scaffold. In any case the cross-beam was missing, for the cart bringing the beam had broken down, and it did not yet resemble a scaffold. The guards ordered to break the swords cleanly over the prisoners' heads sometimes indulged in brutal horseplay and more than one prisoner was thrown to the ground with a gashed head. Then the field ambulance was summoned, and they would be roughly bandaged. In the shadows a small, well-protected group of foreign diplomats, recently arrived to attend the Tsar's coronation, looked on in silence.

At about half past three the ceremony of degradation was completed and the prisoners were issued the striped convict garments, which resembled dressing gowns, and hustled back to their cells. Time was running out, and the officials were showing an increasing nervousness. The distribution of the dressing gowns was done so hurriedly that no effort was made to sort them out; and tall men received dressing gowns which reached only to their knees, short men found themselves enveloped in their long robes, and some were marched off in their underwear. The ceremony had been performed without dignity because for quite incomprehensible reasons the officials had been unable to adhere to the timetable. The Tsar had given the strongest orders that the five condemned men should be executed at three o'clock in the morning, and it was now nearly four o'clock.

Strange things had happened, and stranger things were to happen before the night was over.

During the night the five ringleaders were taken to small cells within the Kronwerk curtain. In these small wooden cells in a vaulted corridor they were permitted to write letters, confess to their priests, and receive their relatives for the last time. Only Sergey Muraviev-Apostol availed himself of this permission, and was allowed to see his sister. She had promised not to break down, but all her promises were forgotten when she entered the cell, and the few minutes he spent with her were devoted to exhorting her to face the inevitable courageously. She fainted away, and had to be carried to the waiting carriage in the arms of the guards.

At intervals during the night the young Mikhail Bestuzhev-Riumin could be heard whimpering, and now Muraviev-Apostol was free to turn his attention to his friend, whom he regarded as a younger brother. There were cracks in the wooden partitions, and he began to talk softly and earnestly about the need to die with great dignity. The whimpering came to an end, and then for a while quietness descended on the cells. Soon Father Myslovsky and Pastor Reinbot came to offer them the consolations

of religion. They knew that the time of the execution was approaching.
Ryleyev sat down and wrote a letter to his wife, commending her and his
daughter Natasha to God, and begging her not to lose courage. The last
words were: "Farewell, I have been ordered to dress." Having comforted
his wife he turned to confront Father Myslovsky, who was visibly pale
and drawn. He took the Father's hand and laid it over his own heart, saying: "Can you hear it? It beats calmly."

They dressed quickly, wearing the new shirts that had been sent to them
by their families and the clothes they were arrested in; and then because
the Tsar still feared they might escape at the last minute, they were hobbled with specially heavy irons. By mistake they were given irons intended for the prisoners who would soon be leaving for Siberia, for the
padlocks were incribed by the locksmiths with messages like "Forget me
not." As they were led out of the Kronwerk curtain by a detachment of
Pavlovsky Guards, all of them were subdued except Ryleyev, who shouted
out in a clear voice which could be heard by some of the prisoners who
had returned from the degrading ceremony on the parade ground: "Farewell, brothers, and forgive me!"

They were not marched straight to the scaffold, but instead were taken
to the dimly lit fortress chapel where a priest in funeral vestments read
over them, with all the proper solemnity, the service of the dead. This, too,
was ordered by the Tsar, who sent his own doctors to watch over them in
case they fainted. The service of the dead left them in better spirits than
before, and as they marched slowly with hobbled feet to the glacis, where
the scaffold was standing and the crossbeam was at last in place, they
walked with deliberate dignity, and they did not flinch at the sight of the
scaffold. When Pestel saw the scaffold, he turned to Father Myslovsky
and said: "They should have given us a better death. It would be much
better if they shot us." Later Father Myslovsky would say of him: "None
showed greater courage. He seemed to me to be ready to bear the weight
of two Alpine peaks on his shoulders."

But if Pestel and the other condemned men were ready, General
Chernyshev and the Governor General Golenishchev-Kutuzov were not.
They were having trouble with the scaffold. Everything had been done
according to rule; the deep pit was dug; beams of the proper size and
width were assembled; ropes of the proper length had been provided from
the military stores; and there was a suitable arrangement for removing
the planks over the pit by pulling on a ring-bar beside the platform. But
no one had taken any precautions against the rain, with the result that
the ropes had shrunk and the grease which was being rubbed into the
rope by the hangman was coming off in his hands. General Chernyshev
was almost beside himself with fury, for he had promised the Tsar that

he would keep strictly to the timetable. He was shouting to his officers and to the hangman, a burly middle-aged snub-nosed Finn, who knew no Russian. There was no time to fetch longer ropes. It was decided to borrow a bench from somewhere and make the prisoners stand on it. There was some discussion about where a bench could be found, and finally they borrowed one from a nearby schoolhouse.

While these discussions were going on, the condemned men were being dressed in white shrouds which reached to the ground, with black cords at the neck, waist and ankles. Their hands were pinioned behind their backs and white hoods were placed over their heads. On their chests were squares of black leather bearing their names and the words: "Criminal, Tsaricide," though they had not in fact killed the Tsar. The fastening of these inscriptions took some time, and afterward it was discovered that Ryleyev and Kakhovsky had each received the other's leather square. General Chernyshev ordered them to be changed.

There was still much to be done to insure a prompt and speedy execution, and it was thought that the condemned might usefully spend their last moments listening to music while being paraded down the line of Pavlovsky Guards. Accordingly the band was ordered to strike up, and the five men bundled in their drab white swaddling bands walked with calculated dignity along the line, as though they were inspecting the parade. They looked grotesque with their white hoods perched on top of their heads, but Father Myslovsky was overcome by their courage. "Why do they do this to us, when they know we have not been frightened by bullets or cannonballs?" Pestel asked; and it was the absurdity and hollowness of the spectacle that oppressed him.

By this time it was about half past four and the scaffold was still not ready. The prisoners were told to sit down on the grass and wait. By twisting their bodies they were able to shake each others' hands in a last farewell. They spoke quietly and simply, like people resting during the intermission of a disturbing play. Kakhovsky was sunk in his own nightmares, and he lay down in the grass a little apart from them.

At last General Chernyshev was quite sure that no further hitch would delay the proceedings, and he gave orders that the hanging should be carried out. Father Myslovsky, who had been watching over his charges, made a sign of protest, but the guards pushed past him, and the prisoners were taken half-stumbling to the platform and then hoisted onto the benches, the Finnish executioner jumping up behind them. Cloth sacks reaching down to their waists were pulled over their heads and the hangman carefully arranged the nooses which were thickly coated with yellow grease. Then, seeing that everything was in order, he jumped off the platform, pulled the ring-bar which released the planks and the benches, and looked up to see the condemned men twirling satisfactorily on the short ropes. Father Myslovsky made a sweeping movement with his hand, and hoping they could still hear him, he cried out in a loud voice: "I absolve and I bless!" Then he fainted. A moment later General Chernyshev saw something that terrified him more than anything had ever terrified him in his life. Three of the bodies had vanished, and three empty nooses were hanging from the crossbeam.

Because the ropes were wet and the nooses did not tighten properly, their heads had slipped free and they had fallen with the planks and benches to the bottom of the pit. Bruised and bleeding, but still conscious, Ryleyev, Muraviev-Apostol and Kakhovsky, were lying huddled together, helping one another. The cloth sacks had fallen from their heads. Ryleyev's face was streaming with blood from a wound in his forehead and another over his ear, where he had struck a bench. One of the officers present, a man called Steingel, said later that he distinctly heard Muraviev-Apostol saying: "My God, in Russia they do not even know how to hang properly."

There was consternation among the high officials who had hoped that their long ordeal would be over before sunrise. The sun was now coming up, and it was necessary to act quickly. The Governor General Golenishchev-Kutuzov rode up and shouted: "Hang them! Hang them again more quickly!" It was easier said than done.

For about a quarter of an hour the officials shouted and wrangled among themselves. Someone, probably a soldier of the Pavlovsky Guards, shouted that it was against the law to hang people twice. The band was ordered to play, so that the soldiers would have something to occupy their thoughts, and now dance music floated over the parade ground which was turning gold in the sun.

The three men who had fallen into the pit were lifted up and laid on the grass slope below the ramparts, while the doctors from the field hospital cleaned up the wounds. They were still bundled up in their coarse white cerements, now bloodstained, with their hands pinioned behind their backs. They lay there quietly, sometimes talking to one another. Ryleyev is said to have shouted to General Chernyshev: "Give the hangman your epaulettes! They are stronger than the ropes!" and to have cursed the Governor General repeatedly, and to his face, as he peered down and gazed through his lorgnettes at his three remaining prisoners. Pestel and Bestuzhev-Riumin were dead, but they were not cut down. No one seems to have thought of using the ropes which had already proved effective.

Benckendorf, disgusted by the spectacle and perhaps unnerved by it, lay flat on his horse's neck with his face buried in the mane. It was said that until the last minute he had hoped for a reprieve, and up to the moment of the hanging he had been looking in the direction where the Tsar's messenger might be expected to enter the parade ground.

At last new rope was obtained, and the two priests accompanied the men to the scaffold, murmuring prayers. This time the hanging was successful, and they died quickly. There remained the problem of disposing of the bodies. A public burial was unthinkable. An official report spoke of the "hundreds of thousands" who would have gathered by the graveside. It was decided to bury them at night in the utmost secrecy on Golodai Island, the northern part of Vasilyevsky Island, and accordingly at midnight a cutter left the Peter and Paul Fortress and made its way along the Golodai Canal until it reached some wasteland near the Smolensk Cemetery and near a guardhouse. Though the grave was believed to be secret, flowers were found on it the next day. For many days people congregated at the graveside, until some agents of the Tsar spread the rumor that the bodies had been thrown into the moat of the Peter and Paul Fortress. Then people came to gaze at the moat, carrying flowers in their hands.

Shortly after the execution a messenger was dispatched to the Tsar, who had spent the night at his palace in Tsarskoye Selo, outside St. Petersburg. He had slept fitfully, for all night, at half-hour intervals, couriers had been arriving with reports from the Peter and Paul Fortress. Pushkin, who moved in court circles during the later years of his life, says he heard from one of the Tsarina's ladies in waiting that the Tsar awoke early and went for a walk in the park accompanied by his Irish retriever. He looked morose and preoccupied. Having nothing better to do, he went down to the lake, and kept throwing his handkerchief in, ordering the retriever to fetch it. He was still playing with the handkerchief when a footman brought him the news that another courier had arrived from the Fortress. Without a word the Tsar strode back to the palace.

The message brought by the courier was signed by the Governor General Golenishchev-Kutuzov. It was quite brief, and read:

> The executions were carried out with proper order and tranquillity both on the part of the troops and of the spectators, who were few. Owing to the inexperience of our hangmen and their lack of skill in constructing the scaffold, at the first attempt three men, Ryleyev, Kakhovsky and Muraviev fell down, but they were soon hanged again and thus received the death they deserved, of which I hereby inform Your Majesty with loyal obedience.

About the same time a message came from General Ivan Dibich, testifying on behalf of the army that the troops had behaved magnificently while the villains behaved villainously; the phrase must have pleased the Tsar, for he repeated it in a letter which he wrote later in the day to his mother, the widow of the murdered Paul:

I am writing, dearest Mother, just these few words in a hurried hand, wishing you to know that everything happened quietly and in good order. The villains behaved villainously, without dignity. This evening Chernyshev will be coming to you, and as an eyewitness he will be able to tell you what happened in greater detail. Excuse this short account, dearest Mother, but knowing and sharing your anxiety, I wanted you to be informed concerning matters known to me.

The Tsar spent the day writing letters and praying in the church, alone with his own thoughts. To please him, the generals who had been present on the parade ground sent him completely fictitious accounts of the acts of contrition and repentance performed by the condemned men in their last moments. They had all accepted their punishment meekly, and their last words were in praise of the Tsar. Even Kakhovsky, the most deserving of punishment, had begged for the Tsar's forgiveness.

For the Tsar it was a pleasing and satisfactory end to a troublesome business.

THE SHINING KNIFE

As the Tsar had foreseen, the execution of the five revolutionaries sent a shudder through Russia. He had acted forcefully and shown that he was master in his own house. Very soon the rest of the conspirators would be sent out on their long journeys to the lonely prisons of Siberia and nothing more would ever be heard of them. The uprising would be a distant memory, and no one now would dare to raise his hand against the autocracy. His government of the empire would continue "with proper order and tranquillity."

As his generals well knew, these were among his favorite words, and he liked to regard the empire as a kind of chessboard where the moves took place in silence and in an orderly, logical fashion. It was, he believed, a very simple matter to rule an empire, provided the people were obedient, did not ask questions, were never informed concerning matters of state, and showed respect for the autocracy. The crime had been committed, the guilty had been punished, and it was now necessary to perform the solemn act of purification which would lay the ghosts of treachery. When he returned to St. Petersburg that evening, it was observed that he was in good humor and smiled easily.

On the next day the thanksgiving service passed off without incident. The church bells pealed, and a portable chapel erected near the monument of Peter the Great was filled with members of the imperial family and dignitaries of state, who knelt as the Metropolitan Serafim read a special litany composed for the occasion, calling upon the faithful to offer prayers to the Saviour, "who vouchsafed to protect and deliver us from seditious tumults aimed at the overthrow of the Orthodox Church, the Throne, and the ruin of the Russian Empire." Afterward, with the Tsar accompanying him on horseback, the Metropolitan in his golden robes moved among the soldiers on guard and sprinkled them with holy water, blessing them and also blessing the Square where all the horrors had taken place. As Count Loebzeltern, the Austrian ambassador in whose house Prince Troubetskoy had taken refuge, observed in a letter to the Austrian court, "the solemnity of the ceremony made a profound impression on the people and its effect was not lost on the upper classes."

That evening the Tsar performed an act of reconciliation by accepting an invitation from the Horse Guards regiment, which had in the past included a number of conspirators. They proposed to entertain him with a feast and a firework display in the park on Yelagin Island, one of a cluster of islands at the mouth of the Neva. It was explained to him that the fireworks would symbolize the brilliance of his reign. He accepted the offer gracefully and he was in good spirits throughout the entertainment. He had put the five hanged men out of his mind. He did not know and could not have guessed that he would be haunted by them for the rest of his long reign.

All over Russia men were haunted by the hanged men. The Decembrist uprising became a legend, all the more powerful and compelling because the government forbade any public reference to it except in tones of stern disapproval. It had entered men's dreams and quickened their hopes, stirred their imaginations and shocked them into a new awareness of the arbitrary cruelties of the autocracy. As Pestel had observed, even if the uprising was put down, it would still be a victory.

Among those who were deeply haunted by the uprising was the poet Alexander Pushkin, then twenty-five and living in exile under police surveillance on the family estate at Mikhailovskoye, far from the capital, for having written poems against the autocracy. Alexander I had especially disliked Pushkin's ode "Freedom" which contained the lines:

> Tremble, O tyrants of the world,
> And you, O fallen slaves, arise!

There were many other poems by Pushkin which had incurred the displeasure of the authorities. Although he was not implicated in the conspiracy, there were some who regarded him as one of the prime movers, for his poems were often incitements to rebellion. Moreover he was on intimate terms with many of the revolutionaries. He was a close friend of Wilhelm Kuchelbecker, and knew Ryleyev well; he had maintained a long correspondence with Alexander Bestuzhev; all together there were at least twenty of the Decembrists in his circle of friends. Yet for all his revolutionary connections he had never been admitted into the inner circle of the conspirators, who distrusted him precisely because he was a poet with a poet's failings. He was not the kind of man who could keep a secret, he was incautious, and he rejoiced in grand gestures. It was generally agreed that he would make a bad revolutionary.

News of the uprising reached Mikhailovskoye in slow stages and was often distorted. More than a week passed before Pushkin had any real conception of what had happened, and it was a month before he could bring himself to write to Vasily Zhukovsky, the poet, who was one of the most assiduous courtiers of the new Tsar and therefore in a position to extend his friendly influence. Pushkin felt rightly that the government knew about his connections with the revolutionaries. "I see in the newspapers that the government intends to punish all those who had information about the conspirators and did not reveal it to the police," he wrote. "But who except for the police and the government did not know about it? People talked about the conspiracy at every street corner, and that is one of the reasons why I am innocent. Nevertheless I am still being watched by the police: it may easily be proved that I held discussions with one or another of the accused, and it is true that many of them were my friends." Zhukovsky showed little sympathy for Pushkin. "You were not implicated in the conspiracy—that is perfectly true," he wrote back. "But your poems were to be found among the books of the conspirators. A poor way to reconcile yourself with the government." He advised Pushkin to remain in the country, to live very quietly, and to attract no attention to himself: it would be madness for him to come to St. Petersburg.

In his anxiety over the fate of his friends Pushkin sent letter after letter to important personages, hoping to learn exactly who had been arrested. His world was falling round him. He wrote well during those months of anxiety, for fear and terror proved to be a spur to poetry, but when he heard that five men had been executed and over a hundred were being sent to Siberia, he was seized with a sense of fury and shame. He drew pictures of scaffolds on his manuscripts, constantly wrote down the initials of the condemned men, and portrayed them hanging at the ends of long ropes. Sometimes he drew them in detail wearing their white shrouds

with their hands pinioned behind their backs, but more often he drew them in thin silhouettes as though he were seeing them from a great distance. While writing the fifth chapter of *Evgeny Onegin*, full of the terrors of winter and presentiments of disaster, he drew the faces of Pestel, Ryleyev, Pushchin and Kuchelbecker on the side of the manuscript so that they crowd the page and spill over into the verses. More portraits of the conspirators appear again in his sketches for a projected tenth chapter of *Evgeny Onegin*, which he never completed. Once again there is the familiar picture of the gallows set on the ramparts. Long-nosed Kuchelbecker is seen beside Bestuzhev-Riumin with the profile of a Roman centurion. All together on a single page there are fourteen recognizable portraits of revolutionaries he had known. The gallows are repeated twice, and so too are the words: *I ya by mog* . . . ("I, too, might have been . . .") Pushkin had intended to visit St. Petersburg secretly during the week when the uprising broke out. He knew only too well that he had escaped arrest only by a series of miracles.

Not long after the execution of the five men he wrote the poem generally regarded as the greatest single verse he ever composed. These lines, written with a fierce and unrelenting passion, were to echo through the remaining years of nineteenth-century Russia like an invitation to revolution. Guilt, terror, shame, and the knowledge of imminent upheaval were strangely commingled in this verse, which should be quoted in full because it conveys the temper of Pushkin's mind at a moment when he seemed to be in possession of prophetic powers:

THE PROPHET

Through the dark desert I came,
With spiritual thirst aflame:
At the crossing of the ways
I saw the six-winged Seraph blaze.
He laid soft fingers on my eyes,
Sweeter than a slumber is:
Like a raging eagle shaken
My prophetic eyes awaken,
And my roaring ears are drowned
In tumult and a thunderous sound,
As though convulsive Heaven had bred
A host of angels in my head,
And green sap rising in each tree,
And monsters creeping in the sea.
Then from my mouth the Seraph wrung
From its nest my sinful tongue,
And took away my idle thoughts
And plucked the evil by the roots.
His hand was dabbled in his blood.

On my decaying lips he laid
The wisdom of a serpent, then
He forced his bloodstained hand within
My yawning flesh to pluck away
My heart, and then he pressed
Live coals of fire upon my breast.
In the dark desert as I lay
Lifeless, God's own voice did say:
"Arise, O Prophet, sing your song,
Give utterance to my fulfilled tongue.
In every land proclaim my Plan—
Lay waste with fire the heart of man!"

Three more stanzas were written, and Pushkin seems to have destroyed them either because they were too dangerous or because he could not pursue the vision with any assurance. Yet he knew very well in what disguise the Prophet would appear among men. He would come in the white vestments worn by the hanged men, and with a rope round his neck, and he would wreak vengeance on the Tsar. Only four lines from the remaining stanzas have survived. They read:

Arise, arise, O Russia's Prophet!
In thy dishonored vestments come,
And with a rope around thy neck
Bring destruction on the Tsar!

Pushkin spent the summer in inner turmoil, though outwardly carefree. Police spies prowled around the estate, and followed him on his occasional journeys. "I learned," wrote the police spy Boshnyak, "that Pushkin appeared at the fair at the Monastery of the Holy Mountain wearing a Russian blouse tied at the waist with a pink sash, a straw hat on his head, and an iron-tipped cane in his hand. They say he is very quiet and prudent, and never talks about the government." He knew he was being watched and was not particularly surprised when on the evening of September 3 a police officer came from Pskov to arrest him. He had just time to sweep some papers from the table into the fire when the officer came into the room. Five days later he was being led into the presence of the Tsar in the Kremlin in Moscow.

Exactly what transpired during that long and painful interview is unknown, for the account that has come down to us has been made up from many different sources written over a long period of time. According to General Dibich, the chief of the general staff, who heard the story from the Tsar, Pushkin was asked where he would have been if he had reached St. Petersburg in time for the December uprising. He answered: "I would have been in the ranks of the rebels." The answer seems to have pleased the Tsar, who liked straight answers.

"Well, have you decided to change your ideas?" the Tsar asked. "Give me your word of honor that you will behave properly if I give you your freedom."

Pushkin gave his word of honor. The Tsar smiled and said: "You have done enough mischief. I hope you will be sensible from now on. There is no reason why there should be any quarrel between us. Send me everything you write. From now on I shall be your censor."

A moment later Pushkin was being led into an adjoining room full of courtiers in uniform. In a loud voice the Tsar said: "Gentlemen, here is the new Pushkin. You may forget the old one."

If the Tsar thought that Pushkin had been converted into an obedient tool of the autocracy, he was mistaken. Pushkin's love of freedom survived the interview with the Tsar, and he continued to write in secret verses in favor of the Decembrists. To the end of his short life he felt a sense of guilt for not having taken part in the battle in the Senate Square.

The Tsar hoped that the Decembrist uprising would fade from the pages of history, but instead it remained vividly alive in the imaginations of the people. Sometimes indeed it escaped from history altogether, to enter the more dangerous realm of legend. Generations of revolutionaries would look back upon the Decembrists with veneration as the first martyrs of the revolutionary faith. They dreamed of revenge: the Tsar toppled from his throne, his courtiers fled, all the panoply of the autocracy tossed aside. The young especially identified themselves with the Decembrists. The poet Mikhail Lermontov was eleven years old when the uprising took place, and he was only sixteen when he wrote a darkly prophetic poem about the coming of an avenger:

> A year will come—for Russia, a black year—
> When the crown so many Tsars have worn, will fall;
> The mob will lose the love it had for them,
> And multitudes will feed on blood and death.
> The law, thrown over, will no longer shield
> The little children and the chaste young wives;
> And Plague from stinking bodies of the dead
> Will roam the streets of mourning villages,
> And silently call victims from their homes;
> And Hunger's teeth will tear at this poor land;
> And reddening skies will make the rivers red.
>
> On that day will appear a powerful man.
> And you will know him, and will understand
> Why in his grasp he holds a shining knife.
> And woe to you! Your weeping and your groans
> Will only make him laugh. And everything
> About him will be frightening and dark,
> Like his black cloak, beneath his towering brow.

PETRASHEVSKY

*Restore the image of man in all its splendor . . . Tear
down the cities and the towns, and use the bricks for
building new cities and towns. Let the shame and grief
and beggary and misery all vanish, and be utterly transformed into perfect joy and riches and harmony.*

—DMITRY AKHSHARUMOV

THE DREAMERS

WITH THE DECEMBRIST UPRISING a revolutionary age had been ushered in, and henceforward there would be no turning back. Although the autocracy was to survive for another ninety-two years, it was
already doomed.

While the surviving Decembrists continued to live in the forgotten
wastes of Siberia, a new revolutionary generation arose. Not all of these
revolutionaries were men of action. Some were philosophers, poets, jour-
nalists, dreamers, authors of manifestoes, ponderers of violence, engineers
of fantasies. There were some who took part in no conspiracies, fought no
revolutionary battles, and if they were arrested and imprisoned, it was not
for any crimes they had committed, but because chance had decreed that
they should earn the displeasure of the police. Sometimes they were the
most dangerous.

There were some, too, without any conspiratorial gifts, who were so determined to bring about the downfall of the autocracy that they dedicated
their lives to a desperate battle of wits, attempting to destroy the state by
the power of their ideas. They were not dreamers, for they had calculated
precisely where the autocracy was vulnerable. They shot out ideas like
cannonballs. Usually they lived abroad, and the cannonballs took the

71

form of illegal pamphlets and newspapers smuggled into Russia under the eyes of the frontier police. In this way for nearly half a century Alexander Herzen, the illegitimate son of Ivan Yakovlev, a wealthy nobleman, attacked the Tsar with a succession of newssheets which were brilliantly designed to goad him and reduce him to imbecile fury. The quiet, well-mannered man in a frock coat was the greatest propagandist of them all. Lenin, who admired him this side of idolatry, described him as "one of those who were most responsible for paving the way to the revolution."

As a boy of fourteen living in Moscow, Herzen was present on the day a Mass of Thanksgiving was sung in honor of the Tsar's victory over the five leaders of the Decembrist uprising. "In the midst of the Kremlin," he wrote thirty years later in *The Pole Star,* "the Metropolitan Philaret thanked God for the murders. The entire royal family was present at the service, the senators and ministers nearby, and in the immense space the close-packed Guards knelt bareheaded and joined in the prayers. Never have the gallows been celebrated with such pomp, as the cannon thundered from the heights of the Kremlin . . . On this spot and before the altar profaned by a bloody prayer, I swore to avenge the victims and dedicated myself to the struggle against that throne, that altar, and those cannon." With his lifelong friend Nikolay Ogaryev he went out into the Sparrow Hills overlooking Moscow and together they solemnly dedicated the history of their lives to the destruction of the enemy. Their newssheet

25 Іюля 1826года.

The Pole Star commemorated a periodical started by the Decembrists themselves. On the cover there was a drawing of the heads of the five men condemned to death. Below there was the date of their execution, 25 July 1826, and an ax, the symbol of vengeance.

Wealthy, immoral, scrupulous in his relations with men, and completely unscrupulous in his relations with women, Herzen left Russia on the eve of the French revolution of 1848 and spent the rest of his days wandering through Europe, usually accompanied by a flock of legitimate and illegitimate children, living the life of the *gentilhomme russe citoyen du monde,* restless always, never striking any deep roots. He wrote angelically—his autobiography *My Past and Thoughts* must be counted among the supreme achievements of nineteenth-century Russian literature—and his interminable correspondence, much of which has survived, remains the ultimate source for many of the strange divagations of the Russian revolutionary movement.

Herzen wrote with power and audacity, for he was a master of language and a vigorous hater. Violence is never far below the surface. In his introduction to *From the Other Shore,* a study of the failure of the French revolution of 1848, he wrote:

> Do not look for solutions in this book—you will not find them. In general modern man has no solutions. What is solved is finished, and the coming upheaval is only in its infancy.
>
> We do not build, we destroy; we do not proclaim a new revelation, we eliminate the old falsehoods. Modern man, that unhappy *Pontifex Maximus,* only builds a bridge—it will be for some unknown stranger in the future to pass over it. You perhaps will see it. Do not, I beg you, remain behind *on this shore.* Better perish with the revolution than seek refuge in the almshouse of reaction.

Though Herzen suffered no more than a few days of imprisonment in his youth, and he had little understanding of the mind of the active revolutionary who pits his strength against the Tsarist police, he remained throughout his life the convinced revolutionary. His motto was the cry of the eighteenth century rebel leader Emelyan Pugachev: "I am not yet the real crow, but only a small one; the real one is still flying in the sky." At the masthead of *Kolokol* (The Bell), the newssheet which he published in London and Geneva with the help of Ogaryev, he wrote: *Vivos voco!* ("I call to the living!") But the bell was tolling for the death of the Tsar.

While Herzen fought with a deliberate purpose and a well-planned strategy from abroad, there were others who fought from inside Russia like sleepwalkers armed with revolvers, with staring eyes and uncertain aim. They formed grandiose plans and involved their friends in grave dangers. When the trap was sprung, all perished.

Mikhail Vasilyevich Petrashevsky was one of those brilliant and eccentric revolutionaries who rejoiced in revolution for its own sake, delighting in all forms of conspiratorial activity. He even dressed like a stage conspirator, in a Spanish cape and a dark broad-brimmed hat. He was a heavy-set man with a thick curly beard which concealed most of the lower half of his face, small melancholy eyes, a high rounded forehead, an air of mournful detachment. He gave his name to a revolutionary movement, but appeared to be curiously unfitted for the role he was called upon to play. He was known to be a landowner with considerable wealth—he owned a number of villages—but in St. Petersburg, where he worked as a clerk in the Foreign Ministry, he chose to live in happy squalor. There was something disarming as well as menacing about him, and perhaps he resembled most of all an unruly, destructive child.

Even in childhood he showed a passion for eccentricity, tormenting his teachers with his calculated insults, and having acquired a reputation as a determined baiter of all those who were placed in authority over him, he surprised his teachers on his last day at school with a superb speech written in their honor. In his speech he enumerated all their good qualities and announced himself as their most grateful servant. The teachers were so pleased with the speech that they had it printed.

He soon fell under the influence of Fourier and was especially taken with the idea of building phalansteries all over Russia. He decided to educate his own villagers in socialism. He liked to steal out at night and read from Fourier's works to the watchmen and beggars who were still abroad, and he would give twenty kopecks to anyone who said he understood perfectly what he had read. He would repeat his readings on another night, and if the peasants understood him the second time, he would give them five kopecks, and when they reminded him that he had previously paid them twenty kopecks, he would explain at some length that they only deserved five kopecks because they had heard it all before and did not have to exert their brains so much. "No, master," they answered. "We should be paid more, for we have been in your service longer." In time he gave up these nightly street-corner readings. It was too expensive, and the peasants seemed to be immune to his teachings.

He did not however give up his interest in Fourier, whom he described as his "sole god," the progenitor of social salvation, and the source of the ideas which would bring the revolution about. "When I read his works for the first time, I seemed to be reborn," he wrote. "I worshiped the immensity of his genius, and I discarded all my previous idols, as a pagan discards his idols when he becomes a Christian." Whether his peasants were agreeable or not, he decided to transform them into loyal members of a phalanstery. The opportunity occurred when one of his villages burned down. He decided to build a new communal village where everything was held in common. There would be common dormitories, dining rooms, cowsheds, stables and coach houses. There were forty families in the village, and at first, as they watched the new village rising on the ashes of the old, the peasants demonstrated their pleasure and agreed to live harmoniously in common. Petrashevsky set off for St. Petersburg to invite a select company of close friends to witness the official opening of the first Fourierist phalanstery on Russian soil. It would be a gala occasion, and perhaps even an event of historical importance. When he returned to the village with his friends, he found the village burned to the ground.

As a clerk in the Foreign Ministry he behaved toward his superiors with the same calculated impudence that had marked his behavior toward his teachers. He wore his hair long over his ears, and when he was told that long hair was hardly in keeping with his position as a clerk and it would be necessary for him to cut his hair or suffer an official reprimand, he gaily went out and bought a woman's wig, returning to the office the next day with hair so long that it streamed halfway down his back. His superior was appalled until Petrashevsky removed the wig and showed that he had obeyed the official command.

Such tricks were habitual with him; they were the greater part of his life, and he was always inventing new and more preposterous ones. Asked to draw up a memorandum on improving the form of government, he replied with a long treatise which was half desperately serious, half an extravagant attempt to laugh the government to scorn. The treatise included discussions on: (a) the advantage of civilizing apes by shaving them; (b) an examination of the guilt of the Russian people who permitted the Moscow fire of 1812; (c) the need to transform monasteries into charitable institutions; (d) an exposition of the true principles of Christian philosophy; and (e) the advantage of introducing the English jury system into Russia. The officials of the Foreign Ministry read the treatise and quietly filed it away.

Some of the ideas in the treatise reappeared in a handbook which Petrashevsky prepared with the innocuous title: A Pocket Dictionary of Foreign Words Adopted in the Russian Language. No pocket dictionary of foreign words existed, and he was able to invoke the blessing of the Grand Duke Mikhail on this new enterprise. Since the Grand Duke was the Tsar's brother, the censor made no effort to prevent publication. Many of the articles contained undisguised attacks on the autocracy, but were so cleverly written that they gave the impression of being merely informative discussions on foreign words like socialism, communism, Fourierism, the constitution, and the opposition. Even the most unlikely words served his purpose. The word "odalisque," for example, opened the way to a discussion on the rights of women, and the word "Negrophile" provided a springboard for a discussion on freeing the serfs. For Petrashevsky and his assistants, Valeryan Maikov and Roman Strandman, the *Pocket Dictionary* provided an inexhaustible source of quiet invective, for there was scarcely a word adopted from foreign languages which could not be used to deride the government. The Russian language was growing richer every day in foreign words. Critique, idealism, authority, oratory, chemistry, anarchy, literature, administration, daguerreotype—all these words, and many hundreds of others, had entered the Russian language with very little change, and suitably offensive articles could be written around them. The first volume of *A Pocket Dictionary*, dedicated to the Grand Duke, was published in April 1845. There were 176 pages with two columns to the page, and some 1,424 foreign words were defined. The book covered the letters A to M, and Petrashevsky immediately went to work on the remaining letters.

The dictionary was neither wildly successful nor a *succès d'estime*. No special attention was paid to it, and there were few who regarded it as a revolutionary attack on the government. The dictionary had in fact defeated its aim by being too clever. But when in the following year Petrashevsky brought out the second volume, which was also passed by the censor, the police took action and quietly confiscated the copies they could lay their hands on. The books were burned, but Petrashevsky went unpunished, protected by the Foreign Ministry and by his reputation as an eccentric philosopher.

Petrashevsky was not particularly dismayed by the failure of his dictionary to subvert the government. He had implicit faith in the power of the written word, and in the peculiar property of words which enables them to say the opposite of what they mean. In 1848 he wrote an essay with the attractive title of *Methods of Raising the Property of Land,* dedicated to the nobility of the Petersburg province. The essay was designed to flatter the nobility, but those who read closely observed that he recommended the general sale of land to the merchant classes, who were permitted to own neither land nor serfs. If, following Petrashevsky's proposal, land was sold to the merchants, the emancipation of the serfs would follow inevitably.

From about 1844 onward he had the custom of inviting his friends to Friday evening soirées in the upstairs drawing room of his house on Pokrov Square, at the western end of St. Petersburg. A rickety wooden stairway lit by an evil-smelling rapeseed-oil lamp led to a plainly furnished room, where the two most prominent objects were a piano and a large samovar. Petrashevsky would usually be sitting on a dingy cretonne-covered sofa, his short legs dangling. He talked continually, rarely troubled to introduce his guests to one another, and had a habit of changing the subject of his discourse with sudden and alarming speed. Around him there congregated a group of devoted admirers. In spite of his heavy beard and his carefully cultivated middle-aged appearance he was still remarkably young. Born in 1821, he was only twenty-three when he began his revolutionary career.

Though eccentric, he was not a charlatan. His father had been a distinguished surgeon, and he liked to speak of "probing problems with a scalpel." His admirers were usually cultivated young men from the provinces, and among them were many who were to become famous or notorious later. The young Mikhail Saltykov-Shchedrin, later to become a great satirist and the governor of a province, attended the meetings briefly. Chernyshevsky heard about them and deliberated whether he could usefully join the movement, but finally decided that they were altogether too theatrical and remote from the problems which consumed him. The young poets Alexey Pleshcheyev and Sergey Durov were frequent visitors. Durov was later credited with forming another circle within the greater circle of the followers of Petrashevsky. A number of Guards' officers joined the group, among them a certain Nikolay Mombelli, a calm dignified man who wore heavy sideburns and a thick drooping mustache. He was already notorious for the fact that he had written an essay suggesting that the Tsar should be forced to eat the same food as the peasants of Vitebsk, whose bread scarcely differed from horse dung.

The most exotic of the revolutionaries was Nikolay Speshnev, an immensely wealthy landowner who was blessed with superb good looks, a quick ironical mind, and a gift for satanic mischief. He had a delicate mustache and wore his long curled hair down to his shoulders. But his courage and resourcefulness belied his appearance, and the small revolutionary circle which was believed to be controlled by Durov was in fact controlled by Speshnev.

If those who met Petrashevsky were fascinated by the intricacy and fervor of his mind, they were even more fascinated by the cool ferocity of Speshnev, one of those rare men who are genuinely intoxicated with thoughts of destruction. He half-despised the abstract intellectual discussions of Petrashevsky, with their literary and moral overtones. He wanted a violent upheaval, a lethal blow at the heart of the government at whatever the cost in suffering and terror.

There was an air of mystery about him, which he deliberately cultivated. He spoke of having abandoned his property in Kursk for a life abroad with a beautiful Polish woman who apparently poisoned herself for love of him, leaving him inconsolable. He lived briefly in Switzerland,

Paris, Vienna and Dresden, always in touch with revolutionaries, and he may very well have met Marx and Engels in Paris. He was the only member of the Petrashevsky circle who had been in touch with the revolutionary movement outside Russia, and for this reason he acquired an extraordinary authority among the young revolutionaries in St. Petersburg.

Petrashevsky seems to have admired, feared and disliked Speshnev, finding him altogether too exuberant in his desire for a thorough cleansing of the Russian state. At a time when revolutionaries considered themselves to be socialists, Speshnev was already announcing that he was an impenitent communist. He proclaimed that a small elite would take power and establish an iron dictatorship. Petrashevsky was horrified. "If a dictator arises," he said, "I shall be the first to raise my hand against him."

The young Dostoyevsky attended some of the meetings of the Petrashevsky circle. Like many others he was charmed by Speshnev, whose "Mephistophelean quality" both attracted and repelled him. Years later, when he was writing *The Devils*, that strange discursive novel in which many different revolutionary groups belonging to different times and places are curiously commingled, he described Speshnev accurately under the name of Stavrogin:

> He did not talk very much, and was elegant without any exaggeration, strangely modest and at the same time very willful and determined, unlike the rest of us. The dandies among us gazed at him enviously, and were all outclassed by him. I was particularly struck by his face. His hair was a curiously intense black, his light-colored eyes were peculiarly limpid and calm, his complexion was unusually soft and white, and the color of his cheeks was a little too bright and clear. Then, too, his teeth were like pearls, and his lips like coral—one would have said he was a paragon of beauty, but there was a hint of something strange and repellent about him. There were people who said his face was a mask, but they were always saying such things about him, and there were some who spoke of his extraordinary physical strength.

Dostoyevsky did not, of course, base the figure of Stavrogin entirely on Speshnev, for many other revolutionaries, including Bakunin and Dostoyevsky himself, went into the making of that formidably nihilistic revolutionary. Stavrogin was given the outward appearance and some of the traits of character of Speshnev. Above all, Dostoyevsky had detected in him an illimitable ruthlessness and a gift for pursuing revolutionary theory to devastating conclusions.

Such was the man who presided over the Durov circle by employing all the arts of seduction. He had an uncanny instinct for selecting weak men who found refuge in his strength. Durov, who was pious, intelligent and curiously colorless, was perhaps the weakest in the group, which never amounted to more than seven or eight persons. Pleshcheyev and

Dostoyevsky were also members. Dostoyevsky, who had borrowed five hundred rubles from Speshnev, with no hope of being able to repay the money in any forseeable future, fell into a fit of neurotic depression during those days when he felt the presence of that strange Mephistopheles beside him. He complained of a sharp pain over his heart and became unusually argumentative and irrational. When his doctor suggested that the depression would soon pass, Dostoyevsky answered: "No, it will never pass, and will always torment me. I have borrowed money from him. I am with him, and belong to him. I can never return the money, and he will never let me return it. So you see, I have my own Mephistopheles now."

Dr. Stepan Yanovsky wrote his memoirs long after the event, but there is no reason to doubt that Dostoyevsky talked exactly in this way. He was deeply implicated in Speshnev's conspiratorial activities, and it is possible that he signed the revolutionary oath which was found among Speshnev's papers after his arrest. "I, the undersigned, do hereby undertake to pledge myself unreservedly to a full and complete participation in the rebellion and the subsequent fighting at such time as the Committee decides to come out in open rebellion, and I further undertake to provide myself with firearms and other weapons . . ."

When Speshnev was interrogated by the police and confronted with that extraordinary document, he laughed it off, explaining that it was nothing more than an exercise in romantic play acting. No one had signed the document; no one had been asked to sign it. The police had other opinions, and there is some reason to believe that all the members of the Durov circle were forced to sign it.

Rebellion was often discussed in the Petrashevsky circle, though usually in the form of an abstract revolt far in the future. One night in November 1848 the discussion, at which Dostoyevsky was present, became more concrete. It centered around the person of Raphael Chernosvitov, a former police official who had become the manager of a gold mine in Siberia. With his bland features and waxed mustache he looked like a prosperous businessman; he was in fact a man with dangerous revolutionary instincts. He told them about a serious revolt which broke out among the peasants on the state properties in the Shadrinsky district of Perm *guberniya*. Some six thousand peasants had rebelled, and the revolt was only suppressed with the arrival of about twelve hundred mounted Cossacks. The ringleaders of the revolt were severely punished. Of course nothing about the revolt, which took place five years before, had appeared in the newspapers, but Chernosvitov vouched for its authenticity: he had himself taken part in suppressing it.

As he spoke in those carefully modulated sentences which Dostoyevsky described as being "exactly like the sentences written by Gogol," Chernos-

vitov opened up new and hitherto unsuspected vistas for the revolutionaries. They had not thought of the vast possibilities of leading a peasant
revolt against the government. The days of Pugachev and Stenka Razin
belonged to the dim past; they were contemplating a revolution which
aimed at the heart of the government. Chernosvitov spoke of a time when
all the peasants of Russia would rise against the government, ensuring its
downfall.

At later meetings Chernosvitov explained how a massive uprising could
be engineered in Siberia, which would spread to the Urals, where four
hundred thousand fighting men with easy access to arms were only waiting
for the signal to march on the capital. He was a persuasive speaker, and he
fired the revolutionaries with his plan of action. Speshnev was especially
taken with him, and together they spoke of launching a vast *émeute,* an
uprising which would extend over the whole length and breadth of Russia.
How they intended to bring this about is not clear, but it is certain that
they were beginning to abandon philosophical theories for direct action.

Meanwhile the Petrashevsky circle was beginning to operate more
effectively under the new sense of urgency brought into the movement by
Chernosvitov. The Friday evening entertainments continued, and became
even more popular, with more and more students and Guards officers taking part. The government had got wind of these meetings, and Count
Orlov, the chief of the Gendarmerie, was already aware that subversive
statements were being made. The problem was how to find a suitable spy
who would penetrate the closed group and report faithfully on their conversations. The task of discovering a good spy was given to Liprandi, an
official in the Ministry of the Interior, who was of Italian descent. He chose
a young teacher in the faculty of philology in the University, who had only
recently taken his degree. His name was Pyotr Dmitryevich Antonelli, and
he was the son of a well-known painter, also of Italian descent. Antonelli's
reports to the secret police were to bring the Petrashevsky circle to its
downfall.

As a spy, Antonelli was well chosen, for he was wonderfully typical of
the young men who gathered around Petrashevsky. He had a long nose,
blond hair, and charming manners. He talked well, had excellent connections, and had already achieved some sort of notoriety from his habit of
wearing red waistcoats. He could be vitriolic in his denunciations of the
government and the Orthodox Church—a little too deliberately vitriolic,
for Speshnev became suspicious, refused to have anything to do with him,
and made sure that he learned very little about the Durov circle. Antonelli
first attended the Petrashevsky meetings in March 1849. His full reports
were sent first to Liprandi, then to Count Orlov, and finally to the Tsar.

The Durov circle was already working in high gear, and in need of more dedicated recruits. Apollon Maikov, the poet, writing nearly forty years later, tells how Dostoyevsky came to visit him in January with a request that he be permitted to spend the night. Maikov agreed, lent his friend a nightshirt, and they talked halfway through the night. In a conspiratorial mood Dostoyevsky suddenly announced that he had been appointed by the secret committee to ask Maikov to join. "What committee?" Maikov asked, and gradually the whole plan unfolded. A secret press was being founded to print subversive manifestoes and all kinds of documents attacking the regime, and as a result of these inflammatory manifestoes a revolution of incalculable proportions would break out. The press had nothing to do with Petrashevsky, who was "an idiot, a mountebank, and a man who talks for the sake of talking, and therefore nothing can be hoped from him."

Maikov was startled, and warned Dostoyevsky that a subversive printing press would only bring ruin to the young revolutionaries. "You and I are poets," he said, "we have no practical sense at all, and therefore we should have nothing to do with these clandestine affairs." And while Dostoyevsky continued to argue the case for the revolution, Maikov smiled and said nothing. "I remember Dostoyevsky sitting up in bed like a dying Socrates among friends," he wrote later, "while he enlarged with all his eloquence on the sacredness of the undertaking, and how it was our absolute duty to save the country, etc. etc., and when he had come to the end of his harangue I burst out laughing and began to joke with him, and then he said: 'You won't join us?' and I answered: 'No, I will never join.' "

The next morning Dostoyevsky left Maikov's house after swearing him to secrecy.

Maikov was under no illusions about the dangers and difficulties of the conspiratorial movement, and he was firmly convinced that the secret printing press was already in existence and perhaps already printing inflammatory manifestoes and pamphlets. The police never found the press, which had been designed by the brilliant and much-loved Pavel Filippov, a student in the faculty of science at the University, in such a way that it could be broken up into many parts and easily concealed. There is some doubt, however, whether anything was actually printed on it, and many years later Dostoyevsky told his wife that the press was never used. He said: "The Socialists sprang from the Petrashevsky conspirators. They sowed many seeds, and among them was everything that was used in succeeding conspiracies, including lithography and the secret printing presses, but our press was never used."

In later years this mysterious press acquired considerable fame, for a great deal depended upon whether it existed. The printing of leaflets against the regime was a capital offense, and only the most determined revolutionaries would dare to employ a press. In fact, the press was finally assembled only a few hours before the police arrested the conspirators. Broken up into its separate parts, it was in the house of one of the conspirators when the police arrived. They failed to find it only because it was lost amid a confusion of scientific instruments. Later, when a seal was placed on the door, some of the conspirators who had not been arrested succeeded in lifting the door off its hinges without breaking the seal and the press was smuggled out.

In April 1849 time was running out for the conspirators, but a few more days were still left to them to discuss the prospects of the revolution and to celebrate the coming of the Golden Age.

On April 7, 1849, the seventy-seventh anniversary of the birth of Charles Fourier, it was decided to hold a solemn celebration in his honor. For this purpose a large portrait of Fourier was especially imported from Paris. It was placed on a table and garlanded with flowers. The celebration took place in the apartment of Alexander Evropeus, and the chief speaker was Alexander Khanykov, a friend of Chernyshevsky. Khanykov was a firebrand who had been dismissed from the University for "unreliable opinions." Petrashevsky and Speshnev were present. Altogether there were only eleven young conspirators attending the banquet in Evropeus's apartment, but the importance of the meeting transcended the small number of guests, for it was the first political banquet to be held in Russia.

Khanykov dominated the assembly and his well-merited reputation as a firebrand received confirmation in a speech of startling violence. "My fatherland is in chains, my fatherland is enslaved," he thundered. "Religion and ignorance—the companions of despotism—have obscured and stifled its natural inclinations!" He went on to address the fatherland in tones of injured and outraged innocence, and at the conclusion of a long speech announced that the time of Transfiguration was at hand. There was general applause, more toasts were drunk, and Khanykov found himself being embraced and kissed.

Then Petrashevsky rose, and in quieter tones announced his undying faith in Fourierism, which alone could organize society according to its needs, and he warned them against experiments in misguided political systems—the warning was probably addressed to Speshnev, who still held to his dreams of a communist dictatorship. Petrashevsky spoke cautiously about the need to adapt Fourierism to a soil for which it was never intended, "the savage and ignorant soil of Russia." At the conclusion of his speech more toasts were drunk, and there were more embraces.

But the most memorable speech that evening came from the soft-spoken and retiring Dmitry Akhsharumov, a student of Oriental languages, a poet of some talent, devoted to the revolution, and consumed with bitterness at the thought of his people trapped within an iron autocracy. His speech echoed the ageless preoccupations of the Russian peasants, with their dreams of the Golden Age brought about by violent destruction. He said:

Restore the image of man in all its splendor and beauty, for which he has lived so long. Liberate and organize his deep harmonious passions, which are now oppressed and stifled. Tear down the cities and the towns, and use the bricks for building new cities and towns. Let the shame and grief and beggary and misery all vanish, and be utterly transformed into perfect joy and riches and harmony. That all the earth shall be covered with palaces and fruit trees and adorned with flowers—this is our high aim, and there is no greater aim on earth.

Akhsharumov was neither the first nor the last to say these things, but he said them with greater simplicity and force than anyone else, and he therefore deserves to be remembered. Out of that same dream came the famous *Revolutionary Catechism* of the archconspirator Nechayev, and it was never very far from the thoughts of Lenin. "Tear down the cities and the towns . . ." "*Razrushit stolitsi, goroda.. . .*" In the Russian the words have a terrible beauty.

As he spoke, Akhsharumov looked directly at Petrashevsky and Speshnev, for he agreed neither with the Fourierism of the one nor the communism of the other, though he shared their desire for a violent revolution. His ideas were more akin to those of Bakunin, and went back to ancient, ancestral archetypes which had long existed in the Russian mind. The tall, slender poet with the pointed beard, the delicate features, and the haunted eyes had made the evening memorable, but only at the expense of Fourier. In his long speech there was in fact not one sentence with which Fourier would have agreed.

Dostoyevsky took no part in the meeting in honor of Fourier, but he was not inactive. He still believed firmly in the coming revolution, and with his brother Mikhail he was deeply involved in the conspiracy. He was in desperate economic straits, with the creditors threatening to foreclose, and he was attempting to complete a long and extremely complicated novel. Yet he still found time to take part in the Friday meetings at Petrashevsky's apartment and at the various other meetings of the Durov circle which were called by Speshnev. He attended the Friday meeting on April 15, where he read aloud the letter which the critic Belinsky had written in a cold rage to the novelist Gogol. Pleshcheyev had obtained a handwritten copy of the letter from Moscow and thrust it into Dostoyevsky's hands, saying: "You must read this—it is the greatest letter written in our age!"

So it was, and for reading it aloud Dostoyevsky was to suffer a punishment so great that it very nearly broke his spirit. The letter, written from a watering place in Germany where Belinsky was attempting to repair his shattered health, was a merciless attack on Gogol for having published a strange little book of essays called *Selected Passages from Correspondence with My Friends*. They were the letters of a sick man pleading with his friends to put wickedness away, to devote themselves to God, and to submit themselves wholly to the autocracy, which Gogol had come to regard as a divinely instituted system of government. According to Gogol it was the task of all men living under the autocracy to discover patiently the precise niches which had been preordained for them. The familiar Gogol of the great plays and novels was lacking. This was a new and alarming Gogol, close to death and damnation, stridently proclaiming that the Kingdom of God had been entrusted to the Tsar. Belinsky spent three days writing his letter of denunciation, in a mood of controlled and exasperated fury. It was the letter of one sick and dying man to another, and it went far beyond the normal scope of a personal letter, for it included a philosophy of action and rebellion and a contemptuous dismissal of everything that Gogol stood for. The letter was painful to write, for there was a time when Belinsky had proclaimed that Gogol stood head and shoulders above living Russian writers.

Although the letter was addressed to Gogol, it was also intended, like all Belinsky's critical writings, for a wider audience. There is a sense in which it has very little to do with Gogol, and very much to do with revolution. For twenty pages Belinsky poured out his determined hatred of the Tsarist government, which was "nothing more than a vast corporation of robbers and thieves," and of the Orthodox Church, which was "the champion of inequality, the enemy and persecutor of the brotherhood of man." The letter, which became a revolutionary classic, should be quoted at some length, because it brilliantly conveys the dominant ideas of the revolutionaries of his time:

> You have failed to understand that Russia sees her salvation not in mysticism, nor in asceticism, nor in pietism, but in the successes of civilization, enlightenment and humanity. What she needs is not sermons (she has heard enough of them!) nor prayers (she has repeated them too many times!) but the awakening of the people to the sense of their human dignity lost for so many centuries amid the dirt and the refuse; she needs rights and laws conforming not with the preaching of the Church, but with common sense and justice, and their strictest possible observance.
>
> Instead of this, Russia today presents the dire spectacle of a country where men traffic in men, without even having the excuse so insidiously exploited by the plantation owners in America, who claim that the Negro is not a man. Russia is a country where no one has a name; instead there are only nicknames like Vanka, Vaska, Steshka, Palashka. It is a country where there are no guarantees of individual freedom, honor and property, where

there is no law obeyed by the police, and the government is only a vast corporation of robbers and thieves. The most vital national problem in Russia today is the abolition of serfdom and corporal punishment, and the strictest possible observance of the laws which have already been passed. This is even realized by the government itself, which is well aware of how the landlords treat their peasants, and of how many landowners are annually killed by their peasants, and all this is proved by the timid and abortive half-measures for the relief of the white Negroes and the amusing substitution of the knout for the cat-o'-three-tails . . .

The Church has always served as the defender of the knout and as the servant of despotism, but why have you mixed Christ up in this? What have you found in common between him and any Church, least of all the Orthodox Church?

Christ was the first to bring the people the teaching of freedom, equality and brotherhood, and He set the seal of truth to that teaching by His martyrdom. And this teaching was man's *salvation* until it became organized in the Church and took the principle of Orthodoxy for its foundation. The Church became a hierarchy, and therefore the champion of inequality, the flatterer of authority, the enemy and persecutor of the brotherhood of man—and so it has remained to this day.

The meaning of Christ's message has been revealed by the philosophical movement of the preceding century. That is why a man like Voltaire who stamped out the fires of fanaticism and ignorance in Europe by ridicule is all the more the son of Christ, flesh of His flesh and bone of His bone, and much more the son of Christ than all your priests, bishops, metropolitans or patriarchs, eastern or western . . .

According to you the Russian people are the most religious in the world. That is a lie! The basis of religious feeling lies in piety, reverence, and the fear of God. But the Russian utters the name of the Lord God only when scratching himself somewhere. He says of the icon: *If it is not good for praying, then it is good for the pot.*

Take a closer look and you will see that the Russians are a profoundly atheistic people, who still retain a good deal of superstition, but not a trace of religious feeling. Superstition passes with the advance of civilization, but religious feeling often survives for a long while. We have living examples of this in France, where even today there are many sincere Catholics among enlightened and educated men, and where many who have rejected Christianity still cling to some kind of God. But the Russian people are quite different. Mystic exaltation is not in their nature. They have too much common sense, their minds are too positive and lucid, and therein lies the vastness of their historic destiny . . .

I shall not speak of your panegyric on the love of the Russian people for their lords and masters. I shall only remark that the panegyric has not met with agreement from anyone and has lowered you in the eyes of those people who would otherwise find themselves very close to your ideas. As far as I am concerned, I leave it to your conscience to admire the divine beauty of the autocracy . . .

As far as I can see, you do not properly understand the Russian people. Its character is determined by the condition of Russian society, which is seething with new forces and struggling to express itself, while weighed down with heavy oppression and without an outlet, weary, apathetic, and filled with dejection. In spite of the Tatar censorship only literature shows signs of life and progressive movement, and that is why the title of author is held in such high esteem among us, and this applies even to writers of small talent. The title of poet and writer has long since eclipsed the tinsel of epaulettes and gaudy uniforms . . . So the people look rightfully on Russian writers as their only leaders, defenders and saviors against Russian autocracy, orthodoxy and nationalism.

In our own day such statements about the Russian autocracy would be subversive. In the eyes of the secret police Belinsky's letter was nothing less than a manifesto directed against the government, to be suppressed at all costs. The revolutionaries intended that this letter should be printed on their secret press and distributed throughout Russia, but this plan, like so many others, miscarried, and it was not printed until nine years later when it appeared in Alexander Herzen's *Pole Star*, although hundreds of handwritten copies were being circulated throughout Russia.

When the reports on this Friday meeting came to him, Count Orlov decided to act. A heavy dossier concerning the Petrashevsky circle had accumulated over the months, and in addition there were the precise reports of Antonelli. He sent the complete dossier to the Tsar with the suggestion that all the members of the circle should be placed under arrest. The Tsar read the dossier attentively and wrote in the margin: "I have read everything. The affair is serious. Even if it is only foolish talk, it is nevertheless criminal and intolerable. They must be arrested, as you recommend."

It was decided to arrest them on the evening of the following Friday. The Tsar, who had shown no mercy to the Decembrists, had already decided on an appropriate punishment: the ringleaders would be sentenced to death.

THE EXECUTION IN SEMYONOVSKY SQUARE

ON THE NIGHT OF APRIL 22, 1849, some thirty-five members of the Petrashevsky circle were arrested in their beds. During the following days eight more were rounded up, and the government was satisfied that all the leading members of the conspiracy were under arrest. Petrashevsky, Durov, Speshnev, Akhsharumov, Mombelli, Khanykov, Evropeus, Dostoyevsky and all the important conspirators were arrested the first night. The police knew exactly where to go and they had obviously been following the conspirators closely.

The orders of arrest as well as an immense quantity of documents concerning the examination of the conspirators have survived. In a file labeled "On Engineer Lieutenant Dostoyevsky," now in Moscow, there can be read the fading handwriting of Count Orlov's order to a certain Major Chudinov of the Gendarmerie, commanding him to arrest Dostoyevsky in the middle of the night. It reads:

BY HIGHEST ORDER

Your Honor is commanded to arrest former lieutenant of engineers and author Fyodor Mikhailovich Dostoyevsky tomorrow, at four o'clock in the morning, at his lodging at the corner of the Malaya Morskaya and Voznesensky Prospect. He is to be found in the house belonging to Shill, on the third floor, in the apartment of Bremer. All his books, papers and effects are to be sealed and delivered into the safekeeping of the Third Division of the Imperial Chancellery.

Many years later, writing in the album of a friend, Dostoyevsky told the story of the strange night when for the first and last time in his life he was arrested by the Tsarist police. April 22 was a Friday, and he had intended to spend the evening with the Petrashevsky circle, but on his way he was caught in a sudden shower and decided to call on his friend Dr. Yanovsky for a change of clothes and to borrow some money for a droshky. The doctor, who had been Dostoyevsky's childhood friend, welcomed him warmly and broke open the alms box which he had specially provided for the more impecunious of his friends. Dostoyevsky left the doctor's house with a fresh suit of clothes and six five-kopeck pieces, but instead of joining the Petrashevsky circle he called on another friend and talked into the early hours of the morning. Then he went home, slipped into bed, and fell asleep. A few minutes later he was under arrest. Here Dostoyevsky describes his arrest:

I was still sleeping when I became obscurely aware that some strangers had somehow entered my room. I heard a saber rattling, knocking against something. It seemed to me very queer, but what exactly was happening? With an effort I opened my eyes, and heard a soft and very gentle voice saying: "Get up!"

I saw a police officer or perhaps a police commissioner with a beautiful beard. He did not speak. Someone else, wearing a blue uniform with the epaulettes of a lieutenant colonel, was speaking.

"What is happening?" I asked, rising from the bed.

"Orders."

I looked, and saw it really was "orders." By the door stood a soldier, also in blue. It was his saber which was rattling.

"What on earth is happening?" I asked myself, and then I said: "Excuse me, what—"

"It doesn't matter, it doesn't matter," the lieutenant colonel was saying, and his voice seemed very beautiful. "Get up! We can wait!"

While I was dressing they rummaged through all my books and tied them together with string. With my pipestem the officer began to rake over the dead ashes in my small stove, but on reaching out for the cornice his grip failed, he fell heavily on a chair and then from the chair to the floor. That was how these intelligent gentlemen came to learn there was nothing in the stove.

On the table there was a five-kopeck piece, old and bent. The officer studied it carefully, and after a while he nodded in the direction of the lieutenant colonel.

"Is it counterfeit?" I asked.

"Hm, well, we'll find out about that," the officer grumbled, and added the coin to the other evidence.

Then we left. At the door the landlady and her servant Ivan said goodbye. Ivan was especially frightened, but he looked grave, as befitted the seriousness of the occasion; certainly, it was not a very festive ceremony.

We drove off to the Fontanka prison by way of the chain bridge and the Summer Garden.

About the same time Petrashevsky was being arrested by no less a person than General Leonty Dubelt, the second in command of the Third Division of the Imperial Chancellery. Petrashevsky's vast library interested the general, who realized that there could be no question of tying up the books with string and carrying them off for examination. This would be done later, on a more suitable occasion. Meanwhile he took some books off the shelves.

"General, for God's sake don't touch them!" Petrashevsky exclaimed.

"Why not?"

"Because every one of them has been banned by the censor. Even if you only glance at them, it will be bad for you!"

"Then why do you keep them?"

"A question of taste," Petrashevsky said negligently, and soon he had removed his exotic dressing gown and was wearing the proper attire for a prisoner under arrest. Without another word he followed the general to the waiting carriage.

The Fontanka prison was merely a way station for the far more dreaded Peter and Paul Fortress. Here the prisoners were interrogated briefly by Count Orlov in the famous "white room," and because it was a bitterly cold night and perhaps also because Count Orlov was in an indulgent mood and pleased with the work of his agents, the prisoners were given a meal with hors d'oeuvres and wine. But merely because Count Orlov and his assistant, General Dubelt, were present in the room, the prisoners knew that the government looked upon the affair with the utmost seriousness.

Among the prisoners was Dostoyevsky's brother Andrey, who had never had the slightest connection with the Petrashevsky circle. He had been arrested in mistake for the eldest brother Mikhail, whose wife had just given birth to a child and had not yet fully recovered. The prisoners were permitted to talk to one another, and so it happened that Dostoyevsky was able to convince Andrey to remain silent and accept an undeserved punishment for a few days, so permitting Mikhail to put his affairs in order before his own inevitable arrest. Mikhail had only a slight connection with the circle, and Dostoyevsky counted rightly on his release. Because Andrey offered to substitute for his brother, Dostoyevsky was eternally grateful to him, and he regarded it as among the few heroic acts he witnessed in his lifetime.

Later in the day all the prisoners were transferred to the Peter and Paul Fortress.

A complete list of the prisoners and the cells they occupied has survived, and so we learn that Petrashevsky and Dostoyevsky were included among the most dangerous prisoners placed in the Alexis Ravelin. Petrashevsky had Cell No. 1, Dostoyevsky had Cell No. 9. Other prisoners were given cells in the Trubetskoy and Zotov bastions and in the Nikolsky and Catherine curtains.

As the police had known for some time, none of the members of the Petrashevsky circle belonged to the nobility. Insofar as there was a conspiracy at all, it was solidly rooted in the middle class. Discussing the difference between the Decembrists and the Petrashevsky circle, Liprandi, the chief of police, wrote: "The Decembrists were drawn exclusively from the nobility, and above all from Guards officers. The Petrashevsky circle, on the contrary, apart from a few Guards officers and Foreign Office officials, consisted of semieducated students, merchants, and even shopkeepers trading in tobacco." Those who were arrested included nine professors and college administrators, ten students, seven army officers, three writers, two artists, one landowner, and one who was described in the official records as "a petty bourgeois." There were eight government officials, none of high rank.

The police were puzzled by what appeared to be a strange mingling of many different occupations and they had some difficulty in finding the core of the conspiracy. They asked interminable questions, interviewed the prisoners at length, and acquired mountains of documentary evidence, none of it very convincing and much of it at cross purposes. The question of the secret printing press was perhaps the most important one, but no conclusive evidence of its manufacture was brought forward. Some prisoners agreed that they intended to make one and had planned to print pamphlets on Fourierism on it, but Fourierism was not in itself seditious, and the Petrashevsky circle, according to the prisoners, was nothing more

than an intimate group of friends who came together for intellectual re-
freshment. Dostoyevsky protested that he had never had the slightest inclination toward a republican form of government, and if he had read
aloud Belinsky's letter to Gogol it was merely because Belinsky was regarded as a great critic whose attack on Gogol must be regarded as a
matter of literary criticism.

Month after month the interrogations went on, while the prisoners remained in their clammy cells. The cells were barren, uncomfortable and
deliberately forbidding. Akhsharumov, who was imprisoned in the Trubetskoy Bastion, has left an account of his cell:

> When I saw my new dwelling place in daylight, there was presented before
> my eyes a small, filthy, narrow dwelling place just over five meters long and
> three meters wide, with a high ceiling. The walls were covered with white-
> wash which had long ago ceased to be white, and all over them were the
> finger stains of a prisoner who evidently had no books to pass the time away.
> There was one window, very large in comparison with the size of the room,
> and the small panes of glass were all painted (except for the topmost row)
> with oily yellowish-white paint. An iron grille covered the window, and
> opposite it there was the massive ironbound door and the large dirty mirror
> of a tiled stove, which could be lit from outside. There was nothing except a
> bed, a small table, a chest provided with a lid; and on the windowsill a jug
> and an earthenware lamp with no oil.

Dostoyevsky's cell in the Alexis Ravelin was very similar: long, narrow,
dark, with only a little light coming through the top of the window. "I
live by that light," he wrote, and in the hours of darkness he gave way to
sleepless despair. He suffered from hemorrhoids and diarrhea, cramps and
sudden fits of nervous exaltation, but on the whole he was a model prisoner, seemingly at peace with himself. He was permitted to receive books
and letters, and he could walk in the small garden within the triangle of
the Alexis Ravelin. He planned three short stories and two novels, but
only one of the stories, called "The Little Hero," was actually written
down, and pehaps it was inevitable that the story should be a strange
description of a boy's growth into adolescence and freedom, with the
action depending on a mysterious letter—a letter of pardon. He read
Shakespeare in Russian and the Bible in French, and these quieted his
nerves. He had been on the edge of a nervous collapse before his arrest,
and sometimes in later years he would regard his imprisonment as a
blessing, for it saved him from himself.

Dostoyevsky in those days was not yet a famous novelist. He was
twenty-seven, without a family, without a regular income, living by
translations and hack work. He had produced two novels *Poor Folk* and
The Double, neither of them of outstanding merit, though Belinsky had
seen much promise in them. As he paced his cell, he knew only too well

that there was little to show for his misspent life, much of it wasted in the years spent in an engineering school. But now at last in his prison letters there can be heard intimations of a voice which would be heard again in his later years. Fear had gone; courage had gone; there was only the quivering nerve, the man alone with himself contemplating the mysteries of human existence.

In the Peter and Paul Fortress many men suffered from prison fever, bouts of near madness, terrible depressions. The revolutionary Vera Figner who was imprisoned there toward the end of the century complained that after several months of silence her vocal chords weakened and her sense of time became hopelessly distorted. When she was released quite ordinary sounds had a paralyzing effect on her, so that when a teaspoon was dropped she had to exert all her will power to prevent herself from screaming. No one imprisoned in the Fortress ever completely recovered from the experience.

Dostoyevsky survived better than most. The student Vasily Katenev went mad and was removed to the prison hospital, where he soon died. The government official Ivan Yastrzhemsky wrote in his memoirs: "I remained in the Ravelin from April 23 to December 23, and if I had stayed there a day longer I would have gone insane." Dmitry Akhsharumov tore a nail out of his bed and kept sharpening it, determined to commit suicide the moment he could endure prison life no more. Petrashevsky nearly lost his reason, and for weeks he trembled on the verge of madness. He wrote to the prison commandant a strange letter in which he spoke of "whispers trying to destroy me," and he begged to have the whispers officially removed. Significantly the prisoners who came closest to madness were all from the Alexis Ravelin or the nearby Trubetskoy Bastion, the most dreaded, the most silent, the most closely watched of all the sections of the Fortress.

The months passed in loneliness and misery. The summer, when the cells were so humid that the prisoners could scarcely breathe, gave place to a damp autumn, when the mists rose over the Neva, and soon it would be winter. Meanwhile the interrogation dragged on. The prisoners would be brought before the examining commission, asked perfectly senseless questions, and then released to the equally senseless silence of their cells.

On the whole the examining committee acted fairly: they asked senseless questions because they were at a loss to understand the nature of the conspiracy and hoped by probing to uncover its mysterious origins. The five men who sat behind the table and cross-examined the prisoners were all men of intelligence, and only one was a bully. This was General Dubelt, known as "the fox," who had a long, lean face, a drooping mustache, and cheeks covered with a dark spider-web of wrinkles. The remaining members of the commission were Prince Gagarin, Prince Dolgoruky, and the two generals Rostovtsev and Nabokov, the last being the chairman of the commission and the commandant of the Peter and Paul Fortress. The two princes were uniformly courteous, and Dostoyevsky felt that they were naturally kind and well-mannered, and had a sincere desire to get to the bottom of the matter. The generals were more crafty and went out of their way to intimidate the prisoners, though with little success.

As everyone expected, Petrashevsky bore himself with grave dignity, assumed the entire blame, held fast to his Fourierist principles, and sometimes lectured the commission on the need to build phalansteries for the salvation of the working classes. He even suggested that the Tsar should finance a phalanstery in France, thereby bringing an end to the class war in Western Europe, and showing himself to be the benefactor of Europe, the moral superior of Napoleon, and the most judicious of Tsars. When Dostoyevsky, who had little sympathy for phalansteries, was asked about Fourierism, he replied that it was obviously impractical in Russia and could be found only in "the uncut pages of a book or in an idyl in twenty-four cantos." Asked about the aims of the Petrashevsky circle, he answered that it had no aim except to perpetuate itself as a friendly debating society, and if sometimes extreme statements were made that was no more than could be expected in any debating society. He asked whether men could be punished for their unspoken thoughts. It was a dangerous question, very close to the heart of the mystery the commissioners were probing. "We should all be guilty," Dostoyevsky told them, "if our intimate thoughts were investigated, if we were held accountable for every word we said to our intimate friends." Dostoyevsky spoke so much about the intimate rights of man that he seems to have reduced the commissioners to incoherence. At one point General Rostovtsev jumped up from the table, shouted: "I cannot look at Dostoyevsky any more!" and marched out of the room.

Finally, when all the interminable cross-examinations were over and all the affidavits had been read, the commissioners knew no more about the conspiracy than they had known in the beginning. The printing press, which might have provided concrete evidence of wrongdoing, had vanished into thin air. Because there was no evidence, the commissioners found themselves involuntarily discussing the ideas which the prisoners put forward until it occurred to them that they were falling into a trap. They could find no subversive pamphlets. There was no revolutionary plan of action, no call to arms. At most there was a debating society, a conspiracy of ideas, a weighing of conflicting theories. Antonelli had heard them expressing dissatisfaction with the government, and there was always Dostoyevsky's reading of Belinsky's letter to fall back upon. What the commissioners found, or thought they found, was evidence of a *potential* crime, which had not yet taken place. At any ordinary time the government might have decided that nothing was to be gained by prosecuting the prisoners, but these were not ordinary times. The revolutions which swept across Europe in 1848 had demonstrated to the Tsar the dangers of the new ideas, and he was determined to put a stop to *thoughts* of rebellion. Nicholas I had severely punished the Decembrists; he would punish the followers of Petrashevsky in the same way.

After eight months of deliberation the sentences were handed down. Of the forty-three men who were originally arrested, one had died, twenty-two were allowed to go free, and twenty remained in the Peter and Paul Fortress. All twenty were condemned to death.

On December 22, when they were escorted out of the Peter and Paul Fortress, the prisoners were in a state of shock. Early that morning they had been told they were condemned to death. Now, at seven o'clock, they were being led out into one of the courtyards of the Fortress and made to enter waiting carriages. They sat four to a carriage, and could see nothing, for the windows were covered with frost. When they asked the guards what was going to happen, they were told: "We can tell you nothing." They were shivering with cold, for they wore only the light clothes they had been wearing when they were arrested in the spring.

Though they could not see outside the carriage, they knew St. Petersburg well and they could tell where they were by the sound of the wheels and the horses' hoofs on the roads—the wooden beams of the bridge, then the cobblestones of the Liteiny, the long street which cuts straight through the heart of the city. The carriages were escorted by mounted gendarmes in light-blue uniforms, with drawn swords. After the Liteiny they were at a loss to know where they were, for the carriages rumbled through the side streets.

When at last the five carriages and their escort came to a halt, they found themselves in Semyonovsky Square, the parade ground of the Semyonovsky Regiment, overlooked by the Church of the Vladimir Mother of God. It was one of the largest squares in St. Petersburg, and was now filled with troops, including a massive detachment of the Moscow Infantry Regiment, Horse Guards, and Guards Chasseurs. They had been chosen because three of the condemned men were officers belonging to these units. The troops formed a square, but there was a break of about a hundred feet to enable a crowd of onlookers to watch the ceremony. According to the police report, there were about three thousand onlookers, and there must have been an equal number of soldiers. On that chilly morning, with two inches of snow on the ground, they were about to watch the execution of twenty men.

The ceremonies of torture and execution fascinated the Tsar, who had carefully arranged the setting, devised the stage properties, and planned a satisfactory denouement. During the previous night workmen had erected a large wooden platform with steps leading up to it and railings all round. Not far from the platform and a little to one side were three thick oak stakes stripped of bark: to these the condemned men would be bound before they were shot. The platform was covered with black cloth which sparkled in the snow, and there was a kind of altar. Here, as on a stage, the ceremonial rites appropriate to condemned felons would be performed in full view of the public. Here the priests would hear their last confessions, swords would be broken over their heads, and they would be dressed in the white vestments of death. From this height they would step down as into a pit, to be executed. The sixteen-man firing squad had already taken up positions close to the oak stakes.

Although everything had been arranged in great detail, with that careful exactitude which the Tsar always demanded of his generals, there were some very curious features about the ceremonies on the Semyonovsky Square, and the most curious of all was that it was wholly a military affair even though only a few of the condemned were military men. In fact it was the presence of serving officers in the Petrashevsky circle which incensed the Tsar and drove him to the furious expedient of ordering a massive public ceremony of execution such as had not happened since the time of Catherine the Great. He had rid himself of the Decembrists quietly; they were never displayed in public; and he thought he had inspired sufficient fear among army officers to prevent them from ever coming out in rebellion again. The strange events on the Semyonovsky Square can be interpreted very largely in terms of the Tsar's realization that the army had not learned its lesson.

At first the prisoners were led round the square on foot, so that the troops could see them in their misery and degradation. Akhsharumov, who later drew a detailed plan of the square and the movements of the condemned men, shows them making the long, slow journey while keeping very close to the lines of troops, and it is evident that this was intended as the first stage of a prolonged punishment. They were made to walk in solemn procession round the place of their death, and they could not have failed to observe the three oak stakes, which were more than twice the height of a man.

When they had walked round the square they were led two by two, up the steps leading to the platform, where they were odered to form in two rows, as though on parade. Petrashevsky, Mombelli and Grigoriev stood at the head of one row, with Dostoyevsky being tenth and last. Mombelli and Grigoriev, being army officers, were given positions of importance immediately behind Petrashevsky.

At first Dostoyevsky could scarcely recognize his companions, for they had visibly changed since they were arrested. Bearded and unkempt, their teeth chattering, their noses blue with cold, their hands numb, they resembled caricatures of themselves. Most of them were very calm, in that strange state of exaltation and exhaustion which comes to those who are condemned to die, but one or two were on the verge of hysteria. The prisoner Nikolay Kashkin, a former government official, was weeping. He had been friendly with General Golovachev, who was in charge of one of the detachments of troops, and when he saw that Kashkin was about to collapse, the general rode up to the platform and said quickly: *"Vous serez graciés tous, tous!"* Only Kashkin and two others heard the words, but there was little comfort in them. They were too numbed, too weary of the sickening ceremony to understand what was happening. The general had violated his oath of obedience to the Tsar, and he may have excused himself with the thought that he had committed only a small crime, inasmuch as he spoke in French and was speaking privately, as man to man, with someone of his own class.

An officer strode onto the platform and began to recite the names of the condemned men, and after each name he repeated the words: "Death by shooting."

Many times in his novels Dostoyevsky would return to those extraordinary moments he spent on the platform in the snowbound square, and there can scarcely have been a day in his life when he did not remember them. In *The Idiot* Prince Myshkin, who is very nearly a self-portrait of Dostoyevsky himself, declares:

> The most terrible part of the whole punishment is not the bodily pain at all, but the certain knowledge that in an hour—in ten minutes—in half a minute—this very *instant*—your soul must quit your body, and you will no longer be a man, and this is certain, certain! That's the point—the certainty of it! Just at the instant when you place your head on the block and hear the sound of the iron grating above your head, there is a quarter of a second which is the most terrible of all!

And Prince Myshkin argues that this ultimate moment of truth is the real punishment inflicted upon the victim.

Many years later Dostoyevsky described the scene to the great Russian mathematician Sonia Kovalevsky, who recorded it in her memoirs. He said:

> I remember how the officer, after he had finished reading our death sentences, folded up the paper and stuffed it in his pocket, and then stepped down from the platform, and at that very moment the sun came out of the clouds and flashed across my face. I turned to my neighbor and said: "It's impossible! They don't really intend to shoot us!" Instead of replying, he pointed to a row of coffins covered by a cloth. When I saw this, I lost all hope, and I was deeply convinced that they intended to shoot us.

I remember I was very frightened, and at the same time determined not to show any fear, and I kept talking to my companion about everything that came into my head. He told me afterward that I was not even very pale, and all the time I was talking about a story I was making up, and that I was very annoyed that I could not write it down. But I remember nothing of this. What I remember is a number of isolated, inconsequential thoughts. Then a priest stepped up on the platform and invited us to make our confessions, but only one did so, though when he held out the crucifix we all touched it with our lips.

For more than half an hour they had been forced to stand in those two rows on the platform, while the crowd watched silently. The priest went on to deliver a sermon on the text "The wages of sin is death," calling upon them to make a true repentance, and when he had finished two men in brilliant kaftans climbed onto the platform and broke swords over their heads as a sign that they no longer possessed any civil or military rights whatsoever. There was a sense in which the breaking of the swords was the ultimate punishment, removing them from a world of honor and dignity: the actual shooting would be almost an anticlimax.

They all knelt as the swords were broken over them, and when they stood up again they were ordered to remove their outer garments and put on the hooded white gowns with long sleeves which would serve as their shrouds. Petrashevsky, one of the few who could still make a joke, said: "What a stupid attire!" Then Petrashevsky, Mombelli and Grigoriev were led down the steps and bound to the posts, and the hoods were drawn over their faces. Swords flashed, a trumpet sounded, there was a roll of drums, and the sixteen soldiers standing sixteen feet away from the three bound men raised their rifles at an order and prepared to take aim.

Dostoyevsky was among the next three to be executed, and he related to Sonia Kovalevsky the thoughts that came to him as he waited for the inevitable end:

> I had, as I supposed, at most five more minutes of life, and I decided to devote them to thinking about myself. I tried to picture to myself how it would all happen. Now I was full of life and consciousness, and in five minutes I would be *nothing*, or *someone*, or *something* quite different. From where I stood I could see the Church of the Vladimir Mother of God glittering in the sun. I remember staring intently at the cupola and the radiance which it gave forth, and I was seized with the fancy that this radiance was my new world, into which I would be absorbed in five minutes. I remember how painful it was, this physical aversion I had for the unknown world which approached nearer and nearer.
> And suddenly there was a strange stir among the men on the platform. My shortsightedness prevented me from distinguishing anything, but I knew something was happening. Suddenly I became aware that an officer was riding full tilt across the Square in our direction, waving a white handker-

chief. This was the imperial messenger bringing the news of our amnesty. Later we learned that the whole affair had been planned; and in truth how could it have been possible to punish with death these twenty youths, some hardly out of their childhood, for offenses so small. The Tsar had made the decision to punish us in order to terrify us, so that we would remember his laws.

If this had been the Tsar's intention, he singularly failed in his objective. He succeeded only in crushing their spirits, and many years passed before any of them recovered.

While Petrashevsky was bound to the stake, he somehow succeeded in shaking off the hood which covered his face. So he was depicted quite accurately in a drawing made by an unknown artist, which shows him leaning forward and staring contemptuously at the soldiers who are aiming at his heart.

The officer riding across the Square brought his horse to a halt beside General Rostovtsev, who was in command of the executions, and delivered the letter sealed with the imperial cipher. Then General Rostovtsev, who spoke with a pronounced stutter, began to read aloud the immensely long letter, which began, like all the official documents of the Tsar, with the recital of the imperial titles:

"By the grace of God, We, Emperor and Autocrat of All the Russias, Tsar of Moscow, Tsar of Poland, Tsar of the Taurian Chersonese, Tsar of Georgia, Grand Duke of Kiev, Vladimir, Novgorod, Lord of Pskov and Grand Duke of Smolensk . . ."

By this time all the prisoners knew that their sentences had been commuted and that the Tsar had deliberately arranged this strange charade in order to torment them. The general, holding the letter close to his face, could scarcely be heard as he recited the new penalties to be suffered by the prisoners. Petrashevsky was sentenced to penal servitude for life, Mombelli and Grigoriev to fifteen years' hard labor, Filippov and Akhsharumov to four years' imprisonment and then to be sent to the Caucasus to fight as common soldiers, Durov and Dostoyevsky to four years' hard labor and then to join the ranks, Speshnev to ten years' hard labor, Khanykov and Pleshcheyev were ordered to join a regiment of the line, and Alexander Palm, who had cooperated fully with the authorities, was given no sentence at all, but allowed to resume his former rank in the army. As for Chernosvitov, who had spoken so ardently of a peasant rebellion from one end of Russia to the other, he was sentenced to imprisonment in the Kexholm Fortress "in perpetuity." To the end of their lives Petrashevsky and Speshnev believed that he was an *agent provocateur* and that the sentence was merely a charitable way of rewarding him for his services to the Crown. They imagined that he would change his name and vanish into obscurity far from the prison fortress to which he was theoretically assigned.

The Tsar was so determined to punish Petrashevsky that he ordered him to be sent straight to Siberia from Semyonovsky Square. "It would have been much better to have shot me," Petrashevsky observed. The irons were placed on his feet, and he was ordered to enter a waiting carriage.

"You forget," he said, "I have still one more task to perform. I must say goodbye to my friends."

Paying no attention to the generals, he limped up to the platform, embraced his friends tenderly, taking his own time, and only when he had spoken to all of them in turn did he leave the platform and enter the carriage.

Now at last the strange cart which had appeared to contain coffins lying under a tarpaulin was opened up. It contained not coffins but enough sheepskin overcoats, fur hats and felt boots for all the prisoners. The gift of clothes was the last ironical gesture of the Tsar before the comedy came to an end. One of the prisoners had to be helped into his clothes. This was Grigoriev, who had gone mad while bound to the oak post.

In time nearly all the prisoners who were sent to Siberia returned to Russia. Dostoyevsky lived out his prison sentence in Omsk and recorded the experience in the first of his great masterpieces, *The House of the Dead*. Only Petrashevsky never returned to Russia. When Nicholas I died in 1855 all the members of the Petrashevsky circle were granted an amnesty, but Petrashevsky himself rejected it, demanding a new trial, which was refused. A brilliant, embittered man, close to madness, he lived more and more within himself. For a while in Irkutsk he was under the protection of Nikolay Muraviev, the liberal Governor General of Eastern Siberia, for whom he wrote pamphlets and compiled statistics, built schools and acted as a political adviser. The agents of the Third Division watched him closely, for they knew better than the Governor General what Petrashevsky's real intentions were. More than ever he thought of the peasant revolution which would sweep across Russia from east to west; he had studied at great length the peasant rebellions in the past, from the Levellers movement in England and the Peasant Wars of sixteenth-century Germany to the revolts under Pugachev and Stenka Razin.

At Irkutsk Muraviev held a small court in which the revolutionaries were allowed to play small roles. Speshnev, Bakunin and Petrashevsky all attended this strange court which was so remote from St. Petersburg that it was almost independent. While Muraviev reigned they could do very much as they pleased, but when he was recalled to the capital in 1861 the liberal influence in Siberia came to an abrupt halt; and Petrashevsky could expect little from Muraviev's successor, General Korsakov, whom he had insulted in the past, calling him a mere post horse. Petrashevsky was banished from Irkutsk, to eat out his heart for the remaining years of his life in obscure Siberian villages, building schools which the children rarely attended, quarreling with all the government officials he encountered, brooding alone through the long nights of Siberian winters. Because he offended everybody, he was continually on the move. He stayed briefly in Minusinsk and Shushenskoye, familiar to historians because Lenin was exiled there many years later, and then he was on the march again. Yeniseisk and Krasnoyarsk received him coldly, and he went to stay in the obscure village of Verkhny Kebezh, but remained only a short while. He had prayed that the peasants would revolt, but the peasants despised him. He had become a recluse, hounded by the police from one small town or village to another.

He died on or about December 7, 1866, in the lost little village of Belskoye, where he had been living alone in a small house on the outskirts. Many stories were told about his death. Some said he was murdered by the peasants, others that he had taken poison. The doctor who arrived two months later found the frozen body where it lay, and pronounced that he died of apoplexy. When the doctor had written out the death certificate, he was buried. There were no mourners at the funeral, which was attended only by two gravediggers.

He died obscurely, but his name lived on. He had written no manifestoes, led no mutinous troops, possessed no large following. He was neither a practical revolutionary nor a theorist of revolution; he had entered into a conspiracy of ideas, and the conspiracy failed because the ideas were never worked out to a logical conclusion. No one ever found any evidence that he seriously hoped to bring about a revolution. It was remembered that he tore the hood from his face when he was bound to the stake on Semyonovsky Square and confronted the executioners with the courage of despair, and throughout his life in exile he fought against the tyranny of the Tsar. His courage, his energy remained to remind future generations of revolutionaries that the cause was not lost. Like the Decembrists he was remembered because he had failed, and the failure was itself a presage of future victory. When Herzen heard of Petrashevsky's death, he wrote in *Kolokol*: "Future generations will honor his memory, for he died for the freedom of Russia." It was the epitaph which he would have liked most of all.

Not long after the trial of Petrashevsky, in a letter addressed to the French historian Jules Michelet, Herzen described the fate of the conspirators in terms of an old Russian fairy tale. He wrote:

The case of Petrashevsky and his friends, condemned to penal servitude for life, being deported in 1849 for organizing revolutionary clubs not ten feet away from the Winter Palace, adequately reveals, both in the insane recklessness of the attempt and in the obvious hopelessness of the cause, that the time for rational reflection is over. There is a popular Russian fairy tale which tells how the Tsar, suspecting his wife of unfaithfulness, ordered her to be placed with her son in a barrel, and then the barrel was sealed and cast into the sea.

For many years the barrel floated on the waters.

Meanwhile the Tsarevich grew not by days but by hours, and his feet and his head began to press against the ends of the barrel. Every day he felt more cramped in those close quarters. One day he said to his mother, "O royal mother, allow me to stretch myself to my full length and know freedom."

"My dear Tsarevich," answered the mother, "beware of doing that—the barrel will burst and you will perish in the salt sea."

The Tsarevich thought for a moment in silence, and then he said, "O royal mother, I will stretch myself. Better to stretch oneself just once and know freedom, and then perish!"

That fairy tale, sir, tells our whole history.

BAKUNIN

Let us put our trust in the eternal spirit which destroys and annihilates only because it is the unsearchable and eternally creative source of all life. The passion for destruction is also a creative passion.

THE IMPROBABLE GIANT

AMONG THE REVOLUTIONARIES who affected the course of the Russian Revolution in the nineteenth century one man stood out above all others, although in fact he had very little influence on the Russian people and his life consisted of a series of dramatic failures. To those who knew him he seemed to be Revolution personified; and sometimes he was more like a force of nature than a man. Eccentric, flamboyant, dedicated, he spent his life in the service of the revolution, and in the end there was little to show for it. He captured, or helped to capture, a few towns in Germany, Italy and Spain. He wrote voluminously, but so unequally that his writings form a kind of Jacob's quilt with some patches of intense brightness and large areas of gray. Unlike Marx, who became his triumphant adversary, he lacked self-discipline and that hard core of fanaticism which enables a man to ride roughshod over the ideas of his age and to change them according to his will.

Mikhail Bakunin, who was born on the family estate at Premukhino some 150 miles northwest of Moscow on May 30, 1814, and who died obscurely in a Swiss hospital sixty-two years later, grew up like Lenin in a nest of gentlefolk. There was nothing in his upbringing to suggest that he would become a fiery revolutionary. His kind and indulgent father, a liberal with charming manners and the air of a *grand seigneur,* had traveled widely. It was said that he was present at the fall of the Bastille, and

101

he had earned a doctorate in philosophy at the University of Padua. After long journeys he returned to Russia to live quietly with three unmarried sisters and his widowed mother on the family estate. He married into the noble family of the Muravievs and sired ten children. His wife Varvara seems to have been a stern disciplinarian, but her discipline was offset by the remarkable gentleness of the father. Mikhail had two elder sisters, Lubov and Varvara, and two younger ones, Tatiana and Alexandra. Then came five more sons. Mikhail, surrounded by adoring and obedient sisters, secure in the affection of his family, and occupying a strategic position among the children, enjoyed an idyllic childhood. A small river, the Osuga, ran through the estate. There were water meadows, fruit trees, an old sawmill, vast expanses where the children could roam at will. On winter evenings they read *Swiss Family Robinson,* and on summer afternoons they filled their hampers and drove out to some especially beautiful part of the estate or went to visit their neighbors.

The idyl ended when he was fifteen and his father decided to send him to the Cadet School in St. Petersburg. He seems to have detested St. Petersburg from the beginning, and he especially detested the Cadet School, where he ran up debts and showed not the slightest inclination for the military life. Dismissed from the school for inattention to his studies, he was posted to a brigade in an obscure town on the Polish frontier. Garrison life pleased him no more than the Cadet School, and after two years of "unendurable misery" he fled to Premukhino and announced that he was too ill to continue his military career. Technically he was a deserter and liable to arrest and imprisonment, but the family connections saved him from the consequences of his folly. He obtained an honorable discharge and set about remaking his life. He was not yet twenty-one, and he had spent five useless years in the army.

In those years he was something of a dandy, with cleancut handsome features, a thick mane of hair brushed back from a broad forehead, with deep-set gray eyes under sweeping eyebrows, a wide nose, a long mouth, and a pointed chin. It was not a face which suggested intellectual distinction. He looked like a young officer of the Guards, big-boned and well-groomed, with the air of a man who remains the thoughtful spectator while living a life of carefree dissipation. Women were continually falling in love with him, but he had in fact very little interest in them, perhaps because he knew them too well. His sisters adored him, and to anyone who cared to listen they would expound Mikhail's philosophy of life until the words "What Mikhail says is . . ." became the chorus of their entire existence. Mikhail, in turn, protected them in his patriarchal way, chased away their suitors, saw that they read the right books, taught them the course of conduct they should pursue, and continually addressed them with words of warning and encouragement. They were his willing slaves, and he took care that they should enjoy their servitude.

There were, of course, many flaws in the young idealist who had been permitted to exchange an army career for a life of gentle indolence. He had a violent temper, a sharp tongue, and a deep-seated restlessness which showed itself in constant visits to Moscow to escape from the oppressive atmosphere at Premukhino, and these visits would be followed by the abrupt return of the prodigal to the bosom of his family. He had come under the influence of the idealist philosopher Fichte, who celebrated the divine harmony of the universe in which the human spirit acts out its destiny by embracing divinity, and in his conversations and letters the words "divinity," "soul," "freedom," "love," and "reality" were almost interchangeable terms. He set about translating Fichte's *Guide to a Blessed Life*, which he never completed, and he completed a translation of Fichte's lectures *On the Vocation of the Scholar*. It was a vocation which he earnestly desired, and throughout his turbulent life he was continually pausing to ask himself whether he should not return to the quiet contentments of scholarship.

Nikolay Stankevich was his mentor in the study of Fichte, as Vissarion Belinsky was to become his mentor in the study of Hegel. Stankevich was a young aristocrat, sweet-tempered and irresolute, doomed to die of tuberculosis before he had left any mark on the world. In the Russian fashion they lived for their conversations, which lasted all night and sometimes continued through the whole of the next day. In the eyes of Mikhail he had only one fault—he fell in love with Alexandra, the youngest and prettiest of the four sisters. Belinsky fell in love with the oldest. Mikhail wanted his adoring sisters for himself, and he went to immense pains to safeguard them from his friends.

Though comparatively wealthy, Mikhail's father had not the least intention of supporting his indolent son. Mikhail would be housed and fed when he returned to the family estate; in Moscow he must house and feed himself. The inevitable consequence was that he led the life of a sponger, mounted up debts which Stankevich sometimes paid, lived off relatives, and quite early in life earned the nickname of "Khlestakov," after the infamous sponger in Gogol's comedy *The Inspector General*. Except for his translations from Fichte he had published nothing, and he was in danger of becoming the perpetual dilettante.

A sister died; his father raged against his useless existence; Stankevich vanished into the Caucasus for his health; there were violent quarrels and reconciliations with Belinsky; he read omnivorously, and sometimes taught mathematics to the children of his rich Moscow relatives; and this was the extent of his life. Clearly it had to change. In the spring of 1840, when he was twenty-six, he decided that he had suffocated enough in Russia and it was time to be educated. Borrowing some money from Herzen, and with the prcmise of an allowance from his father, he sailed from St. Petersburg to Lübeck, and so by coach to Berlin, where within a few days he met the young and impressionable Ivan Turgenev, who now assumed the role previously occupied by Stankevich and Belinsky. They became inseparable, attended the same lectures together, and sat up half the night discussing Hegelian philosophy in all its iridescent ramifications. Something of incalculable importance was happening: for the first time Bakunin was learning to use his brain.

He was not, nor was he ever to become, a philosopher in any recognizable academic sense. He thought of himself as a philosopher, read philosophy interminably, and sometimes indicated that in due course he would claim the chair of philosophy at the University of Moscow. He filled copious notebooks with extracts from philosophical works, and became acquainted with the revolutionary implications of Hegelianism. At last in the summer of 1842 he bestirred himself sufficiently to write an essay in which he attempted to discover his own philosophical position among the Young Hegelians. It was published in Arnold Ruge's *Deutsche Jahrbücher,* a magazine of political opinion, in October, and immediately became a *succès de scandale,* for it expressed with extraordinary cogency one aspect of the Young Hegelian movement which was calculated to send shivers down men's spines, by warning them that the revolution was much closer than they had thought. By a purely dialectical process he came to the conclusion that the task of the philosopher was to destroy everything that hindered the coming of a new heaven and a new earth.

The essay was called *The Reaction in Germany: a Fragmentary Discussion by a Frenchman.* It purported to have been written by a certain Jules Elysard, of whom nothing whatsoever is known. The signature was a transparent fabrication, for Bakunin readily admitted to its authorship. Indeed, he reveled in it, and received the congratulations of his friends with the proper mixture of pride and forbearance. Belinsky and Herzen were both agreeably surprised to discover so much violence in so indolent a man.

Bakunin argues that the thesis (the government) is opposed by the antithesis (the revolution), and that only when the revolutionaries have completely overthrown the government will there arise "the young and mighty world in which all our present dissonances will be resolved into a harmonious whole." The argument is specious, and stated without conviction, for he plays with the Hegelian concepts as though he were perfectly aware that they were being employed out of context. But this play-acting is merely the prologue to an argument in which he demonstrates that both in politics and in philosophy compromise is not viable, that the war between the reaction and the revolution must inevitably be fought to a conclusion, and that the penalty of the compromisers is to be utterly destroyed by the opposing forces. As a somber illustration he gives the example of the Jews in Poland who had supported the Poles and then changed their allegiance to the Russians, with the result that they were hanged by both.

The peroration was among the most memorable things that Bakunin ever wrote:

> All peoples and all men are full of presentiments. Everyone whose living organisms are not paralyzed sees with trembling expectation the approach of the future which will utter the decisive word. Even in Russia, in that limitless and snow-covered empire, of which we know so little and which has before it perhaps a great future, even in Russia the dark storm clouds are gathering! The air is sultry, it is heavy with storms!
>
> And therefore we call to our blinded brothers: Repent! Repent! The Kingdom of God is coming nigh.
>
> Let us put our trust in the eternal spirit which destroys and annihilates only because it is the unsearchable and eternally creative source of all life. The passion for destruction is also a creative passion.

The opening words of the peroration were to be echoed by Marx in the *Communist Manifesto,* written six years later, but they already possessed a respectable ancestry. The romantic spirit envisaged a world haunted by doom, at the mercy of titanic forces, inevitably fated to watch the giants at their fatal conflict. There was the sense of hovering over the abyss or of some vast cataclysmic destruction. The romantic imagination fed on disasters long before the disasters came, and Bakunin was still the romantic philosopher, moving with transparent ease through the revolutionary holocaust which was not to take place until the following century.

The sources of Bakunin's peroration can be easily traced in the German romantic novels of Tieck and the Grimm brothers, and in Goethe's *Faust,* where "the eternal spirit which denies" makes an intermittent appearance. The messianic note was to be found among the socialists of France and Germany; Bakunin was not the only one who wore the camel-skin robe of the Baptist and pronounced that the Kingdom of Heaven was coming nearer every day. He was speaking in the accents of an authentic Western tradition, not as a Russian. Russians, even very intelligent Russians, were puzzled by Bakunin's celebration of the coming storm. They saw no sign of it. The dictatorship of Nicholas I had never been stronger, and it was in no mood to surrender its powers. The "dark storm clouds" would soon be gathering over Paris and the capitals of Central Europe, but they were not to reach Russia for three quarters of a century.

Bakunin never despaired of revolution, though he was not yet certain how it would come about. Always in poverty, spending his life in desultory revolutionary conversations, he led a life of astonishing indolence made tolerable by enduring friendships. He met Georg Herwegh, the revolutionary poet who had been forced to flee to Switzerland after the publication of his book of poems and was now returning to Germany to receive the plaudits of the crowd, and soon Herwegh was occupying the place in Bakunin's affections formerly occupied by Stankevich, Belinsky and Turgenev, who had departed for Russia. Herwegh, three years younger than Bakunin, was the son of a hotelkeeper, but he had the appearance and manners of an aristocrat. Bakunin's more enduring friendships were usually for revolutionaries with aristocratic tempers.

Herwegh's triumphal progress through Germany culminated in an audience with King Frederick William IV of Prussia, who remarked to the young poet: "I like an opposition when it is dictated by principle." Believing himself to be specially favored, the poet then addressed a resounding letter of protest to the King, and was immediately ordered to leave the country. He went to Switzerland for the second time, and Bakunin joined him.

The brief idyl in Switzerland enabled Bakunin to think out his revolutionary philosophy in the company of several young women and a few dedicated revolutionaries, the most determined of them being Wilhelm Weitling, the author of a slender volume called *Guarantees of Harmony and Freedom*. Weitling was that very rare thing—a true proletarian revolutionary. The illegitimate son of a German girl by a French officer quartered in Magdeburg during the Napoleonic Wars, he was a journeyman tailor with a deep interest in creating secret revolutionary societies among craftsmen, and he was now operating in Switzerland. Herwegh gave him a letter of introduction to Bakunin, and they immediately became close friends, with Bakunin threatening to learn a trade and become a craftsman so that he could take part in Weitling's revolutionary organizations.

Weitling had spent some time with Blanqui in Paris, and though he wrote in German, his sympathies were with French revolutionaries. There was a peculiarly French savagery in him. He was all for killing off the bourgeoisie so that a pure form of communism could come into existence. "The perfect society," he wrote, "has no government, only an administration; no laws, only duties to be performed; no punishment, only means of correction." Marx read *Guarantees of Harmony and Freedom* and congratulated the author on the broad sweep of his arguments, and later drummed Weitling out of the communist party. Bakunin too became disenchanted, as he saw that the new state envisaged by Weitling was a soulless mechanical entity, "a herd of animals held together by force and intolerable coercion." In the history of the communist movement *Guarantees of Harmony and Freedom* holds a special place, for it provided the first blueprint of the proletarian communist state.

Weitling went on to write another slender volume called *The Gospel of a Poor Sinner,* which took the form of an autobiographical fragment in which he continually appeared as Jesus Christ, "the illegitimate son of a poor girl Mary," with a program of communism and violence against the state. The manuscript was sent to the printer, but the Swiss police raided the press and Weitling was condemned to six months' imprisonment for blasphemy and political unorthodoxy. Among his papers the police found the name of Bakunin, and they appear to have passed on the information to the Russian Legation in Berne, for soon Bakunin was being officially invited to return to Russia, with the prospect of being imprisoned in the Peter and Paul Fortress as a notorious revolutionary. Instead of accepting the Russian summons, he fled to Brussels, and a few days later to Paris.

Paris was in fact the obvious place for him to be. It was the heart of the revolutionary movement in Western Europe, and one by one most of his friends were making their way there. Arnold Ruge, who had published his article *The Reaction in Germany,* was already there, a refugee from Dresden. Herwegh, who had married into a rich Jewish family, was living there in considerable splendor. Bakunin survived as usual by sponging on his friends, repaying them with lively conversations and magnificent dreams of a world conflagration. He met George Sand, Lamennais, Cabet, the author of the famous utopian pamphlet *Voyage to Icaria,* Louis Blanc, Victor Considerant, Marx, Proudhon, and many others who were engaged in promoting the revolution. He saw a good deal of Marx, but there was little intimacy between them. Bakunin, who was not devoid of personal vanity, was struck by the towering vanity of Marx. He was prepared to admit that Marx had an incisive and forceful mind, never hesitated to carry his conclusions to their extraordinary extremes, and was notably successful in sharpening the fine edge of his sarcasm. There was something petty bourgeois about him—a lack of generosity, an absence of any refinement, a too easy recourse to legalistic arguments—and Bakunin with his aristocratic temper, generous to a fault and impatient of legalistic argument, found no reason to sit at Marx's feet. "Marx called me a sentimental idealist, and he was right," Bakunin wrote later. "I called him morose, vain and treacherous, and I too was right."

Toward Proudhon Bakunin showed a kinder temper and deliberately set himself to learn at the feet of the fiery apostle of anarchy. Bakunin was a physical giant, Proudhon was small and thin-boned. Bakunin could talk for three days in succession, while Proudhon liked to think before he spoke. What they had in common was a lively interest in philosophy and an absolute dedication to overthrowing the existing order; in addition they had gifts of friendship. "I spit on the gods and men, I revere only study and friendship." They were sentiments which were very close to Bakunin's heart.

Bakunin taught Proudhon the elements of Hegelian logic, to such effect that when Proudhon wrote a book in which he attempted to introduce Hegelian terms in his own fashion, Marx scored an easy victory by announcing quite properly that Proudhon had never really understood Hegel and had shown himself to be an ignoramus. Proudhon, who saw no virtue in the Hegelian triad of thesis-antithesis-synthesis, replied that he was unable to understand why the Germans thought a synthesis was always forthcoming. Synthesis, in his view, was the blindfold which German philosophers wore to blind themselves from reality. "Marx," he said, "is the tapeworm of socialism."

With Proudhon Bakunin was always at ease; they talked all night and regarded themselves as fellow conspirators in the revolutionary war. They had found each other's measure, and neither was wanting. To the end of his life Bakunin would regard himself as the disciple of the original French philosopher who asked "What is property?" and answered "Property is theft."

Bakunin did not spend all his days discussing philosophy, and in fact most of his time and energy was spent in amassing the small amount of income and property necessary to keep alive. He wrote very little, lived very simply, and was continually in debt. He kept out of the limelight, and although the French police kept him under observation, they had very little to report. Bakunin, too, found very little to report about himself. He was leading a life of extreme dissipation, for he was dissipating all his energies in talk. The long-expected revolution was as far away as ever, and there was very little to show for his life. Sometimes he was close to suicide.

He thirsted for great dramatic movements, heroic gestures, sudden apotheoses. He saw himself as a revolutionary dedicated to the simple thesis that the state must be put to the flames and that the entire working population of Europe must rise in rebellion against their masters, himself the firebrand uttering the call to arms, but the reality was very different. He was living in a shabby apartment, suffering from fever and hunger, unable to write two consecutive lines of prose, and filled with a desperate yearning to be in Russia amid the familiar sights of his childhood. On the advice of a doctor he had shaved off his bushy mane of hair. He was thirty-two years old, an age when most men have acquired a settled profession and a family, and he had none of these things. It was time he went into action.

The opportunity came in November 1847 when some Polish *émigrés* invited him to attend a banquet to honor the occasion of the anniversary of the Polish insurrection of 1831. He ordered a wig, put on a clean shirt and a clean suit of clothes, and attended the banquet, where he delivered a speech of such extraordinary violence that the Polish *émigrés* sat on the edge of their seats and watched him, spellbound by the splendor of his rhetoric and the thunder of his call to arms. It was one of his most satisfying speeches, and he liked to remember it in the sad days to come. His theme was the undying solidarity between the Polish insurgents and the creative forces of Russia. He spoke of a time when all the Slavs would be united in peace and harmony under a single revolutionary government in which the Tsar would have no place. He attacked the Tsar wholeheartedly, pointing out that he had scarcely a drop of Russian blood, and was more German than Russian, and the Germans were the common enemies of the Slavs. Let the Slavs arise and throw out their foreign masters and put an end once and for all to the reign of despotism. Some fifteen hundred French, Russians and Poles cheered him to the rafters; for the first time he had shown himself to be a masterful orator with the power to summon men to the barricades. An informer brought the substance of the speech to the attention of Count Kiselev, the Russian ambassador in Paris, and a few days later Bakunin was served with an order to leave the soil of France. He returned to Brussels, which he had left three and a half years before.

Brussels was filled with revolutionaries, but they were not the kind of men, he thought, who would ever stand at the barricades. He met Marx and Engels, and drew away from them in horror. He wrote to Herwegh:

> The Germans, those craftsmen Bornstedt, Marx and Engels—especially Marx—are plotting their usual mischief here. Vanity, malice, quarrels, theoretical pride and practical cowardice, high-minded theories about life, action, and simplicity, and at the same time a total absence of life, action, and simplicity. Self-conscious and intelligent workmen and a disgusting playing with them. "Feuerbach is bourgeois" and the word "bourgeois" becomes an epithet boring to the point of nausea through repetition, though they themselves from head to foot are little provincial petty bourgeois. In a word lies and stupidity, stupidity and lies. Impossible to breathe freely in such a society. I keep away from them, and I have explicitly said that I shall never enter their Communist union, and I'll have nothing to do with them.

In this way, like a man resolved to lead a life of virtuous activity, Bakunin cut himself adrift from the abstract theoreticians, especially German theoreticians. There was no common ground between his fiery dreams of destruction and the ferocious abstractions of Marx. That winter, in an obscure lodginghouse in the suburbs of Brussels, Marx composed the *Communist Manifesto*.

Eighteen forty-eight was the year of revolutions. All over Europe, as the year advanced, revolutions broke out like a chain of firecrackers. The first revolts took place in Italy, the second in Paris. As soon as the February revolution broke out in Paris, Bakunin made preparations to go there. He was in a mood of extraordinary jubilation, beside himself with excitement. Paris had changed overnight; there were barricades two stories high, and the workmen manning them had an air of dignity and self-assurance. Bakunin joined their ranks, and helped to organize the workmen's militia from the Tournon barracks near the Luxembourg Palace. He marched in their processions, attended their banquets, delivered bloodcurdling speeches in heavily accented French, and enjoyed himself as never before. "*Quel homme! Quel homme!*" exclaimed Marc Caussidière, the revolutionary Prefect of Police. "On the first day of the revolution he is a perfect treasure, on the next he ought to be shot!" It was a verdict which other revolutionaries learned to share.

Now at last he was in his element, and the thought of other revolutions taking place without his active participation haunted him. Old Europe was breaking up; revolutions or the simulacra of revolutions were beginning to break out all over Central Europe; he wanted to be present at all of them. He rushed to Berlin, but here at least the government was in full control, and he was arrested and escorted under guard to Leipzig. Prague summoned him, and he hastened to attend the Slav Congress announced for the end of May. Congresses are not revolutions, and Bakunin, as the self-elected representative of revolutionary Russia, found himself at odds with the majority, who cared nothing at all for bloody revolutions: they wanted and obtained a manifesto, a suitably watered-down statement of Slav aspirations. Bakunin helped to write the final draft, but nearly all his more exuberant statements were carefully omitted in the published version. The revolution had become "a battle of ghosts." An angry and confused Bakunin found himself wandering aimlessly across Central Europe in search of a cause.

The Russian police were trailing him; Marx was openly attacking him, repeating the *canard* that he was an agent of the Russian secret police; and he was nearly friendless and alone. In June Windischgrätz with a small body of troops quashed the revolutionary insurrection in Prague; a few days later General Cavaignac put an end to the revolution in Paris. Bakunin wrote *An Appeal to the Slavs,* in which he called for the dismemberment of the Austrian empire, but no one listened.

A strange story was told about his journey to Prague. It was said that while he was traveling in his coach he came upon a group of German peasants on the estate of a great landowner. The peasants were milling around the landowner's castle, not knowing what to do. Bakunin jumped out of his coach, and immediately offered the peasants his assistance, wasting no time on idle questioning. Remembering perhaps that he had been a cadet, he formed them into ranks and drew up an order of battle. When he resumed his seat in the coach, he had the satisfaction of seeing the castle burning on all four sides. Then, quietly rejoicing, he drove on to Prague.

The story, which was told by Herzen, is suspect, because it is exactly what Bakunin would have liked to have done. He alone could have told the story to Herzen, and he was not above inventing and embroidering on the truth. He had a pagan passion for fire. He spoke of "the childish, almost demoniac delight of the Russians in fire," and he held throughout his life to the belief that no revolution could be successful until the government offices were smoking ruins. He was perhaps a throwback to those ancient Russians who fought against their invaders from the safety of the forests and marshlands, defending themselves with the simplest of weapons—fire, axes, their bare hands. He approved of the firing of Moscow by the Russians to save it from the Grande Armée of Napoleon, and he found a particular pleasure in contemplating the marauding peasants who set fire to their masters' manor houses. He did not quail before the spectacle of all Europe and Russia reduced to cinders. Only in this way could the new heaven and the new earth be brought about.

The opportunity to fire a city or at the very least its government offices came in the late spring of the following year. As it happened, he was staying in Dresden, when a dispute with the king of Saxony brought the revolutionaries out on the streets. The first barricades went up on May 3, and later in the day the revolutionaries attempted to rush the arsenal and seize all the weapons in it. The troops remained loyal to the government, and fired into the crowd, killing fifteen men. From that moment there could be no turning back.

Richard Wagner was then the conductor of the Dresden opera, and in his moments of leisure he would amuse himself in the company of Bakunin, whose theories on the necessary regeneration of the human race by means of wholesale destruction and devastation seemed to derive from some unknown and wholly improbable mythology. Bakunin would talk for hours about the impending doom which must be visited on the human race, but always with a kind of sweet-tempered gravity, as though he were conferring a blessing by ordering so much destruction. He was childlike, gay, ironical, idealistic, kindhearted. He knew nothing about music, and his sole contribution to Wagner's musical education was the suggestion that he should compose an oratorio in which the tenor sang "Kill them!" and the soprano sang "Hang them!" while the bass sang "Fire! Fire!" without ever pausing for breath. Invited to dine at Wagner's house, Bakunin seized on the cold meats and the thin slices of sausage, and consumed them in a single mouthful. It was the same with the brandy which he consumed by the tumblerful. "He had the greatest antipathy for that celebrated moderation which prolongs the enjoyment," Wagner commented with the air of a man who found it difficult to share Bakunin's gargantuan appetite.

Nevertheless they had much in common, for they were both men with a fierce appetite for living. In their different ways they both stood for the destruction of the old order, the renovation of a world grown gray with weariness. They admired each other and were happy together like children, and there was a bond between them, though neither could have said what attracted him to the other.

On May 4 Wagner met Bakunin in the street as he was threading his way over the barricades, a cigar stuck jauntily between his teeth. They were both on their way to the Town Hall, where the provisional government had just been proclaimed. Wagner thought his companion would be delighted by the turn of events, but Bakunin was in no mood for enjoyment. He complained that the revolutionaries knew nothing about defending their hard-won gains, and the only pleasure he derived lay in the thought that he could wander about the streets at his leisure without being followed by the secret police. Once he arrived at the Town Hall his tone changed. He offered advice, sternly rebuked the leaders of the provisional government for their reliance on political speeches rather than muskets and cannon, and took over the military direction of the revolution, laying out the maps on the table in the Council Chamber and marking out the sites of barricades and defense posts. There he remained during the following days, his beard growing longer, his eyes more watery, as the hours passed and the Prussian troops gradually forced their way into the town. On another visit to the Town Hall Wagner found him lying on a mattress spread out in the Council Chamber, still flaunting a cigar, completely in command of himself, though he had had no sleep for many nights.

The revolution was doomed, for the Prussian troops worked their way through the houses instead of taking the barricades by storm. The rebels were shot out of hand, or thrown into the Elbe. Communications between rebel outposts broke down, and it was clear that the provisional government could survive for only a few more hours. Bakunin tried to persuade his comrades to fill the cellars of the Town Hall with gunpowder and blow themselves up, but the provisional government had prudently removed the gunpowder to a safer place. With the Prussians coming closer to the Town Hall, the remnants of the small revolutionary army slipped out just in time, their last act being to cut down the trees in the Maximilienallee to protect their left flank. The wealthy people living on the avenue protested tearfully against this final desecration. How would they live without their trees? Why were they being deprived of shade? Bakunin vividly remembered their tears, and confessed to Wagner, who also took part in the retreat, that few things had pleased him more than the sight of these wealthy people wringing their hands and weeping copiously. "The tears of the Philistines," he said, "are the nectar of the gods!"

At Freiberg their ways parted. Wagner hurried to Weimar and then to the security of Switzerland. Bakunin and a small band of revolutionaries went on to Chemnitz, in the hope of raising the industrial proletariat to the red flag. Dead with fatigue after five days of commanding a small revolutionary army, he threw himself down on a bed. A few hours later the police rushed into his bedroom, and he was put under arrest.

For eight years he was to remain a prisoner. For thirteen months he was a prisoner in Dresden and in the fortress of Königstein perched high on the rocks. It was a pleasant enough prison, with a splendid view of the mountains. Books were provided, and he was allowed to smoke as much as he pleased. He was permitted to correspond with his friends, and he was even allowed to walk in the courtyard of the cavalry school where he was imprisoned, provided he allowed himself to be chained to two soldiers with fixed bayonets. His trial proceeded slowly, for the judges could make very little of this strange prisoner who defended all his actions by an appeal to the justice of anarchy. He heard himself being sentenced to death, and was only mildly disturbed; it was after all what he had expected.

Removed to a prison in the Hradčin Castle in Prague, and then to the Moravian fortress of Olmütz, he watched, as though from a great distance, the progressive decline of his fortunes, for each prison was worse than the last. At Olmütz he was chained to the wall of his cell. He was almost beyond caring, for it was clear that in its own good time the government would carry out the death sentence. He fell into long fits of brooding. He was remote from the world as in a grave.

He did not fear death. What he feared above all was being handed over to the Russians, and this was precisely the fate which was being reserved for him. At last on May 17, 1851, he found himself at Cracow under guard, and in the dead of night he was given over to the twenty Cossacks and six gendarmes who had been waiting for him at the frontier for seven weeks. His safe arrival on Russian territory was reported to the Tsar, who wrote a single Russian word on the official report. It was *"Nakonets"*—"At last."

Six days after being handed over to the Russians on the frontier, he reached St. Petersburg. Throughout the journey he had conducted himself quietly and sensibly; the gendarmes were kind to him, and he surprised them with his meekness. They had expected a man of towering violence, and instead there was only a bowed, prematurely aged man who spoke charmingly about his experiences in Europe.

The doors of the Peter and Paul Fortress were opened for him, and he was thrown into a dungeon in the Alexis Ravelin.

THE DEPTHS OF THE ABYSS

W HEN BAKUNIN SAT IN HIS CELL in the Alexis Ravelin, he knew he had reached the end of the road. There was no mortal power which could remove him from the Peter and Paul Fortress. The Tsar, who had ordered his arrest and intrigued with the crowned heads of two nations in order to take physical possession of him, was not, nor would he ever be, in a mood to offer a pardon. The prisoner had been plucked out of Saxony and removed bodily to St. Petersburg: the Tsar had shown that his power reached far beyond the confines of his empire. There could be no question of a trial, for Bakunin was a state prisoner, and there was no likelihood that he would be sent to Siberia. He might hope for miracles—the death of the Tsar, the coming of the long-promised age of revolution—but these were small hopes, and a man would be a fool to trust in them. He contemplated suicide: a not uncommon subject of contemplation in the Alexis Ravelin. All the evidence pointed to the fact that he was doomed to die in the prison.

He had changed remarkably since the day, eleven years before, when he left Russia to study philosophy in Berlin. The twenty-five-year-old dandy had become a bent, prematurely aged man with thinning hair, sickly and paunchy, with swollen feet and prison pallor. He could expect to live for two or three years, and then one morning he would be found dead in a corner of his cell. But Bakunin had not the least intention of dying: even in his greatest miseries he was sustained by a huge appetite for life. He would continue to fight back with all the resources of his intelligence, his knowledge of strategy, and his endurance. He had survived two prisons, and would survive a third.

For two months he was left alone in his cell. It was the custom to let prisoners alone for months and sometimes years on end; then in their own good time the police would question them and extract confessions from them. But Bakunin was no ordinary prisoner; he had become a legend in his own lifetime; he must be dealt with in an unusual way. In the middle of July the iron door of his cell was opened to admit no less a person than Count Alexey Orlov, the chief of the Third Division and the principal aide-de-camp of the Tsar. He was a man of sixty-five, very grave and earnest in manner, not without kindness, and he appeared in the full uniform of the court. He explained that he had come directly from the Tsar to convey a personal message from His Imperial Majesty. Bakunin was told that he had nothing to fear since the death penalty no longer existed in Russia: the Tsar was asking him to make a full confession of his sins "like a spiritual son addressing his spiritual father." It was not therefore to be such a document as a criminal prepares in appealing to a judge, but a deeply personal and intimate confession such as a man makes to a priest. Bakunin agreed to write his confession, and the Count departed.

In later years when rumors that he had written a complete confession to the Tsar reached the revolutionaries, Bakunin was attacked as an informer, and the old legend that he was a spy in the pay of the Russian government was revived. But he was neither a spy nor an informer, and his confession was designed with great subtlety to satisfy the curiosity of the Tsar, to educate him, and to provide him, should he so desire, with an excuse for mitigating the harsh sentence already imposed. Bakunin revealed himself as a man who had suffered deeply for his crimes. He divulged no secrets, implicated no one who was not already well-known to the Russian police, and betrayed no one except himself, for sometimes in the rush of his ideas he showed only too well that he was a convinced revolutionary without an atom of true repentance. The document, which covers over a hundred printed pages, vanished into the archives of the secret police, and was discovered in 1919. It was published for the first time in 1921, seventy years after it was written.

Bakunin's confession was one of the most revealing documents he ever wrote, for it describes step by step how he became a revolutionary. He makes no excuses. This happened, he says, and it could not have happened in any other way. "I came out in open revolt against Your Majesty and Your Majesty's government," he writes near the beginning of the confession. "I dared to set myself up as an enemy against Your Majesty, I wrote and spoke against you, and stirred people against you, as often as I could and wherever I could." He goes on to recount his life in detail, and sometimes pauses to describe the characters of the people he loved—Herwegh "that truly pure and noble person possessing a greatness of soul rare among the Germans," Weitling "with his innate intelligence, energy and savage fanaticism, his proud and noble belief in the liberation and the future of the enslaved masses," and Turgenev "who spoke of Russia with love and sometimes with tears." He describes how he came to make a public speech in celebration of the Polish uprising, and how he met the young French revolutionaries in the Tournon barracks in Paris, remembering their exquisite manners and their fierce heroism. But these graceful tributes, like greetings sent out into the world from the silence of his cell, are forgotten when he recounts his adventures in Central Europe and his attempt to overthrow the Kingdom of Saxony, and those other attempts to overthrow the Austro-Hungarian empire, although they scarcely deserved to be called attempts at all, for they were little more than ideas burgeoning in his brain. At the Prague Conference he had hoped to bring about the dismemberment of the Austro-Hungarian empire, beginning with Bohemia. He wrote in his confession:

I hoped to bring about in Bohemia an absolute and radical revolution, which would have brought everything toppling down. Even if it came to grief and the Austrian government proved to be victorious, they would have found nothing in its place. We regarded the fact that the entire aristocracy of Bohemia and all the rich property owners were German as favorable to our cause, for we could send the aristocrats and the hostile clergy into exile and expropriate their property, dividing half of it among poor peasants to win them to our cause, while the other half would be used to create an extraordinary fund to pay the expenses of the revolution.

My intention was to destroy all the castles, and to burn, wherever they could be found in Bohemia, all the dossiers connected with administrative, judiciary, and public trials as well as all charters and titles to property and mortgage deeds, and I would cancel all debts which amounted to less than a certain convenient sum, say one or two thousand gulden. In short, I contemplated a revolution which was unprecedented and terrible, although directed more at property than at people . . .

But my intentions were not limited to the revolution. I intended to transform all Bohemia into a revolutionary camp and build a force capable not only of safeguarding the revolution in its country of origin, but of taking the offensive, to stir up all the Slavs and incite them to revolt, and tear down everything which bore the mark of the Austrian monarchy, and then go to the aid of the Hungarians and the Poles—it would have been a struggle against Your Majesty! . . .

The seat of the revolutionary government possessing unlimited dictatorial powers would be in Prague. With the aristocracy exiled and the hostile clergy deported, the Austrian government would be abolished and its officials dismissed, though a handful of the most important and better informed would be retained at Prague, so that we could seek their advice, treating them as though they were a library from which we could extract useful statistical material. All the clubs and newspapers, all those wordy and anarchic elements would be dissolved, and everyone would be forced to accept the existence of the dictatorship.

Bakunin was taking the Tsar at his word: he was confessing those deepest crimes of intention which were also his most fugitive dreams. In fact nothing at all had happened except the production of a manifesto. When he describes the uprising in Dresden, he no longer has recourse to dreams, but relates the events quietly and accurately in proper order.

What is most disturbing in the confession is the absence of a focus, for the arguments against the Austro-Hungarian empire merge imperceptibly into arguments against the Russian empire. Some of the best pages are devoted to a pitiless examination of the German character, but much of what he has to say could equally be said of the Russians. He will fight the Russian monarchy, but if the Germans should set foot on Russian soil he will turn about and fight them even more strenuously. He believed that the mission of Russia was "to revitalize the decadent Western world," but his opinion of Russia was that it was so weakened by tyranny and poverty that it was almost beyond praying for. "The basic drive in Russia is fear," he wrote, "and fear destroys all life, all intelligence, all generous movements of the soul."

Though the confession is riddled with confusions and never achieves a clear-cut purpose, it wonderfully conveys the exuberance of Bakunin's beliefs and his anarchic character. He says what he thinks, even when he thinks two exactly contrary ideas. He celebrates the absolute freedom which will come about when the revolution is successful, and at the same time he insists on an iron dictatorship, which is the negation of freedom. In one breath he warns the Tsar against expanding his frontiers—"What will it profit Russia if half the world bows down to her?"—and in the next breath he speaks of the vast, untapped power which will accrue to Russia when the enslaved peasants are given their freedom, and then she will become so powerful that no enemy or combination of enemies will ever dare to oppose her. He had nothing but contempt for the Russian aristocracy, whom he described as "debauched and timid souls," but showed a proper respect for the autocratic Tsar: it was a respect that a man offers to a mortal enemy. The Tsar had asked for a confession, which included by definition not only crimes actually committed but all those he had intended to commit if opportunity or chance permitted, and Bakunin had no scruples in describing the supreme crime which he had never been in any position to commit—the destruction of the Russian state. After apologizing for having lost contact with conditions in Russia, and therefore approaching the problem with a certain lack of assurance, he goes on:

I was perfectly prepared to use any or all the means which fell into my hands. Conspiracy in the army, a mutiny of Russian soldiers, the summoning of Russian prisoners to revolt in order to form the nucleus of a Russian revolutionary army, finally a peasant insurrection. In a word, Sire, my crime against Your Sacred Majesty knew neither in thought nor in intention any limits whatsoever. And so once more I thank Providence which drew back my hand in time, before I had committed or even begun a single one of those dreadful acts against you, my emperor, and against my country.

In confessing to the crime of desiring to overthrow the state, Bakunin demonstrated a transparent honesty and a transparent folly. The Tsar carefully annotated the manuscript, and where Bakunin admitted this superb crime and confessed that he deserved the most severe punishment, the Tsar wrote in the margin: "The sword shall not strike off the head of him who confesses such sins. May God pardon him." But this was not to say that the Tsar had pardoned him. The confession only made the Tsar more determined than ever to keep Bakunin in prison. He evidently enjoyed reading the manuscript, which was copied out in the impeccable calligraphy of one of Count Orlov's scribes, and he liked to pepper the margins with "Note well! How true! A striking truth!" but he never made the slightest suggestion that the sentence should be mitigated. Bakunin had revealed himself too well.

When describing his revolutionary activities in Central Europe Bakunin described his own character at some length. "I was both the deceiver and the deceived," he wrote, "and sometimes I was a charlatan in spite of myself." It was a true verdict. For the rest of his life he was to be the deceiver, the deceived, and the charlatan in spite of himself. Sometimes the charlatan would give place to the philosopher of revolution calmly surveying the possibilities of destroying the old order and bringing about a new order in which men would be brothers.

He finished writing his confession in September, and then waited to see what would happen. Nothing happened except as an act of mercy he was permitted to see his father and his sister Tatiana. The Tsar had made his decision: the punishment was imprisonment in the Alexis Ravelin in perpetuity. He would be permitted to read novels and scientific works, even newspapers and periodicals, but he would never again be allowed to endanger the state.

For Bakunin they were years of total despair relieved only by the rare visits of his father and sister, and later of his brother Paul. Occasionally letters came, and on rare occasions he was able to smuggle out a reply in mingled Russian and French, in which he would offer advice, describe his own misery, and lament his lost hopes. He told them that he had abjured philosophy; all those years of studying the Hegelian dialectic had ended only in a profound horror of abstractions. If he could have lived his life again, he would have lived like a peasant. He had hoped in his youth to study everything, and he now realized that those who study deeply live at a disadvantage. In a letter smuggled out to his family at the end of 1852 or the beginning of 1853 he wrote:

The great men of science and knowledge are not made like ordinary men; they are so organized that they are nothing for themselves, everything for others—they become books, abstractions, logical deductions, calculations, lively contemplations, and this is sublime, if you like, but they are scarcely human. In spite of their greatness, and perhaps because of it, they remain incomplete, monstrosities of nature, and their individual existence has always been poor and useless, sometimes even ridiculous.

So he wrote in a letter filled with the milk of human kindness, gently chiding his brother Alexander for not caring sufficiently for the peasants and for loving books more than life, and since there was always the possibility that the letter might be discovered, there were the inevitable appeals to the mercy of a benevolent Tsar combined with protestations of repentance. But the Tsar was adamant: under no account was Bakunin permitted to leave his cell. Some small comforts—a nightshirt lined with squirrel fur, and new trousers and boots—were permitted to reach him from his family, and we hear of two canaries in a cage dispelling the interminable silence of the Alexis Ravelin. When the Crimean War was about to break out, and it was believed that the British and the French might attack St. Petersburg by sea, it was thought advisable to remove him to the safety of the Schlüsselburg Fortress on the shores of Lake Ladoga. Accordingly on March 23, 1854, a small convoy left the Peter and Paul Fortress with the heavily manacled Bakunin, and on the following day after a long train journey he was duly registered as the occupant of Cell No. 7 of the Schlüsselburg Fortress. He was now in a worse situation than ever, for Schlüsselburg had a reputation for brutality absent in the prisons of St. Petersburg. Cell No. 7 was even smaller and darker than the cell in the Alexis Ravelin. He protested, and some months later he was given a larger cell.

He was growing old rapidly; his health was breaking down; he had lost his teeth, suffered from piles and scurvy, shortness of breath and noises in the ears; the huge lumbering giant was swollen and shapeless as he sat in a corner of his cell lost in his dreams or fighting off racking headaches. In the Peter and Paul Fortress there was always the hope that some distinguished officer of the court might visit him and report to the Tsar that "the repentant sinner Mikhail Bakunin" deserved some mitigation of his sentence, but no officer of the court ever visited him at Schlüsselburg.

In February 1855 Tsar Nicholas I died of a severe chill brought about by inspecting his troops in the intense cold. To his son and successor, the Grand Duke Alexander Nikolayevich, he dictated his last instructions, and the warning that the future was dark and burdensome, and a few moments before his death he dictated the dispatch which would be sent to all the cities of the empire—"The Tsar is dying." The Crimean War was still going on. Alexander II had inherited a nation on the verge of defeat.

It is the custom of monarchs when they ascend the throne to offer an amnesty to prisoners, but Alexander II showed no disposition to follow the tradition. The war was still dragging on, there were mounting economic difficulties at home, and political turmoil, far from abating, became increasingly uncontrollable. The new Tsar was relying heavily on the secret police.

Not until February 1857 was there any hint that there might be a change in Bakunin's fortunes. Toward the end of the month he received permission to write to the Tsar. This meant, as he well knew, that he was being invited to appeal to the Tsar's mercy and that every word must be weighed against the known proclivities of the Tsar and his entourage. The confession had been a mistake; he had confessed too much. This time there could be no error. The appeal was obviously written with extraordinary care, revised many times, examined and re-examined until it conveyed exactly the sentiments he wanted to convey, with the result that of all Bakunin's works this four-page letter to the Tsar gives the impression of being the most complete and the most carefully contrived. He abases himself before the memory of the dead emperor, seeks the indulgence of the new, points to the sufferings and humiliations he has endured during his long years in prison, reminds the Tsar that five of his brothers had volunteered for the front, and offers his undying loyalty to Alexander II. He could not quite prevent himself from writing in the tones of a deposed emperor who seeks to reclaim his throne, but he could and did write with a sense of the majesty of the occasion. Describing his life in prison, he wrote:

> This awful solitude possesses at least one great and indisputable advantage: here a man confronts himself face to face. In the turmoil of our earthly existence and in the course of our daily lives, men yield easily to the delights and illusions of vanity, but in the forced inactivity of the prison cell and in the tomblike silence of perpetual seclusion these dreams wither away; and a man who has kept within himself even a solitary spark of the truth must inevitably come to regard the whole of his past life in terms of its true value and real worth; and when his past life has been hollow, useless, and harmful as was mine, then the prisoner becomes his own executioner; and however hard the implacable conversations he exchanges with himself, however poignant the ideas which then arise, this conversation once embarked upon can have no end.
>
> This I know from an imprisonment which has endured for eight years.

Such sentiments were no doubt intended to appeal to the Tsar's sense of pity, but they also came from Bakunin's heart. The Tsar was suitably impressed, and ordered him exiled to Siberia. Bakunin asked for permission to visit the family estate at Premukhino for the last time before vanishing into the icy wastes of exile, and this too was granted to him. There was an uncomfortable reunion with his family, with Bakunin so withdrawn into himself that he could scarcely bring himself to recognize his brothers and sisters, and then within twenty-four hours he was on his way to Siberia under armed guard.

An obscure village in Tomsk *guberniya* had been chosen for his place of exile, but he succeeded in convincing the authorities that he was too ill to travel beyond Tomsk, the provincial capital: it was the first mitigation of his sentence, and there were to be many more. He remained in exile for four years: during every minute he seems to have been fighting for his freedom, demanding more and more privileges, exerting more and more pressure on the officials charged to supervise his activities. He made a living as a tutor, and among those he taught was the pretty eighteen-year-old Antonia Kviatkovsky. He proposed to her, and was immediately accepted. He was forty-four, but looked sixty; his bride looked like a child.

In 1858, the year of this unlikely marriage, General Nikolay Muraviev, the Governor General of Eastern Siberia, concluded a treaty with the Chinese government by which vast areas of the Chinese empire north and west of the Amur river were incorporated in the Russian empire. Muraviev had acted with astonishing adroitness, and for having brought the Russian empire to the bounds of the Pacific, he was rewarded with great honors and great powers. Bakunin's mother was a Muraviev, and he was the second cousin of the Governor General. Such a lucky kinship was not permitted to rest unhonored, and when the Governor General paid an official visit to Tomsk, the former prisoner of the Alexis Ravelin and the Viceroy met on equal terms. Muraviev was pleasantly impressed by the intelligence and bearing of his cousin, and Bakunin was made deeply aware of the liberality and sense of social responsibility of Muraviev. A few months later Bakunin received permission to leave Tomsk and to take up a post as a commercial traveler in the Amur Company at Irkutsk, the Viceroy's capital. The post was a sinecure and paid 2,000 rubles a year. No work was demanded of him, and Bakunin could therefore spend his time in planning to escape from Russia and building up a revolutionary movement abroad or in preparing for the day when he would receive a full pardon and could return to St. Petersburg to stir up revolution in the capital. His revolutionary fervor had grown stronger rather than weaker during the years of imprisonment. At whatever the cost he was determined to bring about the downfall of the Russian monarchy.

Although Bakunin himself was not conscious of any change in his motives, they had changed profoundly in prison. His brother Paul, visiting him in the Peter and Paul Fortress, was one of those who observed the change. He wrote to his sister Tatiana: "Our brother is moved by iron passions. He was the fire in the flame, suddenly torn out of all circumstance and movement, estranged from the world, plunged into sepulchral silence and solitude within and without. Oh, this, too, is a fire. For three years already it has been seething in his soul. Before, it was a flame of life; now it is a flame of death."

Paul's verdict was profoundly true, but it was not the whole truth. When Bakunin escaped from Russia, making his way on an American ship across the Pacific, staying briefly in America—long enough for him to spend a day with Longfellow—and then to England, the revolutionary flame remained undimmed, but it was no longer charged with the old passion. He wrote as violently as ever, conjured up the ancient visions of destructions with the most exquisite impartiality, always the wanderer in search of the spark he could blow into a flame. He invented vast revolutionary organizations which never consisted of more than a handful of people. His passion drove him to Sweden, Denmark, Switzerland and Italy, but in none of these countries was he able to dig deep roots. At bottom he was too chivalrous and too kindhearted, and altogether too disorganized, to be a successful revolutionary; and when he encountered revolutionaries who would stop at nothing, he quailed before them.

When at last he died, weighed down with years and with the respectability that comes from innumerable failures, the police were concerned to register his death in the proper manner. A close friend, remembering that he had once possessed a villa in Switzerland, and not wanting to suggest that he had spent his life as a professional revolutionary, replied: "He was a property owner." The official records state that Mikhail Bakunin, property owner, died in a hospital at Berne on July 1, 1876. It was the supreme irony in a life given over to many ironies.

CHERNYSHEVSKY

You are the best among the best, the movers of movers,
the salt of the salt of the earth.

THE SAINTLY REVOLUTIONARY

ANYONE WHO KNEW NIKOLAY CHERNYSHEVSKY in his youth must have thought him an unlikely candidate for revolutionary immortality. He had none of the rage that stirred in Bakunin's soul, no vindictiveness, no gift for self-dramatization. He was still quite young when he vanished forever into a Tsarist prison, but there never came from him any word of complaint. He was arrested because the Tsarist government feared that he would precipitate a revolution. They regarded this small, quiet, profoundly studious man, who always looked like a candidate for priesthood, as the most dangerous man in Russia.

He was one of those men who seem to move in a cloud of learned dreams. His learning was prodigious: he knew French, German, Latin, Greek, Arabic, Persian, Tatar and Hebrew. His fame in our own day does not depend on his learning, or on his treatises on aesthetics and political science, but on a few brilliant pages written when he was a prisoner in the Alexis Ravelin. In those pages he painted a vivid portrait of the archrevolutionary, "the destroyer of the age." For the first time a ruthless and credible revolutionary was depicted in three dimensions. If he had not been imprisoned, it is unlikely that those formidable pages would have been written.

From the beginning he seemed destined for the priesthood. His father was a priest, a grave and kindly man, who read widely and particularly admired the novels of Dickens and George Sand. He was a liberal, and he read books which the police regarded with abhorrence, like Radishchev's *A Journey from Petersburg to Moscow*. He doted on his son, gave him all the books he wanted to read, and instilled in him a belief in the infinite possibilities of knowledge, with the result that the boy grew up thinking that if he could acquire all the knowledge in existence, he would become a world leader, a kind of intellectual emperor over men's minds and wills. One overwhelming problem tormented him: perpetual motion. If he could discover the secret of perpetual motion, he would become automatically the greatest benefactor of mankind. He spent months designing machines which were intended to capture the forces of perpetual motion. Nothing came of them, and he turned to thoughts of a world encyclopedia to be written in French, "the common language of mankind," which would include every ascertainable fact that had ever been recorded.

The slight bespectacled youth with the fastidious manners and the soaring pride in his own intellectual accomplishments was not a particularly pleasant person. He was vain and pompous as a seminarian at Saratov, and when he entered St. Petersburg University at the age of sixteen, he was still vain and pompous. St. Petersburg changed him. Almost overnight he acquired a new character, as he saw that all his childish dreams of domination only made him ridiculous in the eyes of his fellow students. In Saratov where he was born, he could cut a figure as an intellectual. In St. Petersburg, where everyone was an intellectual, it was a far more difficult matter.

Henceforward he became the most humble of men, charming, diffident, excitable, always eager to pursue learning and friendship. He looked faintly ridiculous, with his brilliant red hair, long neck, and spectacles which gave him an owlish appearance. He had a thin piping voice. More and more he came to resemble his grave, kindly father. It was generally believed that he would become a professor, and in the academic world his mild eccentricities would be pardoned and his learning would be allowed free rein. In fact he never became a professor. For a few years he became a teacher in a provincial high school. For twenty-one years, a third of his life, he was an exile in Siberia.

The first of his works to bring him to popular attention was his master's thesis, *The Aesthetic Relation of Art to Reality*, which appeared in 1855, the year Alexander II ascended the throne. He had been working on it for two years, but its publication had something of the effect of a manifesto to the new age, and in its own way it was a revolutionary document. The acceptable aesthetic doctrines taught in the University were concerned with the sublime, the beautiful, the tragic. Art was the supreme embodiment of reality, and sublimity was the aim of art. Chernyshevsky outraged the professors by insisting that the only reality was life, that tragedy has nothing whatsoever to do with fate or necessity—tragedies are merely the horrible experiences which men suffer for no apparent cause—and beauty, far from being a remote object of contemplation, is everywhere, for "beauty is life." As for the artist, he is merely the pale copier of the beauty which exists all around him. He railed at the German philosophers of aesthetics who studied a Greek statue of a youth and proclaimed it to be the most beautiful object in the world: what about the living youth? We are told about the sublime beauty of the Apollo Belvedere, but no philosophers ever speak about the beautiful people you see every day walking along the streets of St. Petersburg. In this down-to-earth fashion Chernyshevsky demolishes all the problems of aesthetics without understanding them. It was a pleasant youthful exercise, and achieved some small fame because the thesis was bitterly contested by the professors.

The publication of the master's thesis led him into journalism and literary criticism, as one of the editors of *Sovremennik* (The Contemporary.) He was twenty-three, with a growing family to support. He had married a famous Saratov beauty, Olga Sokratovna Vasilyeva, and he was already tolerating her tantrums and flirtations with patience and humility. She adored flirting with young officers of the Guards, dances, horses, country villas. "I wish to have a husband who is completely at my mercy," she said, and Chernyshevsky was perfectly willing to accept the role she had chosen for him, explaining at great length that he could not conceive of marriage unless the partners enjoyed equal freedom. But while being bullied at home, he was himself something of a bully in his writings. He wrote in a harsh, intolerant style, impatient with everyone who did not share his earthy materialism, impatient of authority, and never happier than when he was tearing down some wretched academic philosopher who had dared to believe that Plato's intelligence was greater than that of a sturdy Russian peasant.

After the debacle of the Crimean War Russia entered into a period of reforms. The *Sovremennik* became the spokesman for the liberal party which brought about the emancipation of the serfs in 1861. While the Act of Emancipation satisfied many of the liberals, it left many others with the feeling that the Act evaded the main issue because the peasants did not immediately receive tenure of the land. Chernyshevsky belonged among those who regarded the Act as a fraudulent imposition on the peasants. He did not say so openly—he was too careful and artful a writer to invite the attentions of the police—but his implied criticisms were read and understood by the university students, who admired him and sometimes inveigled him into dangerous discussions. They worshiped him for his saintlike character, his good humor, his devotion to all that was young and fresh in the country, and for his vision of a Russia where all the excesses of authority were exchanged for democratic egalitarianism. Mysterious fires were breaking out in St. Petersburg, peasant revolts were occurring all over the country, and secret revolutionary parties were being formed. Although Chernyshevsky had not written a single word against the government, the police decided to arrest him. He had acquired a position of towering intellectual authority, and they were determined to prevent him from exercising it. On July 7, 1862, three months after *Sovremennik* was banned by the government, Chernyshevsky was arrested, and since he was regarded as a dangerous criminal, he was given a cell in the Alexis Ravelin.

From the beginning he protested vigorously against his arrest. He went on a hunger strike, and was only dissuaded from continuing when he was told that if he persisted, he would never be allowed to see his wife and his two young sons. When he demanded an explanation for his arrest, he was told that the governor of the Peter and Paul Fortress was under no obligation to inform him. He had committed no crime against the state and no legal proof of guilt was ever advanced against him, but he was in no position to summon lawyers to his defense. He could expect to spend the rest of his life in the Alexis Ravelin.

To save himself from going mad, he undertook a vast program of work. He wrote short stories, essays, a full-length novel, innumerable articles, and embarked on a series of translations. He translated two volumes of Macaulay's *History of England,* two of Friedrich Schlosser's *History of the World,* an entire history of the United States, and vast quantities of Rousseau. In four months he wrote the long novel *What Is To Be Done?* The Tsarist police, still searching for a reason for imprisoning him, were inclined to permit him as many books as he pleased, and his small cell became a library filled to the roof with his favorite authors: Lermontov, Gogol, Montaigne, Flaubert, George Sand, Smollett, Dickens, Darwin, and the romantic poets Heine, Fet and Tyutchev.

His writings from prison were published, for the censors regarded them as mere literary exercises. Even *What Is To Be Done?* was published without incident, not because they were incapable of recognizing a revolutionary novel, but because the censor in the Fortress assumed that the government censor would examine it, while the government censor assumed that it had already been examined in the Fortress. The novel was subsequently banned, but not before it had become widely known. It was written during the first winter of his imprisonment, at the time of his greatest sufferings.

One year and eight months after his arrest he was brought to trial and sentenced to eight years of penal servitude and banishment to Siberia.

He was also condemned to undergo the ordeal of "civic execution," the solemn ceremony of public degradation usually invoked only in cases of high treason. The ceremony took place two weeks later, on May 31, 1864. On the Mytny Square just off the Nevsky Prospect and not far from the Smolny Institute a black platform was erected, with an eight-foot-high black post from which chains descended. Here the prisoner would be forced to kneel while a sword was broken over his head, signifying death, and then he would be fastened to the chains, and this would signify bondage. At the time of the "civic execution" of the Petrashevsky conspirators, a more massive choreography had been employed, but the days of Nicholas I were over and a quieter ceremony was demanded by his successor.

The announcement of the public ceremony of degradation was made two days before in the official government gazette, and some hundreds of people gathered in the square in the pouring rain to await the arrival of the carriage from the Peter and Paul Fortress. The platform was surrounded by guards and soldiers to keep the public at a respectable distance. There were many umbrellas up, and people were shouting: "Take the umbrellas down!" It was early morning, and the pale light coming through the low clouds gave an ugly, raw appearance to the scene.

At last the carriage with Chernyshevsky arrived, and as he climbed up on the platform, his face white as a candle, swollen, and nearly unrecognizable, a hush descended on the crowd. An official read out the sentence. It was a very long sentence, for his crimes were enumerated at great length. For nearly a quarter of an hour the official droned on, while Chernyshevsky gazed at the crowd, looking for a familiar face, and sometimes making the faintest of inclinations of his head when he thought he recognized someone. He was bareheaded now, and the rain streaked down his red hair and beard. Over his chest hung a blackboard on which someone had painted in white letters: "Government criminal."

Then it was time to kneel while the sword was broken over his head, and a moment later he was chained to the post. In theory he would then become the victim of the crowd's displeasure and their execrations would be the last sounds he would hear before departing for Siberia. But there was only the hush of the crowd and the sound of the rain pouring on the wooden platform. Chernyshevsky stood very still, waiting. Suddenly an extraordinary thing happened. A bouquet of flowers was thrown at his feet. Two more followed. The police shouted: "Who threw them?" There was no answer, but one of the policemen caught a glimpse of a seventeen-year-old girl in the act of throwing a bouquet and arrested her. All that is known of her is that her name was Michaelis, and that she was banished from St. Petersburg.

When the ceremony was over Chernyshevsky returned to his waiting carriage. The next day he set out for Siberia. He never saw St. Petersburg again.

The strange novel he wrote in his cell in the Alexis Ravelin continued to be read eagerly. There was almost no plot, many of the characters were stereotypes, and it was formidably long. But it had the pulse of life, and portrayed the man of the future. Chernyshevsky chose to describe "the new man" a little evasively, making him a secondary character in the book, with no direct impact on the plot. We are given only a few tantalizing glimpses of him. He hovers somewhere in the background of the novel, emerging briefly to fill the air with his thunder and the lingering smell of saltpeter.

The first time we see "the new man" is at a picnic, where he displays great strength as a wrestler, simultaneously throwing two men down to the ground. A hundred pages later he enters the apartment of Vera Pavlovna and being left alone he takes down from the shelves Isaac Newton's *Observations on the Prophecies of Daniel and the Apocalypse of St. John.* He comments on the phenomenon of a great genius surrendering to religious insanity and pronounces the book a work of singular interest "for those who study the question of the mingling of insanity and intelligence." He is the detached observer, seeing all things in the light of his own intellect, and strong as an ox.

His name is Rakhmetov, the descendant of a thirteenth-century Tatar chieftain who abducted and married the niece of a high officer of the Russian court. Rich and aristocratic, he has inherited four hundred serfs and seven thousand acres of land, but lives the pure ascetic life and subjects himself to intense privations in order to prepare himself for an arduous life of contemplation and action. He had an income of thirty thousand rubles, but spent only a small fraction of it on himself, preferring to give money to promising students or professors—at the age of twenty-two he was paying the expenses for two students at the University of Kazan and five more at the University of Moscow. He lived quietly and modestly in a small apartment in St. Petersburg where the furnishings were those that might be found in a monk's cell. He read voluminously: once he read for eighty-two hours at a stretch, remaining awake on the first two nights by sheer will power and fortifying himself on the third night with eight cups of coffee. His choice of reading matter was dictated by a desire to read only the essential. Accordingly he would read the entire works of Gogol, but only glance at a few pages of those novels which covered the ground which Gogol had already exploited. His motto was: "No luxury, no caprices, nothing but the essential."

Rakhmetov lived by the clock: so much time for reading, so much time for exercise, so much time for aiding others. There was something inhuman and even terrifying about him, for he chose to live in defiance of the laws of normal behavior. For a while he traveled all over Russia, using all available vehicles, and sometimes traveling by foot. He was wandering along the banks of the Volga when he fell in with some boat haulers and acquired the nickname which would always bring a smile of pleasure to his face—Nikitushka Lomov. The first bearer of this name had been a *burlak*, or Volga boatman, of a previous generation, a giant who drew the pay of four men because of his Herculean strength. Rakhmetov was powerfully built, and became a boat hauler as famous as this legendary giant, so that whenever they docked in a town along the Volga he would be followed by people saying: "There's Nikitushka Lomov!" He had trained himself to be strong by living on raw beef and taking a vast amount of exercise. "Strength is necessary," he observed. "It gains the respect and love of the common people."

Sometimes there were trials of strength of a different kind. Once in St. Petersburg he asked a doctor friend for ointment "against cuts from sharp tools." The doctor merely assumed that Rakhmetov was engaged in some arduous carpentry work and gave him a large jar of ointment. The next day a terrified landlady came to the doctor with the news that she had peered through a crack in the door and seen Rakhmetov lying in bed and covered with blood. The doctor rushed to the apartment. He found Rakhmetov bleeding from a hundred wounds, his shirt and the floor under his bed swimming with blood. He had arranged hundreds of inch-long nails on his bed, with the points coming through his felt mattress. "It was a necessary trial," Rakhmetov explained. "Improbable, perhaps, but it had to be done. Now I know what my body can do."

The landlady described Rakhmetov as a man utterly without pity for himself. Vera Pavlovna, the heroine of the novel, described him as a titan, a somber monster, a man possessing uncanny powers. Chernyshevsky himself was not quite sure what to make of his invention, and wrote:

> People like Rakhmetov are scarce. I have met but eight (of whom two were women). They resembled each other in nothing, save in one thing. There were among them the amiable and the stern, the melancholy and the gay, the fiery and the phlegmatic, the impressionable and the imperturbably calm. They resemble each other in only one thing, as I have said, but that is enough to make a special type of them and to distinguish them from all other men. I laughed at those whom I knew, when I was with them; they grew angry or not, but they could not help doing as much themselves. And indeed there were many ridiculous things about them, and it was in that respect that they resembled each other. I like to laugh at such people.

But in fact Chernyshevsky did not laugh at them very much or very often, for he realized that this strange "rigorist," who had entered his novel unbidden, had come to stay. In an autobiographical novel called

The Prologue, by which he meant the Prologue to revolution, Rakhmetov, subtly altered, returns as the professional revolutionary Volgin, who lives according to the same code of honor and the same cold logic. *The Prologue* was written many years later in Siberia, when Chernyshevsky felt very nearly hopeless about the future of the revolution, and Volgin was no more than a pale copy of Rakhmetov. In *What Is To Be Done?* Chernyshevsky had caught the bird on the wing, in all his bright feathers. In countless novels the character of the Russian revolutionary would be examined and described at length, but no one ever produced a more vivid portrait.

The virtue of Rakhmetov was that he was entirely credible in his place and time, and he answered to the needs of the generation which came to maturity in the sixties. Not that they did not quarrel with him: they found him almost too cold, too overbearing, too austere, and at the same time they were fascinated by him. He represented "the new man" who would bring about the revolution by the sheer force of his personality.

Rakhmetov was continually insisting that young revolutionaries should go to the people. He ate what the people ate, worked as the people worked, and suffered as they suffered, but all the time there was a kind of romantic reserve, a sense of distance. He never touched alcohol, never slept with a woman. When told that such an extreme course was unnecessary, he answered: "On the contrary, it is very necessary. We demand that men may have a complete enjoyment of their lives, and we must show by our example that we demand it, not to satisfy our personal passions, but for mankind in general; that what we say we say from principle and not from passion, from conviction and not from personal desire." But principle and conviction are sometimes too cold even for revolutionaries.

It was a question which Vera Pavlovna raised among her revolutionary friends, not always receiving the answer she wanted. To her friend Lupukhov, she said: "I cannot accept a theory which condemns people to a life which is merciless, cold and prosaic." Lupukhov answered by saying that even if the theory is cold, it teaches people how to find warmth. "The theory is merciless," he said, "but if the people follow it, they will cease to be the pitiful objects of idle compassion. The theory may be prosaic, but it uncovers the true motives of life."

Vera Pavlovna was never completely convinced by the theory. She had founded a cooperative sewing circle, full of warmth and gaiety, and felt no need to worship Rakhmetov, the ruthless exponent of unbridled will power. She thought the revolution would come about in some other way, perhaps by transforming all of Russia into a great cooperative, and in her dreams she would see the postrevolutionary world with astonishing brightness. There would be no more hovels, no more poverty. People would live in splendid new hygienic cities; food kitchens would feed whole towns; men would control their own lives, and machines would do their work for them. With so much leisure people would be able to follow the sun, and bask in innocent pleasures, while the peasants sat beneath the trees, drank wine, and waited for the fruit to fall. Utopia was round the corner, and it seemed to her that all that was necessary was a concerted effort by people to bring it about.

The significance of Rakhmetov lay precisely here, for he was one of those who knew that Utopia would be brought about by arduous effort and by the iron determination of a small elite. He was the personification of the harsh revolutionary law, one of those prime movers who appear only at rare intervals. So Chernyshevsky extols him in almost lyrical terms:

> You are few in numbers, but only through you can the life of all mankind come to its full flowering; without you they will wither away. You are few in numbers, but only through you can people breathe; without you they will die of suffocation. There exists a great mass of honest men and goodly people, but you are the rare bouquet of good wine, and from you arises the strength and the aroma. You are the best among the best, the movers of the movers, the salt of the salt of the earth.

In these words Chernyshevsky offers his valediction to Rakhmetov, who replaces Isaac Newton's *Observations on the Prophecies of Daniel and the Apocalypse of St. John* on the shelves and then vanishes from the novel. Of his subsequent life nothing was known for certainty. There were rumors that he returned to his family estate, sold his property, gave a large amount to the seven students he was supporting, and then traveled across Europe, staying in each country only as long as it was necessary to form a true conception of its ideas, customs, and institutions. They said he suddenly appeared in the house of one of the greatest European thinkers of the century with the words: "I have thirty thousand thalers; I need but five thousand; the remainder I beg you to accept." Though the philosopher was living in great poverty, he was not at first inclined to accept the gift, and asked why it was being made. "For the publication of your works," the stranger replied. Of Rakhmetov's further adventures little was known except that he planned to settle down in the United States, "the country I must study more than any other." He had withdrawn himself from Russia, but the implication was clear that he would return in due time to lead the revolution, more austere and more terrible than ever.

Although Rakhmetov appears in only forty pages of a long novel devoted to the social endeavors and the love affairs of Vera Pavlovna, he remains, as Chernyshevsky well knew, the heart and core of the novel, all the more present when he is absent. To the young university students he was a model to be imitated and revered. Thirty years later the young Lenin, then a student at the University of Kazan, came upon the book, and spent a large part of a summer devouring it. He told his friend Celia Bobrovskaya: "It is great literature, because it teaches, guides and inspires you. I read the novel five times that summer, and each time I found new and powerful ideas in it." What inspired him was the figure of Rakhmetov, the stern taskmaster of revolution.

Among those who realized the potentialities and dangers of "the new man" were the revolutionaries Zhelyabov and Sophie Perovskaya, who organized the assassination of Alexander II. There came a time when every town in Russia had its own Rakhmetov. The police in despair were confronted with a fictional character who could not be arrested and placed in the Alexis Ravelin because he was born there and had escaped beyond their reach.

"We are seeking, thirsting, waiting," wrote the critic Dobrolyubov. "We are waiting for someone to tell us what to do."

Chernyshevsky told them what to do—if they would confront the state fearlessly, with absolute dedication and determination, there was nothing they could not do.

ZAICHNEVSKY

We shall kill them in the squares, in the narrow streets of the towns, in the broad avenues of the capitals, in the villages and the hamlets. Remember that when this happens, who is not with us is against us.

YOUNG RUSSIA

In the early summer of 1862 a series of extraordinary fires broke out in St. Petersburg and the provinces. It was a very hot, dry summer, and no doubt some of these fires broke out in a perfectly normal manner. But the people were puzzled by the fact that so many of them were not normal fires, for they often broke out near important buildings. An air of menace hung over the land. Fire followed fire, until it seemed that all the cities of the empire must perish that summer. Between May 28 and June 9 there was one major conflagration each day, not counting hundreds of minor conflagrations. The police suspected the revolutionaries, who had everything to gain by creating an atmosphere of panic. The revolutionaries, in turn, put the blame on *agents provocateurs* from the police, who had nothing to lose by fanning the flames.

What came to be known as the Great Fire of St. Petersburg broke out on the Monday after Trinity, the day of the Holy Ghost, June 9, at about three o'clock in the afternoon. The Apraxin Dvor, an immense market place filled with small wooden booths selling secondhand goods and wooden storage houses suddenly caught fire, and at about the same moment the nearby lumberyards went up in flames. Prince Peter Kropotkin, then a young member of the aristocratic Corps de Pages and not yet a famous revolutionary, was having a late lunch in the Corps de Pages mansion when he looked out the window and saw a cloud of smoke rising

133

over the market. By the time he ran out of the building, the many tongues of flame had become one immense seething flame throwing out tendrils and branches in all directions and threatening the Corps de Pages mansion, the Imperial Bank of Russia, the National Library, the Ministry of the Interior, and the Foundling Hospital, all of which were in the vicinity of the market. There was a narrow lane between the Apraxin Dvor and the mansion of the Corps de Pages; the lane was filled with small shops selling oil, turpentine and groceries, and soon it was nothing but a roaring inferno with great streamers of brilliantly colored flame shooting straight up in the air from the exploding oil drums. There was no wind, otherwise the whole of St. Petersburg would have gone up in flames.

Throughout the afternoon and evening the market and the lumberyard continued to burn, and the people of St. Petersburg watched with apprehension while the police and high officials gathered to debate on the proper measures to be taken. There was no steam fire engine in the city, until some workmen decided to import one from the ironworks at Kolpino twenty miles away on the railroad. There were no fire pumps. The officials lost their heads, and the chief of police, General Annenkov, wandered about in a daze. From time to time a Grand Duke would appear, and then hurry away. Late in the afternoon, when the Imperial Bank of Russia was at last out of danger, the Tsar appeared briefly, announced that the mansion of the Corps de Pages must be saved at all costs, and then he too hurried away. If the Corps de Pages had gone up in flames, the National Library and half the Nevsky Prospect would also have been destroyed. The pages themselves, and all the workmen and spectators they could round up, fought the blaze through the night, and it was not until the early hours of the morning that they were able to report that it was under control. The fire had demonstrated that the bureaucracy and the fire brigades were woefully inefficient. There was now a smoldering ruin in the heart of St. Petersburg.

In high government circles there was an increasing disposition to blame the revolutionaries for the fires. Kropotkin tells the story of how he went to visit his cousin, an aide-de-camp of the Tsar, and found him glowering over copies of the liberal magazine *Sovremennik*, which he had once read with delight even to the extent of admiring the articles of Chernyshevsky. "Well, it's all over now!" the aide-de-camp said. "I never want to read another word of this incendiary magazine!" "These words," wrote Kropotkin, "expressed what 'all St. Petersburg' was thinking."

The reaction had set in, and the Tsar who only a few months before had signed the edict offering freedom to the serfs was becoming more and more convinced that he had made a mistake. He was in no mood to tolerate ideas of reform, even those ideas which had been officially promulgated. It was generally believed in government circles that the final liberation of the serfs promised for the beginning of March 1863 would be indefinitely postponed. Another belief readily accepted in government circles was that there had come into existence a Central Revolutionary Committee with ramifications in all levels of Russian society. This dreaded committee had vowed to overthrow the autocracy and to uproot every vestige of privilege. No one knows whether this revolutionary committee actually existed, and it seems to have been invented by the police for their own purposes.

Quite suddenly the government felt itself threatened by forces over which it had little or no control. Somewhere in the dark depths of Russia a powerful and relentless opposition was gathering in secret, prepared to plunge the whole country into a state of anarchy. The long-delayed revolution was about to take place, but the names, the motives, and the resources of the leaders remained unknown. The government acted blindly, arrested hundreds of young students, banned liberal newspapers and magazines, and set up an extraordinary commission to inquire into the dangerous condition of social order. The extraordinary commission, presided over by Prince Alexander Golitsyn, was granted special powers. It could arrest, interrogate and imprison anyone it pleased, examine whatever documents it pleased, ban any books or journals it pleased, and close down clubs and societies which threatened public safety. The Chess Club of St. Petersburg, founded six months before, was closed down on the grounds that "completely baseless opinions circulate there and have their origin in the Club." The closing of the Chess Club was not entirely unwarranted, for although it had been founded under high auspices for the most innocent motives it was in fact attended by people with revolutionary sympathies. Both Chernyshevsky and Pisarev, a famous revolutionary critic, could be found there sitting quietly over chessboards, while busily engaged in revolutionary discussions.

The police may have exaggerated the power of the revolutionaries, but there was no doubting the revolutionary ferment under the surface. Just a few days before the outbreak of fires a manifesto entitled *Molodaya Rossiya* (Young Russia) had been distributed in Moscow and St. Petersburg. Government officials found it on their desks, others found it in their mailboxes or slipped under their doors. There was no indication of the name of the author or where it had been printed. Just as the Great Fire in St. Petersburg and the many other fires which broke out in the city and the provinces were attributed variously to the police and the revolutionaries, so to this day no one knows whether the police or the revolutionaries wrote the manifesto and circulated it. It was a hair-raising document designed to strike fear in the heart of the government and it succeeded brilliantly in its objective.

Molodaya Rossiya begins with a simple affirmation: "Russia is entering the revolutionary stage of its existence." It then goes on to describe why a corrupt society must be destroyed and replaced by a new society based on the power of the liberated peasantry and of the youth of Russia, "who contain everything that is best in the country, everything that is alive, and they are prepared to sacrifice themselves for the good of the people." The Tsar, his family, and the entire imperial party must be swept away. In the place of the autocratic Tsar there will be a dictatorship formed of a small body of determined revolutionaries dominating the National Assembly. Russia will become a Federal Republic divided into an unknown number of regional governments, with the rural *obshchina* as the basic unit. Everyone will belong to an *obshchina* on equal terms, and every member of the community would be granted land for a term of years, after which it would be redistributed. All other property might be held for life, but it would revert to the *obshchina* at the time of the owner's death.

But it was not for its encouragement of land reform that the manifesto acquires its particular importance. What it possessed to a degree hitherto undreamed of was a vision of a future where all the edges were clear-cut and sharply delineated, all the necessary reforms listed in order, the machinery of government clearly outlined, the rights and duties of the citizens stated without the least ambiguity. With prophetic force it described the future communist state, or at least the programs which the communist state attempted to introduce. All industry was nationalized, the socialized factories being run by elected managers. There would be no army: instead there would be a national militia. Women were to be fully emancipated, and the institutions of marriage and the family were abolished. The rich would be taxed out of existence; education would be a public expense and free to all citizens; prices would be fixed according to "the real value of goods," not to the artificial values demanded by merchants eager to enrich themselves. The socialized factories were responsible to society, and must furnish society with an account of their work. Monasteries and nunneries, "the chief cesspools of corruption," must be closed, but nothing is said about the closing of the churches. Landlords are to be expropriated without indemnity, and no one may inherit property under any conditions, because property is owned by the community and not by individuals.

The author of the manifesto was under no illusions about the bloody revolution necessary to bring the dictatorship to power. It will be "a bloody and pitiless revolution, which will change radically and without exception all the foundations of present society and destroy the partisans of the present order. We are not afraid of it, although we know that a river of blood will flow, and innocent victims will perish. We greet its coming, and we are prepared to lay down our lives for this long-hoped-for event."

According to the manifesto the dictatorship will not be a permanent one; it will exist "for a while," until the new society is completely organized. There will be no free elections, for the party in power will ensure its own election. The manifesto declares:

> We are firmly convinced that the revolutionary party, which will be at the head of the government if the movement succeeds, will have to retain for a while the present system of a dictatorship. This will indeed be necessary in order to bring about political control, and perhaps administrative control as well, so that we can introduce the new foundations of economic and social order in the shortest possible time. The party must seize the dictatorship with both hands, and stop at nothing.
>
> The elections of the National Assembly must be carried out under the guidance of the government, which will see to it that no partisans of the present order, if any of them remain alive, are elected to the Assembly. The French National Assembly showed what happens when a revolutionary government fails to interfere in the elections. Because it did not interfere, the Republic was destroyed and Louis Napoleon was elected Emperor.

In its cadences and a certain directness of statement *Molodaya Rossiya* was remarkably Western. Whoever wrote it was steeped in the revolutionary literature of France and in the Jacobin tradition. While the title of the manifesto derived fom Mazzini's *La Giovane Italia,* the substance derived from those bitter and often anonymous pamphlets written by French and German revolutionaries in 1848, when they saw victory slipping from their grasp. Bakunin was to declare later that *Molodaya Rossiya* suffered from two cardinal faults: a scorn for the people, and frivolity in the face of human emancipation, for instead of elaborating a workable revolutionary program, it moved among vast revolutionary abstractions, ferocious dictatorships, and romantic blood baths. In fact, as the Bolshevik revolution demonstrated, *Molodaya Rossiya* was much closer to reality than anyone suspected.

The peroration of *Molodaya Rossiya* ranks among the greatest passages of revolutionary vituperation, the naked hate leaping from the page:

> Soon, very soon, the day will come when we shall unfurl the great flag of the future, the red flag, and with a mighty cry of "Long Live the Russian Social and Democratic Republic," we shall move against the Winter Palace to annihilate all its inhabitants. It may well be that we shall only have to destroy the imperial family, i.e. about 100 people, but it may also happen, and this is more likely, that the whole imperial party will rise as one man in defense of the Tsar, because for them it will be a matter of life and death. If this should happen, then with faith in ourselves, in our strength, in the sympathy of the people toward us, and in the knowledge of the glorious future of Russia—the country which destiny has ordained to be the first to

bring about the triumph of socialism—we shall cry out with one voice: "Get your axes!" and then we shall attack the imperial party with no more mercy than they have shown toward us.

We shall kill them in the squares, if the cowardly swine ever dare to appear there. We shall kill them in their houses, in the narrow streets of the towns, in the broad avenues of the capitals, in the villages and the hamlets. Remember that when this happens, who is not with us is against us, and who is against us is an enemy, and every method may be used to destroy the enemy.

If the revolution fails, and if we have to pay with our lives for this daring attempt to give men human rights, then we shall go to the scaffold without fear or trembling, and as we place our heads on the block or in the noose, we shall repeat our great cry: "Long live the Russian Social and Democratic Republic!"

The manifesto was signed "Central Revolutionary Committee," and these words were as terrifying to the government as the incendiary contents.

Although there is still some doubt about the author of the manifesto and especially the circumstances in which it came to be written, it is now generally credited to Pyotr Zaichnevsky, the son of a landowner in the province of Orel, born in 1842. A brilliant pupil in the local secondary school, he was seventeen when he became a student of mathematics at Moscow University, where he came under the influence of the writings of Herzen and Ogaryev. There was something of Speshnev in Zaichnevsky —an easy brilliance, great pride, a certain feeling for melodrama. Vera Figner, who knew him when he was still a student, speaks of his "magnetic quality," which drew people effortlessly to him. Impressed by an essay written by Ogaryev defending the Decembrist revolutionaries, Zaichnevsky decided to reprint it on the lithograph machine used by the students for making copies of their lectures. He printed three hundred copies, and sold them, and then went on to reproduce articles by Herzen from *Kolokol*. In this way he satisfied some of the yearning of the Moscow University students for subversive literature, only to discover that their desire was insatiable. By the same simple lithographic process he printed whole books, including Ludwig Feuerbach's *The Essence of Christianity* and Ludwig Büchner's *Force and Matter,* both of them being works which offered simple materialist answers to complex problems. Büchner was an extreme materialist, who regarded everything in the universe as matter acted upon by force, and therefore all problems could be considered in the light of elementary physics. Feuerbach postulated a God who was merely a reflection of human desires. These two books became the bibles of the young students in Russian universities, and by publishing them in cheap lithographed editions Zaichnevsky at the age of eighteen was already exerting his influence on the intellectual life of his time. What profit he made from his illegal publishing house went back into producing more and more books.

As Speshnev had observed long before, there could be no revolution without a revolutionary press. Zaichnevsky's achievement was to have built up a small publishing house, using the primitive tools available; other students followed, and Moscow University was soon full of young publishers. But in Zaichnevsky's eyes it was not enough to publish the books and sell them to students and young intellectuals; the books must be distributed all over Russia; and he proposed that the students themselves should become colporteurs bringing their books and pamphlets to the remotest villages. When the summer holidays came round, he set out on horseback from Moscow to the family estate in Orel, stopping at the wayside inns and preaching the gospel of socialism. According to his own account he was greeted everywhere with enthusiasm, and had no difficulty selling his books. Emboldened by success, he described his triumphs in long letters to his friends, especially his close friend Pericles Argyropulo, a young aristocrat of Greek descent, who shared his sympathies and worked with him in his publishing house. In these letters he openly denounced the autocracy and spoke of how the peasants welcomed his invitations to open rebellion as he explained to them the necessity for marching on the towns, seizing the arsenals, and waging war against the Tsar. The letters were intercepted by the police, and one particularly long one was submitted to the Tsar, who wrote on the margin: "The contents are so criminal and dangerous that I consider it necessary to have both Zaichnevsky and Argyropulo arrested immediately, and they are to be brought here with all their documents. I must find out who they are."

Zaichnevsky and Argyropulo were arrested and lodged in the Moscow prison, together with some of their helpers from Moscow University. Traditionally, the police of Moscow were more liberal toward political prisoners than the police of St. Petersburg, and the students were permitted a good deal of freedom. They could receive visitors, food and fruit were sent in, and they were permitted to read the newspapers, including clandestine newspapers. The prison ward became a club, with students wandering in and out as they pleased, bringing books and writing materials, endlessly debating the next moves in their war against the autocracy; and the prison became a publishing house. Zaichnevsky appears to have been treated with quite unusual leniency, for we hear of him leaving the prison in the company of a guard "to go to a bathhouse." In this way he was able to contact anyone he pleased and to continue to superintend his publishing house.

His friend Pericles Argyropulo died in jail on December 18, 1862, a year and a half after his arrest. His death was attributed to typhus. Shortly afterward there took place the trial of the university students who had helped Zaichnevsky with his publishing ventures. The sentences were comparatively light, for most of the students were released and placed under police surveillance. Zaichnevsky was sentenced to a year of hard labor. Released, he continued to agitate for revolution, and spent the rest of his long life—he died in 1896—in and out of jails. He never attained any great prominence in the revolutionary movement, nor perhaps would he have desired a position of leadership. He was one of those who were dedicated to sapping the foundations of the autocracy, and in his own quiet remorseless way he did as much as any of the more famous revolutionaries to bring this about.

His masterpiece, if indeed he wrote it, was *Molodaya Rossiya*, the most violent of all the manifestoes published up to that time. Many years later he claimed that he wrote it in the Moscow Central Prison with the help of some of his fellow students and had no difficulty in smuggling it out. The manifesto was printed on a hand press belonging to a student who had been sent down from the university and was living in Ryazan province. The first copies were distributed in St. Petersburg at the beginning of May 1862 in order to divert the attention of the police from Moscow. Asked why he had written it, Zaichnevsky answered that he wanted "to make those liberal and reactionary devils violently sick."

There is not the least doubt that Zaichnevsky did write a violent manifesto while he was in prison. What is doubtful is whether the manifesto when it finally appeared was entirely the work of students. Among the students who were rounded up and imprisoned with Zaichnevsky were a number of weak-willed youths who were only too happy to become informers and *agents provocateurs*. We hear of a certain Vsevolod Kostamarov, who collaborated with the police during the entire period of his arrest. Kostamarov gave the police a full account of the revolutionary meetings held by the students, and he readily supplied information about their secret contacts with Chernyshevsky. Kostamarov was in fact responsible for Chernyshevsky's arrest. The police were well aware that revolutionary agitation was becoming increasingly violent, especially in the universities, and their lenient treatment of the Moscow students can be more easily understood if we assume that they deliberately cultivated an atmosphere in which informers and *agents provocateurs* could work unhindered. Zaichnevsky exulted in the fact that he wrote *Molodaya Rossiya* in prison, the last place on earth where the police would search for the author of an incendiary pamphlet, and he claimed that the police never knew that he wrote it. But it is at least likely that they were aware of the pamphlet at every stage of its gestation, aided and abetted its progress, made suggestions about the final form it should take, and through their *agents provocateurs* helped to write it, for it served their purpose. Zaichnevsky was secretive about his editorial assistants, mentioning only the name of the student responsible for the brief passages on the abolition of marriage and the family, but by his own account many others were involved.

Over *Molodaya Rossiya* there falls the shadow of the secret police. The revolutionary movements were honeycombed with their agents, and they knew what the revolutionaries were saying and writing. If we assume that they encouraged the writing of *Molodaya Rossiya* and helped to distribute it, and were themselves responsible for the great conflagrations which broke out in St. Petersburg and the provinces during the following weeks, we are merely assuming what we already knew: they were capable of employing the most fiendish weapons against the revolutionaries who themselves employed fiendish weapons. They were using fire to put out fire. In this desperate game no mercy was shown on either side.

Many revolutionaries suspected that *Molodaya Rossiya* was written by an *agent provocateur* because it served the reaction far more than it served the revolution. As a direct result of the pamphlet the police were given exceptional powers, newspapers and magazines were banned by court order, public reading rooms were closed, and a closer watch was kept on university students and men known to have revolutionary sympathies. Among those who viewed *Molodaya Rossiya* with alarm was the student Pyotr Ballod who was engaged in publishing revolutionary pamphlets and articles on a secret press so small that he called it the Pocket Press. In May 1862, just after *Molodaya Rossiya* became widely known, he wrote and prepared for publication a manifesto warning the people against the idea that the revolutionaries were in love with incendiary violence. On the contrary they wanted to limit violence as far as possible. It was not their aim to embark on a ferocious civil war, but to bring about the downfall of the autocracy with as little bloodshed and as little damage to the country as possible. Not fratricide but fraternal love would bring about the revolution. The manifesto was ready to be set up when other matters intervened. Ballod was in communication with Herzen, and his chief concern was to defend the revolutionary ideas of his master, who was then engaged in a violent controversy with a Baltic baron called Theodor de Fircks, who had assumed the improbable *nom de guerre* of D. K. Schedo-Ferroti, an anagram of his real name. Baron de Fircks was a Tsarist agent with headquarters in Brussels, and the possessor of a considerable gift for vituperation. His attack on Herzen was widely published, and the young intellectual Dmitry Pisarev decided to write a counterblast which would be printed on the Pocket Press.

Pisarev's counterblast was untitled, and is generally known as *Concern-*

ing the Schedo-Ferroti Pamphlet. It was in fact a manifesto addressed to the Russian people, though disguised as an attack on the secret police and its hired publicists among whom Schedo-Ferroti occupied a special place; and as Pisarev recited the crimes of the police and the autocracy, comparing them with the noble and dignified behavior of Herzen, he became more and more violent in his denunciation of the autocracy which permitted these evils to endure. In the last words of the pamphlet he assailed the government with the fury of a man who has reached the end of his patience:

> Look around, Russian people, look at all these goings-on. Consider whether we should tolerate this brutality masked in an ancient aspect of divine law. Look where our literature has come to, look where public education has come to, look what has happened to every good thing undertaken by society or by our youth. Exploiting a few accidental fires, the government has decided to pour everything down its own throat, and it will continue to swallow everything—money, ideas, people—and there will come a time when after a spate of swallowing, it will have swallowed such a vast accumulation of things that the ugly monster will burst asunder. The Sunday schools are closed, the popular reading rooms are closed, two papers have been closed, the prisons are filled to bursting with honest young men who love the people and their ideas. Petersburg has been placed on a war footing, the government is determined to regard us as irreconcilable enemies. It is not mistaken. There can be no reconciliation. On the one side—the government which consists of scoundrels bribed with money squeezed by deceit and violence from the poor. On the other side, the side of the people, there is everything that is young and fresh, everything that is capable of thinking and of going into action.
>
> The dynasty of the Romanovs and the Petersburg bureaucrats must perish. Neither monsters like Valuyev[*] nor writers like Schedo-Ferroti can save them.
>
> What is dead and rotten is ripe for the grave. All that is necessary is to give them the last push and then cover their stinking corpses with mud.

Pisarev had evidently read *Molodaya Rossiya,* but he writes more calmly, without any glorying in bloody revolution. In the final sentence the knife turns slowly in the wound, as he utters the most dangerous of all the curses inflicted on the autocracy.

Such writings could scarcely go unpunished, and when Ballod was arrested and the incriminating document was found in his apartment, the police had little difficulty in discovering that Pisarev had written it. Then, on July 15, 1862, at the age of twenty-one, he followed Ballod into the Peter and Paul Fortress, where he remained for the next four and a half years.

---

[*] Count Pyotr Alexandrovich Valuyev (1814–1890) was not a monster. Becoming Minister of the Interior in 1861, he was largely responsible for the great reforms which took place during the reign of Alexander II.

In the history of the revolutionary movement in Russia Pisarev occupies a place of quite special importance not so much for any of his writings, which were largely devoted to literary criticism, but for a certain attitude of mind, a gaunt skepticism, an intolerance of romantic attitudes, a refusal to come to terms with the fashionable revolutionary cults. He regarded the problems of "hunger and nakedness" as the central problems of the age; if they were not solved, then all the other problems were merely decorations. "A pair of boots is more important than Shakespeare," he wrote, meaning that in the face of hunger and nakedness Shakespeare too was merely decorative and therefore outside the current of life. He regarded Bazarov, the hero of Turgenev's novel *Fathers and Sons,* as the prime example to be followed, for the completely dedicated nihilist, who hoped for nothing except the emancipation of the people through science, was the only *effective* revolutionary in an age given over to ineffectiveness. Bazarov proclaimed: "The scientific dissection of frogs is the highest human ideal." Pisarev replied: "Precisely here, in the dissected frog, there lies the salvation and renovation of the Russian people." What he meant was that even revolution must give way to the detached exploration of science for the benefit of the human race, and especially for the Russians. His faith in science was absolute, and the most famous and memorable of all his statements, often used to defend revolutionary destruction, was in fact a statement describing the scientific method by which all things must be examined, tested, doubted:

> If authority lies, then doubt will destroy it, and this is as it should be. If authority proves useful and indispensable, then doubt will return it into our hands and we shall examine it on all sides and it will resume its former position. In a word here is the ultimatum of our camp: What can be smashed must be smashed; whatever withstands the blow is fit to survive; whatever flies into smithereens is rubbish. In any case, hit out right and left—no harm can or will come from it.

These words were published in the magazine *Russkoye Slovo* in the second part of a long article entitled "Nineteenth Century Scholasticism," which appeared in October 1861. Though the article was censored, and the censor confessed in his diary that he was enraged by it, these words were left uncensored. Pisarev was not talking about the authority of the Tsarist state only; he was talking about every form of authority wherever it is found. Significantly when an English translation of Pisarev's essays appeared in the Soviet Union, the second part of the article was left untranslated.

When Lenin was sent into exile in Siberia, he took with him a small portrait of Pisarev, and in conversation he would often speak of Pisarev's extraordinary profundity and self-assurance as he went to the heart of a problem. In *What Is To Be Done?* which Lenin wrote in 1901, he quoted a long passage by Pisarev on the nature of reality and dreams. There was an art, Pisarev said, in dreaming wildly, and if men worked conscientiously for the achievement of their dreams, then nothing was lost. Great things could only come about through men who dreamed the impossible. It was a lesson which Lenin took to heart.

The portrait which Lenin took to Siberia showed a long, lean face of grave delicacy and charm, almost girlish. The eyes were deepset and brooding, the hair was brushed severely back, he had tiny ears and a thin chestnut beard which curled forward from beneath his chin. It was the face of a young priest; he did not look like a man who wrote withering literary essays from a prison cell. These essays taught a whole generation of students how to think.

Born in 1840 to a family of the petty nobility which had lived for generations in the province of Orel, Pisarev was one of those people who seem to be doomed to self-destruction from the beginning. He wrote with muscle, but in his private life he was at the mercy of his nerves. He was always falling desperately in love. He fell in love with Raissa Koreneva, a beautiful bluestocking who wrote inconsequential novels, and when he heard she was about to marry Evgeny Gardner, a porcelain manufacturer, he was so incensed that he sent the prospective bridegroom a vitriolic letter demanding that they should settle the matter in a duel. Gardner paid no attention to the letter, and married Raissa. A few days later Pisarev chanced upon them at the Tsarskoye Selo railroad station and slapped Gardner across the face. The police came running up, there was a brief inquiry, Gardner placed no charges, and the incident was dismissed as one of those inevitable quarrels which attend the marriages of beautiful bluestockings. On July 15, 1862, exactly two months after he had slapped Gardner's face in the railroad station, Pisarev was arrested by the police for his vitriolic attack on the Tsar in his comments on the Schedo-Ferroti pamphlet. He was thrown into a cell in the Nevsky Curtain of the Peter and Paul Fortress.

Pisarev seems to have welcomed his arrest; he was an unusually quiet and even-tempered prisoner, complaining sometimes of the dreariness of his cell, but happy with the books he was permitted to read and the articles he was permitted to write. In all the four and a half years of his imprisonment only one violent incident is reported. The archpriest Vasily Palisadov, who was in the pay of the police, entered his cell and suggested that the time had come for Pisarev to confess his sins before God. Pisarev seized a book and hurled it at the priest, and then threw him bodily out of the cell. The archpriest did not visit the cell again.

Like Dostoyevsky, who believed that imprisonment saved him from madness, Pisarev recovered his mental health in prison. He never wrote better. Altogether twenty-five full-length essays, some of them amounting to more than 150 pages, were produced in the Fortress, and while some of them are merely extended book reviews, there were others in which he demonstrates a hard, muscular style and a biting wit. All his writings were censored, but surprisingly little was cut out by the censor, for he wrote deliberately in a manner calculated to lull the authorities into believing that he was merely practicing the art of literary criticism. He would write about "popular movements" when he meant "revolution," and in other ways disguise his intentions. "Our life," he wrote, "has no need of powerful individuals; we have more than enough of them. What we need is awareness of reality." His prison writings were a constant striving for the awareness of reality.

He wrote a long essay on scholasticism, by which he meant the academic philosophers who "petrify life into concepts." A long essay on Darwin's *Origin of Species* permitted him to range widely through the animal kingdom, pausing to discuss the institution of slavery among ants, and the strange behavior of Mexican woodpeckers and blue-eyed cats and Egyptian dung beetles, while continually hinting that natural selection could be interpreted in political terms. An essay entitled "Popularizers of Negative Doctrines" offers a witty account of French eighteenth-century thinkers, giving special prominence to Boisguillebert, Voltaire and Rousseau— "negative doctrines" was a phrase devised to put the censor off the scent. He discusses Voltaire with deep affection, and has some caustic things to say about Rousseau, whose sentimentality offended him. Indeed, what is most remarkable about his essays is their dry, lean, uncomplicated character. When he examines a novel, he looks for the skeleton, the solid structure beneath the flow of words, and when he examines history he looks for the solid causes and tosses the decoration away.

One of the most remarkable of his essays is "A New Kind of Man," an examination of Rakhmetov, the towering revolutionary figure in Chernyshevsky's *What Is To Be Done?* Such men, he says, are invaluable and irreplaceable, but he is disturbed by their romanticism. Why must Rakhmetov torment himself? The account of Rakhmetov submitting himself to torture on a bed of nails offends him: why should a man choke in his own strength and display so much superfluous energy? But while distrusting Rakhmetov's romantic asceticism, he celebrated his passion for freedom. He envisaged a time when dozens of Rakhmetovs might arise, and he was saddened by the thought that they might appear in an age of apathy and pass unrecognized. "If indeed such men exist," he declared, "then perhaps the bright future is not so immeasurably distant as we used to believe."

So the years passed in the quietness of his prison cell, while he read omnivorously and wrote continuously. He resembled a monk immured in a monastery rather than a revolutionary immured in a Tsarist fortress. Perhaps it was inevitable that when he was released in November 1866 following an amnesty to celebrate the marriage of the Tsarevich with a Danish princess, the reality which had appeared to be so simple when viewed from a prison cell became too much for him. His health broke down. He continued to write, but the clear vision had faded. A year and a half after his release he spent some days at Dubbeln, a summer resort on the Baltic coast near Riga. One day he went swimming along a deserted stretch of the coast, and vanished. When his body was recovered, he had been dead for many hours.

At his death he was only twenty-seven years old, yet he had left a deep impression on Russian literature. The students who became revolutionaries read his works and cherished him for the violence of his ideas expressed in calm and muscular prose. Above all they cherished him because he insisted that the supreme duty of man was to solve once and for all the pressing problem of the hungry and the disinherited. In the eyes of Pisarev, all the arts, all culture, all systems of government, all the cultivated amenities of life were worthless as long as a single human being remained hungry. It was not a rational philosophy, but it fired the imaginations of three generations of students and helped to bring about the downfall of the autocracy.

KARAKOZOV

*I have decided to destroy the evil Tsar and die for my
beloved people.*

AN ATTEMPT ON THE TSAR

O<small>N</small> A<small>PRIL</small> 4, 1866, Tsar Alexander II spent part of the afternoon
walking in the Summer Garden which lies a little to the east of the
Winter Palace. It was a bright spring day, and he was in good humor.
One of his young nephews and a niece accompanied him, and there were
the usual police guards hovering in the distance, including the portly
General Totleben, the Chief of Police. Through the railings the crowds
were able to see him talking animatedly to his charges, and because he
was a popular Tsar they broke out from time to time with cries of "Hurrah!" and "Long Live the Tsar!" Already he was known as "the liberator
Tsar," for he had brought about the liberation of the serfs by imperial
edict in 1861, and although it was in fact only a partial liberation, and the
peasants were still under heavy obligations to their landlords, there were
many who regarded him as the savior of his country, just as there were
still many who regarded him as a despot. A tall, heavy-set man, with red-
dish side whiskers and a brisk manner which concealed an extreme sensitivity and a grave ignorance, he carried himself well. When at last, around
five o'clock in the afternoon, he came to the ornamental gates where a carriage was waiting for him, the people began to cheer more loudly, and
some prepared to kneel before him in a manner which had become customary in Russia when a peasant found himself in the presence of a lord.
He paused for a moment to salute the crowd, and was about to enter the
black-lacquered carriage with the imperial arms painted in gold when a
shot rang out. Suddenly everyone was shouting and screaming, the police

were dashing through the crowd and clubbing everyone who got in their way, and only the Tsar, who was unharmed, seemed to be unaffected by the scene.

He knew of course that the shot was intended for him, and he had escaped death only because the assassin's pistol was defective or because it was poorly aimed, but he showed no sign of relief. He looked at the crowd with an expression of disinterest, as he would look at a map showing the position of soldiers in a war. No one had been hurt. A man in a shabby brown coat had shot at him from a distance of six feet, but the Tsar had not seen him.

The assassin was able to run only a few yards alongside the railings when the crowd closed in on him. They knocked off his workman's cap and would have lynched him if the police had not come up in time. Streaming with blood, he shouted: "You fools! You fools! I did it for your sake!" He would have gone on to harangue the crowd, but they shouted him down. The police tied his hands with rope, and pushed him toward the carriage where the Tsar was waiting for him. There was a moment of silence while the Tsar looked the prisoner up and down: a thin slight man with high cheekbones, flaxen lackluster hair, weak rounded shoulders, and deep-set blue eyes. It was not a face of any particular nobility. He was a man of twenty-six, but he had the dazed careworn features of a student who always fails in his examinations. There was also something feminine in his appearance, and an incalculable strength.

"Are you a Pole?" the Tsar asked.

"No, pure Russian," the man answered, and looked away, as though the comedy of his arrest and confrontation with the Tsar already wearied him.

"What is your name?"

"Alexey Petrov."

"Where do you come from?"

The man shrugged his shoulders.

Leaning forward, the Tsar said: "Why did you fire with your pistol?"

"Look at the freedom you have given the peasants," the man answered bitterly, and said nothing more, for the police at a nod from the Tsar bundled him unresisting into a carriage and drove off across the Chain Bridge to the Peter and Paul Fortress.

Someone in the crowd pointed to a peasant standing cap in hand near the Tsar's carriage, saying he had struck the assassin's arm, causing the bullet to go wild. The peasant was a middle-aged capmaker from Kostroma called Osip Komissarov. General Totleben at once presented the capmaker to the Tsar, who thanked him, asked some polite questions, and ordered the general to see that he was properly rewarded. For a few weeks Osip Komissarov bathed in the glory of official acclaim. He was presented at court, granted a title of nobility, and regarded as another Ivan Susanin, also a peasant from Kostroma, who had saved the life of the first Romanov by hiding him from the Poles. Osip Komissarov had been a serf until the liberation, and it was thought to be particularly significant that the Tsar's life had been saved by a former serf who thus demonstrated his gratitude. But there were many who believed he had been merely plucked out of the crowd by General Totleben in order to provide a diversion, and the subsequent history of the peasant seemed to confirm the suspicion. When society hostesses praised him for saving the life of the Tsar he would smile vacantly, too drunk to know what was being said, and sometimes he would fall into fits of weeping. At last his behavior became intolerable, and he was sent back to Kostroma, where a few weeks later he drank himself to death.

The prisoner in the Peter and Paul Fortress refused to talk. Unlike Komissarov he had a sharp brain, and knew exactly what was demanded of him. They found nothing on his clothing to suggest his identity. On the day after his arrest Prince Dolgoruky, the head of the Third Division, reported to the Tsar: "Every possible means will be employed to uncover the truth." This meant that torture was being used. One of their ways of torturing him was by keeping him awake until at last out of sheer exhaustion and the desire to sleep, he would be made to speak. Guards were ordered to sit beside him all day and all night, prodding him into wakefulness the moment he dozed off. The guards were relieved every two hours. "He was a cunning man," one of the guards reported later. "He would sit there cross-legged, swinging one of his legs to make us believe he was awake, and then he would sleep for a while with the leg still swinging. We soon caught on to his trick, and we would warn the guards who relieved us. This went on for a whole week."

Two days after his arrest it was decided that religion might be usefully pressed into the service of a police interrogation, and Prince Dolgoruky reported to the Tsar: "He was examined all day without respite—a priest spent a few hours encouraging him to speak." Later another and more persuasive priest was employed for the same purpose.

The prisoner was like a monk who had sworn a vow of silence. A week later they knew scarcely more about him than they had known at the beginning. He would offer them useless scraps of information, and promise that if he was permitted to sleep he would divulge everything he knew, but the Third Division had already taken his measure. In one of his twice-daily reports to the Tsar written about a week after the arrest Prince Dolgoruky wrote:

From the enclosed report Your Majesty may observe what the principal commission of inquiry has accomplished during the second half of the day.

In spite of the fact that the criminal has not yet revealed his true name, and assures me most convincingly that if he is permitted to rest he will write out tomorrow a full account of the affair, and although he is physically emaciated and shows increasing signs of exhaustion, it may be observed that even today he has not made the slightest effort to provide a full confession.

So the days passed, with the prisoner pitting his silence against all the resources of the secret police. Count Muraviev, the butcher of Poland, was entrusted with the task of making him talk. Torture was applied again—"The refusal of the prisoner to speak has placed the commission under the necessity of using energetic measures," Muraviev reported, admitting later that the "energetic measures" had failed. Religion was tried again. Day after day the archpriest Vasily Palisadov, a fashionable society priest who had published a collection of his sermons in French, was permitted to enter the cell and offer spiritual consolation. Palisadov was a middle-aged man of the world, exactly twice as old as the prisoner, with a gift for ferreting out secrets, and he appears to have been more successful than the other agents of the Third Division. Tall and elegant, with long silver-streaked hair reaching to his shoulders, he played so much on the prisoner's religious feelings that he finally succeeded in reducing him to a state of imbecility. The starving and exhausted prisoner spent endless hours on his knees in passionate prayers, begging for divine forgiveness.

Some days after the arrest of the prisoner, the police who had been searching everywhere for a clue to his identity, received a visit from the proprietor of the Znamensky Hotel, who reported that one of his hotel guests had been missing ever since the attempted assassination. He had signed the hotel register as D. Vladimirov. The police checked the room and found the address in Moscow of a certain Nikolay Ishutin. The inquiry was immediately transferred to Moscow. As the days passed, the police were able to congratulate themselves that they had uncovered a conspiracy far more dangerous than the Petrashevsky conspiracy. For the first time they came upon a group of students who were absolutely ruthless and determined to overthrow the government.

Nikolay Ishutin was one of those men who make revolutions. Born in the province of Saratov, in that Volga region which had produced many revolutionaries in the past and would produce more in the future, Ishutin was the son of a fairly well-to-do merchant and a woman from the nobility. His parents died when he was two years old, and he was entrusted to the care of a relative of his father, Vladimir Karakozov, a landowner of no great wealth, who also belonged to the Saratov nobility. Ishutin was the same age as the landowner's son, Dmitry, and they grew up together.

Neither Dmitry Karakozov nor Nikolay Ishutin were good students.

Karakozov was sent down from the University of Kazan, but permitted to return on his promise of good behavior, and studied with no particular talent. Leaving Kazan without a degree he went to the University of Moscow, where he was again sent down, this time for nonpayment of tuition fees, and then worked briefly as a clerk for a nobleman, a labor which he appears to have regarded as beneath his dignity. Ishutin, who was also a student at the University of Moscow, showed no particular interest in learning, and indeed he despised it, saying that the purpose of the University was to produce "generals of culture" who would inevitably become officials or respectable bourgeois leading artificial lives remote from the people. Pisarev had said that the revolution would come about as the result of learning and science; Ishutin replied that it would come about as the result of terrorist activity and by creating cooperative associations among the workmen.

By sheer force of personality Ishutin became the accepted leader of a circle of revolutionaries who called themselves "The Organization." Following Chernyshevsky's *What Is To Be Done?* they organized small cooperatives among tailors and bookbinders, and planned to open their own communal factories. It was a tightly knit revolutionary group, with a terrorist arm known as "Hell." This was a very small group consisting of students who lived communally in the house of a certain Ipatov, and were sometimes known as "the men from Ipatov." They lived by a strict regimen and were vowed to revolutionary destruction. Dedicated to obedience, they inhabited a world which was not the world of the living. "Hell" was the creation of the romantic and thoroughly undisciplined mind of Ishutin, who appears to have derived the idea from his reading of Gothic novels and accounts of the history of the Assassins, those eleventh-century conspirators who were commanded by the Old Man of the Mountain to kill anyone who stood in the way of his own political aspirations in the Moslem world. Ishutin saw himself as another Old Man of the Mountain.

The members of "Hell" studied assassination as an art, and their main purpose was to assassinate the Tsar and other dignitaries. Potential assassins would draw lots, and the man who was chosen would immediately vanish from his usual haunts and take up an entirely new form of life in the capital. Everything was permitted to him: he could steal, murder, denounce perfectly innocent people to the police, as long as he held in view the supreme purpose for which he was sent to St. Petersburg. On the eve of the assassination he would disfigure his face with chemicals; after firing the shot he would take poison. The police would never be able to discover his identity, but they would find on his body a manifesto declaring the reasons which had brought him to commit the act. If the first attempt failed, another "man from Ipatov" would step into his shoes. Ishutin himself would decide when the assassinations would take place.

"Hell" had its own code of laws and precise regulations. As Ishutin described them, they resembled the laws of medieval knighthood or the even more severe laws applicable to a community of monks. A member of "Hell" was never permitted to marry; he must live under a false name; he must surrender his friends and all connection with his family. "In general he must live with one single exclusive aim: an infinite love and devotion for his country and its welfare." In much the same way Nechayev, a later and even more imperious revolutionary, would describe the strange, haunted, passionless life of the revolutionary in his *Revolutionary Catechism*.

Sometimes when Ishutin considered the vast potentialities of "Hell," it occurred to him that it could be adapted to many purposes. "Hell" was not merely a machine for performing acts of terror which would bring about the downfall of the Tsarist regime; it was itself the supreme guide and defender of the revolution, the source of all political directives, the maintainer of revolutionary privilege, the secret heart of the revolutionary process. Therefore "Hell" would endure long after the revolution had been brought into being. In all this Ishutin showed that he possessed a prophetic gift.

The sources are obscure, and it is not certain whether Dmitry Karakozov was ever a member of "Hell." Nevertheless, as the foster brother of Ishutin and as a close friend, he knew all about the movement, sympathized with it, and saw himself as one of those dedicated men prepared to lay down their lives for their country. He was a member of The Organization, and he had been a master in one of the free schools which Ishutin organized in Moscow in the hope, as he said, "of raising a crop of young revolutionaries." Then he fell ill, and could no longer work for The Organization. In his weakened condition he felt that his whole life had been useless, and it only remained for him to perform one final great act of mercy before committing suicide. He bought a pistol and a bottle of poison, and in a mood of religious exaltation went off to spend a few days in the fortresslike Troitsky monastery near Moscow, where Peter the Great had taken refuge and where the most dedicated monks lived in underground cells. It was the most famous and beloved of all the monasteries in Russia, often visited by prayerful men about to make important decisions. When he returned to Moscow he told Ishutin that he had reached an irrevocable decision—he would assassinate the Tsar.

Ishutin did his best to dissuade him. Karakozov was too sickly, too nervous, too frail to undertake such a task with any hope of success. He was in an exalted mood, and cared nothing for the revolutionary society which Ishutin had organized. He would kill the Tsar and die, and this would be his supreme offering to his country.

Other members of The Organization also tried to dissuade him, but in vain. Karakozov slipped out of Moscow and vanished into the underworld of St. Petersburg, living in obscure lodginghouses and run-down hotels, frequently changing his place of residence. According to the code of "Hell," he was expected to write a manifesto explaining his deed and to take poison immediately after firing the shot. The poison was ready, and so was the pistol, but there were no bullets. It took him a little time to find the bullets, and a little more time to write the manifesto, which he distributed with a characteristic disregard for caution near factory buildings and anywhere else where he thought workmen might find it. The manifesto was addressed "To Worker Friends," and was unsigned. There was nothing particularly memorable in his manifesto, which was written quietly and a little sadly in the mood of a man who knows he must carry out his purpose because there is no alternative. There were no fierce romantic gestures, no bloodthirsty denunciations. He wrote:

Brothers, I have long been tormented by the thought of why the simple Russian people have to suffer so much, and my restless strivings have given me no peace. I see the nobility in their idleness, and the swarms of wealthy officials and other privileged people living in their glittering houses, and they produce nothing, while the eternal simple peasant and the laborer in his workshop and at the factory bench work unceasingly. These idlers have climbed on the shoulders of simple folk, and they suck the peasants' blood. I have searched in books for the cause of all this, and I have found it. The man responsible for all this is the Tsar, and all Russian history proves it. Throughout the centuries the Tsars have gradually built up the organization of the state and the army, and they have taken the land and given it to the nobility. If you think carefully about this, brothers, you will realize that the Tsar is the first of the nobles. He never offers his hand to the peasant because he is their worst enemy . . .

I myself have traveled in many parts of our Mother Russia. I have seen the wretched lives of the peasants, and I know they grow poorer and poorer as a result of the measures taken for their "liberation." Soon even the pitiable clothes will be stripped from their backs. I have felt all the grief and sorrow of seeing my beloved people dying in this way, and so I have decided to destroy the evil Tsar and die for my beloved people.

He went on to declare that if he failed, others would follow, and once the Tsar was dead, the people would see how small and powerless were the great officials and landed proprietors once the support of the Tsar had been removed from them. Then there would be real freedom, and the land would be given over to cooperatives, with the income divided equally among all. Russia would no longer be ruled by thieves and exploiters, and everyone would live in plenty.

Though ill-written and repetitive Karakozov's manifesto was a far more human document than *Molodaya Rossiya*. It was evidently written by Karakozov himself without the help of anyone else. He arrived in St. Petersburg in the middle of March, and by the end of the month a copy of the manifesto was already in the possession of the police. The manifesto together with a letter, signed "A student," explaining the circumstances under which it had been handed to him, lay in their files. But the police made no effort to trace the student or the author of the manifesto. They attached no importance to it: it was just one more anonymous pamphlet which had fallen into their hands.

Ishutin appears to have received a copy of the manifesto about the same time. Alarmed by the prospect that Karakozov might kill the Tsar before any preparations for a revolutionary uprising could be made, he sent Pyotr Ermolov and Nikolay Stranden, both members of The Organization and belonging to the minor nobility, to St. Petersburg. They were ordered to prevent or delay the attempt. They had difficulty in finding Karakozov, and when they caught up with him, he refused to obey them, saying that he was more than ever convinced that he must carry out his sacred duty. Ishutin then sent a categorical order that he should return to Moscow. Surprisingly he obeyed, and we hear of a meeting of The Organization held at Ishutin's apartment on April 4, at which Karakozov was present. Four days later he was back in St. Petersburg. Whatever decision was reached during the meeting, Karakozov was still determined to carry out the attempt.

He believed that his act would be welcomed throughout Russia, but in this he was mistaken. The factory workers and the peasants regarded the Tsar with affection, knowing that he was responsible for the liberation of the serfs, which he had ordered in defiance of his advisers. They had no love for the landlords or the government officials, but they had even less love for the young intellectuals and students who could sometimes be heard calling for the destruction of the state. When the police found the scrap of paper with Ishutin's address at the Znamensky Hotel and began to uncover details about "Hell," the most willing informers were to be found among the peasants and factory workers for whom Karakozov was prepared to sacrifice his life.

More than fifty persons were arrested. As usual, the police dragnet included a number of innocent people, who were later released. All together thirty-five were brought to trial, divided into two groups—the first included Karakozov, Ishutin, Ermolov, Stranden, and others who played an active role in the conspiracy, and a larger group consisting mostly of students who were thought to be the dupes of the revolutionary leaders.

The police had little difficulty in dragging out the full story. The prisoners confessed and implicated one another. Ishutin, who had thought of himself as the future revolutionary dictator of Russia, wept as he declared that he had done everything possible to prevent the assassination attempt, and was not believed. Karakozov's role as a self-appointed assassin acting independently of "Hell" became clear many weeks later. Throughout the examination of the prisoners daily reports were sent to the Tsar.

The trial of the eleven principal conspirators took place in the same large room in the Peter and Paul Fortress which saw the trial of the Decembrists forty years before. Once again there was the horseshoe table covered with a red cloth and a half circle of judges in full uniform. The president of the court was Prince Gagarin, an old man with a large nose and a shaggy beard who resembled a kindly wolf, and he was almost as nervous as the prisoners. Karakozov was the first to be brought in. He was too ill, too confused to answer the court's questions intelligibly; and the Prince who had gazed at him first with horror, insisting on using the familiar form of address because it was intolerable that such a villain should be addressed in polite tones, finally spoke to him kindly, his voice scarcely audible when he read out the death sentence. Ishutin, too, was condemned to death. The remaining prisoners were sentenced to long terms of forced labor and exile.

Told that he was permitted to appeal to the Tsar's clemency, Karakozov wrote an ambiguous letter to the Tsar in which he declared that his offense was so terrible that he could expect no alleviation of his punishment, but he swore that he would never have attempted the crime if he had not been in an abnormal state of mind brought about by a deep concern for the welfare of the people. He—or perhaps his lawyer—begged the Tsar's forgiveness "as Christian of Christian and man of man." The appeal reached the hands of Zamyatin, the liberal Minister of Justice, who showed it to the Tsar when they were traveling together by train from St. Petersburg to Tsarskoye Selo. "There was an angelic expression on the Tsar's face," Zamyatin wrote later, "when he told me: 'As a Christian I have long since forgiven him in my heart, but as a sovereign I do not believe I have a right to pardon him.' "

The question of how many conspirators should be hanged was debated at some length. Count Panin suggested that "to hang two is better than one, and to hang three is better than two." At one time the Tsar seemed to be determined to hang Karakozov, Ishutin and Khudyakov, one of Ishutin's chief lieutenants. Finally it was decided that only Karakozov should hang, while Ishutin would suffer the fate of the Petrashevsky conspirators: he would be brought to the scaffold in a shroud, and at the very last moment he would be reprieved.

Another question was keenly debated among the Tsar's chief advisers:

the date of the execution. This was complicated by the fact that Princess Dagmar of Denmark, the nineteen-year-old daughter of King Christian IX, was soon to marry the Tsarevich Alexander Alexandrovich, and it was especially desirable that there should be no hangings during the long weeks of festivities preceding the wedding. Then, too, the hangings could not possibly take place in the week between September 7, the anniversary of the Tsar's coronation, and September 11, the name day of Saint Alexander Nevsky after whom the Tsar was named. Finally it was decided that the hanging should take place on September 15, a Saturday, shortly after dawn, in the Smolensky Field on Vasilyevsky Island, not far from the place where the five Decembrists were secretly buried. All over St. Petersburg there were posters in heavy black letters describing the place and time of the execution of "Dmitry Karakozov, enemy of the state." The Tsar was particularly anxious that there should be a large crowd.

A small house on the edge of the field was requisitioned for the Execution Commission. There the representatives of the Tsar, the Minister of Justice, and the police were gathered to welcome the prisoner and to accompany him to the scaffold, which was erected on a high black wooden platform in the middle of the field. Troops were drawn up round the scaffold. Some American sailors from a squadron paying an official visit to Russian waters were given a privileged position inside the square of soldiers. The two-horse cart which had brought Karakozov from the Peter and Paul Fortress drove across the field to the scaffold. Karakozov was sitting with his back to the horses on a high box, in chains. He looked strangely limp, his face a curious grayish blue, almost lifeless. One of the cuirassiers who was present said later:

> My first impression was that they were bringing out an india-rubber doll to be hanged; that Karakozov was already dead. Imagine that the head, the hands, the whole body were absolutely loose, as if there were no bones in the body, or as if the bones had all been broken. It was a terrible thing to see, and to think what it meant. However, when two soldiers took him down from the cart, I saw that he moved his legs and made strenuous endeavors to walk by himself and to ascend the steps of the scaffold. So it was not a doll, nor could he have been in a swoon. All the officers were very much puzzled by the circumstances and could not explain it.

The explanation was a simple one, being contained in the two words which appeared constantly in the reports sent to the Tsar from the Peter and Paul Fortress—"energetic measures" to make the prisoner speak were being taken almost up to the day of execution.

The well-worn panoply of death accompanied the execution of Karakozov, which was attended with the customary Tsarist refinements. Karakozov stood close to the railings, gazing out at the people who had come to see him die, while a general mounted the scaffold and read out the death sentence in a low voice, his hands trembling, his plumed hat under his arm. Since he represented the Tsar, there was a roll of drums before he spoke, a signal to all the spectators to remove their hats. Then there was silence, as the archpriest Vasily Palisadov in full regalia mounted the scaffold and presented a gleaming gold cross to the prisoner at arm's length. No one heard what Karakozov said, or whether he said anything at all. Then it was the turn of the executioner, who for some reason hastily threw a white hood over the prisoner's head. This was a mistake, for according to the protocol of the time the prisoner must first be dressed in the white shroud with the long sleeves before he is hooded; and accordingly the hood was removed at a signal from the chief of police. To many, and perhaps also to Karakozov, the removing of the hood was thought to mean that he had been pardoned. It was observed that in those few seconds while he stood bareheaded the color came back to his cheeks and he no longer twitched and he seemed to be about to speak. Then the executioner hastily forced his arms into the white shroud and the long sleeves were tied behind his back, and for the second time the hood was thrown over his face. The armless, faceless doll was then lifted up carefully and made to stand on a bench, while a rope was placed round his neck.

All that remained was to kick the bench away, and while he dangled helplessly the drummers beat a tattoo, drowning the groans and prayers of the crowd.

For the rest of the day until long after nightfall the body of Karakozov hung from the black gallows on Smolensky Field. About midnight it was cut down, and carried away to an unknown burial place in a one-horse cart.

The memory of Karakozov lived on, while the names of his fellow conspirators were soon forgotten. The attempt to kill the Tsar had been carried out by a single man against the wishes of his fellow conspirators in a mood of reckless abandon. His failure pointed to a more deadly method. Since the revolutionaries regarded the Tsar as legitimate prey, what was to prevent them from mounting an attack in depth, with many revolutionaries taking part in a well-organized plan and a clear-cut order of battle? Instead of one lonely tormented man, there would be ten or twelve revolutionaries acting in cold blood, calmly and accurately, with a machinelike precision. Any small group, if it were sufficiently determined, would always succeed in breaking through the cordon round the Tsar.

Among the first—perhaps the very first—to think in this way was Pyotr Tkachev, the son of a minor nobleman from Velikiye Luki. His father died when he was young, and he was sent to a boarding school in St. Petersburg. He was sixteen when he was first caught up in the storm of political ideas raging at the time. At seventeen he entered the University of St.

Petersburg as a student of law, and for taking part in student disturbances he was arrested a few weeks later and thrown into the Peter and Paul Fortress. Later he was transferred to the fortress at Kronstadt. Through his mother's influence he was soon released. Expelled from the University, he worked as a journalist and as a literary critic, and in 1862 produced an anonymous pamphlet *What We Want,* in which he vigorously denounced the government and called for a speedy revolution. What he wanted was action—quick, remorseless, irrevocable action, an organized revolutionary party. The police traced the author of the pamphlet, arrested him, put him on trial, and saw that he was sentenced to three months' imprisonment in the Peter and Paul Fortress. He was not considered especially dangerous, and as a member of the nobility he was treated with leniency. He was then only nineteen.

He was released early in 1863 and went to work in the offices of the liberal paper *Russkoye Slovo,* where he wrote articles and book reviews. In a book review written in 1865 he expounded Marx's theory of economic determinism, saying that the theory which had been clearly and accurately expressed by Marx in his *Critique of Political Economy* published in 1859, "has now become the common property of all decent-thinking people, and no intelligent man can find any serious objection to it." He appears to have been the first Russian radical to be influenced by Marx.

Wearing his hair long, his round face decorated with a small mustache, Tkachev looked like the impoverished nobleman he was. His manners were diffident and gentle, his prose violent. His mother had friends in high places, and they were able to expunge the record of his expulsion from the University, and he was permitted to take his degree in law. He now had four careers: he was a lawyer, a journalist, a translator, and a revolutionary conspirator. He translated Ernst Becher's *The Problem of the Working Class in Its Contemporary Significance and the Means to Solve It,* a brief and undistinguished work by a German social philosopher, to which he added a series of notes and commentaries of a violently revolutionary character. He wrote:

> Under the normal order of things political control belongs to those classes which dominate the economic sphere. But the normal order can be temporarily interrupted, and in this way the vicious circle can be broken. It is absurd to expect a natural transition from the old regime to the new, because they are based on diametrically opposed principles. Everyone ought to know that this transition requires a certain leap and everybody must prepare for it.

The translation of Becher's book with the commentary was published in 1865 with the approval of the censor, who evidently forgot to read the final pages. It had an extensive sale, especially among the more radical students in St. Petersburg University. Tkachev's tactic was a clever one, but it had already been employed by Chernyshevsky in his notes to his

translation of John Stuart Mill's *Political Economy*, and it was not therefore original with him. What was original was the conception of "a certain leap." It was an idea which Lenin took strongly to heart.

Among the students who gathered in Tkachev's lodgings to discuss the
forthcoming revolution was the formidable Sergey Nechayev, soon to become a brilliant exponent of revolutionary techniques. Tkachev realized
the potentialities of Nechayev, and together they wrote *A Program of
Revolutionary Action,* which begins with the statement that Russia is "a
kingdom of the mad" and only by a revolutionary leap involving the
destruction of the existing government, mass insurrections by the peasants,
and the establishment of a revolutionary elite, can it be restored to sanity.
The greater part of the program appears to have been written by Tkachev,
but here and there it is possible to discern the characteristic style of
Nechayev, who almost certainly wrote the words: "Members of the organization must give up every possession, occupation or family tie, because families and occupations might distract them from their revolutionary duties." These words reappear with only slight changes in Nechayev's *Revolutionary Catechism.*

The new program envisaged total revolution commanded by a revolutionary elite in close contact with revolutionary movements abroad, with
precise and clearly stated objectives. Exact dates were given. The elite
must be formed by May 1, 1869, the eighth anniversary of the abolition
of serfdom, and the revolution was to take place in the spring of the following year when the blueprint had been worked out to the last detail
and all the revolutionary leaders were at their posts.

This grandiose and menacing document was intended to be nothing
less than the opening salvo of the revolution which would sweep over
Russia and perhaps over the whole of Europe. Intoxicated with visions
of destructive fury Tkachev and Nechayev set about organizing the nucleus of student groups which would provide the intellectual leadership
of the coming revolution.

There were student disturbances in January after the end of the Christmas vacation, and a fairly large number of students were arrested.
Tkachev wrote a manifesto *To the Public,* ostensibly to protest the arrests, but a student reading between the lines would realize that it was an
urgent call for open rebellion. Hundreds, perhaps thousands of copies of
the manifesto were run off a hand press, and some of them fell into the
hands of the police. Once again the authorship was traced, and Tkachev
was arrested and thrown into the Peter and Paul Fortress. Nechayev, who
had been busy organizing the revolution in Moscow, was luckier. He
slipped across the frontier and made his way to Switzerland.

The police were now rounding up hundreds of students. They realized
that there had come into existence a far more dangerous conspiracy than

they had suspected. Only three years had passed since Karakozov had attempted to kill the Tsar, but this new conspiracy was being led by far more ruthless and determined men. The police congratulated themselves that they had scotched the conspiracy just in time.

Tkachev was finally brought to trial in July 1871, and sentenced to sixteen months' imprisonment followed by exile in Siberia. The police had discovered *To the Public*, but knew nothing about *A Program of Revolutionary Action*, otherwise he would have been given a more severe sentence. His mother interceded with the authorities, and when the prison term was over he was permitted to live quietly under police surveillance on the family estate at Velikiye Luki, not far from the Polish frontier. In 1873 he succeeded in escaping abroad.

For the remaining years of his life he conducted himself as a professional revolutionary, quarreling with other revolutionaries, editing his newssheet *Nabat* (The Tocsin) in Geneva, and sternly demanding that the revolutionaries stop talking and instead form hardheaded revolutionary groups determined to seize power with all the weapons of terror. He wrote in *Nabat*: "The struggle can be conducted successfully only by combining the following conditions: centralization, severe discipline, swiftness, decisiveness, unity of action. All concessions, all wavering, all compromises, all division of authority, and decentralization of the fighting arm weaken their energy, paralyze their activity, and deprive the struggle of all chances of victory." These, too, were words which Lenin took to heart.

Once Tkachev spoke of "the terrifying terror which really terrified, and so frightened the autocracy that it gave up the ghost." Lenin approved of these words and quoted them in his early revolutionary pamphlet *What Is To Be Done?* with the comment: "This is majestic."

As the years passed Tkachev found himself increasingly living in solitude. He had only a handful of followers, little money, no prospect of bringing about his fiery dream of revolution. Gradually he went mad. He died of general paralysis at the Hospital of St. Anne in Paris in January 1886.

The Decembrists, Petrashevsky and Karakozov had thought of the revolution in human terms. Even Bakunin, the unregenerate "creator of vast destructions," had regarded revolution as something to be suffered, not practiced by an elite corps determined to employ every ruse and every available weapon to bring the revolution about. With Tkachev and Nechayev the revolution enters a new and more terrible phase, for they placed themselves outside the bounds of morality and human decency. They taught total revolution, the uprooting of the entire state in order to establish a revolutionary dictatorship. They were the masters from whom Lenin learned.

NECHAYEV

Our task is total, terrible, universal and merciless destruction.

THE YOUNG TIGER

NECHAYEV STANDS at the threshold of the modern world—the dedicated terrorist determined to put the world to the flames. But in the rare photographs that survive, there is no hint of the terror he caused. A mass of thick, dark, curly hair, a broad forehead, veiled eyes under level eyebrows, a flat nose, lips that are almost feminine. In one of these photographs he wears the wide-lapelled coat of a dandy, and gazes out of the oval frame with the insolence of an aristocrat. To the end there was something of the aristocrat in him: he disdained danger, spoke on familiar terms with the aristocracy and regarded himself as one born to lead.

He was small and frail, dark-skinned, nearly always hungry. Those who knew him say he was always slovenly in appearance, his shirt falling to ruins, his hair tousled and his beard uncombed. They speak of his strange, quick walk, his broad accent, his habit of biting his fingernails. Men were in awe of his courage. Obstinate, never accepting defeat, forever dreaming of destroying the autocracy, always wandering restlessly, he was like a mad ghost let loose upon the world, a ghost breathing fire and murder. From the beginning he seems to have hated the world, not only the world of the Tsar, but the peasant world from which he sprang. He set himself up against the vast power of the Tsarist police, and continually slipped from their clutches. He was a blackmailer, a murderer, a seducer, and a thief—these were his lesser crimes. His greatest crime was that he lived with a pure thirst for destruction and in different ways influenced both Lenin and Hitler, for the theses he stated were adopted directly by one

161

and indirectly by the other. In his own time he was so important that the conspirators plotting the assassination of Alexander II debated whether the rescue of the legendary revolutionary Nechayev was more necessary than the destruction of the Tsar. In his life he committed only one murder, but he may be responsible for millions of murders; and the single murder he committed seems to have been an act of gratuitous bravado, committed in a moment of madness. His life was a dogged, interminable struggle against the autocracy; and when he was shackled to the wall and there was almost no strength in him, he continued to fight. He was everything that was evil, but even in his evil he possessed a raw, human courage.

Sergey Gennadievich Nechayev was born at Ivanovo, near Vladimir, a hundred miles to the northeast of Moscow, on September 20, 1847. Ivanovo was then a small textile town, hardly more than an overgrown village: it had not yet blossomed into the great manufacturing city of Ivanovo-Voznesensk. His father was an innkeeper, sometime small merchant, artisan, and factotum, who married the daughter of a house painter from Kostroma. After the marriage he followed his father-in-law's trade, became a house painter and was on good terms with the local gentry, attending weddings and putting up the decorations. He was a good worker and much sought after. His wife helped out with dressmaking. She had been a serf and her husband had bought her freedom.

Nechayev spent some of his early years with his maternal grandparents in Kostroma, a city of medieval splendor. Here in the year 1313 the Tatar Prince Chet, the commander of the Golden Horde, saw a vision of the Virgin, was converted to Christianity, and built a cathedral in her honor. Here too the young Mikhail Fyodorovich Romanov, the first of his line, took refuge from a marauding Polish army and received the submission of the boyars. Somewhere on the outskirts of Kostroma the peasant Ivan Susanin was captured by Polish cavalry and ordered to reveal the Tsar's hiding place. Because he refused, he was tortured to death. Glinka wrote the opera *A Life for the Tsar* to celebrate the peasant's heroism.

When Nechayev was four years old there was erected on the main square of Kostroma a huge granite column in memory of the Tsar and the peasant. At the top of the column stood a gigantic bronze bust of the Tsar. Leaning against the column, in the attitude of a slave mourning his master, was a bronze of the murdered peasant. The day of unveiling was a holiday. The bands played the tumultuous choruses from Glinka's opera. A Grand Duke officiated and received the messages of humble loyalty which were duly transmitted to the Tsar; and on the cobblestones the serfs from a hundred miles around knelt to receive the blessings of the Metropolitan. It was a day which people remembered for many years to come. Somewhere in the Cathedral, no one knew exactly where, the peasant had been buried. In no Russian town were the Tsars worshiped with greater devotion.

But Kostroma was dying. It had been dying for a very long time. The old battle flags hung in the Cathedral of the Assumption, which faced north because it was in the north that the Grand Duke Vasily Kostromsky had seen another vision of the Virgin. The flags were falling to dusty ribbons, and the paint was flaking off the great cupolas. Early in the sixties a royal commission was dispatched to Kostroma to inquire into the general decay threatening the palaces and cathedrals of the city, but little was done except to restore the secret chamber where the Tsar had hidden from the Poles. Kostroma lived on with its memories. From the fever of decay, from hallucinations of the medieval past, Nechayev may have drawn a part of his strength.

When Nechayev came to St. Petersburg, he rarely spoke about his youth. We know little about his childhood. He was fourteen when he heard the town crier reading the Act of Emancipation on a cold, blustery morning in the town square of Ivanovo. That night there was a banquet in the town hall, followed by prayers for the safety of the royal family in the churches; and he may have remembered the long procession of ex-serfs making their way through the town with lanterns, singing hymns. Within a week the ex-serfs were wondering what the Act of Emancipation amounted to, for there was no immediate change in their social position.

From being a house painter Nechayev's father became a builder and Sergey, after an unprofitable period spent serving behind the counter of a local shop, became his father's errand boy. Once he was sent out on an errand during a snowstorm with a letter for an important client. The letter was lost. Sergey floundered about in the snow, trying to find the letter, which probably was blown out of his hands. It was very late when he returned home. Asked about the letter, he confessed he had lost it. His father turned on him and cursed him for a good-for-nothing. Much depended on the letter, and the old man was almost out of his wits with hate. He had never inflicted corporal punishment on his son before. For the first and last time his father took down a birch rod and flogged him. Long afterward one of Nechayev's childhood friends remembered the incident as a turning point: from that moment there was a core of bitterness in him.

He learned to play the flute and he played with cardboard soldiers, a game which boys played in Russia well into their teens. The soldiers were painted crudely, red for the Russians, blue for the Turks. Then they were shot down with peas. When he was younger he played the game of "banker" with the gold and silver foil from the tops of wine bottles representing coins and scribbled bits of paper representing paper money. He learned a little French and German, accompanied his father into the houses of the wealthy merchants, became an expert floor polisher, and learned how to paint signs passably well. There is a story that he drank heavily for a while and then gave it up. He was restless and sought out the company of the educated and he despised the merchants. One day he announced that he was determined to be a student. An obscure writer of *feuilletons* named Nefedov gave him some letters of introduction to students in St. Petersburg. A few days later Nechayev left Ivanovo forever. He was twenty-one, and he had wasted the whole of his youth.

For the next four years he lived at an astonishing level of intensity. Within a few months of his arrival in St. Petersburg he was in singlehanded control of a vast network of conspiracy. Superbly confident in his own insolence, plotting destruction, he dominated the Russian revolutionary scene until he disappeared into the silent cells of the Peter and Paul Fortress; but even then, like a dark ghost, he terrorized from behind the prison bars. It was as though he was determined to make up for lost time.

Small and thin, with a long dark face and piercing blue eyes, with no experience of revolutionary activity and almost no schooling—he only learned to read when he was sixteen—Nechayev seems to have arrived in St. Petersburg with his plans already made. From the beginning he talked about overthrowing the dynasty. Was it boredom, poverty, hatred of the merchants of Ivanovo, the memory of Ivan Susanin, the ancient medieval lusts burning in him? No one knows.

From those who survived his revolutionary activities we have brief glimpses of him walking the streets in a threadbare coat, wearing boots too large for him. It is autumn, the snow already falling. He has a job as teacher of religious instruction in a day school. At night he attends lectures at the University. He lives in a small dark room off a courtyard, almost without furniture. There are portraits of Robespierre, Saint-Just and Herzen on the walls, and books everywhere—Carlyle's *French Revolution* in a Russian translation, the works of Blanqui, Robert Owen, and Babeuf, and histories of the Decembrists.

He lived in a student hostel, an old house boarded up into a number of small rooms which resembled caves. The winter damp came through the walls. A small group met in the apartment of Yenisherlov, a rich student who could afford comfortable sofas, bookcases, delicate chairs. There were even two immense tables strewn with books. In the group were Vladimir Orlov, and the two brothers Amethystov: Ivan was a student at the University, Evlampy a student at the Medico-Chirurgical Academy. They were joined a little later by Zemphyr Arbore-Ralli and Prince Cherkessov, the owner of a celebrated bookshop much frequented by students.

There were perhaps twenty others. They were dedicated revolutionaries, prepared to sacrifice their lives in the struggle against autocracy, but in need of leadership. Nechayev provided the leadership. He had a simple solution for all problems. Bring the students out on strike, take over the arsenals, destroy the Emperor. Orlov was put in charge of a scheme for organizing the student movement, while Nechayev maintained over-all control. In December 1868, as head of the "Secret Revolutionary Committee," Nechayev drew up a brief outline of his plans for the coming months:

> Up to the month of May 1869 the activity of our best men should be concentrated in Petersburg, Moscow and all other cities where there are universities. We must prepare for a student protest movement in all universities and high schools. We must demand the right of assembly. At the same time propaganda must be immediately begun among the proletariat, and there should be further propaganda in all cities and towns where the poorer classes are concentrated.

This was not especially illuminating, but Nechayev was merely warming up. In January and February he was sending delegates to Moscow, Kiev, and Kharkov, and he had received the oath of allegiance from ninety-seven students who signed their names to a sheet of paper—the list turned up mysteriously sixty years later in the police archives. Early in February overtures were made to the revolutionary Pyotr Tkachev, whose pamphlet called *To the Public* was being widely read among the students. It was Tkachev who had first announced the possibility of a technique of revolt, and suggested that the revolution should begin from within the universities: Nechayev provided the date, the sense of overwhelming urgency, and the conception of a simultaneous uprising of students and workmen. Nechayev also provided the iron discipline and the threat of the death penalty to anyone who refused to obey the commands of the Central Committee. The movement was growing. It now included Vladimir Cherkezov,* who had been implicated in the Karakozov affair, and a host of serious-minded and determined students. They possessed their own printing press, borrowed from a certain Semyon Serebrennikov who was to play a strange role in Nechayev's later life. The secret printing press was operated by Alexandra Dementieva, the eighteen-year-old daughter of a staff captain, who later became the wife of Tkachev. On the press immense quantities of the pamphlet *To the Public* were printed for distribution during the uprising. Everything was ready. The colleges were seething, but there was still some opposition to united action. Suddenly, toward the end of February, the police pounced on two or three of the emissaries Nechayev had sent to the universities, and Nechayev

* Not to be confused with Prince Cherkessov.

himself was summoned to the police station. He succeeded in throwing the police off the scent, but he knew he was a marked man and would be arrested at the moment of the outbreak. He decided to leave St. Petersburg and seek the safety of Moscow.

Two days later Vera Zasulich, then a young college student at St. Petersburg, received a letter in the ordinary mail. There were two enclosures. One read:

> I was walking in the Vasilyevsky Island this morning and I passed the police cart used for the transport of prisoners. As it went by a hand appeared at the window and I heard the voice of a dear friend: "If you are a student send this to the address given." I feel it is my duty to fulfill what is demanded of me. Destroy this note, in case the handwriting is recognized.
>
> A Student.

The other note, scribbled in pencil, was in Nechayev's handwriting:

> They are taking me to the Fortress. Do not lose heart, beloved comrades. Continue to have faith in me, and let us hope we meet again.

Nechayev's message was in fact a brilliant piece of deception, but there was nothing wildly improbable in the story. He was already a legend, and because the message portrayed him as a revolutionary hero, he was merely reinforcing a portrait that already existed in the minds of many students. Vera Zasulich believed in the message implicitly. She immediately informed Anna Grigorieva, Nechayev's sister, who was also studying at the University, and soon all the young revolutionaries knew about Nechayev's arrest. If Nechayev was in the Peter and Paul Fortress—for his reference to "the Fortress" could hardly mean anything else—then he was the first martyr of the student revolt, and a mass meeting was called to demand his release. The police were puzzled. They knew he was not in the Fortress, but they could find no trace of him. In fact while the police were frantically searching for him and the students were demanding his release, Nechayev was living quietly in Moscow under one of his many aliases. He remained in Moscow for two weeks, and then with the passport of his friend Nikolayev slipped out of the country and made his way to Switzerland.

No one knows why he left St. Petersburg so abruptly. It is possible that he lost his nerve. It is also possible that he intended his bogus arrest as a method of retaining power over the students: though he had failed to lead the revolt, the story of the arrest, and the subsequent stories of his escape, would help him to consolidate his authority. In later years, living under another name, he would tell the story of how he had escaped, pause dramatically and say: "And do you know where this mysterious Nechayev is now? He is standing in front of you. No, I am not Pavlov. I am Nechayev."

It is also possible that Nechayev left Russia because he was convinced that the outbreak in the universities would be ingloriously stamped out by the Russian police, and needed the prestige of someone greater than himself to lead it to success. Leaving Russia, he went straight to Geneva, where the old revolutionary Mikhail Bakunin received him with open arms. He had come, he said, as a delegate of the Russian Revolutionary Committee, with its headquarters at St. Petersburg, to seek the advice and protection of the greatest of all living revolutionaries. Bakunin was overjoyed. He took Nechayev into his house and listened with rapt attention while Nechayev spoke of how he had scaled the fortress walls and made his way from St. Petersburg to the Rumanian border with the police hot on his trail. He had outwitted them; he would always outwit them; and now he demanded only the blessing of Bakunin before returning to Russia and leading the revolt.

If the students had known the real circumstances of Nechayev's escape, they might have torn him limb from limb. The revolt, so carefully planned, broke out on March 19. There were wild speeches, and a good deal of waving of the revolutionary flag. The students refused to attend lectures and marched with banners in the streets. But to the students' dismay the police paid very little attention to them until nightfall; then they swooped down and arrested the ringleaders with the help of student spies. The first arrests took place in the Medico-Chirurgical Academy. These were followed by arrests in the Technological Institute and the Institute of Engineering. The revolt had sputtered out. Even the police refused to treat it seriously, and most of the arrested students were sent home in a few days.

Early in March Nechayev sent a letter to Vera Zasulich explaining in detail how he had escaped from the Fortress. It was all very easy. He had simply put on the coat of a general, and slipped out. He went on to explain that the journey to the border was far more dangerous: he was arrested in southern Russia, and it had been necessary for him to fight one of the guards and one of the officials put in charge of him. He had pushed them out of his way, and then started running, and these Russian policemen were far too slow—he had outdistanced them. These stories, with their circumstantial details, were relayed to the students who were beginning to wonder whether Nechayev had really escaped from the Fortress. In veiled language Nechayev promised to return and this time lead the revolt to success.

The relations between Bakunin and Nechayev were soon intimate. In these early days Bakunin never seems to have distrusted Nechayev's motives. Bakunin had a curious habit of looking in silence at people when he first met them, holding his head quizzically, frowning, muttering to himself, attempting to absorb them into his own stream of consciousness.

First impressions counted. And the impression produced by Nechayev was evidently one of considerable force. Here was the ideal young Russian, the born revolutionary leader, who had come to Geneva just at the time when the old revolutionary was losing all hope of witnessing even the faintest spark of the revolutionary fervor. A few years earlier he had dismissed Russia as a byzantino-tartaro-germanic empire. Nothing could be done with it. The people were too stupid. And here was Nechayev with news of daily revolts springing out of the Russian colleges and universities. Nechayev became his guest. He called Nechayev "Boy," remembering the English he had learned during his brief stay in London. Nechayev called him "Matrena," a diminutive for Maria.* Bakunin seems not to have cared; he seems even to have delighted in the new name; and there is some evidence that the twenty-two-year-old Nechayev seduced the old revolutionary. They were always together. They swore oaths of eternal loyalty to one another. The dead weight of revolutionary frustration lifted from Bakunin's shoulders; he grew visibly younger in the presence of the dangerous and seductive revolutionary who brought him a breath of his native land. Nechayev was introduced to Bakunin's friends. Nikolay Ogaryev was living in Geneva. A poet and a revolutionary with a curious history of tragic love-affairs, a man of immense charm, suffering from epilepsy and given to frequent bouts of drunkenness, he was introduced to Nechayev, and immediately fell under his sway. Ogaryev was so ravished by his new acquaintance that he sat down to write a poem in his honor. It is not a good poem. It was probably the worst poem he ever wrote, but in the original Russian it is recognizably Ogaryev's and moves with considerable passion:

THE STUDENT

To my young friend Nechayev
He was born to a wretched fate,
And was taught in a hard school,
And suffered interminable torments
In years of unceasing labor.
But as the years swept by
His love for the people grew stronger,
And fiercer his thirst for the common good,
The thirst to improve man's fate.

There were two more verses, celebrating the great future opening out before the young revolutionary. Nechayev prized the verses nearly as much as he prized a document dated May 12, 1869, which marked his entry into the World Revolutionary Alliance, and ran as follows:

* This was not the first time Bakunin received a feminine name. Three-year-old Liza Herzen called him "Big Liza" when he stayed with the Herzens in London.

The bearer of this certificate is one of the accredited representatives of the Russian Section of the World Revolutionary Alliance. No. 2771.

MIKHAIL BAKUNIN

This certificate was a wonderful invention, with its seal and flamboyant signature and the suggestion that there were at least 2770 other members. In fact, Nechayev was the only member of a revolutionary organization which seems to have been invented on the spur of the moment. The seal affixed to the certificate bore the words "European Revolutionary Alliance, Central Committee." No one had ever heard of the European or World Revolutionary Alliance, and no one was ever to hear of it again; but it satisfied Nechayev's desire for documentation, and Nechayev could henceforth prove to any doubting Thomases in Russia that he had received the blessing of two famous revolutionaries whose names were known throughout Europe and who were reverenced by Russian students. And just as Bakunin was impressed by Nechayev, so Nechayev was impressed by the constant coming and going of revolutionaries who made their way to Bakunin's disorderly study, with its books piled all over the chairs and the samovar half hidden under monstrous mountains of paper. Nechayev listened to their discussions, which often lasted all night. He was impressed by the perpetual activity. New life was springing in Bakunin. He was losing weight. By dieting he had lost fifty pounds of fat, but he was still eating Gargantuan amounts of beef and drinking by the bucket, and seemed never to be drunk. Herzen, who came to visit him in May, wrote that he was "charging forward like a locomotive which has got too much steam up and has run off the rails." Bakunin would have denied that he had run off the rails, but there was no doubt that he was going full steam ahead; and Nechayev was able to write to friends in St. Petersburg that "our work is seething here: a soup is brewing such as all Europe will be unable to gulp down." Very calmly and happily the conspirators were talking of fanning the flames of Europe from end to end.

Nechayev's letters to St. Petersburg were a source of annoyance to many of the recipients. Nechayev, intoxicated by the prospects of worldwide revolution as seen through the failing eyes of Bakunin, had forgotten to take even elementary precautions. Bakunin wrote openly through the mails. He would use initials or numbers instead of names, but he took no further precautions, arguing that the police were altogether too stupid to understand what he was talking about. In this he was wrong. The police of six or seven nations were trailing him closely, while the Russian police were keeping close watch on the vast correspondence Nechayev was conducting with Russia. Every letter Nechayev wrote seems to have been opened, copied, and carefully weighed as evidence to be brought against him later. Between March and August 1869 the authorities seized 560 letters and pamphlets written by Nechayev, involving 387 persons in St. Petersburg alone. A rather smaller number of letters and documents sent to Moscow were also seized. If Nechayev received no reply to letters which were being held up for examination by the secret police, he would write abusive letters accusing his friends of cowardice or treason or, worse still, indifference to the revolution. It has been argued that he did this in order to compromise the recipients, but this is doubtful. He was puzzled and annoyed by their silence, and deeply hurt, and like Bakunin he refused to believe that the police were sufficiently intelligent to see through his thin disguises. On July 22, 1869, he sent an open telegram to his friend Uspensky, which read:

Monsieur Uspensky, Moscou, Loubianka, Librairie Tscherkezoff
Pour retourner Pavloff envoyez argent, écrivez vite, télégraphiez réponse Genève, quai Seudet, 15.
                                                                        MONSCHAL

Even if this were the only communication to fall into their hands, the police would have learned matters of considerable interest to them. They knew already most of Nechayev's pseudonyms—he called himself at various times Ivan Petrov, Ivan Pavlov, Dmitry Fyodorovich and Captain Panin. The telegram informed them that he was about to return to Russia, was in need of money and had an easily accessible accommodation address. They could have sent their special agents in Switzerland to the address, but apparently no special watch was taken at this time, and the copies of the letters were simply filed and temporarily forgotten.

Nechayev's need of money, vast sums of money, was growing urgent. He was determined to return to Russia and bring the revolution about, and revolutions are expensive. As usual, Bakunin himself was in dire straits. He remembered, however, that the sum of eight hundred pounds sterling had been deposited in 1858 in a London bank in the name of the revolutionary Alexander Herzen. Herzen had spent a few weeks with him in Geneva in May, and taken a violent dislike to Nechayev. The money had been placed in Herzen's hands by a certain Bakhmatiev, an eccentric Russian landowner who had passed through London on his way to found a communist paradise in the Marquesas. Pausing only long enough for some brief discussions with Herzen, he had disappeared forever into the Pacific. The capital was still intact. Ogaryev had a presumptive claim on half of it. Working through Ogaryev, Bakunin suggested that the money could be profitably used in encouraging the Russian revolution which he and "Boy" were about to launch. Ogaryev was soon sold on the idea. He was slowly drinking himself to death, and hardly cared what happened to the money, though he received from time to time little trickles which represented his share of the interest: this was employed to finance the publication of his poems and pamphlets. Under the combined pressure of Bakunin and Nechayev, Ogaryev began a series of begging letters to Herzen in London. At first he asked for the entire sum. Later he begged for half. The correspondence lasted several weeks, and it was not until the end of July that Herzen agreed to surrender one half of the Bakhmatiev fund, amounting to 10,000 francs. Herzen suggested that the money be spent on establishing a revolutionary printing press in Geneva, adding that Bakunin would be better employed superintending a printing press than pursuing nebulous adventures in Russia. The money was solemnly received by Ogaryev, who in turn handed it to Bakunin. Most of it was then transferred to Nechayev.

With the money, Ogaryev's poem, and the slip of paper which announced his admission into the World Revolutionary Alliance, Nechayev was now prepared to return to Russia. He had not been lazy. He had thought out some of the revolutionary problems which would face him when he returned, and with the help of Ogaryev and Bakunin had written a number of manifestoes, projects, and encyclicals. All together eight pamphlets were produced. These were:

Some Words to Our Young Brothers in Russia
To the Students of the University
Two articles contained in The People's Vengeance, No. 1, which appeared
    in the summer of 1869
On the Russian Nobility
The Student (Ogaryev's poem, also called Enlightened Personality)
How the Revolutionary Question Presents Itself
Principles of Revolution
The Revolutionary Catechism

Of these only the first two and Ogaryev's poem were signed. Nechayev's open letter to the students was written in a form somewhat reminiscent of an imperial rescript. He spoke of having scaled the frozen walls of the Peter and Paul Fortress by the grace of divine providence. He had thwarted the dark forces of the Tsardom, and now promised to lead the students in a fight to the death against the evils of reaction. Some Words to Our Young Brothers in Russia was a muddled plea to young students to assume the role of midwives to the revolution:

Dear brethren, I urge you with all my heart to abandon the doomed world of academies, schools and universities, from which you are now being expelled and where you were continually taught to stand at a distance from the people. Go among the people! There you will find your true campus, your wisdom and your lives! Learn from the people how to serve them, and how to help them to their best advantage. Remember above all that young educated people should not be the teachers, benefactors, and dictatorial leaders of the people, but should act as midwives helping to bring about the self-emancipation of the peasants, concentrating their forces and assisting them to employ their true energies.

The pamphlet *On the Russian Nobility* has no particular interest, and the articles in *The People's Vengeance,* almost certainly by Nechayev, covered ground more expertly covered in *Principles of Revolution,* which appears to have been written by Nechayev and Bakunin in tandem, for there are passages which have all the diffused grandeur of Bakunin's style at its best and other passages as incisive as anything Nechayev ever wrote. "We recognize," says the author of *Principles of Revolution,* "no other activity except the work of utter destruction, but we admit that the nature of this activity may assume varied forms—poison, the knife, rope, etc. In this struggle the revolutionary sacrifices everything." This sounds like vintage Nechayev, while the following passage seems to contain both hands:

> Brigandage has always been one of the most honored forms of Russian national life. The brigand is the hero, the defender, the popular avenger, the irreconcilable enemy of the state, and of all social and civil order established by the state. He is the wrestler in life and in death against all this civilization of officials, nobles, priests, and kings . . . He who does not understand brigands cannot understand the history of the Russian masses. He who is not sympathetic with them cannot sympathize with the lives of the people, and lacks the strength to avenge the ancient, interminable wrongs suffered by the people: he belongs to the camp of the enemy, the partisans of the state . . . It is only through brigandage that the vitality, ardor and strength of the people can be established indisputably . . . The brigand in Russia is the true and unique revolutionary . . . He who desires to make a serious revolution in Russia must enter their world. The season is at hand. The anniversaries of Stenka Razin and Pugachev are approaching, and it is time to celebrate these warriors of the people. Let us all prepare for the feast.*

The last and the most deservedly famous of the revolutionary essays composed between March and August 1869 shows all the signs of having been composed by Nechayev, though a few easily identifiable phrases may have been inserted by Bakunin. This is *The Revolutionary Catechism.* In all that has gone before, we are aware that the revolutionaries are playing with revolution: now at last we encounter the gaunt and haggard face of the real thing. In the original Russian it moves at the slow and steady pace of a funeral march—a funeral march over an entire civilization.

The Revolutionary Catechism consists of twenty-six formal articles on the nature of the revolution of destruction. In cold blood, without ever hinting at mercy, Nechayev demonstrates how a handful of men can de-

---

* Stenka Razin's rebellion was crushed in 1671, Pugachev's rebellion in 1773.

stroy a whole civilization. Total destruction is the aim: he does not care if anything survives the flames, and if nothing survives this is a matter of total indifference to the revolutionary. Those who take part in the revolution and those who oppose it are placed in their precise categories. There are ominous underscorings, hints of undisclosed powers, moments when the pen seems about to falter, but Nechayev goes on to the end, depicting with the utmost calm the portrait of the terrorist at the height of his powers.

THE REVOLUTIONARY CATECHISM

The Duties of the Revolutionary toward Himself

1. The revolutionary is a dedicated man. He has no personal inclinations, no business affairs, no emotions, no attachments, no property and no name. Everything in him is subordinated towards a single exclusive attachment, a single thought and a single passion—the revolution.
2. In the very depths of his being, not only in words but also in deeds, he has torn himself away from the bonds which tie him to the social order and to the cultivated world, with all its laws, moralities and customs and with all its generally accepted conventions. He is their implacable enemy, and if he continues to live with them it is only in order to destroy them more quickly.
3. The revolutionary despises all dogmas and refuses to accept the mundane sciences, leaving them for future generations. He knows only one science: the science of destruction. For this reason, and only for this reason, he will study mechanics, physics, chemistry, and perhaps medicine. But all day and night he studies the living science of peoples, their characteristics and circumstances, and all the phenomena of the present social order. The object is the same: the prompt destruction of this filthy order.
4. The revolutionary despises public opinion. He despises and hates the existing social order in all its manifestations. For him, morality is everything which contributes to the triumph of the revolution. Immoral and criminal is everything that stands in his way.
5. The revolutionary is a dedicated man, merciless toward the state and altogether merciless toward the educated classes; and he can expect no mercy from them. Between him and them there exists, declared or concealed, a continual and irreconcilable war "for life or for death." He must accustom himself to enduring torture.
6. Tyrannical toward himself, he must be tyrannical toward others. All the soft and tender affections arising from kinship, friendship and love, all gratitude and even all honor must be obliterated, and in their place there must be the cold and single-minded passion for the work of revolution. For him there exists only one pleasure, one consolation, one reward, one satisfaction—the success of the revolution. Night and day he must have but one thought, one aim—merciless destruction. Aiming cold-bloodedly and indefatigably toward this end, he must be ready to destroy himself and destroy with his own hands everyone who stands in his way.
7. The nature of the true revolutionary excludes all romanticism, all sensitivity, all exaltations and enthusiasms. He must also exclude private

vendettas and personal hatred. The revolutionary passion, practiced at every moment of the day until it becomes a habit, is to be employed with cold calculation. At all times and in all places the revolutionary must refuse to allow himself to be guided by his personal impulses, but only by the total submergence of himself in the revolution.

Relationship of the Revolutionary toward the Revolutionary Comrades

8. The revolutionary can have no friendly feeling to anyone unless, like him, the other is dedicated to revolutionary affairs. His degree of friendship, devotion, and obligation toward a comrade must be determined only by the degree of the comrade's usefulness in the practical work of complete and destructive revolution.

9. It is superfluous to speak of solidarity among revolutionaries. The whole strength of the revolutionary work lies in this. Comrades who possess the same revolutionary passion should, as much as possible, deliberate all important matters together and come to unanimous conclusions. But the revolutionary, in accomplishing whatever plan is finally decided upon, must rely entirely on himself. The contract of revolutionary destruction demands that no comrades should come running up with advice and assistance if this detracts from the success of the plan.

10. Each comrade should have under him several revolutionaries of the second or third rank, i.e. comrades who are not completely dedicated. These should be regarded as portions of a common fund of revolutionary capital, to be expended as he thinks fit. He should expend them as economically as possible, always attempting to derive the utmost possible use from them. He should regard himself as capital consecrated to the triumph of the revolution; and he must not be regarded as expendable without the entire agreement of the fully initiated comrades.

11. When a comrade is caught in a dangerous extremity and the question arises whether he should be rescued or not rescued, the revolutionary must make his decision without recourse to personal feelings, but only in terms of the eventual success of the revolution. Therefore it is necessary to balance carefully the usefulness of the comrade in so far as it is a question of revolutionary strength, and the most careful consideration should be made to decide whether he is worth rescuing.

Relationship of the Revolutionary toward Society

12. Whether a new member, after giving proof of loyalty by word and deed, should be accepted is a matter to be decided only by unanimous agreement.

13. The revolutionary enters the world of the state, of the classes and of so-called culture, and he lives in this world only because he has faith in its speedy and total destruction. He is not a revolutionary if he feels any sympathy for this world. He must not hesitate to destroy any position, any place, or any man in this world—all must be equally detested by him. All the worse for him if he has parents, friends, and loved ones; he is no longer a revolutionary if they can stay his hand.

14. Aiming at implacable destruction the revolutionary can and sometimes must live within society while pretending to be other than what he is. A revolutionary must penetrate everywhere, among the lowest and the middle classes and in the houses of commerce, in the churches, in the

palaces of the aristocracy. He must know the world of the bureaucrats and of the military and of literature, and he must enter into the Third Division and even into the Winter Palace.

15. All the members of this filthy society can be split up into several categories: the first category comprises those to be condemned to death without delay. The comrades should compile a list of those to be condemned, weighing the relative gravity of their crimes against their value to the revolution; and the executions should be carried out according to the prepared order.

16. In the preparation of these lists and in placing the condemned according to the prepared order, no private sense of outrage should be considered, nor is it necessary to pay attention to the hatred provoked by these people among the comrades or the people. But hatred and the sense of outrage must to some extent be made use of, because these things help to incite rebellion among the people. It is necessary to be guided only by the relative usefulness of these executions for the sake of the revolution. Above all those who are especially inimical to the revolutionary organization must be destroyed; their violent and sudden deaths will produce the utmost panic in the government, it will shake the foundations of government and deprive it of the services of its most intelligent and energetic agents.

17. The second group consists of those to whom we concede life provisionally in order that their bestial behavior shall drive the people to inevitable revolt.

18. The third category consists of a multitude of personages or animals distinguished neither for intelligence nor for energy: those who enjoy wealth, connections, influence, and power. These must be exploited in every possible way; they must be implicated and confused; as far as possible their dirty secrets should be found out, so that we can make them our slaves. Their power, influence, and connections, their riches and energy will form an inexhaustible treasure and a precious help in our various undertakings.

19. The fourth category is composed of ambitious people and liberals of various shades. We shall pretend we are following their ideas and give them cause to think we are blindly conspiring with them, while in fact we take them under our own control. We shall root out all their secrets and compromise them to the uttermost, so that there will be no way out for them and they can be used to create disorder in the state.

20. The fifth category consists of doctrinaires, conspirators, revolutionaries: all idle word-spillers who orate before meetings or in front of a piece of paper. They must be constantly driven forward to make violent declarations carefully arranged to agree with our purpose. The majority of these will leave nothing behind but a vast ruin; from a few of them we shall attain real revolutionary gains.

21. The sixth category is especially important: women. They should be divided into three chief divisions. First: those frivolous, thoughtless and vapid women, whom we shall use as we use the third and fourth category of men. Second: women who are ardent, gifted and devoted, but do not belong to us because they have not yet achieved a passionless and austere revolutionary understanding: these must be used like the men of the fifth category. Finally there are the women who are completely on our

side, i.e. those who are wholly dedicated and who have accepted our program in its entirety. We should regard these women as the most valuable of our treasures; without their help it would be impossible to succeed.

The Duties of our Society toward the People

22. The aims of our Society are none other than the entire emancipation and happiness of the people, i.e. the common laborers. Convinced that their emancipation and the achievement of this happiness is brought about only by means of an all-destroying popular revolt, we shall see that society will employ all its power, all its resources towards increasing and intensifying the calamities and evils until their patience is exhausted and they will break out in a *levée-en-masse*.

23. By a popular revolution, the Society does not mean a revolution tailored according to the classic western model, a pattern which is fundamentally restrained by the existence of property and the traditional social orders of so-called civilization and morality. Until now such a civilization has cast down one political form only to substitute another, thereby attempting to bring about a so-called revolutionary state. The only salutory form of revolution is one which destroys the entire state to the roots and exterminates all imperial traditions, the whole social order and all the existing classes in Russia.

24. With this end in view the Society refuses to impose any new organization from above. Any future organization will doubtless work its way through the movement and life of the people: but this is a matter for future generations to decide. Our task is terrible, total, universal, and merciless destruction. (. . . *strashnoye, polnoye, povsemestnoye i bezposhchadnoye razrusheniye.*)

25. Therefore, in drawing closer to the people, we must above all unite with those elements of popular life which, from the very beginning of the imperial power of Muscovy, have never ceased to protest, not only in words but in deeds, against everything directly or indirectly connected with the State: against the nobility, against the bureaucracy, against the priests, against business, and against the tight fist of the extortioner. We must unite with the adventurous tribes of brigands, who are the only true revolutionaries of Russia.

26. To knit the people into a single force which is wholly destructive and wholy invincible—such is our organization, our conspiracy, and our task.

Such is *The Revolutionary Catechism,* which was to have important consequences for the world, since it was read by Lenin and influenced the course of the Bolshevik revolution. This cold and ascetic document, which demanded of the revolutionary such extraordinary qualities of detachment and heroism and a complete self-effacement, was Nechayev's masterpiece. With this he threw down his gantlet. One of the characters of Dostoyevsky's novel *The Possessed* is made to say: "To level the hills is a good idea." In *The Revolutionary Catechism* Nechayev shows succinctly, clearly and almost without emotion how the leveling process can be carried out.

Nechayev's blueprint of revolution was directed at all the classes in Russia except the class which he called *cherno-rabochiyi lyudi,* the "black working people," peasants and laborers, and it would seem that he was not too greatly concerned about them. If they perished in the conflagration, there would still be a handful of people left to create the new society he only vaguely dreamed about, for according to Nechayev the destruction of the outworn society was the immediate task: somehow, by some means unknown, the new society would arise phoenixlike from the ashes. He was not in the least concerned with Zaichnevsky's "social and democratic republic." He was concerned only with imposing a kind of scientific order on the art of destroying an existing society. There are about ten words in Russian which mean "destruction," and he rings the changes on all of them. Everything must be destroyed! No stone must be left standing! In the guise of revolutionaries, the angels of fury and destruction and denunciation have returned to the world, and suddenly it occurs to us that we have heard this voice before—in Isaiah, in Jeremiah, and in the chapters of Genesis describing how the Deluge visited the earth. Behind the stark theses of the *Catechism* lie a fierce religious vindictiveness and a prophet's fervor.

Nechayev portrays the revolutionary in considerable detail. Austere, determined and tyrannical, he wages a cold and unremitting war on the world and on himself. He is the fanatic who dares not let his eyes gleam, for fear of being observed. He is the most dangerous of mortals: the hero dedicated to unheroic ends. His austerity leads to a kind of asceticism. Nikolay Berdyaev, the modern Russian philosopher, has observed that the *Catechism* is unique in its asceticism:

> It is a sort of instruction in the spiritual life of a revolutionary, and the demands which it makes are harsher than the requirements of Syrian asceticism. The revolutionary must have no interests, no business, no personal feelings and connections; he must have nothing of his own, not even a name. Everything is to be swallowed up in a single exclusive interest, by the one idea, the one passion—revolution. Everything which serves the cause of revolution is moral. Revolution is the one criterion of good and evil. The many must be sacrificed for the one. But this is also the principle of asceticism. In such a case the living person is crushed; it is deprived of all the richness of the content of life for the sake of the Revolution-God.

It is unlikely that Nechayev would have approved of Berdyaev's summary, for he was supremely disinterested in philosophical inquiries. What interested him above all was the technique of bringing a successful revolution about, the measures to be taken, the exact points of weakness of the adversary. He demanded from the revolutionary leaders a superb cold-bloodedness and absolute determination rather than asceticism. A handful of ruthless and dedicated men could, he believed, overthrow an entire nation, and he was concerned to show step by step how it could be done.

When Nechayev wrote "Our task is terrible, total, universal and merciless destruction," he meant exactly what he said, but this vision of terror did not originate with him. It had its roots deep in Russian history, in the great blood baths of Ivan the Terrible, and in the violence of the religious schismatics of the seventeenth century who burned themselves en masse to prove a point of Scripture. The revolutionaries of an earlier age had shown an extraordinary tolerance of violence for its own sake. Zaichnevsky and Pisarev had denounced the autocracy, morbidly fascinated by the cruelties and horrors which lay in store for it; and in the manifesto entitled *Molodaya Rossiya* Nechayev found the stern authoritarian tone he employed in the *Catechism*.

Although Nechayev regarded himself as the sole author of the work, which is written in a style he has made authentically his own, it did not spring fully formed from his fertile mind. Many influences can be detected in it. He appears to have combed through the revolutionary literature of his age, borrowing a phrase or an image here and there, fusing them together under the pressure of his violent imagination. Some images were borrowed from school textbooks, and he appears to have read attentively the account of the conspiracy of Catiline by the Roman historian Sallust, who describes the methods with which Catiline hoped to achieve power:

> He taught many kinds of evil to the youths he corrupted. From their ranks he would find men capable of committing perjury or affixing their seals to forged documents, and he thought nothing of damaging their credit and their fortunes or of exposing them to peril; then, when their reputations were ruined and they were stripped of all sense of shame, he made larger demands on them. If he had no immediate motive for committing evil, he would cause inoffensive people to be attacked or killed with as much malevolence as if they had been guilty of injuring him. And rather than allow his students to lose their skill or nerve through lack of practice, he would have them commit needless outrages.

Catiline, too, had observed the advantages of suborning women, especially those who had luxurious tastes and were debt-ridden. "These women, he thought, would do good service in agitating among the city slaves and organizing acts of incendiarism; their husbands could either be induced to join the cause, or be murdered." The savagery of the last three words would have a peculiar appeal to Nechayev, who took over many of the conspiratorial ideas of Catiline and made them his own.

With the *Catechism* completed, Nechayev now decided to return to Russia. He planned to spend the winter organizing his forces. On February 19, 1870, the ninth anniversary of the emancipation of the serfs, he intended to unleash the civil war which would topple the Tsar from the throne. Following the injunctions of the *Catechism,* he had already prepared the list of those condemned to death. At the head of it were General Trepov, the Chief of Police in St. Petersburg, and General Mezentsev, the Chief of the Political Police of the Empire. The life of the Tsar was to be temporarily spared, so that "the free peasantry, having broken the chains of slavery, on the day of vengeance will be allowed to break his head and at the same time pull down the tattered garments of the obsolete imperial system." At that moment not only the Tsar but the whole imperial family was to be destroyed, leaving no trace behind them. And following the example which Bakunin had attempted many times in the past, Nechayev was determined to capture one of the imperial arsenals. His revolutionaries would be armed to the teeth. This was to be war to the death.

Though the Russian secret police had opened his mail and kept sporadic watch on him in Geneva, they showed a curious lack of vigilance at the border. With the help of some Bulgarian and Serbian revolutionaries, Nechayev made his way to Bucharest, then an outpost of the Turkish empire. Then he slipped over the border, and reached Moscow by the middle of September. He spent less than a hundred days in Russia and failed to achieve any of his objectives, but in those three months he carried out one by one all the commands of *The Revolutionary Catechism.*

In the years of the peasant revolts of Stenka Razin and Pugachev, the steppes of southern Russia had resounded with a strange, high-pitched Cossack battle cry: *"Nechayi! Nechayi!"* ("Cut! Cut!") Now a silent Nechayev was returning to Russia, hoping to succeed where his Cossack ancestors had failed.

ON THE EVE

W HEN NECHAYEV RETURNED to Russia, his first task was to gather together the remnants of the revolutionary organization. He soon found his friend Vladimir Orlov, who had sent him money abroad, and Nikolayev, with whose passport he had left the country. They had preserved their faith in him and were willing to obey his orders. In a short time nine cells, each composed of five members, came into being, together with a special group of trusted advisers known as the "Great Russian Section, Moscow." These alone were granted the privilege of knowing Nechayev's real name: to the others he remained Ivan Petrovich. The central organization seems to have consisted of the young nobleman Pyotr Uspensky, who managed the well-known Cherkessov Bookshop; Alexey Kuznetsov, a student of the Petrovsky Agricultural Academy; Nikolay Nikolayev, who had once lived in Ivanovo and was now a student of the same Agricultural Academy; Ivan Prizhov, a forty-two-year-old secretary attached to the college and the author of two books, *The Poor in Holy Russia* and *A History of Russian Taverns;* and Prince Varlaam John Aslanovich Cherkessov, a railway engineer born in Tiflis a year after Nechayev. Two others, a student of the Medical Academy called Alexey Deteils, and the twenty-five-year-old Varvara Alexandrovskaya, the wife of a college professor, seem also to have taken part in the high councils of the secret organization. To these—and to these alone—Nechayev outlined the grand strategy.

The strategy was simple. First, it was necessary to increase the number of cells until all European Russia was covered with a vast network of cells owing allegiance to Nechayev. Secondly, the Imperial Armament Factory at Tula must be honeycombed with agents of the secret organization. Thirdly, on a day yet to be determined by Nechayev all the cells would come out in open revolt, every man armed and disciplined. Inevitably there would be war through the summer, followed by a general congress in October; and Nechayev explained the advantages of an outbreak in the spring by saying that if the insurrection failed in the cities, they would be able to fight along the Volga and the Dnieper with all the advantages of summer weather, and the peasants would be able to find shelter in the forests. As he spoke, his mind moving with delighted incomprehension among the serious problems of revolt, it seems never to have occurred to him that he possessed no military training; and if it had occurred to him, it would not have disturbed him any more than it disturbed Trotsky. He had appointed himself commander in chief, and he already claimed to have agents in the Imperial Armament Factory. The number of cells in St. Petersburg was increasing daily. Money was beginning to flow into the revolutionary coffers. Tula was being "cased." Soon Nechayev was able to report to Kuznetsov and Uspensky that "our main strength is not in Moscow but in Tula where we have fifty men in the arsenal on our side" and some time later he reported to Prince Cherkessov: "The men at the arsenal are all ready and we can take over Tula any time we like."

Our knowledge of these statements comes from reports which appeared in the *Records of the Moscow High Court,* which began an inquiry into the mysterious affair at Tula at the end of the year. The report entitled *The Affair of the Conspirators Sergey Nechayev, Nikolay Nikolayev, Ivan Prizhov, and Others* offers a strange jumble of overheard conversations, excerpts from the reports of police spies, and references to a secret notebook, otherwise unidentified, which contained an account of the comings and goings of the revolutionaries. From this report we learn that the police were well aware of Nechayev's alias Ivan Petrovich. They knew that Nikolayev went under at least three aliases: Alexander Vasilyevich Belkov, Belkin, and Yegor Anisimov. But on the whole the report tells us very little about Nechayev's activities and the travails of the conspirators that early autumn. We know that Nechayev claimed 150 members in Moscow and some of his most loyal adherents belonged to the Petrovsky Agricultural Academy, where Ivanov, Dolgov, Ripman, and Kuznetsov were students. Among these students Nechayev was always known as Ivan Petrovich. To other students in Moscow he was Pavlov, which seems to have been the name he maintained in all his dealings with Moscow University. We know there were endless intellectual discussions which were often stormy. We hear of occasional attempts to blackmail members in order to swell the coffers of the revolutionary organization. A young army officer in St. Petersburg was ordered to arrest a former member of the group and blackmail him into signing a promissory note for 6,000 rubles. It was an unpleasant incident, and though the promissory note was signed, the 6,000 rubles were never collected.

There seem to have been continual financial difficulties, but everyone spoke of Nechayev's amazing optimism. While the revolutionaries waited upon his favor, and while Nechayev continued to tell disarming lies about Nechayev, sometimes saying that he had died in Siberia, at other times referring to "the famous and melancholy occasion when our Nechayev was shot by the police on the road from Tambov to Perm," Nechayev himself was never at a loss. He held authority by reason of the mystery surrounding him. Who was he? No one seemed to know. Was he really the Nechayev whose name was spoken with bated breath? Meanwhile, Nechayev was certain the revolution would break out in the spring. He sent messengers to Bakunin, announcing that all was well and he hoped shortly to be able to summon the old anarchist back to Russia. To the messengers he explained that if Bakunin asked questions, they must be answered evasively. If Bakunin asked about Nechayev, they must say: "Nothing is known." Nechayev exclaimed: "The old man is the most inquisitive devil in the world. Don't trust him!"

One of the reasons why we know so little about those days in spite of the voluminous evidence brought forth at the trials is that Nechayev trusted no one, continually wore disguise and lived in a world of pseudonyms. He would summon meetings, usually arriving late, explaining that he had just come from a town five hundred miles away. There would be a short discussion, Nechayev would present the orders of the mysterious Society of which he was at once the chief executive and the legislature, and then he would be off again to Tula or St. Petersburg. Dostoyevsky has described such meetings in *The Possessed,* giving them a curiously hysterical air, but in fact Nechayev's meetings with his fellow conspirators seem to have been strangely quiet. We hear of meetings in which Nechayev said: "Prepare yourselves. In the spring everything will be different. Don't disturb yourselves. Wait for the signal." He was waiting with buoyant optimism for the moment when the Imperial Armament Factory at Tula would fall into his hands.

Everything was going well for the revolutionaries when an incident occurred which was to destroy all Nechayev's carefully laid plans. It was a small incident at first, no more than a clash of temperaments. Once or twice before he had given way to bouts of senseless anger. He slept badly. He was continually rushing from one place to another. Now he gave an order of no importance whatsoever, and when it was disobeyed he flared up, murdered the culprit who disobeyed him and then ran for his life. In a sense he was running from this murder until the day he died.

It began so quietly that afterward the conspirators had difficulty remembering exactly how it happened. Kuznetsov said later that he thought it began on November 4. Nechayev, Kuznetsov and Ivanov were having a secret meeting. Nechayev had brought along some leaflets he had written recently. These leaflets were inflammatory incitements to rebellion, written under the title *From Those Who Are United to Those Who Are Scattered.* In brusque tones Nechayev ordered Ivanov to post them on the walls of the students' dining hall and of the library of the Agricultural College. Ivanov demurred. He explained that it would only lead to the closing of the dining halls, police raids, the arrest of innocent students. This may have been exactly what Nechayev intended. There was a long pause. Ivanov said nothing at all. He could see Nechayev's anger, the lips pursed, the eyes glaring.

"I tell you," said Nechayev, "the Society has ordered it. Are you disobeying the Society?"

"I refuse to listen to the Society when it tells me to do completely senseless things."

"Then you refuse to submit to the Society?"

"Yes, when it behaves stupidly."

Nechayev turned on his heel. His face was white. He wanted certainties, absolute obedience to commands, the knowledge that everyone was submitting to his will. Ivanov had been a trusted member of the group. It flashed through Nechayev's mind that the police seemed to know far more about the mysterious Society of the Ax than they should ever have been allowed to know. Ivanov was always smiling. He was handsome, well-built, an excellent student. Nechayev had taken to him, but seems to have doubted his loyalty for some time. And then, too, no one had ever dared to accuse Nechayev of stupidity before. The brief conversation rankled, and Nechayev came to the conclusion that Ivanov's refusal must be regarded as an act of rebellion. It was as though Ivanov was saying: "What is all this about the Society of the Ax? Who gives you the right to issue orders? Every time you go away and consult the Society, you come back and tell us that the Society has endorsed your views. I don't believe the Society exists."

After the meeting with Kuznetsov and Ivanov, Nechayev disappeared. Presumably he was in Tula, where there was constant coming and going of revolutionaries. He returned two weeks later with the announcement that he had obtained a new printing press. There were more discussions with Nikolayev and Kuznetsov about Ivanov's "act of treason." Nikolayev was startled. He had not regarded Ivanov as a man capable of committing treason. Nechayev asked what should be the punishment of a stool pigeon. There followed long theoretical discussions, but according to Kuznetsov, who was present at many of them, they came to no agreement. On November 19 there was a meeting between Ivanov and Prizhov. At the trial Prizhov said they discussed nothing of any particular importance, but this is unlikely: it would seem that Prizhov was sounding out Ivanov, and he later reported on the meeting to Nechayev, who now concluded that Ivanov must be punished. Accordingly he asked Nikolayev for a revolver and a knife, and ordered Nikolayev to summon Ivanov to a meeting in a grotto of the Petrovsky Park. Ivanov was to be told that the new printing press was hidden there, and Ivanov himself would be placed in charge of it. By this time Nikolayev was fully aware that Nechayev planned to murder Ivanov in the grotto.

The Petrovsky Park lay on the northwest of Moscow, on the outskirts of the city. Some fifty years before it had been a haunt of the aristocracy. Here the nobility had built little painted Swiss chalets, danced beside the lake and admired the flowers. Prince Razumovsky had built an enormous palace overlooking the gardens, but in 1861 the palace was bought by the government, pulled down, and the site offered to the University. The aristocracy had deserted the park, and wealthy merchants built their suburban houses where there had once been painted chalets. The gardens were going to waste. It occurred to the officials of the University that the

site of Prince Razumovsky's palace was admirably located for an agricultural school with botanical gardens and model farms. Accordingly, in
place of the palace, there arose in 1865 the Petrovsky Agricultural Academy, of which Ivanov was one of the few, carefully-selected students.
There were only 150 students. Ivanov knew the gardens well, and he
would have no difficulty finding the grotto. It was a winding grotto, the
kind often frequented by lovers, and it overlooked a small pond.

It was a dark night with low scudding clouds and thick snow on the
ground. The lakes and ponds in the gardens were covered with a thin
sheeting of ice. Ivanov, accompanied by Nikolayev, made his way to the
grotto. It was dark inside, with no light anywhere. Nechayev was waiting
outside. So, too, were Kuznetsov and Uspensky. Prizhov was standing
beside Nechayev. He said later that he did not enter the grotto, but others
remembered that he followed Nikolayev. It was going to be a very simple
murder. The only weapon Nechayev had on him was the knife, given to
him by Nikolayev, which he slipped inside his heavy boots. Suddenly
Kuznetsov, standing outside, heard shuffling sounds followed by a scream,
but it was not the scream of Ivanov. Nechayev, blundering in the dark,
had put his hands round Nikolayev's neck, and would have strangled
him if he had not recognized the voice in time. All Kuznetsov knew for
certain was that there was a nightmare within the grotto, whispers, scuf-
fling sounds, sudden pleadings. Then there was another scream; this time
it came from Ivanov.

"So the murder is about to take place," Kuznetsov whispered to himself. "In the dark grotto—"

But the murder did not take place within the dark grotto. Ivanov
hurled himself out of the grotto, screaming at the top of his voice, followed by Nechayev, who was wildly waving his arms. Nechayev pushed
Ivanov down to the ground, grappled with him and finally sat on him.
Prizhov, standing some twenty paces away, said it was so dark that all
he could see was a black shuddering mass, and out of the shuddering
mass there came Nechayev's clear voice shouting: "Give me the revolver." Both Prizhov and Nikolayev claimed they remained in the grotto.
It was probably Kuznetsov who provided the revolver. Ivanov was still
fighting for his life. In the death struggle he succeeded in biting Nechayev's thumb. Suddenly there was a shot, and soon Nechayev was turning
the body over to search in the pockets, and then there came Nechayev's
voice again, shouting for stones. No one understood what he wanted the
stones for until he explained they would all have to help carry the body
to the pond. It was all confusion, people running about in the dark, whispering, and then came Nechayev's authoritative voice, telling everyone
exactly what to do. He fired another shot into Ivanov's head, presumably

because Ivanov was still alive, and then he shot wild, and Prizhov, who felt the bullet whistling past his face, screamed. He had an odd idea that Nechayev was going to kill them all. He kept shouting his name, saying: "I am here! Don't shoot!" He was a simple-minded man, and seems never to have understood what was happening. But when Nechayev ordered him to help carry the body to the pond, with heavy stones tied at the neck and feet, Prizhov went running along with them. "I didn't feel strong enough to help carry the body," Prizhov said later. They dropped the body in the pond. Even then Nechayev bungled, for he suddenly pushed Nikolayev into the pond, and Nikolayev came out cursing, wet through, wondering whether Nechayev had pushed him in deliberately and not daring to ask. Then, the murder accomplished, they all went to Kuznetsov's apartment. Nikolayev dried his clothes, Nechayev bandaged his bleeding thumb, and they all sat up half the night discussing their success in putting an end to the life of an obvious informer.

In *The Possessed* Dostoyevsky based his account of the murder of Shatov on the published reports of the murder of Ivanov, with significant variations. Oddly enough, though Dostoyevsky mentions the grotto, he makes no use of it; three conspirators jump on Shatov in the light of three lanterns and almost at once Peter Verkhovensky shoots at Shatov's forehead. A moment later he is going through Shatov's pockets, and giving instructions for getting the stones and tying them to Shatov's neck and legs; and then the conspirators, awed, argumentative, and giving way to sudden senseless screams, carried the body to a pond. But Dostoyevsky's account of the murder is at considerable variance with what actually happened. Characteristically, he makes his conspirators far more hysterical than they were. They scream; they indulge in fights among themselves; the swinging lanterns light up a scene of madmen dancing wildly in circles, some with handkerchiefs stuffed in their mouths to prevent them from shouting, others crowding round the dead body and still others running around in a wild panic. In fact, when Ivanov was killed, the conspirators appear to have been remarkably quiet and undemonstrative, and though there was some purposeless running about, most of them stood quite still, regarding it with considerable detachment like figures on a darkened frieze. It was Nechayev's responsibility, and they felt little responsibility of their own.

We know nothing about the further incidents of that night, but Nechayev's speech to the conspirators in Kuznetsov's apartment may very well have corresponded to the speech which Dostoyevsky puts into the mouth of Verkhovensky:

> Gentlemen, we can now disperse in the knowledge that we have all fulfilled our duty, a duty which we have each of us undertaken without feeling

any sense of compulsion. And if you feel unhappy about the matter, may I remind you that you will feel still unhappier tomorrow, and there is nothing shameful in such feelings. . . As for danger, I cannot foresee any. It would never occur to anyone to suspect any of you, particularly if you behave reasonably and make no foolish mistakes . . . You understand, you have been called upon to bring new life into an organization which is dying of stagnation. Remember this, and may it bring you courage. From now on we have only one aim. We must bring everything down with a crash. The State will fall, and all its moral standards will fall with it. We alone are left, we who have prepared ourselves to take over the government: we shall bring the intellectuals over to our side, and as for the fools, we shall let them carry us on their shoulders. . . . Tomorrow we shall not meet, gentlemen. I shall go into the country for a while. You will hear from me the day after tomorrow. Meanwhile I think it would be better if you spent tomorrow at home, and if you made your way to your own houses tonight going by different routes, two at a time.

In some such way Nechayev must have spoken to the conspirators who were now beginning to regard him with hatred, though they took pains to conceal it. He was at the height of his power. He was determined to show that he was impervious to moral principles. Covered with blood, his hand bitten by Ivanov's teeth, he had led his party of revolutionaries away from the first engagement with the enemy, and accounted himself victorious. It seems never to have occurred to him that Ivanov was innocent of the crime of being a police spy, and in later years he would talk proudly of having committed "a political murder."

Nechayev had previously arranged to go to St. Petersburg immediately after the murder. He left by train the next day. The cells he had established were behaving in a way which gave him no pleasure. The students were making no effort to suborn the military or to take over power. Instead they were engaged in endless theoretical discussions. "Remember Karakozov! Go out and murder the government!" He contemptuously dismissed the theoretical discussions as the ravings of incompetent children, and drew up new plans for taking over the state. He told them there was good news from Tula: they would soon have arms. But in fact there was little news from Tula, and Nikolayev, who went to Tula about this time, had nothing to report. Five days later the newspapers announced the discovery of the body of the young student Ivan Ivanovich Ivanov. The body had risen to the surface of a pond not far from the Agricultural Academy. It was a small item in the newspapers, and the revolutionaries in St. Petersburg paid little attention to it. Nechayev himself thought he had covered his traces, for he returned to Moscow a few days later. He did not know that Uspensky had already been arrested, and that the police were on his trail. Worse still, Ivanov had left a number of documents in his room which clearly pointed to a revolutionary conspiracy, headed by a certain Pavlov. The police were already familiar with Pavlov. Telegrams were exchanged with St. Petersburg. Uspensky, the most intelligent of the conspirators, was beginning to talk. Nechayev went into hiding. It was rumored that he slipped out of a police net by wearing women's clothes. On December 3 Kuznetsov and Prizhov were arrested. From that moment the traces of Nechayev disappear until about the middle of the month when Prince Cherkessov paid a visit to Tula to see the twenty-six-year-old Varvara Alexandrovskaya, then busily occupied in the conspiracy to take over the armament factory. He told her that Nechayev was in extreme danger, and needed her help. He must go abroad again. In Switzerland, or elsewhere, he would obtain money to advance the revolution and help those of the conspirators who were in danger of arrest. Varvara Alexandrovskaya agreed. Early in January, with a false passport, disguised as a woman, with Varvara Alexandrovskaya at his side, and pretending to be her sister, Nechayev slipped out of Russia and made his way to Bakunin in Switzerland.

When he returned to Russia, he came as a prisoner of the Tsar.

THE RESTLESS YEARS

B AFFLED BY DISEASE, the perfidy of his friends, his wife's infidelity, and above all by the constant pressures of the secret police, Bakunin had grown weary of Geneva. He complained of the smells in the street and the curiously pervasive bourgeois character of the town. It was a place where nothing happened. People played cards, the taverns were crowded with amateur chess players, there were the endless Sunday morning promenades: it was enough to drive you mad. Bakunin thought of going to Italy, but he had already taken part in two attempts to seize power in Italy, and he had no longer any strong attachment for Garibaldi. Accordingly he decided to live in Locarno, on the Italian frontier, where living was cheap and where he hoped to dream away the last years of his life. The fight had gone out of him. He wrote to Ogaryev that he was not in the slightest interested in the possibility of a revolution in France, though he was to change his mind later. "I have absolutely no desire to see a great display of fireworks," he wrote shortly after he had set up his establishment in Locarno, in a letter to Herzen. But Herzen was dying, and the old order was passing. An exhausted Bakunin gazed over Lago Maggiore, dreaming about what might have been, spending odd moments during the day racking his brains over a translation into Russian of an obscure work of "economic metaphysics" by Karl Marx. At intervals he read Proudhon and Comte and continued to work on a leaflet on the subject of suppressing the State.

When Nechayev reached Geneva, he learned to his dismay that Bakunin had fled. He stayed with Ogaryev and disinterred some of the pamphlets they had written the previous year. He gave them to Varvara Alexandrovskaya and bade her return with them to Russia immediately, explaining that the fire of the revolution must be fed. The truth was that he was getting tired of Varvara, who immediately made her way back to Russia and was arrested by the police on the frontier, with the pamphlets intact. Nechayev still had considerable sums of money. In addition to the money he found in Ivanov's pockets there were the dues paid by the members of the secret society. And when Ogaryev pointed to the swollen thumb, Nechayev answered proudly that he had once more been arrested by the police as he slipped over the frontier, he had clubbed the policeman over the head, but there had been a terrible fight. Ogaryev was impressed, and to impress him still further Nechayev explained that wealth was pouring into the coffers of the secret society and all of Russia was on the verge of revolution. He proposed to spend only a few days in Switzerland: soon he would return and "light the faggots under the Tsar's throne."

Early in February Nechayev made his way to Locarno. Herzen had just died and Bakunin, still suffering from the shock, greeted his young friend with open arms. "Boy" had not changed. If anything, Nechayev was more dauntless than ever. He repeated the stories of great wealth which would soon be flowing into his hands, about the mysterious Russian nobleman who was on the point of selling his estate and handing it over to the Society, about the vast prospects of revolution. When Bakunin pointed to the wounded hand, Nechayev told how he had fought off a whole battalion of police officers singlehanded. He had returned, Nechayev said, for one last consultation with Bakunin before ordering the revolution.

The long idyl with Bakunin continued as before, but there were problems to be solved. Nechayev's money was running out; there was delay in obtaining the large sums which were due to arrive from Russia; Bakunin was complaining against the drudgery of translating *Das Kapital* for which he had received an advance of 300 rubles against a total fee of 1,200 rubles to be paid on completion of the work. The 300 rubles were already spent, and Bakunin had translated only the introductory chapters.

Nechayev offered to relieve Bakunin of the responsibility of finishing the translation. On "official" notepaper, bearing the name of the Society of the Ax in red ink, with an ax, a dagger, and a revolver drawn roughly on the paper, he sent off a letter to a certain Lyubavin, a Russian student then studying at a university in Germany who had acted as intermediary and persuaded a Russian publisher to make the advance. Lyubavin was told he had committed a monstrous crime. Bakunin was a revolutionary whose life was devoted to the revolution; to demand that he should exploit his talents by hackwork showed an amazing ignorance of affairs. The student was peremptorily commanded to telegraph to Bakunin a release from his obligations. If he refused, the Society of the Ax would take appropriate measures. The letter was unsigned, and Lyubavin concluded that it had been written by Bakunin and immediately wrote an insulting letter to Bakunin, recapitulating the contents of the letter received from the Society of the Ax. Bakunin was alarmed. At bottom, he had the bourgeois instincts: he always paid his debts. He immediately wrote to Lyubavin, announcing that he accepted his obligation and would repay the 300 rubles as soon as circumstances permitted. He regretted however that he saw no likelihood of ever being able to complete the translation of *Das Kapital*. Then he turned on Nechayev and asked for an explanation. Nechayev laughed. He had simply taken the most obvious course, and he was sorry the old man took it amiss. Soon the matter was forgotten, for new problems were arising every day. The fate of the 300 rubles owed to the Russian publisher Polyakov could be relegated to the future. The Russian revolution, too, could wait. The most pressing problem was that the Swiss government had received an extradition order for Nechayev's arrest, and for the first time in his life Nechayev was alarmed. As Nechayev explained with admirable simplicity: "Money is never a problem. If we want money, all we have to do is to hold up the Simplon post. But when the Swiss police are on our track, we have to work much harder."

What happened then could easily have been predicted: Nechayev set Bakunin to work. Writing to Ogaryev on February 8, Bakunin complained bitterly about the amount of work Nechayev had made him do:

> I am late in replying to your letter because Boy is making my head whirl with all the work he sets before me. This morning I had to write an article on the subject of the courtesy of the police who place themselves at the service of foreign powers and go running after thieves, forgers, and brigands so-called . . . The situation of the Russian refugees in Europe imposes upon us the necessity to do everything we can, without losing a moment, to win the public over to our side. Unless we do this, every single one of us may be extradited as though we were the worst kind of thieves and assassins.

Already there were rumors that Nechayev had murdered Ivanov. Nechayev denied them glibly. A little later he was admitting the rumors and explaining that the murder was purely political, and unavoidable: Ivanov had been found guilty of a crime against the revolution. Bakunin was aware there was nothing to prevent the Swiss police from arresting Nechayev on an extradition order. Fearing for his own life and also for Nechayev's, he set to work on a pamphlet which later became the celebrated plea entitled *The Bear of Berne and the Bear of St. Petersburg*, which purported to have been written by a Swiss citizen. It was a heady document, accusing both governments of tyrannical practices, and it did nothing to make Nechayev's position less vulnerable. By this time Bakunin was beginning to lose that perfect faith with which he had accepted Nechayev's least utterances in the past. Nechayev stayed with Bakunin less than ten days and returned to Geneva. There at least he could be sure of complete acceptance of his views. Ogaryev, far more than Bakunin, had fallen under Nechayev's spell.

The idyl between Nechayev and Ogaryev was interrupted by a further idyl between Nechayev and the elder daughter of the "poor, dear, feckless" Herzen, who had died in Paris on January 21. Natalie Herzen, who was known as Tata, was present at her father's death. Shortly afterward she hurried to Geneva to comfort Ogaryev, once her father's alter ego. She had inherited a small fortune. She painted well. She had the fine, strong features of her father. She could speak four languages, and she was filled with revolutionary fervor. Ogaryev began to think of a match between Nechayev and Tata Herzen, which would link the foremost of practicing revolutionaries with the family of the great apologist for a Russian revolution. And when, after a visit to Paris in February, Tata Herzen returned to Geneva, Bakunin was thinking in the same terms.

There is no reason to believe that Tata Herzen ever fell in love with Nechayev. But Nechayev lived under Ogaryev's roof, Tata was always by his side, and he set her to work addressing envelopes. Bakunin had been complaining that Nechayev had grown lazy, but the fit of laziness soon passed. Since no money was coming in, the letters to Russia consisted largely of appeals for funds to aid the revolution. Most of these letters fell into the hands of the police, and almost no money came out of Russia. Remembering Tata's skill in drawing, Nechayev suggested that she draw designs for making banknotes. Tata groaned: she had no experience in drawing banknotes and no intention of trying. The problem of money was growing urgent. In March Bakunin arrived in Geneva with the bland suggestion that Tata should help the cause by marrying into a rich family. She was pretty; she was gifted; in what better way could she serve the revolution than by selling herself to a rich admirer? It was not one of

Bakunin's more brilliant suggestions and sounds suspiciously like the kind of idea which would occur to Nechayev. For Nechayev was not totally devoid of ideas. He suggested a literary alliance between Tata Herzen and himself; together they would edit the revolutionary magazine *Kolokol*, which had been founded by her father. Tata threw herself enthusiastically into the plan. Between April 2 and May 9, six issues of *Kolokol* appeared with the names of Natalie Herzen and Sergey Nechayev on the masthead. Neither of the editors had any experience of producing a revolutionary magazine. It was excessively tame, full of praise for Herzen and subdued attacks on Bakunin. There were unsigned open letters written in Nechayev's worst style, and there was none of the fire which characterized the brief pamphlets which Nechayev had begun writing from the moment he first stepped on Swiss soil. Only two assumptions are possible: either Nechayev was deliberately bowing to Tata's more liberal revolutionary ideas, or he was simply using the magazine as an instrument to advance his claims on Tata's fortune. She seems to have admired and feared him by turns, and to have resisted his attempts to seduce her, and she was fond of him to the very end. But she never submitted herself to the orders of the mysterious society which Nechayev claimed to control and seems to have realized very early in their relationship that it had no existence outside Nechayev's brain.

There remained the Bakhmatiev fund. Since the death of Herzen the fund came under the control of Ogaryev, who could dispose of it as he pleased. Under Nechayev's promptings he decided to give the greater part of it to Nechayev's Society of the People's Vengeance. To give an appearance of legality to the transfer, Ogaryev summoned a meeting of revolutionaries; and in the presence of Tata Herzen, her young brother Alexander, Natalie Ogaryev, and a few other Russian exiles, the money was handed by Ogaryev to Bakunin, who handed it to Nechayev. Both Ogaryev and Bakunin retained small sums for themselves. As usual Bakunin showed his notorious respect for contracts and demanded that all those who witnessed the transfer of the money should sign an affidavit. He had not counted upon Nechayev, who refused on the grounds that such an affidavit involved his honor as a revolutionary. There the matter rested until later in the year when Karl Marx announced that all the money had fallen into Bakunin's hands. Bakunin was so aroused on a point of honor that he drew up a manifesto to be signed by Ogaryev. The manifesto, a wonderful tissue of truth and incomparable falsehood, read:

I, the undersigned, do hereby declare that all the moneys contained in the Bakhmatiev fund were placed in the hands of Nechayev, to be given over to the Russian Committee of which the aforesaid Nechayev is the foreign representative, according to the documents and statements in his possession.

Bakunin had no right whatsoever to dispose of the funds, and did not in fact do so. The right to dispose of the fund belonged exclusively to Herzen and me; and after Herzen's death I alone possessed the right to dispose of it. Bakunin himself took no part in the transfer of the capital sum to Nechayev, which took place in the presence of only two people: Natalie Alexandrovna Herzen and myself.

Unfortunately, on this occasion, I made an unpardonable omission. Having absolute confidence in the revolutionary faith of Nechayev, I did not ask for a receipt. It was only later, when my opinion of Necheyev changed for the worse, that I decided to ask him for a receipt . . . Nechayev refused, offering the pretext that the Russian Committee never acted in this manner. This dishonest attitude on the part of Nechayev only confirmed my suspicion that ideas of morality were completely foreign to him.

The part which Bakunin played in this affair was as follows. After the death of Herzen he persuaded me to give the money to Nechayev as the representative of the Russian Committee, as the single designated revolutionary who could be said to represent the Russian revolution abroad. To this man the total sum contained within the Bakhmatiev fund was given. It was not difficult to convince me that this was the best course to adopt, for I shared with Bakunin an absolute faith in the existence of the Russian Committee, and both of us regarded Nechayev as its chief representative abroad.

Such was Bakunin's contorted apologia with its truths, half truths and lies so inextricably mingled that even now we can hardly disentangle them. The only thing that is certain is that the greater part of the Bakhmatiev fund, amounting to 10,000 francs, disappeared in Nechayev's pockets. Some of the money may have been expended on the cost of publishing *Kolokol*. A good deal of it must have been kept by Nechayev. Bakunin in the affidavit takes care to repeat twice that he received none of the money, so arousing the suspicion that he received a considerable share of it. But the mystery of the Bakhmatiev fund remains.

There are other mysteries concerning Nechayev's brief stay in Switzerland. There is, for example, the mysterious figure of Vladimir Serebrennikov, of whom nothing is known except that he was always to be seen by Nechayev's side. Bakunin regarded him as a rogue, but never enlarged on his crimes. He seems to have attached himself to Nechayev and to have been his constant messenger and confidant. We know more about another revolutionary called Semyon Serebrennikov, a friend of Ogaryev who was one of the witnesses who attended the transfer of the money to Nechayev.

On May 9 Semyon Serebrennikov was standing outside Ogaryev's house when three plain-clothes men hurled themselves upon him. There was a short struggle, Serebrennikov heard the words, "Camperio . . . Nechayev . . ." and then his arms were twisted behind his back and tied with cord. Protesting, he was removed to the police station, threatened with a revolver and kept waiting until the superintendent arrived. His papers were taken from him: passport, letters, money, banknotes. When the superintendent arrived, Serebrennikov was formally accused of being Nechayev. He was shown a photograph of Nechayev with the usual police description underneath. He pointed out that Nechayev's hair was dark, his own blond, and kept asking to see Ogaryev. He had difficulty in making himself understood. He knew no French and could not speak German with ease. He was thrown into a cell and given ten francs to buy food.

The next day there was a formal interrogation. Once again he attempted to explain that he was not Nechayev. He said he was a poor student, the son of a peasant, born in the village of Znamienka in Ilguinsk district in the government of Irkutsk. Asked to account for his movements during the previous five years he said he had spent the greater part of his time studying in St. Petersburg. In April 1869 he left Odessa for America by way of Vienna, Berlin, and Hamburg. In America he had gone under the name of Guy Ore. He had stayed there only a few months. He was back again in Europe in December, studying at the Polytechnic College in Zurich. Asked whether he knew Nechayev, Serebrennikov answered that he had encountered a student of the same name in St. Petersburg, but at the time of the murder he was safely in New York living with a Russian called George Leger, 148 Lawrence Street, in the house of a certain Mr. Rietzel, a teacher of music. This could be checked by the authorities of New York. Asked to account for his more recent movements Serebrennikov shrugged his shoulders and said he arrived in Geneva five days ago.

Serebrennikov was kept in prison for a further ten days. The fourth interrogation occurred on May 20. After the interrogation he was led into a courtyard. A mysterious visitor was watching him from a window above, evidently someone who knew Nechayev well and who could recognize him. But the recognition evidently failed, for on the next day, a Saturday, Serebrennikov was suddenly released. He had been accused of no crime. There was not enough evidence to link him with Nechayev. Serebrennikov was furious. He complained that while he was in prison the only reading matter allowed consisted of two or three twenty-year-old newspapers, a novel published in 1781, and a French grammar printed about the same time. Serebrennikov was of the opinion that they were deliberately conspiring to reduce him to a state of insanity with these old books and newspapers. The novel particularly annoyed him. "It would have been useful to a peasant," he said, "but I am a student and deserve better."

With this, Serebrennikov disappears from the scene, as an authentic "figure of mystery." He was not quite as innocent as he made out in the pamphlet which he printed at the end of the month. The pamphlet was entitled *L'Arrestation de S. Sérébrénnikov par la Police de Genève,* and purported to show that the Swiss police were completely out of their minds, and should pay him a large sum as damages for unlawful arrest. In fact, Nechayev knew him well and he had played a small role in Nechayev's revolutionary activity. In St. Petersburg Serebrennikov had possessed a small printing press, and, as we have seen, it was on this press that Alexandra Dementieva printed the copies of Tkachev's inflammatory pamphlet summoning the students to revolt. The printing press was to be mentioned at great length during the trial of the *Nechayevtsi* the following year. For the Russian government the arrest of Serebrennikov was an expensive mistake. On the day of the arrest the Swiss police forwarded a telegram to St. Petersburg, announcing the capture of the dreaded Nechayev, with a full description. The Russians were wary and immediately sent two men to Switzerland to identify the prisoner. One was a watchman attached to St. Petersburg University, the other a watchman attached to the Andreyevsky College, the day school where Nechayev had once taught theology. When they failed to identify Nechayev, Serebrennikov was released. The Russian police caught up with Serebrennikov four years later when he was working in Prussia. He was extradited, put on trial and sent to Siberia.

Meanwhile Nechayev was still hiding in Geneva and the surrounding villages. He was always on the move, always a little ahead of the police. Ogaryev in his mysterious way continued to keep in touch with him. Once when Nechayev was staying in the little mountain village of Le Locle in the Jura, Tata Herzen was sent on a secret mission to him. A little while later she hid him in her house for a week. It was now known that the Russian government had supplied the Swiss with an extradition order, accusing Nechayev of being a common criminal. Bakunin sent an endless stream of letters and telegrams to Nechayev warning him that he was in danger of imminent arrest. There were letters on May 2, 4, 6, and 9 and two telegrams were sent on the fifth and the seventh. "Why are you silent?" Bakunin complained in one of the letters written from Locarno. "If you have received my letters, why don't you reply? I know nothing of what is happening and understand less." Probably Nechayev could not have replied to the letters even if he had received them. He was on the run. Bakunin rushed to Berne, hoping to head off any action by the Swiss police. He consulted lawyers and buttonholed judges. The lawyers Adolf and Gustav Vogt offered to work on behalf of Nechayev. The *Bundesrath* Knusebeck explained that although the Federal Council would probably refuse extradition if the case was brought to their attention, there was nothing to prevent the Cantonal Council of Geneva from obeying the order of the Russian police. At least ten Russian agents were searching for Nechayev, and they were well supplied with funds. In panic Bakunin drew up an open letter to his friends in Geneva, begging them to act quickly. He urged all Russian *émigrés* to sign a memorial in defense of Nechayev. Many signed, though some afterward regretted their signatures and explained that they signed against the evidence and without conviction. "Beware of falling asleep on the task," Bakunin wrote. "Apply yourselves! Give the largest possible publicity to this act of cowardice on the part of the Swiss! Use every weapon open to you—pamphlets, articles in the newspapers, private correspondence! Keep up an unrelenting pressure!" In the midst of Bakunin's furious efforts to save Nechayev there arrived from Moscow a young revolutionary called Lopatin who asked casually why anyone should trouble to defend a common murderer. Lopatin had an unimpeachable revolutionary background. He had seen Nechayev at work in Switzerland and in Russia. He poured scorn on Nechayev as the valiant revolutionary. The story about the escape from the Peter and Paul Fortress was untrue. There was no vast revolutionary society in Russia waiting to obey Nechayev's orders. The scars on Nechayev's thumb were death marks left by Ivanov's teeth. "There is absolutely nothing that can be said in his favor," Lopatin explained; and though Bakunin refused to believe Lopatin's report as it was recounted to him by Tata Herzen, it is clear that his faith in Nechayev was shaken.

While Bakunin was attempting to move heaven and earth to save Nechayev from the Russian police, an obscure quarrel broke out between the two revolutionaries. All we know is that the quarrel involved Ogaryev and related to some conditions which Bakunin laid down. Writing to Ogaryev on June 14, Bakunin refers haltingly and in veiled tones to the causes of the rupture which now seemed inevitable:

> . . . I now feel it is my duty to state clearly and categorically for the benefit of Neville [Nechayev] the conditions I have already mentioned to you. My mind is made up, I shall not and cannot take back my words, I refuse to make a single backward step. Whether he accepts my conditions depends very much on your attitude toward me. He will accept them if you tell him to, as you will if you come to the conclusion that it is just, useful, and necessary to lend me your support. I have done my best to convince you, and I have given you all the information I have. All I can do now is to wait for your reply and for his . . . Of course "Boy" is obstinate, and I too, once I have made up my mind, have not the habit of changing it. *Ergo*, a rupture with him, at least from my side, now seems inevitable. If we all agreed, acting with complete unanimity, we might be able to make some impression on his pigheadedness; on the other hand we might fail completely. In any event we must put an end to the affair once and for all.

Neither Nechayev nor Bakunin has left any clues about this sudden alteration in their relations. Already in February Bakunin had written to Ogaryev about "the conditions on which he could give himself up to the cause." He told Ogaryev that he had overcome all false shame. "Up to this

moment we have acted as pure idealists: we have served the cause only
with our aspirations, our desire to perform great deeds, occasional pieces
of propaganda. But if anyone wishes to perform on a large scale, he must
know a great deal and dare splendidly." Bakunin added that it was also
necessary to have control over considerable resources. But it is unlikely
that the estrangement arose as the result of Nechayev's failure to support
Bakunin financially. Their differences lay much deeper. Both were impoverished, bitter, remorseless in their desire for power. In their different
ways they had outlived the need for one another. Generosity was a quality
which Bakunin retained to the end: it was not a quality we can associate
with Nechayev, who felt no gratitude to Bakunin and no generous impulses toward any man. There came a blunt letter from Nechayev announcing he would arrange a rendezvous at a time and place to be determined later. Then there was silence.

A week later Bakunin heard that Nechayev had slipped out of Switzerland. He had taken with him a box containing Bakunin's entire international correspondence, hundreds of private letters and letters of introduction written many months before. There could be only one reason for the
theft. Horror-stricken, Bakunin wrote to his friend Talandier in London:

Neuchâtel, July 24, 1870

MY DEAR FRIEND,

I have just heard that N. has visited you, and you have given him the
address of our mutual friends (M. and his wife). I am forced to the conclusion that the two letters which O. and I sent to you, warning you to keep
him away from your doors, failed to arrive in time. Without the least exaggeration I believe this delay to have been an absolute disaster. And if it seems
strange to you that we are warning you against a man to whom we have
given letters of introduction, letters written in the warmest terms, then remember that these letters were written in May, and since then we have
been confronted with some grave incidents—incidents which have made us
break off all relations with N. At the risk of appearing to be out of our
minds, we believe we have the sacred duty to warn you against him. And
now I shall try to tell you very briefly the reasons why we have changed our
opinion of him.

It is perfectly true that N. is the one man most persecuted by the Russian
government, which has covered the whole continent of Europe with a cloud
of spies determined to find him in whatever country he can be found. It is
true too that the Russian government has demanded his extradition from
Germany as well as Switzerland. It is also true that N. is one of the most
active and energetic men I have ever known. When he serves what he calls
the cause, he never hesitates, stops at nothing, and is as merciless toward
himself as toward others. This is the chief quality which attracted me to
him, and it was this which made me over a long period of time seek out an
alliance with him. There are some who say he is simply a fraud. This is a lie!
He is a dedicated fanatic, and a very dangerous fanatic: with him an alliance
can only be disastrous. And this is why: there was a time when he did

actually belong to a secret organization in Russia. This organization however no longer exists. All its members were arrested. N. is alone now: alone he represents what he is pleased to call the Committee. With the Russian organization decimated, he is busy preparing a new one abroad. All this would be natural, legitimate, and extremely useful, but his methods are reprehensible. Deeply impressed by the disaster which destroyed the secret organization in Russia, he came to the conclusion that if he was to form a true and indestructible society, he would have to base it on the political principles of Machiavelli and adopt the motto of the Jesuits: "Violence for the body, lies for the Soul."

Truth, mutual confidence, fast friendships—these can only exist among a dozen individuals who form the inner sanctum of the Society. All the rest must be no more than blind instruments of the Society's will, expendable according to the whim of the twelve, who are bound together by the sternest oaths. It is perfectly permissible to deceive, compromise and steal from the underlings: it is even permissible to lose them. He is wholly the conspirator. And so, now that you have received N. because we sent our own letter of recommendation, and you have given him your confidence and recommended him to your friends—to M. and Mme. M. in particular—what will happen when he has entered your world? Let me tell you. First, he will tell a host of lies in order to increase your sympathy and confidence in him, but this is not all. The sympathies of lukewarm men, by which I mean men who are not wholly dedicated to the revolution, men who have other interests, men with family ties and love affairs and friendships and social relations —such men he regards as unworthy, and he will do everything he can to submit them wholly to the cause, and quite without your knowing it, he will try to take over your whole life. To do this, he will spy on you and attempt to get possession of all your secrets, and if left alone in a room in your absence, he will open all your drawers, read all your correspondence, and if he finds a letter which in some way compromises you or your friends, he will steal it and guard it carefully for his own purposes of intimidation. He has done this with O., with Tata and other friends, and when we faced him with the charge, he dared to say: "So I did it? Well, that's our system. That is how we treat enemies—we have to compromise *everyone* who is not completely with us." By this he means all those who are not completely convinced of the complete validity of his system and have not promised to apply it themselves.

Then, too, if you introduce him to a friend, his first aim will be to sow dissension, scandal, and intrigue between you. If your friend has a wife or a daughter, he will attempt to seduce her and get her with child, forcing her beyond the limits of conventional morality and so place her that she is compelled to make a revolutionary protest against society.

Every personal tie, every friendship, everything . . . all these he will regard as evil, and he will do his best to destroy them, and he will do this because these things weaken the effectiveness of his secret organization. Do not, I beg of you, cry out that this is an exaggeration! All this has happened and can be proved. When he is unmasked, this poor N. is so childlike, so simple in spite of his systematic perversity—he even thought he could convert me and begged me to develop this theory in a Russian journal which he wanted me to publish. He has betrayed the confidence of us all, stolen our letters, horribly compromised us—in a word, he has behaved like a villain. His only excuse lies in his fanaticism! Without knowing it, he is terribly ambitious, because he has come finally to the conclusion that the revolutionary cause can be identified with his own person, and so leads the life of a martyr, full of privations and unbelievable hard work: therefore you cannot call him an egoist in the worst sense of the word. He is a fanatic, and fanaticism has led him into becoming an accomplished Jesuit—there are moments when he is no more than a beast. Most of his lies are white lies. He plays the Jesuit game as others play the game of revolution. But in spite of his naïveté, he is extremely dangerous, because *every day* he commits crimes, abuses confidences, acts treacherously; and it is all the more difficult to prevent these things from happening because one hardly suspects their possibility. In spite of all this he is a force to be reckoned with, because he has immense energy. And so it was with immense sorrow that I broke with him. I thought of how service to our cause demands immense reserves of energy, and how rarely we come upon anyone so richly endowed with pure energy. But after thinking the matter out, I came to the conclusion that no other course was open to me, and now that we are apart, I must keep fighting him to the bitter end. Believe it or not, his last project was to form a group of thieves and bandits on Swiss territory, evidently with the intention of bringing about a revolution. I have prevented that by making him leave Switzerland, and it is quite certain that if he had continued with his project, this group of bandits would have been captured within the space of a few weeks—he would have been lost, and everyone else would have been lost with him. His friend and companion S. is an outright scoundrel, a brazen liar, without the excuse or the saving grace of fanaticism. He committed innumerable thefts of papers and letters from me. And these are the fellows whom M., even though warned by J., has thought of introducing to Dupont and Bradlaugh. The evil has been done, and we must do what we can to put it right, making as little noise as possible and without scandal.

1. In the name of your peace of mind, the peace of your family and your own dignity, I beg you to shut your door to them. Do this without any explanations: simply cut off all connection with them. For many reasons we do not want them to think we are waging war on them all along the line. They must think these warnings against them are coming from our enemies —and this statement might very well be true, since there have been some very energetic accusations against them stemming from the general council in London. Please do not unmask us too prematurely. They have stolen our papers, and we must get them back somehow.

2. Persuade M. that the safety of his whole family depends upon breaking with them. Warn them about how he will systematically try to corrupt and seduce young women, and in this way wield power over the whole family. I am distressed beyond words at the thought that they have got M.'s address: they will publicly denounce M. They told me quite openly, and in the presence of witnesses, that they are perfectly prepared to denounce their enemies to the secret police; and by enemies they mean those who are only lukewarm to the revolutionary faith; and they regard denunciation as a perfectly legitimate means to an end. To take over a person's family secrets and thus hold a whip over them—this is one of their most important weapons. I am so terrified at the thought that they have M.'s address that I beg him

to move to another lodging, and so avoid discovery. And if M. continues to be infatuated by his own judgment and continues his relations with these gentlemen, then I am sure that there will be terrible consequences, and these will arise as a consequence of his own blind vanity.

3. You and M. must warn all our friends to be on their guard against these gentlemen. N., the most obstinate of players, will lose the game—the other is lost already. None of our friends must be allowed to fall into the general pattern of ruin. It is all very sad and humiliating, especially since I recommended them, but truth is the better part and the greatest remedy against all evils.

Bakunin was quite capable of writing fifty-page letters, and this letter to Talandier is by no means the longest he wrote. Yet it is one of the most illuminating and certainly the most despairing of all his letters. Written in bile, in the extreme assurance that he had at last seen evil face to face, he paused long enough to offer Nechayev a tribute of baffled admiration. He was bemused, as he had never been bemused before; it was beyond all comprehension, he said, and yet there was nothing performed by Nechayev which he had not himself encouraged and performed a hundred times. Even the name of his friend terrified him; he dared not write it down in full; and he went bitterly complaining against the injustice of "Boy" to anyone who cared to listen to him.

Meanwhile Bakunin had performed a useful service to humanity. The letter to Talandier provides the perfect summary to the nihilist character, and belongs to the great series of "Characters" written during the seventeenth and eighteenth centuries. Bakunin saw the danger and recoiled in horror. The huge terrifying insolence of Nechayev frightened him, as later it pleased Lenin; and what is apparent throughout this long letter is a kind of envy of Nechayev, a deep love, and even an understanding; it is as though Bakunin is saying, "He is terrible beyond words; he has compromised me; but he is singularly great in his terrible way." Bakunin had only been playing with destruction; this was the real thing. He had written once: "The passion for destruction is also a creative passion." He had only half believed it. Now for the first time he saw this belief parading in the flesh.

Stung into fury by his loss, Bakunin writes with quite extraordinary penetration of the nihilist character. Himself a nihilist or nearly a nihilist, he is able to relate the construction of the nihilist mind when projected to its ultimate extension. So Dostoyevsky describes Kirillov with immense understanding, and Hitler (though he was pretending to be doing something else) described his own nihilism in a speech he delivered after the blood bath of 1934. Mostly, it is only the nihilists who write convincingly about the nihilist character. Bakunin was so frightened of Nechayev that he remained in hiding for six weeks. He knew he was not innocent. He expected the vengeance of Nechayev. Strangest of all is the underlying quietness and composure of the letter. It is as though Bakunin was setting about the task of stripping Nechayev of his adornments quietly, tenaciously, knowing that the task was necessary, and not only because it was necessary to warn Talandier: it was also necessary that he should himself be warned.

The letter to Talandier was only one of many. He wrote to his friend Mroczkowski in London, begging for every scrap of available information about Nechayev. What had Nechayev told him? Where is he? Who is he staying with? Had Bradlaugh and Dupont been warned against him in time? To another correspondent he wrote urging that every effort should be made to steal back from Nechayev the papers which Nechayev had stolen from him. "I beg you to break off all relations with Nechayev and his little friend Woldemar S.,* and afterward do everything you can to destroy your traces." From Locarno he wrote to Ogaryev on July 28, admitting that the worst had happened. His letters of warning had been received too late. Mroczkowski had introduced Nechayev to "that iconoclast Bradlaugh" and to Dupont, an influential member of the International Workingmen's Association. Nechayev was planning to publish *The Bell* in London. Everything was going badly, but thank heaven, Ogaryev had sent him a packet of tea. We can leave Bakunin as he brews the tea and commiserates with himself on the loss of his secret journals.

In London Nechayev fared badly. Within a few weeks Bakunin's letters caught up with him. He seems to have quarreled with Vladimir Serebrennikov, and with immense difficulty he produced two numbers of a new Russian periodical called *The Commune* (*Obshchina*) which purported to be the organ of the Russian Socialists. The first number appeared under the date line September 1, 1870, but probably came out some weeks later. It contained a veiled attack on Herzen, "the grand old man of the revolution who only knows how to play at liberalism." It also contained an open letter to Bakunin and Ogaryev, accusing them of being reactionaries, revolutionaries "of the most incompetent kind" and men who had mismanaged the funds entrusted to them. In the open letter Nechayev demanded the balance of the Bakhmatiev fund, but unknown to Nechayev, Bakunin had signed on July 21 a statement to the effect that he was borrowing 450 francs from the fund and proposed to return the money within three weeks or at the latest on the fifteenth of August. It can be assumed that Ogaryev and Bakunin now regarded the fund as their own private repository, to be used as they thought fit, and there was not the least likelihood that they would entrust the balance to Nechayev.

* Vladimir Serebrennikov, who accompanied Nechayev to London. He used the name Woldemar Sallier.

There was little Nechayev could do in London. In January 1871 he was in Paris. In March he was once again in Zurich, working with a Serbian passport as a house painter. There were rumors that he visited Lyons during the few days when Bakunin placed himself at the head of the Committee of Public Safety during the Commune, but Bakunin found no trace of him and it is unlikely that Nechayev, whose French was always poor, could have made headway in France. He returned to Zurich because he was known there, and still had a handful of friends. It was the time when the International Workingmen's Association was at the height of its power, and the First International had no sympathy for Nechayev's methods. He lived secretly, and was often penniless. Serebrennikov remained in London, and it sometimes pleased Nechayev to send messages to Serebrennikov who would then transmit them to Switzerland, giving the impression that Nechayev was still in England. Penniless, desperate, going under half a dozen different names, living with obscure Rumanian and Serbian revolutionaries, Nechayev still planned a revolution and he was still surrounded by a loyal but improvident band of followers, but the original impetus was wearing thin.

At the beginning of July 1871 there opened in St. Petersburg the trial known as "the trial of the *Nechayevtsi.*" Some eighty-four of the followers of Nechayev had been rounded up. The courthouse was open to the public; the newspapers were encouraged to publish full reports of the proceedings. Nearly everyone who had come in contact with Nechayev in Russia was under arrest. Nechayev's chief lieutenants, Orlov, Nikolayev, Prizhov, Uspensky, Kuznetsov and Mme. Dementieva were brought to the witness stand, and gave full accounts of their dealings with Nechayev. From diaries, documents, and telegrams the police were able to fill in a complete history of the hundred days Nechayev had spent in Russia. The public was appalled by the extent of the revolutionary society and by the extreme youth of the conspirators: their average age was just over twenty-two. Many had been kept in prison for nearly two years. One had committed suicide; another had gone mad. They included the sons of peasants and members of the nobility, the widow of a general, the cousin of a famous composer, the son of a Finnish landowner, a number of students from Turkestan with names like Djavad Ishkhanov, and an obscure Frenchman with the extraordinary name of Pajou de Moncey. At the trial *The Revolutionary Catechism* was read out at length together with Ogaryev's poem and most of the documents which Nechayev produced with Bakunin's assistance in the early days of their friendship. The bourgeois were fascinated and terrified by the emergence of "the Nechayev monster." An alarmed public prosecutor described the conspiracy as "a dagger thrust at the heart of the monarchy." It was more than a dagger.

It was a threat which was to hang over the dynasty to the very end, and the witnesses for the prosecution took pains to point out how close Nechayev had been to raising the standard of revolt. But not all the evidence pointed toward a strong revolutionary movement. Asked by the president of the court how many cells of conspirators there had been, the prisoner Dolgov could remember only four: there were, he said, cells around Kuznetsov, Ivanov, Nechayev, and himself. When he was further asked whether the organization was a strong one, he answered: "No, it was very, very weak."

Weak or strong, Nechayev's influence was dreaded by the Tsar, who asked for daily reports and held special meetings at which the implications of *Nechayevshchina,* all that could be understood by the portent of Nechayev, were discussed at length; and at some time during the trial he ordered the arrest of Nechayev even if it meant taking "extraordinary measures."

Some of the witnesses at the trial pretended to an ignorance they clearly did not possess. Some like Semyon Kuznetsov pleaded not guilty. Others like Ripman pleaded "guilty to belonging to a secret society whose aim, known and accepted by him, was a social uprising among the people." Those who had taken part in the murder of Ivanov related the incident at length to a hushed court, holding nothing back; and in the fading pages of the journals of that time we can read the details of the murder as seen by the four participants—only Nechayev's own account is lacking. But the death of Ivanov was neither the main nor even the most important subject to be aired at the trial. The main subject was Nechayev, whose absence only made him all the more present, a ghostly mocking criminal who defied the might of the Tsarist police to arrest him. Who was he? Where did he obtain his strength? This man who called himself Pavlov and Ivan Petrov, Dmitry Fyodorovich and Captain Panin, who wore his disguises well and sometimes appeared in women's clothes, the chief of the Narodnaya Rasprava, the People's Vengeance, or those other societies which proliferated around him, the Society of the Ax, the Society of the Five, who was he? And if you arrested him and tortured him to death, how could you be certain that he would not arise again?

The mystery of Nechayev was not solved at the trial; it is still unsolved. The witnesses confessed that they had never understood him, but they feared the powers he wielded, those mysterious threats which he called down in the name of vengeance. But there were strange omissions at the trial. Very little was said about Nechayev's attempt to capture the arsenal at Tula, and the president did not press too hard in his inquiries about how Nechayev had hoped to take over supreme power. Dolgov was asked by the president whether the aim of the Society was to prepare an uprising among the people. Dolgov answered evasively: "Nechayev said the people were ripe for an uprising and we must help them in every possible way." The president reminded Dolgov that they had been talking about an uprising. What kind of uprising? "Well," said Dolgov, "I thought deputies would come together from various places and introduce new laws." But everyone else knew that the uprising would not consist of an assembly of lawyers.

Later the government regretted that it had held the trial in public. Three hundred had originally been arrested: these had been winnowed down to eighty-four. The jury decided to acquit all but those who had been close to Nechayev and those who participated in the Ivanov murder. Alexey Kuznetsov, who had spent a year and a half in jail, was sentenced to ten years' hard labor, while his brother Semyon was acquitted. Prince Cherkessov was sentenced to deprivation of all rights and permanent exile in Tomsk. (As a member of the nobility he could not safely be sentenced to prison.) Shortly afterward he escaped abroad, dying in London in 1925. Uspensky received the sternest punishment, fifteen years' imprisonment. Nikolayev, who had taken part in the expedition to Tula and given Nechayev the knife with which Ivanov was stabbed, received only seven years and four months' imprisonment. Prizhov received a sentence of twelve years' imprisonment to be followed by permanent exile in Siberia. He survived his years of imprisonment and died in Siberia in 1885. Of the others who received short terms, Pyotr Tkachev escaped abroad in 1873 shortly after completing his sixteen months' sentence. Later he married Alexandra Dementieva, who was released from jail in January 1872 and ordered to live in Novgorod under police surveillance. A short while afterward she received permission to leave Russia "without the right to return," and she was present at Tkachev's bedside at the Hospital of St. Anne in Paris when he died in 1886. Alexandra survived him by forty years. Deteils received four months' imprisonment and five years' police surveillance. The president, addressing those who had been found not guilty, reminded them that they were in the same position as all other honest citizens. Nothing had been proved against them, and therefore they could hold their heads high.

The trial was over, but the mystery of "the Nechayev monster" remained. Frightened by the possibility that the monster would emerge again, the Tsar repeated his explicit instructions for Nechayev's arrest, and incensed by the conduct of the president at the trial, he discussed with Count Pahlen, the Minister of Justice, how such trials should be conducted in future. In the following year there appeared over Count Pahlen's signature a new law withdrawing political cases from the ordinary tribunals. Henceforth political trials would be judged by special tribunals composed of senators appointed by the Emperor alone.

The trial had left the public with mixed feelings. There was the pleasant shiver of apprehension at the mysterious spectacle of "the Nechayev monster," the spider in the midst of an endless web. There was the pleasant knowledge that the police had once more been defeated: as the result of a trial lasting from July 1 to September 11 the police, far from proving their capacity to nip revolts in the bud, had only shown an amazing incapacity to understand what was happening beneath their eyes, and they had failed to arrest Nechayev, whose audacity delighted many, even though the details of the murder of Ivanov were singularly depressing. Vera Figner, who was in Switzerland at the time of the trial, recalled reading about it in the newspapers. "I read about them every day," she wrote later, "but I must say that it was only the murder of Ivanov, described in all its tragic detail, which made any impression on me—all the rest was inexplicable and passed me by." But Dostoyevsky read the published reports avidly. He knew one of the defendants, a relative of his wife. He had begun to work on *The Possessed* in 1867, but he could make no headway with it. By January 1871 he had written only two chapters. When the trial opened in July, he hurried to St. Petersburg and he was one of the spectators in the public gallery. The figure of Nechayev intrigued him, and under various disguises Nechayev appears in the novel, now as Shatov, now as Kirillov, now as Pyotr Verkhovensky. From the Nechayev trial he borrowed names, incidents, complete situations, though later he went to some pains to deny that the influence of Nechayev was present in the novel. In *The Diary of a Writer* he wrote: "I myself am an old Nechayev, or else—perhaps—might have been a follower of Nechayev, I am not sure. In the days of my youth it might certainly have happened." And in the notes which he wrote while planning the novel he would sometimes write the name of Nechayev where he had intended to put the name of Verkhovensky.

Nechayev's presence in the novel is profoundly evident in the scenes where Verkhovensky summons the millennium for the benefit of Stavrogin. Speaking in the authentic accents of Nechayev, Verkhovensky announces the destruction of the civilized world:

> Culture is unnecessary! We have had enough of science! Without science we have material enough for a thousand years, but one must maintain discipline. The only thing that is lacking in the world is discipline. The thirst for culture is an aristocratic thirst. The moment you have a family or fall in love you get the desire for property. We will destroy that desire: we will make use of drunkenness, slander, spying. We will make use of incredible

corruption. We'll stifle every genius in its infancy. Everything must be brought to one common denominator: complete equality.

While Dostoyevsky was busy writing *The Possessed* and the brooding image of Nechayev still hung over St. Petersburg, the physical Nechayev was wandering restlessly over Switzerland, searching desperately for a hiding place. He lived from hand to mouth. He made occasional sums of money by sign painting. Very few people knew where he was staying. Vera Figner, who was in Zurich at the time, said that hardly anyone suspected his existence among them. A few who met him begged him to leave the country for his own sake. Nechayev replied that he chose to remain, and in any event those who wanted to get rid of him were clearly doing so for selfish reasons: in a country brimming over with small clandestine revolutionary organizations, they were afraid Nechayev would take over. Lonely, embittered, still dreaming of future conquests, still talking about a revolutionary society which would overthrow the Tsar, Nechayev lived in one garret after another.

One day in the spring of 1872 Nechayev appeared in Zemphyr Arbore-Ralli's house in Zurich. Arbore-Ralli had been one of Nechayev's first associates at St. Petersburg in 1869. He had been arrested in March 1870, after the failure of the first student uprising. Released a few days later, he was arrested again in Kishinev and thrown into the Peter and Paul Fortress, but no evidence of any consequence was brought against him and in October 1871 he was released and sent into exile. By the end of the year he had escaped abroad, and now he was studying quietly, with no particular passion for revolutionary activity. Nechayev's visit surprised him. It was the first time he had seen Nechayev outside Russia. Nechayev asked for shelter, and stayed at the house for a few days. As Arbore-Ralli describes him:

> He had changed a good deal. There he was—thin, of medium height, nervous, biting his nails to the quick, and his eyes were burning and he kept making sharp gestures with his hands. He was not a good talker and he spoke Russian with a broad Vladimir accent. He had still learned no French conversation, though he could somehow explain himself in the language and he read the language with only a little use of the dictionary. All he had when he came was a small handbag and two books—the *Confessions* of Rousseau and the *Mémoires Authentiques* of Robespierre. During his stay with me neither of us spoke about Ivanov. He knew why I said nothing, for it was I who had introduced Ivanov to Uspensky during my stay in Moscow.

Arbore-Ralli had been a friend of Karakozov and an intimate of Nechayev's. He had listened approvingly in the days when Nechayev spoke of "the destruction of those monsters in gleaming uniforms sprinkled with the blood of the people." He had introduced Nechayev to all his friends, but he had learned to regret his admiration for the revolutionary, and after a few days he reminded Nechayev that the police were on his trail. Nechayev made his way to La Chaux-de-Fonds, high up on a plateau in the Jura Mountains, where some anarchists had established cooperative workshops. It was a small town, and according to Prince Peter Kropotkin the least attractive of all Swiss towns, for "there is no vegetation there, and it is open to bitterly cold winds in winter, when the snow lies as deep as in Moscow, and melts and falls again as often as in St. Petersburg." Here Nechayev settled under the name of Linders, working at odd jobs, still resolutely dreaming of revolution. Vladimir Serebrennikov was in London, and some days later Arbore-Ralli received through the mail a mysterious letter from London written on notepaper decorated with the sign of the Ax and "The People's Vengeance" in red ink across the top. Together with the letter were a number of pages in cipher, which Arbore-Ralli was ordered to send to Nechayev. Amused, Arbore-Ralli wrote to Nechayev at La Chaux-de-Fonds and suggested it would be much simpler if Nechayev wrote directly to Serebrennikov: there was no purpose in playing this conspiratorial game of ciphers, and in any event Arbore-Ralli had no desire to act as intermediary. Nechayev had previously begged Arbore-Ralli to come to La Chaux-de-Fonds. The invitation was refused. Unknown to Nechayev, Arbore-Ralli was in touch with Bakunin. Soon an alarmed Bakunin was sending Nechayev urgent warnings to leave the country. Remembering the pamphlet which Bakunin had once composed in defense of Nechayev's right to stay on Swiss soil, Nechayev replied with his accustomed pride: "I too have friends in Berne, and they would have warned me if I was in danger."

The danger was drawing closer. From time to time Nechayev slipped into Zurich. More and more he was coming to see a great hope in the young Polish revolutionaries. He met one of them called Turski, also a refugee, and a member of the Polish Socialist party, at that time containing no more than twenty members. At the head of the party was a certain Adolf Stempkowski, who was the secretary of Greulich, the leader of the Swiss Socialists. He had escaped from Russia after the Polish uprising in 1863. He spoke Russian with a Polish accent, and was well known among the Russian *émigrés* in Switzerland. Like Nechayev, Stempkowski worked as a sign painter. Once long ago he had the reputation of being a stool pigeon, but he worked so hard on behalf of so many revolutionary organizations that he was now in everyone's good graces. Turski arranged a meeting between Stempkowski and Nechayev. For three weeks Nechayev had been receiving urgent warnings from Bakunin to leave Switzerland. "This is no longer 1870," Nechayev answered. "It's only the Bakuninists who want to get me out of the country." In this he was wrong: the Russian police also wanted him, and Stempkowski was their paid agent.

As usual Nechayev had laid his plans deeply. He had discussed at length the possibility of infiltrating into Bakunin's organization. It was Turski's opinion that Stempkowski would be able to provide any information about Bakunin that Nechayev wanted. "He detests Bakunin," Turski said, "but superficially they are on the best possible terms. See him. He will give you all the information you want." Nechayev hurried to the rendezvous in a Zurich restaurant. Stempkowski was all affability. Suddenly he raised his hand, making a beckoning sign, Nechayev thought he was summoning a waiter. Immediately two plain-clothes detectives pounced on Nechayev, removed his revolver and dragged him screaming out of the restaurant. Some Russian and Serbian students were outside the restaurant. Nechayev called to them. There was a brief struggle, and for a few minutes Nechayev was free. The police however were determined to arrest him, and the students were not particularly concerned about Nechayev's fate. "It would have been very easy to have saved Nechayev," a witness said later, "but no one really wanted to. We remembered the murder of Ivanov, and we thought he deserved punishment. We even helped the police to arrest some of Nechayev's would-be rescuers."

A few hours later Nechayev was removed from the Zurich prison and handed over to Russian police officers on the Bavarian frontier. It was August 14, 1872.

The Swiss police officers had acted in good faith. From St. Petersburg there had come an extradition order drawn up with all the proper codicils and an outline of the evidence against "one Sergey Nechayev, student, charged with the murder of Ivan Ivanov, student, on November 24, 1870." The date was wrong, but that was of small consequence to Nechayev as he made his way back to Russia.

A few days after Nechayev's arrest Vladimir Serebrennikov, Nechayev's strange alter ego, appeared at Arbore-Ralli's house. The documents stolen from Bakunin had been preserved intact. Serebrennikov offered to sell them for 400 francs. Hiding his eagerness, Arbore-Ralli bought them and a few days later, with the help of Armand Ross, the seasoned revolutionary who had been Bakunin's secretary for many years, he set about examining the documents. Among them was found the letter in which Bakunin promised to submit himself entirely to Nechayev's will, even if Nechayev should order him to forge banknotes. There was a copy of The Revolutionary Catechism, faithfully copied out in Bakunin's handwriting. There were diaries, letters, manifestoes, cuttings from newspapers with Bakunin's annotations, complete lists of Bakunin's visitors, and a copy of the numerical cipher which Bakunin employed in his correspondence. It was all there, down to the last telegram. Presumably the documents were handed to Bakunin. From this moment they disappear from sight.

With Nechayev under arrest, Bakunin showed himself astonishingly free from bitterness. He had good reason to hate Nechayev. It was not only that Nechayev had repeatedly maligned him, stolen his documents and laughed in his face. There was also the matter of the celebrated letter which Nechayev had written to Karl Marx's publisher. Marx was vengeful, and at the height of his power. He had watched Bakunin's growing popularity within the International with alarm. At the Congress of the International in Basel in 1869 Bakunin had been the figure who stood out among the revolutionaries as the one most likely to capture the International for his own purposes, but in the Congress which took place in London in September 1871 Bakunin was absent and Marx was in full control. He ordered a full inquiry into Bakunin's relations with Nechayev. *The Revolutionary Catechism* was now well known and Marx believed or pretended to believe that it was the work of Bakunin. A certain Utin, who later became a contractor to the Tsarist army during the Turkish war of 1877, was asked to prepare a full record of the Nechayev trial and of Nechayev's relations with Bakunin, and this document was formally presented to the Congress of the International at The Hague the following year. On the insistence of Marx Bakunin was drummed out of the International. Bakunin was deeply perturbed, stung to the quick by "this germano-judaic complot against me." But he refused to express any horror at Nechayev's perfidy, and could think only of the days when Nechayev came to him and he welcomed the boy with open arms. He wrote to Ogaryev in November:

> Some secret voice tells me that Nechayev who is utterly lost and certainly knows it—this Nechayev who is so confused and vitiated—is far from being banal. This time his heart will reveal all his old courage and primitive energy. He will perish like a hero, and this time he will betray no one and nothing.
>
> So I believe, and soon we shall know whether I am right. I do not know what you feel, but for my part I am deeply sorry for him. In all my life no one has done so much harm to me—so much premeditated harm—but I am sorry for him nevertheless. He is a man of rare energy, and when I met him for the first time, his heart was burning with love and compassion for the poor oppressed people of Russia: his soul was stamped with the true suffering of the sickness of our age. Only his outward aspect was unclean; inside he was pure . . .

From the day when Nechayev was handed over to the Russian police, he behaved as Bakunin had prophesied.

THE TIGER CAGED

C APTURED, NECHAYEV was still a force to be reckoned with. Legends hung about his name. The police officers who guarded him and kept him shackled in specially reserved compartments of the train which brought them by a roundabout route through Smolensk to St. Petersburg, and so to the Trubetskoy Bastion of the Fortress of Peter and Paul, wondered at the power of the legend. There was the young revolutionary with the straggly beard and the deep-set eyes, looking no more dangerous than any young Russian student, but at every station it was necessary to send off telegrams to Count Levachov indicating the exact time of arrival and the probable time of departure, and the condition of the prisoner. It was assumed that he would attempt to escape. At every station armed guards were sent to watch over the train. He was not only heavily shackled and fettered, but two policemen were chained to him. At moments amused and tolerant, at other moments wildly facetious and brutally angry, Nechayev watched the policemen with the supercilious air with which he regarded all authority. It was as though he were saying throughout the journey: "All these shackles are quite useless. I shall escape. I possess an idea which is far stronger than your chains." The telegrams sent to Count Levachov are still preserved. We know the exact time to the minute when Nechayev's train passed through the towns on the railway. Finally—and we can almost hear the sigh of relief which went up in government circles in Moscow and St. Petersburg—we know that he was received in the Peter and Paul Fortress at exactly nine o'clock on the morning of October 19, 1872, and that shortly afterward he was interviewed by Count Levachov.

The interview appears to have been brief. The Count was affable. He explained that there might be "a certain mitigation of your fate" if Nechayev gave the Russian government a complete outline of his organization. Nechayev parried, and suggested that he was in a position to make conditions. Among these conditions was a sweeping change in the nature of government authority, with Nechayev himself as "a special adviser."

Nechayev talked for some time about the inevitability of the revolution and hinted at his own commanding position among the revolutionaries. Levachov said afterward that Nechayev's conditions were "brilliant and profitable for him, and very bad for us." After a while Levachov called his bluff and reminded Nechayev that he had been captured in secret, no one knew what had happened to him and he was at the complete mercy of the government. Nechayev answered: "You can take my life away, but not my honor." He was still playing the game of the powerful revolutionary, though he possessed hardly a single disciple. Levachov seems to have been convinced that Nechayev, though not so powerful as he pretended, was still a formidable adversary.

The meeting with Count Levachov took place in a cell in the Trubetskoy Bastion. Count Levachov hinted that Nechayev would be thrown into the Alexis Ravelin unless he cooperated with the government. Nechayev knew that he was being treated with the implacable vengeance reserved for an archenemy of the state.

In his damp cell, lapped by the waters of the Neva, Nechayev waited. He shouted abuse at his guards and ordered them to bring the prison superintendent into his presence, and when the superintendent arrived, Nechayev pointed out that he had been captured illegally; he had abjured his Russian nationality; he was an *émigré* like all the other *émigrés;* and he should be freed unconditionally. He asked for pen and paper, to write a letter to the Tsar. Neither paper nor pen were given to him, and while the prison superintendent took note of all Nechayev's remarks, and full reports on Nechayev's behavior were sent to the Tsar, he remained in the silence and loneliness of his cell.

October passed, and then November, and Nechayev was still alone in his cell, fed three meals a day—the allowance for food was 50 kopecks— and every afternoon he was allowed out of his cell for a short walk while a guard cleaned it. The walls were damp and thick, very dark, and there was a small heavily grilled window eight feet from the floor. An iron bed, an iron table, a commode, a paper-thin woolen coverlet, a Bible, a kerosene lamp which was kept burning all night: nothing else. The food was slops. The damp air brought on asthma. Iron rings, rusted but still immensely strong, were fixed to the walls: to these the prisoners were chained. But more terrible than the privations of the prison was the ghostly autumn mist which penetrated the cells and hung over the high walls, a mist which blocked out the light. And through the mist came the silent warders in their black uniforms, always walking in pairs and under orders never to talk with the prisoners.

In this silent world anything might happen. A man might freeze to death, or be bludgeoned by a warder in the corner of his cell, and no one would know or care. At various times in the past it had been rumored that prisoners had been quietly hanged or poisoned at the whim of the prison governor. But under Alexander II, who desired to know everything that happened in the vast domains of his empire and spent his days brooding over interminable reports, the Peter and Paul Fortress had become a hive of bureaucratic efficiency. Daily reports were sent about each prisoner to the head of the Third Division; many of these were placed on the Tsar's table. Nechayev did not know for certain, though he may have guessed, that an endless stream of reports on his behavior was being sent out from the prison offices. Officials in the highest circles of the land were busily poring over reports and debating his fate.

But what should be done with the prisoner? Should he be killed quietly, without anyone being the wiser? Should he be left to rot inside the Fortress? In an audience with the Tsar, Count Levachov pointed out the advantages of a well-staged public trial: it would help to destroy the legend Nechayev had created around himself and it would intimidate the revolutionaries by showing them they were powerless in the face of the Russian secret police. Accordingly the Tsar agreed to a trial early in the New Year, and at five-thirty on the afternoon of December 22 Nechayev found himself under a police escort, with Major Remer in command, outside the walls of the Peter and Paul Fortress. He had been told only that he would be put on trial in Moscow.

The usual fantastic precautions were taken. Once again he was chained to two police officers, and once again telegraph messages were sent to Count Levachov whenever the train passed through a station. Near Moscow the train was shunted into a siding, and a heavy guard surrounded him as he descended from the train.

The trial opened on January 8 at twelve o'clock, with President Dreyer as the presiding official, a jury, and a court of assessors. It was brief and explosive. Nechayev's attitude to the court was calculated to offend. He hammered away at the greatest weakness in the prosecutor's case—he had been arrested illegally, in a foreign land. He saw himself as the heroic defender of freedom, refused to answer questions, hurled abuse at the prosecutor and defended the killing of Ivanov as "a purely political matter." He played deliberately to the gallery. With his hands thrust in his pockets he glared at the president and shouted: "I do not recognize this court! I am an *émigré!* I do not recognize your emperor or your laws!" Shortly afterward the president ordered him to be removed. As Nechayev marched out, there was sympathetic applause from the gallery, and Dreyer firmly reminded the audience that if there was another outbreak he would order the police to remove them from their seats.

When Dreyer considered that Nechayev had had time to cool his heels, a message was sent to him saying that if he promised to behave he would be allowed to enter the chamber. Nechayev marched back. He had promised nothing. The prosecutor began to ask leading questions. To all these questions Nechayev shouted: "Hurrah for the Zemsky Sobor!" This reference to the States-General established by Peter the Great and then abandoned was calculated to inflame the audience, and once more there were sympathetic murmurs from the audience. Dreyer decided to take the matter in his own hands. He asked Nechayev point-blank whether he regarded himself as guilty of the murder of the student Ivanov. Nechayev answered that he was being tried according to the laws for common criminals, whereas the murder of Ivanov was clearly of a political character. The medical reports read at the trial of the *Nechayevtsi,* with details of how Ivanov had died by bullet wounds, strangulation, and drowning, were now read out again as important parts of the evidence against Nechayev. Nechayev assumed an air of profound indifference. He leaned forward on his elbows, pouted, rolled his eyes at the gallery, pushed out his lips and pulled at his beard. At times he sat with arms akimbo. An observer during the trial described him: "He is about twenty-five, not tall. He wore a black silk jacket, breeches and a dirty waistcoat. Nothing extraordinary about his face—you will see such faces commonly among young dandies. Thick, but not long chestnut-colored hair. Rather narrow, deep-sunken eyes. A thin prickle of hair on his upper lip. His profile is sharply outlined, but when you see him full face the broad forehead makes the face look square and rather vulgar." Evidently he was not a prepossessing person at his trial, but he had no intention of being prepossessing. His aim was to show derision of his judges, and in this he succeeded.

All through the indictment, the reading of the evidence and the cross-examination, Nechayev clowned. He beat time with his left hand, looked vaguely at the public gallery as though he were searching for someone, and then for long periods he would sit quietly, twisting his beard and his thin mustache, forming the hairs into braids, or else smoothing his hair or silently playing an invisible piano on the ledge in front of him with his right hand. When the prosecutor had completed a long speech of denunciation, Nechayev remarked quietly: "It is humiliating to defend myself against such obvious calumnies. All Russia knows that I am a political criminal. I repeat what I have already said to Count Levachov—the government can take my life away, but not my honor!" Then he smote himself on the breast.

For this behavior he was once more dismissed from the court. What happened then is not clear. According to Nechayev he was taken to an empty room and set upon by police officers. The police officers denied beating him, but they may have been so angered by his contempt and impertinence that they could hardly prevent themselves from beating him. Police officers, then as now, regarded the beating of prisoners as a conventional exercise. When Nechayev was again allowed to enter the court he was in a fiery temper and began to denounce the officers. He was silenced by the reading of the verdict. He was sentenced to twenty years in Siberia, and he was dragged from the court, shouting: "Long live the Zemsky Sobor! Down with despotism!"

On the next day in his Moscow prison Nechayev called for paper and ink and wrote a letter to Count Levachov:

Count!

When I was sitting in my cell in the Peter and Paul Fortress, you came to me and asked me to explain the real purposes of my activities. You said that if I told the truth there would be some "mitigation of my fate." At that time I refused to furnish you with any explanations. But now my fate is decided, and the time has come when I think I can partly satisfy your wishes and place the facts in proper perspective. The words of a man condemned to twenty years' imprisonment in Siberia should convey only the desire for the truth—no one should doubt the truth concealed in them. In this letter I propose to give you the information I promised long ago.

In the following, I shall base myself only on facts, but the facts I have in mind have scarcely anything in common with the administrative system as practiced in this uncivilized country. While talking of facts, let me tell you of one fact of considerable importance. Yesterday, in the Hall of Justice, applause broke out. As a result the president decided to throw me out of the chamber. I was dragged into a corridor and then into an empty room, where a police officer began to beat me over the back and legs. The atrocious behavior of the officer was all the more shocking because I never showed any enmity toward him and was always coldly polite and well-mannered. For myself, I do not believe that any government can take pride in the fact that it has these knights of "club law" among its officers. I know that the reforms of three or four years ago were meant to make "club law" impossible . . .

But you asked me about my activities. Count, my fate is decided or almost decided. I shall go to Siberia, and this is why I must speak the truth, and it seems to me that you in your high position deserve only the truth, and nothing else will have any meaning for you. The high government post which you hold gives you the opportunity to see things as they are. And so, putting aside all dreams of Utopia, I urge you to consider that Russia is on the eve of a political revolution. Everywhere the desires straining within society are assuming more radical and more destructive channels: everywhere there are small conspiracies and plots against the overpowering strength of the government, but these small conspiracies can coalesce into large conspiracies, and these in turn to furious revolutions. But I do not want these things to happen. Freedom from above is better than freedom from below. Above all, I believe it is the task of our time to work for constitutional revolutions rather than the bloody revolution which tears down a whole people.

Myself, I am a son of the people! My first and only aim is the happiness and well-being of the people. Here we see Stenka Razin and Pugachev once more ascending the scaffold, as in France they would be ascending the guillotine, and on the other side we see the people being fired on and put to inconceivable suffering. But I know that in the end the people have the power to put the people in power. The task of all men of good will in this stormy age is to avoid that inevitable terror which will come about if the people decide to tear down the thrones of the mighty.

You asked me to describe the purposes of my activities. These are the purposes.

Nechayev signed the letter *"Emigré* Sergey Nechayev, transformed by Mezentsev from a political into a common criminal." Underneath the signature he wrote a postscript: "I shall go to Siberia with the deep assurance that millions of voices will soon be shouting: 'Long live the Zemsky Sobor!'"

The letter is a complex document: many purposes were inextricably woven into it. Nechayev seems to have had considerable regard for Count Levachov and some hope that he might be able to bring about constitutional reforms. Levachov was close to the Emperor. He possessed a singularly brilliant mind, and had treated Nechayev fairly, if distantly. The letter formed an apologia for his own actions and at the same time, since the Count was bound to be informed of Nechayev's behavior at the trial, it demonstrated that Nechayev was in full command of his faculties. By implication Nechayev was saying: "I clowned during the trial, and did so deliberately, to show my contempt for your jurists. But I have a mind that can see clearly, and you should use me as a consultant." As always he was playing for high stakes.

It was the custom when prisoners were sentenced to long years of imprisonment in Siberia to hold a ceremony of public degradation. The authorities doubted whether the ceremony would serve any useful purpose in the case of Nechayev. There was the danger that he might be rescued by the mysterious friends he was always hinting at. There was the very real possibility that a few determined revolutionaries might, if they succeeded in capturing Nechayev, use him as a symbol of resistance against the government. If anything, he had by his contempt of authority during the trial increased his own legendary stature. But by January 20 it had been decided that the government would risk the ceremony of public degradation. On that day Count Shuvalov wrote a memorandum to Prince Dolgoruky, the Governor General of Moscow:

> Although existing laws and regulations must be carried out to the letter, I have the honor to inform you that the daring behavior of the prisoner at his trial demands that the complete observance of the law shall be accompanied by extraordinary measures of security to prevent anyone from recognizing him or helping him to escape.

Nechayev was in prison in the Sustcherskaya district north of the river. Count Shuvalov's memorandum referred to the difficulties of transporting Nechayev from the prison to the Horse Parade south of the river. The Horse Parade was the usual place for the public degradation of prisoners.

It was decided that the ceremony should take place at night, with as few witnesses as possible. Major Remer, Lieutenant Popov, and a sergeant accompanied Nechayev in a closed carriage at eleven o'clock at night for the journey south of the river. The idea of taking Nechayev in a carriage was not a very good one. He made several efforts to escape. At the Horse Parade the carriage was met by a military escort. Alone and fettered, standing under a symbolical gallows, surrounded by a hollow square of soldiers and policemen, Nechayev faced his accusers. His sentence was once more read out to him. Drums rolled. A solemn prayer was read by a priest, for the ceremony involved a kind of symbolical execution and at the end of the ceremony the prisoner was supposed in some mysterious way to have passed out of life altogether, his long exile in Siberia to be accounted no more than a passage to limbo. Usually the prisoners were too awed by the ceremony to make speeches. Nechayev was not awed. While the drums rolled, he shouted at the top of his voice: "The guillotine will soon be standing where I am! It will lop off all your heads! Don't fear, in two or three years your turn will come!" A little later he shouted: "Down with the Tsar! Hurrah for freedom! Long live the Russian people!" When he was being lifted into the carriage he was still shouting: "I am on my way to Siberia! I know millions of people are on my side! Down with despotism! Hurrah for freedom! I am a political prisoner, but I am being treated like a common murderer! I have received no trial—only a mockery of a trial!" Soon afterward his voice was drowned by drums.

Nechayev had every reason to believe he was about to make the long journey to Siberia. From Siberia, however, too many prisoners had escaped. The Tsar ordered him imprisoned in the Alexis Ravelin of the Peter and Paul Fortress.

The journey from Moscow to St. Petersburg was made in secret and by a roundabout route. He left Moscow by train at 8:05 in the morning of January 26. It is possible that an attempt to rescue him was made at the Nikolayevsky Railway Station, but the reports are confused. At Smolensk the following night Major Remer telegraphed the usual report to Count Levachov. A lawyer, passing along the platform, was told by some railwaymen that "the famous conspirator Nechayev" was on the train. The secret therefore was not so well kept as Count Levachov had hoped. The train swung west to Vilna and then to Tsarkoye Selo. At 9:45 on the night of January 28 Nechayev passed through the gates of the Peter and Paul Fortress for the last time. The clothes he wore during the trial were removed from him and he was put into prison garb. The prison records of the Fortress, remarkable for detail, list the clothes taken from him: a hat of lambs' wool, a black cloth coat, a jacket, half boots, thick cloth trousers, waistcoat, shirt, drawers, and a pair of copper shirt studs.

From now on his life was to be a ceaseless fight with the prison. The Tsar, who regarded him as a mortal enemy, had decided to discredit him by annihilating him. For years no word would ever be heard from him. For years no one knew whether he was alive or dead. The Tsar himself sent a message to the military governor of the Fortress: "Put Nechayev discreetly and forever in the Fortress." Many years later, after the Bolsheviks had come to power, there was found the original order written by the governor of the prison, Bogorodetsky. The order is dated January 29, 1873, the day after Nechayev had been admitted into the Fortress. It reads: "I command that Sergey Nechayev, deprived of all rights and imprisoned yesterday under the orders of His Majesty in the Alexis Ravelin, shall be placed in Cell Number 5 in the greatest secrecy and guarded with the greatest vigilance. His name is never to be pronounced, and he is to be known only by the number of his cell."

The achievement of Nechayev had only just begun. He fought a long war against authority even when he was chained in a cell so small that if he stretched out his arms he could touch both sides. From the first he was a nuisance. He asked for books, demanded a retrial, hinted at the powerful forces who were even then determined to rescue him. When Count Levachov suggested he might become an informer, he refused abruptly and turned his back on the Count, just as he had turned his back on President Dreyer at the trial.

By order of the Tsar a weekly bulletin on Nechayev's health, and how he spent his time, was prepared by the prison officials on the basis of daily reports. In these reports the prisoner's name is never mentioned.

On February 9, 1873, the first report was issued:

> The prisoner in cell number 5 of the Alexis Ravelin has from February 2 to February 9 behaved quietly and courteously. He wakes each morning at 7, and has gone to sleep at 9:30 except on February 2 when he woke at 7:45 and went to bed at 11:30. He sleeps well.
>
> During the day he reads the *War Gazette* of 1869, and often walks about the cell, rarely lying on the pallet. Recently he has been behaving more affably than usual, his expression is happier and he is beginning to look people in the eyes where previously he avoided a direct gaze. Previously he answered everyone roughly in a cutting voice, dropping his eyes.

These strange bulletins were prepared until the day Nechayev died. The first two bulletins are known to have been read by the Tsar, and it is probable that Alexander II continued to read them until he was killed by terrorists when returning to the Winter Palace after a review. The first bulletin hints at explosions of temper during the first week of Nechayev's imprisonment. These explosions were rare. From early in February he decided to fight the government with a cool brain and all the weapons at his command. He decided to keep his body and brain active. Though chained, he practiced gymnastics in his cell. He asked for books—the list was endless, and included John Stuart Mill's *Political Economy*, Gervinus' *History of the XIX Century*, Louis Blanc's *History of the French Revolution*, Jules Clarétie's *History of the Revolution of 1870–71*. For some weeks nothing was done. The library of the Alexis Ravelin was not so well served with books as the library of the Trubetskoy Bastion, and there was some doubt whether interlibrary loans were permissible. In the end permission was obtained from Count Shuvalov to let Nechayev read all the books he listed except Louis Blanc's *History of the French Revolution*. Nechayev was not too downcast. He had already read the book in Switzerland.

On the twenty-third of February a second bulletin was sent to the Tsar:

> The prisoner in cell number 5 of the Alexis Ravelin has from February 16 to February 23 behaved quietly. He is now reading the *War Gazette* for the year 1871 and is generally cheerful. Exception is made under the date of February 19, the first day of Lent. Given Lenten food, he remarked: "I have no belief in God and none in Lent. So give me a plateful of soup and some meat, and I'll be satisfied." On February 21 he walked about continually, often lifted his hands to his head, was thoughtful and went to sleep only at 1:30 in the morning.

This bulletin was written by Major Remer, who seems to have been permanently attached to Nechayev.

Nechayev suffered no ill consequences following his refusal to eat a Lenten supper. He announced that he intended to compose a history of the Tsardom, and asked for pen, ink and paper. These were given to him. He began a long war against the stupidity of librarians and asked to be allowed to have a complete library in his cell, saying that it was impossible to compile a worthy history of the Tsardom without a vast number of books. He asked for Robert von Mohl's *Geschichte und Literatur des Staatswissenschaften*, a surprising demand since he knew almost no German. The continual demand for books served a double purpose: it occupied his time, and the reading of the books sharpened his brain: also, he was patiently devising a code formed by making small pencil marks under letters, and in this way hoping to communicate with other prisoners. Many years later, when Olga Natanson was imprisoned in the Fortress, she came upon the penciled code marks. "I knew Nechayev was in the fortress and not in Siberia by the marks he left in the library books." But during the early years of Nechayev's imprisonment no one except the prison officials and the Tsar knew he was there.

Nechayev's plan was simple. He would insert a small wedge, and then see whether he could push it deeper. Already, even in those early months, he was beginning to exert an extraordinary influence over his guards. He would ask them simple questions. They would refuse to reply. But all the time Nechayev was watching them closely. He observed their eyes. He devised questions which they could hardly fail to answer. Once they had spoken to him they were at his mercy. Little by little he was driving the wedge deeper. He used the same tactics with the prison officials in charge of the library. When he saw they were sympathizing with his desire for books, he sprang the trap by asking them to communicate with his sister and fetch "the small library, now in my sister's house, which belonged to me when I was an *émigré.*" He never received these books, but the attempt showed his audacity.

Life in the Fortress continued silently and without change. The prison records say that May 16, 1873, he was transferred to Cell Number 7 for a few days. The official reason was the removal of the double winter windows and their replacement by summer windows. Presumably someone in authority had demanded a thorough search of the prisoner's cell. On October 2 the river rose and the Alexis Ravelin was threatened with flood water. The officials held their breaths. No orders had been received about what should be done to Nechayev if his cell were threatened with flood water. For a few hours, until the following dawn he was removed secretly to the Trubetskoy Bastion. Then the waters subsided, and Nechayev spent the winter alone with his books in his clammy cell.

At some time during the second year of his imprisonment Nechayev shared his cell with a certain Shevich, a former guards officer who had been involved in a scandal at court. The reasons for making Nechayev share his cell are obscure, and nothing is known about Shevich except that he was white-haired, had long been considered insane and had been a prisoner of the Alexis Ravelin for more than twenty years.

Reports on Nechayev's behavior were still being sent to the Tsar and to the head of the Third Division. The report for April 19, 1874, read: "No change has been observed in the prisoner in cell number 5 of the Alexis Ravelin. He behaves very quietly, and spends his time reading and writing." But Nechayev was not quiet. In his own way he was stirring up trouble. By this time he was on good terms with the guards, who were already calling him admiringly "our eagle." By whispers and subtle hints he had conveyed to them that he was an important personage, of royal blood. The guards, remembering the fate of Alexis, half believed him. They slipped food into his cell. Some years later they were to give him a plan of the Fortress and send messages out for him, but in these early years he was still the young tiger calculating how to force a passage through the bars and he had not yet learned that the simplest way was to force the keeper to unbolt the gate.

The years passed slowly. The ferocious revolutionary ferment which was to arise in Russia in the late seventies had already begun. The movement known as "To the people" was spreading like an epidemic, and in 1873 was in full progress. All over Russia young college students were working in villages and factories, disguised as laborers and farmers. They forged passports, scattered revolutionary pamphlets and spoke in quiet, educated voices of putting the court and the government into the hands of the executioners. They modeled themselves on the young Rakhmetov, the hero of Chernyshevsky's *What Is To Be Done?* who lived the pure ascetic life and subjected himself to intense privations as a preparation for revolutionary activity. Young doctors appeared mysteriously in obscure villages, saying they had come to serve the people. They demanded no payment. They modeled themselves on the portrait of Bazarov in Turgenev's *Fathers and Sons,* which had appeared in 1862, though they disputed many of Turgenev's judgments. They disputed in particular Turgenev's statement that the nihilist "refuses to bow down to authority, and will never accept any principle of faith, however much that principle may be revered," claiming that they had faith in the people, and that was enough. Soon the small group of convinced terrorists known as the Narodnaya Volya ("the People's Will") would hurl itself in single combat against the powers of the government. Meanwhile there were daily arrests and the prisons were filling with young students. Throughout Russia the revolutionary ferment was increasing. Ironically, Nechayev knew nothing about it.

In the third year of Nechayev's imprisonment a strange incident occurred. As usual, he was behaving quietly, immersed in his books. Suddenly the door of his cell was flung open and he was confronted with General Potapov, chief of the Corps of the Gendarmerie. The general had come with a renewed offer to Nechayev: if he would outline all the ramifications of his conspiratorial activity and serve the Third Division as a spy, he would be given his freedom. Nechayev was incensed. He struck the general fiercely across the face, drawing blood. The guards hurled themselves on Nechayev in time to prevent a second blow. Bleeding from the mouth and nose, Potapov left the cell. Nechayev himself recorded later that he received no punishment for his attack on the general.

This incident occurred in January 1875. Six months later, in July, the prison governor, alarmed by the increasing revolutionary activity in Russia, had a long interview with Nechayev. In the course of the interview Nechayev offered to write a detailed letter to the Tsar outlining the measures he thought necessary to bring the revolutionary activity to an end. A letter to the Tsar, supposed to have been written by Nechayev at this time, has come down to us, but it is written in a style so unlike his usual style that it appears to be a forgery. But on January 30, 1876, Nechayev did write a letter, which he addressed to "His Imperial Majesty Alexander Nikolayevich, Lord and Emperor of the Russian People," and there is not the slightest doubt of its authenticity. It is a long letter, written in the familiar hard, unrelenting style. He begins with the assertion that he has been arrested illegally and imprisoned without trial, and goes on to accuse the Tsar of deliberate duplicity. He asks why he has never been told "the conditions agreed upon with the Swiss government, by which I, the émigré Sergey Nechayev, was handed over to the judgment of the Russian court." He goes over the familiar ground. He remembers that he was removed from a prison in Zurich at night, unexpectedly and without warning, and was not aware he was to be handed over to the Russian police until he had crossed the frontier and was greeted by Police Inspector Sevastyansky. All the old griefs are set out. Once again he refers to the murder of Ivanov as a purely political crime. Why should he be sentenced to perpetual imprisonment? He has done nothing worthy of the punishment. He has offered repeatedly to help His Imperial Majesty to put an end to the revolutionary ferment in the country. The Tsar must realize the unforgivable nature of his crime. Nechayev demanded an immediate trial as a political prisoner and hinted that if this was not brought about he would shake the throne of the Tsar of All the Russias to its foundations.

With this letter Nechayev sealed his own fate. The long honeymoon was over. The Tsar read the letter. On February 7 he summoned the head of the Third Division to his presence, and gave orders for condign punishment. Two days later there was a meeting of the prison officials to inquire how the orders should be carried out. On February 14, while Nechayev was making his usual daily walk in the prison garden, guards rushed into his cell, searched it thoroughly and removed all the writing material and all the books. When he returned to the empty cell, he was told that the books and paper had been removed as a punishment. He stared hard at the bare walls and said in a clear voice: "Very well." The bulletin issued at the end of the week goes on to say: "He was strangely quiet during the rest of the afternoon, but at four o'clock he began to scream." Four o'clock is the time when darkness falls over St. Petersburg in February.

As a further punishment he was made to wear the fetters on his wrists which he had been allowed to discard when writing.

For nearly two years he felt the full force of the Emperor's vengeance. Though he was eventually allowed to read again, all writing materials were refused him. Now more than ever he came to resemble the old, shaggy ferryman in Tolstoy's *Resurrection* who lived on the bank of a Siberian river and who was so angry at all things and all men that he refused to bear a name, to recognize any authority, or to bow to any man.

The long fight for books and paper and a modicum of freedom had been lost. The years had aged him. His face was lined, and he suffered from prison pallor. His name was still dreaded, and there were still prison officials who trembled in his presence. But the young tiger suffered from fits of shivering, and at night he could be heard singing, in a cracked voice, strange melancholy songs. He slept badly. Some thought his mind was already unhinged. But he had the courage of despair, and gradually he began to exert authority over the guards. He was not defeated yet. He had still seven years to live, and in the course of those seven years he was to exert a strange, invisible power over the prison and over the revolutionaries of Russia.

THE SHAKING OF THE BARS

I F IT WERE desired to reduce a man to nothingness," wrote Dostoyevsky in *The House of the Dead,* "it would be necessary only to give his work a character of uselessness." In the gray twilight of his cell Nechayev was slowly dying of the disease of uselessness. Once a day a guard entered and silently removed the drawer of the commode; three times a day he was handed food through the bars; the bells of the cathedral chimed every day with terrible regularity; every day there was the dull boom of the noon gun and every midnight the bells in the cathedral spire chimed "God save the Tsar." And so it would go on until the day when the guards would find him lying dead in a corner of his cell.

From the beginning Nechayev had decided to fight back, but there was little strength left in him. The skin at his wrists and ankles was suppurating. His face had the pale-blue color of prisoners who have been long buried in their cells. His lips quivered uncontrollably. Everything in the cell, the narrow iron bed, the brick stove, the commode, even his own body, was chained or bolted to the walls; he had become no more than an extension of the cell. Yet he was determined to fight on. At the first sign of government weakness, he would pit all his remaining strength against his enemies. He was waiting for a momentary accident, a moment of in-attention when the warders were occupied elsewhere, but this moment was long in coming.

It was the misfortune of Nechayev that he represented in the eyes of the autocracy all the mysterious forces which were known by the name of terrorism. Alone, with only his cunning to guide him, he had inaugu-rated a secret society with ramifications through all strata of society. That the secret society had no further existence after Nechayev's arrest seems never to have occurred to the Tsar's ministers: they suspected its influence everywhere, and every new outbreak of terrorism was attributed indirectly to Nechayev.

But his greatest misfortune was that the years of his imprisonment co-incided with a remarkable resurgence of revolutionary activity in Russia, and while the revolutionary activity was at its height, he could neither hope for redress nor exert his power over the movement. The years 1876–1879 marked the culmination of vast and carefully contrived outbreaks of terrorism. Bakunin died in July 1876. He had never enjoyed a very great influence in Russia. He belonged to an age when revolutionists thought the battle could be waged by inflammatory manifestoes alone. Now the time of the scientists and the engineers of revolution had come: the key-word was organization, and among the revolutionaries were the most knowledgeable experts on high explosives. Instead of Nechayev with his *Revolutionary Catechism* and his strange power over young students were men like Zhelyabov and Kibalchich, both experts in the use of explosives, the one a superb organizer, the other the possessor of one of the finest sci-entific brains then known in Russia. Now for the first time it began to seem possible that the Tsar might be overthrown. His whole palace might be blown up, his train hurled off the railway lines, his lines of communi-cation and his very existence at the mercy of the revolutionaries who planned his destruction coldly, poring over maps and timetables and books of analytic chemistry. The romantic period was over, or nearly over, for there were still a few revolutionaries prepared to employ Nechayev's methods: conspiracy, bluff, intimidation, the threat of vast peasant up-risings. Such a threat was employed in 1875 by Yakov Stepanovich, who took the name of Dmitry Naida and secretly showed the peasants a Golden Charter printed in gold letters on satin, and ostensibly signed by the Tsar. The charter purported to be an appeal by the Tsar to his faithful peasantry, urging them to kill their landlords and live in an anarchist para-dise. For some months peasants in the Chirigin and Cherkassy districts swore to follow the Tsar's precepts, but the movement came to an end when a drunken peasant revealed the whole story to a soldier.

For a government on the defensive the behavior of young students who went about educating the peasants was more worrying. In 1876 and 1877 the police arrested more than a thousand of these students, keeping them in jail over long periods. Finally in September 1877 a public trial of 193 students was held, all that were left after the winnowing process had been carried out. Eighty prisoners had died in jail, while others had committed suicide. All the 193 were regarded by the police as dangerous revolutionaries.

The trial, which lasted until January 1878, was conducted with intense bitterness on both sides. The defense pointed to the sickly faces of the accused, who had been starved in prison. They recalled the names of the prisoners who had died under arrest. They listed the crimes of the autocracy and went over to the offensive. In the eyes of the revolutionaries the hero of the trial was Ippolit Myshkin, the son of a noncommissioned officer, arrested for a bold attempt to rescue the philosopher Chernyshevsky from his prison in Siberia. "This court," Myshkin shouted, "is worse than a brothel where girls sell their bodies to earn a living! Here are senators who out of cowardice and servility, and the hope of promotion and decorations, sell other people's lives, sell truth and justice to the highest bidder—" In the crowded courtroom the president's bell was continually ringing for silence. When the trial ended the autocracy had lost again. Only ninety-four of the prisoners were sentenced, mostly to short terms of imprisonment. The Tsar was infuriated by the obstinacy of the jury in bringing in such verdicts. In his memorials and in the annotations he wrote on the margins of police reports he described the revolutionaries as "ridiculous," "headstrong," "men without character or principles." He seems never to have understood that they were intelligent, ruthless, and determined people, and he continued to place in positions of authority men who were completely incapable of dealing with the problem.

Among these was a certain General Trepov, the Chief of Police in St. Petersburg. The singer Chaliapin, who came to know him well, has described him as a dandy who scented himself, wore immaculate gold-braided uniforms, continually twirled a small blond mustache and behaved with studied brutality at all times. He was handsome, widely interested in the arts, and seemed unaware that his face was pitted with smallpox. He had a habit of inspecting prisons and houses of detention. At these places he allowed his brutality free play. Encountering a political prisoner called Bogolubov, Trepov ordered him to remove his hat. Bogolubov refused. Trepov was incensed, rushed at the prisoner, gave him a blow across the face and demanded an apology, and when the prisoner refused, ordered him to be beaten with birch rods.

Such incidents had happened frequently, and the revolutionaries were powerless to prevent them. This time it was agreed that General Trepov must be punished. Various groups of revolutionaries discussed methods of punishing him, but it was the young revolutionary Vera Zasulich, then living under police surveillance in a village near Moscow, who decided to take the matter in her own hands. She hurried to the Gendarmerie. On the excuse that she wanted to present a petition, she was allowed into the general's office. There she whipped out a revolver and shot him. He was severely wounded, but recovered in time for the trial. The Emperor had suggested that it would be dangerous to hold the trial in public. Count Pahlen replied that her guilt was undeniable, and in any event she had confessed to the crime and the jury could hardly contravene her evidence. The Emperor seems to have been satisfied with the reply and made no further attempt to interfere in the trial.

Vera Zasulich was defended by one of the best advocates of the time. Once again the defense went over to the offensive. Not Vera Zasulich but General Trepov was being tried. The defense listed the general's crimes, spoke of the young girl's idealism and defended the revolutionaries against the police. Against all the evidence, the jury brought in a verdict of Not Guilty. There was wild applause, and the judge had no alternative but to order her release. While Vera Zasulich was being mobbed in the corridors of the court, General Trepov signed an order for her immediate rearrest. He was too late. The crowd surged round her. She was lifted into a carriage driven by a young artillery officer, Sidoratsky. Suddenly a shot rang out. Sidoratsky fell dead. In the confusion Vera Zasulich slipped out of the carriage and was carried through the crowd to safety. A week later she was on her way to Switzerland.

The Tsar was incensed, but there was little he could do. Immediately after the attempt on Trepov's life, he summoned General Mezentsev, Chief of the Political Police of the Empire, and discussed methods of dealing with the terrorists. It was Mezentsev who suggested that the sentences imposed on the convicted prisoners in the Trial of the 193 be severely increased. Mezentsev also suggested that crimes against the state be dealt with by summary courts. There was provocation enough. Arrests continued all summer. Mezentsev sent telegrams to all the governors urging the implacable punishment of all revolutionaries. At nine o'clock in the morning of August 4 General Mezentsev, accompanied only by an aide, was walking through one of the main streets of St. Petersburg when a fast carriage pulled up beside him. Out of it leaped a former artillery officer, Sergey Kravchinsky, with a naked sword in his hand. He killed Mezentsev and then jumped back into the carriage, having left the sword firmly embedded in the general's body. The carriage was being driven by the fastest horse in St. Petersburg. Kravchinsky escaped into hiding, and soon afterward disappeared from the country. On the same day there was printed a pamphlet composed by Kravchinsky under the title *A Death for a Death*. In the pamphlet he explained at great length why he had killed Mezentsev, set out the general's crimes, and detailed the consequences if the government determined upon revenge. "Our aim," said this remarkable pamphlet, "is the destruction of the existing economic structure and the removal of social injustice." Under the name of Stepnyak, Kravchinsky continued his revolutionary activity from abroad.

The killing of Mezentsev by Kravchinsky was the turning point. Henceforth the revolutionary movement in Russia was to become increasingly violent and to move closer to Nechayev's conception of what a revolution ought to be.

Nechayev was still guarded closely. The small empire which he wielded over the guards, the secret meetings with high officials, his studied insolence and his furious determination, all those hidden resources which he guarded as he guarded over his own sanity had led him nowhere. He was so much a prisoner of the Tsar that he was unable to smuggle a single letter out of the Fortress.

How well the Alexis Ravelin was shut off from the outside world can be seen from the testimony of Tolstoy. In 1878 he applied to the governor for permission to visit the Ravelin where a distant relative, Prince Volkonsky, a prominent Decembrist, had been imprisoned many years before. The governor offered to show him all over the Fortress: all, except the Alexis Ravelin. "You must understand the terribly stringent rules which have been laid down for the Ravelin," explained Baron Maidel. "There are only three people who are allowed to enter the Ravelin and leave it alive: they are the Emperor, the Chief of the Gendarmerie, and myself." Tolstoy was puzzled. He had served under Baron Maidel in the Crimea. He could see no real reason why his innocent request should be refused. "It is the order of the Emperor," said the Baron. "No prisoner shall ever leave it alive."

Later, these rules were apparently changed. A prisoner who went mad was removed to an insane asylum. A few—a very few—prisoners were allowed to leave the Ravelin for Siberia later, when the Fortress was jammed with prisoners following the wave of revolutionary unrest in the eighties. But until the spring of 1879 rigorous laws were still applied to the Fortress: and when the laws were changed, it was only because the government had no alternative.

That spring, an unprecedented number of new prisoners entered the Fortress. They were the prisoners whom General Drenteln, the new Chief of the Third Division, regarded as too dangerous or too important to be sent into ordinary prisons. The Fortress officials accepted the new prisoners with ill grace. "We will have to take them, but we do not want to take them," Baron Maidel wrote to the Minister of the Interior. With this new influx, it was no longer possible to put prisoners into isolation cells, for the only way in which men could be isolated in the Fortress was by placing them in cells surrounded by two empty cells. Originally, Nechayev had been placed in a cell which had one empty cell beside it, the other being occupied by a madman. Soon it would be necessary to put other prisoners close to him. Meanwhile the prison guards, overworked by the presence of increasing numbers of prisoners, silently rebelled. And when in April 1879 the young revolutionary Solovyev shot at the Tsar outside the Winter Palace, sending the Tsar running to the shelter of the nearest doorway, running not in a straight line but in zigzags, avoiding death by a singular display of acrobatics, the guards brought the news to Nechayev, who appeared strangely unmoved.

"I've told you a hundred times that it would happen," Nechayev told the guards. "I myself belong to the Party of the Succession. I cannot tell you what position I hold in the society, but it is an extremely high one. Solovyev was one of our recruits. Remember, the Party of the Succession will eventually come to power. Make no mistake, there will be many more attempts against the Tsar by the party, of which I have the honor of being a member."

Nechayev's Party of the Succession was as nebulous as all the other political parties he had fathered, and considerably more aristocratic, for among its members he included many Grand Dukes and some ministers of the government. In the name of the party Nechayev promised high rewards to the guards who helped him. They would learn in time that he had been fighting for them, not for himself. All those wasted years he had been trying to reach out to them, and now at last they were beginning to treat him far more seriously, their new-found trust in him mingled with a sense of guilt because they had not sufficiently helped him in the past. It was only when he claimed partial responsibility for Solovyev's attempt on the Tsar that they began to fear "our eagle." "I have been suffering here without ever having committed a crime," he told them. "I have worked only for the peasants, for you and your fathers. I tell you, there will be a revolution, an end to the Tsardom. It will happen as it happened in France. We will take the land from the landowners. The factories will belong to the nation." Once more he hinted that he was a prince of the royal house. Since no one knew his real name and he was always referred to as "the well-known state prisoner," and since many princes and counts had been imprisoned in the Alexis Ravelin, the guards hardly dared to dispute his claim.

Toward the end of the year the revolutionaries attempted to derail the imperial train on the Moscow-Kursk railway. Once again Nechayev took credit for the deed. He prophesied that very shortly the whole of the Tsar's family would perish. There was evidence that the revolutionary movement was gaining impetus. For the revolutionaries 1879 was a good year. Early that year Prince Dmitry Kropotkin, Governor General of Kharkov, a cousin of the anarchist Prince Peter Kropotkin, was shot and killed as he left the theater. On April 25, a month later, an attempt was made on General Drenteln, the Chief of the Third Division. On August 26 the Executive Committee of the Narodnaya Volya formally condemned Alexander II to death. Martial law was declared through all European Russia, unlimited discretionary powers were given to the governors general, and exile by administrative process was for the first time authorized by the Tsar. But the vast powers placed in the hands of the police were often misused, and the stupidity of the police was equaled by the cunning of the revolutionaries. One of their most cunning and most adroit plans concerned an attempt to blow up the Winter Palace itself.

In the autumn of 1879 a young peasant, Stepan Nikolayevich Khalturin, was working as a carpenter in the Winter Palace. He was a joiner and polisher, had been employed in several St. Petersburg factories and was an excellent workman; he was also a member of the Executive Committee of the Narodnaya Volya. He had founded the Northern Workers' Union. When the union was crushed, Khalturin vowed vengeance upon the Tsar, and sought the permission of the Executive Committee to enter the palace as a common workman. Gradually he would accumulate singlehanded a sufficient store of dynamite to blow up the palace. All he needed was the dynamite, which he stored under his pillow in his sleeping quarters in the cellar. Though heavy guards were placed at the entrance to the palace, there were no guards at the gate through which the workmen and servants entered. Accordingly, he accumulated a large store of dynamite. The problem was then to discover when the Tsar would be in the palace dining room—it was decided to fire the dynamite when the royal family was sitting down to dinner. Khalturin pretended to be weak in the head. He was always scratching his neck and asking innocent questions and was a great favorite among the other workmen and the guards who occasionally visited the cellar.

In November 1879 the police arrested a revolutionary, discovering on him a plan of the palace in which the dining room was marked with an ominous red cross. A detachment of soldiers was thereupon sent to search the palace. Khalturin showed coolness during the search. His luggage was examined, but none of the soldiers thought to look under his pillow. A post of gendarmerie was established permanently in the cellar. Khalturin went about his work as usual, and was particularly admired by the corporal of gendarmes, a man called Petrotsky. He continued to pick his nose, scratch at his neck and tell droll pointless stories. He played the part so well that Petrotsky one day brought his daughter to the cellar and explained to Khalturin that she would make an admirable match. Khalturin laughed slyly. "I'm just a peasant," he said. "I just don't know what I'd do with her." Everyone laughed. A few days later the Tsar himself passed through the cellar on a quick tour of inspection. Khalturin remarked bitterly: "I'd have killed him if I'd had a hammer handy." One day Khalturin had a long discussion on the subject of terrorism with Petrotsky. They were two or three feet away from the hidden store of dynamite. "I'm just a stupid peasant," Khalturin said. "All this talk about terrorists—I don't understand. Tell me, please, what does a terrorist look like?" Petrotsky laughed: "Oh, they're easy to recognize—desperate-looking fellows with wild eyes! You can tell them at once!" Suffering from migraine headaches which came from the fumes of dynamite under his pillow, Khalturin took immense pains with his plan, and until long afterward no one suspected him; and he failed in his purpose by a hairbreadth. He had every reason to believe that the Tsar was in the dining room when he exploded the dynamite. In fact the Tsar had been delayed by an audience with Prince Alexander of Hesse, and he was just about to leave for the dining room when the dynamite exploded. It was twenty minutes past six o'clock on a dull February evening. All the lights went out. There were screams in the dark. For half an hour it was believed throughout St. Petersburg that the Tsar was dead within the ruins. But the royal family had escaped. The explosion killed ten soldiers, wounded thirty-three more, and injured twenty-three civilians. The floor of the dining room was wrecked and all the windows were broken. The next day there appeared all over St. Petersburg placards announcing that the Executive Committee of the Narodnaya Volya regretted the deaths and injuries of the soldiers and civilians but took entire responsibility for the attack. The Executive Committee promised to continue a relentless struggle with the dynasty, until social reforms were carried through. Khalturin himself escaped to Rumania. Two years later, in March 1882, he returned to Russia, killed General Strelnikov in the streets of Odessa, was arrested on the spot and was executed a few days later.

The explosion in the Winter Palace filled Nechayev with renewed hope. He told the guards: "We have failed this time. Watch out! The next time we shall succeed!"

Of all the years which Nechayev spent in prison, the year 1880 was the happiest. Once more his influence was being felt among the guards. An immense hope welled in him. The explosion in the Winter Palace had led, as the revolutionaries had hoped, to an effort of reconciliation by the Tsar. Exactly a week after the explosion Loris-Melikov, a convinced liberal, was given semidictatorial powers, and for a brief period there was instituted a "dictatorship of the heart." The revolutionaries took full advantage of the new government's weakness and pursued their attacks relentlessly.

Meanwhile in prison the battle of the books went on. The policy of the prison governor changed with each passing month. There would be weeks in which Nechayev would be allowed to read only journals, other weeks in which all the resources of the prison libraries were thrown open to him. If he was found to have written messages in code, the books would stop. With innocent eyes, Nechayev would ask why he received no books, and the prison governor was in no position to offer explanations to his most insolent prisoner. One day at the end of March 1880, Nechayev, after his daily walk in the prison garden, returned to his cell to discover that once more all his books had been removed, with the exception of a single issue of the *Official Journal*. He was outraged, summoned the guards, demanded his books and wept when they explained that they were helpless in the matter—the order had come direct from the prison governor. Nechayev waited a few days, then one night he carved a letter to the Tsar with a broken teaspoon on the walls of his cell. To make the letters stand out more clearly, he filled them with his own blood. The letter read:

> To His Imperial Majesty, Lord and Emperor,
> Alexander Nikolayevich.
> Your Majesty!
> At the end of my eighth year of solitary confinement, the Third Division, without any provocation whatsoever on my part, has deprived me of my last means of exercising my mind—the reading of new books and journals. Not even General Mezentsev, who tore me to pieces with a flogging two years ago, dared to deprive me of this occupation. Evidently the Third Division is determined that I should spend my days in a state of debilitating idleness. Evidently they have determined to destroy my mind by inactivity. My strength has declined during many years of suffering in prison. I believe they are firmly of the opinion that they can drive me down the road of madness or suicide.
> I have no desire to share the fearful fate of my unhappy neighbor in the prison, whose insane screaming gives me no peace at night.
> I have the honor to inform Your Majesty that the Third Division of the Imperial Chancellery may deprive me of my mind only by depriving me of my life: not otherwise.
>
> Palm Sunday, 1880
> S. Nechayev

According to the prison records he was still complaining that he received no journals on July 21, but by the end of July the stream of books opened up again, and until the following year when it was decided to let him rot to death he was allowed to read as he pleased. This was the year when he came to maturity, swiftly extending his influence. His guards presented him with a plan of the prison fortress and smuggled notebooks, paper, maps, and forbidden journals into his cell. Except for the freedom which he desired above all things, he needed only the presence of a revolutionary companion to make him happy; and in November even this gift was given to him.

Stepan Grigorievich Shirayev was originally a peasant from Saratov. He had studied at the Saratov gymnasium, and spent two years studying veterinary science at Kharkov. In 1876 he emigrated, and worked as a smith in Paris and London. Returning to Russia, he joined the Narodnaya Volya and became a member of its Executive Committee. Because of his expert mechanical knowledge he was one of the conspirators chosen for the task of setting mines under the Moscow-Kursk railway over which the imperial train was due to pass. The mines failed to explode. Arrested on December 4, 1879, he was brought to trial only in October of the following year. He was condemned to death, but the Tsar commuted the penalty to imprisonment for life. On November 10 Shirayev was thrown into Cell Number 13 of the Alexis Ravelin.

Nechayev was overjoyed. Letters were passed between their cells. For the first time Nechayev learned the details of the revolutionary organization of the Narodnaya Volya. Here at last was a revolutionary party he could respect. He learned that the members of the party had the utmost admiration for him and would listen to any advice he gave them. They exchanged secrets. Nechayev broached the most cherished of all his plans: a plan to take over the Peter and Paul Fortress on the day when the imperial family attended a service at the Cathedral. Then the Tsar would be captured and the successor proclaimed. Shirayev was skeptical, but he offered to submit the idea to the Executive Committee if any means could be discovered to send messages outside the Fortress. On this subject Nechayev was an expert. There were now enough guards in his power, and he arranged with a certain Andrey Orekhov, one of the prison warders, that a letter written by Nechayev should be smuggled outside the Fortress and given to a certain Dubrovin, who lived nearby. Dubrovin, like Shirayev, came from Saratov. He was a revolutionary who belonged to the Chorny Peredyel party, worked on the periphery of the revolutionary movement, and was prepared to risk his neck for Nechayev. The message sent to Dubrovin was given to Grigory Isayev, a member of the Executive Committee of the Narodnaya Volya. The effect was electric.

Vera Figner has told in her memoirs the extraordinary impression produced by the letter. One evening in January, 1881, she was sitting in her apartment in the Voznesensky Prospect, waiting for Isayev. It was a time of terrible strain among the revolutionary organizations, because an attempt on the life of the Tsar had been planned, the police were already suspicious, and few of the revolutionaries thought they would survive the attempt. There were two other members of the Executive Committee with Vera Figner. It was ten o'clock. Suddenly Isayev burst into the room, his coat covered with snow. He placed a thin sheaf of papers on the table and said quietly, as though it were a matter of no importance at all: "A message from Nechayev—from the Ravelin."

"Are you sure?" Vera Figner asked.

"Yes, quite sure," Isayev nodded, and then there was a long awkward silence. It was as though the redoubtable Nechayev, the most legendary of revolutionaries, had sprung into the room beside them.

Vera Figner was stunned. At twenty-nine she was an experienced revolutionary. She had grown up with the revolutionary movement, and knew all the active revolutionaries of her time, but she had never set eyes on Nechayev, who belonged to the generation immediately before her own. She had read the interminable accounts of his trial, and bitterly regretted the death of Ivanov. In 1872 she left Russia for Switzerland, and she was in Zurich at the time when Nechayev was arrested by the Swiss police. She knew a good deal about Serebrennikov and many of Nechayev's friends. Serebrennikov, indeed, had been her favorite, and she remembered how he had been arrested and was later released, when a watchman from the Andreyevsky Academy declared that Serebrennikov did not in the least resemble Nechayev. But in Switzerland Nechayev seems to have had almost no connection with the Russian émigré students at the University: he belonged to the past and was almost forgotten. And now he had suddenly emerged from the grave. Spirited back to Russia, he had disappeared so completely that no one knew where he was imprisoned or whether he was still alive.

In silence the revolutionaries read Nechayev's long letter. As usual he wrote crisply, in a businesslike way. He wrote as "a revolutionary removed from the main stream of the revolution should write to the comrades who are still in freedom." He spoke of his overmastering desire to escape from the Fortress, and he talked succinctly about the way the revolution had immeasurably broadened its base since his arrest. Listening to Nechayev's letter, Vera Figner was aware of a sense of guilt. She had hated him in the past. Now it seemed to her that all the dark stains in Nechayev's character could be explained and washed away. The blackmail, the extortions, the murder of an innocent man, all these could now be explained as deliberate inventions by his enemies. Above all, he showed himself resolute, determined to help the members of the Narodnaya Volya and the possessor of a fantastically pure revolutionary imagination.

More letters came. In these letters Nechayev revealed what had happened to him during the long years of his imprisonment. He had fought off despair. Hands and feet chained, living in a dark cell alone, he had succeeded at last in exerting his influence over his jailers. He told how he had examined minutely the character of every soldier and warder who was brought into contact with him. "I observe incessantly, notice everything and store my memories." He was full of praise for the work of the Narodnaya Volya. He spoke of how the prison authorities had offered him his freedom if he turned informer, and how he was flogged and placed in solitary confinement when he refused. He said he had only one desire: freedom to work for the Executive Committee.

If Nechayev had written the letter a few weeks earlier the subsequent history of Russia would have been different. At this moment the Executive Committee was immersed in a plan to assassinate the Tsar. To attempt to liberate Nechayev from the prison would involve a complete change of plan. There is a story that the Executive Committee wrote to Nechayev and offered to abandon the attempt to assassinate the Tsar and instead concentrate on efforts to release him. The story, though sometimes denied, may well be true, for there exists a long letter from Nechayev to the Committee in which he outlines two methods by which he could escape: one method involved a long pipe which would somehow be thrust through the soft earth under the Fortress, coming out into the open in the small garden where Nechayev took his daily walks. Down this pipe Nechayev would slide to freedom. It was a wonderful, fantastic and probably impractical idea. The second method involved the large-scale bribing of the officers and guards at the Fortress. There survives a letter from Nechayev which says: "Forget about me for a time and go about your own affairs. I shall watch from afar with the deepest interest."

But this was only the last of a long series of letters in which Nechayev exhorted his revolutionary comrades to deeds of daring and resource. Andrey Zhelyabov, a stern, patient, and superbly gifted executive, dealt with the correspondence. Nechayev formed an excellent opinion of Zhelyabov's capacities, and at one time suggested that Zhelyabov should become the revolutionary dictator. His old impudence and joy in life returned. He suggested that the Narodnaya Volya should distribute millions of copies of a false proclamation, ostensibly from the Tsar:

> We, Alexander II, Emperor and Autocrat of All the Russias, Tsar of Poland, Duke of Finland, etc. etc. on the counsel of Our Most Beloved Consort, Her Imperial Majesty the Tsarina, and also at the entreaty of the Princes and Grand Dukes, etc. etc. and in consequence of the repeated requests of the entire Nobility, have thought it fitting to return the peasants to serfdom, to prolong the period of military service, and to overthrow the houses of prayer of the Old Believers etc. etc.

This proclamation was never issued. Undeterred, Nechayev sketched out a secret *ukaz* ostensibly from the Holy Synod, to be issued after the assassination of Alexander II:

> Almighty God having seen fit to put Russia to this supreme trial, we have the misfortune, O Brethren, to inform you that the new Tsar, Alexander III, suffers from a confusion of the mind and no longer comprehends affairs of State. Therefore the loyal clergy are in duty bound to offer secret prayers at the altar for his miraculous return to health; and let none of you confide this secret to anyone.

These letters were smuggled out through soldiers, prison guards, and servants employed in the Fortress. In return the Narodnaya Volya sent him long coded letters, money, even food. He was not always pleased with the letters from the Executive Committee and occasionally complained against their tone. "Do not thank me for any compliments I may have written," he wrote. "The success of your organization cannot spring from a bourgeois conscientiousness. Our enemies will grow fat on it. By being scrupulous, you will make your task more difficult. It may even cost you hundreds and thousands of deaths."

In time the messengers from the Fortress came in direct contact with the revolutionaries. They did not of course know them by name; but they knew "the dark one," "the red-haired one," "the one who is broad and fat, wears a little black beard and has his lips turned up at the corners." About a hundred letters were exchanged in a period of a little more than two months. Then the blow fell.

On March 1 Grinevitsky hurled the bomb which killed Alexander II. A few days previously Zhelyabov, who had organized and planned all the complex aspects of the assassination, was himself arrested. On him there was found 25 rubles, five copies of the newspaper of the Narodnaya Volya, and a number of letters in code written by Nechayev. On March 10 a further windfall came into the hands of the police—more letters and a list of names, pseudonyms and addresses, found in the possession of the revolutionary Sophie Perovskaya. The code names were easily translated: Andrey Orekhov became Petukh, a certain Shtiklov became Shtulov. The conspiracy within the Peter and Paul Fortress was soon scotched, and to add to Nechayev's miseries Baron Maidel, the governor of the Fortress, died. In his place there was appointed the stern and sharp-featured General Ganetsky, the hero of Plevna.

On the day when the news of the assassination of Alexander II reached the Fortress, Nechayev addressed his guards: "Now you see I was speaking the truth. We have killed him. I was the first to warn you. I told you the Tsar would be killed if he did nothing for the peasants."

It was almost the last act of the outrageous drama which Nechayev had been playing. From now on he could hope for no mercy, and no mercy was ever shown to him. Slowly, impenitently, fighting tooth and nail almost to the last breath, mocking his accusers and certain of his revolutionary vindication, of the triumph of his desperate desires, he went down to his death.

THE TIGER DIES

Throughout the spring and early summer of 1881 the Tsarist police worked as they had never worked before. Implacable in their determination to root out the terrorists, they made wholesale arrests and winnowed out their prisoners at their leisure. The "dictatorship of the heart" had been proved a failure. By May 11, Loris-Melikov had resigned. In his place there came the more forceful Count Ignatiev. The power behind the throne was the Procurator of the Holy Synod, Konstantin Pobedonostsev, who hoped "to drown the revolution in Jewish blood." "I will force one third of the Jews to become Christians, another third I shall force to emigrate, and I shall see that the remaining third starves to death." It was as though Hitler and all his legions were alive on Russian earth.

At some time between March 20, when Baron Maidel died, and July 19, when Adjutant General Ivan Stepanovich Ganetsky sent a strange letter to Plehve, the recently appointed Chief of the Gendarmerie, Ganetsky for the first time visited the Alexis Ravelin and addressed his prisoners. He was seventy years old, but his voice was strong and vibrant. He had in his possession the evidence proving that Nechayev had suborned the guards; and he was determined that there should be no repetition of the offense. The speech he made as he stood at the great iron door leading into the casement was directed mainly at Nechayev. He threatened dire punishment for any infraction of the regulations. Nechayev, his nerves at breaking point, subsequently wrote a complaining letter to the Tsar:

Sovereign!
    The new commandant Ganetsky, immediately after his assumption of power over the Fortress, made a speech to the prisoners in the Ravelin con-

cerning the events of March 1. The character of his speech and all the circumstances surrounding it were entirely improper. The speech was not delivered in a room specially prepared, but in the corridor and not far from the casemate door. The speech, which was spoken in a thundering voice, was chiefly destined for my ears—this was quite clear from the contents. It was delivered in such a way that I heard every word clearly. This intimidating speech failed in its aim. The oblique threats made by General Ganetsky did not terrify me; on the contrary they showed me that under the pressure of recent events, the officers of the administration are going out of their minds; and having lost their wits, they are in process of losing their dignity.

The Alexis Ravelin is a secret prison—no inspectors ever penetrate here. Formerly there were abuses, such as one might expect in a prison remote from the world. The late commandant, the respected Baron Maidel tolerated the swine warder Philimonov, but while fulfilling his austere duty, the Baron set his face against allowing the prisoners to be tortured. Now, after hearing Ganetsky's speech, this swine of a Philimonov shamelessly snatches away our last morsels of hope and declares that he is doing this in accordance with instructions received from the commandant. I have therefore begged the commandant that I should be fed from the guards' canteen with coarse tea and porridge—in spite of the inadequacy of such meals, they would be altogether preferable to the meals from the precious store supplied by Philimonov!

All those who are in any way employed in the Ravelin are now of the opinion that they can oppress the political prisoners to their hearts' content. Since the arrival of the new commandant the guards have become impertinent and provocative. The time allowed me for exercise has been reduced from two hours to twenty minutes. Worse still, for a whole month I have not been allowed out of this stifling casemate. Ganetsky has even ordered the ventilation passages to be closed. Apparently his purpose is to prevent me from making ink out of the soot. The glass in my high window was clean in the old days: through this glass I could see a little space of sky. What terrors assail the heart of a prisoner alone in his cell, condemned to perpetual imprisonment, deprived of the consolation of watching the clouds in their progress and the gleaming of the stars at night.

Two commandants: General Korsakov and Baron Maidel, six chiefs of gendarmes beginning with Count Shuvalov and ending with General Cherevin, and President of the Supreme Council of Ministers Loris-Melikov—all these have visited me, and all these have seen the clean windowpane, and not one of them was of the opinion that a clean windowpane threatened the safety of the state, and it is a fact that I . . .* under investigation over many weeks and months. But I was not a prisoner "under investigation," and it is now ten years since I was first deprived of my liberty: the burden of watching over me apparently involves no high political principles, but being completely arbitrary and impersonal has been entrusted to the prison authorities.

I had one personal enemy—General Mezentsev. He kept me in chains for two years, but he did not shut out my view of the sky. I had another enemy —General Potapov, whose face I once struck. He had the right to hate me, but he took no revenge on me. He knew well enough that to take revenge on a man deprived of his freedom is to have the soul of a beast. General Pota-

---

* Some words are indecipherable in the manuscript.

pov behaved like a man. I do not know whether General Ganetsky possesses any of those feelings which are properly called human, but I do know—judging by his visit to the Ravelin and how he stood for an hour by the casemate door and gazed approvingly upon the misery of the prisoners through a crack—that he finds a good deal of satisfaction in contemplating the suffering of others, and this is a satisfaction which can hardly be called human. Of course he has no desire to hurl me into an abyss of despair. He sees the tears and torments and the baffled rage of the prisoners, and no doubt he listens to the wild screams of frenzy which come from my poor companion in misery imprisoned in the casemate beside mine, a poor devil sentenced to solitary confinement to the point of madness. Oh no! I gave Ganetsky no satisfaction —he did not see me in tears. I want him to live on, and when the time comes for him to be dragged to the scaffold, we shall see whether he shows a hundredth part of my own peace of mind, my own self-control.

In the year 1875 I wrote a detailed letter to the highest authority in the land, in which I demonstrated to your august father that Absolutism had had its day. I said that the foundations of an absolute monarchy were shattered beyond recall. Only by granting a Constitution can our ruler save Russia from the horrors of revolution. I said it was necessary to introduce without delay a liberal representative system, and unless this was done, there would be no way of avoiding internal unrest, and there would continue to be insolent attempts on his life by men prepared to suffer nothing to come in their way. I said that in a few years it may be too late. The turn of recent events has only confirmed my prophecy. The reaction after the catastrophe of March 1 was inevitable. It was in the order of things . . . but the scale of the reaction and the way it has been prolonged will inevitably result in oppressions, and these oppressions in turn will further endanger the rule of the people who think they can govern the country.

I am a victim of a gross injustice. I was placed on trial in Moscow, deprived of all my fundamental juridical rights. They not only did not allow me to choose defending counsel, but they refused to furnish me with copies of the evidence taken in open court. I was not informed of the charges. Sentenced to twenty years' imprisonment on the basis of unproven accusations hurled at me by the prosecutor—accusations which are clearly against all the evidence, as everyone in Russia knows—I was denied the right of appeal. Further, I was deprived of every possibility of exercising my rights, for they gave me no copy of the judgment and refused to give me ink and paper so that I could complain to the proper quarters. I was taken in the depths of the night from the scaffold and then by roundabout ways, traveling halfway across Russia, to the Peter and Paul Fortress. There I was buried alive, placed in solitary confinement, deprived of everything. I do not expect the new governor to lighten my woes, and I would not be surprised if this letter made everything worse.

Louis XVI only understood the terrible sufferings of prisoners when he was himself given over to the mercy of the Bastille.

Nowhere in the world are administrative officials so strict as they are in Russia; nowhere else are those who govern more shamelessly determined upon vengeance.

Without shame, I have accounted it my duty to acquaint Your Majesty with the conditions of my life in prison. The utmost punishment has been inflicted on me in the name of Your Majesty. But is this Your Majesty's true desire? I shall suffer all these privations willingly, if I could know that this was the intent of Your Majesty's imperial purpose. But to be a victim of Your Majesty's will and to be deprived of humanity and to be silent . . .

I am at the end of my tether. Written in blood, with a nail.

This was the last letter Nechayev wrote to the Tsar, and probably the last that he ever wrote. With its hesitations and ambiguities, its desperate pleadings, the fierce hammering on single themes, it shows Nechayev at his best—and his worst. As he recalls the injuries inflicted on him, the hurts are magnified, and there are swift changes of perspective, sudden alterations of mood, immense gaps. His mind, slowly eaten away by the corrosive poisons of loneliness and the bafflement of a man who once had power within his grasp, pleads insistently: so does his body: but the pleadings turn in different directions and recoil upon themselves. At the very end he demonstrates his most secret desire: some recognition by Majesty. But it was the peculiar privilege of the Tsar that he could be more powerful when he was silent than when he spoke, and in the long-drawn history of Nechayev's imprisonment nothing is so remarkable as the prisoner's determination to be heard in a void of silence, and the Tsar's determination to use silence as his most formidable weapon.

A copy of Nechayev's letter, written in lampblack, reached Ganetsky, who was a soldier and therefore was not likely to have any sympathy for Nechayev's diatribes against the Tsar. Only two things in the letter concerned him, as prison governor—the fact that Nechayev was able to write at all, and Nechayev's accusations against the quality of the food. On July 19, 1881, Ganetsky sent a copy of the letter with a covering note to Plehve. Presumably no one had warned him not to mention the prisoner's name: for the first time in years a communication from the prison boldly avoided the familiar words, "the prisoner in Cell Number 5." Ganetsky wrote:

> Prisoner Sergey Nechayev, who has been deprived of all rights and is kept in the Alexis Ravelin, has been found writing a complaint to His Majesty. The writing is in lampblack which would appear to be mixed with kerosene.
>
> I am enclosing a copy of the document for Your Excellency's attention, and I have the honor to inform you that Nechayev is in the highest degree unstable, rude, and insolent to all those who have official dealings with him. His pretense at finding the food unsatisfactory merits no attention whatsoever. I can testify personally to the great care which is taken in the Alexis Ravelin for keeping the food fresh, and that it is of the highest quality . . .

It is unlikely that Ganetsky wrote with his tongue in his cheek. Well-intentioned, an excellent officer who had earned the affection of his men in the battles against the Turks, he occasionally visited the prison kitchens, tasted the food and was always remarking on its high quality. If the Tsar ever read the letter, he would have smiled contentedly. It had taken a good many years, but at last they had Nechayev where they wanted him: squirming, begging for mercy, insolent as always, but with the knowledge of eventual defeat written in every line of the monstrous and wonderful letter. There was no abject surrender, but then no one had ever hoped to see Nechayev surrendering abjectly. The long processes of expiation were beginning to bear fruit; and those who were watching Nechayev carefully from the shadows could reflect that a *mea culpa* would soon be heard from the remote cell in the Alexis Ravelin. They could have killed him. Instead they demanded an interminable act of expiation; and for them the importance of Nechayev's letter must have resided in the knowledge that Nechayev was perfectly aware what was demanded of him.

Suffering from scurvy and dropsy, his lungs choked by the foul air of the Ravelin, his mind the prey of doubts and sudden paralyzing dreams of grandeur, Nechayev was slowly losing the one thing he valued more than his physical body—his will power. At the beginning of the year he had the guards at his mercy and was corresponding freely with friends outside the prison. By midsummer he was saying: "I am at the end of my tether." He was closer to the end than he could ever have suspected.

In the heat of the St. Petersburg summer the obscure madman Beidemann, who had kept Nechayev awake on so many nights, was removed from his cell. Beidemann had been regarded as a harmless eccentric who suffered from nothing more serious than prison fever, but at last he was seen to be quite mad, and on July 3 Ganetsky gave orders for him to be removed to an asylum.

The relief which followed Beidemann's removal was followed immediately by the shock of Shirayev's death. Shirayev was in Cell Number 13, and Nechayev had maintained contact with him through the prison guards. Dr. Gavril Wilms, the prison doctor, announced Shirayev's death in his usual dry and unilluminating manner. He wrote in his report of August 18, 1881:

> The prisoner suffered during the spring from a light catarrh complicated by occasional hemorrhages. In spite of the medical assistance given to him, there appeared signs of tuberculosis in the left lung at the beginning of July. He died at six o'clock this morning.

Dr. Wilms had no particular incentive for keeping the prisoner alive, and seems to have botched his work. He was sixty years old, stoop-shouldered, "gray as the moon and dry as a stick." Polivanov said of him that "there was something in his manner and his voice so repulsive and impertinent that he was entirely unlike anything you expected to see in a doctor." The death of Shirayev was a blow to Nechayev, for it cut at the roots of his communications with the outside world, and it was some time before he was able to announce to the Narodnaya Volya the passing of one of their chief lieutenants. Later the Narodnaya Volya announced that Shirayev died in September, and it is possible that Nechayev himself did not know the exact date of Shirayev's death.

Into Shirayev's cell came the prisoner Leon Filippovich Mirsky, and with his coming Nechayev's fate was sealed.

Mirsky was the pure amateur of revolution, where Nechayev was the ardent professional. On March 13, 1879, Chief of Gendarmerie Drenteln was driving through the streets of St. Petersburg. He was Mezentsev's successor as chief of the Third Division. Mikhailov, the revolutionary leader of the Narodnaya Volya, had selected him as a proper target for the revolutionaries, and was arranging for his execution when Mirsky, the twenty-year-old son of a Polish nobleman, riding a beautiful white racehorse, suddenly took it into his head to kill the chief of the gendarmerie himself. He followed the general's carriage, fired several shots through the window and then made off. The general was wounded, but gave orders for the driver to give chase. When his white horse stumbled and fell, Mirsky with superb presence of mind simply beckoned to a policeman and said: "My good man, this horse is hurt; just look after it while I go and get the groom." Then he took a droshky, went straight to Mikhailov's hiding-place and announced with an air of bravura: "I have just killed Drenteln, and now, my dear fellow, have the kindness to inform my mistress where I am hiding."

Mikhailov was shocked, but there was little he could do. Drenteln had not been killed. The attack had been bungled. Worse still, Mirsky, an aristocrat to the finger tips, had attacked the general out of bravado. Mirsky's mistress, Elena Kestelmann, who went by the name of Lilia de Chateaubriand, was informed, brought to Mikhailov's hiding place and immediately went into hysterics. Mirsky was still wearing the impeccable riding clothes which he always wore on horseback, and seemed not in the least perturbed by the trouble he had caused. He was perfectly prepared to ask Mikhailov to produce another horse from Tattershall's, and then he would ride back to his own home and perhaps kill another policeman on the way. With great difficulty Mikhailov succeeded in convincing him that he must go into hiding. He slipped out of the city, and made his way to Taganrog.

Meanwhile, Elena, who was bearing his child, was being closely watched, and Mikhailov had to change his hiding place. A good number of St. Petersburg women, who regarded the morning ill spent if they had not been able to observe through their lorgnettes the familiar young nobleman riding past, wept into lace handkerchiefs. The revolutionaries cursed in silence. They tried to make him go abroad, but he refused; and some months later he was arrested. The house where he was staying was surrounded; he tried to fight his way out, was wounded, arrested, and placed on trial.

In the courtroom he wore a black morning coat and white tie. He was contemptuous of legal assistance, smiled impassively and was courteous to everyone. He admitted the crime. The newspapers reported that "he presented a very gentlemanly appearance," and there was a gasp of horror in the court when he was sentenced to death.

But Mirsky was not hanged. Instead he was taken to the Peter and Paul Fortress. The trial at the military court had lasted two days. Within three days Drenteln was being asked whether he thought the prisoner could be used in a manner "suitable to the advantage of the government," and within a month it was decided to remove Mirsky from the Trubetskoy Bastion where he was originally placed to the Alexis Ravelin. It was explained to him that as an officer and as a loyal subject of the Tsar he could serve his country by reporting on the prisoners. Mirsky agreed, and at half past two in the morning of November 28 he was taken to Cell Number 1. On the same day General Schmidt who was temporarily in charge of the Third Division, wrote two reports: one to the Tsar saying that Mirsky had been taken to the Ravelin, the other for the files saying that he was being sent that night to Siberia.

As a stool pigeon Mirsky was incompetent. No information of value was received from him until the early autumn of 1881 when the police, having checked through the mysterious documents in cipher found in the possession of Sophie Perovskaya at the time of her arrest, came to the conclusion that they represented the code names of the guards in the Peter and Paul Fortress. They realized at last that Nechayev had been communicating with the outside world. Mirsky was informed. He was ordered to report any conversations between Nechayev and his guards, and he was also asked his opinion about the meaning of the code words. Nechayev, who had previously taken a sharp dislike to Mirsky, now began to talk with him openly. By December the police were in complete possession of all the information they wanted. The guards were put on trial. Nechayev himself was removed to Cell Number 1, and fed on bread, water, and a little soup. Except for one last appeal to the prison governor, nothing more was ever heard from him.

The prolonged trial of the guards revealed Nechayev's secret power in the prison. An astonished governor learned that half the warders in the Fortress were in some way implicated in efforts to free Nechayev, or to carry messages for him, or to bring him recruits. Four officers and thirty-five warders were involved. All were summarily punished, and sent to Siberia.

Of the last year of Nechayev's life almost nothing is known. Chained to the wall, never allowed out of the cell, his tongue turning black, suffering from scurvy, he was left to rot. The scurvy may have been the worst. The Fortress was full of prisoners who had been arrested in the roundups following the attack on the Tsar in March: these prisoners clamored for sugar, lemons, and milk in the hope of warding off the scurvy. Ganetsky inspected the prisoners and came to the conclusion that something had to be done, and we have full records of the number of lemons and the number of bottles of milk bought for the prisoners in the Alexis Ravelin during this time. In July 1882 thirty-one lemons were bought, and sixteen bottles of milk. In August there were thirty lemons and thirty-eight bottles of milk. In September the bottles of milk shot up to 108, but in November only fifteen lemons were bought. Nechayev's scurvy was so bad that Dr. Wilms ordered for him a half bottle of milk and half a lemon every day.

On June 1, 1882, Ganetsky wrote to Plehve:

> The prisoner in Cell Number 1 in the Alexis Ravelin, formerly held in Cell Number 5, has requested a Bible and the presence of a spiritual counselor. I regarded this as a strange development, for the prisoner has never previously shown the slightest desire for instruction in the true faith.

Plehve replied that neither the Bible nor a spiritual adviser should be given to Nechayev. He knew the risks. Somehow, by means that Plehve could only suspect, Nechayev would use the paper of the Bible for writing messages and the priest for distributing them. From this time nothing more was ever heard of Nechayev. His punishment was now absolute: no books, no light, no air. He was to be left severely alone; no one must talk to him, while his body slowly decayed, with festering sores at the ankles and wrists.

On November 21, 1882, Dr. Wilms stepped into the quiet cell, having been summoned by an astonished warder. Nechayev was lying dead in a corner. Dr. Wilms made a brief examination, and wrote on official notepaper his usual brief report:

> I have the honor to inform you that the prisoner in Cell Number 1 in the Alexis Ravelin died in the morning of November 21 around 2 o'clock. His death was caused by dropsy complicated by scurvy.

In such simple terms did Dr. Wilms sign the death certificate of the man who had put terror into the heart of the Tsar. Ganetsky, who could hardly believe the news, came to examine the body. It was certainly Nechayev, but no one who had known him during his revolutionary days would have recognized him. He was swollen monstrously, as people swell when they

are starving, and his skin was a strange blue color. Ganetsky gave orders
for the chains to be knocked off and then dispatched a message to Plehve,
informing him of the death and asking for orders. Plehve decreed that the
body of "the well-known prisoner" (he did not mention the name) should
be buried secretly in the dead of night, and that all his clothes and possessions should be burned.

That night, at one o'clock, Nechayev's body was taken from the Fortress
to the Preobrazhensky railway station and removed to an unknown burial
ground. On the same night there was a bonfire of Nechayev's effects. These
consisted of a pair of trousers, a fur cap, a short fur coat, a summer coat
and a summer jacket, a warm flannel shirt, a pair of drawers, a cravat, a
bowler hat, chamois gloves, mittens, a pair of woolen stockings, one pair
of half boots, and two handkerchiefs.

It was exactly twelve years to the day since the murder of Ivanov.

The secret of Nechayev's death was well kept. For some months already
the revolutionaries thought he was dead. When in March 1882 Alexander
Mikhailov and Morozov were thrown into the Fortress, they made inquiries about Nechayev, but though he was then only a few yards away
from them, they could learn nothing. They assumed that he was dead already. It was rumored that he had been taken to Schlüsselburg and murdered on the way, and for years afterward it was believed that he had
been hanged in the corner of his cell. There were circumstantial stories
about how Ganetsky had given him poison, and other stories about how
Nechayev had beaten his brains out against the walls of his cell. The secret
was kept until 1917, when the Social Revolutionaries who had inherited
many of the qualities of the revolutionaries of the Narodnaya Volya,
opened the records of the secret police. Then for the first time it became
known that Nechayev had died in a way no one had suspected—of starvation.

Nechayev was the most obstinate, the most astute in attracting legends
to his name, and the most potentially dangerous of the revolutionaries
who fell into the net of the Tsarist police. Others were to follow—Zhelyabov, Sazonov, Kaliayev, a hundred thousand more. Slowly, patiently, often
with immense courage and resource, they sapped away at the foundations
of the Tsarist state. None of them ever guessed that the followers of Karl
Marx and Engels would inherit the state they were attempting to overthrow. In the year of Nechayev's death, the members of the Executive
Committee imprisoned in the Peter and Paul Fortress smuggled out a
message to the people of Russia. Called *From the Dead to the Living* the
letter repudiated the violence of the early revolutionaries:

> Brothers and sisters, we are sending you from our graves what may be
> our last greeting, our testament. On the day of our triumph do not soil the

glory of the revolution with any acts of cruelty or brutality against the vanquished foe. May our unhappy fate not only be the price of Russian freedom, but may it also serve to bring about a more peaceful and more humane society. We salute our country, we salute all mankind.

This letter, written in the same month that Nechayev was calling for a Bible and a spiritual counselor, was signed by Morozov, Isayev, Alexander Mikhailov, Kolotkevich, Kletochnikov, Aronchik, and Trigoni. They are names now, and few people are concerned with them. They were survivors of a small revolutionary group which changed the course of Russian history, for they brought about the death of the Tsar Alexander II and were indirectly responsible for the tormented years of reaction which followed. The acknowledged leader of this group was Andrey Zhelyabov, who once said of Nechayev: "He was the greatest of them all." Lenin said of Nechayev: "People completely forget he possessed unique organizational talent, an ability to establish the special techniques of conspiratorial work everywhere, an ability to give his thoughts such startling formulations that they were forever imprinted on one's memory."

ZHELYABOV

History moves too slowly. It needs a push.

THE REBELS

EVERYTHING IN Russia will one day end in a dreadful uprising, and the autocracy will fall in ruins because so many people are crying out against the Tsar."

The words were written by the Hanoverian ambassador shortly after Peter the Great tortured the Tsarevich Alexis to death in the Peter and Paul Fortress, but they might have been written at almost any epoch in Russian history. The fear of a dreadful peasant uprising was deeply rooted in the autocracy; so too was the fear of assassination, though the Tsars usually died in their beds. Alexander II was the first Tsar to fall at the hands of an assassin coming out of the people, his murder planned and directed by Andrey Zhelyabov, the son of a peasant.

No one ever looked less like a peasant than Zhelyabov. The long face with the wide arching brow resembled the intellectual. Tall, well-built, with rosy cheeks and lively blue-green eyes, he could be taken for a doctor or a lawyer, or even for a professor. When he had money, he dressed well. He was proud of his long dark curly beard, his fine hands, his ability to mix well and inspire devotion. He was riddled with ambition, and was rarely humble for long. Women adored him, and the blue-blooded Sophie Perovskaya, the daughter of a governor general of St. Petersburg, became his mistress and seemed to recognize in him something of her own aristocratic sensibility. Magnificently virile, contemptuous of weakness, strangely impersonal so that often we have the impression of a man watching himself in the hope of detecting his own flaws, he was, as Lenin said, "the true mechanic of revolution and one who never lost his nerve." Vera

245

Figner spoke of him as "our leader and tribune," and it is clear that he dominated the Executive Committee which pronounced sentence of death on the Emperor and on high officials. Others detected an aristocratic note of casualness in him. The young terrorist Rysakov said he was "completely fascinated" by Zhelyabov's presence, the quick mind, the sense that Zhelyabov was standing at the hub of history. The blue-green eyes, the richness of his voice, the way he would sometimes in the middle of a long discussion start roaring like a schoolboy, reminding everyone not to be too serious while remaining himself deadly serious, his habit of stroking his long beard or passing his hands over his hair, his extraordinary composure at moments of crisis—all these things were remembered afterward with affection and gratitude. Nechayev was called "the eagle": always remote, always strangely condescending, so that even when he was drawing up plans for destroying half of Russia he seemed to be conferring a favor. Zhelyabov was called "Taras" after the swashbuckling hero of Gogol's *Taras Bulba*. The name fitted him, though he had little talent for swashbuckling. He was heroic and larger than life; a rich sap flowed in his veins; he knew what he was doing. In all this he was singularly different from Nechayev who seemed so often to be at the mercy of his obsessions.

Zhelyabov was born in 1850, the son of serfs, at Sultanovka in the Crimea. At the age of four he was sent to live with his grandparents. His grandmother, who was born a free Cossack, taught him Cossack songs. He never forgot the songs and would sing them in a clear, deep baritone, even when the police were on his track and he had to be asked to keep silent for fear that the police would recognize his voice. He was proud of his Cossack blood; and the memory of the great revolts of Stenka Razin and Pugachev burned in him. He learned to read at an unusually early age, and fell in love with Pushkin's poetry, especially the rich, gilded poem called "Golden Fish." From his grandfather, a sectarian, he learned to read Church script. Then for a while his father's master took an interest in him, taught him and then sent him as a boarder to a school in Kerch in the Crimea. Tall and thin, quick-tempered—he was always getting into scrapes —he developed a passion for reading, and was counted an unusually good scholar: he was good enough to receive the school's Silver Medal, and with this he was entitled to entry into the civil service. If he wanted to, he could go on to the University with a small scholarship—the first wave of reform under Alexander II had produced a sudden need for educated men, and it was beginning to be considered both by rich merchants and by the landed aristocracy that the endowment of scholarships was a proper tax on income. Zhelyabov received a bursary amounting to 30 rubles a month from the estate of a certain Lududaki. He had been born a serf; he had spent part of his childhood as a groom on the estate of his father's master; and he was now well on his way to becoming an educated man.

All accounts of those early days speak of his gaiety. His friend Chudkovsky described him as "above medium height, with rosy cheeks, large smiling eyes which are extraordinarily expressive, and with black wavy hair." The veteran revolutionary Breshkovskaya remembered him as "tall and rosy-cheeked, with large lively ever-gay eyes," the possessor of "a vigorous figure and beautiful face, radiant with happiness." His eyes, which were described as being the color of the Black Sea, meaning that they were a luminous blue-green, seemed sometimes to be lit by interior fires. He danced well, but a little too vehemently. He had a passion for riding the swings in the public park and liked to make the complete circle, forcing the swing up until he was sailing high above the crossbar. And even his poverty—for the small scholarship was hardly more than the wage of an unskilled laborer—was something to be dismissed with a smile. Wherever he went he was perfectly at ease, and he gave the impression of a man who took a dancing delight in life.

Zhelyabov left the Kerch gymnasium in June 1869 and entered the law school of the Novorossisk University at Odessa with the fall semester. It was a brand-new university founded only four years before, while the city itself was new and gleaming: it had been founded by Catherine II in 1794. With its port and naval base and great gardens, it was growing faster than any other city in the Empire, overflowing with the Greeks, Jews, and Armenians who came to make their fortunes.

We know very little about his life at the University. Though he had only one suit, he never complained of poverty. Poverty was something that an ex-serf could expect according to the nature of things. He seems to have been free with his money, and occasionally gave lessons. He took his meals at the *Kuhmisterka,* the canteen provided for young students at the University where meals could be bought at cost price or less. We know that he spent the long vacation of 1870 as a tutor to a rich family near Simbirsk on the Volga. If he received any salary, he must have spent it shortly after returning to the University, for the University records note that in October 1870 he was excused from paying attendance fees on the grounds of poverty, and a little while later he received from the University authorities a special grant of 350 rubles from a fund founded by the same Lududaki who had originally granted him a scholarship. He was well-behaved in classes, and he was constantly being praised for his diligence in his studies.

The year 1871 was unusually exciting for Russian students in Odessa. It was the year of the Paris Commune, the trial of the *Nechayevtsi,* and of Count Dmitry Tolstoy's educational reforms. It was also the year when American grain competition was felt for the first time, resulting in a decrease of grain exports and a general lowering of the standard of living in Odessa, which had become by this time the fourth-largest city in Russia. The effect of the grain competition was a disastrous pogrom, in which the shops of Jewish merchants were looted and burned. Zhelyabov, as a Cossack, seems to have had no sympathy for the Jews, though he took no part in the pogroms.

Count Tolstoy's educational reforms were based upon an attempt to eradicate all revolutionary tendencies in the schools and colleges. Discipline was to be stricter. New curricula were announced, with an emphasis on the classics, Latin and Greek. Such dangerous subjects as history, Russian literature, geography, and the natural sciences were severely curtailed. The inevitable result of the new laws imposed by the Minister of Public Instruction was to send floods of students to the universities abroad, where learning was encouraged and Latin and Greek were not prescribed as a kind of mental hygiene. And throughout Russia young revolutionaries now began to hold secret classes in the courses which Count Tolstoy regarded with such horror.

With the help of three friends, Zaslavsky, Zhelyesnak, and Goldstein, Zhelyabov decided to ignore the new law and opened a secret college for girls. The girls adored him and flocked to his lectures on Russian literature; other students lectured on physics, geometry, and arithmetic. Zhelyabov was acquiring a talent for oratory and a passion for reciting poetry. He would recite Pushkin's poem "Winter" or a translation of Hood's "Song of the Shirt," and afterward explain the social implications of the poems—the desperate winters faced by Russian peasants, the miseries of factory life, though he knew nothing about factory life and there are no desperate winters in Odessa. It was the time when the movement to the people was at its height, and there was nothing particularly outstanding in Zhelyabov's determination to educate a number of middle-class girls. Later he was to acquire some experience of the real "To the people" movement. Dressed as a peasant, he worked sixteen hours a day on a farm, while attempting to instill revolutionary principles in the peasants' minds. It was an unsatisfactory experience. "From the moment they wake up to the moment they go to sleep not a single thought ever enters their heads," he complained. "All they have is their zoological instincts. You can't do anything with the peasants: we shall have to rely on the industrial proletariat."

With the illegal school thriving and his own legal studies progressing normally, Zhelyabov could look forward to a pleasant career as a lawyer known for his slight radical tendencies. He might have remained a lawyer all his life if it had not been for a professor with the unlikely name of Valtazar Vlassievich Bogishich.

Professor Bogishich was a Czech who spoke Russian badly and suffered from an unruly temper. He was nervous. He had only recently come to the University. He disliked the informality of Russians and preferred the staid formality of the Austrian universities. Professor Bogishich saw the student Avram Baer lounging on his bench and shouted: "Do you think you are in a tavern? If you can't behave better, get out!" The student attempted an explanation and a muttered apology. Bogishich thought he was being impudent or misunderstood what the student was saying, and suddenly screamed: "Get out! Silence! Get out!" Then Bogishich came down from the podium and pushed the student out of the lecture hall. Some students thought they saw the professor kick the student, but there is some doubt about this. After a brief delay the professor returned to the podium and continued the lecture.

The matter might quite easily have ended there. Bogishich was not disliked. Professors have been known to flare into sudden tempers, only to apologize at the end of the lecture. But when the students came to talk about the matter afterward they decided they had good cause to punish Bogishich. He had used too much force and he had used the word *kabak*, which implied a low-class tavern, rather than the less vulgar word *traktir*. Also, he had failed to offer any apology. The appropriate punishment followed. Four days later, on October 20, when Bogishich was due to deliver his next lecture, there were no students in the classroom, but the corridors were crowded. Students hissed, whistled, and whispered comments on his behavior, as he passed by them. Bogishich was outraged and sought the advice of the vice-rector, who offered to meet with the students the following day. Expecting to find only the students who had attended the professor's class, the vice-rector was surprised to find a mass meeting. He called for representatives from among the students to discuss the matter. Zhelyabov, who had never attended any of Bogishich's lectures, was one of the delegates. There was a conference with the rector, which Bogishich was invited to attend. The professor bore no grudge; the representatives of the students were conciliatory; it was believed that with a simple apology the whole matter would pass over.

On Saturday, October 23, Bogishich's classroom was well attended, but there was no sign of the professor. Thinking it over, he had come to the conclusion that he would lose too much face by making an apology. The students were in an uproar. Someone began singing a bawdy song. Bogishich had made two mistakes: he had failed to keep his promise given to the student representatives; he had also failed to understand the student temper. There were shouts: "Bogishich, resign!" The matter was getting out of hand. The students refused to return to classes unless an apology by Bogishich was forthcoming. The rector ordered the immediate convocation of the University Council. The derisive shouts and songs of the students could be heard during the conference. Nervous professors began to imagine there would soon be riots. It was agreed that the ringleaders must be put on trial before the University court and an expression of profound regret should be sent by the faculty to the injured professor. The faculty members wrote a memorandum to Count Dmitry Tolstoy, who deliberately misread their liberal protestations and telegraphed:

> Am in entire agreement with the University Council. Request Governor General take strictest measures to put swift end to disorders. Expelled students to be banished immediately from Odessa.
>
> COUNT TOLSTOY

With the blessing of the Governor General and the Minister of Public Instruction, the rector decided upon a full investigation. The examination of witnesses lasted a week. The evidence of Zhelyabov and more than fifty others was heard, and soon the punishments were handed down—one student was expelled for a year, though allowed to continue his education elsewhere, and two others including Zhelyabov were expelled without the possibility of continuing their education. Colonel Knoop, the head of the Third Division in Odessa, thought the punishments too severe. He regarded the students as innocent and blamed the professor, saying that Bogishich was deliberately making a mountain out of a molehill. A certain Professor Sechenev announced boldly: "Professor Bogishich is the single cause of all our present disturbances." But the verdict of the rector was final, and on November 11 Zhelyabov was arrested and placed on a ship sailing for Kerch. A crowd of admirers came down to the docks, waving flags, singing songs, loudly protesting Zhelyabov's innocence. About this time, feeling that the whole affair had gone beyond the bounds of reason, Bogishich himself tendered his resignation, and it is possible that the matter might have ended there if it were not from the very beginning evident that Count Tolstoy wanted an excuse to put the students in their place. Floods of telegrams were exchanged between Odessa and Moscow. Bureaucrats sitting nearly a thousand miles away were passing judgment on matters about which they knew nothing. Against his will Colonel Knoop was ordered to see that the decisions taken in Moscow were rigorously carried out; and when the police learned on November 15 that Bogishich had accepted a post at Warsaw University, they ordered him to remain at Odessa. A weary Bogishich resumed his lectures on November 17, and the incident was closed.

Zhelyabov had learned his lesson: anyone who stands up against established authority must be prepared to pay for the crime. He was not particularly bitter. At the last moment the vice-rector had summoned him into his office and offered to let him resume his studies in the following year. The vice-rector had not however taken account of the authorities in Moscow, and when Zhelyabov applied for re-entry on the following September, Moscow played a Jesuitical trick. Zhelyabov had been banished for a year. He could therefore not return to the University until November, and it was clearly impossible for a student to enter the University so late in the scholastic year. Thereupon Zhelyabov gave up the struggle, and made no more effort to enter a university.

At the age of twenty-two he had few qualifications for earning a living. He had studied Latin, French, and German in the Kerch Alexandrovsky Gymnasium; he had read widely in Russian literature; he had a smattering of the law. At best he could become a tutor. And when he returned to Odessa at the expiration of a year's banishment, he hoped to settle down as a teacher in some rich family. But he was too famous or notorious in Odessa; no jobs were forthcoming and he made his way to Kiev. There he was employed as tutor in the house of a certain Yahnenko, a businessman who had made a small fortune in sugar and lived on the outskirts of the city. Yahnenko had two daughters, Tassi and Olga. Zhelyabov promptly fell in love with Olga, the younger and prettier one.

If Semyon Yahnenko had been a little less good-natured and a little less indulgent to his favorite daughter, the marriage might not have taken place. His sympathies were liberal. He liked Zhelyabov, who was presentable, charming, and altogether the kind of young man he wanted to have in his family. Zhelyabov was not an intellectual, but he would make a good manager of a sugar factory. Olga was hopelessly in love. She was gay, quick, talented, and sang well, though Tassi sang a little better, and at one time the family had thought of making her a concert singer. Olga was the apple of her father's eye, and when she announced in the spring of 1873 that she was going to marry Zhelyabov, her father merely asked whether she had chosen the date of the wedding. She said they would be wed in the summer, and would then return to Odessa, a far more modern and progressive town than Kiev. Olga was just twenty, her husband twenty-three.

The marriage was ill-starred from the beginning. Zhelyabov had married her because she was pretty, affectionate, confiding, and easily swept off her feet by his stories about the need to serve the people. Olga believed him implicitly, and never ceased loving him, though she missed the comforts and luxuries she had enjoyed at home. She missed her grand piano and her singing lessons, and the little house parties on the Kiev estate where the landowners gathered and listened to Olga accompanying herself on the piano. "All you do is to delight the ears of plutocrats and aristocrats," Zhelyabov said bitterly. "Now we must get down to work." Work consisted of lessons in midwifery for Olga and a teacher's job in an orphanage for her husband. With his Yahnenko connections he could have entered an excellent career, but he chose to do otherwise. There seems to have been no bitterness between Yahnenko and Zhelyabov. They understood one another, and if the boy wanted to live in poverty and serve the people, that was his affair. If the young couple needed money, they knew where to find it.

Olga was shocked by poverty. Zhelyabov, who knew poverty well, simply laughed. One of his friends, Semenyuta, has described their living conditions. "It was a shabby dark room on the outskirts of the town. Two or three chairs, a rickety table and an unmade bed with a mattress like a pancake." But they were out most of the day, and they were still too much in love to be unduly perturbed by the appearance of the room. And though Zhelyabov felt an insistent need to serve the people, and had chosen the job at the orphanage largely because it brought him in contact with the poor, neither possessed revolutionary leanings. Zhelyabov had learned his lesson. He was determined to attract as little attention to himself as possible. He would not be a great lawyer. He would spend his days humbly serving the people.

It had not always been like that. Occasionally, when he was living on the Yahnenko estate, he would slip away and meet the young revolutionaries of Kiev, who were forever discussing the social and political theories of Lavrov and Chaikovsky. Groups of students, who called themselves members of the "Chaikovsky Circle" would meet secretly, discuss books, ponder the corruption of the government, and attempt to hammer out a program for the future. It was not yet a full-blooded revolutionary movement, for no general program had been agreed upon; and Prince Peter Kropotkin who entered one of the groups of the Chaikovsky Circle in 1872 speaks of meetings at which nothing more serious than Stanley's expedition to Africa in search of Livingstone was discussed. But the innumerable Chaikovsky Circles were close-knit, foreign books on the labor movement in Western Europe were being studied, and Alexander II was credited with the belief that these discussion groups might one day overthrow his throne. He once remarked that he wished he could corral all the members together in a single town, where he could keep watch on them. But the idea of the concentration camp had not yet reached Russia, and he merely imprisoned any members he could lay his hands on.

In Kiev the discussions of the Chaikovsky Circle were held in secret, usually in an unfurnished house. Ekaterina Breshkovskaya paid a visit to one of these meetings where Zhelyabov was present. Axelrod, a young revolutionary who later became a close friend of Karl Marx, had summoned the meeting in a house which the builders had not yet finished building. They had to walk through the dark streets in the outskirts of the city to find the house. They found a plank table, oil lamps, benches, nothing more. Present were Axelrod, a rich landlord called Dalinsky who had returned from abroad to make inquiries about the possibility of revolution through the Chaikovsky Circles, a man called Emme who was the acknowledged leader of the group in Kiev, and another young revolutionary called Rashevsky. Dalinsky had brought Zhelyabov with him. They discussed whether they should open schools in the villages. Emme and Dalinsky felt schools were a waste of time; they needed their energies for more exciting endeavors. The speeches were long, slow, and hesitant. Breshkovskaya maintained that even if they introduced no program for opening schools in the villages, at least they should make an effort to educate the older children. Histories of various educational experiments were recited. At one point Axelrod pointed to Zhelyabov approvingly, saying he had been born a serf and had done brilliantly as a university student—what more proof was needed to demonstrate that education was necessary? Various resolutions were passed. Zhelyabov was restrained and respectful, and hardly opened his mouth. At last Breshkovskaya and Axelrod fell soundly asleep, and the discussion went on without them. Writing forty-five years later Breshkovskaya was slightly patronizing. It was her opinion that Zhelyabov must have been "astonished by the interest we took in him, and obviously pleased to see the sincere joy with which the intelligentsia welcomed and accepted a comrade who had risen from the people." It is much more likely that Zhelyabov was amused by a good deal of talk which led to nothing.

Except for these rare visits with Emme and Dalinsky in Kiev, Zhelyabov had shown no particular interest in the revolutionary ferment of his time. Even in Odessa, when he was living in the slums, he took part in none of the liberal movements. He liked fishing. He associated with his old friends at the University. He developed an interest in chemistry, and asked his friend Semenyuta to give him lessons. Semenyuta refused, saying he was altogether too clumsy with his fingers to play about with test tubes. The conference in Kiev must have had some effect on him, for he began to spend the evenings giving free classes to workmen. Early in 1874 he seems to have been on the fringe of a Chaikovsky Circle instituted by a certain Makarevich, a student who posed as a shoemaker. When Makarevich was arrested, Zhelyabov sent a letter in cipher to Madame Makarevich, telling her about the arrest and urging her to get from her parents the money to bail her husband out, and gave directions for forwarding the money. The police intercepted the letter. Zhelyabov was arrested, and brought before Colonel Knoop. His explanations were apparently satisfactory, for the colonel wrote in response to enquiries from St. Petersburg:

Zhelyabov cannot possibly be accused of belonging to the Makarevich circle. He has explained the whole situation to me with complete frankness. His part in the affair arose solely from his chivalrous acknowledgment of the claims of personal friendship. His personal character and social position—he recently married the daughter of a highly respected municipal councilor— make his guilt extremely unlikely.

Knoop added that he had authorized the release of Zhelyabov on bail of two thousand rubles, but St. Petersburg, remembering the troubles at the Novorossisk University, had already placed the finger of suspicion on him. Knoop received a telegram: "Arrest Zhelyabov immediately." Accordingly Zhelyabov was committed to prison, where he remained for four months, while Yahnenko and Knoop together attempted to pull strings to release a man who was only too obviously innocent. It was four months later before Knoop received the authorization to release Zhelyabov from prison on a bail of three thousand rubles. It was a beautiful spring day in March. Zhelyabov had entered the prison with his usual gay demeanor; when he came out his jaws were set and the sparkle had gone from his eyes. "From that day," he said afterward, "I became a revolutionary."

Yahnenko, the municipal councilor and owner of innumerable sugar factories, had paid the bail, and did not let his son-in-law forget it. Olga was still in love, but the marriage already was breaking up. Zhelyabov gave lessons and went out on long silent fishing expeditions. This was the time when the Slavs were rising against the Turks in Bosnia and Herzegovina. Zhelyabov collected funds for the rebels, and he would have joined the revolutionary movement against the Turks if he had been allowed to go abroad, but being on bail, he was under police surveillance, and not allowed to leave Odessa.

There was nothing in the law to prevent him from going out on the Black Sea in his fishing boat or talking to the young naval officers of the port. Though moody, he still made friends easily; and at some period during the two and a half years when he was out on bail, the dedicated revolutionary became a close friend of a dedicated officer of the Russian Imperial Navy, a man who was infinitely loyal to the Tsar. At that time Lieutenant Rozhdestvensky was a young torpedo-boat commander who liked nothing better than to show Zhelyabov around his gleaming torpedo boat and take him out on trials. Tall and well-built, with a biting tongue, a quick mind and an abiding interest in social problems, the lieutenant was a model Russian naval officer. Strict with his men, he demanded and received their affection. He was already famous for his physical courage. Thirty years later Rear Admiral Rozhdestvensky, Chief of the Naval Staff and Commander in Chief of the Second Pacific Squadron steamed halfway round the world to meet a shattering defeat at the hands of Admiral Heihachiro Togo in the Strait of Tsushima. By that time Zhelyabov's revolutionary adventures were only a memory, and a whole new school of terrorists had arisen to terrify the Tsar.

Zhelyabov admired the torpedo boats and would sometimes go out for four or five days. From the officers he gained a considerable knowledge of high explosives. Once he nearly blew himself up, and at another time, when a torpedo exploded prematurely, he received a splinter in the arm which prevented him from bending his elbow for some weeks. Through the naval officers he met some of the officers at the Artillery Academy. From them he learned about shells, emplacements, parabolic arcs, and range finding. He was an apt pupil. Sometimes he would lead the conversation toward social questions. Once an officer offered to devote his whole time to the revolutionary movement. Zhelyabov, already regarding himself as a revolutionary, answered: "Stay where you are! You will be of much more use to us in the army." Then for long periods he would disappear from Odessa—police surveillance had been relaxed—and would go to Kerch and work on the farms, exhausting himself with physical labor, singing Cossack songs to his baby son who was born in 1876, living quietly, so quietly indeed that the Yahnenkos thought all ambition had been burned away in him. He had been in prison, and the prison had poisoned him. He was only one more of the quiet, bitter students without jobs, rootless and hopeless, who were beginning to see that the country was in desperate need of a revolution. Except for his student speeches against Bogishich he had received no prominence, and he was a little puzzled when in September 1877 he was ordered to surrender his bail and found himself once more in prison. What had happened was that the government had decided upon a general roundup of revolutionary elements, and a mass trial (which came to be known as the Trial of the 193) was about to take place in St. Petersburg. As the least important of the prisoners, Zhelyabov was almost the last to be arrested. The trial ended in January 1878. Zhelyabov was acquitted, and immediately made his way back to Odessa, where he was faced with the almost hopeless task of earning a living by tutoring. He almost decided to spend the rest of his life working with peasants on a farm. He had a police record; he was regarded as a young firebrand who had escaped a long term of imprisonment only by a miracle; and his future could hardly have looked darker.

In prison he had met Sophie Perovskaya. It seems to have been only a brief meeting, but Zhelyabov was deeply impressed by her. Small and graceful, with a delicate nose, full lips, and light-blue eyes below a high arching forehead, she belonged to the highest aristocracy. Her grandfather had been Minister of Public Instruction, her father had been Governor General of St. Petersburg at the time when Karakozov attempted to assassinate the Tsar in 1866. For his inexcusable carelessness in allowing the attempt to take place, the Governor General was summarily dismissed from his post. He had enjoyed great power. Frustrated, he made the lives of his family miserable, and Sophie hated him. She hated his political views, his continual bullying of the servants, his boasting and his debts; and she possessed a fierce love for her mother, a woman of great beauty. Sophie was sixteen at the time of the Karakozov affair. Three years later, when the general fell ill and went abroad to take the cure, Sophie remained in Russia, staying with family friends.

Among these friends were members of the Chaikovsky Circle. She listened to them. She had a deep contempt for talk, and cried out for action. Living alone, studying for the diploma which would enable her to earn a living by teaching, refusing all aid, translating and copying to pay for her rent, wholly absorbed in the revolution, she was a thorn in the flesh of the students who were happily content to spend the rest of their lives discussing the revolution. Sophie wanted revolution now. She was nineteen when she was arrested for the first time, for agitating among workmen on the Nevsky Prospect. She spent a year in prison, and was then released on bail with orders to remain on the family estate in the Crimea. Prison only quickened her revolutionary ardor, and in the general roundup which preceded the Trial of the 193 she was among the first to be arrested. Acquitted at the trial, she went underground. Alone among the prisoners at the trial Ippolit Myshkin had received a heavy punishment. Sophie immediately embarked on a plan to rescue him while he was being transferred from one prison to another. Failing in this, she went to Kharkov, to organize the release of prisoners there. The attempt failed. The police were now on the watch for an extraordinary slip of a girl who seemed to be wielding vast powers among the revolutionaries, and they trapped her one day when she was secretly visiting her own estate in the Crimea. She was exiled to Archangel province, two thousand miles away. She seems to have enjoyed the journey and was on good terms with the guards, who treated her politely, so politely that when she had a chance to escape between Simferopol and St. Petersburg she decided to remain with them because she did not want them to be punished if she escaped. Later she changed her mind. When they were nearing Archangel and were spending the night at a small railway station, Sophie slipped out of the room and quietly boarded a train for St. Petersburg. She had no money. When the inspector asked for her ticket, she pretended to be a giggling peasant girl on her way to the capital for the first time. In fact she often resembled a peasant girl, and Vera Figner who knew her well once remarked on the peasant quality of her face. "With her short

The Peter and Paul Fortress

The Alexis Ravelin

Gateway to Peter and Paul Fortress

Cathedral of St. Peter and St. Paul

The Senate Square, St. Petersburg, 1810

Prince Sergey Trubetskoy

Alexander Bestuzhev

Kondraty Ryleyev

Pavel Pestel

The Uprising of December 14, 1825.
From a painting by K. I. Kolman
made in the 1830's.

Nikolay Speshnev

Mikhail Petrashevsky

Fyodor Dostoyevsky

Dmitry Akhsharumov

Scene on Semyonovsky Square, on December 22, 1849. A reconstruction by an unknown artist made a few years later. Petrashevsky is on the extreme right.

Alexander Herzen

Nikolay Dobrolyubov

Dmitry Pisarev

Nikolay Chernyshevsky

Chernyshevsky at public ceremony of degradation on Mytny Square, May 31, 1864. From a painting by Y. M. Kozmichev.

Vissarion Belinsky

Mikhail Bakunin

Khalturin

Tkachev

Dmitry Karakozov

Sergey Nechayev

The Assassination of Alexander II on the banks of the Catherine Canal, March 1, 1881. A contemporary drawing from the Illustrated London News.

Yegor Sazonov

Sophie Perovskaya

Alexander Ulyanov

Ivan Kaliayev

[ABOVE] *Andrey Zhelyabov, a drawing made during his trial.*

[RIGHT] *The execution of the assassins of Alexander II. From a contemporary drawing by A. A. Nasvetevich.*

Kibalchich   *Sophie Perovskaya*   *Andrey Zhelyabov*
From a drawing made at the trial by K. Makovsky.

Alexander Kerensky

flaxen braids, her light-blue eyes and her childishly rounded cheeks, you would have thought her a peasant until you saw the high sweep of her forehead." Breshkovskaya, who was also one of the prisoners at the Trial of the 193, presents a slightly different picture:

> She was as pure and calm a figure as if she had stepped out of the classic drama of ancient Greece. Her young fresh face expressed peace of mind, calm wisdom, and superiority over her surroundings. Even her smile was as serious as that of a mature man. She was very small and very youthful, and had a round, fair face, rosy cheeks and delicate features.

There was one other prisoner at the Trial of the 193 whose life was to be intimately associated with Zhelyabov. He was the young scientist Nikolay Kibalchich, the son of a parish priest, a man with a smooth rounded forehead, deep-sunken eyes, a fine Greek nose, a short black beard and the look of a dedicated intellectual. His wide-ranging mind was already occupied with problems of flight and jet propulsion. He spent two years at an engineering college and then transferred to a medical school. He knew German, French, and English, and was already immersed in social problems. He took little exercise, often forgot to eat, and studied technical journals all day. One day he was caught giving a prohibited book to a peasant and was thrown into prison for three years. At the trial he was sentenced to a further two months' imprisonment and then released. The damage had been done. He might have lived out his life quietly as a brilliant research professor. Instead he became the revolutionaries' expert on high explosives.

By arresting so many young students and then being compelled to acquit nearly all of them, the government showed itself incompetent to deal with the revolutionary situation. Instead of heading off the revolt, it had only made the revolt more certain. Exasperated students cried out for a rallying point. Their hero was Ippolit Myshkin, but Myshkin was in jail. There was no leadership, only a host of discussion groups and a handful of ineffective revolutionary societies. The Trial of the 193, however, consolidated the opposition, and gradually the secret society which called itself Zemlya i Volya (which may be translated Land and Freedom, though *zemlya* implies the physical earth and *volya* has a vast range of meanings including those of "will" and "the pure determination to achieve an object") began to assume the ascendancy. It was not a powerful society. In December 1876 it held its first demonstration outside the Kazan Cathedral in St. Petersburg. They had planned to organize thousands of workmen in great processions, but no more than two hundred people gathered to listen to the fiery speeches of the nineteen-year-old Georgy Plekhanov. The police did not even trouble to disperse the small crowd; they sent a few hoodlums to heckle the speaker and beat up the crowd, and then arrested the ringleaders at their leisure. Plekhanov escaped abroad. Among those who were left was a certain Alexander Mikhailov, a nineteen-year-old student at the Technological Institute whose passion for secret conspiracy entitles him to be regarded as the *éminence grise* of the early revolutionary movement. His hand is visible in many of the attacks on government leaders during the next two years. He was connected with the assassination of Mezentsev in 1878 and with Mirsky's attempt on Drenteln in 1879, and he was close by when Alexander Solovyev fired five shots at the Emperor on the morning of April 2, 1879. In the early days of the Zemlya i Volya he assumed the role which Savinkov was to play after the turn of the century.

Mikhailov had a passion for order, a clear mind, and a contempt for nervous and excitable revolutionaries. He usually distrusted Jews and Russians from southern Russia. He lived alone, very quietly, attracting no attention to himself and pouring scorn on the young nihilists who wore blue spectacles and long hair. He was the mechanic of revolution. For days on end he wandered through the streets of St. Petersburg, taking careful note of all the dark alleyways, the police stations, the escape routes. He constructed careful maps and sometimes gave the impression of a general about to take over the city. He spoke in a clipped, matter-of-fact voice, and refused to play the Russian game of talking for talking's sake: when visitors came, he opened a bottle, poured out a glass of vodka for each guest, and then replaced the bottle in a cupboard. He would allow a few minutes for drinking, then collect the glasses and insist that the members get down to business. A party member given the task of copying addresses complained that it was bad for his eyes. "Excellent," said Mikhailov. "You can carry on until you go blind." He had Nechayev's brand of obstinacy and Nechayev's wide understanding of political forces, but his words were tempered with gentleness.

Among other things Mikhailov gave himself the task of organizing the finances of Zemlya i Volya. The party was poor. It lived on the small contributions of students, each gift rarely amounting to more than two or three rubles. Recently, however, the position had changed with the appearance of Demetrius Lizogub, who had returned to Russia from eleven years of study at Montpellier in France. Lizogub's father and mother had died in quick succession, and he was now very rich and singularly without any ambition except to serve the revolution. He was tall, pale, slim, with a long beard which gave him an apostolic appearance. His blue eyes were shaded by long lashes, and he spoke in a slow, well-modulated voice. Entirely unassuming, he wore old clothes and tried not to spend any money on himself—everything must go toward the revolution. But in August 1878 his land agent, a certain Drigo, decided to denounce him.

Lizogub was arrested at Kharkov, but succeeded in bribing a police official and escaped to Odessa, where the police again caught up with him a few days later. With Lizogub in prison, Mikhailov's task was to establish communication with him and obtain power of attorney over the few thousand rubles which remained of Lizogub's estate. There was some doubt about where Lizogub was imprisoned, and it was a long time before there was any communication between the two revolutionaries. Finally, in May 1879, Mikhailov established communication with Lizogub in Odessa, and a few days later he met Zhelyabov.

The meeting between Mikhailov and Zhelyabov had profound consequences on the revolutionary movement. They recognized each other's strength. Mikhailov came out of the gentry, while Zhelyabov came from a family of serfs; but they had the same general attitude toward the revolution, the same distaste for what Mikhailov called "the Russian nature," and the same calm determination to free Russia from the autocracy of the Tsar. Mikhailov suggested that Zhelyabov join Zemlya i Volya, explaining frankly that the party was a terrorist organization committed to the assassination of the Emperor. Would Zhelyabov join? Zhelyabov pondered the idea, and then said he would join on one condition: he would take part in a single assassination attempt and then retire from the scene. He had no desire to commit himself to lifelong servitude to a party, and he seems to have accepted Mikhailov's suggestion with the air of a man saying: "Well, I'll try it out once, and if it's no good, I'll get out." He knew there was a chance that he might be killed or executed and offered to divorce his wife, but Olga was still in love with him and she refused to entertain the idea. He was not very good at hiding his emotions. He told her he had come to hate her, but the words were not altogether convincing; and when he left on his mysterious errands in the north she firmly believed he would eventually come back to her.

About this time Mikhailov had decided to summon a conference of revolutionaries. The government had acted sternly after Solovyev's attempt on the life of the Tsar. The death penalty was being exacted on revolutionaries even when they had merely given money to the revolutionary organizations—Lizogub was hanged in August 1879, after refusing to defend himself at his trial. He had died bravely, smiling, very quiet, on a scaffold erected in a public square in Odessa, gazing on the crowd which had assembled in the burning heat of a summer day as though he were a priest blessing them. There had been a wave of such executions.

Mikhailov summoned the conference of revolutionaries at Lipetsk, then a famous and expensive watering place, the last place the government would expect to find them. Under false names, with false passports, Zhelyabov and Mikhailov arrived on June 13, 1879. A few days later the other delegates arrived. These included Tikhomirov and Morozov, two intellectuals who later shouldered most of the burden of providing the intellectual foundation of the Narodnaya Volya. Another delegate, self-appointed, was Grigory Goldenberg, who had been responsible for the assassination of Prince Dmitry Kropotkin in Kharkov earlier in the year. There were altogether about twenty delegates who met secretly in the forests surrounding Lipetsk. They would go in small groups with their picnic baskets and later meet in some remote part of the forest. And it was in these forests with their mineral springs and their memories of the hunting parties of Peter the Great that Mikhailov and Zhelyabov hammered out a new statement of revolutionary policy. It was not enough to make sporadic attacks on individual governors, ministers, and chiefs of the gendarmerie. They must overthrow the whole government and prepare to produce a new government in its place.

Up to this moment no one had dared to face the inevitable issues. They had played at revolution. Now, according to Zhelyabov, the time had come to "use all possible weapons." Among those weapons was the terror which would be brought about if the Emperor were executed. From that moment Zhelyabov and Mikhailov were committed to killing the Tsar.

The conference at Lipetsk was followed by another at Voronezh attended by Plekhanov, Sophie Perovskaya, and the two Figner sisters. Plekhanov had been responsible for the abortive demonstration outside the Kazan Cathedral, and was at that time a moderate socialist. He refused to take terrorism seriously. Reading from one of Morozov's pamphlets calling for widespread revolt, he asked whether anyone in the audience could possibly believe such arrant nonsense. He expected to hear murmurs of approval: instead there was silence, and shortly afterward he left the conference, saying he had more important things to do than discuss revolutionary policy with hotheads.

Plekhanov was not alone in the view that the revolution could be brought about by discussion groups. There were more conferences. Finally it was agreed that there could be no compromise between the two groups, and the party which had originally been called Zemlya i Volya disbanded, to become two parties. The moderates henceforth went under the name Chorny Peredyel, meaning the Black Partition, the party being dedicated to the division of the black earth among the peasants. The extremists took the name of Narodnaya Volya, meaning The People's Will. Each party had taken one part of the original double-barreled name for its own. During its brief existence the Chorny Peredyel floundered. It was never a popular organization, and its members found difficulty in obtaining recruits. It published only one issue of its newspaper. The Narodnaya Volya went from strength to strength, at the mercy of police spies and traitors, but never having difficulty in obtaining recruits. At its head were five resourceful and determined revolutionaries: the intellectuals Tikhomirov and Morozov, and the "bomb throwers" Zhelyabov, Mikhailov, and Sophie Perovskaya.

On August 26, 1879, the Executive Committee of the Narodnaya Volya formally sentenced the Emperor to death.

THE YEARS OF FAILURE

T HE FIRST ACT of the Narodnaya Volya was to pass sentence of death on the Emperor; the second was to draw up a charter. Zhelyabov was responsible for the sentence of death. Tikhomirov and Morozov together hammered out the charter and then presented it to the Executive Committee, which discussed it interminably and finally passed it with a few slight amendments. The charter read:

A. We are socialists and *narodniki* by conviction. We believe that it is only through socialist principles that humanity can attain liberty, equality, fraternity, general well-being, the full development of the human personality and of progress. We are convinced that the people's will alone gives sanction to the emerging social forms, and it is only in this way that freedom is incarnated in life and so enters into the consciousness of the people. The welfare of the nation and the popular will—these are our two sacred principles, never to be separated from one another.

B. When we contemplate the conditions under which people live and have their being, we observe a nation submerged in economic and political serfdom . . . We observe the present bourgeois government maintaining itself in power by the exercise of brute force: the army, the police and the officials rule, exactly as they did in the days of Genghiz Khan. We observe the entire absence of popular approval of the government. We see a government which has nothing in common with the aspirations and ideals of the people. We see ancient traditions still living among the people—the right of the people to own land, communal and local autonomy, the idea of federated states, liberty of conscience and of speech. These principles are capable of far-reaching development . . .

C. We believe that the popular will can be established by calling into existence a Constituent Assembly elected by free and universal suffrage. Though this is far from being the ideal form by which the popular will may be manifested, it is at the present time the only possible and practical solution. Our aim is therefore to remove the power from the existing government and transfer it to the Constituent Assembly.

D. While wholly submitting ourselves to the will of the people, we nevertheless as a party believe it to be our duty to put forward a program for the benefit of the people. We intend to continue making propaganda for our program up to the outbreak of the revolution, we shall continue to recommend it during the electoral campaign and we shall defend it in the Constituent Assembly itself. The program follows:

1. A popular government with full power to decide all relevant issues.
2. A wide degree of local self-government.
3. The independence of the *mir* as an economic and administrative unit.
4. The land to belong to the people.
5. All factories and workshops to be put in the hands of the workers.
6. Complete freedom of conscience, speech, press, right of assembly, and the right to agitate during elections.
7. A universal electoral law, without class or property qualifications.
8. The existing army to become a militia.

We intend to proclaim this program, believing that none of these demands can be separated from one another and only the acceptance of the entirety of these demands will bring about political and economic freedom for the people and the correct development.

E. With these aims in view, we believe that the party must develop along the following lines:

1. *Propaganda and agitation.*
   Our propaganda must aim to popularize among all classes the idea of a democratic political revolution by means of socialist reforms, and to popularize the existing program of the party . . .
2. *Destructive and terrorist measures.*
   By terrorist activity to destroy the more harmful members of the government, to protect the party from espionage and to punish the official excesses and cruelties committed by the government and the administration. These measures will have the aim of weakening the strength of the administration and of demonstrating the possibility of an unrelenting fight against the government, thus strengthening among the people a belief in our ultimate success. Finally, by terrorist acts we shall develop a proper and suitable combat strength.
3. The organization of secret societies to be centralized . . .
4. Contacts to be formed in the administration, the army, society, and among the people . . .
5. The organization and fulfillment of the revolution . . .
6. Electoral agitation to choose members for the Constituent Assembly . . .

The five paragraphs of the charter of the Narodnaya Volya do not seem particularly remarkable today, but in their time and place they came with shattering force. For the first time there was a social program combined with a revolutionary method. The social program was simple, the revolutionary method direct; and there seemed every possibility that the revolutionaries might succeed in their aims. The terrorists stated openly that they were determined to "destroy the more harmful members of the government and punish official excesses and cruelties." It was decided to destroy the Tsar as he returned in the imperial train from his summer palace in the Crimea.

On October 1 Zhelyabov went to Alexandrovsk. It was a small town largely inhabited by Mennonites from western Prussia, slow, cautious men who spoke German, not particularly enamored of the Russians. Zhelyabov chose the place for many reasons: the lay of the land offered excellent prospects for burying land mines under the railway tracks, the Mennonites were not likely to report any suspicious activity to the government, and it was once the capital town of the Zaporogian Cossacks, and indelibly connected with the name of the Cossack hetman Taras Bulba. Zhelyabov went under the name of Cheremisov, a merchant of Yaroslavl. He spoke of setting up a tannery. He visited the local merchants, became friendly with the chief of police and the town councilors. He thrived on his disguise, gave parties, told innumerable stories about the Cossacks and was regarded as a man who would certainly make his mark on the town. His landlord was also of Cossack descent, and they swore eternal fealty to one another. Zhelyabov possessed an inexhaustible knowledge about the workings of tanneries, and liked nothing better than discussing the operations of the imaginary factory. Afterward people remembered the endless discussions and marveled at the strange way in which they had accepted him, for no factory was ever built and there was not even any decision about its site.

Zhelyabov spent his days in the town; at night he worked on the railway track. It rained continually. With Zhelyabov were two young revolutionaries, Okladsky and Tikhonov. They worked up to their ankles in mud. The plan was to bury two land mines under the track as it wound along an embankment cut into the slopes of the mountain. When the land mines exploded, Zhelyabov hoped the imperial train would be hurled off the embankment into the valley below. Most of the work was done by Zhelyabov who suffered from night blindness, and was forced to proceed with painful slowness. There were continual difficulties. Because it was known that the imperial train would soon be returning, the line was being inspected by a patrol which passed along the embankment every three or four hours. Once Okladsky fell asleep while he was on sentry duty. Zhelyabov was heartsick. For a moment he thought of shooting the man, for were not the revolutionaries at war with the government? He told himself revolutionaries who fall asleep at their task are exactly like soldiers who fall asleep in battle. In the end he decided to say nothing about the matter to Okladsky. He was in a high fever. The embankment was a quagmire. He was afraid of being observed during the frequent lightning flashes.

He had to dig out a long underground chamber, but the roof kept caving in. On November 16 he learned that the imperial train was due to pass two days later. The night of the seventeenth was pure nightmare. He had one cylinder in place, and he was about to insert the second in its place immediately below the rails when it slipped out of his hands, fell down the embankment and was lost in the mud below. He succeeded in finding it, placed it in its proper position, attached the wires leading to an induction coil, and returned to his house in Alexandrovsk. He was now very ill. The strain of playing a double game over a period of two months was beginning to tell on him. He had hoped for a coded telegram which would give him the order of the coaches in the imperial train; no telegram came, and he knew he would have to guess which coach the Emperor was in. It was raining when he went out in a farm cart to a place he had carefully chosen beforehand. The wires led to the cart. From the train he would appear to be a farmer driving to market. No one would suspect him. But when he pressed the switch as the fourth coach passed over the cylinder, there was no explosion and the train puffed slowly toward the north, out of sight.

Zhelyabov was downcast, and cursed his lack of mechanical ability. He knew a good deal about explosives, but he had always been clumsy with his hands. The day after the train passed through Alexandrovsk, the snow fell. In the mud he had been able to plunge about at his heart's content, but the line inspectors would easily pick up the traces of his footprints in the snow. He decided to leave the cylinders under the embankment. It might, after all, be possible to blow up the Emperor's train the following year.

The attempt at Alexandrovsk was only one of three attempts to wreck the imperial train during its northward journey. All the attempts failed. Land mines were laid under the train at Odessa and just outside Moscow. Only one exploded, and that destroyed a luggage car. With twelve revolutionaries gathered along the line, all of them armed with large quantities of dynamite, the Emperor had passed through unscathed.

On November 22 the Executive Committee published a proclamation to the people:

> On November 19 near Moscow, on the Moscow-Kursk railway, an attempt was made upon the life of Alexander II by the order of the Executive Committee. Land mines were placed under the train. The attempt failed. At the present time we do not propose to go into the causes of the failure.
>
> We believe that our agents and all the members of our party are in no way discouraged by the failure. From the present failure they have learned a lesson which will be of service to us in further attempts against his life. We shall go forward with renewed faith in our strength and the possibility of bringing our war to a successful conclusion.

Turning to all Russian citizens who honestly desire to follow the road to freedom, we affirm once again that Alexander II is the personification of hypocritical despotism, a bloodthirsty coward ever reaching out towards greater and greater deeds of violence . . . Instead of truth, justice and freedom, we are presented with a violent and warlike dictatorship . . . He has deserved the death penalty by the pain he has caused and the blood he has shed . . .

But our concern is not with the Emperor alone. Our aim is to fulfill the people's will, the people's good. Our task is to free the people and to offer them the largest possible control over their own fate. If Alexander II were to recognize the terrible evil he had brought down upon Russia, and if he refused all power for himself, and handed power over to a General Assembly chosen by the free vote of the people, then and only then would we leave Alexander II in peace and forgive him his crimes.

Until then there must be war! Implacable war!

The mood of the Executive Committee was not entirely shared by all the members of the party. The failure hurt them. A single bomb could have brought down the dynasty; and to have failed when all the advantages were on their side was to admit a fatal lack of proper organization. In a mood of profound bitterness an anonymous contributor to the journal of the Narodnaya Volya wrote "a story for children":

Once upon a time there was a very, very good Tsar. The evil people wanted to kill him, and they even put a bomb under the railroad on which this excellent Tsar was traveling. They failed to kill him. The chief of police in the very ancient capital was summoned. He made every kind of excuse for having failed to penetrate the intentions of the evil people who laid the bomb, which did not in fact destroy the Tsar though it came very close to it. At the sight of his terrified entourage the Tsar decided to show mercy. "None of you are guilty," he said. "I am guilty, because I am too good." Everyone was deeply moved. A triumphant and prolonged silence ensued. Everyone felt a certain awkwardness.

That night the Tsar was restless, and he fell asleep only toward morning. His old servant heard him murmuring in his sleep: "The courage of a King . . . convoy . . . Providence has preserved me . . . carriages must be armor-plated."

For a long time after the event the people continued to pray for the safety of the Father of the Country, and for a still longer time the priests zealously endeavored to assure the people that this was the best of all possible Tsars.

The people however don't give a damn. The people are very rough, and all they can think about is bread.

From this time onward ill-luck was continually dogging the revolutionaries. The police were alert. They succeeded in capturing the printing press, and though a new press was promptly bought, and given the name of "flying press of the Narodnaya Volya," the revolutionaries were continually faced with difficulty in running it. The police attempted to check their source of ink and paper supplies. It was ordinary black ink, and

ordinary notepaper, moistened to take print. In December Stepan Shirayev was arrested and thrown into the Peter and Paul Fortress; there, later,
Nechayev came to know him through messages circulated by the warders.
Shirayev was a member of the Executive Committee and was one of those
who organized the attack on the Tsar's train. A more serious loss occurred
when Grigory Goldenberg was arrested in November. Though he had
assassinated Prince Dmitry Kropotkin the previous February and attended
the Lipetsk Conference, he was not a member of the Executive Committee. He was arrested at Odessa, and found in possession of dynamite. He
was a Ukrainian Jew, thin and dark, with blazing eyes and an immense
wide forehead, a weak chin and a curiously shaped mouth. Though passionately convinced of the need for revolution, and with a long record of
revolutionary activity, for which he had been punished by being exiled
to Archangel, he was not generally liked by the revolutionaries, and in
prison he talked. The police played on his vanity. They recognized him
as the murderer of Prince Kropotkin, and could therefore put him on
trial and execute him whenever they pleased. Goldenberg was gradually
convinced that his greatest service to the state would consist of arranging
a truce between the Emperor and the revolutionaries. He received assur-
ances that no harm would come to the revolutionaries, compiled a list of
their names and pseudonyms, and revealed most of the party secrets. The
police found themselves in possession of a hundred names and descrip-
tions of conspirators. Goldenberg was assiduously complimented and
made to feel important. For the first time they learned the extent of the
revolutionary conspiracy against the state. In the end, Goldenberg realized
that the police had hoodwinked him, that there was no intention of bringing about a truce, and the police had simply used him as a stool pigeon.
In utter despair, he committed suicide. The journal of the Narodnaya
Volya announced shortly afterward in the pathetic black-bordered list
which accompanied all its issues: On July 15, 1880, in the Peter and Paul
Fortress, Grigory Goldenberg ended his life by suicide, strangling himself
with a towel.

The harm was done. The party members grew more desperate. Another
attempt to blow up the Emperor as his carriage was passing through the
streets of Odessa failed. There followed a scheme to blow up the Stone
Bridge over the Ekaterininsky Canal in St. Petersburg while the Emperor
was riding over it. The bridge was never blown up because one of the
conspirators, who had no watch, arrived too late on the scene. During a
period of eight months, six separate attempts were made on the life of the
Emperor, and all failed. As the result of Goldenberg's confessions the
police were hot on their trail. They had a few thousand rubles, a printing
press, about twenty devoted followers, almost nothing else. Yet the Narod-

naya Volya was headline news in the St. Petersburg and Moscow newspapers. Its manifestoes were widely read, and the power of the revolutionaries to terrorize the dynasty was slowly increasing.

In the months of despair which followed the failures, Zhelyabov and Mikhailov kept the party going by the sheer force of their good humor. Nothing daunted them. They were always on the verge of arrest, and always escaped. Occasionally Zhelyabov would fall into fits of depression, but they were short-lived. "It doesn't matter if we fail now," he would say. "We must keep on hammering. If we continue relentlessly to hammer at the same target, we shall break through." The young Sophie Perovskaya was not quite so hopeful of seeing the revolution in her own time. "It will take two generations," she said once, "and few of the terrorists will see it, but it will happen." She dressed like a workingman's wife, in a cotton dress with men's boots, her head covered with a kerchief. She would carry on her shoulders the two pails of water she had dredged up from the Neva. No one would have recognized in her the young society beauty who had once danced in the fashionable ballrooms of St. Petersburg. And gradually she was falling in love with Zhelyabov. She had half-despised men in the past. "A woman's man," she had said of a young revolutionary known to Prince Peter Kropotkin, and Kropotkin remembered ever afterward the biting tone in her voice. She had a sharp tongue, and was often strangely prim, and could not abide slovenliness. It has been suggested that she would have made an excellent schoolmarm, but this is unfair: she was born to be a Minister of Health and Social Affairs in some revolutionary government.

By the summer of 1880 Zhelyabov and Sophie Perovskaya were living together in a small apartment in St. Petersburg off the Ismailovsky Boulevard. It was a two-room apartment with a small kitchen, very bare. The windows had muslin curtains, the cushions were stuffed with straw, and the samovar had a broken handle. Sophie did the housework and the marketing. They lived on the money coming into the party funds, and on odd jobs. Both of them called meetings among university students and among the officers stationed at St. Petersburg, and they began to extend their influence among the workmen. By the end of 1880 the party claimed some 250 members in its Workers' Section in St. Petersburg and another thousand elsewhere.

In the fall of 1880 came the great crop failure in the Volga. Prices skyrocketed. Starvation was widespread, and the peasants were flocking to the towns, away from the barren fields. It occurred to Zhelyabov that there was hope for a peasant insurrection. Himself a peasant, he was appalled by the stories of conditions in the south; and at the first meeting of the Narodnaya Volya he announced his determination to go south.

"I believe I have the qualities for leading the revolt," he said. "I'm convinced that this is the best way to make the government aware of the people's need for relief. You may think that by going south I have put aside all thoughts of assassinating the Emperor. No, you are wrong. I merely propose to postpone the attempt."

But the meeting broke up without any conclusion being reached, and the promised peasant rebellion was postponed indefinitely. The party had neither the physical resources nor the money needed for a peasant revolt. It was agreed that it would be best to concentrate their attention on assassinating the Emperor.

In the winter of 1880 the young revolutionaries had many things on their minds. Kviatkovsky and fifteen other members of the Narodnaya Volya were put on trial before the St. Petersburg Military Court in October. All of them used the court as a forum for their revolutionary views. The trial was notable for the severity of the punishments. Kviatkovsky and Presnyakov, who had taken part in the attempts to blow up the railways, were sentenced to death, and were executed on November 4. At this trial, too, there was mentioned for the first time a phrase which was to become only too familiar later. "The red terror of the Executive Committee is the answer to the white terror of the government." The words were spoken by Shirayev who, though arrested the previous year, was not brought to trial until the police had enough evidence to convict a solid batch of revolutionaries. The words were quoted against the revolutionaries. Worse was to follow, for a few days after the executions Alexander Mikhailov visited a photographer to pick up photographs of Kviatkovsky and Presnyakov. The police had warned professional photographers in St. Petersburg that something of the kind might happen, and he found himself trapped. Now only Zhelyabov remained of the two leaders who had dominated the party from the beginning.

Now more than ever Zhelyabov was determined to put an end to the Emperor. This time he would so arrange his forces that it would be impossible for the Emperor to escape. They had kept a close watch on the Emperor's movements. They knew that he often passed along the Malaya Sadovaya, and when Zhelyabov learned from Sophie Perovskaya that a shop overlooking the road was for sale, he took her along to inspect it. The landlord's agent was suspicious. The tall, black-bearded intellectual who called himself Kobozev hardly resembled the kind of man who would normally open a cheese shop, though Zhelyabov spoke about cheeses as fluently as he had spoken about tanneries in Alexandrovsk. The landlord's agent communicated his suspicions to the police. They discovered the address of the Kobozevs and learned that their passports were made out in Voronezh; they then telegraphed to Voronezh and learned that passports had in fact been made out to two people called Kobozev. The police were examining hundreds of passports a day. There seemed to be nothing wrong, the passports had the proper number and gave the proper description. It was no more than a routine action. The landlord's agent was informed that the Kobozevs were a reputable couple. On January 1 Zhelyabov paid the first quarter's rent of 250 rubles. The next day he had a sign painted for 35 rubles. Then it was necessary to lay in a stock of cheese. Mining operations were in progress by the end of the week, with most of the revolutionaries taking part.

It was a hard winter, with sleet and snow muffling the sound of their picks and shovels. January was a month of wild excitement. This was the month when the famous letter was received from Nechayev. Breathlessly, nine or ten revolutionaries, taking turns, all consumed with impatience, were at work digging a gallery under the road. At night the lights of the cheese shop would be left burning before an ikon, while the conspirators broke through a concrete wall and pondered the problem of the iron waterpipe which barred their way under the road. They had difficulties in getting rid of the earth; and when they had settled the problem of the waterpipe by working round it they were confronted with the problem presented by an ancient wooden drainpipe. They decided to cut through it, only to discover they were cutting through a sewer. The smell was overpowering, and nearly gave them away. They were exhausted by their work in the gallery, and they lost six more of their adherents by arrest, including the handsome Kletochnikov, who had spent the last two years working at a desk in the police offices and was therefore able to warn them about most impending actions against them by the police. The strain was beginning to tell. A weary hopelessness settled upon Zhelyabov, and he would talk about the day when all the St. Petersburg terrorists were under arrest, and who would carry on? He had no great faith in the theory that terrorism would bring about swift changes in the government. Loris-Melikov had instituted the "dictatorship of the heart" and with painful slowness the government was turning toward a more liberal program. Zhelyabov was a terrorist now only because he had been a terrorist before: it had become a habit, and he was perfectly aware that it was a dangerous one. "There is something terrible about being a terrorist," he observed about this time, and added without intending any irony: "It dominates your mind so much that it affects your freedom of judgment."

That winter the wildest plans were debated. With the help of the naval officers who were secretly attached to the party they planned to bring the fleet up from Kronstadt and bombard St. Petersburg. There was more talk of peasant revolts. A writer in the party journal spoke in February of "the need to give the signal of revolt to millions of starving peasants." Nothing came of it. To friends from Moscow a weary Zhelyabov, with the exhaustion of despair written over his face, was saying: "If we fail, then

Moscow must continue the fight." It was as though he knew in his bones that the revolutionaries in St. Petersburg would be wiped out.

On February 20 a meeting was held in an apartment in the Telezhnaya. Present were Zhelyabov, Sophie Perovskaya, Kibalchich, Ignaty Grinevitsky, Timofey Mikhailov, Nikolay Rysakov, and Ivan Emilyanov. Grinevitsky, who was known as Kotik, was twenty-four. He was a Catholic, the son of a small landowner near Grodno, with a round, pleasant face and a studious manner. Timofey Mikhailov was twenty-one, the son of a Smolensk peasant. He had a broad forehead, eyes set wide apart, a firm chin, and could not be taken for anyone but a peasant, though he was a metalworker by trade. Rysakov was an eighteen-year-old student from a poor family, quiet and dreamy, and for a revolutionary unusually religious. He came from Tikhvin in the south; his father worked in a lumberyard and gave him a small allowance to help him to make his way through technical school. Most of the allowance went into the treasury of the party. Emilyanov was nineteen. He had been brought up by his grandfather who was employed at the Russian embassy at Constantinople, and he spoke with a heavy Bessarabian accent. These four, all of them closely attached to Zhelyabov, who had been consistently recruiting through the winter, had offered to be bomb throwers.

The meeting in the apartment in the Telezhnaya was to put the finishing touches to their plans. The gallery under the Malaya Sadovaya was now ready to receive the cylinders of dynamite. Kibalchich explained the nature of the hand bombs. They were like heavy hand grenades, exploding at the moment a glass vial broke inside them, and weighed five pounds. All that remained was to choose the day for the explosion. It was decided that the attack should take place on Sunday, March 1, when the Emperor made his usual morning journey to the Riding School to review the honor guard. If the Emperor's carriage passed through the Malaya Sadovaya, then he would be blown to pieces by the underground mine. If he escaped, the bomb throwers would be waiting for him. Zhelyabov himself would give the signal.

Perovskaya was unusually nervous during these last days, and seems to have suffered from forebodings. There were rumors that the cheese shop was about to be raided. They worked in an atmosphere of exhaustion and relentless pressure. Zhelyabov was usually in good humor, but the strain could be seen in his too-easy laughter. Once Sophie was observed holding his hand and looking up at him with an expression which suggested they would not be long together. There were constant conferences. Kibalchich was insisting that the bomb throwers should practice throwing bombs in a deserted quarry outside the city; he complained that they were behaving like amateurs. So far there were no arrests, and no evidence that the police were watching them. One evening Zhelyabov called a conference with Perovskaya, Rysakov, Timofey Mikhailov, and Grinevitsky. Zhelyabov looked ill, slept badly and complained of severe headaches, but his eyes were glowing. He informed them that in less than a week a Tsar would be dead. On the next day, at half past seven in the evening, when he was calling on a friend, the police pounced on him. They were too quick to give him time to draw his revolver. One of the policemen had been present at the Trial of the 193 and had recognized him.

"So you're Zhelyabov," the policeman exclaimed.

"Your very humble servant," Zhelyabov answered, "but it is not going to help you in the least."

Everything had been arranged so that the attempt could proceed without Zhelyabov. On the morning of the twenty-eighth none of them knew of Zhelyabov's arrest. Kibalchich said he was probably busy; there were a hundred possibilities to explain his absence. He took his bomb throwers to the Smolny Monastery near the Cathedral of the Redemption. They found a gravel pit and practiced throwing dummy bombs. Finally Timofey Mikhailov threw a live bomb. It was a small one, but it gave off a good deal of smoke and flame. The next morning they were to meet in the apartment on the Telezhnaya, and as far as Kibalchich knew there was nothing to prevent the attack from being successful.

On the afternoon of February 28 the police became once more suspicious of the cheese shop. They sent round a general from the Corps of Engineers disguised as a municipal surveyor. The general poked around. The conspirators had concealed the entrance to the gallery. There was a pile of coke in one corner of the store room. The general kicked at it. If he had kicked a little harder, he would have discovered the entrance to the gallery, where the cylinders were already in position. He asked about the deep layers of straw on the floor. They explained that the straw was used for packing cheese. He failed to see the earth piled under the bed. It was a perfunctory examination. Suddenly a cat came into the room, rubbed itself against the general's boots, and everyone was smiling. They talked about the cat for a while, and soon the general left.

The next morning the news of Zhelyabov's arrest was known. Alone, with two bombs on her lap, Sophie Perovskaya drove in a carriage to her appointment with Grinevitsky and Rysakov. A little while later Kibalchich, also with two bombs, drove to his rendezvous with Emilyanov and Mikhailov. The last instructions were given. It was agreed that all the bomb throwers should be in their places by noon.

Shortly after Grinevitsky woke up, he wrote a letter to be given to his comrades in the event of his death:

> . . . Alexander II must die. His days are numbered. I or another will bring about this last terrible blow; and the sound of the blow will be heard

all over Russia and the echo of it will penetrate into the most distant corners
—it cannot be long delayed.

He will die, and with him we shall die, his enemies, his executioners . . .
What of the future?

How many more victims will our dear and unhappy country demand before we have achieved our freedom? I am terrified by the thought, as I
stand now with one foot in the grave, that after me there will be many beloved sacrifices, many men killed, in the final death struggle with despotism
. . . History shows that the luxurious tree of freedom needs blood to
quicken its roots.

It is not my fate that I shall take part in that final battle. Fate has revealed for me an early death, and I shall not see our day, our hour of victory; and never shall I know the blazing light of our triumph. But I believe
that by dying I am doing all that is in my power to do, and no one on earth
can demand more of me.

A few hours after writing this letter Grinevitsky was dead. So was the
Tsar.

THE DEATH OF AN EMPEROR

A T EIGHT-THIRTY on the morning of March 1 Tsar Alexander II rose
in his bedroom in the Winter Palace overlooking the Neva. It was
a cold day with thick snow on the ground, but the sky was clear. It was
Sunday. Bells were ringing. He was not oppressed by any sense of coming
disaster. On the contrary he was exhilarated by the brightness of the day
and by the prospect of spending the afternoon leisurely with his young
wife, the Princess Yurievskaya, whom he had married morganatically
after the death of the Empress. His only official task for the day consisted
of reviewing a guard of honor at the riding school called the Manège, just
off the Mikhailovsky Square.

Afterward his children remembered that he was in good humor when
he took them for a walk in the palace gardens. Then there was divine
service in the royal chapel, followed by a light breakfast. Around ten
o'clock the Emperor went to his study for his usual meeting with Loris-
Melikov. For some time they discussed a proposed draft law for the
establishment of a commission to report on the laws passed by the State

Council. It was widely believed that this draft law would herald a new constitution. The majority of the members of the State Council approved of the law, but serious criticisms had been raised against it and the Emperor had for some weeks postponed a final decision. At some time shortly after eleven-thirty, sitting in his study with the wide windows looking out over the frozen garden, Alexander II formally accepted the draft law and ordered it published in the *Official Gazette* and in the newspapers. He gave the signed document to Loris-Melikov and soon afterward went to the boudoir of Princess Yurievskaya, exclaiming that he had at last signed the law and hoped the people would now believe he intended to grant everything in his power. He spoke very solemnly, and Princess Yurievskaya remembered afterwards that he made the sign of the cross as he said: "Yes, tomorrow it will be published in the newspapers—this is my order." He stayed only five minutes with the Princess. As he was leaving, she said: "I beg you not to ride along the Nevsky Prospect. I would be so much happier if you went by the Ekaterininsky Canal."

"So I shall," the Emperor answered, and those were the last words she ever heard from him.

In fine humor, at exactly 12:55, the Emperor entered a covered carriage for the journey to the Manège. The review passed off creditably. There were no incidents. The Emperor was observed to be unusually gracious to the officers, and he complimented the troops. Afterward he made the short journey to the Mikhailovsky Palace, where he took coffee with the Grand Duchess Ekaterina, the daughter of his uncle the Grand Duke Mikhail and the Grand Duchess Elena Pavlovna, who had been one of the leaders of the movement which led to the freeing of the serfs in 1861. Both uncle and aunt were dead. The Emperor was particularly devoted to the daughter. Over coffee he told her about the new draft law, smiled and seemed completely at ease. He stayed with her only fifteen minutes, then ordered the coachman to return to the Winter Palace by way of the Ekaterininsky Canal. It was now a few minutes past two o'clock.

The clear sky of the early morning had given place to heavy clouds. The streets were drab and gray, the snow turning to slush and the wind whistling. All along the Inzhenernaya were heaps of piled up, dirty snow. The streets were crowded with worshippers returning from church. As the Tsar's carriage bowled along, Cossack outriders on either side and a Cossack guard riding ahead, with two horse-drawn sleighs filled with policemen following behind, the Tsar could reflect that he had safely avoided all the dangers Princess Yurievskaya had pointed out to him, and yet it had been an entirely memorable day: a new draft law had been formally approved, he had spent a delightful hour at the riding school, and soon he would sit over a light lunch, there would be another walk in the garden with the children, and then there would be the usual leisurely Sunday evening interrupted only by another short service in the royal chapel.

The carriage flashed down the Inzhenernaya and then turned sharply along the Ekaterininsky Canal. Fifty yards further on Rysakov threw the bomb. He lobbed it under the carriage, hoping to bring the carriage to a stop. If the Tsar survived the bomb, Rysakov was prepared to shoot him. There was a sheet of flame and a loud explosion. The carriage, however, held together: the back axle was damaged, and the seat, sides and back were torn by bomb fragments. The horses bolted, the coachmen whipping them on, and swaying a little from side to side, the carriage followed. The Tsar shouted: "Stop!" A hundred yards further on the coachman succeeded in bringing the horses to a halt. For a few moments the Tsar remained inside the carriage. Then the sleigh with Colonel Dvorzhitsky, the Chief of Police, drove up. Dvorzhitsky jumped off his sleigh and ran to the battered carriage and opened the door, expecting to find the Tsar wounded or perhaps dead. He was delighted and surprised when the Tsar stepped out, looking pale but unhurt. Dvorzhitsky said something about his gratitude for the Tsar's escape and advised a quick return to the palace. For some reason the Tsar wanted to return to the scene of the explosion. He could hear a child screaming in the distance. There were groans from some of the Cossacks who had been wounded by fragments. He looked strangely preoccupied, like a man compelled to move toward an inevitable destiny. By this time two marines had thrown themselves upon Rysakov. They held him, waiting for the police. The second sleigh, containing Police Captain Koch, had already veered round. The two marines shouted that they had caught the terrorist. Sulphur-yellow smoke was still rising over the place where the bomb had fallen, and the Grand Duke Mikhail, who heard the explosion and saw the smoke from a nearby street, came running up. The Emperor was limping as he walked along the narrow pavement beside the parapet which overlooks the Canal. He was unguarded, for all the Cossacks except those who were wounded were still mounted, and Colonel Dvorzhitsky followed some paces behind, not knowing what to do and hardly caring, for the matter was out of his hands: the Tsar was determined to walk to the scene of the explosion.

By this time Captain Koch had searched Rysakov and found his revolver.

"Who are you?" Captain Koch shouted.

Rysakov shrugged his shoulders. He was sweating profusely. The two marines and some more policemen who came hurrying up were pressing him against the parapet, and he was almost exactly in the same spot from where he had thrown the bomb.

The crowd which had formed mysteriously after the explosion was out of hand. Everyone was shouting and screaming. Everyone was fighting for a good position to see Rysakov or to see the yellow stain left in the snow by the explosion or to see the two people who were lying in the street, wounded and writhing. One was a Cossack of the escort, the other a baker's boy, Nikolay Maximov, fourteen years old, who only a few moments before had been walking down the street with a basket of bread balanced on his head. The boy was dying. He screamed incessantly in a pool of blood. One of the few Cossacks who had not remained on horseback came running up when the Tsar was close to the boy and said: "Your Majesty, the crowd is too big. It would be safer if you didn't go among them." The Tsar answered: "You need not worry. I want to get a little closer." The Cossack then went to Dvorzhitsky and said: "My Colonel, the crowd is far too big. It's dangerous, and we must get the Tsar away." Dvorzhitsky waved the Cossack away. Suddenly one of the officers of the guard called out in alarm: "Where is the Tsar?" "I am safe, thank God," the Tsar replied, and pointed in the direction of the dying boy. At that moment Rysakov, who was being pommeled by the police and the marines, shouted: "We shall see yet whether you are safe." Afterward Rysakov denied making the statement, but it was a likely thing for him to say and it was reported by careful observers. There was a stunned silence. The Tsar walked straight up to Rysakov and said: "So you threw the bomb?"

"Yes."

"What is your name?"

"Glasov, artisan."

"A fine fellow," the Tsar said contemptuously and then moved away, calling to Dvorzhitsky to show him where the bomb fell.

Dvorzhitsky was in a strange, careless mood, his mind dulled by the excitement and the shock of the explosion. As Princess Yurievskaya complained afterward, he behaved throughout with all the simple-minded alacrity of a footman and completely forgot his duty as commander of the Tsar's security guards. It was not his task to open the door of the battered carriage for the Tsar to get out. This could have been done as well by any one of the Cossacks. His task was to protect the Tsar even against the Tsar's expressed wishes. He should have insisted that the carriage be driven to the palace and he should have prevented the Tsar from mingling with the crowd. With Dvorzhitsky hanging on the heels of the Tsar and Koch guarding the terrorist although there were a number of army officers who could have taken charge of Rysakov, the situation was out of hand. Everyone seemed to be sleepwalking. The Tsar was dragging his left leg and gazing about him with a strange, strained expression. Afterward blood was discovered inside the carriage, and it is possible that he was severely cut by shattered glass at the time of the explosion and did not know he was wounded.

The crowd was now so thick around the Tsar that Dvorzhitsky had to force a way along the pavement. Grinevitsky was leaning against the parapet, having come up from his position at the intersection of the Malaya Sadovaya and the Italyanskaya. Pale and smiling, wearing a fur cap, his hands crossed over his chest, he waited until the Tsar was only two feet away and then he hurled the bomb with all his strength at the Tsar's feet. Once again there was a huge yellow fountain of stone, snow, fire, and smoke. There were screams and groans, then a terrifying silence. When the smoke lifted, twenty people were dying in the snow. Dvorzhitsky was unrecognizable, blood streaming from sixty separate wounds, though they were mostly surface wounds, since he had been behind the Tsar when the bomb exploded and the Tsar's body took the full force of the explosion. All round him were pools of blood and pieces of torn flesh. Someone was shouting: "Help! Stop him! Over there, in the garden!" The words made no sense. Grinevitsky was lying close to the Emperor, and he too was unrecognizable, hardly more than a mess of bloody pulp.

The Tsar's body had been flung against the parapet. He was still alive, but the blood was pouring from his shattered legs. Lying on his back, with his head against the parapet, his eyes closed, breathing heavily, he had never looked less like a Tsar. His military cap had been blown off, his uniform was in rags, his sword had gone, and blood streamed from every part of his body. For a while he kept murmuring words which no one could understand, then he whispered to Dvorzhitsky: "Help me," and then a little later: "It's so cold, so cold." Some cadets, returning from a parade, rushed up. They threw a cadet mantle over the mangled body and put a cadet cap on the Tsar's head. The Grand Duke Mikhail, the Tsar's brother, forced a way through the cadets and bent over the dying man:

"Alexander, can you hear me?"

"Yes."

"Tell me how you feel."

"Hurry. Take me to the palace."

The cadets, who seem to have been afflicted with the same tendency towards sleepwalking as the police, began to lift the body toward Koch's police sleigh. Someone shouted that it would be much better to remove the Tsar to a nearby house where his wounds could be attended to immediately.

"No, to the palace," the Tsar murmured in a voice distinctly heard by the Grand Duke, the cadets, and the two Cossacks who had taken charge of the sleigh under Cavalry Captain Kulebyakin.

Kulebyakin ordered the cadets away. The Cossacks were ordered to drive the sleigh to the palace. There was no stretcher. Bleeding profusely, the Tsar was sitting up in the sleigh between Kulebyakin and the Grand Duke. The crowd was screaming. Now everyone knew the Tsar was dying and nearly everyone wanted to dip a handkerchief in the bloody snow. Someone was singing the national anthem. More people came running up. The Tsar opened his eyes, and saw the blood on the cavalry captain's sleeve.

"So you are hurt too, Kulebyakin?"

"It doesn't matter. We are only concerned with Your Majesty."

The Tsar made a gesture which indicated that he understood, then his head fell back and he closed his eyes. Some Cossacks had been sent on ahead to prepare the palace for the Emperor's arrival. "Hurry—the palace. I want to die there," the Tsar murmured, and then was silent. They were the last words he ever spoke.

In the palace Princess Yurievskaya was already dressed in a fur hat and a fur cloak for the afternoon promenade in the garden which the Tsar had promised her. Suddenly from downstairs there came a cry: "The Tsar is ill!" Immediately the Princess imagined he was suffering from one of his recurrent attacks of asthma, and she thought of the oxygen balloons. She ordered a servant to carry six or seven balloons to the Tsar, and she had one in each hand as she flew down the stairs. At the foot of the stairs she paused. The door was opening, and some Cossacks were bringing into the palace a strange unrecognizable object, all scarlet. She could make nothing of this until one of the Cossacks shouted that it was the Tsar. The body was taken up the marble steps, and then along a corridor leading to the Tsar's study, where it was placed on a couch near the desk. The Princess followed. When she realized at last that it was her husband lying there, she hurled herself on him, fondled him, cried out to him, kissed him, held his head in her hands, her fingers moving so frantically that she seemed to be pulling out his hair. All the time she kept screaming: "Sasha! Sasha!"

When Count Baranov murmured: "Courage, courage, Princess! He is still alive!" she let go and allowed others to attend the Tsar.

Two *valets de chambre* began to undress the Tsar, to make him ready for the doctors who had been summoned, but what remained of his uniform was in rags and sticking to his flesh and could not be unbuttoned. They slit the uniform with a pair of scissors down the back.

When Dr. Kruglevsky, Surgeon Extraordinary to the Tsar, arrived in the study, the bleeding was still going on. He made a brief examination. He found that the right leg had been torn off, the left leg was shattered, and there were more than two hundred separate wounds. One eye was shut, the other expressionless. The handsome head, once the blood was washed off, was still recognizable.

"I have come too late," the doctor said. "Nothing can be done."

"No, no, you must do everything you can to save him!" the Princess exclaimed.

In a dead silence Dr. Kruglevsky began to bandage the wounds to prevent the blood from flowing on the carpet. He asked how the Tsar had been transported to the palace, and when told of the sleigh ride he groaned. Was there no stretcher? Was there no way to prevent the jolting?

The Grand Duke Mikhail whispered, hardly knowing what he was saying: "I was there! I saw it happen!"

Princess Yurievskaya turned on him sharply and said: "If you were there, then how did you let it happen?"

"I was too late. I could do nothing."

The room was crowded. The Tsarevich Alexander took his place by the couch. The Emperor's remaining eye was wide-open, unseeing. There was almost no pulse, almost no breath coming from the lungs. The Princess sprinkled water on his face and rubbed ether into his temples and put the oxygen balloons close to his lips and nose. Dr. Botkin suggested a blood transfusion, but there were no instruments available. Kruglevsky suggested that as soon as the Emperor returned to consciousness, his legs, one shattered, the other hanging to the thigh only by ligaments, should be amputated. The Princess agreed. She said later: "If God had let him live even without his legs, he would still have been my beloved, and he would have belonged to me all the more, for then he would have had to relinquish the throne."

The chief of police arrived, saluted smartly and said he had compiled a full report of the tragedy. No one paid any attention to him except the Tsarevich who looked at him coldly, and then returned to contemplate his dying father.

The Tsar was behaving strangely. His head kept nodding from side to side. The expressionless eye was still staring fixedly. Dr. Kruglevsky had his fingers on the Tsar's pulse. Someone said: "Silence, please. The end is near."

The last sacraments were administered by an archpriest whose hands shook so violently that he dropped the golden spoon holding the sacramental mixture of bread and wine. Dr. Kruglevsky was still holding the Tsar's hand. Suddenly he let it drop.

"The Tsar is dead," he announced in a loud voice. It was 3:35 P.M.

The Princess screamed and fell to the floor, and two guardsmen were summoned to carry her to her private quarters.

The new Tsar was standing by the window. Powerfully built, six feet tall, with huge hands which could tear a pack of cards in two, he alone seemed to show no signs of grief. When the chief of police strode up and asked whether the Tsar had any orders to give, Alexander III snapped: "Orders? Yes, of course. The police have apparently lost their heads. The Army will take charge of the situation. I shall confer with my ministers at once in the Anichkov Palace." Shortly afterward the new Tsar abruptly left the room.

Such was the end of a Tsar who had ruled despotically. His murderer survived a few hours longer. Grinevitsky's mangled body was removed to a hospital. He had as many wounds as the Tsar. The police kept watch by the bed, hoping he would talk in delirium. For a few moments before ten o'clock he regained consciousness. A police inspector asked him his name, and he answered in a clear voice: "I know nothing," and died shortly afterward.

When Grinevitsky threw the bomb, Emilyanov was running in the direction of the Ekaterininsky Canal. He had heard the first bomb, and he was only twenty paces away from the Emperor when the second bomb was thrown. He did not act like a revolutionary, and he was puzzled by his own behavior. When he saw the Tsar fall, he ran with the crowd to help him, his bomb still wrapped in paper under his arm. He risked being arrested on the spot, and perhaps being torn to pieces by the mob, and he was one of the first to reach the Tsar's side. He stayed with the crowd for a while, and then with Timofey Mikhailov made his way to the apartment on the Telezhnaya where the conspirators had agreed to meet.

That night St. Petersburg was a nest of rumors. No official or unofficial statements were issued by the police. Rysakov refused to divulge his identity. It was widely believed that Alexander II was assassinated at the orders of high officials determined to maintain the autocracy at all costs. The mysterious behavior of the Tsar, the incompetence of the Cossack escort and the police, the silence of Grinevitsky, the strange accident by which the Tsar's death occurred just at the moment when he had signed a draft decree designed to give greater freedom to the country—all these things suggested that the assassination had been brought about by members of the "Court party"; and even when on the next day the Narodnaya Volya issued a manifesto to the workers of Russia, claiming full responsibility for the murder, suspicions were not dissipated. The manifesto read:

Today, March 1, Alexander II, the tormentor of the people, has been put to death by us, socialists. He was killed because he did not care for his people, burdened them with unauthorized taxes, deprived the peasants of their land and surrendered the workers to the mercy of plunderers and exploiters. He did not give the people freedom: he did not listen to their griefs and their tears. He defended only the rich and lived himself in the utmost luxury, while the people went hungry. The Tsar's servants, from the village police to the high officials, plundered the people and barbarously maltreated the peasants; and these servants of the Tsar were especially protected and rewarded by the Tsar. Those who stood out for the people he hanged or exiled to Siberia. So he was killed. A Tsar should be a good shepherd, ready to lay down his life for his flock: Alexander II was a ravening wolf and a terrible death has struck him. Now a new Tsar, Alexander III, climbs to the throne. He must not be allowed to behave like his father. May he proceed to hold general elections in the villages and towns and in all the factories. May he recognize the sorrows and deep needs of the people, and go forward into the truth! . . .

By the time this manifesto appeared, Rysakov was beginning to crack. He had been confronted with Zhelyabov in prison on the night of the assassination, but though they quietly celebrated their triumph, neither revealed the names of accomplices to the police. On March 2 Rysakov was examined again, at greater length. Dark-faced and thickset, with unruly hair, and a look of peasantlike stolidity, he was an easy prey for Colonel Dobrinsky, the most brilliant of the police officials in charge of eliciting information from captured terrorists. The usual promises of lenient treatment were made. The enormity of his crime was constantly repeated to him. He was told that the Tsar had signed the draft law a few hours before the assassination. Rysakov said little, but what he said was enough to start the police on a singularly successful effort to round up the whole band of terrorists. From Rysakov the police learned about the apartment in the Telezhnaya, and that night they sent a detachment to the apartment. Gesya Helfman and Nikolay Sablin were asleep when the police began to break down the door of the apartment. Sablin awoke, realized he would have to shoot his way out and took up a position near the door, firing through it, so that the police were forced to scatter and find hiding places on the landing. Then there was a long pause, followed by a single shot and a woman's screams for help. Sablin had shot himself through the head and Gesya Helfman had gone insane with grief. When the police broke in, they found Gesya Helfman standing motionless by the body of Sablin, unable to say anything at all except that she wanted the bombs to be carried to safety—she seems to have been afraid that a police bullet would set off one of the bombs. The police found two live bombs, a plan of St. Petersburg with pencil marks drawn around the Malaya Sadovaya and the Ekaterininsky Canal and another rough plan drawn on the back of an envelope. They removed Gesya Helfman to the House of Preliminary Detention, and kept watch over the empty apartment.

They did not have to wait long. Around eleven in the morning Timofey Mikhailov entered the house, climbed up the dark stairway and paused before Apartment 5. The police pounced on him. Mikhailov was heavily built, and was able to shrug them off. When he explained that he was searching for a cab-driver friend, the police almost believed his story, but told him to wait and gave him a chair inside the apartment where the bloodstains were still fresh on the bed. They thought Mikhailov would break under the strain of seeing the familiar apartment deserted by the conspirators and ringed round by the police. Mikhailov did not break. He suddenly jumped up, pulled out his revolver and began to shoot his way out, wounding two policemen before being disarmed. The police never explained why they had not searched him for weapons. Rysakov's hint about the apartment in the Telezhnaya was disastrous. It led to the suicide of Sablin, the death on the scaffold of Timofey Mikhailov and the death in prison some eighteen months later of Gesya Helfman.

There remained of the major conspirators Sophie Perovskaya and Nikolay Kibalchich.

Perovskaya was on the run, hiding in different apartments each night, wandering the streets during the day. She seemed totally impervious to the danger of being abroad in a city hung with black flags, with trigger-happy Cossacks stationed at every corner, and the police embarking on a wide-scale search of all the houses where the conspirators might be hiding. She was walking boldly down the Nevsky Prospect on March 3 when she bought a copy of a newspaper announcing that Zhelyabov had confessed to being the organizer of the assassination. She turned pale, but did not lose her self-control, and went walking down the street with the newspaper hanging in her hand, her face to the ground.

Those who saw her at the time say she was still beautiful and was full of a strange, elated tenderness. She was pale, with black rings under her eyes, and her voice, usually clear and sweet, had become a hoarse whisper, but otherwise she was unchanged. She kept talking about plans to rescue Zhelyabov. The conspirators still had secret channels in high places, and Perovskaya seems to have known exactly how far the examinations of Zhelyabov and Rysakov were progressing. Told to leave St. Petersburg and go into hiding, she refused, saying that if she left the city there would be no more hope of rescuing Zhelyabov; and thinking continually of Zhelyabov, so that the assassination of the Tsar and the arrest of Rysakov occupied only a small part of her mind, she was, according to one who knew her well, "like a bird who sees a hawk flying above her head, a hawk which has stolen her young."

We have only one clear glimpse of her in those days. One evening—it must have been March 6 or 7—Perovskaya slipped into Vera Figner's apartment on the Voznesensky Prospect, and asked whether she could spend the night there. Vera Figner was startled. The conspirators had sworn an oath to help each other. Why, then, should Perovskaya hesitate to ask for so small a thing as a night's lodging?

"I don't understand," Vera Figner said. "Why do you ask?"

"I ask because if the police raid the apartment and find me here, they will hang you as well."

"I have a revolver, and if they come, then I will shoot, whether you are here or not."

Perovskaya was strangely quiet that night. They talked about the past, about Zhelyabov and about the correspondence they were still carrying on with Nechayev. Perovskaya smiled often, but it was a sad little smile, and Vera Figner came to the conclusion that she knew she was doomed and was not even trying to escape. On March 10 the police caught up with her, and a week later they arrested Kibalchich. All of the major conspirators were now accounted for.

In the eyes of the Russian government a conspiracy to kill the Tsar could only come out of the depths. To the surprise of the jurists at the trial, the prisoners formed a cross section which included all elements in the Russian scene. There was Zhelyabov, born out of the peasantry, though he looked and behaved like a practiced administrator. There was Kibalchich, the son of a priest, with his black beard and dark penetrating eyes, a brilliant scientist who knew as much about explosives and jet propulsion as anyone then living. There was the weak-willed Rysakov, born out of the lower middle classes, though there was a good deal of the peasant in him. Timofey Mikhailov was a laborer, and Sophie Perovskaya was the pure aristocrat, with the aristocrat's sense of responsibility. Finally there was Gesya Helfman, the daughter of a rich Jewish manufacturer who left her home and deliberately worked as a seamstress in Kiev during the "To the People" movement.

Under arrest, the terrorists behaved according to character. Zhelyabov assumed full responsibility for the assassination and parried all efforts to incriminate others. Kibalchich read scientific treatises, and knowing he would die, did everything possible to see that his theories were carefully considered in scientific circles. Rysakov broke down completely, pleaded for mercy, incriminated everyone and to the very end hoped he would be allowed to lead a detachment of prison officers to the hiding places of the terrorists who were not yet arrested. Timofey Mikhailov sat quietly in his cell. Gesya Helfman, pregnant with the child of her husband, Nikolay Kolotkevich, did nothing to help the authorities arrest him, and he survived in freedom for a few more months until he was finally arrested. Perovskaya lived only for the moments when she could see Zhelyabov in the courtroom, but she was sufficiently aware of her appearance to ask her family to send her new clothes.

The fighting strength of the Narodnaya Volya had been broken, but the movement continued. On March 10 there appeared a long and carefully composed letter written ostensibly by the Executive Committee to the new Emperor Alexander III. The letter, which was actually composed by Tikhomirov, is an important document in the history of the Russian revolutionary movement. Many, perhaps all, of the demands made to the head of the state are applicable to the Russia of today. The letter covers six closely printed pages in that vast compilation of revolutionary documents known as *Literatura Narodnoi Voli,* and is so important that it is here quoted at considerable length:

A LETTER FROM THE EXECUTIVE COMMITTEE
TO ALEXANDER III
YOUR MAJESTY!

While the Executive Committee fully comprehends the deep sorrow you must feel at the present moment, it does not feel justified in postponing an explanation simply on the grounds of natural delicacy. There is something higher than the most legitimate personal sentiments, and this is the duty we owe to our country, the duty to which all citizens must sacrifice themselves and their feelings and even the feelings of others. In obedience to the all-powerful demands of duty, we have decided to address you immediately, not waiting upon events, just as the whole historical process now threatening us with rivers of blood and terrible convulsions also refuses to wait upon events.

The bloody tragedy of the Ekaterininsky Canal was not an accident, nor was it in any way unexpected. The events of the last decade have made it absolutely inevitable; and herein lies its deep significance for the man who has been placed at the head of the government. Such occurrences can be explained as the result of individual acts of malignity or as the work of evilly disposed "gangsters,"* but only by those who are incapable of analyzing the life of a nation. Through the last ten years we have seen how, in spite of strong persecution and the denial of all liberties, in spite of the Tsar's total lack of interest in his own dignity and in spite of the absolute sacrifice of everything in order to suppress the revolutionary movement, this movement has obstinately extended and has attracted to itself the best elements of the country, the most energetic and self-sacrificing people of Russia, and for three years the revolutionaries have carried on a desperate war with the administration.

You must know, Your Majesty, that the government of the late Emperor was not lacking in energy. It hanged the innocent and guilty among us and filled prisons and remote provinces with exiles. It caught dozens of so-called "revolutionary leaders" and hanged them: they died with the courage and tranquillity of martyrs, but the movement did not cease—on the contrary, it grew and strengthened. No, Your Majesty, the revolutionary movement does not owe its existence to individual conspirators. It is a process of the social organism, and the scaffolds raised for the more energetic exponents of this process are as powerless to save the outgrown order of things as the Crucifixion of the Saviour was powerless to save the ancient world from the reforming triumphs of Christianity.

The government may well be able to arrest and hang an immense number of individuals. It can suppress a great number of revolutionary groups. It

* Tikhomirov uses the word "sheiks."

may even destroy the most important of existing revolutionary organizations. But the issues remain unchanged. It is the circumstance of the age that creates revolutionaries, a whole nation's discontent, the urge of all Russia toward new social forms. It is impossible to exterminate a whole nation; it is just as impossible to stifle discontent by repression: discontent flourishes in such a soil. So, whenever a revolutionary dies, his place is immediately taken by others who come out of the people in ever-increasing numbers, but now they are more deeply angered and more energetic than before. In order to carry on the war these people organize themselves on the basis of the experience derived from their predecessors. So the revolutionary movement has grown stronger in numbers and in the quality of its men. And all this is evident from the history of the last ten years. . . .

If we look back clearly and dispassionately at those grief-stricken years, we shall be able to prophesy accurately the future progress of the revolutionary movement if the policy of the government remains unchanged. The revolutionary movement will continue to grow and to extend; acts of terrorism will increase in frequency and intensity; the revolutionary organism will constantly be bringing forward new and altogether stronger forms to replace those which have been destroyed. Meanwhile there will be increasing numbers of discontented people in the country; confidence in the government will decline; and the idea of revolution, its possibility and inevitability, will establish itself in Russia more and more firmly. A revolutionary earthquake, a terrible explosion, a tremendous bloody upheaval will complete the destruction of the ancient order.

Upon what, then, depends this terrible and lamentable prospect? Yes, Your Majesty, the words "terrible and lamentable" are written here deliberately—they are not an empty phrase. We understand better than others the lamentable destruction of so much talent and energy—so many losses in bloody skirmishes and in the work of breaking down so much that possessed strength which under better conditions might have been expended in creative labor in developing the intelligence, the welfare, and the social life of the Russian people.

Whence comes this lamentable necessity for bloody conflict?

It comes, Your Majesty, from the lack in Russia of a real government in the true sense of the word. A government in the very nature of things *should give outward form to the aspirations of the people and give effect to the people's will.* But with us—excuse the expression—the government has degenerated into a camarilla and deserves to be called a set of "usurping gangsters," a title more appropriate to the government itself than to the Executive Committee . . .

These are the reasons why the Russian government exerts no moral influence and has no support among the people. These are the reasons why Russia brings forth so many revolutionaries. These are the reasons why the murder of a Tsar excites in so many people only joy and sympathy. Yes, Your Majesty, do not be deceived by the reports of flatterers and sycophants—the murder of a Tsar is popular in Russia.

There are only two ways out of this state of affairs—revolution, absolutely inevitable and not to be averted by any punishments, or a voluntary transfer of supreme power to the hands of the people. In the interest of our country and in the hope of averting a useless waste of energy and in the hope of preventing the terrors that always accompany revolutions, the Executive Committee begs Your Majesty to proceed along the second course. Rest assured that as soon as the Supreme Power ceases to rule arbitrarily and accedes to the demands of the people, you may without fear discharge the spies who disgrace your administration, return the guards to their barracks, and burn the scaffolds that are demoralizing the people. At that moment the Executive Committee will voluntarily terminate its own existence and the organizations formed around it will disperse, so that the members may devote themselves to cultural work among the people.

We address Your Majesty as men who have disregarded all prejudices, setting aside the distrust created by the government throughout a century. We forget you are the representative of the authority which has so often deceived and injured the people. We turn to you as a citizen and a man of honor. We trust that no personal bitterness will cause you to forget your duty or extinguish in your mind a desire to know the truth. We too have cause for bitterness. You have lost your father. We have lost fathers, brothers, wives, children, and our dearest friends. We are ready to suppress our personal feelings if the good of Russia demands it. We expect the same from you.

We set no conditions for you: do not therefore allow these propositions to embitter you. The conditions prerequisite for a transfer from revolutionary activity to peaceful labor are not imposed by us, but by history. In our belief there are two conditions:

1. A general amnesty for all political crimes: because they were not crimes, but rather the fulfillment of social duty.
2. The summoning of representatives of all the Russian peoples to consider the existing social and economic order, and so to remodel it in accordance with the people's desires.

But we believe it necessary to remind you that the representatives of the people can come together to legalize the Supreme Power only if the elections are perfectly free. Such elections should be held under the following conditions:

1. Delegates should be sent from all the existing classes of society without distinction, and in number proportionate to the number of inhabitants.
2. Canvassing on the part of the delegates and the elections themselves should be absolutely unrestricted, and therefore the government, pending the organization of the National Assembly, should authorize as temporary measures:
   a. Complete freedom of the press.
   b. Complete freedom of speech.
   c. Complete freedom of public meeting.
   d. Complete freedom in election programs.

This is the only way in which Russia can return to the path of normal and peaceful development.

We declare solemnly before the people of our country and before the whole world that our party will submit unconditionally to the decisions of a National Assembly elected in this manner, and we will never allow ourselves to offer violent resistance to any government that the National Assembly may sanction.

And now, Your Majesty, decide. Before you are two courses: you must make your choice between them. We can only beg of fate that your judgment and your conscience will lead you to choose the only course consistent with the welfare of Russia, with your honor and with your duty toward your country.

Tikhomirov had had no contact with the revolutionaries in prison when he wrote his letter to the Emperor, but he had discussed his views with them frequently. The letter, too long for effective propaganda, too short for a revolutionary handbook, and lacking in the grotesque imaginative leaps which make Nechayev's *Revolutionary Catechism* so memorable, achieved the opposite of what Tikhomirov hoped to achieve. The new Emperor read it, and was enraged. Through the whole of his reign he was determined to govern Russia with implacable absolutism.

THE JUDGMENT

W ITH THE PRISONERS under arrest the government set about arranging a trial which would be brief and salutary. Now at last, having committed their greatest crime, the terrorists had been rounded up, and they could expect no mercy. There would be a number of swift executions, followed by a long silence in which the country, warned of its errors, would realize that only obedience to the autocracy would lead to a few small social improvements. The autocracy, instead of being weakened, had been strengthened. Hardly anyone doubted in court circles that the main strength of the terrorist movement had collapsed. All over Russia in those early days following the assassination the grief of the people was evident. Then gradually the wheel turned full circle, and soon the memory of the dead Tsar as a paternal overseer of his people gave place to memories of his excesses: from being murderers the prisoners became heroes. Zhelyabov and Perovskaya especially were regarded as heroic figures. People recoiled at the thought that these legendary figures should be condemned to hang.

Throughout his life Tolstoy made many pronouncements concerning the government, but he rarely caught the mood of the people. One evening, two weeks before the trial, he threw himself down on the leather

sofa of his study and tried to think out all the implications of the trial
and the inevitable executions. He was tormented by the thought that the
punishment of the prisoners would lead to a hardening of the movement
for social reform. Good must be returned for evil; nothing is gained by
vindictiveness; only Christian charity can dare to reap a reward. Best to
forgive the Tsar's murderers: give them money and send them away to
America; and if they must be fought, then they should be fought with
spiritual weapons. Their fate haunted him. He imagined Sophie Perovskaya standing on the little tabouret underneath the gallows, involuntarily
adjusting the noose until the knot lay under her windpipe, "and then when
the tabouret was pushed away and the cord pressed the soft gristle of her
throat and the hard vertebrae of her neck, she felt a sudden rush of blood
to her head and her whole body writhed, and then, slowly suffocating
under the black cap, her face turned blue and the eyes popped out of
their sockets."

For Tolstoy, as for thousands and perhaps millions of Russians, the fate
of Perovskaya was so terrible, so unnecessary and so much a part of the
tragedy of the times that he imagined every detail of it long before it
happened. He could not forget it. Thinking of Perovskaya, he remembered how he was once attacked by a bear. "I lay under the bear and
looked into the large warm mouth with the wet, white, glistening teeth.
He breathed over me and I saw him turning his head to get into a position
where he could bite into both of my temples at once, and then hurrying
or simply because his appetite was excited, he made a trial snap in the
air and again opened wide his mouth—that red, wet, hungry mouth, dripping with saliva."

Half-dozing on the sofa, in a waking nightmare, all the tragedy of the
trial came to Tolstoy with terrible force: it seemed to him that it was not
Alexander III, the judges, and the hangman, who were sentencing Perovskaya to death, but Tolstoy himself. As soon as he awoke he began to
write in white heat a letter to the Tsar.

In this letter, the most extraordinary that he ever wrote, Tolstoy begins
haltingly, deferentially, hardly knowing to what extremes he would dare
to go. He began by announcing himself as an insignificant, weak and
worthless person, who lived deep in the country and received news only
through the newspapers, and he realized how strange and audacious it
was that he should bring himself to advise the Tsar. Nevertheless his conscience could not rest. He put aside all flowery introductions and demanded the right to speak to the Tsar as man to man. And then he went
on at once to beg for an unprecedented act of mercy—the Tsar should forgive his father's murderers. There followed an extraordinary outline of
the history of the revolutionary movement in which Tolstoy finds himself

standing at a point midway between the autocracy and the revolutionaries, judging and excusing both. He wrote:

There appeared about twenty years ago a group formed mostly of young
people who had set their hearts against the existing government. They
imagined a new social order, or even no order at all, and by all manner of
godless and inhuman means, by incendiarism, robberies and murders, they
attempted to destroy existing society. For twenty years there has been war
against these people, but instead of dying out, this war only increases in
violence, and these people have reached a most terrible state of cruelty,
which is indeed harmful to the state.

Those who fought against this plague have employed two methods: one
method was to cut out the canker by severe punishments, the other was to
allow the disease to follow its course. But there is a third way: that of Christian forgiveness, and this has not yet been employed.

Today, your position is that of a sick man at the height of a critical illness.
One false application of remedial measures, one mistake in diagnosis, and
the patient will be dead! . . .

By some fatal and terrible error these revolutionaries were the victims of
a fearful hatred of your father, and so this outrageous murder was committed. The hate harbored by these revolutionaries may die with them. As
for you, though they die, you are the innocent victim of your exalted position. On your hands is no blood. Nevertheless you stand at the parting of the
ways. In a few days it may be that those who believe Christianity is no more
than talk, and blood must be spilled and death must reign in the political
ways of life—it may be that these men will triumph; and then it will happen
that you will pass forever from that blessed state of purity and life in God
and enter into the pathways of state necessity, where everything is justified,
even the breaking of the law of God and man . . .

O Monarch, forgive them! Call these people to you: give them money:
send them away to America, and let there be written in your hand a manifesto beginning: "I say unto you, 'Love your enemies.' " I do not know how
others would feel, but for my part I would become your willing slave! I
would weep with emotion every time I heard your name, as I am now weeping! What am I saying? I do not know how others . . . But I *do* know! I
know that with these words love will pour like a flood over Russia.

By killing and destroying the revolutionaries you cannot contend against
them. It is not only their numbers which are important, but their ideals. To
struggle with them without spiritual weapons can lead only to defeat. They
demand enough for all, equality and freedom. To contend against them, you
must bring forward an even higher ideal. Only the ideal of love, forgiveness,
and the return of good for evil is sufficiently strong to contend with them.
Should you offer them your forgiveness, then I say that all Russia will melt
like wax before the image of the Emperor who follows in the law of Christ.

No one had ever dared to address the Tsar in these tones, and Tolstoy
was well aware that he would have immense difficulty in bringing the
letter to the Tsar's attention. He wrote to Pobedonostsev, the Procurator
of the Holy Synod, begging him to show the letter to the Tsar, and to his

friend Strakhov he sent another copy, asking Strakhov to see that it was put in the hands of Pobedonostsev. But the head of the Holy Synod, a former tutor of the Tsar, refused to have anything to do with it. Taken by devious routes the letter was handed to the Grand Duke Sergey, himself to be assassinated many years later. No reply was received from the Tsar. But Pobedonostsev wrote to the Tsar a letter in which he pleaded that nothing be allowed to interfere with the executions. In reply Alexander III reassured him: "Be calm. No one will dare to come to me with such proposals. I guarantee that all six shall be hanged." But Tolstoy had dared, and all over Russia there were people who hoped for an act of forgiveness.

Some weeks after the executions Pobedonostsev wrote a letter to Tolstoy in which he said: "My Christ is not your Christ. Mine is a man of strength and truth, healing the weak; yours has the features of one who is weak-willed and needs to be cured." It is just possible that the words were Alexander's message to Tolstoy.

Loris-Melikov originally planned to put Rysakov and Zhelyabov on trial together. The trial would be very brief, and followed by immediate execution. But as Rysakov gave more and more information, and there emerged the hope that the whole apparatus of the Narodnaya Volya might be rounded up, it was decided to wait. Meanwhile the Tsar took the precaution of absenting himself from St. Petersburg. The Ruler of All the Russias disappeared in his country palace at Gatchina, giving orders that trenches should be dug all round the palace to guard against mining by the revolutionaries. The destruction of the dining room in the Winter Palace was still a vivid memory.

The date of the trial was set for March 26. On the day before, Zhelyabov made an announcement in which he demanded trial by jury and urged that he could not be tried by the court of the Senate, which consisted of paid functionaries of the government. He had attacked the Tsar as the head of the government. It was up to the people to decide who was guilty. This was a warning to the authorities of the attitude he was likely to take; they rejected his demand and discussed the possibility of a summary execution of the criminals, and then rejected the idea only because they were afraid of the inevitable popular clamor. A short trial was best. The evidence must be conclusive, and the prisoners, though they would be allowed to speak, would be given comparatively little opportunity to use the dock as a forum for expressing their political views.

The prisoners were strangely subdued. They knew they would be executed. The trial was merely a formality. Sophie Perovskaya wrote to her mother, asking for cuffs and collars. Her dress had been torn, presumably in the struggle at the time of her arrest. She asked that the collars be rather narrow, and that there should be buttons to her cuffs. Her mother hurried from the country with the collars and cuffs and sought from Loris-Melikov permission to visit her daughter. After deliberately keeping her in the corridor outside his office, Loris-Melikov at last permitted her to enter the room. Scowling, he ordered Madame Perovskaya to obtain from her daughter the names and addresses of her accomplices, and the old lady answered that it was completely impossible for her to persuade Sophie against her own convictions. Loris-Melikov was tempted to refuse the permission she requested, but he finally allowed her to see her daughter in two brief interviews, with a sentry and police officer in attendance. Neither the mother nor the daughter had much to say to one another. Vera Figner speaks of how Sophie "lay with her head on her mother's knee like a sick, tired child, motionless and speechless." Occasionally they murmured a few words to one another, and once Sophie said: "I am not your only child, and so you have the others to care for." After the second interview Sophie wrote to her mother:

> My darling. I implore you to be calm and not to grieve for me. My fate does not affect me in the least and I await it with complete tranquillity. I have long expected it, and known that sooner or later it must come. And then too, my dear Mamma, my fate is not such a mournful one. I have lived according to my convictions, and it would have been impossible for me to have done otherwise. So I wait here with a tranquil conscience. The only thing that oppresses me is the thought of your grief, my adored Mother. It rends my heart.

The dilemma of the "sensitive murderers" has been expressed at greater length and with more subtlety by others, but until the time of Kaliayev no one ever expressed it so simply or so honestly. When Sophie entered the courtroom there was a small smile playing at the corners of her lips.

The trial began at eleven o'clock on the morning of March 26 in a courtroom packed with officials, the doors locked, the prisoners shackled, the old jurist Fuchs acting as president, sitting with a number of assessors representing the Estates of the Empire—a hand-picked rural headman represented the peasants. The assessors were silent and took no notable part in the trial. Fuchs himself had already received a message from the Tsar urging condign punishment for the accused, and though he behaved with strict legality it was clear that he was prepared to obey the Tsar's order to the letter.

When the six prisoners were led in, the order they were compelled to assume was significant. First came Rysakov, the weakest. He was followed by Mikhailov, Helfman, Kibalchich, Perovskaya, and Zhelyabov. One by one the prisoners were ordered to state their names, ages, religion, and occupation. At first Zhelyabov refused to answer. He declared that the manner in which the charge had been drawn up was vague and ridiculous, he denied the right of the court to put him on trial and he would refuse to answer questions put to him by hired assessors who would inevitably agree with the government's case. There was a long and involved argument between Zhelyabov and Fuchs. Finally Zhelyabov relented. He would answer questions so long as he was allowed to state his own case. Wearily, the urbane Fuchs allowed him the privilege of stating his case after he had answered the introductory questions:

"What is your name?"

"Andrey Ivanovich Zhelyabov."

"Your age?"

"Thirty."

"Your religion?"

"I was baptized into the Orthodox Church. However, I reject orthodoxy, although I admit the teachings of Jesus Christ—this teaching has an honored place among my moral convictions. I believe in the truth and justice of that teaching, and I solemnly declare that faith without works is dead. I believe that every true Christian should fight for the truth and for the rights of the oppressed and of those who are too weak to assert their rights; and I am prepared to suffer for them. Such is my creed."

The solemn admission of reverence toward the teaching of Jesus startled the assessors. The police dossiers indicated that Zhelyabov was an atheist. Then why this sudden conversion? The question was never answered. The philosopher Berdyaev later confessed to being deeply moved by Zhelyabov's tribute to Christianity. It is possible that Zhelyabov was merely paying a momentary tribute to "that moderate democrat Christ" who was worshiped by Pushkin.

Gaunt, severe, towering above the other prisoners, Zhelyabov behaved in court like an ideal witness. Unlike Nechayev, he stated his case under cross-examination simply, without rodomontade and with no appeal to the gallery. He was occasionally rebuked by the president, but usually for nothing more serious than a misunderstanding of the law. He admitted he was a member of the Executive Committee of the Narodnaya Volya, spoke about the years he had spent in peaceful propaganda among the peasants and told how he had inevitably come to the conclusion that the Russian bureaucracy was the enemy of all social growth. Fuchs demanded a retraction of the statement, but none came. Zhelyabov simply shrugged his shoulders, and was then allowed to continue. He found fault with the charge. The six prisoners in the dock did not form a secret society according to the terms of the indictment, and in any event Mikhailov had nothing to do with the matter. Asked his occupation, he said that for some years his main occupation had been the liberation of his fellow countrymen.

Muraviev, the Public Prosecutor, informed the court that he proposed to read the depositions of Colonel Dvorzhitsky and two other witnesses wounded in the explosion. Zhelyabov countered by demanding that depositions be taken from two political prisoners, but the request was ruled out of order on the grounds that political prisoners always distort the issues. The long, involved, and often inaccurate deposition of Dvorzhitsky was read. Inevitably, Dvorzhitsky put himself in the best light, speaking about his honor, his love for the Emperor, and how he had wished that his life had been taken rather than that of the Emperor. Captain Koch was called as a witness. The captain explained at one point that he had had to draw his sword to shield Rysakov from the vengeance of the mob. The claim is unlikely. In any event he had no business defending Rysakov. Zhelyabov pounced on the captain's words and asked for further elucidation. Exactly how and where and against whom had the redoubtable Captain Koch drawn his sword? In the end the captain admitted that he had drawn his sword, but a moment later he had returned it to its sheath, for there had been no occasion to use it.

The examination of nineteen witnesses lasted most of the day. Zhelyabov could not be silenced. He was always jumping up and demanding elucidations, guidance in matters of procedure, quarreling with the president, demanding straight answers to straight questions. An artist in the public gallery made hurried drawings of him. The one reproduced here shows Zhelyabov in a mood of quiet watchfulness and the artist has drawn in the eyes with a heavy pencil, as though to emphasize his alertness, but the same artist made other drawings which emphasize the half-mocking smile, and there is one which shows Zhelyabov as the stern accuser, more like a judge than a prisoner about to be sentenced.

Of the other prisoners only Kibalchich had much to say, and most of what he said was technical. Proud of his knowledge of explosives and of Russia, he protested when the military experts insisted that the bombs were made of some substance imported from abroad, and he referred the military experts to an article in the *Russian Artillery Journal* for August 1878. There, if they cared to read, they would find the formula for the bomb which had killed the Emperor. And when General Fedorov said that the mine in the Malaya Sadovaya would have torn a hole in the earth twenty feet in diameter, killing anyone walking on the pavement and breaking all the windows of the houses in the street, Kibalchich gave a meticulous lecture on the explosive effects of mines, proving that eighty pounds of high explosive would have done very little damage except to the carriage immediately above the mine—the only danger outside the area would come from falling fragments. The trial droned on. Muraviev was waiting for his great moment, and he could be seen drumming on his table, his eyes lifted to the ceiling. His moment came on the third day, as he launched into an impassioned plea for justice—justice for the present Emperor and for the memory of the dead Emperor "who was martyred in the Calvary of the Ekaterininsky Canal." Zhelyabov laughed at the impassioned oratory, but he would have been well-advised to keep silent, for Muraviev turned upon him, lifted an accusing finger, tossed back his head and said: "A nation mourns, but Zhelyabov laughs and mocks the greatness of the departed." It was the kind of thing Muraviev could do with considerable effect, and like another Cicero pointing to another Catiline he continued to address the court in long rhetorical passages. He was less concerned with justice than with the majesty of his own rhetoric, until the time came for him to point once more at the benches where the accused were sitting. "Where," he asked dramatically, "shall we find the men who had the audacity to cut down the great oak under whom we all were sheltered? Who killed the Tsar? I can answer in a few words. They are there, in front of you, and only condign punishment can wash away the evil they have committed. Let us then root out the venomous weeds; let us have done with them; and then breathing the air of freedom, let us follow in the hallowed footsteps of the One, the Invincible, the Sacred Hope, the August Leader who has succeeded to the Throne!"

Once Muraviev referred to Zhelyabov as a bandit chieftain, which must have seemed improbable even in that court where many improbable statements were being made. He read from Morozov's more violent editorials in the newspaper of the Narodnaya Volya—five copies of the newspaper had been found on Zhelyabov when he was arrested, but the Third Division possessed a complete set in their files. Yes, it was all there: Morozov was inciting all Russians to revolt. These despicable intellectuals were not expressing the great things of the soul; on the contrary, they were expounding the sentiments of murderers, thieves, the dregs of society. They were men whose lives must be snuffed out so that good citizens could sleep soundly in their beds. Against the weight of Muraviev's speeches, the defending counsel could do little, and while they spoke Muraviev watched them scornfully, as though he could hardly believe anyone could have the temerity to defend such evident scoundrels.

Gerard, who defended Kibalchich, did his superb best. He spoke quietly about Kibalchich's early years and reminded the government that the scientist had spent three years in prison for giving a harmless book called *The Tale of the Four Brothers* to a peasant. The Trial of the 193 became the major theme of Gerard's defense: the trial was put on trial. Gerard was gravely warned against his references to the police, who had gone about indiscriminately making arrests of innocent students. He was told that the actions of the police were beyond the jurisdiction of the present court.

Then it was Zhelyabov's turn to speak. He had refused the services of counsel and could therefore make a speech in his own defense. The court debated upon the validity of allowing Zhelyabov to defend himself, but he was legally entitled to the right, and Fuchs bowed to the inevitable, after explaining at length to Zhelyabov that he must keep strictly to the point, and the court would not admit a harangue in which Zhelyabov justified his actions by an appeal to political principles. And then Zhelyabov spoke, very quietly at first and then in tones of rising indignation, jerking his head sharply whenever he was interrupted by the president and glowering at the public galleries whenever the claque murmured in disapproval. Patiently he explained how the Narodnaya Volya had been brought into existence and how the excesses of the government had inevitably brought about the emergence of a terrorist party. He said:

> To understand our present use of weapons, you must understand our history. Our history—for we have a history—is short in years, but rich in experience. Gentlemen of the Court, if you will look into the records of political trials, you will find that the Russian popular parties have not always used bombs, and we too as a Party have had our days of youth and shining dreams. It is not our fault that those days have passed . . . We have searched for means by which we could help the people, and we chose to act as common working people propagating our socialist ideas peacefully. This surely was doing no harm. What happened? We were thrown into prison and sent into exile. Originally we were an entirely peaceful movement, we opposed violence, we detested the thought of revolution—and so we were crushed . . .
>
> Originally there was not one of us who approved of violence, but when I was thrown into prison I became a revolutionary . . . Then we saw that the "movement to the people" led nowhere, and we looked around us and discovered that there was much in the Russian popular tradition we could build on . . . We took to deeds, not words. Action meant using force, but even then we were not convinced of the need to employ force sternly. So it went on until 1878. Then it was that we decided to cut the Gordian knot. The movement which began with the cry "To the people" ended inevitably in the tragic affair of March 1. Eighteen seventy-eight was the determining year. That was the year of *A Death for a Death*.* Circumstances were forcing this conclusion on us, but as for myself I spent the summer of that year quietly propagandizing in my village. That winter there was still no solution, and I spent the next spring in the south—a time of anxiety and distress . . .
>
> The prosecutor accuses me of killing. But our efforts were not so narrow: we had other aims. We wanted a revolution, and we were preparing to form a revolutionary party on the widest possible scale . . . As for myself, my personal task was to work for the common good, and when I found I could not do this by peaceful means, I turned to violence. But I would willingly abandon violence if there was the least possibility of serving my ideals by peaceful means.

* The pamphlet written by Kravchinsky (Stepnyak) to celebrate the assassination of General Mezentsev.

Zhelyabov had hoped to be able to make his speech without interruptions, but the president was continually ordering him to keep to the point, to speak only of his own actions, to refrain from any discussion of the party. Zhelyabov found himself talking more and more about the party. Indeed, he could hardly help himself, for he *was* the party.

And then at the end, the defendants were allowed to make their "final statements." Rysakov, terrified, denied that he had ever taken part in the terrorist movement. Timofey Mikhailov mumbled something about his lack of education. He was too nervous to be able to make a clear statement. Kibalchich lectured the prosecutor on the idiocy of solving all government problems by the rope and the knout. There must be social progress and there must be some way in which the aspirations of the people can be expressed. He spoke dryly, professorially, and without visible emotion. Gesya Helfman spoke more passionately, but most of her speech was devoted to showing that she was in no way humbled by the prosecutor's charges. Characteristically, Perovskaya was concerned with the good name of the revolutionaries. The prosecutor had charged them with being the dregs of society, living immoral lives, and she answered:

> The prosecutor has hurled a number of charges against us. With regard to his statements of fact I will say nothing: I dealt with them all during the preliminary investigation. But I and my friends have been accused of immorality, cruelty, and contempt for public opinion. Against such charges I must protest. Those who know anything about our lives and the circumstances in which we have had to work will not reproach us either with immorality or cruelty.

Zhelyabov was allowed to speak once more. He said only that the prosecutor had used his statements for his own ends, twisting them, and now he regretted having spoken in court. In fact, he regretted none of it, and this was his last ironical jab at his accusers.

At midnight the court rose and the prisoners were removed to their cells. At three o'clock in the morning they were brought back to listen to the verdict. All were found guilty, but Rysakov was only nineteen and there were long discussions about whether the death sentence could be applied to a minor. At last the president decided that the death sentence was appropriate even to a minor. The prisoners were then condemned to be hanged. The sentence on Perovskaya, who belonged to the nobility, would be submitted to the Emperor for his approval. The rest were given two days in which to appeal.

The news that the prisoners were condemned to death was published in the newspapers, and the government announced that a vast number of telegrams approving the sentence had been received.

Except for Rysakov who made a last desperate appeal to the Tsar and Mikhailov who wrote a reasoned petition, none of the prisoners asked for mercy. After the trial they remained quietly in their cells, receiving visits from lawyers and priests. Kibalchich immersed himself in the problems of flying machines. Zhelyabov read history books and newspapers. Mikhailov read the Bible. Perovskaya was strangely calm and spent her days leaning against the walls of her prison cell, lost in her dreams. Of the six prisoners the calmest of all was Gesya Helfman who announced three days before the hanging that she was pregnant. A medical commission was immediately appointed by the prison superintendant to examine her. They discovered that she had been pregnant since January, and as a result her death sentence was commuted to imprisonment for life. She lived only until September 1882, dying insane.

As always in prisons where there are condemned prisoners, the guards caught the mood of quietness and were observed to be especially gentle with their charges. There were clear spring days. Once every morning and again in the afternoon the prisoners were led out into the courtyard. They were allowed to talk to one another for a few moments. At these meetings Zhelyabov and Perovskaya were always together. Afterward it was said that they rarely spoke: it was enough that they should be together.

On the evening of April 2, shortly before eight o'clock, priests entered their cells to receive their confessions and offer the Sacrament, but Perovskaya and Zhelyabov refused to see them and turned their backs to them when they insisted on staying. Timofey Mikhailov confessed, but refused Communion. Kibalchich spent more than an hour calmly discussing religion with the priest, but he refused to confess or receive the Sacrament. Only Rysakov, now broken and almost unrecognizable, confessed and received the Sacrament.

According to the guards all the prisoners were asleep by midnight.

At six o'clock in the morning of April 3, when the sun had already risen, the prisoners were awakened. They were given cups of tea and told to dress, and were then taken to the prison waiting-room, where the black clothes they would wear for the execution were laid out for them. These clothes were made in the prison. Drab and shapeless, they were intended to mock the humanity of the prisoners. While putting on her black robe, Perovskaya broke down. Timofey Mikhailov found her weeping a few minutes later and said: "Keep your chin up, Sophie." She brightened, smiled, and paid no more attention to the shabby black dress which resembled a vast maternity gown. A few moments later a prison official was placing large oblong placards, held up by a string round their necks, against their chests. The placards, on which the word "Tsaricide" was written in black ink which had run, so giving the appearance of dripping black blood, were made of thin sheets of wood. Exactly similar placards were tied round the necks of prisoners sentenced to death for high treason in the middle ages.

In the prison courtyard the tumbrels were waiting. They were ordinary springless peasant carts on which a kind of platform had been constructed. The prisoners were made to sit on benches on the high platform, their backs to the horses. They were handcuffed, their hands behind their backs, and their feet fettered. In the first cart were Zhelyabov and Rysakov, the man who had organized the assassination and the one who had thrown the first bomb. Rysakov kept looking at Zhelyabov, but though they were chained close together, Zhelyabov pretended to be completely unaware of Rysakov's existence. In the second cart Perovskaya sat between Mikhailov and Kibalchich.

The prison gates opened a few minutes before eight o'clock, and the small procession came out into the warm spring air. The two tumbrels were followed by a carriage with priests, and then in turn by a cart with five unpainted coffins. Behind these came part of the military escort. Some Cossacks rode beside the carts, and beside the tumbrels marched the drummers who were ordered to drown out any speeches made by the prisoners to the crowds in the streets. Troops lined the approaches to the vast Semyonovsky Square, where the scaffold had been erected since early the previous evening.

Many stories were told of the slow journey from the prison to the Semyonovsky Square, and the behavior of the prisoners. Vera Figner tells the story that when Perovskaya was being lifted onto the cart, her hands were tied behind her back so tightly that she complained: "Loosen the cords a little, they hurt me." The guard is supposed to have replied: "You'll feel worse in a little while." It seems unlikely. Vera Figner also tells the story of how later in the morning she sat next to a well-dressed young man on a streetcar and noted the gleam of excitement in his eyes, and how everyone in St. Petersburg reflected in some way an awareness of the terrible joy which comes over people who have watched prisoners going to their deaths. All eyes were on Perovskaya. They watched her silently and with compassion, admiring her composure, yet admitting the inevitability of her execution. The correspondent of the *Kölnische Zeitung* noted that Kibalchich and Zhelyabov were very calm, Timofey Mikhailov was pale but firm, Rysakov liver-colored, and Perovskaya's cheeks were still rosy and she still looked beautiful. None except Mikhailov attempted to address the crowd, and Mikhailov's voice was soon drowned by a roll of drums.

That morning there was a misty white haze, and the first thaw was beginning, the streets gleaming silver with puddles of melted snow. All of St. Petersburg seemed to be in the streets along the route to the Semyonovsky Square, and in the square itself over 80,000 people were assembled. The scaffold stood at the dead center of the square. It consisted of two uprights and a crossbeam with six hooks dangling beneath, set on a large wooden platform about four feet high and solidly built. Everything, the scaffold, the platform and the steps leading up were painted black. There were railings along one edge of the platform and three wooden posts were set securely at some distance from the scaffold, with manacles and chains already attached. Foot Guards and Cossacks were drawn up in ranks around the platform, and there were Cossacks distributed all over the square. The drummers stood immediately below the scaffold.

The executioner was a drunken ex-prisoner called Frolov, famous for bungling. He was short and squat, with a heavy red face; he resembled a punch-drunk boxer. He had been waiting there, testing the ropes with the help of his assistants since half past seven. He had a good deal of time, for the tumbrels containing the prisoners did not arrive until half past eight and it was three quarters of an hour later before the first prisoner was brought to the gallows.

When the tumbrels rolled into the Square, a huge murmur rose from the crowd. The prisoners were taken down from the carts. Zhelyabov, Perovskaya, and Mikhailov were chained to the three wooden posts, while Kibalchich and Rysakov were chained to the railings. The long sentences were read out. Zhelyabov and Perovskaya were seen to be whispering together. The drums were muffled. The reading of the sentences included a summary of the crimes, and took nearly half an hour. There were other formalities to be observed: documents were signed by men in frock coats and top hats who stood beside a table and seemed in no hurry to conclude the entertainment. The five priests who had visited the cells the previous evening climbed onto the platform and held out crosses to the prisoners, who kissed the crosses, received the priests' blessing and then watched the priests descend from the platform. Zhelyabov's long hair was blowing in the wind. The executioner removed their chains. It was the time for their last farewells, before the white cowls were slipped over their heads. Handcuffed, his feet fettered, Zhelyabov moved across the platform toward Perovskaya and kissed her. He was followed by Kibalchich and Mikhailov. Rysakov then came toward Perovskaya, but she turned her head away. His dark face grew darker and he was trembling with fear. Then all five were placed under the gallows, the cowls were fastened over their heads, and Frolov removed his coat.

The order of the hanging was deliberately designed: those who had committed the greatest crimes in the eyes of the government were to be hanged last.

Kibalchich was the first to climb on the tabouret, the rope already fastened round his neck through a slit in the cowl. Frolov pushed the tabouret away, and at the same moment there came a loud and prolonged roll of drums. Kibalchich died quickly, without struggling, and apparently without any pain. It was now Mikhailov's turn. He was heavily built, taller than Zhelyabov, and he may have hoped his weight would bring about a merciful quick death. He had been hanging for a minute when the rope broke. He fell on his face on the platform. He was still alive, still conscious. Because his hands and feet were tied, he could not lift himself up. The crowd screamed. Some of them were shouting: "Glory to God!" believing a miracle had occurred, for it was impossible to believe that the executioner could proceed with the hanging. Frolov lifted him up. It was observed that Mikhailov still had enough strength to mount the tabouret unaided. Then the tabouret was kicked away again, and he hung for a minute and a half on another rope until this, too, broke. He fell on his chest. The crowd was appalled. "Poor Russia!" someone shouted, and this time the crowd began to shout out to the high functionaries on the platform, saying he must be released, the farce could not be continued, it was time they showed mercy. For a few brief moments the crowd began to sway and jostle and quiver as though it was preparing to rush the protective ranks of the guards. Mikhailov was still conscious, but he could not walk any more and had to be lifted onto the tabouret. Frolov ran another length of rope to the hook intended for Gesya Helfman. With two ropes round Mikhailov's neck there was a chance that he could be hanged finally. Frolov was standing on a ladder. The ladder teetered. Among the crowd of high officials on the platform were three or four who murmured in disgust, but mostly they were silent, nervous, afraid of the crowd and still more afraid of the punishments the Tsar would inflict on them if the executions were bungled. The third hanging was successful, though for some minutes Mikhailov writhed in terrible convulsions. When a military doctor protested, Frolov turned on him and began cursing.

It was then Perovskaya's turn. Because she was shorter than the others, she looked very frail even in her heavy shroud as she was led to the tabouret. A great sigh went up among the crowd when the tabouret was kicked away. The convulsions were very brief, and she died almost as quickly as Kibalchich. Zhelyabov died slowly. Frolov had taken the precaution of tying a double knot in the noose. Zhelyabov's convulsions seemed endless.

To the very end Rysakov had hoped for a pardon. More nervous than the others he was seen to jump up and down and to hop from one leg to the other as he stood on the platform. When Frolov indicated that his time had come, he screamed and somehow dug his feet behind the railings and had to be pulled away. He was struggling up to the moment when the tabouret was kicked away, but his convulsions were brief.

By half past nine there was no longer any sign of life in the five white-hooded bodies hanging from the crossbeam. The sun burned through the morning haze, shining on the sea of faces. Then the bodies were taken down, the doctors examined them and signed the death certificates and the prefect announced that justice had been done. By 9:58 the bodies had been loaded onto two waiting carts, to be driven to the railway station, and two minutes later the prefect gave the order for the scaffold to be torn down. With a pair of scissors, Frolov was snipping off short lengths of rope to be sold to the highest bidders.

The bodies were taken to the Preobrazhensky Cemetery. There, many years later, a caretaker pointed to an abandoned corner thick with rubble and weeds and said that Zhelyabov and Perovskaya were somewhere underneath. Today there is no one who knows where they are.

The history of the Narodnaya Volya ends with the hanging of the conspirators who brought about the assassination of Alexander II. For a few more years the party survived. There were more assassinations and more desperate attempts on the part of Tikhomirov to hammer out a policy of revolutionary action, but with the arrest of Zhelyabov and Alexander Mikhailov the party lost its two greatest leaders and never recovered its power. Mikhailov was imprisoned in the Peter and Paul Fortress: and it was perhaps no accident that he died in the famous Cell Number 1 in which Nechayev died. Dr. Wilms wrote in his medical report on March 18, 1884: "The prisoner Alexander Mikhailov died at twelve this morning of inflammation of the lungs and edema."

On April 29, 1881, the new Emperor Alexander III issued a manifesto in which he announced the end of all reforms:

> In the midst of Our grief the voice of God commands Us to stand bravely at the helm of government, trusting in Divine Providence and with faith in the power and truth of the Absolutism We are called upon to defend; and We are determined to strengthen the State against any attempts to weaken Our power, and this We do for the benefit of Our people.

Alexander was saying no more than his ancestor, the Emperor Nicholas I, who addressed a manifesto to Europe, beginning: "Submit yourselves, ye peoples, for God is with Us."

All power was now concentrated in the hands of the autocracy. The revolutionaries were weary and could no longer fight back with their old strength. The murder of Alexander II was like a vast explosion that had exhausted their energies. They needed time to prepare a new onslaught on the dynasty. At the end of his classic account of his life as a minor revolutionary Vladimir Debogori-Mokrievich wrote sadly that he could see no hope of any more organized outbreaks: "It seems to me that from 1881 onward the Russian revolutionary movement went into a decline. Men cannot endure to live in a state of perpetually mounting excitement. They cannot perpetually be asked to sacrifice themselves for the revolution, for such sacrifices demand spiritual resources which are not met with every day."

Twenty-two years later the Social Revolutionaries, who had inherited the program of the Narodnaya Volya, once more introduced the weapons of terrorism against the autocratic state.

ALEXANDER ULYANOV

I have no faith in terror—only in systematic terror.

A NEST OF GENTLEFOLK

T HE FAMILY OF His Excellency Ilya Nikolayevich Ulyanov was among
the most respected in Simbirsk. They had a large house on Mos-
kovskaya Street, a large garden, orchards, servants, a carriage, and the use
of a small country estate. A private income supplemented the salary of
the head of the family, who had been raised to the nobility when he
became the inspector of schools throughout the entire province. The
name Ulyanov appears in the register of the Simbirsk nobility in the
seventeenth century, but Ilya Ulyanov, the son of an obscure tailor in
Astrakhan, was respected chiefly because he had risen from poverty to a
position of high eminence in the scholastic system. He was not descended
from the nobility, but on the contrary he reached up to it, and was proud
of his rank as an Actual State Councilor and the possessor of the Order
of St. Vladimir.

He was a slight, slender man with a bulbous forehead, deep-set eyes, a
small nose, and a bristling beard, who behaved throughout his life with
the decorum proper in a man devoted to the Tsar and to his family. His
studies at the University of Kazan were concerned chiefly with mathematics and meteorology, and there was something precise and scientific in
all his actions. He was thirty-two when he married Maria Blank, the
daughter of an eccentric doctor and landowner of Swedish and German
descent. The doctor was something of a crank and wrote a pamphlet

303

called *As Thou Livest, So Heal Thyself* on the medicinal virtues of water. He encouraged his daughters to wrap themselves in damp sheets when they went to bed, "in order to strengthen their nerves," and this regimen, which might have proved disastrous, seems to have had no effect on Maria, who lived to be nearly eighty.

Six children were born of the marriage, and in the family circle it was generally agreed that Alexander, the eldest, was the most gifted, the most charming, and the one most likely to leave a mark on the world. All the virtues were showered on him at birth. He was kind and gentle, devoted to his brothers and sisters, and he possessed a wide-ranging intellectual curiosity. History, which pays scant attention to family virtues, has forgotten him, preferring to remember his young brother Vladimir, who became Lenin.

Alexander grew up to become a long-faced, lean-boned youth with fine eyes, full sensitive lips, and a mop of unruly hair. He was quiet and reserved, in this way differing from Vladimir, who was four years younger, and very boisterous and assertive. They liked each other, but there was an undercurrent of tension between them. Alexander had a passion for telling the truth, while Vladimir sometimes told lies, and while Alexander was unfailingly respectful to his parents, Vladimir was sometimes disobedient and rude. We hear of sudden bouts of temper, as when they were playing chess and their mother interrupted the game to remind Vladimir that he had not carried out an order. Engrossed in the game, he replied rudely, telling her to go away. She repeated the order and again he replied rudely, mocking her. This was too much for Alexander, who said sternly: "Unless you do what Mama tells you to do, I shall never play chess with you again."

Other similar stories were told about them, but there was no lasting antagonism. Vladimir had the gift of mimicry, and it amused him to imitate his brother's gestures, and also to copy his behavior. When faced with a problem, he would ask himself: "What would Sasha do?" Their tastes and talents differed, and they were never very close, but they were also never far apart. Alexander enjoyed Dostoyevsky, while Vladimir took to reading Turgenev until his eyes were almost falling from their sockets. Alexander enjoyed the intricacies of fretwork, the careful manipulation of things, scientific experiments, while Vladimir had no talent for experiments and was clumsy with his hands. Alexander became a dedicated biologist, while Vladimir never studied any of the sciences and was indifferent to them; his preference was for languages, especially Latin, and for literature. The temper of Alexander's mind was classical and detached, operating within the realm of the possible, while his unruly brother demonstrated from childhood that he possessed a romantic temper and enjoyed pushing ideas and actions to daring and impossible conclusions.

Very few of Alexander's early writings have survived, but the little that remains suggests a calm, sensible and gifted mind. In a school essay on the subject "What does a man need in order to make himself useful to society and the state?" he wrote:

> To be useful in society, a man should be honest and he should devote himself to unremitting toil, and if his work is to yield the greatest possible results he needs intelligence and a knowledge of his own affairs . . . From his earliest youth he should cultivate honesty and a sound view of his responsibilities toward his neighbors, and these beliefs will determine the work he chooses to do, whether he will be guided in his choice by his usefulness to society or by an egotistical desire for personal advantage. . . .
>
> This love of work should extend to trivial and insignificant matters, and also to matters which at first sight seem absolutely impossible to perform. To be a really useful member of society, a man should become accustomed to hard work, refusing to be daunted by any difficulties or obstacles, whether they arise from external circumstances or are due to his own failings and weaknesses. To do this he must exercise self-control and develop a determined and steadfast character.

Alexander's school essay written when he was sixteen describes his own character: he was the serious dedicated student with "a determined and steadfast character," who never doubted that he had been called upon to perform acts useful to society and the state. When he went to St. Petersburg University to study science in August 1883, he continued to behave in the same sensible way. He was supported by his father, and felt that the least he could do in return was to use the money sparingly, work without respite, pass all his examinations honorably, and achieve a reputation as a great scientist. It was a simple code, but it was not an unusual one, for Russian students nearly always took their responsibilities with the utmost seriousness and they were accustomed to living on almost no money at all.

Alexander was not simply the dedicated scholar immersed in his books and his scientific experiments. Though quiet and reserved, he made many friends, visited the theater, joined the Volga Society which was made up of students who had come from Kazan, Simbirsk and the other towns on the Volga, and it was remembered that he had a passion for poetry and listening to music. At such times his grave, earnest face would become still more grave, still more earnest, as he sank deeper and deeper into a world where no one could follow him. His mother had taught him to play the piano, and like all the members of his family he was musical.

During the summer vacations he returned to Simbirsk to spend nearly three months with his brothers and sisters. Some part of the vacation was always spent on the estate at Kokushkino, where they would spend their time leisurely boating on the river or reading in the garden. Inevitably the children paired off according to their ages: Alexander with the studious Anna, Vladimir with the beautiful Olga, Dmitry with Maria, the ugly duckling and the youngest in the family. From time to time their father, who was busy establishing new schools wherever they were needed—he had the reputation of having established more schools in a shorter space of time than anyone else in Russia—came to spend a few days or a whole week with them before leaving on one more of those expeditions which led him into the remotest regions of the province. Then the whole family would go swimming, boating or hunting together. It was a nest of gentlefolk, rich according to the standards of the time, with their own carriages, servants, and retainers.

The summer of 1885 was the last which the whole family enjoyed together. Alexander came down from St. Petersburg, resplendent with the glory of having won a gold medal for a thesis on the habits of sea spiders. From the age of twelve he was determined to be a biologist, and now his determination was bearing fruit. He surprised his father by handing him eighty rubles saved from his allowance of forty rubles a month, explaining that it was perfectly possible to live on thirty rubles a month. Ilya Nikolayevich remonstrated with him. It was absurd, he said, for the son of an Actual State Councilor to live like a poor student and starve himself when the money was available. Alexander said nothing. He had worked out a careful budget and he was determined to abide by it. A few months later his father suggested he should come to spend Christmas with the family at Simbirsk. Alexander replied that it was scarcely worth the expense for such a brief vacation, and he remained in St. Petersburg. It was a decision he had cause to regret.

When he returned to St. Petersburg after the summer vacation, his sister Anna accompanied him. She had decided to become a primary-school teacher and intended to study in a teachers' training college. That summer the fifteen-year-old Vladimir had been more than usually rebellious and disobedient, and Alexander had announced that he was now thoroughly tired of his brother's unruly temper. "Vladimir is certainly talented, but we don't understand each other any more," he said sadly.

In January Ilya Nikolayevich died. His death was completely unexpected, for he had been in good health until the day before he suffered a heart attack. A telegram was sent to Alexander. Of all the children he was the closest to his father, and seems to have suffered the most. The shock wounded him so deeply that he thought of suicide. Grief tormented him, and for weeks he went about like a man in a nightmare, not knowing where to turn to escape from the burden of his sorrow. The consolations of religion were denied to him, for he had abandoned churchgoing at the age of fourteen or fifteen, saying quite simply that he was no longer a believer and it would be a waste of time to try to convert him.

In the summer after his father's death he returned to Simbirsk for the last time. It was noted that he was even more reserved than usual. Returning to St. Petersburg for his fourth year, he seemed to have changed character. The man who had been perfectly content to spend the greater part of his days bending over a microscope or reading voluminously in Russian, German, English and French—according to a friend his favorite book was Herbert Spencer's *Principles of Biology,* which he regarded with a feeling akin to reverence—now sought out the small revolutionary groups among the students and plotted to assassinate the Tsar. His calamitous revolutionary career was one of the shortest on record. It lasted little more than a hundred days, and it ended two months later on the scaffold.

Alexander first came into prominence among the student societies when he helped to organize a procession to the grave of the socialist writer Nikolay Dobrolyubov on November 28, 1886, the twenty-fifth anniversary of his death. Since the students were evidently planning a massive political demonstration and would have to cross the whole of St. Petersburg to reach the Volkovskoye Cemetery where Dobrolyubov lay buried, the police banned the march. Nevertheless the students persisted. Some six or seven hundred set out to the cemetery, carrying banners and wreaths. The police locked the cemetery gates, arrested ten students, took down the names and addresses of the more vociferous, and dispersed the rest. On the following night some forty students were arrested. The University was in an uproar. For the first time the students had attempted to measure their strength against the police and they had failed ignominiously.

They salved their consciences by collecting money for the arrested students, issued and distributed a hectographed account of the "Dobrolyubov affair," and discussed the next steps to be taken. These included a mass meeting in the square outside the Kazan Cathedral or outside the Winter Palace, disorders in the educational establishments in St. Petersburg, the bombing of police headquarters, and the assassination of Gresser, the Chief of Police, "and even someone of greater importance." So Orest Govorukhin, a student of St. Petersburg University, who later escaped abroad, describes the discussions of the student leaders after their failure to mount the protest march to the grave of Dobrolyubov, and it is clear that their rage derived less from their failure to pay tribute to the memory of a brilliant writer than to a growing sense of frustration. The time had come for a direct confrontation with authority.

As Govorukhin tells the story, describing how the students passed quickly in a few hours from the contemplation of meetings, disorders and bombings to a calm acceptance of the necessity to assassinate the Tsar, he is completely convincing. It was in just such a way that the Petersburg students would discuss political events, taking refuge in extremes. But in such discussions there would always be a fanatic to tip the scales in favor of the most extreme and dangerous course, and such a fanatic was found in Pyotr Shevyrev, the twenty-three-year-old son of a shopkeeper in Kherson. Shevyrev was dying of consumption. Imagining himself to be the inheritor of the revolutionary tradition of the Narodnaya Volya, he possessed the fanaticism of the sick and the dying. He had a high white forehead, deep-set eyes, a weak chin; his face resembled a skull. Except for his voice, which was musical, there was very little in him to attract the attention of other students; he was one of those men who operate best in the company of a stronger and more resourceful man. The combination of Alexander Ulyanov and Pyotr Shevyrev was a remarkable one, and soon many students were flocking to join them. Shevyrev had written the inflammatory account of the "Dobrolyubov affair" which was hectographed and distributed all over St. Petersburg, and Alexander had been deeply impressed by the violence of its tone. He had himself come to some firm conclusions about terror. According to Govorukhin, he used to say: "I have no faith in terror—only in systematic terror." In his schoolboy essay he had celebrated "the determined and steadfast character," and he was now applying it to a subject about which he knew nothing at all.

Although he knew nothing about terror and proved to be a remarkably inefficient terrorist, Alexander was one of those men who were quite incapable of stopping in mid-passage. Once he had embarked on a program of action, he would inevitably continue to the end. All through December there were secret meetings. Most of them seem to have taken place in Alexander's lodgings at 21 Alexandrovsky Prospect, not far from the Peter and Paul Fortress. Among the first to join the conspiracy was Joseph Lukashevich, a young nobleman from Vilna who had founded at his own expense a student restaurant and a revolving fund for poor students. Others were Vasily Generalov, the son of a Don Cossack, and Pakhomy Andreyushkin, who came from the Kuban. Very few of the conspirators were Great Russians; all came from the outlying provinces or from Poland and Lithuania. Through the student Mikhail Kancher, the son of a post-office official, the terrorist group came in contact with some young Polish students, who proved to be useful in obtaining nitric acid and otherwise helping with supplies. Two brothers were involved in the conspiracy—Joseph and Bronislav Pilsudski. Joseph was to become Marshal of Poland and dictator of his country, but in those days he was a dedicated socialist. For being implicated in the conspiracy he was later arrested and sentenced to five years' penal servitude in Eastern Siberia, but there is some doubt whether he really knew what was happening. At the trial he denied all knowledge of the affair and expressed his absolute detestation of terrorist methods, and it is possible that he was innocent. The prosecution was able to prove that he had sent a coded telegram to Vilna and that an illegal printing press was hidden in the apartment he shared with his brother.

In January Alexander was still reading up in the University library on how to make bombs. It was a subject he had never studied before, and he came to it with all the innocent high-mindedness of the amateur. He devised an infernal machine of a novel kind, for around the solid-packed core of dynamite there were hollowed-out leaden pellets containing strychnine. Strychnine was easily available through a pharmacist friend, but they had some difficulty in obtaining the dynamite and the nitric acid which would trigger the explosion. Alexander seems to have designed the bomb himself, without the aid of any professional manufacturers of weapons.

Toward the end of February most of their preparations were completed, and Shevyrev, living in a state of exaltation, was all for immediate action, taunting them because they were so slow, because they had not already brought about the downfall of the Tsar. A stubborn, impudent, strangely unsympathetic man—so Govorukhin describes him—he was evidently in no state to command a terrorist attack on the Tsar, and they were relieved when he suddenly left for the south to improve his health. Alexander was then left in complete command.

At his trial he formulated his ideas on the necessity of the attack very clearly and simply, as though he were reading from a long prepared text, but those who worked with him report that he was never very clear about what would happen after the attack. He would say: "The present state of affairs leads us inevitably to perform acts of terrorism," but when he contemplated the consequences of these acts he was aware that there were two quite different possibilities. The first possibility was that the government might introduce far more repressive measures than any used hitherto, and this would inevitably bring about more assassinations. The alternative was that the government would make concessions, perhaps very small concessions. Alexander's attitude was that terror was "a completely reasonable method for bringing about more concessions," and it never seems to have occurred to him that the government was unlikely to concede to the terrorists and that "very small concessions" were hardly worth contemplating.

It was decided to kill the Tsar on March 1, the anniversary of the assassination of Alexander II.

On February 16 they were sufficiently advanced in their plans to go through the first practice runs. On that day, or the following day, they went into the country and made some experiments in exploding dynamite and fulminate of mercury. These appear to have been successful. There remained the question of false passports to enable them to escape abroad, but the passports had not yet arrived from Vilna, and they were in some doubt whether they would arrive in time. On February 18 all the bombs were ready, and it remained only to decide on a plan of operation and to draw up the manifesto. Four days later there was a meeting at Kancher's apartment where Alexander read out the manifesto he had written and they discussed who would throw the bombs and how they would be thrown. It was decided that the bombs should be entrusted to Osipanov, Andreyushkin and Generalov, with Kancher and Gorkun as the observers who would give the signal for the attack. A second terrorist group, consisting of workmen, would step in if the first attack failed, but this group seems not to have been organized in time. Osipanov was twenty-six years old, and the oldest of the conspirators. He was chosen because he was regarded as the most experienced and reliable.

He was no more experienced or reliable than the twenty-year-old Andreyushkin, who had written to a student friend in Kharkov a letter which was a long hymn in praise of terrorism. "I shall not enumerate the advantages and significance of the Red Terror," he wrote at the end of January, "because it would take me centuries to do so, considering that it is my *dada,* and it is what keeps me hating the Social Democrats." He went on to proclaim that within a few days or weeks all of Russia would learn that there were revolutionaries capable of introducing a merciless terror. "We have it in our power to introduce a truly merciless terror," he wrote, "and I firmly believe that it will take place in a very short time."

The police intercepted the letter on January 15, but nearly six weeks passed before they were able to identify the sender, who had taken the precaution of signing it with another name. By that time Andreyushkin and his fellow terrorists were already prowling the Nevsky Prospect preparing for the moment when the Tsar would drive out of the Winter Palace on one of his tours of inspection, and Alexander's revolutionary proclamation had already been printed and prepared for distribution. On February 26, and again two days later they reconnoitered the Nevsky Prospect. The police had by now identified Andreyushkin, and they kept him under surveillance. The police report dated February 27 noted that they were behaving oddly, carried bulky parcels, and had been followed from midday to five o'clock in the afternoon. The conspirators apparently did not know that the Tsar was not staying at the Winter Palace. The following day was the sixth anniversary of the assassination of Alexander II. The Tsar who had been staying in his vast six-hundred-room palace at Gatchina arrived by train in St. Petersburg and immediately drove to the Winter Palace. This was the opportunity the terrorists had been looking for, but the police forestalled them. They pounced on Osipanov, Andreyushkin and Generalov. Osipanov was carrying a bomb in a hollowed-out copy of Grinberg's *Dictionary of Medical Terminology*. This bulky volume was taken from him. The others were also disarmed on the spot. Osipanov had another bomb in his pocket, and at the police station he suddenly hurled the bomb on the floor in the hope of destroying the entire police station and everyone in it. It failed to explode, and a general of ordnance later testified that all the terrorists' bombs were badly designed, ineffective, and quite harmless.

The proclamation of the executive committee of the terrorist organization was found in Osipanov's possession. From the proclamation the police learned that the revolutionaries were acting on the assumption that the entire social order in Russia would disintegrate with the killing of the Tsar. It had not happened when Alexander II was assassinated, and the only possible explanation seems to be that they were all living in the unreal world of Shevyrev's fantasies.

As soon as the three bomb throwers had been interrogated, a report was sent to the Tsar. He wrote on the margin: "This time God has saved us, but for how long? I congratulate the officials and the police who have been on guard and acted so effectively." Considering that they had intercepted a letter six weeks before and had ample time to arrest the conspirators, they scarcely deserved the Tsar's commendation.

Of the three bomb throwers Generalov was the weakest, and he was induced to talk freely. He implicated most of the other conspirators. A search of his apartment produced two kilograms of revolutionary literature and a revolver. The police went to Alexander's apartment on the Alexandrovsky Prospect, but found only his sister Anna, who was immediately arrested. Alexander was arrested a few hours later in an apartment on Vasilyevsky Island. Since he was recognized as the leader of the conspiracy, he was kept in solitary confinement to prevent him from having any contact with the others. Fifteen of the conspirators were arrested within a few hours. They included nine students, a seminarian, a pharmacist, two midwives, a man who was described as a petty bourgeois, and a young woman who was described as an instructress in a primary school. This was Anna, who had not yet received her diploma and was not an instructress. During the following days forty-nine more people were arrested. Most of the arrested came from the lower middle classes, although there were some notable exceptions—the Pilsudskis descended from a long line of Lithuanian nobility and Gorkun was the son of a major.

It remained only to discover Shevyrev, who was arrested in Yalta a week later. Brought back under armed guard to St. Petersburg, he proved to be an evasive witness, repeatedly declaring that he had little or nothing to do with the conspiracy and putting the blame on everyone else. Alexander, on the other hand, accepted the entire blame for the attempted assassination and did his best to convince the judges that he alone was responsible and the others had only acted on his orders. At the trial he whispered to Lukashevich: "If you need to, put all the blame on me." His sister Anna said later: "He would have liked to be hanged twenty times over, if it would help the others."

Alexander's purposes were obscure, and have never been satisfactorily interpreted. He described his small terrorist organization as the terrorist wing of the Narodnaya Volya, but in fact the Narodnaya Volya had ceased to exist, dying a natural death after the arrest and execution of the assassins of Alexander II. He never belonged to the Narodnaya Volya, and according to Govorukhin he disagreed with their basic beliefs. At his trial he insisted that no other course was open to him, but in fact many courses were open to him. He appears to have embarked on the venture in a mood of despair, knowing that he was doomed from the beginning. In his speech to the judges he celebrated terrorism at considerable length, and by affirming the right to commit acts of terrorism he signed his own death warrant.

The news of his arrest reached Simbirsk a few days later in a letter addressed to Vera Kashkadamova, a schoolteacher. The letter was written by a relative living in St. Petersburg. "When I received the letter, I sent to the school for Vladimir and let him read it," she wrote later. "He knitted his brows and stood silent for a long time in deep thought. He was no longer the happy boy I knew so well, but a grown man. 'This may be very serious for Sasha,' he said." He lived through the tragedy stoically, continued his studies as usual, but became increasingly reserved and thoughtful. Once when he was asked about his brother, he is reported to have said: "It was not the path we shall take. It is not the right way."

It was decided that Vladimir should be the first to give the news to his mother. He returned slowly to the house and gave his mother a full account of the letter. Understandably she wanted to see the letter for herself, and in less than half an hour she was standing in Kashkadamova's apartment with the letter in her hands. She decided she must go at once to St. Petersburg and left that same day, after sending Vladimir to find someone who would accompany her on the coach to Syzran, the nearest railroad station. By this time everyone in the town seems to have known she was the mother of two arrested terrorists charged with attempted regicide, and her 'liberal' friends feared to be seen with her. In a rage Vladimir watched his mother set off alone.

According to Nadezhda Krupskaya, the failure of the 'liberals' in Simbirsk turned his thoughts to Marxism. "He began to think hard," she relates, "and Chernyshevsky's writings took on new meaning for him, and he looked to Marx for an answer to his questions, finding among Alexander's books a copy of *Das Kapital*, which had proved difficult reading in the past, though now he attacked it with new zest." But this sudden conversion did not take place, and many months passed before Vladimir fell under the influence of Chernyshevsky and later of Marx. It is unlikely that Alexander possessed a copy of *Das Kapital*, and recent attempts in the Soviet Union to prove that he was a convinced Marxist appear to be based on a misreading of the evidence.

In St. Petersburg the widow of the Actual State Councilor Ulyanov set out to save her son's life with absolute dedication. She had relatives in high places, and used all her influence to mitigate the inevitable sentence. She petitioned the Tsar for permission to see her son, and on the margin of the petition he wrote: "I think it would be advisable to let her see him so that she can see for herself what kind of person this precious son of hers is." On April 12, 1887, she was taken to his cell in the Peter and Paul Fortress. He wept on seeing her, but quickly recovered. When she asked him what she could give him, he asked only for a volume of Heine's poems.

As a special favor she was permitted to attend the trial. Seventy-two persons had been arrested, but only fifteen were brought before the court. The defense was conducted by lawyers who proclaimed their lack of sympathy for the accused. They attempted to prove that the defendants were misguided youths who scarcely knew what they were doing, but when Alexander was called upon to make his last speech before sentence was passed on him, he indicated that he knew only too well what he was doing. He made no defense. Instead he embarked on a dissertation on the subject of terror, speaking in the manner of a professor addressing students who failed to understand the problem and were perhaps deliberately misunderstanding it. He astonished his mother, who had never heard him speak in public before, and she whispered: "How well he speaks!" A few moments later, unable any longer to contemplate the sight of her son tying the noose firmly around his neck, she hurried out of the courtroom.

Alexander's speech represents a turning point in the history of the Russian revolutionary movement in the nineteenth century. Whenever Zaichnevsky, Bakunin and Nechayev spoke of terror, they endowed it with a panoply of romance, with the oppressed taking vengeance on their oppressors. They thought of the Winter Palace in flames, the blood streaming in the streets, the knife and ax working against the autocracy. When Alexander speaks of terror, it is an abstraction coldly and scientifically deduced from a set of circumstances which are equally abstract, cold and scientific. He does not speak like a revolutionary; he speaks like a logician. He said:

The facts have been fully and correctly established, and I do not deny them. Therefore the right of defense consists exclusively in the right to present the motive of the crime, that is, to present the processes of thought which led me of necessity to commit the crime.

I can discern in my early youth a vague feeling of dissatisfaction with the social system, and this penetrated more and more deeply into my consciousness and finally led me to the conclusions which have guided me in the present instance. It was only after studying the social and economic sciences that the belief in the abnormality of the present system came to me with full force, and the vague dreams of freedom, equality and brotherhood took shape for me in the strictly scientific form of socialism. I realized that a change in the social system was not only possible, but inevitable. Every country develops spontaneously according to definite laws, proceeds according to a strictly defined phase, and inevitably arrives at a certain social organization. This is the inevitable result of the existing system and the contradictions contained within it. But if the development of a nation's life is accomplished spontaneously, then it follows that separate individuals cannot bring about changes within it, and only those who are intellectually strong can serve the ideal, bringing light into the consciousness of society and being fated to influence the course of social events.

There is therefore only one correct way of development—this is the way of words and the press, and of scientific published propaganda, because every change in the social system arises as the result of a change in the consciousness of society. This proposition is clearly and fully formulated in the program of the terrorist group of the Narodnaya Volya, and this is exactly the reverse of what was said by the Prosecutor. As he explained to the court the processes of thought which lead people inevitably to commit acts of terror, he described them in the following way: Everyone has the right to express his own convictions, and consequently they have the right to implement them by force.

Now, there is no connection between these two premises, and the syllogism is illogical and can scarcely be justified in any way. If I say I have the right to express my convictions, this means only that I have the right to demonstrate their truth, that is, to make true for others what is true for me. If these truths fail to register, then the majority will stand against them, and in that case there can be no question of imposing them by force . . . That is why I am firmly convinced that the only right way of influencing the life of society is by words and by the pen.

But when we regard the government's attitude toward the intellectual life, then not only socialist propaganda but every form of cultural propaganda becomes impossible; and the scientific examination of problems is made immensely difficult. The government is so powerful, the intelligentsia so weak, so concentrated within a few cities, that it is in the power of the government to deprive it of its only resource—the last vestiges of free speech . . .

Our intelligentsia is physically so weak and disorganized at the present time that it cannot embark on open warfare. Only the terrorist is in a position to defend the right to think freely and the right to participate intellectually in the life of society. Terror, as a form of warfare, originated in the nineteenth century; it is the sole defensive weapon which a minority can resort to when it is only strong spiritually and when it is conscious of fighting for justice against the majority's knowledge of its own physical strength. Russian society is so constituted that we can defend our rights only in these duels with the state power . . .

Among the Russian people you will always find ten persons so loyal to their ideas and so filled with the misery of their country that it is no sacrifice for them to die for a cause. Nothing can frighten such people.

In this way Alexander pleaded his case before a judge who was impatient of trivialities and regarded him as an imposter who used ideas to disguise a murder. Ordered to explain his motives, he replied: "I shall not speak about my personal motives, but about the bases of society." He asked for permission to discuss the question whether terrorism produced beneficial results or not, and was cut short. The judges observed that he slipped easily from a discussion of abstractions to hints at his own personal motives, but these personal motives were never made clear. He seemed throughout his speech to be hovering over some guarded and nameless secret. He blamed society, and saw himself as the avenger, while arguing that there could be no avenger because society moved according to its own inevitable laws, in which the individual had no place. There was pride in him. Once he remarked: "As far as my moral and intellectual participation in the affair is concerned, it has been complete, and I have given it all I could of my capacities and the power of my knowledge and convictions." When the transcript was shown to the Tsar, he noted in the margin: "Such frankness is touching!"

The Tsar's sarcasm, for it was nothing less, was misplaced, for Alexander's speech with all its appeals to socialism and the popular ideology of the time possesses a raw nakedness and honesty which were not to be dismissed so easily. Countless thousands of intelligent students were thinking in the same way, hoping against hope that the government would introduce a more liberal policy. They hoped the government would introduce sweeping reforms and move away from its attitude of stultifying remoteness. In the eyes of Alexander terror was not merely one of the available weapons: it was the *only* weapon. At the end of his speech he said:

I wanted to show that terror was the unavoidable consequence of the existing conditions, of the existing contradictions in life. We know we can develop our intellectual capacities, but we do not have the opportunity of placing them at the service of our country. Such a scientifically objective examination of the causes of terror, however strange it may appear to the Prosecutor, will be much more useful for those who reject the idea of terror than mere indignation. That is all I wanted to say.

There was no question of his guilt, for he had proclaimed it to everyone who cared to listen. He was sentenced to be hanged, and the same punishment was handed out to Shevyrev, Osipanov, Andreyushkin, and Generalov. Joseph Pilsudski was sentenced to five years' penal servitude in Siberia, his brother Bronislav to fifteen years' penal servitude on the island of Sakhalin. Lukashevich and Novorussky, who played minor roles in the conspiracy, were sentenced to eighteen years in the fortress at Schlüsselburg. Another prisoner, Ananin, who played an even less important role, was sentenced to twenty years' exile in Uzbekistan. Anna, the future primary-school teacher, was sentenced to five years' exile in Siberia, but after her brother's execution the sentence was commuted to police surveillance on the family estate at Kokushkino. The remaining prisoners received various terms of imprisonment in Siberia.

On May 17 the condemned men were taken to the Schlüsselburg fortress. They were hanged three days later. Andreyushkin, Generalov and Osipanov were hanged first. An eyewitness reported that Andreyushkin's last words were "Long live the Narodnaya Volya!" Generalov had only strength enough to say: "Long live . . ." and was then silent. Osipanov shouted: "Long live the executive committee!" and perhaps these words were addressed to Alexander and Shevyrev, who were made to stand in the great courtyard of the fortress and to watch the hanging of their comrades. This was their punishment, for they were the ringleaders, and in the eyes of the Tsar it was not enough that they should be hanged, but they must watch every detail of their friends' deaths to their last dying convulsions. So for half an hour they stood in the courtyard, and then they mounted the scaffold.

There will always be some mystery about Alexander. That brief career in terrorism was to have untold consequences, for Lenin was deeply influenced by his brother's ideas and his brother's fate. Alexander's death was the spur which drove him to action; it was the crime which had to be avenged at all costs. The brothers had not understood each other, nor had they been particularly close to one another, but there is no doubt that a spiritual bond existed between them. As a child and as a youth Lenin always imitated his brother, and when he returned to St. Petersburg thirty years after Alexander's death he was still imitating him. The imitation took the form of a terrorist attack on the entire state.

The mystery of Alexander lies in the strange disparity between the man and many things he said at his trial. He spoke as though he had succeeded in his aims, modeling himself on Zhelyabov and Perovskaya, but in fact his terroristic exploits were childishly unsuccessful. "I have given it all I could of my capacities and the power of my knowledge and convictions," he said proudly, but he had planned the attack on the Tsar in such a way that it was bound to fail. The bombs were defective; the pistol he gave to Andreyushkin was defective; nothing worked. Even the manifesto which he wrote as though it came from the nonexistent terrorist wing of the Narodnaya Volya had a curiously immature quality, as of one who proclaims himself to be in possession of powers he does not possess.

Zhelyabov and Perovskaya acted with skill and determination. Alexander, considerably more intelligent than either of them, acted unskillfully and without determination. Almost it was an act of suicide. He had changed remarkably since his father's death. At that time he had contemplated suicide. A year later he embarked on a course so suicidal that it seemed to be merely the prolongation of the original impulse to kill himself. Death haunted him; it was the landscape he walked in; and his scientific detachment was perhaps merely the mask for the working-out of a private grief.

There was another element in him which also worked toward his own destruction—his pride. He was aware of his intellectual distinction, the gold medal he had earned for his thesis at the University and the other gold medal he had earned at school in Simbirsk. He knew he towered over the other students of biology. He had not the least intention of becoming a schoolmaster; he was aiming for higher things. Govorukhin reports that when his name was found on a slip of paper which had fallen out of the pocket of one of the students arrested during the Dobrolyubov affair, Alexander feared that he might be sent down from the University and forced to live under police surveillance in Simbirsk. "What a terrible prospect!" he declared. "To live in some Godforsaken place like Simbirsk, where one becomes quite dull. No books, no people!"

SAZONOV

The savages are coming into their own. For ourselves there is only one task: to stand up to them, to fight every act of human degradation and every dishonor.

THE ATTACK RENEWED

I N THE EARLY SPRING of 1904 a wealthy "Englishman" settled in a small apartment in St. Petersburg with his mistress, valet, and cook. The apartment was on the first floor of a house in Zhukovsky Street owned by an elderly German widow who lived on the floor above. The "Englishman" had selected the house with considerable care. It had a wide view of the street, and there were two separate ways of escape from the back. He called himself Charles Harley, carried himself well, wore immaculate clothes and spoke Russian with a pronounced English accent. Every morning the porter brought him his mail, and the landlady, who was sometimes able to thumb through the mail before it reached him, observed that it consisted of business letters from abroad and catalogues containing announcements of the latest models of bicycles and automobiles. The landlady was well content with her tenants, and she would talk delightedly to her neighbors about the satisfaction of serving an Englishman who had answered her advertisement in the *Novoye Vremya*.

Every morning at the same hour the business man set out with his portfolio to his office in the center of St. Petersburg. Every evening he returned to the supper his mistress had prepared for him. The landlady, who spent half her life on the stairs eavesdropping on her tenants, observed their affectionate greeting. They were evidently deeply in love with each other. During the day she occasionally found a pretext for entering the rooms and would talk to the girl about the handsome Mr.

Harley who spoke Russian with a formidable accent. She was a little puzzled. Mr. Harley possessed all the virtues—he was rich, suave, and dignified—but he was living in sin. She wondered why he refused to marry the girl. Had Mr. Harley given her any jewelry? Had he deposited money in her name in the bank? When the girl replied that he had done none of these things, and she was deeply in love with him and wanted nothing except his love, the landlady began to speak of a German wine merchant who might be inclined to offer her marriage, jewelry, and a safe-deposit box. Then the girl laughed and explained that she wanted nothing in life but "my Charles" and the freedom to continue her singing lessons.

The landlady made inquiries about the valet and the cook. The cook, Darya Kirilovna, was an old, bent, peasant woman with a deeply lined weather-beaten face. She hovered between the kitchen and the porter's lodge, rarely going out. She liked warming her old bones by the kitchen stove; the porter spent most of his spare time with her; she had a fund of old jokes and stories, and suffered from heart trouble. Jacob, the valet, also spent a good deal of his time in the lodge, though in the mornings he would often accompany his mistress on shopping expeditions. He was tall, red-cheeked, dark-haired, and he laughed easily. He was twenty-five, but looked twenty. He treated the "Englishman" with the exaggerated respect required of valets and spoke of "the great affairs which my master is accomplishing in the business world." He hinted that very soon factories producing bicycles and automobiles would be built in St. Petersburg and he hoped his master would allow him to work in the factories "because it is necessary that men should improve themselves." The landlady had a particular fondness for Jacob. Skillful with his hands, he could be called upon to mend a leaking pipe. He had bushy eyebrows, and when he laughed his eyebrows would shoot up and he gave an impression of extraordinary enjoyment of the world around him.

Sometimes in the evenings the "Englishman" dismissed his servants, who went off on their own errands. A droshky would be waiting for him, and soon he would come down the narrow stairway with his mistress on his arm, explaining that he was attending a dinner given by one of his business associates or a ball offered by one of the princes he had met in the course of his business affairs. When the droshky had passed down the street, the landlady let herself in the apartment with a passkey. It amused her to wander through the deserted apartment. There were photographs in silver frames, the piano stood near the window, English books filled the bookcases, and on Mr. Harley's desk in a corner of the living room lay the neat piles of his correspondence, and in the drawer below lay his British passport stamped in blue and gold. Once when the police called and inquired about Mr. Harley, the porter replied: "Are you fools? He is a rich English businessman, and if you annoy him you'll hear about it from the British Embassy."

The British Embassy knew about the existence of Mr. Harley, but they would not have recognized this particular Mr. Harley. At the moment the passport had been borrowed by the revolutionary Boris Savinkov, who was being hunted by the Russian secret police. There was a price of ten thousand rubles on his head. Savinkov was a little alarmed by the price. He thought he was worth at least a hundred thousand rubles.

In the ménage which he kept at 31 Zhukovsky Street, nothing was what it seemed to be. His twenty-four-year-old mistress was not his mistress. She was an expert on explosives, a student of medicine, and a dedicated revolutionary. Her name was Dora Vladimirovna Brilliant, and she was the daughter of a rich Jewish family from the Chersonese. Pale and slight, with dark hair and enormous black eyes, she had been studying obstetrics with the desire to serve as a registered midwife in a remote village until she decided she could serve the world better as a terrorist. She had been living in a student garret in St. Petersburg when Savinkov found her, undernourished, earning a precarious living by singing at the café concerts, absorbed in terrorist activities which never came to anything, with sticks of dynamite and gelignite in her battered suitcase. She had worked with passionate intensity in her garret; she worked with the same passionate intensity in her fashionable apartment.

As for the old cook with the kerchief round her head, she was better known among revolutionaries as Praskovya Ivanovskaya. She had been sentenced to long terms of imprisonment, had been exiled to Siberia and had spent forty of her sixty years in revolutionary activity. She was the link with the past, with the great days of the eighties when the nihilists had first emerged to threaten the government with terror. No one seeing her as she clambered slowly up and down the stone staircase would have guessed the power she still wielded in revolutionary circles.

The landlady was always trying to find a legitimate husband for Dora Brilliant. She was also concerned to find a good wife for Jacob, the valet, who was well paid and remarkably pleasing to women. Half the servant girls in the house were finding excuses to go to the porter's lodge, where Jacob could often be found sitting round the wood fire.

Jacob's real name was Yegor Sergeyevich Sazonov. He had already spent a year and a half in the Butyrky prison, had been exiled to eastern Siberia for five years, and escaped to Switzerland. He was eighteen when he came to Moscow to study medicine at the University. Like Dora Brilliant he had hoped to become a village doctor, serving the peasants.

As a student Sazonov showed no interest in revolutionary activity. A monarchist, deeply religious, he hung ikons and portraits of the Tsar on his walls in Moscow. His father was a rich lumber merchant, eminently respectable, a future town councilor. "Pay no attention to the young hot-heads at the University," his father warned him. He was an obedient son. He argued with the hotheads and demonstrated a lofty indifference to their discussions of the coming revolution. During his second year at the University he called himself an "aesthete" and proclaimed that he was interested only in the good and the beautiful. But in 1901 the students declared a strike. Several hundred were herded into the huge courtyard of the Riding School and turned over to the mercy of mounted Cossacks who flogged them with knouts. Some girl students were raped. Sazonov was caught up in the strike, thrown into prison, expelled from the University and banished to his native town, where he was held under police surveillance. In prison he read revolutionary literature for the first time. He was seething with hatred, his mind made up. "My friends know well," he wrote, "with what difficulty I have reached my present conclusion. It is not easy to reject the fundamental laws of humanity, but I have been forced to it. From now on I dedicate myself to open warfare with the government and I know that once decided upon my course, I shall go on to the end." In Ufa he instituted study classes in his home. The police swooped down on him. The man dedicated to revolution was once more in prison. As he sat in the porter's lodge, his hair cropped short, his red face and his hazel eyes merry with laughter, he sometimes paused and stared into space. At such times he was thinking about Siberia and the desperate deeds he was determined to accomplish. By his own calculation he had only a few more weeks to live.

The four revolutionaries living in the heart of the fashionable quarter of St. Petersburg were surprised by their luck. No one had penetrated through their disguise. They spent long hours hiding behind the curtains and looking out on the dimly lit snow-covered street, and they discussed at interminable length the problem of maintaining their disguise. Savin-kov would discuss with the instinct of a master the exact way in which Sazonov was to accept the tips which he, Savinkov, would grandilo-quently toss into the porter's lodge the next day. Dora Brilliant had no liking for finery—she liked to wear black cotton dresses and low-heeled shoes—and Savinkov, as part of his revolutionary duty, set about teaching her to wear perfume and to put curlers in her hair. He was the same age as Sazonov, but looked older. He wore a small dark mustache under a long aristocratic nose, and there were pouches under his eyes. He wore a monocle. His hair was brushed straight back from the forehead, and he walked a little stiffly and pompously, as befitted a young Englishman with so many business interests. One evening he saw some plain-clothes men standing on the opposite side of the street. He gave the signal for immediate evacuation and then relented. There was something strange about the behavior of the plain-clothes men. They stood there in the snow, very brazen, making no effort to conceal themselves. They remained there for a week. Savinkov wondered whether the police had invented a new form of torture. Then one evening, while Sazonov was sitting in the porter's lodge, he saw the familiar face of the lawyer V. V. Bernshtam coming through the gate, followed by the plain-clothes men. Sazonov's heart went to his mouth. He was sure they had come to make an arrest. Later he learned that the lawyer was simply visiting another lawyer in the house. Both lawyers were under suspicion, because they were visited by students and were known to possess considerable libraries. But the police seemed satisfied after a desultory inspection, and soon they left. The conspirators breathed a sigh of relief.

The main task assigned to the band around Savinkov was to kill Plehve, the Minister of the Interior, then at the height of his power. Plehve was responsible for the pogrom at Kishinev, the arbitrary arrest of thousands of young students, and he was identified with the actions of the secret police. With his heavy bland Germanic face, his thick eyebrows, his heavily lidded eyes, his pince-nez, and his horde of mistresses, he represented the accumulated power of the reaction. Kill him, and the whole power of the reaction might be destroyed.

The conspirators went about their work quietly. They were in contact with half a dozen other revolutionaries in St. Petersburg. These others were mainly scouts. The conspirators regarded themselves as the striking force. Dora Brilliant and Sazonov were each determined to be Plehve's murderer.

Savinkov had no illusions about the difficulty of killing the Minister of the Interior. Plehve was surrounded by armies of police spies and special agents, and had spent many years combatting terrorists. Behind his bland face he concealed an extraordinarily quick mind and unusual cunning. When he drove through the streets, it was always at a reckless speed.

"The only way we shall ever kill him," Sazonov suggested one day, "is by throwing ourselves under the carriage with the bombs."

The idea was characteristic of Sazonov, whose hatred of the Minister had increased from the moment when he was sentenced to Siberia. He told himself he could not live in the same world as Plehve, and spoke of hearing voices which whispered: "Strike him, strike him!" during those long days when he made his way back from his Siberian prison. He said: "I could not live in peace any more. When I thought of all the things he had done to Russia, I felt that any ordinary life would be alien to me. I must kill him or be killed by him."

Savinkov quickly rejected the idea of allowing Sazonov to throw himself under Plehve's carriage. He wanted to move cautiously. The scouts reported on all the Minister's movements. They knew at exactly what hour he left his house on Aptekarsky Island in the north of St. Petersburg. They knew when he arrived at the Ministry of the Interior on the Fontanka. They knew every detail of his Thursday morning journeys to the Tsar at Tsarskoye Selo. They knew when he attended cabinet meetings at the Marinsky Palace. Savinkov, Sazonov, Dora Brilliant, and Ivanovskaya acted as their own scouts, and were helped by three resourceful assistants, Dulebov, Kaliayev, and Matzeyevsky; to this group the young Borishansky was added a little while later.

Of these assistants the one closest to Sazonov was Yegor Dulebov, a twenty-four-year-old peasant from the railway shops in Ufa. He had already made his mark in revolutionary circles, for in May 1903 he was one of the two members of the Socialist Revolutionary party who shot and killed Bogdanovich, the Governor of Ufa. Bogdanovich had given orders to his troops to fire on strikers. Twenty-eight had been killed, and some two hundred wounded, and it was inevitable that the Terrorist Brigade should order his execution. Dulebov had been chosen for the task because of his sense of dedication. He had written a long letter on the night before the killing, justifying the action, saying that he had prayed all his life for an opportunity to do good to his fellow men, and now at last he had been given the privilege he desired above all others. At Ufa he had worked as a locksmith, but after the assassination he wandered around Russia, always in hiding, and sometimes the revolutionary organization lost track of him. There was talk of sending him abroad, but he explained that he was a peasant and there was nothing he could do for the revolution while abroad. He talked the same language as Sazonov, whose workingmen's study circles he had attended at Ufa. Both were determined, relentless, and experienced revolutionaries.

Yosip Matzeyevsky and Ivan Kaliayev had less experience. They were both excitable, and at first sight lacked the heroic qualities of Dulebov and Sazonov. Matzeyevsky and Dulebov acted as drivers. They had cabs and were continually driving through the streets of St. Petersburg in the hope of coming upon the Minister's carriage, while Kaliayev acted as a peddler, wearing drab clothes and carrying a tray slung over his shoulders. In the tray there would be apples, pencils, writing paper. As a peddler, in full command of the peddler's jargon, Kaliayev was more useful to the organization than the two cab drivers. He could go anywhere, join any crowd, wander right up to the edge of the Minister's palace. He grew a beard. With his shambling gait and his burst of quick laughter whenever he made a sale, he was popular among the other peddlers. It was Kaliayev who usually learned first about any change in Plehve's movements. Writing about him later, Savinkov said: "He would observe the most minute changes in the streets. He could tell just by a change in the atmosphere whether Plehve was on his way. He could see whether the Minister was coming by the way the policemen were standing, by the way they grouped themselves together, or simply by the way they looked at one another. He had an almost mystical understanding of what was passing through Plehve's mind. He described everything: the footboards, the door handles, the harness, the lamps, the coach box, the axles, and if there was any change in these, he would deduce the reasons for the change. And he knew the names and the appearance of the police spies who always congregated around the Minister."

In all this Kaliayev had an advantage over the other scouts. The cab drivers were always being moved on by the police or having to accept fares. Savinkov himself had to be careful. He was the businessman interested in automobiles and bicycles, and therefore kept close to the business part of the city. Ivanovskaya hobbled around, too old and too ill to help them watch Plehve's movements. Dora Brilliant spent most of her time in the apartment on Zhukovsky Street, though she would make occasional forays abroad.

Life in the apartment on Zhukovsky Street continued as before. None of the minor conspirators ever visited it. They lived at widely separated places in St. Petersburg. Kaliayev, for example, lived with four other young peddlers in a single room in a tenement. But occasionally life in Zhukovsky Street was disturbed by the arrival of important visitors from abroad. Among them was Evno Azev, who stayed there for ten days in the early spring. To the landlady it was explained that he was a distant relative who was visiting the city on matters of business.

Of all the revolutionaries the plump, round-shouldered Azev, with his gray eyes and swarthy yellowish cheeks, thick lips and large square teeth, was the most unprepossessing. In theory he was in command of the Terrorist Brigade, receiving his powers from the Executive Committee of the Socialist Revolutionary party. He leaned heavily on the advice of Savinkov, but no attempt at assassination took place unless he was fully warned, and unless the full details of the attempt were explained to him. He selected the targets and decided which revolutionaries should take part in the attempt. He supplied money, revolvers, and dynamite. All the time he was a paid agent of the Tsarist police, his sympathies divided between the autocracy and the revolution. For no reason which anyone has ever discovered, it pleased him to play with the hunters and the hunted. He disliked Plehve, and therefore put no obstacles in the way of the assassination attempt; he seems to have liked Stolypin and Dubassov, with the result that attempts on their lives failed, for the police received prior warning. Power amused him; he had the conjuror's delight in performing continual miracles, standing in front of the mirror, admiring himself, knowing that a single mistake would mean death.

Gorky described Azev in a short story called "Karamora" as a man who played the double game "simply for the sake of variety," and so it may have been. When Azev visited the house in Zhukovsky Street, he was already a legendary character, a man who had supervised a host of attacks upon government officials. Sazonov and Savinkov trusted him completely. It was Azev who insisted that bombs must be thrown, and he refused to tolerate any plan which involved knives or revolvers. He dismissed out of hand Sazonov's idea of throwing himself with the bomb under the carriage. No, the proper way was the simplest: four terrorists walking forty paces apart. The first was to cut off the Minister's retreat, the second was to throw the bomb, the third would throw another bomb if the other failed, the fourth was to throw his bomb only in case of dire necessity. With luck the first and fourth would survive the attack and be able to report to headquarters. They must come to the help of a terrorist if he was attacked, but it was unlikely that they would be needed for throwing bombs. Azev explained that he would send the bombs just before the attack. Shortly afterward nearly all the conspirators left St. Petersburg. Their plans were laid. It was necessary that the enemy should be unconscious of their existence. Azev and Sazonov went to the Volga. Savinkov went to Sestroretsk, a watering place along the coast northwest of St. Petersburg, where there was a small armament factory and immense rolling parks laid out in the English fashion. Ivanovskaya made her way to Vilna, and there soon afterward all the conspirators came together for their last reunion before the attack on the Minister. Here Azev would give them their final instructions.

The terrorists spent a week in Vilna. "In a small dimly lit room," Ivanovskaya recalled, "sat thoughtful men whose fate was already sealed, exchanging trivialities. Azev alone seemed calm, attentive, and unusually kind." When it was time for them to return to St. Petersburg, Azev kissed them farewell. Years later, when the terrorists placed him on trial and accused him of being an *agent provocateur*, Azev said: "Believe me, when I kissed Sazonov, it was not the kiss of Judas."

The house in Zhukovsky Street had been given up. All the details were agreed upon. The terrorists knew where to meet and how to dispose of the bombs immediately after the attack and where they should go if they survived. Azev had vanished, but everyone else was back in St. Petersburg. It was decided that Plehve should be killed on July 8, 1904, when he was on his way early in the morning to the Baltic Station for the journey to Peterhof, where the Tsar had his summer palace on the shores of the Gulf of Finland. Three days earlier they had been joined by a new recruit, a young leatherworker from Byelostok called Schimel Leiba Vulfovich Sikorsky. He spoke Russian badly; he was awkward and thin-boned; he had a shock of dark hair which fell over his small forehead; but he had long ago decided to offer his life for the revolution. As a Jew he detested Plehve; as a Pole he detested the Tsar. Borishansky knew him well and vouched for his courage. He was to be given the fourth place in the line. Kaliayev was to go first, followed by Sazonov and Borishansky. Dulebov was placed in charge of the bombs and would distribute them at the proper time.

For some reason which was never made clear Sazonov failed to receive his bomb in time. Plehve's familiar carriage drove past on its way to the Baltic Station, no one suspecting that an attack had been averted by a failure in timing. It was decided to repeat the attempt a week later on the occasion of Plehve's next journey to Peterhof. There was another meeting in Vilna, another leave-taking with Azev, and then the conspirators returned to St. Petersburg.

On July 15, a few minutes before nine o'clock, on a bright summer's day, Sazonov hurled the bomb.

THE DEATH OF A MINISTER

I N THOSE DAYS the streets of St. Petersburg always seemed to have an air of emptiness, except in the evenings and the early mornings when people hurried to their business. But this morning the streets were crowded with policemen. Some were disguised as beggars, others as officials. There were policemen on horseback, in uniform, and in plain clothes. At every turning in the road a plain-clothes man was waiting.

Savinkov was appalled by the number of policemen in the street. Someone had evidently warned the police of an imminent attack on Plehve. He caught a glimpse of Sazonov's beautiful quick loping stride as he hurried along the Ismailovsky Prospect, his brass buttons shining, his peaked cap a little to one side over an expressionless face. Sazonov was carrying something in the crook of his elbow. For a moment he disappeared from sight, then Savinkov saw him again, still striding along in the direction of the railway station—a railwayman late for his work, and no one would ever have guessed otherwise. He did not look worried, though in fact he was more perturbed than he had ever been. He was afraid someone would nudge him. A quick shove, and the bomb would fall to the ground. He was forever making little dancing steps to avoid contact. Once he saw a plain-clothes detective bearing down on him, but he quickly disappeared into the crowd.

Savinkov was still keeping a close watch, trailing behind. By now the police were alert. In the sudden excitement two things were evident: someone had warned the police, and the Minister's carriage would soon be coming down the road. People were being searched. At street corners especially the police were watchful. They asked questions and motioned people down alleyways where they could be searched more efficiently. There was that trembling in the air which announces the coming of an important personage. It was as though even the buildings were suddenly alert and watchful. Savinkov caught a last glimpse of Sazonov hurrying over the bridge which soars over the Obvodny Canal; there was the gold band round his railway porter's cap glinting in the sun, and then he was gone.

"We're too late," Savinkov muttered. "We should have come out earlier, and prepared better."

A moment later Plehve's black carriage with the two black horses came bowling down the street. The liveried coachman, wearing a top hat and a cockade, sat in the driving seat. The coach, like the coaches of all the ministers and court officials, was armored with thin steel plates. It was heavy and possessed remarkable momentum. The police were saluting smartly. Occasionally Plehve would bow to the people in the street, but mostly he held himself stiffly, very stern and upright, his white face gleaming in the dark interior of the coach. Near the back wheel a secret-service man on a bicycle was peddling furiously. Another cab came up in the rear, filled with detectives. The police were saluting smartly and the Minister's coach was slowing down because a droshky had swung into the road.

Kaliayev was crossing the bridge when he saw Sazonov disappearing in the crowd. Savinkov had already lost track of him.

It was impossible to imagine that Sazonov would ever emerge from the crowd to toss the bomb. Intoxicated with failure, Savinkov decided that there was nothing further to be done; he would meet Sazonov according to arrangements in the Yusupov Gardens and he would himself kill the Minister on his return from Peterhof. But a few moments later he saw, as in a dream, a tall man in the blue uniform of a railwayman darting out of the crowd in front of Plehve's carriage. Sazonov's timing was fantastically accurate. He stood in the middle of the street with the bomb poised in his hand and he waited for the carriage to swerve past him. In that brief instant he recognized Plehve, and it seems that Plehve recognized that he was about to be attacked, for he suddenly changed his position. Then Sazonov flung the bomb straight at the carriage window. It seems to have exploded on Plehve's lap. There was the sound of a steel plate shuddering under a hammer blow. Sazonov remembered nothing more, for he was thrown ten feet in the air by the force of the explosion.

From his vantage point on the brow of the bridge Kaliayev watched a thin sulphur-yellow cloud, black at the edges, rising from the place where the carriage had been. He heard the clatter of broken glass from a thousand neighboring windows. There was no sign of Sazonov or of Plehve; the carriage itself had been shattered into fragments, with only some sticks and fragments of the wheel hoops still attached to the shafts. The crowd was screaming. Everyone was running away. The horses, wounded in the explosion, were driving madly across the street, dragging the smashed wheels with them, and soon they made straight for the bridge. The thin column of sulphur-yellow smoke puffed out and filled the width of the street; it was like a curtain drawn over the death of the Minister.

Savinkov was inquisitive. He wanted to see exactly what had happened. If he went straight up to the place where the explosion had occurred, he would be reasonably safe, for hundreds of curiosity seekers, who at first had run away, were now returning to look for souvenirs. Someone was shouting: "Don't run up there! There may be another explosion!" The words suggested that Plehve had escaped. Everyone knew that the terrorists worked in pairs, and if the first bomb failed, there was always a second in reserve. There was a stiff wind and the smoke was being winnowed away. Passing the Warsaw Hotel, Savinkov observed that the crushed remnants of the carriage were burning fiercely. This, too, was unexpected: from the force of the explosion he had hardly expected to see anything of that massive carriage. There was no sign of Plehve, but Sazonov was lying in the roadway, about four feet from the sidewalk, his left arm flung out on the cobblestones, his face rigid and pale with little streams of blood trickling over his forehead and cheeks. His cap was blown off. His thick hair lay wet and tangled over his brow. His eyes were half open, and he was breathing with difficulty; and as he lay there, spread-eagled in the road, not moving nor stirring in any way, Savinkov assumed he was dead or dying. There was blood streaming from a wound in the abdomen, forming a huge widening pool at his feet. Savinkov bent over and studied the unconscious face, and then he heard a voice saying: "Well, they say the Minister has escaped." The voice belonged to Police

Captain Perepelitzin. Savinkov recognized him, as he recognized all the other police captains because it was his business to recognize them, and together with the other conspirators he had formed a complete mental dossier of their behavior and characteristics and personal appearance. Perepelitzin seems to have thought Savinkov was just one more curiosity seeker. His jaw was working, he was deathly pale and he kept fluttering his white-gloved hands. "Move along, please," he said. "It's none of your business, sir. Keep moving."

For Savinkov it was all a nightmare, and he made his way to the Warsaw station hardly knowing where he was going. He had brought the nightmare on himself, but when he remembered Sazonov, the tangled hair, the dark blood welling out of the abdomen, the head strangely bent toward the right shoulder as though in his last moments Sazonov was turning his face toward the bomb he had held so precariously, he was overcome with a feeling of inexpressible grief. Some bricklayers, covered with dust, ran screaming past Savinkov. All he could think of was: "The Minister is alive, Sazonov is dead." In his excitement he had failed to observe the body of Plehve lying close to Sazonov among pieces of the carriage furniture. The body was terribly mangled, without arms or legs, the face crushed and unrecognizable. When Sazonov awoke to consciousness the first thing he saw appeared to be a red cloak such as those worn by generals. It was lying near the gutter, and for some idiotic reason people were staring at the red cloak from the sidewalk. The red cloak was Plehve.

Savinkov wandered through the city until he came to the Technological Institute. Dulebov, Sazonov's closest friend, was waiting outside in his cab. Savinkov climbed in.

"What happened?" Dulebov whispered.

"They say the Minister escaped."

"And Yegor?"

"Dead or dying."

There was a long pause. The cab was racing over the cobblestones.

"What do we do now?" Dulebov asked, tears streaming down his cheeks.

"We carry out the plan. The Minister will be returning from Peterhof at four o'clock. At three o'clock I'll hand the bomb to you. You'll be waiting for me outside the Technological Institute."

At a busy cross street Savinkov climbed out of the cab and made his way on foot to the Yusupov Gardens. Once he had to hold on to a wall for support. He had almost fainted when the thin sulphur-yellow cloud rose, and then again when he was bending over Sazonov. He hoped Kaliayev was safe and had not thrown his bomb away, but even if Kaliayev had panicked, or been caught by the police, there was always the hope that with Dulebov's assistance he would be able to kill the Minister in the afternoon. He expected to find Kaliayev in the Yusupov Gardens, but there was no sign of him. There was no sign of Sikorsky, either. Savinkov was perturbed. If Plehve was alive, both Kaliayev and Sikorsky might well have been arrested by now. Savinkov wandered in the empty gardens for a while, and then made his way to a bathhouse in the Lane of the Cossacks, where he rented a room, stripped, bathed, and stared at the ceiling. It was now ten o'clock. When he emerged at noon, he bought a newspaper. The front page had a thick black border, a portrait of Plehve and an account of the assassination which had occurred, according to the correspondent, "at the hands of an unknown terrorist who was critically wounded in the explosion." Savinkov could make little of this. It had never happened to him before that he had been so deadly wrong in his interpretation of a terrorist action. He slipped the newspaper in his pocket and walked straight back to the Ismailovsky Prospect, determined to discover exactly what had happened by talking with people who had witnessed the explosion.

A few moments after Savinkov was told to move on by Captain Perepelitzin, Sazonov awoke from his stupor, gazed around and breathed a deep sigh of relief, and this was followed by a terrible groan, for as he looked across the empty street and saw no sign of the carriage or the two black horses, he assumed that the Minister had escaped. He remembered everything vividly. It astonished him that he was still alive. He tried to get up, but he seemed to have no body. He saw that one of his feet had been smashed and that the blood was running out of a great wound in his stomach. He succeeded in raising himself on his elbow and thinking he was about to die he shouted: "Long live freedom!" He had the feeling that his enemies would soon be after him and it was necessary to make an escape. He thought: "I must be careful. I may get delirious. It would be much better to commit hara-kiri like the Japanese than to fall into the hands of the filthy policemen." He tried to remove his revolver from his pocket, determined to defend himself or shoot himself through the brain. He had not observed Captain Perepelitzin, who had been studying him carefully. When the captain saw Sazonov making an effort to take the revolver from his pocket, he knew he was face to face with the assassin. Perepelitzen knew a great deal about wounds. He knew that this terrorist was far from being dead. There was still a possibility that he would escape. He removed the revolver. Sazonov, recognizing a plain-clothes policeman, screamed and tried to get to his feet. Perepelitzin pressed him down. More policemen came running up. They had recovered from the shock and like Perepelitzin they had come to the conclusion that they had found the assassin. Enraged, they began to beat him. They used their fists, boots, and the butts of their revolvers. It did not occur to them that Sazonov was dying, or at least desperately wounded. He must be made to pay for his sins. And it did not occur to them that Sazonov was beyond suffering and could not feel the butt ends of the revolvers which fell across his face, until his face was no more than a mass of blood and both eyes were badly damaged. Sazonov heard someone shouting: "Be careful! Where's the bomb—the other bomb?" Weakly, while they were still flogging him, Sazonov said: "Please leave me alone. I haven't got another bomb." There was a brief discussion between the policemen. It was decided to take him off the street.

"Where the devil shall we take him?" someone shouted.

"Take him to a hotel—anywhere."

There was a hotel a little way down the street, and after some more discussion it was agreed to take him there until official instructions were received from headquarters. A messenger had already been sent to inform Muraviev, the Minister of Justice. There was a further discussion about how he should be taken, until someone decided that the simplest way was the best: they dragged him by the feet with his head bumping against the cobblestones, leaving a long gleaming smear of blood behind him. At the hotel he was told to climb up the stairs to the only vacant room on the third floor, but he was now too weak even to stand, and with a blanket thrown over him he was carried up to the hotel room and thrown down on the floor, where his clothes were torn off and he was again beaten. None of this beating affected him. He watched it all drowsily, as though from a long way away, in the peace of approaching death, noting that the room seemed to be unaccountably filling with smoke. More and more policemen and officials came in, until there was hardly room to move about. They were all talking in loud voices. Someone came up to Sazonov, knelt down, felt his head and murmured: "He'll live. Better not hit him any more." Then he was taken down the bloodstained staircase, and he remembered nothing more until he woke up in a hospital.

At the hospital one of the policemen remembered that Sazonov had made a curious gesture, putting his hand quickly to his mouth. They were not sure, but it was possible that he had taken poison. Sazonov woke up just as a tube was being pushed down his throat. This, too, seemed to be happening to someone else, in some other place. No poison was dredged up by the stomach pump. It was agreed that he was still too weak to be questioned. He was put under chloroform while the doctors probed in his body for bomb splinters, sewed up the gash in his stomach and amputated two of his crushed toes.

It was evening when he came round. Once again he remembered what had happened on the Ismailovsky Prospect. He wanted to sing for joy. He heard strange voices coming from a long way away. The voices were soft and faint. He felt hideously thirsty and asked for water. Someone was saying: "Tell me your name." Sazonov kept asking for water. "We'll give you water if you tell us your name. Just tell me your name—"

"Why?"

"We have to know. You're in a hospital. We're nurses."

Sazonov laughed deliriously. It was incredible that they should talk like that.

"If you're nurses," he said, "then why aren't you at the front? It's an absolute scandal, eh?"*

The nurses had to shout to make themselves heard. The savage kicks in the head had made him deaf.

Soon water was brought to him. Another voice, deep-toned, said: "We want to help you. We have no other aim. Let us start by being friends."

About this time Sazonov was aware that he had either gone blind or his eyes were bandaged. He lay very still. He refused to talk. He kept telling himself: "Whatever happens I must not let them know my name."

The voice said: "I am the examining magistrate. You are charged with the assassination of Minister Plehve. You are required to tell me your name and the reasons for your act."

"I can tell you nothing," Sazonov answered softly, "except one thing—"

"And what's that?"

"I am a member of the Terrorist Brigade."

There was a long silence. He heard the doctors whispering, and then the heavy footfalls of the examining magistrate as he left the room. Soon the examining magistrate returned; presumably he had received new instructions.

"I must know your name."

"I can't tell you."

"And the names of your accomplices?"

"You are an idiot if you think I will tell you."

The examination went on for two or three hours. When Sazonov fell asleep he was prodded awake. The doctors were still afraid he would die before being brought up to trial. Once he asked the name of the examining magistrate. There was no answer. He learned later that the magistrate was the Minister of Justice, Muraviev, and when he left the room it was presumably to contact the Tsar. The Minister shrugged his shoulders and said: "He may speak better in prison," and gave orders that everything the prisoner said in delirium should be written down.

The next morning Sazonov was removed from the Alexandrovsky Work-

---

* Russia was at this time at war with Japan.

men's Hospital to the prison hospital attached to the Kresty, a large and recently modernized prison overlooking the river. Here there began the long battle to extract information from a singularly silent prisoner.

The man placed in charge of the incessant cross-examination was a police official named Gurovich, who later became an important functionary under the Bolsheviks.

Sazonov knew what to expect. He had slept well, and some of his old braggadocio returned in the prison hospital. Gurovich had a friendly voice as he bent over the bed. Sazonov was in sharp pain, for the effects of the chloroform had worn off, but the pain kept him awake and helped to distract him from the investigation.

Gurovich began pleasantly with a long speech full of phrases about the misdirected heroism of the terrorists, how it was possible to honor them and at the same time regret their foolish extremism. He explained patiently that the government would always be stronger than the terrorists. The prisoner had been prepared to sacrifice himself for his beliefs, however wrong-headed, and "to a certain degree" had behaved in a praiseworthy manner. Then the tone changed. There were hints that Gurovich was in a position to help.

"I am a doctor," Gurovich explained. "Doctors are concerned with the welfare of humanity. Like you, they want everyone in Russia to be happy. I shall look after you to the best of my ability, but you understand I shall need your cooperation. You have committed terrible crimes. It is a small thing perhaps to have killed Minister Plehve, but what about the others— the man who was just standing nearby, and the old woman and the two-year-old child? There were very many people killed. These are the only ones we have been able to recognize."

Sazonov told himself this was a trick, but the doctor went on relentlessly, talking about the old woman and the child, mentioning casually that altogether twenty-nine people had died in the explosion and there were many others who were not expected to live. He mentioned their names and spoke of how all Russia was in mourning for their deaths. People had sometimes praised the terrorists in the past; now they were universally execrated.

"You must have known it would happen," Gurovich went on. "At half past nine in the morning, on the Ismailovsky Prospect, it is always crowded—people going about their affairs, shopping, taking the air. And so you chose the very worst time of the day, and the most crowded street. That's why people are calling you 'traitor.' I don't altogether share their view. They say the two-year-old child was very beautiful."

For an hour Sazonov listened to these lies. Every few minutes Gurovich asked some pointed question about the terrorists' organization, saying:

"You must help us—it is so shameful," or "You have already mentioned many names in your delirium. Why don't you tell me the rest?"

Gurovich had a long experience in dealing with prisoners. He was probing the wound. The torture continued. He discovered that whenever he talked about the dead child, the prisoner stiffened and sweat poured over the bandaged face. Sazonov's calm braggadocio gave place to terror. He held onto the doctor's hand and screamed: "Don't call me a traitor! Call me anything, but never a traitor!" Then he lost consciousness. When he awoke Gurovich was still there. When Gurovich began to speak, Sazonov said quietly: "It's no use. I won't listen. Go away, or I'll shout for help. You're not a doctor. You're a police agent."

When Gurovich left the cell, a real doctor took his place. There were intervals of quiet when new bandages were put on or the bed sheets were changed. The new doctor explained the nature of the wounds and said there was hope of a complete recovery. Then, though Sazonov was aware that others were in the cell, the doctor bent low and whispered: "We're absolutely alone. Let me help you. Would you like messages sent to your friends? Just tell me who to send the messages to." Sazonov half believed him until he said: "The police already have a great deal of information about you. They know one of your comrades threw a bomb in the Neva. They say the boatman who took him out on the Neva was a terrorist, too."

This was the first time the police had shown they knew anything positive about the plot. The comrade who tossed his bomb in the Neva was probably Sikorsky. Presumably the boatman had also been arrested. Sazonov was afraid he had mentioned Sikorsky's name during his ravings. Gurovich had spoken of a second explosion. When he was alone, Sazonov tried to dovetail the pieces together. Two bomb explosions? Sikorsky and the boatman arrested? Twenty-nine people killed? He was still feverishly attempting to understand what had happened from the limited information which reached the cell in the Kresty Prison when Gurovich came and told him there was bad news: Ten more people had died as a result of the explosion, bringing the death roll to thirty-nine. Sazonov refused to believe him. Gurovich gave details, names, addresses, occupations, the kinds of wounds they had received, until Sazonov screamed himself into delirium.

Long before the attack on Plehve the terrorists had discussed the possibility of their arrests. They had promised to believe nothing the police told them. They had sworn an oath to reveal nothing to the police. In prison they would have to fight the same silent deadly war they had fought outside. There were long intervals in which Sazonov remained extraordinarily calm—calm even in delirium. He wrote afterward: "I believe I can remember everything I said in delirium, and this is not at all difficult if you take the proper precautions." He did not reveal what pre-cautions he took, but he seems to have steeled himself to unusual feats of silence. But he could not always remember his ravings and he was not always silent. He wrote in another letter: "My sufferings from wounds were nothing compared with the moral torment of the investigation. Heaven knows what I may have said in delirium. I cried out for death to deliver me, death which had touched me so closely and then so terribly betrayed me. Better not to have been born than to bring disgrace and ruin on our cause, betray my comrades and disturb their faith in me." Gradu-ally a deep sense of guilt was awakened in him: guilt because he may have betrayed the revolutionaries, guilt because he may have been re-sponsible for forty deaths, and then the guilt which came when he faced his own inadequacy in parrying the relentless questioning of the investi-gators.

The Russian secret police were past masters at extracting confessions. Even in these early days they employed moral torture almost to the ex-clusion of physical torture. The policemen who attacked Sazonov on the ground had acted in hot blood and in anger: most of them knew they would be punished for not having guarded Plehve against assassination. Prince Peter Kropotkin mentions in his reminiscences the shock of horror when he heard that Karakozov was physically tortured in the last days before his execution, and how even though there seemed to be no bones in his body, and his head and hands hung loose, he made strenuous efforts to climb the scaffold unaided. Torture had not prevented Karakozov from dying well. There is no evidence that Nechayev was ever tortured. Sazo-nov had no fear of physical torture, but he was beginning to be desper-ately afraid he would talk too much.

For three weeks he remained in his cell in the hospital, bandaged and blind. From the moment he awoke to the moment he fell asleep there was an interrogator by the bedside. He heard no voices except the voices of the young assistant doctor and of Gurovich. Gurovich's hard bluster would be followed by the soothing sermons of the doctor, the tough and the soft, an age-old technique still pursued by the police. In the end it usually succeeds. Gurovich announced that Sikorsky had confessed and told a strange tale about a meeting with an old woman in Vilna shortly before the assassination, and then he went on to say that another Jew, "whose name I do not have to acquaint you with, for you must know it already—he is a man who wears an English coat," had also confessed under arrest, and this man was another comrade from Byelostok. By this time Sazonov realized that Sikorsky, who was once a leatherworker in Bye-lostok, must at least have stated his name and place of residence. There were few other consolations to be derived from listening to Gurovich. He was in great pain, and though the thought of having killed Plehve gave him, as he declared later, "a moral satisfaction so great there is nothing in the world to compare with it," the thought of the thirty or forty innocent people who might also have been killed remained to torment him, so that he had no desire to live and wished desperately he could put himself out of his misery. "Everyone has heard of your revolutionary mottoes," Gurovich said one day. "I applaud them! What noble sentiments! Truth through Blood. Joy and Pride. Beautiful mottoes, until you think of the young mother cut down in her womanhood and the small child still holding a doll, though there is a bomb splinter as large as your fist in her throat."

There were other things that tormented Sazonov. He remembered dimly that when the examining magistrate questioned him in the Alexandrovsky Hospital about whether he had known Pokotilov, killed when experimenting with a bomb in his room in the Northern Hotel, he had replied that he knew Pokotilov well; and when asked about the aims of the Terrorist Brigade he had launched out in semidelirium in a long, militant discourse, describing these aims in detail. This was weakness, though no harm had been done. In talking at all about a member of the Brigade, he had disobeyed a cardinal rule of the organization: the terrorist must be silent when faced with his accusers. When he tried to rationalize his own weakness, he put it down to the terrible thirst which must have arisen as a result of shock. He asked for water. They refused to give it to him. In the end, when the thirst became a raging fever, he had thrown out these tidbits of entirely useless information. But what if it should happen again? He told himself he must beware of giving information away when in a state of shock, for they could produce a state of shock whenever they wanted to. He was at their mercy, fed by strange hands and with a bandage over his eyes. He thought they might be able to induce shock by drugs mixed with his food, but the shock came three weeks and five days after the arrest when the bandage was taken from his eyes. He had thought he had been alone with Gurovich or the doctor. Now he saw, arranged along the four walls, the silent impassive gendarmes who had stood guard in the cell throughout his imprisonment.

"Why don't you tell us your name?" the young assistant doctor asked. "What harm can it do?"

In a weak moment Sazonov answered: "All I can tell you is that my name begins with S."

Two days later he was told: "We know who you are. We have discovered everything. You are Yegor Sergeyevich Sazonov."

During his trial which began on November 30, four and a half months after the assassination of Plehve, Sazonov smuggled a letter out of prison addressed to the surviving members of the Brigade. At the time he thought he would be sentenced to death, and the letter was at once an apologia and a final farewell to his friends. He wrote:

> Believe me, the enemy is contemptible without limit. One should never surrender oneself to them alive. Please tell this to all our comrades. Farewell, dear ones! I salute the dawn of liberty! . . .
>
> Let me tell you of my unpardonable crime. I cannot tell you why, after three weeks of silence, I revealed my name. Comrades, I beg you not to judge me too harshly. If you knew how much I suffered, and how I still suffer, remembering how I sometimes talked in my delirium. I was helpless. What could I do to save myself? Bite off my tongue? But I had not even enough strength for this. I was terribly weak. I wanted only to die or to recover quickly. And then too I remember how I sometimes spoke about the aims of the party, and then I remember that I may not have explained them adequately. As you know, my conception of terror springs from the Narodnaya Volya and so to some extent I disagree with the program of the Terrorist Brigade. When I appeared before the court I felt I was in a false position. I should not have spoken of my personal views. I should have spoken exclusively of the views of the Brigade. Did I commit a sin against the Brigade? Please forgive me. Tell the party to announce my errors publicly, tell them to say they are not responsible for the words spoken by individual members, especially one who is ill. I have still not recovered. The blow on my head was too strong. So I am weighed down with a sense of sin, and I want to confess my errors to you, my dear comrades. And if I am the only one who has wronged our cause, let this too be known. I have tried so consciously to lessen the importance of my errors.

At the trial those who had known Sazonov could hardly recognize him. The youthful apple-cheeked face had gone forever. He was pale and nervous, and had difficulty in collecting his thoughts. His brow was deeply furrowed, and he seemed to have aged by twenty years. He walked on crutches, complained of intolerable headaches, and sometimes stared round the court with a vacant expression. It was whispered that he had been drugged, but in fact he was still suffering from a sense of his own intolerable guilt.

Sikorsky was placed on trial with him. The twenty-year-old leather-worker from Byelostok who spoke Russian so badly that his replies had to be translated in court had behaved with remarkable incompetence. He had been ordered to hire a boat in Petrovsky Park, row out across the lake and then drop the bomb carefully in the water. Instead he had hired a boat on the Neva and in full view of the workmen building a battleship in a dockyard overlooking the river he had hurled the bomb into the river. The boatman was alarmed, and when Sikorsky stuffed a ten-ruble note in his hands, he grew still more alarmed. When he returned to the shore the boatman took his prisoner straight to a police station. Sikorsky denied everything. For some days he held out, refusing to give his name; then he told the rambling incoherent story about the meeting with the woman in Vilna which was communicated to Sazonov. Some time in the autumn some fishermen found the bomb in their nets and handed it to the authorities. It was assumed by the police that at least six people must have taken part in the assassination, but neither Sikorsky nor Sazonov revealed the names of their associates.

During the trial Sazonov learned for the first time that the assassination of Plehve had completely altered the atmosphere of Russia. The Liberal statesman Prince Svyatopolk-Mirsky succeeded Plehve and announced a program of liberal reforms and a relaxation of the censorship. The Holy Synod proposed to convene a Church Assembly to discuss the restoration of the Patriarchate, a sign that the Church was already aware of a change in the weather of the autocracy. Vast plans were afoot for altering the basic structure of government. While the trial was in progress, plans to assemble a Council of Ministers to introduce a legally appointed government and to abolish the extraordinary powers of the Tsar were being widely discussed, and in fact the Council of Ministers met shortly after the trial was concluded. Unknown to Sazonov, his deed had been applauded over large areas of Russia, and when the Liberal lawyer Kazorinov who defended him said: "The bomb was loaded not with dynamite but with the tears and sufferings of the people," there was general assent. Sazonov, who had expected to be tried by a military tribunal and hanged immediately after sentence was handed down, found himself the hero of the hour.

The trial was the quietest of all the trials in which the terrorists took part. There were no loud declamations. The judge treated Sazonov with considerable respect. Though the judge laid down the rule that Sazonov could make no apologia at the trial, Sazonov was in fact allowed to speak at some length. He spoke badly, often lost the thread of his ideas, paused lengthily and sometimes seemed unaware that he was in court. He had, however, written out a statement which he intended to produce at the trial. In this speech, which was never delivered, he said:

> I wish to explain that our party cannot be described as one which acts by violence. It is by its very nature inimical to every kind of violence . . . We are not forcing our ideals upon the people: we wish only to speak the truth . . . We hate and despise violence, and we are convinced that violence is powerless against ideals. But all our attempts at peaceful activity have been met by ruthless persecution on the part of the government. We are subjected to the humiliation of corporal punishment, beaten by knouts, trodden upon by horses, and shot down as soon as we declare our desires and our purposes. We are deprived of the protection of the law and declared to be enemies of the people . . .
>
> Yes, the government made me a revolutionist and a terrorist, though orig-

inally I prayed only for peace. When I escaped from Siberia, I felt that red ghosts were creeping behind me, never leaving me all day and all night, and they whispered in my ear: "Go and kill Plehve!" Since I began to understand the work of the Ministers of Russia, I felt I had no right to enjoy a peaceful and happy life. So in killing Plehve I acted according to the dictates of my conscience.

Sazonov had so completely confessed his crime that the jury had no alternative but to judge him guilty. He was sentenced to life imprisonment with hard labor and deprivation of all rights and property. Sikorsky was sentenced to fifteen years' hard labor. The same day the two prisoners were removed to the Schlüsselburg Fortress.

Like Nechayev, Sazonov in prison was almost more formidable than when he was plotting assassination. He was already a legend. In the five years that remained to him he became a more formidable legend and in the end he sealed the legend with a fantastic suicide.

THE SENSE OF GUILT

IN TSARIST RUSSIA there were two completely different kinds of prisons. There were the great fortress prisons of Moscow, St. Petersburg, and the provincial capitals, with high stone walls, great courtyards, and small damp cells. These prisons were governed by iron laws and were under continual scrutiny by the officials of the Minister of the Interior. From the most important of these prisons went daily or weekly reports to the Tsar. Such prisons were for the aristocrats among prisoners, those who had most dangerously offended the autocracy, and very few had ever escaped from them. In these prisons most of the prisoners were lifers and they could expect to die in their cells.

The fortress prisons were made of stone; on the other hand the Siberian prisons, though often surrounded by a high stone wall, were made of wood. The Ministry of the Interior had little influence in these remote regions. The prison governor was a law to himself, and if he chose, he could make the lives of his prisoners tolerable and even pleasant. Usually the Siberian prisons resembled immense cattlesheds. They were very long one-story buildings set down in some isolated place far from civilization, two or three hundred miles from any cities or railroads. The cells were arranged against the long prison wall and the corridor between the two rows of cells was the common meetingplace. Quite often there was little formal discipline. The prisoners took their meals in their cells which they shared with three or four others. They were locked into their cells at night. But they were generally allowed to walk whenever they wanted in the prison courtyard and they could talk and study. In summer they were allowed to wander in the woods under guard or on parole. They could receive newspapers and could send as many letters and telegrams as they pleased. The prisoners' families lived in villages which grew up around the prisons, and the men were occasionally allowed to spend the night with their wives, while children and wives could enter the prison at will. Political prisoners sentenced to hard labor rarely performed hard labor; nor—after 1900—were they shackled. The young revolutionary Maria Spiridonova tells how she arrived at Arkatui prison and thought she was in "a guesthouse under republican management." The prison governor spoke to her kindly, and she was invited to attend a welcoming party in the prison courtyard: there were speeches at a long table set with flowers and loaded with food. Under the liberal regime of Prince Svyatopolk-Mirsky prison life in Siberia became a holiday. But Sazonov lay in the Schlüsselburg Fortress, and hardly hoped to be sent to Siberia.

The assassination of Plehve heralded a vast change in the climate of Russia. Two months after Sazonov was sentenced to life imprisonment, on January 9, 1905 (old style), "Red Sunday," a solemn procession of workingmen with their wives and children marched in procession through St. Petersburg, singing hymns and bearing ikons. Led by the priest Gapon, they made their way to the great square facing the Winter Palace, intending to lay a petition at the feet of the Tsar. At the approaches of the Winter Palace they were met by armed police and Cossacks who took fright and fired into the procession and then proceeded to execute a formal massacre. This was only the beginning. There followed a series of disasters so violent that by the end of the year Russia was within an ace of being a republic dominated by soviets. In February there were widespread strikes in the universities and high schools, and the peasants were coming out in open rebellion. Kuropatkin's army was defeated at Mukden, and in May Rozhdestvensky's Russian fleet was destroyed at Tsushima. In June came the mutiny of the cruiser *Potemkin*. In August the peace treaty with Japan was signed at Portsmouth. By October the whole country was caught in a general strike, and the first soviet, the St. Petersburg Council of Workers' Deputies, had already emerged with Trotsky as its presiding genius. On October 17 Count Witte issued a manifesto promising far-reaching reforms. It was almost too late. The sailors revolted at Kronstadt;

the Soviets defied the government; for ten days the streets of Moscow were littered with barricades. But the Manifesto of October broke the cutting edge of the revolt and by the new year the fire had burned itself out. A scorched and shuddering Russia faced a burning future.

Through all that year Sazonov remained in the Schlüsselburg Fortress. His wounds healed, he was treated well and recovered some of his old jauntiness, but he had been close to death and the thought of death was never far from his mind. Guilt still plagued him. In the letters to the Terrorist Brigade which he smuggled out, doubt and grief and exaltation can be seen struggling together. Toward the end of the year he wrote:

> Dear comrades! A year and a half has passed since I was removed from your ranks, but though physically separated from you, I have not for a moment ceased to live with you in my thoughts. While the thunder of the revolutionary storm has swept across the country, I have listened for the authentic voice of the Terrorist Brigade, and have not failed to hear it above the great chorus of revolutionary voices. The terrorists know the proper answer to life. With what exaltation have I greeted your victories, and with what sorrow have I grieved over your failures; and yet all these must be expected by the nature of our work, which is truly great and living. With immense humility, with love and adoration I bow before the graves of the fallen.
>
> The end is not yet. I believe the terrorists have still great things to accomplish on the historical scene. Remembering the tasks which still remain for us, and the sacrifices which are still demanded of us, it pleases me to remember, dear comrades, how happy I am when I recall the trust you placed in me on July 15. It would have been a thousand times worse than death if I had betrayed your love . . .
>
> I feel the need to repeat again and again that there must be no misunderstandings between me and those who may one day be called upon to sacrifice themselves. It is absolutely necessary for my happiness to feel identified with you on all matters pertaining to the life and the program of our party.
>
> To those doomed to die I send a special greeting, and it is my prayer that they will go out and honor the banners of our party in firmness and in good health. I greet you, dear comrades, with the knowledge that your courage will be crowned with success. And let us soon arrive at the time when it will no longer be necessary to employ terrorism. Let us pray that the time will come soon when we can foster our socialist ideals under conditions more commensurate with our human strength.

In the early spring of 1906 Sazonov learned that he was to be sent to Siberia. His mood changed. The letters of this period are no longer concerned with death and thoughts of betrayal. In March he was moved secretly to Moscow and lodged in the Butyrky prison, the clearinghouse through which political prisoners passed on the first stage of their exile to Siberia, Turkistan, or the Arctic. He was placed in the Pugachev Tower, reserved for the most important prisoners and there, to his intense delight, he found Gershuni, another member of the Terrorist Brigade. On the Trans-Siberian Railroad they made the journey together.

Arkatui lay then, as it does now, at the end of the road, ten miles from the Mongolian border and some two hundred miles from Serensk, the nearest railhead. The village lay in a barren landscape, bald hills overlooking marshy earth and the endless bare steppes where everything made by man looked unbelievably small against the vastness of sky and earth. There were two rows of ragged wooden huts clinging to the side of a hill —this was the village. Beyond the hill, in an immense grove of beeches and birches, lay the white-walled prison with its red church. Flowers grew everywhere. There were flowers at the foot of the birches, and in the courtyards. The tall wooden gateway was smothered with flowers. "I did not believe I had come to a prison," wrote Spiridonova, who reached Arkatui a month after Sazonov. "To me it was like something seen in a dream, and I gazed upon it with wide uncomprehending eyes." There were children in gay clothes, dancing and singing. There were welcoming committees—the words "We welcome you, dear comrades" were painted in bright red letters across the prison gate, but you could hardly see the words for the flowers. Banners and ropes of flowers were strung between the trees. There was almost no sign of any prison guard. And here, for some reason no one understood, a scented wind came over the steppes.

At the beginning Arkatui was as near paradise as any prison could be. Gershuni and Sazonov were its most distinguished inmates, and they rapidly took charge. Gershuni, with his bright blue eyes and trim beard, organized classes in history and law. Prosh Prozhian, an Armenian revolutionary who later became a member of the first soviet only to fight a relentless battle with the Bolsheviks until his early death in 1919, taught science. Sazonov taught medicine, literature, and law; he also taught in the elementary classes given to young workmen. Gershuni's lectures were the most avidly attended. The warders and prison officers listened and took notes, discreetly standing in the corner. There is no evidence that they ever showed their notes to higher authority; they had come to learn, not to spy. There were choir practices held in the prison courtyard and round-table discussions, and anyone who wanted to deliver a lecture had only to scribble a note and pin it on a notice board. Arkatui resembled a junior university even to its code of manners and its strict morality: no drinking, cardplaying, fighting, or sexual irregularities were allowed Prisoners sentenced to a lifetime of hard labor could be heard bitterly complaining that their bodies were wasting away because they were never allowed to perform any physical labor. In winter it was bitterly cold; in summer the heat came in waves against the wooden walls of the prison cantonment; spring and fall were idyllic.

For a year and a half Sazonov enjoyed a calm carefree existence. There was an atmosphere of intellectual excitement, of intense and puritanical striving after the perfect life. Gershuni, with his immense learning, his determination to sacrifice himself for a cause, his deadly logic, and his air of casual superiority over his guards, was a pillar of strength. Born to riches, Gershuni entered the revolutionary struggle from above; and like Lenin, who belonged to a family of the minor aristocracy, he possessed a relentless will and the intellectual mastery which enabled him to exert his will to the uttermost. He had organized the assassinations of Sipyagin and Bogdanovich, Plehve's two predecessors in the Ministry of the Interior. He was one of the original founders of the Social Revolutionary party, and had been sentenced to death. He was determined to escape from the prison. Two early attempts failed because the rendezvous in the forests north of Arkatui was somehow mistimed. There was no great difficulty in escaping from Arkatui provided a rendezvous was carefully arranged. All that was necessary was to slip past the guards and then vanish in the birch forest and make contact with friends who had ridden secretly from Serensk or Chita. Once Gershuni escaped for several hours, but failed to find his friends. At another time, when the prisoners were temporarily forbidden outside the walls, a tunnel was dug. Unfortunately a guard pacing outside the walls tripped over the soft earth where the tunnel was coming to the surface; the secret was out; and the beautiful tunnel with its floorboards and birchwood supports and wooden panels along the wall had to be abandoned.

Finally the prisoners decided that Gershuni should hide in the cabbage cellar under the prison governor's house. From the cellar there was the usual corridorlike tunnel leading to open ground outside the walls. Guards kept watch on the cellar. Gershuni was placed in a cabbage cask liberally sprinkled with brine, and left there toward nightfall. He wore a metal helmet to protect him from a bayonet thrust by one of the guards who were on the lookout for just such adventures, and he breathed through two rubber tubes which led to two holes cut in the bottom of the cask. The cellar was ice-cold, and Gershuni suffered from cramps. The space between the cabbages was poisoned with carbonic acid gas from the brine. It was a small cask, and he was doubled up like a snake, and in considerable pain, because it was necessary to avert suspicion by tossing the cask roughly into the cellar. Over his head a sheet of leather had been fastened, and he had to cut through the leather with a knife to free himself. He was almost unconscious when he emerged, his face and clothes torn by the nails inside the cask. He had a revolver, a small bottle of ether, and a knife—he only lacked a bomb to have the four essential pieces of a terrorist's equipment. When he climbed out of the cellar at last it was nine o'clock on a bright October morning with thick snow on the ground. By chance one of the prison officers' children came running past him, chasing a dog. Gershuni froze. The child ran past, but the dog kept sniffing the brine and started barking; he thought the game was up, but soon the dog went wandering away. He had to pass close to the small wooden houses where the prison officials lived. He pretended to be making snowballs and then ran across the road which led to the birch forest. No one saw him. Then there was the long journey through the silent forest, along the banks of a river, into deep valleys, and over the bald mountains toward the place where friends with a small cart were waiting for him. A storm came up. Blue-black clouds raced low over the earth, and the wind was so cold that Gershuni nearly abandoned hope of reaching his rendezvous. Even when he found his friends, Gershuni had little hope of completing the journey. For hours they were lost in the storm. He was running a temperature. The wolves howled. He was sure the prison officials were already pursuing him, and they must by now have given warning by telegraph to the neighboring towns. There would be roadblocks and police investigations at the hotels. But some of the telegraph wires had fallen in the storm and they passed through three towns unharmed. Within twenty-four hours he had reached his friends' house. He was given some beggar's rags to wear and put on a coach bound for the Far East. Once a gendarme struck him for pushing his way onto the coach, contaminating the fine gentlemen there with his beggar's rags, and Gershuni commented afterward: "No one will ever know the pleasure I derived from that hard blow." Five days later he was on his way to Japan, and from there he reached the safety of Switzerland.

Gershuni's escape on October 13, 1906, heralded a change of policy toward the prisoners, and Sazonov, who had been Gershuni's intimate friend, received the full force of the rigors of the new administration. The prison governor at Arkatui was dismissed. In his place there came a more hardened governor called Subkovsky. New orders came to the prison. All prisoners must henceforth be chained, they must sleep on straw and not on bed linen, their money must be taken away, and for the least infraction of discipline the most rigorous punishment must be meted out. The prison governor had orders to shoot at the first sign of disturbance, and he was warned that his resignation would be demanded unless the terms of the new orders were carried out. He was ordered to transfer the women at Arkatui immediately to another prison at Malzev, forty miles away. It had been a bad winter and now a blizzard was raging. Many of the women were ill. They had no heavy clothes to protect them. Spiridonova was ill, suffering from tuberculosis, in no state to make a winter journey. The women prisoners decided to defy the authorities by barricading themselves in their cells. Subkovsky was terrified by the women's display of ruthless determination, and telegraphed to the governor of the local prison system: "Cannot obey order because of lack of clothing. Please name my successor." He invited a medical commission to examine the prisoners. Spiridonova and some others were pronounced unfit to travel. Subkovsky might have prevailed against his superior if another prison governor had not appeared on the scene. This was the infamous Borodulin, governor of the Algashi prison, which lay some thirty miles to the west. A heavy-set man with a brutal humor he invaded the women's section of Arkatui at the head of a column of soldiers and ordered them to leave immediately. If they were cold, they could wear blankets. Spiridonova was all for obeying the order. The alternative was bloodshed and rape. She succeeded in arranging a meeting between Borodulin and Sazonov, who was too stunned to say anything except that he entirely disagreed with her acquiescence to the new orders. The prison was seething with revolt. Sazonov had merely to give the order and at the cost of perhaps a hundred lives the soldiers might be overwhelmed. In the end Spiridonova's insistence won him over. "As the sledge drove us away from Arkatui," she wrote, "I could not forget Sazonov standing at the door of his cell, tall and thin and his shoulders bowed down a little. His face was not pale but gray, and his features were strangely fallen and his eyes were closed."

A few days later Sazonov wrote to his mother:

> The worst is happening. Borodulin has taken over; the prison is full of his armed soldiers. We heard Borodulin saying: "Be utterly merciless. Shoot at the first sign of protest, and be careful not to hit the guards." In the presence of one of our representatives he kept toying with his revolver. He said: "I am an expert at cleaning up prisons. I know, of course, that I may be killed. I'm not afraid of death as long as I can first walk over your dead bodies."

It was believed that a closer watch could be kept on the prisoners if they were at Algashi. So Sazonov and fourteen others, regarded as the most dangerous elements in Arkatui, were sent off to Algashi, Borodulin's private preserve. They were put into prison uniform, their heads were shaved, and they were forced to take off their caps and stand at attention whenever they were spoken to. Borodulin was out to break their spirits. He threatened mass floggings, endless tortures. Some of the prisoners refused to have their heads shaved. At the time Borodulin said nothing, but at midnight they were summoned into a large bare room, soldiers with bayonets standing guard against the wall. Afraid the prisoners would fall upon him, Borodulin concealed himself behind the soldiers, and while the prisoners were half-blinded by glaring lights, he shouted: "Remove their caps, strip them naked, then shave their heads by force." Prisoners who refused to obey had their clothes torn from them and were clubbed over the head, while Borodulin kept shouting: "You're not at Arkatui any longer! Before we have finished with you even your bones will have been lost sight of."

From the very beginning there had been a demon of rebellion in Sazonov, but when he assassinated Plehve he was pitting himself against the powerful symbol of autocracy. In his Siberian prison he could only pit himself against mindless brutality. There was no glory to be won from Borodulin, who attempted to reduce everyone to his own mindless level. There had been brutality in the Siberian prisons before, but mostly it had been the aroused brutality of frightened guards. With Borodulin the inhuman, mechanical monster of punishment appeared for the first time. He was the ancestor of the prison officials of our own day in Nazi Germany and Soviet Russia, determined to stamp out the recognizable features of the prisoners, impatient of all common humanity, in love with death. Sazonov saw the menace and determined to pit his whole strength against it.

There was little he could do. He could only make his protest and then die under the blows of the executioners. He seems to have guessed that prisons were to become even more anonymous and infinitely more destructive of human honor. He was enraged because the prisoners were addressed in the second person singular. Borodulin treated everyone like vermin, even his own soldiers. Prison, Sazonov thought, had become an intolerable offense against human dignity, and it was time this offense was punished.

On the first night at Algashi, March 4, 1907, Sazonov urged the prisoners to embark on a campaign of nonviolent resistance. They would refuse to obey commands, refuse to remove their caps when addressed by Borodulin, and when addressed in the second person singular they would refuse to listen.

That night the prisoners were in a mood of somber defiance. Some burst out singing. For some reason these melancholy defiant songs nearly unnerved Sazonov, who buried his head in a mattress and prayed for the singing to end. They were all locked up in a large common cell. They expected Borodulin to enter, order them to their feet, and flog them when they refused. They would go on refusing, and soon some would have been flogged or clubbed to death. They were desperately determined upon rebellion. All night they took turns standing on guard. Sazonov could not sleep, and, after debate with himself, decided to commit suicide in the hope that his voluntary death, which would be immediately known in Moscow, would save the others. He had a phial of morphine sewn in his clothes. He swallowed it. He awoke some hours later with a feeling of nausea, a bad headache, and that was all, save the knowledge that he had now lost the last of his possessions.

All day they waited, but Borodulin made no appearance. On the second day a young terrorist called Rybnikov encountered Borodulin in the corridor. Ordered to remove his cap, he refused. Borodulin ordered him to be led to a dark cell. A few moments later pandemonium broke loose. The prisoners shouted and threatened to batter down the door unless Borodulin appeared with Rybnikov, and when Borodulin arrived with an escort but without Rybnikov and ordered the prisoners to stand at attention, they refused sullenly. In a rage Borodulin ordered two prisoners selected at random to be removed to the dark cell. "Club them over the head if they disobey!" he shouted. Then began the slow deadly game of passive resistance, with the prisoners linking their hands and forming a human chain, while the soldiers struck them over the head with rifle butts. Soon three prisoners were wounded: one with a broken skull, another with a smashed face, and the third clubbed in the chest. The soldiers surrounded one prisoner and led him off to the dark cells, and Borodulin, still hiding behind his soldiers, announced that the prisoners would be punished by being deprived of hot meals, bed covers, and exercise. As a further punishment, the pots filled with excreta would remain in the cell throughout the day.

Sazonov wrote in a letter:

> Evidently he can do anything he likes with us: there is no limit to his tyranny. Borodulin is attempting to curry favor with the criminals, hoping to set them against the politicals, but their sympathy is with us. The only way out is to force this butcher to kill us. Yet a prison revolt would cost too much blood. As for ourselves, we dare not hope for a happy outcome, but we are at peace with ourselves—the peace with which condemned men await their deaths. But to die in an active war is not the same thing as falling beneath the tyranny of Borodulin.

That Sazonov was able to write a letter in which he recounted the whole incident at length and smuggle it out of prison with the intention that it should be read in the Duma shows that the administration and atmosphere of prisons in Russia have since changed vastly. No such thing would now be possible. What he described was a small incident, which has since been endlessly repeated. The public conscience was still tender. Uspensky, a Social Revolutionary member of the Duma, read portions of Sazonov's letter to the tribune. There was a storm of protest; the government was compelled to make a special investigation about the three obscure political prisoners who had been clubbed with rifle butts, and a month later the Duma received the results of the investigation in an atmosphere of derision. The government maintained that the prisoners had behaved so contemptuously toward the prison governor that he had been compelled to use a minimum of force. All over Russia Borodulin's name was now ironically identified with "those who use a minimum of force." On May 28 the military governor of the Nerchinsk Katorga, who had been responsible for the original orders, was shot at Chita by a young terrorist.

Borodulin's days were now numbered. He was not the worst of prison governors. Taunted by the revolutionaries, he had behaved stupidly and brutally, but his brutalities compared with those of our own day were of small consequence. There is no record that anyone was killed during his administration. But the revolutionaries had recognized the machine-like inhumanity of the man, all the possibilities of prison terror and murder latent within him, and they were determined that the government should take warning. In half the provinces of Russia young students were busily plotting ways to assassinate him.

It was a deadly game, played for high stakes. In the end the Borodulins won, but in 1907 the revolutionaries still believed that victory was in their grasp. They had two weapons, assassination and civil disobedience, and it never seems to have occurred to them that these weapons were incompatible.

One day Borodulin invited Sazonov to the governor's office. Sazonov kept his cap on his head, and Borodulin was careful to address him in the second person plural. According to Sazonov, who wrote down the conversation immediately afterward, they talked roughly as follows:

BORODULIN: It occurs to me that I shall soon have to ask the political prisoners to perform repair work in the prison. I accept the fact that they will probably resist my orders. Then I will have to punish them, and that probably means force.

SAZONOV: You must understand one thing—political prisoners have never nourished the false hope that their lives are safe.

BORODULIN: I insist that their lives are in no danger. You completely misunderstand me. If we go on living together, you will learn I am not a beast. Why are you so bitter against me? I merely carry out orders.

SAZONOV: You give orders.

BORODULIN: No, I carry them out. I obey my superiors, and I take the consequences. I do what has to be done, so that the prison can achieve its purpose.

SAZONOV: Then there is nothing more for you to say—

BORODULIN: Yes, there is one thing. I know quite well that the revolutionaries are now determined to kill me. I am not afraid. But before I die, I would like to know what my crime is.

SAZONOV: All Russia knows your crime, and so do you.

BORODULIN: Very well, then. Why don't you write to the revolutionary authorities and ask them to kill me soon? It's distressing to have to wait. Much better to get it over with. Write the letter, and I give you my word of honor that it will go through.

SAZONOV: All you are saying is that you consider you deserve to die. My letter will change nothing. You know you are guilty. You chose to commit a crime, and the consequences follow. As to whether you will be killed, this is a matter for the people outside and does not concern the prisoners.

BORODULIN (*with a faint smile*): Then I understand. I suppose it is time
I ordered a coffin and dug a grave behind the hill.

There was no answer from Sazonov, who left the governor's office
shortly afterward. A few days later Borodulin journeyed to Irkutsk,
where an attempt was made on his life. Barely escaping, he asked for a
month's leave of absence, presumably to put his affairs in order, and
traveled to Pskov in western Russia. The terrorists were hot on his heels.
His movements were carefully watched, and it was decided to assassinate
him on the last day of his holiday. He was leaving the house of the local
prison governor when he observed two strangers making their way to his
carriage. One leaped up and caught the horses' reins, bringing the carriage to a stop. The coachman shouted: "What's the matter, eh? Let go,
you little fool!" Then the coachman heard a single shot. It was fired by
another terrorist who had jumped onto the carriage step, aiming at
Borodulin's heart from a distance of twelve inches. The prison governor
died instantly. Only one of the terrorists was caught. He was tried summarily, sentenced to death and hanged the next day.

By using terror the terrorists had hoped to alleviate the miseries of
Russia. Singularly successful when they murdered Plehve, they were less
successful at all other times. The assassination of Borodulin resulted in
the appointment of a still harsher governor. Ismailov, the new governor,
was the worst kind of Cossack officer. He enjoyed brutality, whereas
Borodulin had merely placed himself at the service of brutality. It was
rare for a prison governor to beat a prisoner with his own fists, but when
a prisoner refused to remove his cap in the governor's presence, Ismailov
struck him repeatedly. It was July 1907. The reaction was in full swing.
When the politicals protested, Ismailov ordered them all to be flogged.
He ordered that he should be addressed as "Your Excellency." When they
refused they were carried to the dark cells. He regarded attendance at
church services as imperative. Those who refused were forced into the
chapels at the end of a bayonet. The old penalties were revived: the
prisoners must sleep without bedding, they could receive no visitors from
outside, and no food could be sent to them from the neighboring villages.
Ismailov introduced a refinement of torture: a prisoner locked in a dark
cell could see through the narrow eye slit a whip hanging in a brightly lit
corridor.

"There is absolutely nothing we can do against him," Sazonov wrote in
a mood of profound dejection. "He is like some huge and elemental force
of nature. One must submit to him, or die."

More and more Sazonov found himself thinking of death. There came
to him at times a desperate need to expiate his own crime. He had failed
to kill himself with morphine; then he must kill himself in some other

way and by so doing attract the attention of the world to the plight of the prisoners. On July 25, largely on Sazonov's pleading, the prisoners decided to go on a hunger strike. It was a hopeless gesture. No one believed it would succeed in changing Ismailov's attitude. Sazonov sent a message to Ismailov: "You have beaten us with rifle butts and flicked your whips over our heads. Now we have nothing to hope for except death. We have resolved to starve until conditions are improved or death frees us from our torturers."

The news of the hunger strike reached Moscow five days later. There were newspaper editorials. Was Russia, a civilized country, to be known throughout the world as a place of barbarism? In England there was uproar; and Cunninghame Graham, speaking in Trafalgar Square, pointed to the imprisonment of Spiridonova and Sazonov, and the beatings they had received, as symptoms of the disease of autocracy. It was the time when governments were still tenderhearted. On the seventh day of the hunger strike Sazonov, who had fallen into a waking stupor, was awakened by a heavy knock on the door. One of the guards entered the cell. He said: "His Excellency the prison governor has been relieved from his post." It was not quite true. Ismailov had been given extended leave of absence, and returned to his post at Algashi some months later. But the government had bowed before the fury of the newspaper editorials, at least temporarily, and from Moscow there came orders to send Sazonov to the prison at Gorny Serentui, where the regime was less harsh and where it was hoped the rebellious prisoner would be forgotten.

The government might have known better. Sazonov had found in the prisons the Archimedean point where a lever could be inserted, and he continued to throw all his weight upon the lever to the end.

THE PROTEST

I N A MOOD of prophecy Sazonov wrote to his father: "I have a feeling I shall never leave this prison alive. Everywhere about me there is only death. The truth is I am not a good prisoner and I doubt if I shall ever accustom myself to this slow maniacal existence in which every effort is made to destroy the personality of the prisoner."

Sazonov wrote often in this strain, but he also wrote many letters in which he described the occasional delights of prison life. On sunny days fresh air and sunlight streamed through the four large windows, through which he could see the bare blue hills in the distance. There were interminable discussions with prisoners who lived together in a large cell—Sazonov said it was ten paces wide, thirteen paces long and only six feet high, but he was a tall man with a large stride and other prisoners have described it as being the largest cell in the place, and the most comfortable. Then there were the new arrivals, and he found most of them delightful—"They are so good, my dear father, that I am altogether lost in brotherly affection for them"—though he complained that the cell was filled to overflowing. The walls were whitewashed, very clean. There was a table set across the whole length of the room where the prisoners studied. Along the walls were benches heaped with bedding. On sunny days the prisoners fought for places near the windows, but they did this with good humor. Though they were half-famished and lived on broth, tea, black bread, and three or four lumps of sugar a day, they were remarkably full of animal spirits and as noisy as schoolboys, so that Sazonov, whose deafness had given place to an acute sense of hearing, complained that "they keep howling all day long, so that it is completely impossible for me to work during the day, and as you know my best times for working are late at night and early in the morning, but these are precisely the times when they are most noisy." But he liked these people even though he was always shouting to them to keep quiet, and he wrote to his mother:

> It is impossible for me to tell you how much I admire them. In spite of walls and imprisonment, in spite of the terrible diet and the knowledge that every one of us has friends and relatives in the outside world pining for him, there is so much resilience of spirit, so much human strength, that whenever you contemplate it, it strengthens your hopes for the future. Your own sufferings disappear when you realize how much they are suffering with you. If you only knew how splendid it is to feel part of this living whole; to be completely without possessions, having no gold and no bread entirely your own. Best of all, we have lost the sense of our own separateness and all our joys and sorrows are held in common. If you would really understand and feel this, then you would know the secret which keeps us so fresh and green.

Gorny Serentui was the headquarters for the whole complex of prisons on the Mongolian border, and was something of a show place. The prison governor lived there in a large house, outside the white walls of the prison. Here, too, was an excellently equipped prison hospital. Intended for 300 prisoners it contained three times as many, but for the prisoners in their cramped quarters there were advantages in numbers. The governor was lenient. From August 1907 to July 1909 there was only one incident which alarmed Sazonov, and for this he could hardly blame the prison governor, who was a model of fairness.

In December 1907 Spiridonova fell ill at Malzev. She had been ill ever since her arrest, but the illness took a turn for the worse. Sazonov was attached to her. He had admired her when they were fellow prisoners at Arkatui, and by smuggling letters they had kept up a continual correspondence. At Malzev there were almost no hospital facilities. A young medical assistant, Sarra Dantzig, herself a prisoner and in the last stages of tuberculosis, was the only person allowed to treat the prisoners. The governor was in no mood to deal leniently with his prisoners and refused to allow Spiridonova to be transferred to Gorny Serentui. He wanted her under his own eyes. Once he suggested that he would willingly allow Spiridonova to be transferred on condition that two sick prisoners now in the hospital were brought back to Malzev. One of these prisoners was the Social Revolutionary Dora Kaplan who later made a determined attempt to kill Lenin. Spiridonova refused. She had no desire for special treatment, and seemed resigned to her approaching death. She had not counted on Sazonov.

As soon as he heard that Spiridonova was so ill that she was thought to be dying, he demanded an interview with the prison governor at Gorny Serentui. The governor was sympathetic and immediately offered to have Spiridonova transported to the hospital, provided that the officials at Malzev agreed. The officials at Malzev refused. Prosh Prozhian and Sazonov debated the matter and decided upon a hunger strike. Once more they hoped to reach the headlines of the Moscow newspapers. At the threat of a hunger strike the governor at Gorny Serentui used his wide powers to bring Spiridonova to the hospital, only to learn that the governor of Malzev had appealed directly to the provincial government headquarters at Chita. A telegram was received from Chita demanding the immediate return of Spiridonova to Malzev. Reluctantly the governor of Gory Serentui was compelled to send her back.

Sazonov was now convinced that the authorities at Malzev were determined to kill Spiridonova. He wrote to his father: "She is going out like a candle, and every day she is approaching closer to death. They want her to die, and they are deliberately provoking her death. As for us, what can we do? Must we be indifferent spectators of her murder? Our hands may be tied, and we are powerless to rescue her, but at least we can die with her!"

Before leaving Gorny Serentui, Spiridonova was allowed a last interview with Prosh Prozhian and Sazonov. The interview was stormy. Sazonov kept talking about "those murderers at Malzev," and Prosh Prozhian with his mastery of argument almost convinced her that she would be a renegade to the revolution if she moved an inch from where she was standing. She was suffering from hemorrhages and fever, but the excitement was worse. She wanted to be left alone, and hardly cared whether she was at Malzev or at Gorny Serentui.

"You are making it a matter of tragic importance," Spiridonova said, "but it is really not very important. I want to rest, and I don't care where I rest. I'm too ill to become a bone of contention. Please leave me alone."

Sazonov and Prosh Prozhian exchanged glances. Sazonov was now for silence, but Prozhian resumed his dialectical arguments, insisting that the revolution needed her presence at the hospital and it was above all necessary to fight against the officials at Malzev.

"We absolutely insist that you see the matter in its revolutionary aspect," he said, and he would have gone on to invent more arguments if Spiridonova had not conveniently fainted.

She was allowed to rest. By nightfall she seemed better and on the next day returned to Malzev. When the prisoners discussed a new hunger strike, Spiridonova wrote that they were behaving foolishly and she urged them to safeguard their health.

In July 1909, orders reached Gorny Serentui from Moscow demanding that the prisoners should no longer be treated in the old lenient way. Prisoners must be warned that if they approached the windows in the evening, they would be shot by the guards stationed outside. They must no longer smoke cigarettes or receive food from outside. The number of books they were allowed to receive must be severely curtailed. Punishments must be severe. Chemodanov, the prison governor, was warned that he had behaved too leniently and was now under the watchful eye of inspectors sent by the government. The governor obeyed the new orders reluctantly for nearly a year and a half. He respected and liked the prisoners, and had a particular fondness for Sazonov. He was a humane man and had nothing but contempt for guards who humiliated the prisoners. "I am doing my best to hold on to my post," he told Sazonov, "for the man who replaces me will be an infinitely worse taskmaster." Sazonov half guessed the terror would begin the moment Chemodanov was replaced.

Early in November 1910 it was announced that a new governor, General Vissotsky, was on his way. Of all the prison governors Sazonov had known by reputation, Vissotsky was the worst. As governor of the prison in Perm, he had an unenviable reputation for ordering prisoners to be beaten at the slightest provocation.

A few days before Vissotsky arrived Chemodanov went to see Sazonov in his cell. Usually Sazonov would rise to greet the governor with a quick smile. This time there was no smile. Sazonov was pacing the cell, his brow furrowed, his eyes glazed with suffering.

"You're foolish to give way to anxieties," the governor said quietly.

Sazonov halted. He turned on the governor sharply.

"Why foolish? Don't you know that the hangman of Perm is on his way?"

"Why do you say that? It's only a rumor—"

"Rumor! Do you think we don't know these people? When he comes here, he will flog us and murder us—there will be no end to his floggings and murders."

"But not for you, Sazonov. After all you have only three more months' imprisonment since your sentence has been reduced. I have given you a separate cell because you have been a model prisoner, and I shall point out your good behavior to my successor. The three months will pass quickly."

Sazonov smiled and shook his head.

"No, they will be very long," he answered. "I don't believe they will ever let me leave here. I know, as well as you do, that there's some connection between Vissotsky's arrival and the fact that I am shortly to be released. I've seen the newspapers. They talk about the unpardonable laxity of our treatment here. Well, there will soon be an end to 'unpardonable laxity.'"

On November 21 Vissotsky arrived with an escort of soldiers and with his own trained warders.

Sazonov had discussed the possibility of a reign of terror in the prison ever since the previous July. In interminable talks with the prisoners he had outlined a course of action to combat the terror. If the new governor refused to treat the prisoners as human beings, he must be killed, and if it was impossible to kill him, then the only alternative for Sazonov was suicide. A message was sent to Spiridonova, asking for her opinion. She argued that it was better to knuckle under temporarily. The important thing was that the lives of the revolutionaries should be preserved for the sake of the coming revolution. Nothing was so important as to preserve a nucleus of revolutionaries ready to take over when the reaction had exhausted itself in fruitless punishments and killings. Sazonov replied: "They have an enormous appetite for these horrors and they will go on indefinitely unless we stop them in their tracks. More decisive measures are needed." Spiridonova disagreed, and when Sazonov wrote about "the insults they offer us," she replied: "Remember, they cannot insult us." These letters were exchanged during the later part of 1909, when it was rumored that Chemodanov was about to be removed. Now in November 1910 they were confronted at last with the enemy they had long feared.

For the first few days Vissotsky kept out of sight. He was in conference with Chemodanov, arranging the last details for taking over the prison. Three days after his arrival the prisoners learned from the chief warder that Vissotsky had dispatched two of his lieutenants for two cartloads of whips. Chemodanov sent messages secretly to the prisoners warning them of what was in store, begging them to behave toward the new governor with exaggerated respect, and he confirmed the story that the two cart-loads of whips were on their way. Henceforth all prisoners must wear the drab prison uniform supplied by the government and have their heads shaved. These were two of the ordinances which Chemodanov had re-fused to enforce. An atmosphere of hysteria and terror settled over the prison.

By this time Sazonov had already decided that if a single brutal punish-ment was inflicted on a prisoner, he would take his own life.

On November 23, he wrote three letters: to his parents, to his brother Zot, and to his fiancée Maria Alexandrovna Prokofieva. In his letters he explained that he could see no other way out. Henceforth the prison was to be given over to "a wild beast, who has no respect for the human per-son." From Vissotsky nothing could be expected except death, humilia-tion, and torture. It was true that he could probably live out the remaining three months of his imprisonment by toadying to the new governor, but he had decided against this course for reasons which should be perfectly clear. He wrote:

> I believe that my suicide, deliberately committed, will arouse the attention of the public to the horrors of the Siberian prisons, and from the better members of society there will come a shout of protest. My comrades in prison will then know that voices are being raised against a government that makes torture and death common occurrences in prison life.

In the same letters Sazonov wrote of the kindnesses he had received from Chemodanov, and he insisted that he was not acting so much against Vissotsky as against a whole system. Above all, he hoped to justify his life by his death.

These letters were the end product of a long process of self-examination. Ever since the attack on Plehve, Sazonov had been afflicted by a towering sense of guilt. He wanted desperately to expiate his guilt, which sometimes embraced the guilt of others, so that when he met the young revolutionary Karpovich, who had assassinated the former Minister of Education, Bogo-lepov—the least defensible of all the assassinations committed by the ter-rorists—Sazonov wrote: "The thought frightens me that in some way I too am morally guilty of murdering Bogolepov." At another time he wrote of himself as "one who has committed the greatest of all crimes," and went on desperately to try to fathom why he, who had dreamed of striving peacefully for the sake of suffering humanity, should have the mark of Cain on his brow. "We took up the sword," he wrote in extenuation of his conduct, "because the enemy compelled us, and only after terrible strug-gles and agonies and under the pressure of tragic necessity." Now the pressure of tragic necessity was driving deeper, and against Spiridonova's advice he resigned himself to suicide.

On the night of November 25 the prison was formally handed over to Vissotsky by Chemodanov.

In a low room reached by an iron staircase the prisoners were introduced to the new governor. Behind a table heaped with documents and complete lists of the prisoners and their prison records sat Chemodanov and Vissotsky. Chemodanov was nervous, flicking over the pages of the documents in front of him. Vissotsky, small, wiry, with a face that was strangely gray and with a small waxed mustache, gazed hungrily at the prisoners as they were brought before the table. A paraffin lamp hung over the table and a prison clerk stood a little to one side. A prisoner shuffled to the table.

"The prisoner Akimov," shouted the clerk.

"Well, what are you sentenced for?" Vissotsky said, glaring. He had used the familiar second person singular.

There was no answer from Akimov.

"Why don't you speak?" Vissotsky said, jumping up, his small eyes gleaming with light from the paraffin lamp.

"I don't choose to speak when I am addressed in that way," Akimov answered, and then he felt a blow over his heart.

"Take him away!" Vissotsky said. "Throw him in the dark cells!"

Then he turned toward Chemodanov and said: "They're all vermin! You have to know how to deal with them."

More prisoners were brought up. Vissotsky talked to all of them in the same way. He roared and thumped the table and made speeches. When a prisoner explained that he was a political, Vissotsky said: "I make no distinction between criminals. Believe me, I shall stop at nothing to make you obey my orders." Halfway through the interrogation Chemodanov could stand it no more, remembered that his coach was waiting, made his abrupt farewells to the new governor and departed. He wrote later that he went away with the absolute certainty that the prison would be a holocaust by the next day. Also, he knew that the prisoners were in possession of a revolver and three steel files sharpened to a razor's edge.

By midnight nine prisoners were in the dark cells, but no one had been flogged.

Sometime during the night Vissotsky visited the special cells where the more important prisoners were guarded. Sazonov was waiting for him, his hands behind his back.

"So you dare to have your hands behind your back when I come to your cell?" Vissotsky barked.

Sazonov placed his hands at his sides.

"I see I am going to have trouble teaching you obedience," Vissotsky went on. "I have heard all about you. Make no mistake, you will soon be screaming for mercy."

"I have survived Borodulin," Sazonov answered, and Vissotsky was perfectly aware of the threat. He marched out.

Two days later a small incident precipitated the holocaust. The long debate was nearly over. The carefully laid plans to murder Vissotsky were abandoned. Vissotsky ordered a criminal to pose as a political in one of the dark cells. The subterfuge was soon recognized, and Mikhailov, a Socialist Revolutionary, objected strongly. Vissotsky had expected such objections and marched up to the cell, flung open the door, flicked his whip and ordered Mikhailov out. Mikhailov refused to step out. Vissotsky grew more threatening. He barked that Mikhailov was to receive twenty strokes for impertinence and for refusing to obey orders. Before the warders could jump on the prisoner, he had taken strychnine, and a moment later, because the strychnine had no immediate effect, he took morphine. Even then he was conscious. He asked for some nitric acid. This was given to him, and at last he fell to the floor. When he reached the hospital there was a gaping hole in his stomach. He died shortly afterward.

All Sazonov's fears were now seen to be well-founded. Vissotsky regarded the politicals as instruments for the exercise of his sadistic desires. Slomyansky, a former soldier, refused to eat the black bread which was thrown to him in his dark cell. Knowledge of the hunger strike was brought to Vissotsky, who ordered Slomyansky to receive thirty strokes. When Slomyansky was stripped and bound to the whipping bench, a doctor was sent for. The doctor declared that Slomyansky was suffering from heart disease and would probably die under the blows.

Vissotsky said: "I'll give him something to cure his heart disease."

Slomyansky was beaten until the blood ran, and he was unconscious when he was taken to the prison hospital.

The doctor who had said Slomyansky should not be beaten was ordered to receive thirty-five strokes "for showing his ignorance of medicine." Manacled, the doctor thrust out at the guard with his chained hands. By a new law any attack on a guard could be punished by summary death. Vissotsky decided to prolong the agony. He ordered that the doctor be given a thrashing with rifle butts and then beaten.

Sazonov had come to the end of his resources. Ahead there stretched unending years of brutality in Siberian prisons. He counseled the others to remain alive; for himself he chose death in a supreme act of protest. He had written once to Spiridonova: "The savages are coming into their own. For ourselves, there is only one task: to stand up to them, to fight every act of human degradation and every dishonor. Unless we do this, the savages may summon from the depths of our unconscious the ancient habits of slaves and kill the revolutionaries in us." Now had come the time to make the only effective protest he knew against the savages. Shortly after three o'clock on the morning of November 28 he took morphine, blew out the lamp and prepared for death. It was exactly three months to the day when he was due to leave prison.

An hour later the night guards heard him coughing and moaning. They rushed in, but he was already dying. The warders discussed whether to awaken Vissotsky and tell him the news. There were long discussions about whether the hospital doctor should be informed. Nothing was done until six o'clock, and it was half an hour before the doctor arrived. By then it was too late, and by seven o'clock Sazonov was dead.*

Told about the suicide Vissotsky remarked: "It's nothing at all to worry about. I don't mind how many of them commit suicide. Suicides by day, suicides by night! Well, there's no point in nursing them. Tell the assistant doctor on duty that neither he nor anyone else is allowed to attend the prisoners at night. He can see them well enough during the day."

Three other prisoners took poison that night, but the prison doctor gave them antidotes and their lives were saved. Petrov, the young doctor who had gone to the help of Slomyansky, attempted to kill himself by pouring paraffin over himself and then setting light to it. He, too, survived.

Except for a letter smuggled to Spiridonova at Malzev, none of the letters written by Sazonov during the last days of his life was ever received. They were confiscated, sent to police headquarters in Moscow and gathered dust until the revolution. But though the prison officials did everything possible to conceal his death, it was known the next day in Moscow. Russia was reeling with the death of Tolstoy, which had occurred mysteriously at Astapovo only a few days before. To the 30,000 students who came out on strike, the two deaths were strangely symbolic. For three years the revolutionary movement had been dying. Now the ghosts of Tolstoy and Sazonov arose to give a new, strange and peculiarly lasting vitality to the movement. The strike lasted three weeks, and the movement did not col-

---

* Whittaker Chambers has described in *Witness* the reasons which brought about his conversion to Communism. He recounts his overwhelming admiration for three revolutionaries: Felix Dzerzhinsky, Eugen Levine, and Sazonov. Of the third he writes:

"The Russian was not a Communist. He was a pre-Communist revolutionist named Kaliayev. (I should have said Sazonov.) He was arrested for a minor part in the assassination of the Tsarist prime minister, von Plehve. He was sent into Siberian exile to one of the worst prison camps, where the political prisoners were flogged. Kaliayev sought some way to protest this outrage to the world. The means were few, but at last he found a way. In protest at the flogging of other men, Kaliayev drenched himself in kerosene, set himself on fire and burned himself to death. That is also what it means to be a Communist. That is also what it means to be a witness."

It is doubtful whether a more muddled and inaccurate account of Sazonov has ever been written.

lapse until 1918. For years afterward it became a legend that the two apostles of passive resistance had died at the same hour and on the same day.

From Ufa, Sazonov's father sent a telegram to Stolypin, the Minister of the Interior:

> I learn with sorrow that my son, Yegor Sazonov, has died in the prison at Gorny Serentui. I most humbly request permission to go to Siberia and bring his body home for Christian burial. The mere permission to bring his body to Ufa, to be buried according to the unchanging rites which have come down from our ancestors, will bring consolation to his grief-stricken parents.

Stolypin's reply was brief:

> Minister of Interior regrets impossibility to comply with your wishes received in letter dated December 5. STOLYPIN.

Vissotsky remained in charge of the prison at Gorny Serentui for some years. But after Sazonov's suicide he received an official reprimand, the power to inflict corporal punishment on political prisoners was removed from him, and most of the political prisoners were sent to outlying prisons. From then until the Bolsheviks came to power, political prisoners were generally treated with remarkable leniency.

During the October Revolution of 1917 the Social Revolutionaries made their bid for power. The surviving members of the party met in St. Petersburg under an immense banner which showed the young Sazonov in the prime of his life. From the rostrum Spiridonova made a speech against the Bolsheviks:

> They talk all the time of terror, but we who have known terror and practiced terror know that the time of terror is over. We have taken power from the old feudal autocracy and the Revolution has been won. Let us talk now of love.
>
> We stand under the banner of Sazonov, who proved in his life that love has its own laws. We honor him as one who struggled for the happiness we all desire. In prison most of us were inhumanly bitter, but Sazonov knew how to create joy in the midst of suffering.

Eight months later the headquarters of the Social Revolutionary party was captured by the Bolsheviks and its members were scattered to the winds.

KALIAYEV

Everything is beautiful. The stars and clouds and flowers and people and—death is beautiful, too.

THE POET

H E HAD A LONG and delicate face, a broad forehead, a firm chin, bright-blue eyes which would smolder and change to a darker blue when he was excited and an almost feminine mouth which curled easily at the corners. He was more Polish than Russian, and to the very end he bore traces of a soft, musical Polish accent. Savinkov called him affectionately "our poet." Sazonov described him as "a precious iridescent stone," and wondered how so slight a person could conceal such power. Shy, incurably quiet, given to long periods of silent meditation, Ivan Kaliayev came to terrorism by way of a luminous faith and a desperate desire to sacrifice himself for the salvation of mankind. He joined the Terrorist Brigade in 1903; two years later he was hanged for the assassination of the Grand Duke Sergey, and no one ever died more gladly.

With Kaliayev we are confronted with the revolutionary in the purest form. Believing in the infinite value of each human life, he was prepared to kill, but only on condition that he sacrificed his own life, his death at once an offering to the revolutionary cause and the sign of an overwhelming love for his fellow men. He found no particular delight in terrorism. He regarded murder as inexcusable and at the same time necessary, and he never escaped from that tragic dichotomy. Nechayev, and Lenin after him, embraced violence with passionate conviction: it was the air they breathed, the atmosphere they carried with them, the stimulus which kept them alive; it was, almost, their food. Kaliayev detested violence. He would go out and kill because he hoped that with one single clean-cut

361

blow he could force the enemy to surrender. He killed scrupulously, plagued by doubts, never entirely convinced of the need to murder but wholly convinced of the need to sacrifice himself. Like Sazonov, whose sense of guilt he shared, he was determined that the war should be waged chivalrously according to the rules he was always having to make up because there were no guidebooks for sensitive murderers. Once, talking to Mikhail Gotz, the most practical and least visionary of the revolutionaries, Kaliayev said: "You understand, when we offer ourselves as a sacrifice, then it is necessary that we should be absolutely pure and chaste. We should not offer up a life we have already grown weary of." For him the terrorists who were prepared to abandon their lives for the sake of others were "knights of the spirit" (*ritsari dukha*), employing a phrase beloved of Kierkegaard, though Kaliayev must have found it among his memories of his Polish ancestors.

In his brief revolutionary career Kaliayev demonstrated so little willfulness and was so transparently dedicated that when he was dead it seemed inconceivable that he had ever existed. Even when he was living people felt he was too unreal, too good, too virtuous altogether to be included among the revolutionaries. He dressed elegantly. He wrote superb poetry. He liked the fine things of life. He had a strange deep rolling laugh which would come on at the most unexpected moments. He had a habit of looking at you with his deep-set penetrating eyes in a way which made you reveal things about yourself you were prepared to tell no one but yourself. He was a Shelley set loose in the tortured world of midnight conspiracies, a Shelley who not only wrote poems against Castlereagh but set out to kill without compunction, violently, quickly, and cleanly, the man he had already murdered in his poetry.

What was his secret? Perhaps we shall never know, but occasionally he hints at it. He belonged to the past. He spoke a language his fellow revolutionaries did not always understand, a language in which the words chivalry, knighthood, purity, were not just counters but possessed depths of meaning so real to him that he could hardly understand why they were meaningless to the other revolutionaries. He complained of the boredom of revolutionary discussions. For him there was only one problem—to kill cleanly. A revolutionary must regard himself as a soldier, but one overwhelmed with a sense of honor. He must have a conscience of a knight-errant, giving all the advantages to the adversary, and he must explore every punctilio of conscience before infringing on the lives of others. It is the matador's code, the delicate swerve of the veronica, the impulse to live close to death only in order to value life more highly. "He is more like a poet than a revolutionary," Sazonov said when he first set eyes on Kaliayev. In fact Kaliayev was more like a knight-errant whose only desire was to serve his princess to the end, and for him the princess comprised all suffering humanity.

When Kaliayev arrived in St. Petersburg in 1903, he was already fully formed. His past tells us little. He was born in Warsaw on June 24, 1877, his father a small landowner and a former officer in the Kiev Regiment, his mother a Polish beauty known for her charities and her love for the poor. His father seems to have been one of those stern, impractical, retired officers who are the commonplaces of Russian novels. From his mother he learned about the Polish uprisings against the Tsar, the blood spilled on the streets of Warsaw.

He was eleven when he was sent to the Apukhtinsky Gymnasium in Warsaw, then celebrated because it produced Polish students fanatically loyal to the Russian crown. In 1896 he left the gymnasium. He had immersed himself in Polish and Russian literature, and already regarded himself as a poet. The next year he went to Moscow, attending lectures in philology and history at the University. By chance he came upon a thin pamphlet written in Polish and printed in London describing socialism. He immediately joined the Polish Socialist party, but apparently without any intention of leading the life of an agitator. He had still no idea how he would earn a living. Abandoning philology and history, he left Moscow and in the fall of 1898 became a law student at the University of St. Petersburg. In the spring of 1899 student disorders broke out, directed against the excesses of the regime. Kaliayev suddenly found himself in the midst of political activity. He made speeches, wrote manifestoes and helped to organize the students. Almost inevitably he was arrested. He spent three months in prison and was then exiled to Ekaterinoslav in southern Russia, where he lived under police surveillance. His interest in a law career had by now completely vanished. He decided to become a teacher of history and philosophy, and one night he slipped out of Ekaterinoslav and made his way to Lvov, where he attended courses at the University, gave lessons (but not enough to stave off hunger), read subversive political magazines and kept up a tremendous correspondence. During a journey to Berlin he was arrested. Several copies of the revolutionary magazine *Iskra*, which had first appeared on December 21, 1900, were found on him. He was summarily arrested and thrown into the Warsaw Citadel, but was released soon afterward, though once more he was sent to live under police surveillance at Ekaterinoslav. In 1903 he went abroad again. By this time he was in close touch with the Terrorist Brigade. It was Savinkov's influence which propelled him into the revolutionary movement, for Savinkov too was born in Warsaw and they had known each other since childhood.

Kaliayev did not look like a revolutionary; nor for that matter did Savinkov, who resembled with his high forehead and sharp, intelligent face, the sharpness occasionally masked by an appearance of polite boredom, a member of the minor aristocracy. Viktor Chernov, who was to become President of the Constituent Assembly which the Bolsheviks dissolved in January 1918, knew them both, and for him Savinkov always resembled a kind of Mephistopheles, while Kaliayev reminded him of "young green leaves still sticky from birth." There was in Savinkov the weariness of the conspirator who sees every incursion into the landscape of danger as an incentive to still closer brushes with death, until death became a commonplace, something he knew so well that he rarely paid it the tribute of fear. For him conspiracy was a kind of intellectual game. He had no deep convictions. He became a terrorist for the joy of watching himself playing, admiring his own expertness, delighting above all in assembling around himself the disciples whose lives he gambled with as he gambled with his own, for the highest stakes. And Kaliayev with his pale feminine face with its delicate lines, the bright eyes which would sometimes lose their fire and smolder with a strange sadness, the slim figure in the clothes that were always a little too tight for him, the boy who resembled nothing so much as a young prince, in love with life and death at their sharpest points, was the perfect foil for Mephistopheles. Chernov said it was the most extraordinary sight to see them together. They seemed in some strange way to belong to one another, and yet when you saw them together you were aware of irreconcilable differences. Nearly all the terrorists, when they met Kaliayev for the first time, found him wonderfully strange; he was always talking about the symbolist poets, Blok, Balmont, and the rest, and he was always carrying dog-eared copies of the poets with him. One cannot imagine Nechayev reading any poet with pleasure, unless it was the terrible little poem written by Ogaryev in honor of the enlightened personality of Nechayev himself. Kaliayev wrote poetry because he had to. It was revolutionary poetry, reminiscent of Shelley's revolutionary poems, but a Shelley who had read Pushkin:

> So now my soul blazes in a fierce tempest
> And my heart shouts with a fierce courage!
> Soon we shall see the purple fire of freedom
> Piercing the darkness of an ancient violence.
> The mask of lies will be torn from the face of evil,
> And from ourselves we shall tear our deathly fear . . .

Kaliayev belied his name, for in Russian *kalit'* means "to temper"; but like all poets he was intemperate. He could not understand why everyone in Russia was not a revolutionary, and half pitied the millions of Russians who did not have the good fortune to belong to the Terrorist Brigade. Once, talking to Savinkov, he said: "I wish to heaven I was in Macedonia.

They say everyone is a terrorist there. And with us? Five or six, no more. How on earth can one be a revolutionary, and not be a terrorist?" And then a little later: "Soon enough we shall see the flames! The peasants will get hold of the bombs, and then—the revolution!" For him the revolution was a white flower which would suddenly burst open, and nothing in the world could be as exciting as the opening of the flower. Though he thought in this way, there was a deep unconcious stirring of religious feeling in him, and Savinkov was probably right when he spoke of Kaliayev's "completely religious" attitude to terror.

When Sazonov was stalking Plehve through the streets of St. Petersburg, Kaliayev, dressed in a railway porter's uniform, was only a little way behind him, carrying a bomb wrapped in a handkerchief. They had all paused briefly in the square which faces the Church of the Protection and Intercession of the Virgin, and while Sazonov sat on one of the benches, explaining quietly to Sikorsky how he should get rid of the bomb if the attempt failed, Savinkov had caught a glimpse of Kaliayev solemnly crossing himself before the ikon which hung on the church gate. Kaliayev had removed his hat. He was still holding the bomb as he crossed himself. Savinkov went over to him and told him it was time to go. It was now twenty minutes to ten. A few moments later they all left the square, Savinkov cutting across the Sadovaya, while the others went in the direction of the Warsaw Station. Borishansky went first, followed at a distance by Sazonov, Kaliayev, and Sikorsky. Kaliayev was smiling and walking with an easy, beautiful gait.

To reach the Warsaw Station it is necessary to cross the bridge over the Obvodny Canal. The bridge swung high over the canal. Kaliayev was on the bridge when he saw the great clouds of smoke rising from the explosion. The bloodstained horses, dragging the remnants of the carriage, came racing past him, and he knew Plehve was dead and there was no need for him to throw his bomb. Sikorsky was behind him. He decided to turn round, explain what had happened and then get rid of the bomb. As he slipped down a side turning a janitor stopped him. Nearly all the janitors in St. Petersburg were police spies, and for a moment Kaliayev thought he would be arrested.

"Well, what happened?" the janitor asked.

"I don't know."

"Didn't you come from there?"

"Yes."

"Then why don't you know?"

"How could I know? They say someone fired a gun."

The janitor seems to have been satisfied with the answer. It had been a peculiarly dull explosion, the sound absorbed by the high houses on the

Ismailovsky Prospect, and soon Kaliayev was racing away, hoping to find a pond where he could sink the bomb before someone asked him what he was carrying in his handkerchief. Then he took the noon train to Kiev.

It was all much simpler and far more terrible than he had imagined. The horses ripped with bomb splinters, the mangled carriage rushing past, the heavy sulphur-yellow cloud rising out of the street, the sudden frightening appearance of the janitor—all these things were to haunt him for the rest of his short life. He had had no time to see whether Sazonov was dead, but he had already lost hope of ever seeing Sazonov alive. Savinkov, too, was convinced that Sazonov was dead. It was more than a week before the news leaked out that Sazonov was alive.

With Plehve dead, the conspirators planned to meet in Geneva and hold a conference to decide the next step. They had all fled from St. Petersburg in different directions—all except the unlucky Sikorsky. Savinkov took the night train to Warsaw, hoping to meet Evno Azev, but there was no sign of the archconspirator there. It occurred to Savinkov that it was unlikely that the search was being extended to Kiev, and he decided to join Kaliayev. There were disturbing rumors that Sikorsky had been arrested, and together they decided to make the journey to Byelostok, which was Sikorsky's birthplace and the place where accurate news of him was most likely to be found. But at Byelostok there was no news at all, and in despair they decided to make for Geneva, traveling through Germany. At Eydtkuhnen on the German border there was usually a quarter of an hour's pause while passports were examined. Savinkov had no passport. When the German frontier guard asked for his passport, Savinkov thrust the little green book which all Russians must carry when they are traveling inside Russia into the guard's hands. The guard seemed satisfied; the train rolled on; and within three days they were in Geneva, basking quietly in the sun, while newspapers all over the world were commenting on the death of the Russian Minister, who was now no more than a memory to the conspirators who had killed him. According to Savinkov the Terrorist Brigade had proved itself, and there remained only one problem: who was the next to be shot down?

One by one the conspirators made their way to Geneva. Schweitzer, Borishansky, Dulebov, Dora Brilliant, perhaps three or four others. Savinkov was so proud of the recent exploit that he demanded autonomy for the Terrorist Brigade. It should have its own treasury, its own high command, its own power to make decisions. There were excellent reasons for this. In theory the Brigade was no more than the fighting arm of the Social Revolutionary party. In fact it was the most widely known revolutionary movement in Russia, and though comprising only a handful of men, was the most feared and the most respected. It was waging war against the government itself while the other revolutionary parties were waging war among themselves; and though Savinkov's claim to autonomy was rejected by the party, he seems to have convinced all the members of the Terrorist Brigade that henceforth they must behave autonomously, whatever the opinion of the party. In this he was aided by Mikhail Gotz, the foreign representative of the Terrorist Brigade, then lying ill at Geneva. It was Gotz's task to provide finances, high explosives, shelter for escaping terrorists, and whatever intellectual sustenance the Brigade needed. Unassuming, with penetrating dark eyes, a thin high-pitched voice, a manner of almost excessive gentleness, Gotz acted as chief of staff to Evno Azev. There was no sign of Azev in Geneva. As usual, Azev was on one of his mysterious journeys. Except for a brief account of the killing of Plehve, which was written by Kaliayev, nothing of importance seems to have been done by the terrorists during the summer. They rested, compared notes, fussed over Gotz, and prepared for the party conference in Paris in the autumn. Azev's absence was perhaps the reason why no program was agreed upon. Mysterious, remote, never present when his presence was necessary, Azev was still in the eyes of the party the chief of the Terrorist Brigade, and no one yet suspected that he was an *agent-provocateur*.

In Paris, at conferences over which Savinkov presided, it was decided to destroy the main stronghold of the monarchy. Those who were most fervently loyal to the Tsar were to die. Among those who were marked for death were the Grand Dukes Vladimir and Sergey, Kleigels (the Governor General of Kiev), Trepov (the Governor General of St. Petersburg), Bulygin (the new Minister of the Interior), and his assistant, Durnov. For this purpose the Terrorist Brigade was split into three groups: Schweitzer was to go to St. Petersburg, Savinkov to Moscow and Borishansky to Kiev. Schweitzer knew that in the Peter and Paul Fortress there would be a memorial service in March 1905 commemorating Alexander II, killed by the revolutionaries twenty-four years earlier. During the service he hoped to kill the Grand Duke Vladimir, Bulygin, Durnov, and perhaps Trepov. In fact the two expeditions to St. Petersburg and Kiev failed, and in the lengthy roster of people on the death-list only the Grand Duke Sergey, Governor General of Moscow and uncle of the Tsar, paid the penalty.

The conspirators left France and made their way back to Russia by roundabout routes, with false passports, in November.

In that desperate winter the revolutionary fires were burning high. Never had there been a time when Russia was so ripe for rebellion. In the Far East the Russian army had suffered one reverse after another. On January 1, 1905, it was learned that Port Arthur had fallen. On January 9 Father Gapon led his famous march of unarmed men, women, and children to the gates of the Winter Palace. It was a bitterly cold day, with snow and piercing winds. When the Cossacks fired into the crowd, the die was cast. From that moment there could never be any doubt that the autocracy would fall. In a manifesto to the Tsar written shortly after the shooting, Father Gapon wrote:

> The innocent blood of workers, their wives and children lies forever between thee, O soul-destroying Tsar, and the Russian people. Now is the time for bombs and dynamite, terror by individuals, terror by the masses, and this must be, and so it shall absolutely come about. An immense sea of blood shall be shed, and because of thee, because of the evil wrought by thy family, Russia may perish! Understand and remember: it would be better if thou didst abandon the throne of Russia and suffer thyself to be placed on trial before the Russian people. Do this, and pity thy children, thou who hast offered peace to other countries but drinkest the blood of thine own children.

Now is the time for bombs and dynamite, terror by individuals, terror by the masses . . .

Since they were determined to kill the Grand Duke Sergey, the most important problem facing the conspirators was to discover his whereabouts. They knew he had three palaces—the Governor General's official palace on the Tverskaya, another official palace set in the gardens of the Neskuchny Park, far away in the southeast of Moscow, looking over the Moskva River, and a small private palace, the gift of the Emperor, within the Kremlin walls. Which one was he living in? There was only one way of finding out. The conspirators, disguised as coachmen and street peddlers, wandered about the city, made inquiries, stationed themselves outside the various palaces of the Governor General, and, in general, kept discreet watch on all his movements. They found to their astonishment that the Grand Duke was visiting all his palaces, but usually spent the night in the palace in the Neskuchny Park. This was surprising, because it meant a long journey to the official residence along roads that could be easily watched. It was as though everything was being made easy for them.

Kaliayev wore the disguise of a coachman. Over his coachman's livery he wore a heavy fur coat with a red silk belt. He looked prosperous, his horse had a sleek coat, the sleigh was well kept. In the livery stables he deliberately assumed the air of a young coachman determined to fleece his customers, miserly, proud, a little pompous and more than a little pious, always crossing himself. It was an odd character for him to assume, but he played it to the hilt. He would tell the coachmen in the stables long stories about his early life as a waiter in St. Petersburg—mercifully few of the coachmen knew St. Petersburg, and he was never questioned. Moiseyenko, who was also under orders to keep watch over the Grand Duke's movements, played the role of a coachman too poor to care for his horse. His sleigh was secondhand, falling apart at the seams. Where Kaliayev was garrulous, Moiseyenko was mute. He rarely spoke to the other coachmen, and simply refused to answer questions about himself. Strangely calm, inscrutable, methodical and completely reliable, he was probably the most determined and most courageous of the small band of conspirators around Savinkov.

There were three other members of the group. There was a young, recently recruited schoolteacher from Baku called Pyotr Kulikovsky, who had no experience of terrorism but possessed a desperate desire to show himself as a resolute revolutionary. There was Tatiana Leontyeva, the daughter of the vice-governor of Yakutsk Province, a blond-haired and statuesque young woman who moved in court circles, dined with Grand Dukes, and observed the decay of the Tsardom from close quarters. Tatiana Leontyeva was also a recent recruit, and if they had been in touch with her earlier they would have had less difficulty in discovering the Grand Duke's movements. Finally, there was Dora Brilliant, who posed as Savinkov's mistress.

Savinkov was so busy planning the attack on the Grand Duke that he did not learn until long afterward that just before the famous day when Father Gapon led the procession to the Winter Palace, the Grand Duke had resigned from his post as Governor General, and was gradually arranging for his furniture to be transferred to the small Nicholas Palace in the Kremlin. He had resigned ostensibly on the grounds that he did not believe he had acted firmly enough during the strikes and the student riots, and he was losing his interest in politics. He had been Governor General since 1891. He was tired, and wanted to rest. Not knowing all this, Savinkov was puzzled by the visits to the three palaces. In fact the Grand Duke Sergey was simply collecting his papers, disposing of his furniture and training his successor.

Through the newspapers it was learned that the Grand Duke would attend a performance at the Bolshoy Theater on the night of February 2. It was decided to throw the bomb as he drove up to the theater. Kaliayev was to take up his position with a bomb on Vozkresensky Square, and Kulikovsky was to stand at the entrance to the Alexandrovsky Gardens. From the Kremlin to the Bolshoy Theater was only a short ride. The Grand Duke would have to pass through the Nikolsky Gate, past the Alexandrovsky Gardens on the left, and then swing into the Vozkresensky Square. The conspirators would therefore be on both sides of him as he passed through the gate.

Kaliayev was overjoyed. Now at last he would be able to demonstrate his faith in terrorism. He wrote to a friend a few days before the attack: "Today I am as carelessly happy as the joyful sun, which calls to me from the blue canopy of a tender and gracious sky. I wander aimlessly in the streets. I gaze at the sun and at people, and I marvel how all my wintry anxieties have fled." To Savinkov he said: "I do not believe there is a past—only a present. It seems to me that Zhelyabov is still alive, and Sazonov is not shut up in the Schlüsselburg Fortress. They are with us. Surely you feel their presence! They are here, all round us!"

In a mood of wild elation, Kaliayev waited on the Ilynka for Savinkov to deliver the bomb into his hands. All that day a storm had been threatening, and by six o'clock in the evening there were flurries of snow in the air and the wind whipped the walls of the Kremlin. Just after seven o'clock Savinkov drove up in a sleigh, handed him a bomb wrapped in a handkerchief, and then vanished down the dark street, to give another bomb to Kulikovsky, who was waiting at the corner of the Varvarka. From the Ilynka Kaliayev walked to the steps of the Duma. It was only a five-minute walk, and he took his time. He was in no hurry. The square outside the Duma was empty. There were no carriages in sight, no sleighs, only the vast emptiness of the square with a few peasants wandering in the direction of the Kremlin as they did at all times of the day and night.

Kaliayev repeated to himself all the details of what had to be done. He must get close enough to the carriage to recognize the Grand Duke, but of course there would be no difficulty. Really, it was not necessary to recognize the Grand Duke at all. It was enough to have recognized the bright green carriage lights, the imperial crest on the carriage door. There was still no one else in the square. It was absurdly cold, and he felt lost and lonely.

"It's impossible," he murmured. "Absolutely no sign of him. Of course he may send someone else to represent him at the theater. Anything may happen—"

He stamped his feet in the snow. The moon was shining. He looked at his watch. He heard shouting coming from some other part of the city. He was strangely at ease, strangely calm. He knew exactly how he would throw the bomb when the carriage came in sight. He had practiced it a hundred times, and he was quite certain he would be able to hurl it through the window, darting out of the shadows so quickly the driver would have no time to swerve, no time to jump down from the driving seat, no time to grapple with him. He was sorry for the driver, but there was a possibility that the driver would only be wounded. And if the Grand Duchess Elizaveta was with the Grand Duke, then he would have to kill her too. He was sorry, but so it had to be. She was after all the sister of the Tsarina, and by killing her he would put terror in the heart of the autocracy. But best of all if the Grand Duke was alone in the carriage! Then there would be no guilt on his hands. It was a few minutes past eight o'clock.

Suddenly Kaliayev stiffened. A carriage was coming through the Nikolsky Gate. He smiled, gripped the bomb a little tighter, and waited for the carriage to come closer. He was sure it was the Grand Duke's carriage. It was a large, old-fashioned closed carriage, with bright green lights and white harness, an astonishingly heavy vehicle. When the carriage was half way across the square, Kaliayev darted out. He thought he recognized Rudinkin, the Grand Duke's coachman, but this was not so important as the fact that he had already recognized the Grand Duke, a tall, heavy, broad-shouldered man with a small beard trimmed close, wearing a dark-blue uniform, his chest covered with medals.

"The time has come," Kaliayev whispered, and he dashed across the path of the carriage and he was already whirling the bomb over his head when he saw the Grand Duchess Elizaveta sitting beside the Grand Duke, while facing them were two dark-haired children—the son and daughter of the Grand Duke Pavel, who had left Russia in disgrace when, after the death of his wife, the Grand Duchess Alexandra, he married morganatically and without the permission of the Emperor. The children were extraordinarily handsome. Kaliayev whirled the bomb above his head, paused and let his hand fall. The coachman had seen Kaliayev, and he now whipped the horses to a faster gallop, shouting at the top of his voice, but there were no policemen in sight and Kaliayev simply disappeared into the shadow of the Duma before making his way to the Alexandrovsky Gardens, where Savinkov was waiting for him.

"What happened?" Savinkov asked.

He had expected to hear an explosion. Kaliayev was sweating and trembling, and he was still carrying the bomb wrapped up in a handkerchief.

"I couldn't throw it," Kaliayev said. "I think I've done the right thing. How can one kill children?"

"What children?"

"The Grand Duchess Maria and the Grand Duke Dmitry. They were traveling with the Grand Duke Sergey. I couldn't kill them."

There was a long silence. Kulikovsky, who had been waiting in another part of the Gardens, came to join them. He had seen the carriage passing in the distance. He was almost out of his mind with anxiety. Until he was face to face with Kaliayev he believed that Kaliayev must have been arrested.

"It's astonishing," Savinkov said. "We never once raised the question, never brought it up before the Committee. You understand, you might

have been arrested with the bomb in your hand. It was terribly dangerous. The whole organization is endangered. You understand, if you had
been arrested, the whole attempt would probably have to be postponed
indefinitely."

Kaliayev nodded miserably. He believed now that he had done wrong.
He had placed the terrorist organization in jeopardy.

"Let the Committee decide," he said. "Let us decide now between ourselves. If you agree, I'll throw the bomb when the Grand Duke leaves the
theater. It all depends upon whether you decide to kill the whole family.
Tell me what you want me to do."

"Killing the whole family is quite out of the question," Savinkov
answered, and he went on to ask Kaliayev whether he was absolutely sure
he had recognized the Grand Duke, the Grand Duchess, and the children. It was just possible that the Grand Duke had traveled alone in one
carriage, and the Grand Duchess with the children and some high officer
of the court had made the journey in another. It was known that the
Grand Duke and Grand Duchess had their separate carriages. It was decided that Kaliayev should prowl outside the theater and see whether
there were two carriages, while Savinkov made inquiries at the theater.
Then they learned, as they had suspected, that the Grand Duke and his
whole family had arrived at the Bolshoy in a single carriage at exactly
the time corresponding to the passage of the carriage across the square.
Kaliayev sighed with relief. He was more than ever convinced that he had
done the right thing.

They waited outside the theater until the performance was over. Once
they went for a stroll along the embankment of the Moskva. Kaliayev was
depressed. He walked with his head bowed, still clutching the bomb.
When the performance came to an end, they returned and silently
watched the Grand Duke and the family entering the carriage.

Half the night they discussed their failure; they were sick at heart, in-
tensely excited, and aware that they might be followed. Years later the
Grand Duchess Maria, who was fifteen and could remember many details of those terrifying days, said she could remember nothing about this
first attempt. It seemed to her that they had simply raced in the carriage
through the darkened streets of Moscow. Savinkov was still perplexed.
He was not completely convinced of the rightness of Kaliayev's actions.
Dressed as an elegant Englishman, he was accompanied by two bearded
peasants. He thought of taking them to the apartment, but it was necessary to keep the police off their tracks, to disappear entirely into the vast
night of Moscow. There were some disreputable bathhouses open all
night, but these were often watched. He settled on a restaurant called
The Alpine Rose on the Sofiyka. The restaurant was closed. Savinkov sum-

moned the porter, gave him a large tip and begged him to bring down the manager, who could make nothing of the studiously insolent Englishman accompanied by two peasants who seemed to be drunk. At last a warm room at the back of The Alpine Rose was prepared for them, and once more in hushed whispers Kaliayev recounted how he had jumped across the loneliness of the immense square and had already whirled the bomb high above his head when he saw the two children. They warmed themselves over the stove. Kulikovsky was ashen-faced, shivering. Once, when they were wandering along the banks of the frozen river, Kulikovsky faltered and almost lost consciousness as he leaned back against one of the granite pillars which supported the embankment wall. Savinkov and Kaliayev had passed on ahead. They heard a rustling sound, and turned just in time. Kulikovsky, the sweat streaming down his face, was moaning: "Take the bomb. I'm going to let it fall." Now he shivered uncontrollably. They had entered The Alpine Rose shortly before twelve o'clock. By four o'clock in the morning Savinkov decided it was time to leave, and by this time all arrangements were made for the next attempt on the life of the Grand Duke. They were too weary to make the attempt immediately. They decided to wait. It was the early morning of Thursday, February 3, and by the end of the week they confidently expected that the Grand Duke would be dead, and his death would be followed by the revolution.

"I am sorry I shall not live to see the revolution," Kaliayev said a few weeks earlier. Now with the knowledge of his approaching death and the thought that almost singlehanded he would bring about the end of the dynasty, he walked out of The Alpine Rose into a snowstorm, saying over and over again that he was ready to do the work entrusted to him and rejoiced in the thought of laying down his life for Russia. He would rest in the country for a day. On Friday he would return refreshed.

That night Savinkov returned to his apartment alone. He had darted back once before to return the bombs to Dora Brilliant, who was responsible for connecting and disconnecting the fuses, a task at that time of quite extraordinary danger and difficulty. When asked her opinion about the failure, she said, lowering her eyes: "The poet did what he had to do." Dora Brilliant's words comforted him. It was after talking with Dora Brilliant that Savinkov felt absolutely convinced that Kaliayev had behaved rightly.

For the rest of the night Kaliayev and Kulikovsky, who had separated, tramped the streets of Moscow. Early in the morning Kaliayev set off by train for a small village in the outskirts of Moscow. Kulikovsky went to another village. They had agreed upon a meeting place for the 4th. It was expected that the attempt would take place some time in the afternoon while the Grand Duke was driving between his palaces. Throughout

Thursday Savinkov rested. The strain was beginning to tell. He remained alone in an obscure hotel. Dora Brilliant was staying at the Slavyansky Bazar Hotel on the Nikolskaya. It was the best hotel in Moscow, and outrageously expensive, but no one would pay much attention to a woman coming out of the hotel carrying a blanket in her hands. She would even be expected to be carrying a blanket, to wrap round her knees when she entered a sleigh. At exactly one o'clock Dora Brilliant stepped out of the hotel and gave the blanket to Savinkov as he dashed up in Moiseyenko's sleigh. The bombs were concealed in the blanket. It was a clear winter day, the frost sparkling. There was no hitch. All the previous night Savinkov had been afraid Dora Brilliant would have an accident with the bombs. Pokotilov had been killed; Schweitzer would be killed later; none of the revolutionaries really knew much about bombs. But as he drove off in the sleigh, Savinkov was well pleased with himself. It was a pleasant sensation to be driving through the brilliant frosty streets, holding the bombs on his lap. Suddenly Moiseyenko was saying: "Tell me, have you seen our poet today?"

"Yes," said Savinkov, remembering that he had met Kaliayev briefly during the morning.

He was puzzled by Moiseyenko's tone: there was something ominous in the way he put the question.

"But you haven't seen Kulikovsky?" Moiseyenko went on.

"No, of course not. I made no arrangements to see him."

"How's the poet?"

"He's perfectly all right."

"I'm glad, but Kulikovsky is in bad shape. He's breaking up. He came back this morning, and told me he hadn't the strength to take part in the assassination. After what happened the day before yesterday, he says he will have to give up terrorist work."

Savinkov frowned. It meant that all their plans would have to be revised. The plan had always been to have two men ready to throw bombs, in case one was wounded or failed to hurl the bomb. Dora Brilliant desperately wanted to throw the bomb, but Savinkov was determined to refuse her wish. As for Moiseyenko, who wore the uniform of a cabdriver and whose papers were all written out with an imaginary cabdriver's name, his arrest would only lead to the discovery of their methods. It would be necessary for Moiseyenko to sell the sleigh and acquire new papers before he could be entrusted with the bomb. As Savinkov explains all the reasons which made it impossible for him and for Moiseyenko to assassinate the Grand Duke on that day, we are aware of hesitations, excuses, somber *arrière-pensées,* and concealment of motives. It would have been perfectly possible for both of them to discard their disguises; throw the bomb; vanish; but if they did this, the small tightly knit organization would probably evaporate. At the moment Savinkov was commander in chief, a position he delighted in. Dora Brilliant was the chief of staff, and the two soldiers remaining were Moiseyenko and Kaliayev. There was no Sazonov, who gave meaning to the struggle by his mere existence. One by one the incompetents had been discarded. As Savinkov turned the problems over in his mind, he saw only one recourse: postponement.

He had not counted upon Kaliayev, who wanted nothing better than the single glory. He would throw the bomb alone. To all Savinkov's strained arguments he had a counterargument. Had he not been alone on the night of February 2? Kulikovsky had chosen the least likely of the two places from which the bomb could be thrown, and now Kulikovsky had failed them, and so it was right and proper that Kaliayev should complete what they had begun. Savinkov raised the question of a premature explosion. Well, that was something that they had to face at all times; why stress it now? As for employing two men, that surely increased the danger —there were no advantages to be derived from posting two men in different places, when it was quite certain that the Grand Duke would make the journey from the Nicholas Palace in the Kremlin to the headquarters of the governor general on the Tverskaya. No: enough of these arguments. "Failure is quite impossible," he said. "I shall kill the Grand Duke, and that's certain." He was blazing with enthusiasm, with the imminence of self-sacrifice. They were standing on the road beside the sleigh, and Moiseyenko turned and said quickly: "It's getting late. Hurry up, and make up your mind."

"Very well, Ivan Platonovich," Savinkov addressed himself to Kaliayev. "You shall do it alone."

Kaliayev smiled. It was a moment he remembered afterward with acute precision, the moment of his triumph. They walked on for a while, embraced and separated. Kaliayev was now strangely calm. In front of him, he thought, there was only the moment of death, calmly considered and deliberately chosen. He did not think he would survive the explosion. If he did, he was sure to be hanged. It never seemed to have occurred to him that he might be wounded in the explosion or that he might be sent on one of those green prison trains with cross-barred windows to a penitentiary in Siberia, where Sazonov was already installed. Two o'clock had struck while he was talking to Savinkov. Now Savinkov was walking slowly to the Nikolsky Gate, passing under the Spassky Tower and so into the Kremlin with its red walls and piles of golden cupolas blazing in the winter sun, the black Romanov eagles outstretched against the sky. For a while Savinkov paused before the statue of Alexander II. From there he could see the Nicholas Palace where the Grand Duke Sergey was living;

he could see the coach, a closed brougham, and he thought he could recognize the coachman, Rudinkin. Soon the Grand Duke would be making the usual afternoon journey to the governor general's palace, and in fact, at that moment the Grand Duke was solemnly discussing with the fifteen-year-old Grand Duchess Maria the purchase of a mandolin. Someone suggested that it was dangerous for the Grand Duke to make the journey alone; it would be better if he did not go alone. The Grand Duke was a man of violent prejudices, insanely autocratic in temper, but he possessed considerable physical courage. Brusquely, he refused the offer of a companion and stepped into the carriage. Savinkov, walking casually, had already passed the Grand Duke's palace and was now making his way to a pastry shop on the Kuznetsky Bridge where he had an appointment with Dora Brilliant.

The Grand Duchess Elizaveta was preparing to spend the afternoon in her workshop in one of the remote palaces of the Kremlin where the titled ladies of the court rolled bandages and prepared dressings for the soldiers of the Russo-Japanese War. She had already called for her sleigh to be brought closer to the steps. The children were in the schoolroom which looked out over the square. In one corner of the schoolroom Fräulein Hase, the Grand Duchess Maria's German teacher, was quietly reading a book. Time passed slowly. The sounds of Moscow were muffled by the snow. For the children it was an afternoon like all the winter afternoons in Moscow, when dusk comes early.

Suddenly there was an explosion; all the windowpanes rattled, and at the same moment a flock of crows began to wheel madly around the painted steeple of St. Ivan's Cathedral, Fräulein Hase rushed to the window. She was followed by an old professor of mathematics, and then by the fifteen-year-old Grand Duchess Maria. The snow-covered square was filling with people. It was impossible to see what had happened. Dmitry came running into the schoolroom. Maria imagined that one of the old Kremlin towers must have fallen in under the weight of snow. She sent a servant to see whether her uncle had left the palace. The servant returned, saying he thought the Grand Duke was still there. He spoke solemnly and evasively, and went away, while the children crept again to the window.

Across the square two sleighs were driving through the crowd. The Grand Duchess Maria was already reconstructing in her mind the whole incident. It seemed to her that the sleighs were filled with policemen and a good number of struggling young terrorists, their clothes in disorder, hair blowing in the wind. These terrorists seemed to be haranguing the crowd, but the windows were closed and she could hear no words. Everything seemed to be happening as though in a dream.

Down below they saw the Grand Duchess Elizaveta, wearing a blue dress, a fur coat flung loosely over her shoulders, jumping into her sleigh, followed by Mlle. Hélène, the governess of the children. In her haste Mlle. Hélène had picked up a man's coat, and like the Grand Duchess she wore no hat. The sleigh drove at a wild gallop and disappeared into the crowd. The children waited, their noses pressed against the window.

After leaving Savinkov, Kaliayev made his way to the Chapel of the Tverskaya Madonna and for a long while he gazed at the ikon set in a glass frame. Reflected in the glass frame he could see the road leading from the Nikolsky Gate and every detail of the Grand Duke's progress from his palace. As usual he wore peasant clothes, high boots, a long coat, and a thick fur hat. His beard was uncombed. Then he walked slowly through the Nikolsky Gate in the direction of the courthouse. He had already seen the carriage driving away. He waited. The road once again was deserted. When the carriage came past, he hurled the bomb at a distance of four paces straight into the window. He was caught up in the explosion, the wild spray of snow and smashed timber and broken flesh. The heat of the explosion seared his face. For a moment he was stunned. When the cloud lifted he could see only the twisted rear wheels of the carriage. His cap was torn off. Splinters stung his face. Curiously, he was still standing, and at the moment of the explosion he had the presence of mind to turn his face away. Of the carriage almost nothing remained: the twisted wheels, a little heap some eight or ten inches high, mingled with pieces of clothing and scraps of flesh, and that was all. Of the Grand Duke Sergey's body there was almost nothing recognizable except one hand and part of a leg which had been broken in half, with the foot torn away. The right arm still clung to part of the torso, but the head, neck, and most of the chest were smashed to pulp. Kaliayev was dazed by the fumes. About ten feet away he saw his cap lying in the snow. He went to pick it up and put it back on his head, and then he saw that his coat was seared in places and there were little slivers of wood hanging on it. Blood was streaming from his face. There was still no one else on the square. He thought of escape, but he knew it was useless, and he was not surprised when a police sleigh bore down on him from behind. A policeman called Leontiev jumped off the sleigh and pressed down on Kaliayev's shoulders. More policemen hurled themselves at him. A man whom Kaliayev recognized as a police spy, with a small ugly face, kept shouting: "Hold him! See whether he is armed! Glory to God, I wasn't killed!" Kaliayev was aware of a growing feeling of nausea which had nothing to do with the naked lumps of Grand Duke Sergey's flesh lying in the snow. The nausea was directed at the police spy. He had not brought a revolver, but he wished now he could kill the little plain-clothes police spy. He said: "You don't

have to hold me. I won't run away. I've done everything I wanted to do."
As he said this, he realized that he was still deafened by the explosion.
Someone was shouting for a cab. At last a cab drove up, and Kaliayev was
thrown into it, shouting: "Down with the damned Tsar! Long live freedom! Down with the accursed government! Long live the Social Revolutionary party!" At the police station in the Kremlin Kaliayev walked up
the stairs with surprisingly firm steps. He was wildly excited, brazen, and
insolent, and laughed at the policemen. When a little later he was transferred to the Yakimovsky police station he fell at once into a profound
sleep.

While the policemen in the sleigh were hurling themselves upon Kaliayev, the Grand Duchess Elizaveta was making her way through the crowd.
She knew what had happened. She was hysterical and at the same time icy
cold. She saw people standing around, gazing at the bits of flesh which
were sacred to her and she began to gather them up and make a neat pile
of them. Most of the people standing around still wore their hats. It
seemed to her an unpardonable affront to the dead, and to herself as a
member of the imperial court. She began to shout to them to remove their
hats, and soon Mlle. Hélène was ordering everyone to doff his hat in the
presence of the Grand Duchess Elizaveta Fyodorovna. Mlle. Hélène's face,
usually scarlet, had turned blue. Her eyes were glazed. Because she wore
a man's coat, people said afterward that the Grand Duchess was accompanied by her valet. There was a strange silence. Once the Grand Duchess
looked up and said: "You ought to be ashamed to be standing there. Go
away." No one paid very much attention to her. There was confusion everywhere. At three quarters of an hour after two o'clock a bomb had exploded, and this was the only fact that could be generally agreed upon.
The sleeves of the Grand Duchess' blue gown were gleaming with blood,
there was blood under her fingernails. She found the medals her husband
wore on a chain round his neck, and clutched them, and carried them
about with her as she picked up the mangled fragments of flesh. From her
own workshop someone brought a common army stretcher and the pieces
which had once formed the body of His Imperial Highness the Grand
Duke Sergey Alexandrovich formed a very small pile, which disappeared
altogether when a coat was thrown over the litter.

From the lawcourts where all the windows were shattered by the explosion and where a trial was in progress, an assistant prosecutor drove
up in a cab. He made two or three feeble attempts to examine the
smashed carriage, and then went on his way.

About this time Mlle. Hélène returned to the palace. When she reached
the children's room she was breathless, hysterical, and almost out of her
mind, her lips violet and her eyes staring. With immense difficulty she

succeeded in conveying to the children that they must come out into the square. Trembling, the children put on their coats, and they would have gone running out if General Laiming, the Grand Duke's aide-de-camp, had not prevented them, saying he had received word from the Grand Duchess that they must move away from the window and on no account enter the square.

At a quarter past three an honor guard of soldiers appeared. After roping off the place where the assassination had occurred, they carried the litter on their shoulders to the Monastery of the Miracle, where they laid it down gently before the altar. The monastery was next door to the Grand Duke's palace. Here shortly afterward came Count Shuvalov, the new governor general of the city, himself to be assassinated a few months later by Kulikovsky who in this way proved to himself that he was still a member of the Terrorist Brigade. At last the Grand Duchess summoned the children, and long afterward the Grand Duchess Maria remembered the frightened face of the priest, the ghostly light of the candles, the blood dripping from the litter and the strange hallucinated face of the Grand Duchess who knelt beside the litter in the candlelight, her sleeves still red with blood.

When Savinkov became a legend, the story was told that he was sitting in the Café Filipov when he heard the explosion, his face hidden behind a newspaper. Suddenly he rose, carefully folded the newspaper, slipped it in his pocket, remarked casually: "What terrible times we are living in!" and sauntered out. The story is almost certainly untrue. According to his own account he was still hurrying to meet Dora Brilliant at the pastry shop on the Kuznetsky Bridge when he heard a muffled roar, brief and not particularly loud. He paid no more attention to it; such a sound could have been made by a steam engine or by the ice on the river. He hurried on, met Dora Brilliant and walked quickly back along the Tverskaya. A street urchin came running up, shouting: "The Grand Duke is dead! His head's blown off!" They went faster. At the Nikolsky Gate, which leads into the Kremlin, there was a huge crowd. All of Moscow seemed to be congregating there. Savinkov and Dora Brilliant tried to make their way through the crowd, but they were beaten back, and it was Moiseyenko, driving up in a sleigh, and pale as death, who shouted out to them that the Grand Duke was dead. They jumped onto the sleigh and drove off. Suddenly Dora Brilliant collapsed, her head fell on Savinkov's shoulders and she shook uncontrollably as she whispered over and over again: "I—I—I killed the Grand Duke."

Many others believed they had killed the Grand Duke. The Grand Duchess felt she was in some obscure way responsible. General Laiming, his aide-de-camp, tormented himself with the thought that the assassination would not have occurred if he had been in the carriage. Savinkov, who had planned the details, thought he was responsible. Behind Savinkov there was the infinitely sinister figure of Evno Azev, the *agent-provocateur*. Behind Azev was Mikhail Gotz, the foreign representative of the terrorists, with his bright eyes and superb intelligence, still lying on his sickbed in Geneva.

It is possible, however, that none of these was as directly responsible for the assassination as the Grand Duke himself. He almost asked to be assassinated. Warned repeatedly against making the journey between the Nicholas Palace and the governor general's headquarters on the Tverskaya at the same hour and along the same route, he was too proud to believe he would not survive an attack by the terrorists he despised, and too much in love with autocracy to believe that autocracy was doomed. More than any of the other Grand Dukes he urged the Tsar to be uncompromising. The journeys he made were useless. It was not necessary that the son of an emperor should take upon himself the task of superintending the removal of furniture from one palace to another. A bitter, proud man, he died unloved by anyone except his wife. On the evening of the assassination the young Grand Duke Dmitry stood by the window with his sister, looking over the dark square. The ramparts and roofs of the Kremlin were blue in the snow. The dark steeple of St. Ivan's Cathedral stood out like a somber black bar against the sky. "What do you think?" asked Dmitry. "Will we be happier now?"

During the following days flowers were heaped on the place where the Grand Duke died, and a search was made for remnants of his body. A finger with a gold ring still attached was found on the roof of one of the neighboring houses. A piece of scorched and bloodstained cloth was found on the other side of the square. Then the spring rains came, and whatever fragments of him remained became part of the earth of Moscow.

Eleven years later, on December 29, 1916, the young Grand Duke whose life Kaliayev had spared himself became an assassin. In Prince Yusupov's palace facing the Neva three conspirators inveigled Grigory Rasputin to a feast. They gave him poisoned cakes, and when these failed to kill him, they shot him in the courtyard, sewed him up in a sack and dropped the body through a hole in the ice of the Neva. The three conspirators were the Grand Duke Dmitry, Prince Yusupov, and Dmitry Purishkevich, an obscure rightist member of the Duma. The wheel had turned full circle.

THE FULL CIRCLE

T HE GRAND DUCHESS Elizaveta Fyodorovna was the granddaughter of Queen Victoria and the daughter of Ludwig IV, Grand Duke of Hesse-Darmstadt. The Empress of All the Russias was her sister. Another sister was Princess Irene, the wife of Prince Henry of Prussia. A third sister was Princess Victoria of Battenberg. Tall and slender, with blond hair and gray-blue eyes, Elizaveta possessed to perfection the imperial manner of her ancestors. She loved the Grand Duke Sergey, always slept with him in the great double bed and seems never to have doubted that he was a pillar of strength to the Empire. When he died, her life ended. Her remaining days were spent in the shadows, as the abbess of the Convent of Mary and Martha belonging to the order of the Sisters of Pity. Those who visited her found a strange, distracted, saintly woman who sometimes peered over their heads and muttered about ghosts.

Perhaps she had been muttering about ghosts from the very beginning. In the curiously fabricated life of the Russian imperial court, the Grand Duchess seemed always slightly remote. She had no great affection for her sister, the Empress. She adored clothes and jewelry and spent long hours every afternoon interminably choosing among a thousand dresses the one she would wear in the evening. She liked gazing at herself in mirrors. She liked the glint of rubies and emeralds, which the Grand Duke bought for her in immense quantities. She hated familiarity; when the young Grand Duchess Maria once kissed her admiringly on the neck, the child was rewarded with a look so cold it chilled her. Childless, she could make nothing of the children who entered her household when the Grand Duke Pavel married a commoner, though occasionally Maria would be allowed to hand her a piece of jewelry. She refused to recognize the Grand Duke Pavel's marriage even when his wife, Olga Pistolkors, became ennobled and received the title of Countess Hohenfelsen, which was later changed to Princess Paley. She spoke Russian badly and read the language with difficulty. Once one of her ladies in waiting read to her Dostoyevsky's *The House of the Dead.* She ordered the doors to be closed, so that no one else in the palace would overhear the terrible, searching words. It is permissible to wonder what she made of the book. What did she say when she heard the words: "The man and the citizen disappear forever in the tyrant," or: "The characteristics of the executioner appear in almost every modern man." She preferred English novels. French books with yellow covers she detested. She painted amateurishly, rode well, collected *bibelots*, and was never happier than when she was attending some court function which allowed her to wear the richly-brocaded costumes and jeweled headdresses which were handed down to the Russian court from the court of the emperors of Byzantium. Ice-cold, with a chaste, thin-lipped beauty, she seemed to have none of the instincts of a living woman but to have been carved out of some rare stone. But in the days which followed the assassination of the Grand Duke Sergey she twice showed there was a woman buried beneath the marble surface.

At six o'clock on the night of the murder she went to the hospital where Andrey Rudinkin, her husband's coachman, was dying of his wounds. There was little left of him and no hope of survival. His body had been gashed wide open, gangrene had set in, and he was barely conscious. She was afraid to frighten him, and so wore the same gay blue dress she had worn in the afternoon. When Rudinkin murmured: "How is the Grand Duke?" she answered bravely: "The Grand Duke sent me here himself to inquire after your health." Rudinkin died peacefully during the night.

On the evening of the next day, in deep mourning and driving in a carriage draped with crape, she visited Kaliayev in his cell. She asked to be left alone with him. The prison governor could only obey.

At first Kaliayev failed to recognize the woman who entered his cell, pale as chalk, dressed in black, with tears streaming down her face. She walked with slow shuffling steps, and suddenly she looked up, gazed straight into his eyes and said: "I am his wife." There was a moment of silence. She sat down on a chair. Her head was bent, and Kaliayev had the feeling she was gazing deliberately at his hands, those hands which had committed the assassination.

"Your Highness," said Kaliayev, "please do not weep."

There was a long silence. Kaliayev kept thinking: "It had to happen. Why come to me? What is she doing here?"

"You must have suffered so much to have done this terrible thing," the Grand Duchess said, and it was perhaps the worst thing she could have said at that moment. Kaliayev was furious. He seems to have thought she was being condescending, when it was more likely that she was showing a rare understanding.

"What does it matter whether I have suffered or not?" he replied sharply. "Yes, I have suffered! But I suffered with millions of other people.

Altogether too much blood has been spilled, and we have no other means of protesting against a tyrannical government and a terrible war. Why do they come and talk to me only after I have committed the crime? Listen! When I was a boy, I thought of all the tears that are shed in the world, and all the lies that are told, and sometimes it seemed to me that if I could, I would shed enough tears for everyone, and then the evil would be destroyed! But what could I do? If I went to the Grand Duke and showed him all the evil he had done, the misery of the people, why, he would have sent me to a madhouse or—and this is much more likely—thrown me into prison, like thousands of others who have suffered for their convictions. Why didn't they let the people speak?"

Kaliayev was excited. It was the ultimate moment of revenge: the terrorist confronted with the royal house. He remembered afterward that he once waved his arms about in his overwhelming excitement, and once he paused sharply, as though daring the Grand Duchess to interrupt him.

The Grand Duchess said: "I'm sorry you did not come to us, and then we would have known you earlier."

Kaliayev was suddenly convinced she spoke out of her heart, without any concealed motives, but he remembered how the workers of St. Petersburg had set out along the Nevsky Prospect from the miraculous Virgin of Kazan to offer a petition to the Tsar. They had been shot down by the hundreds.

"So you think it is easy to go to you?" he went on. "Then look what happened on the ninth of January, when they tried to see the Tsar. Do you really believe such things could go unpunished? Then there is this terrible war which the people hate so violently. Well, you have declared war on the people, and we have accepted the challenge! As for myself I would give a thousand lives, not one, if only Russia could be free!"

The Grand Duchess murmured impatiently: "You should think of the honor of our country—"

"Oh, the honor of our country!" Kaliayev replied ironically, and there was a long pause.

The Grand Duchess was baffled by the young prisoner. She had expected to find him appalled by his crime; instead, he was jubilant. Dimly she saw that he regarded himself as the spearhead of the popular movement against the autocracy. He had talked about the Russo-Japanese War, about the suffering of the people, about his detestation of the autocracy. Now she reminded him that the autocrats also had their burdens. She said quietly: "You think you are the only ones to suffer. I assure you we suffer too, and we want only good things for the people."

Kaliayev was pitiless.

"Yes, you are suffering now," he answered, "but as for giving good things to the people, you give with one hand and take it back 'with the back of the knife.' "

The conversation was getting nowhere. Across abysses of history and custom they spoke to one another. For a while they were both silent. The Grand Duchess had taken a chair: in respect for her Kaliayev had remained standing. Now, as the Grand Duchess began to lose herself in memories of her husband, he sat down. She complained that the Grand Duke had not deserved death; he was powerless; he was no longer governor general when he died; he was good to everyone.

"I beg you not to talk about the Grand Duke," Kaliayev answered. "I have absolutely no desire to talk about him. Everything I have to say will be said at the trial. I killed him with a full sense of responsibility—he was a man who played a powerful political role and knew exactly what he was doing."

"To me he never spoke about politics," she answered, and suddenly she seemed to be very calm and remote. "I came to tell you the Grand Duke forgives you," she went on, and from the folds of her gown she drew out a small ikon and presented it to her husband's murderer, saying: "I beg you to accept this little ikon in memory of him. Yes, and I shall pray for you."

Kaliayev accepted the gift of the ikon. In a way it was a symbol of his victory over the royal house.

"My conscience is clear," he said. "I am sorry I have caused you so great a sorrow. I acted with a deep sense of my responsibility, and if I had a thousand lives, I would give them all, not only one. And now again I will say how sorry I am for you, but still I did my duty and I'll do it again to the very end, whatever happens. Goodbye. We shall never see each other again."

The Grand Duchess left the prison. On her return to the palace the children questioned her, but she said nothing. Years later the Grand Duchess Maria wrote that Elizaveta visited Kaliayev out of an impulse of Christian self-abnegation. More likely she went as one goes to a mystery and to look into Kaliayev's burning eyes.

Kaliayev himself was aware of the mystical character of their confrontation.

"I confess that we gazed at one another with a strange sense of mystery," he wrote. "We were like two mortal beings who have remained alive—I, by the accident of fate: she, because the organization had so willed it, because I had willed it, for we both desired to avoid unnecessary bloodshed. And I, gazing at the Grand Duchess, could not fail to see on her face an expression of gratitude, if not to me, then to that accident of fate by which she had escaped complete destruction."

For Kaliayev the intoxication was complete. Nothing could have given him greater joy. He almost certainly failed to understand why the Grand Duchess came to his cell. The autocracy was now humbled, and Kaliayev had achieved his purpose. In the few days that remained, he lived on the wave crests. In a long poem written shortly after the meeting with the Grand Duchess, he wrote:

> O joy and terror and torment and unrest!
> O storm of spirit and foaming stream!
> The air is filled with voices of anger.
> True to my battle vow, I with my hands
> Was insolent and proud before the enemy.
> I smiled at them, seeing their fear
> And took revenge with my derisive speech.
> The lightning plays upon my heart of storm,
> And the wild echoes scream against the heavens.
> My soul, intoxicated with purest wine,
> Drinks from the sweet cup of victory . . .

In a more somber mood, and still in exultant happiness, he wrote to his friends:

I often think of the last moment; I should like to die immediately. It is an enviable fate. But there is a still greater happiness—to die on the scaffold. Between the act and the scaffold there lies a whole eternity. It is perhaps the supreme happiness of man. Only then does one know and feel the whole strength and beauty of the Idea. To commit the deed and later to die on the scaffold—it is like sacrificing one's life twice.

Between the act and the scaffold there lies a whole eternity! . . . No prisoner had ever been more eager for the hangman's noose. Yet outwardly Kaliayev showed little signs of his devouring excitement. The prison guards found him quiet and remarkably self-possessed. He wrote letters or sat over the books he received from outside. Taken to the Butyrky Prison, he was lodged in the Pugachev Tower, and this pleased him, for the great rebel Pugachev had been imprisoned there and it was a sign that the government feared an attempt to rescue him. To his friends he wrote that he would be faithful to them to death. The letters are written calmly in a mood which suggests that all his perplexities were at last resolved:

MY DEAR FRIENDS AND UNFORGETTABLE COMRADES:
    You know how I did everything I could on February 4 to bring about victory. And now within the confines of my own consciousness, I am happy in the knowledge that I have fulfilled my duty toward Russia now lying in a pool of flowing blood.
    You know how intensely I hold to my convictions and the strength of my feelings, and let no one grieve over my death.

I have given myself wholly to the fight for the freedom of working people, and for me there can never be any concession to autocracy. If in the end it should happen that my heart's aspirations have shown I am worthy to lead the protest of mankind against oppression, then let my death crown the cause I fought for with faith in the purity of an idea.

To die for one's convictions—what is this but a call to battle? Whatever the sacrifices needed to liquidate autocracy, I firmly believe that our generation will put an end to it forever . . . And this will be the great victory of socialism, throwing open the windows of a new life for the Russian people who have suffered so long under the yoke of Tsarist oppression.

With all my heart I am with you, my beloved, dear and unforgettable ones. You held me up when times were hard: we shared together our joys and troubles; and when one day the people celebrate their triumph, then remember me, and let all my labors as a revolutionist be regarded as no more than the expression of inspired love for the people and profound respect for you. Take my work then as a tribute of deep devotion to the party, the bearer of the testament of *The People's Will* in all its immensity.

My whole life seems as strange as a fairy story, as though everything that ever happened to me was already foreseen in the days of my childhood, coming to birth within the secret recesses of my heart until it burst into a flame of hatred and revenge for all.

I should like to name for the last time all those who are close to my heart and infinitely dear to me, but let my last breath be my final greeting and a fierce clarion call summoning you to victory.

I embrace and kiss you all.

A few days after the Grand Duchess' visit Kaliayev heard through the mysterious grapevine which operated throughout all Russian prisons that it was now widely believed he had sought the Grand Duchess' pardon, had knelt at her feet with tears in his eyes and begged her to intercede with the Tsar for his life. Immediately Kaliayev wrote a letter to the Grand Duchess demanding an apology and a retraction. There was no reply. He wrote a second letter. There was still no reply, for the letters were intercepted by her family and never shown to her, and in any event it is unlikely that she would have answered them if she had seen them. The rumors about the original meeting were now widely believed, and in despair Kaliayev wrote a third letter to the Grand Duchess in the tones of an emperor demanding the presence of one of his subjects. It is an unpleasant letter, full of the bitter taste of triumph, and it is entirely unlike anything else that Kaliayev ever wrote:

GRAND DUCHESS!
Since the day of our meeting, I have twice asked to see you and both times I have failed to receive a reply. I shall not enter here into the motives of your refusal to see me, although I must be permitted to say that your refusal of a second meeting hardly recommends your intense desire to see me when you first visited my cell . . .

I believe it is the duty I owe to honor and conscience to explain in this letter all the reasons which have led me to demand another meeting with you.

Your visit on February 7 was completely unexpected. You came to me. You came to me with your sorrow and your tears, and I did not refuse you, I did not expel this visitor from the enemy's camp. You were so helpless in your grief. Perhaps it was the first time you had heard the screaming voice of terror which encompasses us all. You were so weak before the annihilation of all you held dear, in the face of destiny's torments.

For the first time a member of the royal dynasty has bowed her head before the vengeance of the people and acknowledged the crimes of the royal family.

Remember, if you had been in the carriage, you would have been destroyed. But it was not the intention of the Terrorist Brigade to deprive you of your life, and your death (as far as we are concerned) would have been a needless accident. It was in the interests of the Brigade therefore that at the moment when I caught sight of you in the carriage, I should put aside all my detestation of the ruling house and "pray for you." But that you should remain alive—that, too, was my victory, a victory which after the death of the Grand Duke has filled me with overwhelming joy.

And surely you recognized all this at the moment when you came to visit me, wearing the aspect of perfect Christian humility, your soul lit with the earthly gleam of gratitude for the fate which has preserved your life . . . I did not ask you to come. You came to me of your own accord, and the responsibility for the consequences of the visit are entirely yours. Outwardly, at least, we can say that our meeting took place in an atmosphere of intimacy. It was not intended that it should be published to the skies, but for our own sakes alone. We met on neutral ground, as two human beings facing one another. And so you yourself defined it: we were both to enjoy the honor of incognito. How else am I to understand the disinterestedness of your Christian sentiments? I trusted in your nobility. I believed your exalted station and your honor would suffice to guard us against slander, and you are now yourself involved among the slanderous tongues. But you have not feared to be touched by those hands, and my confidence in you has not been justified by events. For there is no other way to explain what has happened: the slanders and the misinterpretations of what happened between us . . .

You may ask: who is guilty? For myself I can only say that my convictions and my attitude toward the ruling house remains unaltered. I myself have nothing in common with the superstitions of slaves and their hypocritical rulers.

I admit I was wrong. I should not have sympathized with you and I should have refused to speak with you. I behaved with kindness, momentarily suppressing the natural hatred I felt for you. I have revealed the motives which moved me: you have proven unworthy of my generosity. I cannot believe otherwise than that you are yourself the source of the slanders which have been published about me. How else could our meeting have been made known? Who would have dared to reveal what we said unless it was you? (The press reports are inaccurate. I never said I was a believer. I never spoke about repentance.)

Kaliayev seems to have regretted the letter shortly after he wrote it. It was altogether too personal, too violent, with too keen an edge of malice. There had been a strange brightness in her eyes; he could not forget the long spatulate fingers, the widow's weeds, the hint of authority in her tone. Shortly afterward he must have received a message from the other members of the Terrorist Brigade, warning him and explaining the vast damage which had occurred to the Terrorist Brigade as a result of the newspaper reports in which he was described as a repentant sinner. He wrote to Savinkov:

> I beg you to forgive me for any harm I have done. Nothing can cause me greater pain than to know that you do not approve my conduct. Now that I stand on the edge of the grave, I have only one consideration—my honor as a revolutionary. This shall be my link with the Terrorist Brigade after my death.
>
> Within the four walls of my cell nothing is so difficult as to distinguish between the significant and the insignificant things of life. There are times when I fear that I shall be libeled after my death. At such times I feel I would like to live on in order to avenge myself against those who libel me.
>
> I have balanced my accounts upon this earth. I loved you, suffered with you, and prayed with you. Therefore defend my honor. Perhaps I have been altogether too frank in talking about my soul, but you know I am not a hypocrite. Farewell, my dear, my only friend. Be happy! Be happy!

The trial which opened before the Court of the Senate on April 5, 1905, took place in an atmosphere of secrecy. The doors were locked. Only high government officials, magistrates, and police officers were allowed in the public galleries, though special permission was given to Kaliayev's mother to be present. The Grand Duchess, of course, was absent. She sent no one to represent her, and had long ago lost interest in the fate of Kaliayev. There was no doubt of his fate. Like Zhelyabov, he proposed to employ the few hours of his trial in a vigorous defense of his actions. Once again the government itself would be placed on trial.

The preliminaries were soon over. The witnesses testified to the fact of the Grand Duke Sergey's death. General Major Zabudsky, an expert on high explosives, testified that the explosion had taken place inside the carriage: from thin splinters found on the scene of the crime he concluded that the bomb was contained in a tin canister, and from an examination of pieces of clothing from the bodies of the Grand Duke and the coachman he concluded that the bomb was packed with kieselguhr. Police officers described Kaliayev's arrest. At first he had refused to reveal his name, though he admitted that he belonged to the Terrorist Brigade. He was found to be carrying a passport in the name of a certain Andrey Shilnik, resident of Vitebsk. The passport was evidently false. He had shown no desire to conceal the fact that he had killed the Grand Duke; had shown indeed considerable satisfaction. Nothing was said about the visit of the Grand Duchess to his cell. There was a passing reference to the superficial wounds and scratches on the face of the prisoner at the time of his arrest. Then there was the testimony of the police officers who made the arrest. Shortly afterward the prosecutor launched on a panegyric in honor of the royal house, and once again there was heard in the Court of the Senate the strange, deep laughter of a prisoner already condemned to death.

Kaliayev was defended by the best lawyers of his time. Bernshtam was vice-president of the St. Petersburg Lawyers Association, a famous liberal and a man who was known to be in sympathy with many of the aspirations of the revolutionaries while at the same time receiving the respect of the official classes. He was ably assisted by Zhdanov, who made an impassioned plea for mercy. Bernshtam spoke more quietly. He went over Kaliayev's history: how he was arrested as a student, how he entered the party and was arrested for the second time in Silesia on the German border, only to be handed over to the secret police. He spoke of the "iron inevitability" which led young students to join the revolutionary organizations. Nothing could stop it. They were caught up in a wave of history; and must a swimmer be punished because he is swimming in an evil sea? But it was Kaliayev's speech in his own defense which was remembered afterward. Surprisingly, President Dreyer allowed him to read out a long speech in which he denounced the whole fabric of the trial, saying that he refused to recognize himself as a defendant—he was simply a prisoner, a man who had been arrested or captured by his enemies. They belonged to opposite camps. "Mountains of corpses divide us," he said. "Hundreds of thousands of broken lives and a whole sea of blood and tears flooding the nation in torrents of horror and resentment. You have declared war on the people, and we have accepted the challenge!"

Kaliayev's speech, very long and very carefully composed, was at once a vindication of his action in killing the Grand Duke and an attempt to vindicate himself in the eyes of the Terrorist Brigade. He refused to admit that "the gentlemen of the court draped in their senatorial togas" were worthy to judge him; the true judges were "the martyred people of Russia"; and he repeated the accusation which Zhelyabov flung in the teeth of the government: "You cannot judge because you are a party to the dispute." And he went on:

> You dare to sit in judgment not only on what I have done, but also upon its moral significance. You do not call what I did an act of killing. You call it a crime, an evil thing. Who gave you this right? It comes strange from you, O most pious dignitaries, who have killed no one, but support your rule with bayonets, and with the force of the law, and with arguments of morality.

There was a certain famous professor of the time of Napoleon III who was quite prepared to acknowledge the existence of two standards of morality. One was for ordinary mortals, and said: "Do not steal," "Do not kill." The other was for politicians, and this law permitted them to do anything they pleased. And you really believe you are above the law and no judgment will ever be passed on you!

Look around you! Everywhere there is blood and tears! War outside and war within the nation! Two worlds, uncompromisingly opposed to one another, have come into furious collision: the flowing waters of life and the stagnant wells, civilization and barbarism, brute force and freedom, absolutism and the people. And what is the result? The unheard-of shame of the defeat of our military strength, the financial and moral bankruptcy of the state, dissolution of the political foundations of the monarchy, the nations on the frontiers of our state each developing a passion for independence, and everywhere a rising discontent, the growth of opposition parties, open revolt of the working people ready to throw themselves into a prolonged revolution carried on in the name of socialism and freedom and—in the background of all this—acts of terrorism! What does it all mean?

It is the judgment of history upon you! It is a wave of new life arising out of the gathering storm—the death agony of autocracy. And a revolutionary does not have to be a utopian to know what things are being dreamed of nowadays! He makes his summaries, seeks out a common denominator, gives expression to the awakening maturity of the new life around him, and hurls his hatred into the enemy's teeth with a single battle-cry: *I accuse!*

About this time the long-suffering president of the court suggested that Kaliayev should answer the direct question: Was he guilty or not guilty of the murder of the Grand Duke?

"I recognize that the death of the Grand Duke occurred at my hands," Kaliayev answered, "but I do not therefore regard myself as having committed a crime."

"Explain your statement," the president snapped; whereupon Kaliayev explained the reasons why the Grand Duke had to die:

The man we killed was a prominent leader of the reactionary party now ruling over Russia. The party dreams of a return to the dark days of Alexander III: his name has become a cult. The influence of the Grand Duke Sergey has been felt throughout the reign of Nicholas II, from the very beginning. The terrible catastrophe on the Khodinskoye Polye* and Sergey's role in it were only the prelude to this unhappy reign. In his investigation of the causes of the catastrophe Count Pahlen said irresponsible people had no

* The tragedy at the Khodinskoye Polye occurred just after the Coronation of Nicholas II. On this immense plain on the outskirts of Moscow, thousands waited at night to receive the gifts of painted porcelain cups filled with sweets. There was a stampede at the moment when the gifts were given out, and 1,400 men, women and children were trampled to death. Sir Donald Mackenzie Wallace, who arrived on the scene the next morning, said "it was a sight more horrible than a battlefield." Against the advice of Trepov, the Grand Duke Sergey had ordered the police away; Count Pahlen's strictures at the subsequent inquiry were widely believed to be directed at the Grand Duke.

right to occupy responsible positions. And so the Terrorist Brigade of the Social Revolutionary party was compelled to make the Grand Duke, irresponsible in law, responsible before the people.

Of course, in making himself liable to revolutionary punishment, the Grand Duke had to amass a whole heap of crimes. First, as Governor General of Moscow . . . he made the city his own feudal principality, interfered with all cultural work, suppressed educational organizations, tyrannized over poor Jews, attempted to pervert the workers, and prosecuted all the opponents of the existing order—I am mentioning only a few of the activities of the dead man, that little autocratic ruler over Moscow. Secondly, as one occupying a high position in the governmental machine, he stood at the head of the reactionary party, the inspirer of its most repressive measures, and the patron of the chief protagonists of a policy of violent suppression of all popular and social movements . . . Finally, there was his personal influence on the Tsar. The "friend and uncle of the Tsar" acted always as the most merciless and unbending upholder of the interests of the monarchy.

Against him the revolutionary organization decided to fight, and indeed it had no alternative. The dynasty and its representatives had aroused the widespread hatred of the masses, and now at last the dynasty is paying its accounts. The deaths of three high officials—Bogolepov, Sipyagin,* and Plehve—provided the autocracy with three deliberate warnings, and the death of Sergey gives still greater point to the warnings already received . . .

My enterprise was successful. Against all the obstacles thrown against us, I know that my party will go forward, and crown itself with still greater victories. This I believe, and nothing will change my belief. Already I see the advancing hosts of freedom and the advent of a new Russia, the workers and the people all enjoying a new form of life. I am glad, I am proud to die for her in the consciousness of having done my duty.

So concluded Kaliayev's speech, but the president could not prevent himself from remarking ironically: "I am led to the conclusion that you regard yourself as an important member of this party you have spoken about. You are proud?"

"No," Kaliayev answered proudly. "As for myself, I have no importance."

"But you keep talking of your great accomplishment?"

"I did my duty, and I would do it again."

The prosecutor was Shcheglovitov, a lawyer with a reputation for liberalism who was to become Minister of Justice in the following year. He was a man who enjoyed power and conspiracy—in 1914 when the war was already three months old he presented a secret report to the Tsar urging an immediate peace with Germany—and he enjoyed his role as defender of the dynasty. He urged that society could only protect itself against the terrorists by implacable vengeance, and demanded the death penalty.

* Bogolepov, Minister of Education, was shot by Pyotr Karpovich in 1897. Sipyagin, Minister of the Interior, was shot by Stepan Balmashev in 1902. Both the assassins were young students.

When the judgment was handed down, separate penalties were awarded on the three charges on which Kaliayev had been arraigned. For belonging to a secret society determined to overthrow the dynasty: eight years' hard labor. For "bringing to an end the life of the Tsar's cousin, His Imperial Highness the Grand Duke Sergey": deprivation of all rights together with the death penalty. For killing, even though by accident and without conscious deliberation, the driver Andrey Rudinkin: deprivation of all rights and imprisonment at hard labor for fifteen years. The sentence was announced at three o'clock in the afternoon. Kaliayev was asked if he had anything to say before sentence was passed on him.

"I rejoice at your verdict," he said. "I hope you will have the courage to carry it out as openly and publicly as I executed the sentence of the Social Revolutionary party. Learn to look the advancing revolution straight in the eyes."

Then it was all over, and he was taken to his cell. Once, long ago, he had sung an old Polish song for Savinkov:

> *Niech pójda dumni,*
> *Niech wróca tlumni.*
>
> May they go forth proudly,
> May they return triumphantly.

So it had happened, and the triumph was sweet to his taste. It had cost him so little. At the trial he had said that within ten years the revolutionary forces would overthrow the dynasty, "and not with secret weapons, but openly." And it pleased him that he had concealed nothing and spoken openly throughout.

In prison Kaliayev was haunted with the sense of glory which came to him every time he thought of offering his life for the revolution. It seemed to him at moments that he had many lives, and all of them were to be gladly given away. In a sense he had died when he murdered; he had died again under cross-examination; he would die finally on the scaffold. The thought of all these deaths freely offered captivated him, and of all the young revolutionaries he was the one who seemed most content in the death cell. He wrote a few days before his death an extraordinary poem in which he demonstrated that he had no regrets, only a towering delight in his achievement. It is a strange poem. In the original Russian it moves with the effect of hammer beats, of a sustained and solemn grandeur:

> *Like a proud lion I waged this holy war:*
> *The incorruptible testimony of the Ancients was by my side.*
> *O terrible was my impetuous wrath!*
> *I killed: the pompous enemy fell,*
> *But fate returned the gift of life to me.*

Then once again I, worthy of these chains,
Hurled at my enemy still another blow,
Quietly rejecting the life he offered me.
Then for the third time I summoned my enemy
To war with my incorruptible mind.
Now he trembles before his destiny
While I await in prison—an unassailable prisoner.

Kaliayev never made clear what he meant by "an unassailable prisoner." Perhaps he meant that he had survived unharmed, and could never be harmed. Those who saw him in prison were impressed by a strange quietness about him. His death meant nothing to him. He would talk about it as though it had already occurred. He seemed to be saying that he belonged to the past, had already entered history and saw no reason why anyone should be concerned with his fate.

He refused to appeal. There was therefore nothing to delay the execution. He remained in the Peter and Paul Fortress until May 9, when orders were received to convey him by police launch to the Fortress of Schlüsselburg overlooking Lake Ladoga. He had already changed into the black clothes prescribed for condemned prisoners. Handcuffed, his feet fettered, he was carried onto the motor launch and kept below decks. He was taken to a cell in the fortress. Troops were stationed on the road leading to his cell. Wherever he looked the windows were closed—orders had been received that every window in the neighborhood must be closed, and all the women and children in the place must keep away from the streets.

His cell in the Schlüsselburg was known ironically as "the workroom." No one knew why this room had been set apart for the last hours of prisoners condemned to death. It was a small room, unfurnished except for a bed. Through the windows he could look out on a wooden fence and on two small flower beds which were being tended by the prison guards.

It was a cold day with a high blue sky and a great wind whipping the ice on the lake. The guards paced outside the "workroom" in the sunlight, but no sunlight fell into Kaliayev's cell. After lunch he lay down on the bed and drew the thin prison blanket over himself. A guard stood watching him in the corner. Kaliayev saw the guard's half-mocking smile and snapped: "You are quite wrong. I am not shivering with fear. I'm cold, and I would be glad if you would get me another blanket."

He rested for a little more than an hour and spent the afternoon writing. He wrote at great length, covering a large number of sheets of paper, but shortly before his death he crossed out everything he had written except a famous quotation from Peter the Great's speech before Poltava: "As for Peter, know that his life is not so dear to him as Russia's happiness." Visitors came to his cell. According to Chernov a last-minute effort was made to make him sign an appeal for clemency. His own attorney entered the cell eight times, each time with some new reason why Kaliayev should throw himself on the mercy of the Emperor, and each time Kaliayev refused. He was asked whether there was anything he wanted. He answered that he would like hot tea and food, and for the rest wanted to be left alone with his thoughts. This wish was not granted. The celebrated Father Florinsky entered, saying he wanted to discuss religion with Kaliayev. Kaliayev answered that he had other things to think about. Around nine o'clock the prosecuting attorney, accompanied by the commander of the fortress, entered. Kaliayev was told he would be executed that night, just before dawn. Kaliayev showed no signs of emotion, asking only that his own attorney be allowed to witness the execution. For some reason this request was refused.

Around ten o'clock Father Florinsky again entered Kaliayev's cell, to receive his confession and administer the sacrament. Kaliayev explained patiently that he had no need of a priest, refused to recognize the ritual of the Church, and was content to die. He had affirmed in court that he considered his death a supreme sacrifice in a world of blood and tears, and saw no reason to change his belief. There seems to have been a further effort to make him sign an appeal and it is possible that if he had signed, his sentence would have been commuted to life imprisonment, but there is no record that Father Florinsky spoke of anything except religious matters. Kaliayev was moved by the evident goodness of the priest and said: "Let me kiss you because you are a good man." They kissed and soon afterward the priest left the cell. They were to see one another again on the scaffold.

At midnight Kaliayev requested that the execution should take place immediately. This request was refused.

An hour later, sitting in his cell, Kaliayev wrote his last letter to his mother:

> DEAR, BELOVED MOTHER!
>
> Soon I shall die. I am happy because I am in full control of myself, and so I shall remain to the end. Let your sorrow, Mother, Sisters, Brothers, overflow with the shining radiance of my triumphant spirit.
>
> Farewell! Greetings to those who know and remember me. I beseech you all to preserve the purity of our Father's name. And never grieve nor cry. Once more—farewell! I am always with you!

At two o'clock in the morning the commandant of the fortress and the hangman entered the cell.

According to custom the hangman was dressed in red, with a red blouse, red breeches, a red cap. He wore a rope round his waist. From the rope hung a knout. The hangman was Alexander Filipiev, who had murdered seven people. He was reprieved upon his offer to act as hangman. Now as he entered the cell, he smelled strongly of vodka. He smiled good-humoredly and asked Kaliayev to hold his hands behind his back: then Filipiev quickly roped the hands together. The commandant looked more nervous than the prisoner or the hangman. Kaliayev was led into the courtyard, wearing a black suit, a black felt hat, no overcoat. The commandant went in front, Filipiev was in the rear. Only a few lamps shone; the gallows itself was veiled in darkness. As usual the scaffold was painted black and so was the small platform with the three steps leading up. In the courtyard were the privileged officials, a detachment of foot guards with fixed bayonets, and the commissioned officers who were free from prison duties.

Kaliayev stood motionless during the reading of the sentence. Father Florinsky held out a cross. Kaliayev refused to kiss it, and said: "I have already told you I have finished with life and I am prepared for death." The priest moved away.

The hangman approached, slipped the shroud over Kaliayev's head, threw the noose over his neck and then kicked the tabouret away, while the drummers in the small courtyard drowned any sounds made by the man who spun at the end of the thin rope. Hardly three minutes had passed since Kaliayev hurried across the courtyard.

The body dangled for thirty minutes before it was cut down. In the courtyard no one moved. The doctor pronounced that he was dead. As dawn came up at last, the body was placed in a wooden coffin, and the soldiers buried it outside the fortress walls, in the prisoners' burying ground between the mound that surrounds the fortress on one side of the lake and the King's tower. After the Bolshevik revolution, when an attempt was made to find the grave, they found only a wooden marker which had almost rotted away. The body itself seems to have slipped away into the lake water.

Kaliayev survived his own death. He was remembered as the handsomest, the most talented, and the most superbly dedicated of the small group of Russian revolutionaries who threatened the Tsardom at the beginning of the century. Of them all, he alone had thrust cleanly, never plagued by doubts except when he saw the young children in the Grand Duke's carriage. Slight and fair-haired, speaking in a soft musical voice with a Polish accent, he brought to the revolution an idealism which seems to have vanished after his death. Once, talking with Savinkov on Vassily Island Kaliayev said: "Everything is beautiful. The stars and clouds and flowers and people and—death is beautiful, too." In a sense it had always been as simple as that.

For the Grand Duchess there were no simplicities—only a long agony. She attended her husband's funeral in the Monastery of the Miracle on the morning of February 23, and she must have observed that neither the Tsar nor the Tsarina had dared to attend. Of the many Grand Dukes who were invited only three had the courage to come. One was a distant cousin, another was the young Dmitry, the third was Dmitry's father, the Grand Duke Pavel, who had received a special dispensation from the Tsar permitting him to return from abroad. Others accepted the black-bordered invitations and at the last minute found excuses.

From the day when the remains of the Grand Duke Sergey were buried, the Grand Duchess gave herself to good works. She painted her bedroom, which was once mauve, in various shades of white, hung it with ikons and set up her own private chapel. When the First World War came she was still abbess of the Convent of Martha and Mary, and she still kept the small Nicholas Palace. It was as though she refused to be separated from the ghosts of the past.

By a strange turn of fate she was herself partly responsible for the death of Rasputin, who was believed by many to be responsible for the misfortunes of the war. The Grand Duke Dmitry had watched the growing power of Rasputin with horror. For some time he had been thinking of putting an end to the horror, but before committing himself he decided to seek his aunt's counsel. The Grand Duchess Elizaveta had no idea that Dmitry was about to take part in a plot against Rasputin's life, but when he asked her whether she considered he was a danger to the monarchy, Elizaveta agreed only too fervently. She painted a dark picture of Rasputin's influence over her sister, the Empress. She saw no hope for Russia while Rasputin remained alive. Dmitry returned to St. Petersburg. Within a few days Rasputin's body was dropped into the ice of the Neva.

The Grand Duchess remained in Moscow throughout the revolution. She was not interested in politics. She lived in a world of her own. In June 1918 she was arrested by the Bolsheviks. She had hoped to be allowed to continue working in the hospital. She described herself as a simple abbess whose only use in the world lay in her skill in tending the wounded. But in a mood of violent hysteria and cynical revenge, Lenin had given orders for the extermination of the entire royal house. Had not Nechayev spoken of "terrible, total and merciless destruction"? Once, long ago, someone had asked Nechayev which of the members of the imperial family should be destroyed. Nechayev had answered immediately: "Why, the whole responsory!" meaning all those members of the royal house for whom prayers were said in the churches. Now the shadow of Nechayev fell over the saintly Grand Duchess. For a few weeks she disappeared from sight, then it was learned that she was living in the obscure village of Alapaievsk in the government of Perm. With her was Prince Vladimir Paley, the son of the Grand Duke Pavel by his morganatic wife. There were also the three sons of the Grand Duke Constantine, Ivan, Constantine, and Igor, and the Grand Duke Sergey Mikhailovich, who had been given the responsibility of building up an air force for the Tsar. With Elizaveta was her maid Varvara. They lived quietly. None of them knew what was in store.

On the night of July 16 the Tsar and his whole family were shot to death in the cellar of the house of the engineer Ipatiev in Ekaterinburg. The bodies were then thrown on a truck and driven to a deserted mine shaft. Elizaveta was not so lucky. With the other members of the royal house at Alapaievsk she was driven to a mine shaft, shot and thrown into the mine. When voices were heard from the bottom of the mine, heavy stones were thrown down. It was said that their voices could be heard for a whole day; afterward there was silence. On April 24, 1920, a strange report appeared in newspapers all over the world:

PEKING IS MYSTIFIED BY RUSSIAN BURIALS

Seven bodies, four of them said to be members of the Russian Imperial Family, arrived in Peking from Harbin yesterday and were buried in the Russian cemetery, outside the city wall. The whole proceedings were surrounded with the greatest secrecy, even the Russian Legation receiving scant information of the circumstance.

The bodies were declared to be those of the Grand Duchess Elizabeth Feodorovna, the Grand Duke Serge Mikhailovich . . . It is alleged that they were killed and their bodies thrown into a coal mine near Perm.

KERENSKY

Be careful! Out of this chaos, like a phoenix out of the ashes, there will come a dictator—and it will not be me! . . . You are recommending childish prescriptions —arrest, kill, destroy! What are you—socialists, or the police of the old regime?

THE END OF REVOLUTION

THE MORNING OF March 11, 1917, broke white and cold over St. Petersburg. The snow glittered brilliantly in the frosty sunshine, and only a few people were walking through the icy streets. Across the Neva the slender gold spire of the Peter and Paul Fortress shone against a perfect blue sky, and all the white palaces gleamed in the wintry light. Here and there a few dark figures were making their way hesitantly across the icebound Neva. From time to time mysterious convoys moved through the city, and it was observed that machine guns were being posted on some of the rooftops in the more fashionable streets.

It was a strange morning—not at all the morning which General Khabalov had been expecting. During the previous days there had been mounting disorder—riots, workers' processions, sporadic fighting. The workers were on strike and becoming increasingly turbulent, the housewives in the bread queues were muttering against the autocracy and especially against the Tsarina, "that German woman," and the rumor factories were busily disseminating propaganda against the government. General Khabalov had very good reason to be disturbed by the mounting tension. On the previous evening he had received a telegram from the Tsar: "I command you, not later than tomorrow, to put a stop to the disorders of the capital, which are intolerable in this grave time of war with Germany and Austria. NICHOLAS II."

General Khabalov, the commander of the military district of St. Petersburg, did not know that this was the last order he would receive from the Tsar, and very nearly the last order the Tsar gave to anyone. The telegram alarmed him, as well it might. He said later that it came "like a thunderbolt," he had no alternative but to obey it—the disorders must be put down by force "not later than tomorrow." "What was I to do?" he said some months later. "How was I to put a stop to the disorders? When they said, 'Give us bread!' we gave them bread—and that was the end of it. But when the banners said, 'Down with the autocracy!'—how could you appease them with bread? But what could you do? The Tsar had given his orders. We had to shoot!"

As soon as he received the telegram, the general summoned his staff and worked out a plan for dispersing any large crowds in the city. To the regimental commanders and local chiefs of police he suggested that the crowds should be given a triple warning; if, after three quite separate warnings, they refused to disperse, the troops and the police were given authority to open fire. Before a map of St. Petersburg he showed the most likely places where the crowds would accumulate, and where dispositions would be taken accordingly. All known troublemakers were to be rounded up. That night police patrols caught most of the active Bolsheviks in the city, and the leaders of other revolutionary parties were also arrested. To help put down the expected disorders two brigades of cavalry were being sent to St. Petersburg from the front, but they would not arrive for several days. General Khabalov was therefore able to use only the military and police forces available in the city. While the police were reliable, the soldiers were less dependable. Most of the soldiers in the barracks were trainees, young and untried, and some of them—the general did not yet know how many—were infected with revolutionary propaganda. Like the women in the bread queues they wanted an end to the autocracy, a new government, popular suffrage, an elected parliament.

General Khabalov was a calm, sensible man, a veteran of many wars, who took no enjoyment in the prospect of bloodshed. St. Petersburg in the third year of the war was in a sullen mood, with violence lurking just beneath the surface. There were still bodies lying in the snow, after the clashes which occurred during the previous days. Soon there would be more bodies. The question was whether the violence could be contained, or whether all of St. Petersburg would be engulfed in it.

As the morning advanced, more and more people came out on the sunlit streets, not in massed crowds, but simply as people going to church or enjoying a Sunday-morning promenade. The streets wore a holiday appearance, and in the heart of the city all was quiet. Here and there a mounted patrol made its leisurely progress, and small groups of policemen paced the streets. There was nothing to suggest that revolution was in the air.

Deceived by the superficial calm, General Khabalov sent a jubilant telegram at about eleven o'clock to General Headquarters at Mogilev. It read: "Today, February 26, all is quiet in the city this morning. KHABALOV."* A few minutes after the telegram was dispatched, reports began to come in from all over the city indicating that the calm was about to erupt. Crowds were beginning to form along the Nevsky Prospect. Workmen from the Vyborg district, prevented from reaching the center of the city across the bridges, were making their way over the ice, carrying red banners and shouting: "Down with the autocracy!" General Khabalov ordered the officers and the police—both the military and the police forces were under his command—to be on the alert.

Shortly before noon a huge crowd gathered in Znamenskaya Square near the Nikolayevsky railroad station. They were being addressed by revolutionaries, but no one was paying very much attention to the speakers. It was a casual, unorganized crowd, waiting to see what would happen, and happy to be in a strategic position, for the square commanded the whole length of the Nevsky Prospect. A training detachment of the Volhynia Regiment was drawn across the Nevsky Prospect, and the commanding officer, Subcaptain Lashkevich, was ordering the crowd to disperse. Few heard him, and the crowd was in no mood to listen. His instructions were to give the warning three times, and if the crowd did not disperse he was to order his troops to fire. Just before the station clock struck twelve, the first volley was fired. There were three or four more volleys, but they did no harm, for the trainees by common accord fired into the air. Some officers then turned a machine gun on the crowd, and the slaughter began.

Before the eyes of the soldiers the entire crowd seemed to disintegrate. Screaming and panic-stricken people were running in all directions. They crowded into the courtyards of neighboring houses, climbed over walls, huddled in small groups in doorways. When the shooting was over, forty people were lying dead in the snow, and there were as many wounded. Soon the ambulances were coming up to remove the wounded to hospitals, and the dead were being carried off to the morgue. By four o'clock in the afternoon there was no sign that anything of any importance had happened in the square, for the blood was strewn with fresh snow. The square looked as it might appear on any Sunday evening. The trains still disgorged their passengers and the droshkies still drove up with passengers eager to catch their trains.

* February 26, Old Style, corresponds to March 11 according to the Gregorian calendar adopted in most of Europe.

With that burst of machine-gun fire on Znamenskaya Square the Russion Revolution began. From this point there was no turning back. The ordinary people of St. Petersburg, the workers and the middle classes—for the distinction between the proletariat and the bourgeois had not yet come into existence—knew that they would have to fight back.

There was sporadic shooting during the rest of the day, with the mounted police patrols breaking up any small crowds with bursts of gunfire, and there was some sniping from the roofs. During the evening a company of the Pavlovsky Regiment came out into open mutiny, but the mutiny was quickly suppressed. Some twenty soldiers with their rifles slipped out of the cordon and joined the people, while the remaining soldiers in the company were placed under arrest. Nineteen of them were taken to the Trubetskoy Bastion of the Peter and Paul Fortress to face a court-martial. They were regarded as the ringleaders, and expected to be sentenced to death.

While General Khabalov was congratulating himself that all disorders had been quelled, Rodzianko, the President of the Duma, realized that the disorders were only beginning. He was in touch with the political parties, and knew that the patience of the people had reached breaking point. That night he sent a telegram to the Tsar at Mogilev. "The situation is serious," he wrote. "There is anarchy in the capital. The government is paralyzed. It is necessary immediately to entrust a person who enjoys the confidence of the country with the formation of the government. Any delay means death. I pray God that in this hour responsibility will not fall on the sovereign." Neither this telegram, nor a still more urgent one sent the next morning, had the slightest effect on the Tsar, who told Count Fredericks, the minister of the court: "The fat Rodzianko has written a lot of nonsense, and I won't reply to it."

The fat Rodzianko had in fact written some sound good sense. There was little movement in the streets during the night of March 11, but it was the calm before the storm. Sporadic shooting continued, and a few more ringleaders were arrested by the police, but there were only a few incidents to disturb the strange quiet which had gathered around the city. The hurt and horror of the machine-gun burst on the Znamenskaya Square seemed to have left the people numbed, frightened, and indecisive. In fact the counterattack was already being prepared.

At six o'clock in the morning, when it was still dark, the trainees of the Volhynia Regiment which had taken part in the shooting on the Znamenskaya Square held a secret meeting in their barracks. There were all together some 350 men, all eagerly discussing the events of the previous day. Their arguments were brought to an end by one of those remarkable figures who always appear in revolutionary times, making important decisions and briefly assuming command, and in so doing changing the course of history. Such men appear for a few days and then vanish completely from the stage of history. The man who suddenly stepped forward and addressed the company was Sergeant Timofey Kirpichnikov, who belonged to no political party. He said the time had come to mutiny, and if the officers got in the way, they would have to suffer the consequences. Subcaptain Lashkevich, who had given the order for the shooting on Znamenskaya Square, heard of the meeting, decided to investigate, and made his way to the hall where the men were assembled. Here he was greeted with a deafening round of applause. Since he was unpopular with the soldiers, he was aware that this was cause for alarm and turned angrily to a sergeant nearby and asked the meaning of the outburst. "It means," said the sergeant, "that we do not intend to obey your orders." For a few more minutes Lashkevich tried to restore order, but when the soldiers shouted: "Get out while you are still alive!" he left the room and ran down a corridor. He was still running when a soldier shot him in the back. He had survived the shooting in the Square by a little more than eighteen hours.

Sergeant Kirpichnikov took command of the company, and marched the men out of the barracks. With standards flying and firing joy-shots, they made their way to the nearby barracks of the Preobrazhensky and Lithuanian regiments, which joined the revolt. The Decembrist uprising had begun in the same way, with the soldiers marching out of their barracks and joining up with other mutinous regiments. But this time there was no day-long parade on the Senate Square. Instead they took possession of the city by continually milling through the streets in automobiles or on foot, shouting in a frenzy of exaltation, shooting into the air, joining the mobs which sacked the police stations, or spilling over the river to Vyborg, the workingmen's quarter, and fraternizing with the workers. The Moskovsky Regiment, which had been the first to come out in favor of the Decembrist uprising, was one of the last to join the February Revolution, joining the revolutionaries only after a short sharp battle on the Liteiny Bridge. Then one by one all the remaining regiments joined the people: the Oranienbaum machine-gun regiment, the crack Semyonovsky and Ismailovsky regiments, and finally the Cossacks. By the end of the day about 127,000 soldiers had come out in open revolt against the autocracy. The capital was in their hands, and they had not the slightest idea what to do with it.

The whole day was spent in continuous upheaval and mounting excitement. The soldiers broke into the Kresty Prison, stormed the arsenal, and captured the Peter and Paul Fortress. The building of the High Court went up in flames. Police stations were set on fire, and many policemen perished in the flames. The soldiers crowded round the Tauride Palace, where the Duma was in session. They shouted themselves hoarse, sang the "Marseillaise," demanded that the deputies come out and address them, and when they wearied of speeches they marched through the streets, fired more joy-shots, killed more policemen, set up barricades around the palace, and debated incessantly about what should be done. Long before nightfall the guns of the Peter and Paul Fortress were trained on the Winter Palace and the Admiralty, where the troops still loyal to the Tsar had taken refuge. They amounted to some fifteen hundred men.

On that night, the first night of the revolution, the red glare of burning buildings lit the sky, and the searchlights from the Admiralty tower made the Neva as bright as day. Soldiers huddled over campfires at street corners, and occasionally there came the rattle of machine guns and rifle fire. The city slept fitfully. With the coming of dawn the last of the loyal troops slipped away and vanished into obscurity.

The victory was complete, and it had been accomplished in a single day. That the Tsar was still on the throne and that orders were still being issued in his name were matters of indifference; he would abdicate quietly a few days later. What was of far greater importance was the fact that the February Revolution had no guiding hand, no program, no clear-cut aim. Lenin was to say later that it was born in "chaos and enthusiasm," and so it remained until Lenin himself seized power in November.

Among those who rose to prominence in the days immediately after the February revolution the most outstanding was Alexander Kerensky, a lean, intense lawyer with a remarkably penetrating voice and a superb gift of oratory. He was a sick man, having only recently recovered from an operation for the removal of a tubercular kidney; his pallor and the strange jerkiness of his movements and the headlong rush of his words set him apart from other men. Among the revolutionaries, chiefly Mensheviks, who hastily formed a Soviet of Workers' and Soldiers' Deputies modeled on the soviet which sprang into existence during the revolutionary days of 1905, he looked out of place, because there was nothing about him to suggest the hard-bitten revolutionary. He had the grace of mind, wit and inner detachment which went with the successful lawyer, and in fact he was famous for defending revolutionaries in the courts. And there seemed to be no place for him in the Provisional Government made up of aristocrats and middle-class professional men which came into existence at the same time, because he was too fiery, too romantic, and too earnest to sit easily beside these men who behaved as though they were attending the board meeting of a company on the verge of bankruptcy. Yet Kerensky was a member of the Soviet of Workers' and Soldiers' Deputies and successively Minister of Justice, Minister of War, and Prime Minister in the Provisional Government. The two organizations were competing for power and dangerously at loggerheads. He was the bridge between them, the maverick who somehow succeeded for a few months in giving purpose and direction to the revolution.

Alexander Kerensky was born in 1881 in Simbirsk, which was also the birthplace of Lenin. The family was another nest of gentlefolk, deeply religious, quietly content, with simple tastes. The father, Fyodor Kerensky, was one of those brilliant school-teachers who went out of their way to make the lessons exciting for their pupils, and he was remembered as a man with the gift of making even Latin enthralling. They were comparatively wealthy, for in addition to the father's salary there was a large inheritance from the maternal grandfather, a Moscow merchant.

At the age of six the boy Alexander was struck down with tuberculosis of the hip, and spent the next six months with his right leg encased in an iron brace. Forced to remain in bed, he devoured book after book, developing a passion for Lermontov, Pushkin, Tolstoy and Dickens which never left him. He had a quick, eager mind and an ungovernable temper, but the temper subsided whenever he was in reach of a book. Like many school-teachers' sons he acquired habits of scholarship early in life.

Suddenly, when he was eight years old, the settled life in a cultured provincial town was exchanged for life on the frontier. Fyodor Kerensky took up a teaching post in Tashkent, the capital of Turkistan, and brought all his family with him. Tashkent had been conquered by the Russians only twenty-four years before, and this was still virgin territory. There were no gentry longing for the restoration of serfdom, no reactionary officials parading their power by issuing absurd orders. The old Moslem civilization continued side by side with the Russian. The city was like a garden, with the snow-capped Pamirs in the distance, and there were all the advantages of frontier life, with the government too far away to be oppressive. Here the boy spent the ten most formative years of his life. In later years he would look back on those carefree years with a sense of nostalgia, but also with the knowledge that by living in Turkistan he had been saved from the social and political dogmas engrained in Russian youth during a reactionary time. The full weight of the absolutist monarchy could be felt in St. Petersburg. In Tashkent, 2,200 miles away, it could be scarcely felt at all.

When he was eighteen he decided to study at St. Petersburg University. It was a time when the students were in turmoil, at odds with the government and with themselves. In February 1897 Maria Vetrova, a student imprisoned in the Peter and Paul Fortress had burned herself alive after pouring kerosene on her clothes. She was the illegitimate daughter of a notary and a peasant woman, and for a while had been a devoted follower of Tolstoy. Then, abruptly, she had abandoned her pacifist principles and engaged in revolutionary activity among the workers. She was setting up an illegal printing press when she was arrested and thrown into the Trubetskoy Bastion, where she seemed for a few days to be resigned to her fate. Then, according to the prison records, she began to behave strangely, raving and screaming all day and all night. The prison authorities sent a doctor and a midwife to calm her, without effect. Her mind was unbalanced, and she was quite mad when she seized the lamp, poured the kerosene over her clothes, and set herself on fire. She died in agony four days later. She was only seventeen.

The commandant of the Peter and Paul Fortress did everything he could to prevent the news of her suicide from reaching the outside world. In this he was unsuccessful. The rumor spread through the student body that she had set herself on fire in an act of protest against the autocracy, and a wave of meetings swept over every university in the country. Five thousand students tried to crowd into the Kazan Cathedral in St. Petersburg when a requiem mass was being held. Afterward there were demonstrations in the square outside the cathedral, and the crowds were dispersed by the police. Hundreds of students were arrested.

The story of Maria Vetrova left an indelible impression on Kerensky's mind, and he was soon taking part in minor conspiratorial activities. He was stirred again in February 1901, when a student called Pyotr Karpovich, twice expelled from the university, shot the Minister of Education, Nikolay Bogolepov. In the eyes of the student body Karpovich had acted justly, and they regarded his willingness to die as proof of his moral heroism. Kerensky shared this belief and looked forward to the time when he too might kill one of the great ministers of state, or even the Tsar. When Sazonov killed Plehve, the Minister of the Interior, three years later, he was overjoyed. The simple, direct philosophy of the Narodnaya Volya pleased him, and he regarded the terrorists as champions of freedom.

By this time he had received his law degree and was happily married. He delivered his first public political speech during a summer vacation in Tashkent; no one paid the slightest attention to the speech. He knew himself to be a revolutionary orator and a potential terrorist; he was looking for a revolution. He nearly found it on that January day in 1905 which came to be known as "Bloody Sunday." By chance he was walking near the Winter Palace square when the long columns of workmen led by Father Gapon marched up to the palace to present a petition to the Tsar, and the cavalry at the orders of the Grand Duke Sergey opened fire. He knew then that the autocracy was doomed. It was a knowledge he shared with hundreds of thousands of other people, and there were many who hoped to be the instruments of justice. He did not know and could not have

guessed that there would come a time when the fate of the Tsar would be
in his hands.

That year he joined a conspiratorial organization which called itself the
Organization of Armed Rebellion. The organization published a biweekly
sixteen-page bulletin called *Burevestnik* (The Stormy Petrel), to which he
contributed. Printed on an illegal printing press, *Burevestnik* claimed to be
the official organ of the Social Revolutionary party and was filled with
violent denunciations and proclamations against the autocracy. On Christmas Eve, late at night, while he was decorating the Christmas tree for his
eight-month-old son, the bell rang and the police entered the apartment.
They were good-humored and apologetic as they searched every nook and
cranny of the apartment. At last they found under a pile of old newspapers
a bundle of manifestoes printed for the Organization of Armed Rebellion,
and Kerensky was immediately placed under arrest and taken off to the
Kresty Prison. After four months in prison, he was sentenced to exile in
Tashkent.

The sentences of prisoners were often capricious, and depended on the
mood of the prosecutor or a prisoner's connections in high places. For
some reason the authorities did not regard the Organization of Armed
Rebellion as being particularly dangerous—it consisted of about six hot-
heads, none of whom possessed anything more lethal than a pocket knife
—and there was an old friend of the family who possessed excellent connections with the chief of police. Within six months Kerensky was back
again in St. Petersburg. He became a trial lawyer, a member of the Duma,
a figure in the political life in St. Petersburg. Eventually he became the
head of a small party which called itself the Trudovik or Workers' party,
an offshoot of the Social Revolutionary party. Although it was a very
small party, it exerted an influence out of all proportion to its numbers.
The most powerful weapon of the Trudovik party was Kerensky's golden
voice, which could drop to a fiery whisper or blaze across a parade ground
with a sound like machine-gun fire.

In a sense the voice was the man. It had then, and still has, extraordinary warmth and resonance, and no one who has received a telephone call
from him or listened to him expounding the history of the February revolution is ever likely to forget the fire in the voice. With the voice went a
wide-ranging experience of revolutionary Russia. He knew the world of
conspiracy, he had been in prison and in exile, he was in touch with revolutionary movements from St. Petersburg to Tashkent, and he knew everyone. The man who came to the forefront after the February Revolution
was a highly skilled revolutionary agitator, whose roots were in the Narodnaya Volya tradition of the eighties.

It has become the custom to regard the February Revolution as a spon-

taneous uprising by the people. So perhaps it was, although there are in-
dications of many plots and counterplots taking place in the shadows.
Lenin once observed that "war arises in great secrecy" and that "revolutionary organizations are helpless in the face of a war when it is really
impending." It is the same with revolutions, which are sometimes trig-
gered by obscure men acting in obscure ways. Subcaptain Lashkevich appears to have belonged to an extremist military organization; Sergeant
Timofey Kirpichnikov seems to have acted on his own responsibility. He
was later decorated by General Kornilov, and after the Bolsheviks took
power he escaped to Constantinople and died obscurely in Bulgaria. By
bringing the Volhynia Regiment, or a small part of it, out in open rebellion, he precipitated the revolution, and never again disturbed the pages
of history.

In his memoirs Kerensky hints at a Masonic plot in which high officers
of state were involved. Among the members of the plot there appear to
have been Prince George Lvov, a number of generals—Krymov, Alexeyev,
Kornilov, and Gurko—Ekaterina Kuskova, and Kerensky himself. Some
members of the Tsarist government, who also belonged to the same Masonic lodge, may have been implicated. But although Ekaterina Kuskova
has written about the plot at some length, and some generals have insisted
in their memoirs that a small group of Masonic conspirators was responsible for the February uprising, there is no reason to believe that the plotters
had any decisive effect on the revolution. There were many semicon-
spiracies, and they appear to have been as ineffective as the Organization
of Armed Rebellion. From the moment Subcaptain Lashkevich gave the
order to fire on the crowd in Znamenskaya Square, there could be no turning back.

In the Provisional Government Kerensky asked for and received the
portfolio of Minister of Justice. In peaceful times such a portfolio carries
no great burden of responsibility; in revolutionary times it can be made
to carry almost unlimited responsibilities. A revolutionary Minister of
Justice may become the legislator of the revolution; he may open the prisons and make arrests at will; the accumulated files of the police fall into
his hands, and the revolutionary police act at his bidding, while the members of the deposed government become his prisoners. In the days following the February Revolution two important members of the Tsarist
government were saved from summary execution only because Kerensky
interposed his own body between the ministers and the howling mob. The
Tsar, too, became the captive of the new Minister of Justice, who ordered
him to be detained in a wing of his palace at Tsarskoye Selo with all the
members of his family.

One of the minor tasks of the revolution was to dispose of the Tsar in a manner which would effectively prevent him from exercising any further power. Kerensky had no illusions on the difficulty of the task. When King George V offered the Tsar asylum in England, Kerensky decided that the offer should be accepted, and in a speech delivered before the Moscow Soviet, he declared that he would himself escort the imperial family to Murmansk because it was absolutely necessary to avoid bloodshed for the good name of the revolution. "I will not become the Marat of the Russian revolution," he said. It was, in its time and place, an ill-advised remark, but it went a long way toward describing the kind of revolution which Kerensky hoped to bring about. The country which had produced Pushkin, Dostoyevsky and Chekhov was too civilized, he believed, to afford the luxury of drowning its enemies in blood.

In that mood, working twenty hours a day, speaking everywhere, now addressing the sailors of Kronstadt who had stomped their commanding officer to death and urging them to obey the orders of the new government, now calling upon the soldiers at the front to continue the war with Germany, now interviewing the Tsar and cross-examining the Tsarina, now presenting his astonished colleagues with the secret treaties removed from the secret files of the Foreign Ministry and negotiating with the Swedish banker Ashberg for loans in order to carry on the war and the revolution simultaneously, he became the personification of revolutionary fervor. He looked the part well. With his bristling close-cropped hair, his deathly pallor, for he had still not recovered from his illness, his infected right hand resting in a black sling, the voice as vibrant as ever, he raced across Russia like a whirlwind. If courage and generosity could have saved the revolution, he would have saved it. But from the very beginning it was almost beyond saving.

On the night of March 14 there occurred in one of the rooms of the Tauride Palace, where both the Provisional Government and the Soviet of Workers' and Soldiers' Deputies had taken up residence, an extraordinary event which was to have widespread repercussions. A Menshevik lawyer, Dmitry Sokolov, famous for his successful defense in many prewar political trials, was busy drawing up a seven-point resolution on the rights and duties of the revolutionary soldiers in St. Petersburg. He was surrounded by a throng of soldiers who were arguing enthusiastically about the form and content of the resolution, dictating clauses, editing clauses which had already been dictated, and generally conducting themselves as conquerors laying down the law. All military power was vested in the Soviet of Workers' and Soldiers' Deputies, and within the regiments and companies the soldiers' and sailors' committees had complete control of rifles, machine guns, armored cars and every other form of military equipment, which must not under any condition be allowed to pass under control of the officers. Compulsory saluting was abolished when off duty, and the titles "Your Excellency" and "Your Honor," with which the soldiers customarily addressed their officers, were banned. Officers must no longer be allowed to address the soldiers with the familiar "thou." Clause 6 declared that soldiers must observe strict military discipline when in military formation and when performing military duties, but the remaining clauses only emphasized that the officers were powerless and that military discipline depended on the decision of the soldiers' committees. The soldiers were the masters of St. Petersburg, and the seven resolutions were a lawyer's brief for revolutionary anarchy. When Sokolov had written out the resolutions to the satisfaction of the soldiers, someone suggested that it should be called "Order No. 1."

The order was addressed to the St. Petersburg garrison, and no very great harm would have resulted if it had been restricted to the garrison troops. Unfortunately it was broadcast to the army at the front, and disintegration immediately set in. And since the February Revolution by overthrowing the monarchy and existing government institutions had the effect of weakening all the chains of command, so that the country was no longer being ruled efficiently, the defection of thousands upon thousands of soldiers from the front as a result of "Order No. 1" had equally fateful consequences. This order, so casually composed on the second day of the revolution, was to influence the course of events for many months to come.

A revolution is never predictable, and the course of the Russian Revolution was especially unpredictable. When Lenin arrived at the Finland Station a month later, no one could have predicted that in eight months he would seize power. He was living in Switzerland when the February Revolution broke out, and to reach Russia it was necessary for him to pass through Germany. He had been in touch with German agents, he was financed with German money, and he had no objection to furthering the cause of the German army, which wanted a detente on the eastern front so that they could throw overwhelming forces on the western front. He was not a German agent and his aims were vastly different from those of the German government, for what he wanted was nothing less than a world socialist revolution.

Lenin had been only a few weeks in Russia when evidence of his connections with German agents fell into the hands of the Provisional Government. It was decided to proceed cautiously and not to publish the documents immediately; he was to be permitted enough rope to hang himself. He was watched closely and there was an especially close watch on his communications with Ganetsky, who acted as the intermediary with the German Foreign Office. By the middle of June Lenin was openly advocating a Bolshevik seizure of power, and when at the First All-Russian

Congress of Soviets, the Menshevik minister Tseretelli made a speech saying that there was no political party in Russia prepared to take power, Lenin answered: "There is! No party can refuse this, and our party does not refuse it! We are prepared at any moment to take over the entire power!"

"I have not the least doubt of that," Tseretelli said dryly.

Then Lenin rose and delivered a curiously meandering speech, accusing the Provisional Government of throttling the revolution, of fighting on behalf of the imperialists, of failing to hang the capitalists, of embarking on a program which would end by sending all the revolutionaries to Siberia. Why had not Finland and the Ukraine been given their freedom? Why had not the war been brought to an end? Why were the Russian soldiers not permitted to fraternize with the German soldiers? He was very pale, shaking with emotion, and as he spoke his own intentions became clear, for he came back again and again to the need to hang all the enemies of the revolution. There must be a blood bath at home, and friendship with the Germans. There must be an end to the imperialist blood bath, and the war of classes must begin. Kerensky cut him short.

"You want to take the road of destruction," he said. "Be careful! Out of this chaos, like a phoenix out of the ashes, there will come a dictator—and it will not be me! . . . You are recommending childish prescriptions—arrest, kill, destroy! What are you—socialists or the police of the old regime?"

Lenin appealed to the chairman of the Congress, saying: "You should call him to order!" but Kerensky refused to be silenced. He declared that the war with Germany would continue because this was the will of the Soviet of Workers' and Soldiers' Deputies, and because revolutionaries were entitled to defend their own country, and were in no need of the advice of the Bolsheviks. He swung round and addressed the Bolsheviks directly: "At the front I have always defended your right to express your ideas."

"Thank you," said the Bolsheviks ironically.

"I have no need for your 'thank you,'" Kerensky replied. "I did this to teach you to fight like honest men with the weapons of truth."

It was a significant exchange, for the Bolsheviks had no illusion about the source of their strength—they were a minority which intended to seize power by violent means and to impose a dictatorship on the majority. Nor had Kerensky any illusions about the nature of the Bolshevik threat. As the long summer went on, he pinned his hopes on the gradual restoration of governmental power over the country and especially in the army where, in spite of "Order No. 1" and the soldiers' committees, there was an increasing sense of discipline. The Bolsheviks, although supplied with ample funds from the German government, had little influence at the front.

Kerensky, now Minister of War, decided that the time had come to mount the long-promised offensive to relieve the pressure on the western front. On June 31 the offensive opened along a forty-mile front in Galicia, and for two weeks the Russian army moved steadily forward. Kerensky was at the height of his popularity; it seemed for a moment that an invincible revolutionary army had been created. On July 16 German shock troops struck back, and the Russian army collapsed.

On that day Lenin made his first bid for supreme power by ordering the Kronstadt sailors, heavily infiltrated by the Bolsheviks, to seize St. Petersburg. Kerensky had left for the front in the hope of rallying the fugitive army; the Provisional Government and the Soviet of Workers' and Soldiers' Deputies were paralyzed by the defeat, and there was no authority capable of exercising power in the capital. Lenin, who had been in hiding, emerged to address the sailors from the balcony of the Kshesinskaya Palace, the Bolshevik stronghold, but he was ill, or had lost his nerve, and his words carried no conviction. The sailors could have arrested the Provisional Government and seized all the government buildings; the city was at their mercy. But the attitude of the garrison troops was still uncertain, and he had no guarantee that he could hold the city. The *coup d'état*, lacking direction and purpose, and with almost no popular support, came to nothing. "It was more than a demonstration and less than a revolution," said Lenin, but it was in fact a resounding defeat for the Bolsheviks. Lenin fled into hiding in Finland, not to emerge until shortly before the Bolshevik uprising.

For Kerensky the defeat of the Russian army in the field was of more importance than an *émeute* in St. Petersburg. But while Lenin had temporarily lost his influence on the workers, Kerensky had lost his unrivaled position as a revolutionary leader, for he no longer possessed control over the army, which was in retreat, and his authority in the capital was undermined by the failure of the "Kerensky offensive." A few days before his portrait had been carried through the streets of St. Petersburg by cheering crowds. When he returned, the people were in a sullen mood. Yet he was still the acknowledged leader of the revolution, the only man who could be trusted to save the revolution from defeat. Power was slipping from him; and the vivid days of February were forgotten in the miseries of the long hot summer.

On August 21 the German armies broke through the front at Riga, and St. Petersburg itself was menaced by the enemy. It was a time for drastic action, for one last attempt to regroup the army and infuse it with a desperate determination. Unhappily it was too late. The military were preparing a *coup d'état* of their own under the command of General Kornilov, who saw himself as a military dictator vested with the powers of an absolute monarch. Kornilov had decided to lead the counterrevolution, and he was prepared to make use of every available stratagem. He had the audacity to declare in his manifesto: "The Provisional Government, standing as it does under the pressure of the Bolsheviks in the Soviets, works in full agreement with the German General Staff." When an agent from Kornilov's headquarters confronted Kerensky with an ultimatum, Kerensky called Kornilov on the telephonograph, pretending to be the agent and demanding confirmation of the ultimatum, which was readily given. Kerensky knew then that he had to deal with a large-scale counterrevolution, and called for a *levée en masse*. Workers, soldiers, railroad men and postal officials armed themselves and cut off Kornilov's headquarters from the rest of the country. But Kerensky had given hostages to fortune; the armed workers hid their rifles and came more and more under the influence of the Soviet of Workers' and Soldiers' Deputies. The Provisional Government never recovered its authority. The Soviet, infiltrated by the Bolsheviks, acquired the power which the Provisional Government had lost. Its fighting arm, the Military Revolutionary Committee, organized by a young Social Revolutionary, was soon honeycombed with Bolsheviks. The way was open for a Bolshevik *coup d'état*.

It was intended that the Peter and Paul Fortress, directly facing the Winter Palace where the Provisional Government was sitting, would play an important role in the *coup d'état*. To capture the Fortress and to direct its guns against the Winter Palace was regarded by the Military Revolutionary Committee as one of its prime objectives. The Fortress commanded the Troitsky and Nikolayevsky bridges, the thick walls provided safe cover from rifle fire, and there were reputed to be large stores of ammunition and guns in the Fortress—there were in fact 100,000 rifles in the Kronwerk arsenal. But the soldiers' committees in the Fortress had shown no disposition to obey the orders of the Military Revolutionary Committee. Some were inclined to be loyal to the Provisional Government, others to be neutral. Trotsky, now in effective control of the Military Revolutionary Committee, decided that he owed it to the revolution to win them over to his side. He slipped quietly into the Fortress during the afternoon of November 5 and addressed the soldiers in a fiery speech. It was a daring maneuver, and entirely successful. The soldiers acclaimed him, arrested their commanding officer, promised to obey the orders of the Military Revolutionary Committee, and gave out 10,000 rifles to the Red Guards.

Although Trotsky won over the Fortress almost singlehandedly, and although it was given a place of importance in the elaborate table of operations drawn up by the Military Revolutionary Committee, it played almost no part in the *coup d'état*. It was arranged that a red signal lamp hoisted on the Fortress flagstaff would signal the beginning of the revolt, that the cruiser *Aurora*, moored near the Nikolayevsky Bridge, would then fire blank shells at the Winter Palace while an ultimatum was being delivered to the Provisional Government. If the ultimatum was not accepted within twenty minutes, both the Fortress and the cruiser would open fire with live shells. It was expected that the Provisional Government would vanish in the rubble of the Winter Palace.

The table of operations proved to be unworkable, and nothing happened as the Military Revolutionary Committee had planned. Because the Peter and Paul Fortress had acquired over the centuries those legendary qualities which made it the source of power, and because it occupied a strategic position opposite the Winter Palace, no one doubted that it would be a decisive factor. Blagonravov, the Bolshevik commissar who had been placed in charge of the Fortress, spent the day delivering speeches and inspecting the troops. He believed that the success or failure of the revolt depended on him. At the last moment it was learned that all the three-inch guns in the Fortress were defective, and though they were trained on the Winter Palace, none was fired. Nor was he able to find a red signal lamp.

The morning of November 7 broke gray and cold on the dispirited and war-weary city. One by one the important buildings were occupied by small detachments of troops and Red Guards during the night. The banks were closed, but some shops were open; the newspapers appeared as usual; the trams were running. No one would have guessed that before the day was over a new age would be ushered in.

The Provisional Government had known for some days that a coup was being prepared, but it was now without any effective weapons. Most of the loyal troops were at the front. Those remaining in St. Petersburg could be divided into three groups of roughly equal proportions: those who were loyal to the Provisional Government, those who were neutral, and those who were determined to wrest power from the Provisional Government in the name of the Soviet of Workers' and Soldiers' Deputies. If there was to be a successful coup, it would come about only if the neutral troops could be won over to the revolt. On these for some days the Bolshevik and Socialist Revolutionary agitators had been working, and had proved to be remarkably successful.

At about ten o'clock in the morning Kerensky left the city, hoping to reach the northern front, rally the troops in the field, and lead them back to St. Petersburg. It was a daring move, and under any other conditions might have proved successful. He was to discover that the generals were divided among themselves, incapable of realizing the urgency of the situation, and in no mood to save the city. He needed no more than five thousand troops, for the garrison troops were ill-trained and incapable of putting up an effective resistance against troops seasoned in battle. On that slender balance hung the fate of the city and of Russia.

In later years, when he looked back over the events of that summer and autumn, Kerensky recognized that many mistakes had been made. His gravest mistake was to have joined the Provisional Government; he could have served the revolution more effectively by remaining within the Soviet. He had hoped the Soviet and the Provisional Government could work hand in hand, but from the beginning they were at odds with one another. He realized, too, that more effective measures should have been employed to destroy the power of the Bolsheviks after the July uprising. They formed a small conspiratorial party working largely outside the Soviet; their stronghold was the proletarian quarter of Vyborg on the north bank of the Neva. Only by sending troops into Vyborg and rooting out the Bolshevik agents could he hope to destroy them. There would have been street battles, and many innocent people would have been killed. He was not prepared to launch a civil war on the city. If this was regarded as weakness, he was content to accept the verdict. Of one thing he was certain: he would not be the Marat of the revolution.

When he found that the generals were divided among themselves, incapable of forming a concerted plan to capture the city or even to give him the handful of troops which would have swung the balance in favor of the Provisional Government, he went underground. It would have been better if the Provisional Government had done the same. Instead, they convened in the Winter Palace, now isolated and defended only by a Women's Battalion and a company of Cossacks. There they deliberated all day, making endless telephone calls during the morning but very few during the afternoon, for one by one their telephone lines were cut. To the end, however, they remained in telephone communication with the army through a secret line. By midafternoon they knew that the army would not come to their rescue, that there was no hope, and that in their own good time the conspirators who formed the Military Revolutionary Committee would come and arrest them.

At ten o'clock in the morning, just about the time that Kerensky was leaving for the front, Trotsky announced that the Provisional Government had fallen. It had not fallen; the announcement was an act of bravado, a propaganda ruse designed to put heart in the Military Revolutionary Committee, which was still undecided about the best means to attack the Winter Palace. At four o'clock in the afternoon the first troops from the disaffected regiments began to form outside the Winter Palace, but it was not until late at night that the first infiltrators made their way into the palace. There was no battle, only a few desultory skirmishes with the Cossacks and the Women's Battalion, and perhaps eighteen persons were wounded and killed. The defenders of the palace melted away. At one o'clock in the morning, eight hours after darkness had fallen, the fifteen members of the Provisional Government sitting in a small inner room of the palace were arrested. The man who arrested them was Vladimir Antonov-Ovseyenko, later to be shot by Stalin. He was a small red-haired man wearing pince-nez, and he looked more like a poet than a former officer in the Tsarist army. He announced that all power was now vested in the Military Revolutionary Committee of the Soviet of Workers' and Soldiers' Deputies. In fact all power was now vested in the Bolsheviks, for Trotsky had captured the committee.

Soon the members of the Provisional Government were being led through the dark muddy streets to the Peter and Paul Fortress.

In this way the Bolsheviks came to power, and the events of that disorderly day were to be known in history as the October Revolution. It was not a revolution but a *coup d'état* executed by the desperate conspirators who formed the Military Revolutionary Committee. There was no popular uprising, no siege of the Winter Palace, no revolutionary call to arms. In silence the conspirators had stolen into the Winter Palace and arrested the government, leaving a vacuum which Lenin and the Bolshevik party were only too eager to fill. On that day the long history of Russian revolutions came to an end.

BIBLIOGRAPHY

Baedeker, Karl. *La Russie*. Paris, Paul Ollendorff, 1902.
Bakounine, Michel. *Confession*, translated by Paulette Brupbacher. Paris, *Les Éditions* Rieder, 1932.
———. *Correspondance de*. Paris, Perrin et Cie., 1896.
Belinsky, V. G. *Selected Philosophical Works*. Moscow, Foreign Languages Publishing House, 1956.
Bienstock, J. "Un Précurseur des Bolsheviks: Nétchaiev," *La Mercure de France,* tom. 137, pp. 5-27. Paris, 1920.
Bowman, Herbert E. *Vissarion Belinsky, 1811–1848*. Cambridge, Harvard University Press, 1954.
Breshkovskaia, Katerina. *Hidden Springs of the Russian Revolution*. Stanford, Stanford University Press, 1931.
Bruford, W. H. *Chekhov and His Russia*. New York, Oxford University Press, 1947.
Carr, E. H. *Michael Bakunin*. New York, Vintage Books, 1961.
———. *The Romantic Exiles*. Harmondsworth, Penguin Books, 1949.
Chaliapin, Feodor. *Man and Mask*. New York, Garden City Publishing Co., 1932.
Chernyshevsky, N. G. *Selected Philosophical Essays*. Moscow, Foreign Languages Publishing House, 1953.
———. *What Is To Be Done?*, translated by Benjamin B. Tucker. New York, Vintage Books, 1961.
Coquart, Armand. *Dmitri Pisarev*. Paris, Institut d'Études Slaves, 1946.
Daniels, Guy. *A Lermontov Reader*. New York, The Macmillan Company, 1965.
Dobrolyubov, N. A. *Selected Philosophical Essays*. Moscow, Foreign Languages Publishing House, 1956.
Dostoyevsky, Aimée. *Fyodor Dostoyevsky: A Study*. New Haven, Yale University Press, 1922.
Field, Cecil. *The Great Cossack*. London, Herbert Jenkins, n.d.
Figner, Vera. *Memoirs of a Revolutionist*. New York, International Publishers, 1927.
Footman, David. *Red Prelude*. New Haven, Yale University Press, 1945.

417

Gifford, Henry. *The Hero of His Time*. London, Edward Arnold, 1950.

Guillaume, James. *L'Internationale: Documents et Souvenirs*. Paris, Société Nouvelle, 1905–1910.

Hare, Richard. *Pioneers of Russian Social Thought*. New York, Vintage Books, 1964.

Herzen, Alexander. *From the Other Shore and the Russian People and Socialism*. New York, Meridian Books, 1963.

——. *Selected Philosophical Works*. Moscow, Foreign Languages Publishing House, 1956.

Kaminski, H. E. *Bakounine: La Vie d'un revolutionnaire*. Paris, Éditions Montaigne, 1938.

Kerensky, Alexander. *Russia and History's Turning Point*. New York, Duell, Sloan and Pearce, 1965.

Kropotkin, Peter. *Memoirs of a Revolutionist*. Boston, Houghton Mifflin Co., 1899.

Laferté, Victor. *Alexandre II: Détails inédits sur sa vie intime et sa mort*. Basel, 1882.

Lampert, E. *Sons against Fathers*. Oxford, Clarendon Press, 1965.

——. *Studies in Rebellion*. London, Routledge and Kegan Paul, 1957.

Leffler, Anna Carlotta. *Sonya Kovalevsky*. London, T. Fisher Unwin, 1895.

Malia, Martin. *Alexander Herzen and the Birth of Russian Socialism*. New York, Grosset and Dunlap, 1965.

Marie, Grand Duchess of Russia. *Education of a Princess*. New York, The Viking Press, 1931.

Maximoff, G. P., editor. *The Political Philosophy of Bakunin*. Glencoe, The Free Press, 1953.

Maynard, Sir John, *Russia in Flux*. New York, The Macmillan Company, 1948.

Mazour, Anatole G. *The First Russian Revolution, 1825*. Stanford, Stanford University Press, 1937.

Merezhkovsky, Dmitri S. *December the Fourteenth*, translated by Nathalie A. Duddington. London, Jonathan Cape, 1923.

Mosse, W. E. *Alexander II and the Modernization of Russia*. New York, Collier Books, 1962.

Nikolajewsky, Boris. *Azeff the Spy*. New York, Doubleday, Doran and Co., 1934.

Nomad, Max. *Apostles of Revolution*. Boston, Little, Brown and Co., 1939.

Perris, G. H. *Russia in Revolution*. New York, Brentano, 1905.

Pisarev, Dmitry. *Selected Philosophical, Social and Political Essays*. Moscow, Foreign Languages Publishing House, 1958.

Rambaud, Alfred. *Histoire de la Russie*. Paris, Librairie Hatchette et Cie., 1918.

Sack, A. J. *The Birth of Russian Democracy*. New York, Russian Information Bureau, 1918.

Savinkov, Boris. *Memoirs of a Terrorist*. New York, Albert and Charles Boni, 1931.

Serebrennikov, Semeon. *L'Arrestation de S. Sérébrénikoff par la Police de Genève*. Geneva, 1870.

Shub, David. *Lenin: A Biography*. Garden City, New York, Doubleday and Co., 1948.

Simmons, Ernest J. *Dostoevski: The Making of a Novelist*. New York, Oxford University Press, 1940.

——. *Leo Tolstoy*. New York, Vintage Books, 1960.

Slonim, Marc. "Le Précurseur de Lenine," *Revue Universelle*, tom. 62 (1935), pp. 684–705.

Steinberg, I. *Spiridonova: Revolutionary Terrorist*. London, Methuen and Co., 1935.

Steklow, Georg. *Michael Bakunin*. Stuttgart, J. H. W. Dietz, 1913.

Stepniak (Kravchinski). *Nihilism as It Is*. London, T. Fisher Unwin, n.d.

——. *Underground Russia: Revolutionary Profiles and Sketches*. New York, 1883.

Venturi, Franco. *Il populismo russo*, 2 vols. Turin, G. Enaudi, 1952.
Wallace, Sir Donald Mackenzie. *Russia*. New York, Henry Holt and Co., 1905.
Wilson, Edmund. *To the Finland Station*. New York, Doubleday and Co., 1940.
Yarmolinsky, Avrahm. *Road to Revolution*. London, Cassell and Co., 1957.
Yaroslavsky, E. *History of Anarchism in Russia*. London, Lawrence and Wishart, n.d.
Zetlin, Mikhail. *The Decembrists*. New York, International Universities Press, 1958.

WORKS IN RUSSIAN

Arbore-Ralli, Zemphyr. "Sergey Gennadievich Nechayev (iz Moikh Vospominanii)."
In *Byloe*, No. 7 (1906).
Belchikov, Nikolay. *Dostoyevsky i Protsesse Petrashevtsev*. Moscow, Izdatelstvo Akademii Nauk, 1936.
Breitfus, Andrei. "Iz Vospominanii o Kazni 3-go Aprela 1881 goda." In *Byloe*, No. 25 (1924).
Chernov, Viktor. *Pered Burei*. New York, Chekhov Publishing House, 1953.
Dostoyevsky, F. M. *Pisma*. Moscow, Gosudarstvennoe Izdatelstvo, 1959.
Elizarova, Anna. *Zhizn Alexandra Ilyicha i ego Uchastie v Dele 1 Marta 1887 g.* Moscow, Gosudarstvennoe Izdatelstvo, 1927.
Gambarov, A. *V Sporakh o Nechayeve*. Moscow, Moskovskii Rabochii, 1926.
Gernet, M. N. *Istoriya Tsarskoi Tiurmi*. Moscow, Gosudarstvennoe Izdatelstvo, 1961–62.
Gotz, Mikhail. "I. V. Kaliayev (iz Vospominanii)." In *Byloe*, No. 7 (1908).
Grabar, Igor. *Istoriya Russkovo Iskusstva*. Moscow, I. Knebel, 1909–1918.
Klevensky, M. M. *Ishutinskii Kruzhok i Pokushenie Karakozov*. Moscow, Izdatelstvo Vsesoyuznovo Obshchestva, 1931.
Korolenko, Vladimir. *Istoriya Moevo Sovremennika*. Moscow, Izdatelstvo Vozrozhdeniye, 1922.
Kozmin, B. P. *Nechayev i Nechayevtsi: Sbornik Materialov*. Moscow, Gosudarstvennoe Sotsialno-ekonomicheskoe Izdatelstvo, 1931.
———. *P. G. Zaichnevsky i "Molodaya Rossiya."* Moscow, Izdatelstvo Vsesoyuznovo Obshchestva, 1931.
——— and Rakitnikov, N. I., editors. *Pisma Yegora Sazonova k Rodnym 1895–1910 g. g.* Moscow, Istoriko-Revolutsionnaya Bibliotek, 1925.
Krasnov, G. V., editor. *N. A. Dobrolyubov: Stati i Materiali*. Gorky, Gorkovskii Gosudarstvennyi Universitet, 1965.
Literatura Sotsialno-Revolutsionnoi Partii "Narodnoi Voli." No publisher, 1905.
Nechkina, M. V. *Vosstanie 14 Dekabrya 1825 g*. Moscow, Izdatelstvo Akademii Nauk, 1951.
Pisnaya, V. N. "Studencheskii Godi Zhelyabova." In *Byloe*, No. 32 (1925).
Pospelov, P. N., editor. *Vladimir Ilyich Lenin: Biographiya*. Moscow, Institut Marksizma-Lenina, 1960.
Prokofiev, V. A. *Petrashevsky*. Moscow, Molodaya Gvardiya, 1962.
Ropshin, V. (Savinkov). *Kon Bledniy*. Nice, M. A. Tumanov, 1913.
Savinkov, Boris. "Iz Vospominanii ob Ivane Kaliayeve." In *Byloe*, No. 7 (1908).
Segal, Elena. *Sophia Perovskaya*. Moscow, Molodaya Gvardiya, 1962.
Semenyuta, P. "Iz Vospominanii ob A. I. Zhelyabove." In *Byloe*, No. 8 (1906).
Shchegolev, P. E. *Alexeyevsky Ravelin*. Moscow, Izdatelstvo Federatsia, 1929.
Shchegolev, P. E. "S. G. Nechayev v Alexeyevskom Raveline (1873–1883)." In *Krasnii Arkhiv*, 1923–1926.
Smirnov, V. *Z. N. G. Chernyshevsky: Izbranniye Pedagogicheskie Proizvedeniya*. Moscow, Izdatelstvo APN, 1953.

CHAPTER NOTES

THE PETER AND PAUL FORTRESS

The chief source for any study of the Peter and Paul Fortress is the five-volume *Istoriya Tsarskoi Tiurmi* (History of Tsarist Prisons) by Mikhail Gernet. Well illustrated and well documented, written without any specific bias, these volumes describe the history in detail of all the Tsarist prisons, but inevitably the Peter and Paul Fortress is given pride of place. Gernet's father was imprisoned in the Fortress at the time of the Karakozov affair, and the five volumes take the form of a monumental salute to his father's memory.

Gernet tends to see the prison as a whole, as a living organism, with its own strange and stupefying mode of existence, so that he sometimes gives the impression of a clinician examining the tissues with exquisite detachment. But very often he will drop the clinical mask and tell stories about the prisoners like a novelist. He had unrestricted use of the documents of the Tsarist secret police when the files were opened after the 1917 revolution, and he made such good use of them that it is unlikely that anyone will ever have the desire or the patience to go over the same ground. Gernet died at the age of seventy-nine in 1953, having published more than 350 books and articles, mostly on penology. He worked on his history for nearly fifty years.

The chief source for the architectural history of the Fortress is to be found in the fifth volume of *Istoriya Russkovo Iskusstva* (History of Russian Art) by Igor Grabar, which contains extensive plans and photographs. There is an admirable plan of the Cathedral in Baedeker's *Russia*.

THE DECEMBRISTS

A vast and increasing library of books on the Decembrists has appeared in the Soviet Union, especially since the death of Stalin, but so far as I know only two scholarly accounts of the unsuccessful uprising have appeared in English. They are Anatole Mazour's curiously mistitled *The First Russian Revolution, 1825,* published in 1937, and Mikhail Zetlin's *The Decembrists* which appeared in 1958. While Mazour is inclined to view the revolt from a fastidious distance, Zetlin, who is equally scholarly, comes to grips with the characters of the protagonists and succeeds in conveying the excitement of the times. I am heavily indebted to this wonderful and little-known book written by a scholar who died before he could see it through the press.

Dmitry Merezhkovsky's novel *December the Fourteenth* resembles all his historical novels. There are dazzling insights, long passages of superb description, and many scenes depicted with subtle accuracy; then, unaccountably, the machinery breaks down, the characters change character, the scenery is suddenly out of focus. There is no explanation for the failures, just as there is no explanation for his triumphs. Yet this novel is still perhaps the best introduction to the Decembrists for the English-speaking reader.

Of the Russian works consulted I found M. V. Nechkina's *Vosstanie 14 Dekabrya 1825 g* (Uprising 14 December 1825) the most useful, even though it is written from the conventional Communist standpoint. I have also consulted the superbly produced volumes of *Literaturnoye Nasledstvo* (Literary Legacy), dealing with the Decembrists as writers. Since most of them were writers who wrote voluminously, and since the editors have taken pleasure in reproducing their writings at great length, with portraits in color and innumerable facsimiles, it is possible to meet the revolutionaries on their own terms. These volumes are to be counted among the most magnificent works of scholarship produced in the Soviet Union.

P. 46   (In the name of the Father . . .)
           Anatole G. Mazour, *The First Russian Revolution, 1825*, p. 187.
P. 63   (The executions . . .)
           Byloe, No. 3 (1906), p. 226.
P. 64   (I am writing . . .)
           M. N. Gernet, *Istoriya Tsarskoi Tiurmi*, Vol. II, p. 157.
P. 68-69   The text of the two quotations from Pushkin is given in A. S. Pushkin, *Sobranie Sochinenii* (Moscow, 1960), Vol. II, pp. 149, 549.
P. 70   Guy Daniels, *A Lermontov Reader*, p. 73.

PETRASHEVSKY

The most useful introduction to Petrashevsky is given by V. A. Prokofiev, *Petrashevsky*, which appeared in Moscow in 1962. This book, one of a series of "Remarkable Lives" originally edited by Gorky, sometimes reads like a novel with extensive conversations quoted verbatim, but all, or nearly all these conversations can be found in the memoirs of the conspirators or of their friends. Prokofiev, who also produced a biography of Zhelyabov, always writes authoritatively with a feeling for atmosphere and for people. The book has a large number of photographs and some admirable maps.

Dostoyevsky's involvement in the conspiracy has been well documented in his own writings. N. F. Belchikov's researches led to the discovery of the entire dossier relating to Dostoyevsky, which he published in his book *Dostoyevsky i Protsesse Petrashevtsev* (Dostoyevsky and the Trial of the Petrashevtsi). No really satisfactory account of the conspiracy has yet appeared, and there are still a number of unsolved problems. It appears that there was more than one informer, and that Chernosvitov was an *agent provocateur* deliberately inciting them to revolt.

P. 73   (Do not look for solutions . . .)
           Alexander Herzen, *From the Other Shore and the Russian People and Socialism*, p. 3.
P. 78   (He did not talk very much . . .)
           Dostoyevsky, *The Devils*, Part 1, Chapter 2.
P. 83   (Restore the image of man . . .)
           Leonid Grossman, *Put Dostoyevskovo* (Moscow: N. A. Stollar, 1928), p. 76.
P. 84–86   (You have failed to understand . . .)
           V. G. Belinsky, *Selected Philosophical Works*, pp. 537–43.
P. 87   (BY HIGHEST ORDER . . .)
           M. N. Gernet, *Istoriya Tsarskoi Tiurmi*, Vol. II, p. 215.

P. 87–88   (I was still sleeping . . .)
            Dostoyevsky, *Pisma*, Vol. IV, p. 337.
P. 90   (When I saw my new dwelling . . .)
            M. N. Gernet, *Istoriya Tsarskoi Tiurmi*, Vol. II, p. 218.
P. 95   (The most terrible part . . .)
            Dostoyevsky, *The Idiot*, Vol. I, p. 5.
P. 95–96   (I remember how the officer . . .)
            Anna Carlotta Leffler, *Sonya Kovalevsky*, pp. 337–38.
P. 96–97   (I had, as I supposed . . .)
            Ibid, pp. 338–39.
P. 100 (The case of Petrashevsky . . .)
            Alexander Herzen, *From the Other Shore* . . . pp. 206–7.

BAKUNIN

The anarchic character of Bakunin is reflected in the anarchic character of his literary remains. No complete or even partially complete edition of his works has been published, and there are reasons for believing that none will be published in the foreseeable future. Meanwhile the useful six-volume edition of his works published by Stock in Paris around 1910 is already disintegrating, the paper crumbling in the hands as you turn the pages.

The best available life is *Michael Bakunin*, by E. H. Carr, who had very little interest in Bakunin's ideas, and therefore found himself compelled to present him as though he were a vacuum wandering in search of air. It is wonderfully readable, but the essential Bakunin rarely appears and his voluminous writings are rarely mentioned. A lengthy chapter in E. Lampert's *Studies in Rebellion* deals adequately with Bakunin's ideas, while G. P. Maximoff's *The Political Philosophy of Bakunin* suggests the immense range of his thoughts.

I have used the French translation of his *Confession,* which has an admirable introduction by Fritz Brupbacher and some authoritative notes by Max Nettlau.

P. 105   (All peoples and all men . . .)
            E. H. Carr, *Michael Bakunin*, pp. 115–16.
P. 116   (I hoped to bring about . . .)
            Michel Bakounine, *Confession*, pp. 207–10.
P. 117–118 (I was perfectly prepared. . . .)
            Ibid., p. 176.
P. 119   (The great men of science . . .) "Lettre à ses parents: Michel Bakounine," *La Critique Sociale*, December 1931, p. 161.
P. 120   (This awful solitude . . .)
            Michel Bakounine, *Confession*, pp. 288–89

CHERNYSHEVSKY

A vast literature has arisen around Chernyshevsky in the Soviet Union, perhaps because he received the approval of both Marx and Lenin. Marx spoke of him as "a great Russian critic and scholar who deserves our high respect," while Lenin, who tended to describe even those people he most admired in blunt and straightforward terms, grows almost lyrical when he describes Chernyshevsky. Yet his writings, except for his letters and one great novel, are very difficult to read. He rambles, rarely keeps to the point, and in the nineteenth-century manner speaks authoritatively on many matters of which he was ignorant.

The present account is based on V. Z. Smirnov's lengthy biographical preface to *Izbranniye Pedagogicheskie Proizvedeniya* (Selected Pedagogical Works) and M. Grigorian's introductory essay in *Selected Philosophical Essays,* published in English in Moscow in 1953. I am also indebted to the long chapter on Chernyshevsky in Richard Hare's *Pioneers of Russian Social Thought.*

P. 129   (People like Rakhmetov . . .)
             N. G. Chernyshevsky, *What Is To Be Done?* p. 224.
P. 131   (You are few in numbers . . .)
             Ibid., p. 241.

ZAICHNEVSKY

The best introduction to Zaichnevsky is given by B. Kozmin in his book *P. G. Zaichnevsky i "Molodaya Rossiya,"* which also contains in a fourteen-page appendix the full text of *Molodaya Rossiya.* A brief account of the conspiracy is given by the same author in *Katorga i Ssylka* in 1930, and there is an illuminating discussion by Franco Venturi in *Il populismo russo.* By the nature of things Zaichnevsky must always remain a rather shadowy figure, and it is exceedingly hard to measure his influence. Yet there is no doubt that he influenced Nechayev and therefore belongs to the mainstream of the Russian revolution; what is in doubt is whether he knew what he was doing.

P. 137   (We are firmly convinced . . .)
             B. Kozmin, "Kruzhok Zaichnevskovo i Argyropulo," *Katorga i Ssylka,*
             1930, p. 7.
P. 137–38   (Soon, very soon . . .)
             Ibid., pp. 8–9.
P. 142   (Look around, Russian people . . .)
             Pisarev, *Sochineniya,* Vol. III, pp. 125–26.
P. 143   (If authority lies . . .)
             Ibid., Vol. I, p. 135.

KARAKOZOV

Shchegolov devotes a whole chapter to Karakozov's imprisonment in the Fortress in his *Alexeyevsky Ravelin,* and Gernet provides many details which Shchegolov omits. The main source for the Ishutin affair is to be found in M. M. Klevensky, *Ishutinskii kruzhok i pokushenie Karakozov.* Venturi has an excellent account in *Il populismo russo.* Karakozov was the unintellectual revolutionary, the revolutionary who acted out of passion and sympathy for the people, and he has not yet received the place in history which he deserves. As far as I know, there is no book devoted to him.

P. 149–150 (From the enclosed report . . .)
             M. N. Gernet, *Istoriya Tsarskoi Tiurmi,* Vol. II, pp. 363–64.
P. 153   (Brothers, I have long been tormented . . .)
             Franco Venturi, *Il populismo russo,* Vol. I, p. 564.
P. 156   (My first impression . . .)
             Peter Kropotkin, *Memoirs of a Revolutionist,* p. 169.
P. 158   (Under the normal order of things . . .)
             Tkachev, *Sochineniya,* Vol. I, p. 410.

NECHAYEV

There exists no definitive study of Nechayev in Russian or English, and no collection of his writings has ever been assembled, although such a collection was once ordered by Lenin. P. E. Shchegolev's account of his last days in the Fortress is reasonably complete, and his book *Alexeyevsky Ravelin,* which also includes accounts of Prince Trubetskoy, Chernyshevsky, and Karakozov, is one of the very few satisfactory works dealing with the Fortress. There are abundant monographs on various aspects of Nechayev's career in *Katorga i Ssylka, Byloe, Krasny Arkhiv* and *Borba Klassov.*

In *Borba Klassov*, Nos. 1–2, 1924, there can be found the text of *The Revolutionary Catechism* and an explanation of the rather simple code in which it originally appeared when found by the Tsarist police.

I am especially indebted to P. Shchegolev's account of the little-known Tula episode, which provides the clue to much that happened later. This appeared in *Krasny Arkhiv* at intervals between 1923 and 1926. The article which appeared in *Byloe* in 1906 on Nechayev's imprisonment in the Alexis Ravelin is the chief source for the rather lengthy account in this book. For Nechayev's childhood there is N. C. Belchikov's brief monograph *S. G. Nechayev v Sele Ivanove v 60–e gody*, which appeared in *Katorga i Ssylka* in 1925, and for an authoritative study of *The Revolutionary Catechism* there is A. A. Shilov, "Katechesis Revolutsionera k Istorii Nechayevskovo Dela," which appeared in *Borba Klassov* in 1924. I have based the present translation of *The Revolutionary Catechism* on the version printed in *Pravitelstvenniye Vestnik* at the time of the trial. Other issues of the newspaper, which is available at the Library of Congress, give verbatim accounts of the trial of the Nechayevtsi, from which it is possible to reconstruct the murder of Ivanov. The depositions of the prisoners at the trial of the Nechayevtsi are given in B. P. Kozmin, *Nechayev i Nechayevtsi*. I have delved into the memoirs of Arbore-Ralli and M. P. Sazhin (Armand Ross) for details of Nechayev's activities in Switzerland, and I owe a special debt to Bakunin's correspondence with Ogaryev. For the rest it is only necessary to add that Nechayev dominated the thoughts of most of the terrorists who lived at the end of the last century, and nearly all of them have recorded minor details of his exploits.

P. 172   (Brigandage has always been . . .)
         James Guillaume, *L'Internationale: documents et souvenirs*, Vol. I, p. 63.

P. 173–76   (THE REVOLUTIONARY CATECHISM)
         Pravitelstvenniye Vestnik, July 11, 1871 (from microfilm supplied by Library of Congress).

P. 177   (It is a sort of instruction . . .)
         Nikolay Berdyaev, *The Origin of Russian Communism* (London: Geoffrey Bles, 1937), p. 63.

P. 178   (He taught many kinds . . .)
         Sallust, *Conspiracy of Catiline*, II.

P. 185–86   (Gentlemen, we can now . . .)
         Dostoyevsky, *The Possessed*, III, 6.

P. 189   (I am late in replying . . .)
         Correspondance de Michel Bakounine, pp. 301–2.

P. 195   (I now feel it is my duty . . .)
         Ibid., pp. 318–19.

P. 196–99   (MY DEAR FRIEND . . .)
         Ibid., pp. 324–30.

P. 204–05   (Culture is unnecessary . . .)
         Dostoyevsky, *The Possessed*, II, 8.

P. 208   (Some secret voice tells me . . .)
         Correspondance de Michel Bakounine, p. 365.

P. 213–14   (COUNT! When I was sitting . . .)
         P. E. Shchegolev, *Alexeyevsky Ravelin*, pp. 196–97.

P. 216   (The prisoner in cell . . .) *Ibid.*, p. 218.
P. 217   (The prisoner in cell . . .) *Ibid.*, p. 219.
P. 229   (To His IMPERIAL . . .) *Ibid.*, p. 249.
P. 234–37   (SOVEREIGN! The new . . .) *Byloe* (7) 1906, p. 165.
P. 242–43   (Brothers and sisters . . .) *Literatura Narodnoi Voli*, p. 924.

ZHELYABOV

The classic account of Zhelyabov's career is given in A. K. Voronsky's *Zhelyabov* (Moscow, 1925). Voronsky writes exceedingly well, and paints in the background with a consummate sense of artistry. A more extensive account of Zhelyabov's childhood and the early influences which went to form his character is given in V. N. Pisnaya's article in *Byloe*, 1925, entitled "Studencheskie Godi Zhelyabova." David Footman's *Red Prelude* (Yale University Press, 1945), while largely based on Voronsky, contains considerable additional material and an excellent bibliography. *Byloe* and *Katorga i Ssylka*, the two magazines devoted to the revolutionary past, have a good number of articles which throw sidelights on the important and peripheral figures in the conspiracy. There are many detailed accounts of the assassination of Alexander II, and though they differ in minor details they are in general agreement about the course of events. There is an especially well-written four-column article on the accomplishments of the terrorists in *The New York Times*, March 15, 1881, immediately after the assassination.

Two recent Russian books in the "Remarkable Lives" series should be noted. They are V. A. Prokofiev, *Andrey Zhelyabov* (1960), and Elena Segal, *Sophia Perovskaya* (1962). They are both useful and solid works, well documented and well illustrated.

P. 264–65   (On November 19 . . .)
              Literatura Narodnoi Voli, p. 167.
P. 279–80   (Today, March 1 . . .)
              Ibid., p. 899.
P. 283–86   (A LETTER FROM THE EXECUTIVE COMMITTEE . . .)
              Ibid., pp. 903–6.
P. 288   (There appeared about twenty years ago . . .)
              Ernest J. Simmons, *Leo Tolstoy*, pp. 10–12.

ULYANOV

The chief source for a study of Alexander Ulyanov is *Zhizn Alexandra Ilyicha Ulyanova i Ego Uchastie v Dele 1 Marta 1887 goda* (The Life of Alexander Ilich Ulyanov and His Part in the Affair of March 1, 1887), edited by his sister Anna Elizarova, where all the documents connected with the trial are published *in extenso*. The book is inevitably a partisan account, and Elizarova's comments are not always helpful. There is no effort to explain the psychological background, and the transition of Alexander from a dedicated student to a dedicated revolutionary is never made clear.

Govorukhin's accurate and exceedingly spirited reminiscences appeared in *Proletarskaya Literatura No. 42*, and do much to redress the balance. They were written while the memory of Alexander Ulyanov was still fresh, in the winter of 1887, and were then given to Vera Zasulich, who in turn gave them to Anna Elizarova ten years later. Her comments, added in footnotes, suggest that there were some differences of opinion between them, but Govorukhin is always convincing while Anna Elizarova on her own admission is given to special pleading. Nevertheless the two accounts admirably supplement each other.

Lenin himself rarely wrote about his brother, but there are affectionate glimpses of Alexander in the memoirs of his two sisters and his brother Dmitry. Very little has been published about Alexander in the Soviet Union, perhaps because it was felt that his amateurishness reflected little credit on his family. Also, the brothers did not really like each other.

P. 305   (To be useful in society . . .)
              P. N. Pospelov, *Vladimir Ilyich Lenin*, pp. 6–7.

P. 314–15　　(The facts have been fully . . .)
　　　　　　　A. I. Elizarova, *Zhizn Alexandra Ilyicha* . . . , pp. 338–40.
P. 315　　　 (I wanted to show . . .)
　　　　　　　Ibid., p. 343.

SAZONOV

The source of most of our present knowledge of Sazonov is contained in an extensive collection of letters edited by B. P. Kozmin and N. I. Rakitnikov under the title *Pisma Yegora Sazonova k Rodnym 1895–1910*. The account of his years in Siberia is derived from two articles which appeared in *Katorga i Ssylka* in 1921 and 1922 by V. Pirogov. I have also used the brief sketch which appears in *Vestnik Russkoi Revolutsii* (Geneva, 1905). A brief and informative account of Sazonov, dealing particularly with his last years, is to be found in I. Steinberg, *Spiridonova: Revolutionary Terrorist*. Like Nechayev and Zhelyabov, Sazonov became a legend in his own lifetime, and many brief and illuminating references to him can be found in the revolutionary memoirs of the period.

KALIAYEV

I have relied largely on Savinkov's memoirs and the memorial volume *Ivan Platonovich Kaliayev* published by the Social Revolutionaries in Switzerland in 1905. It is a small, closely printed book, little more than an extended pamphlet, but it contains most of Kaliayev's verses and nearly all of his surviving letters together with an account of his execution, a summary of his life and some excellent photographs. I have also used the article on him which appeared in *Byloe* in 1908, and I have sometimes consulted Savinkov's short novels which describe, sometimes incisively, but nearly always with a curious diffuseness, the workings of the terrorists' minds. I am also indebted to Boris Nikolajewsky's study of Azev, which illuminates many dark corners.

P. 364　　　 (*So now my soul* . . .)
　　　　　　　Ivan Platonovich Kaliayev, p. 41.
P. 385　　　 (*O joy and terror* . . .) *Ibid.*, p. 14.
P. 385–86　　(MY DEAR FRIENDS . . .) *Ibid.*, pp. 41–42.
P. 386–87　　(GRAND DUCHESS . . .) *Ibid.*, pp. 9–11.
P. 389–90　　(You dare to sit . . .) *Ibid.*, p. 30–31.
P. 392–93　　(*Like a proud lion* . . .) *Ibid.*, p. 41.
P. 394　　　 (DEAR, BELOVED MOTHER . . .) *Ibid.*, p. 45.

KERENSKY

Although fifty years have passed since the October Revolution, the exact sequence of events is still a matter of debate. Kerensky's own account in *Russia and History's Turning Point*, published in 1965, has been severely edited by his publisher with the result that there are far too many gaps in the narrative and it is not always possible to account for his actions at any given time. In discussing the February Revolution he insists that it is still necessary to draw a veil of secrecy over the conspirators. Since the Communists have drawn a similar veil of secrecy over many of the events of October, it is unlikely that we shall ever know the full story.

In this chapter I have drawn on conversations with Kerensky, and attempted to weigh the accounts of Whites and Reds. Blagonravov's account of the last days of the Peter and Paul Fortress is given in *Petrograd, October 1917*, a useful collection of reminiscences published in Moscow in 1957. It is obviously tendentious, and he continually seeks to present himself in a favorable light, while admitting that the Fortress which he commanded took almost no part in the uprising.

CHRONOLOGICAL TABLE

(All dates are given in the Old Style, which in the nineteenth century was thirteen days earlier than the Western calendar.)

May 27, 1703	Peter the Great lays the foundation of the Fortress and the city of St. Petersburg
June 26, 1718	Murder of the Tsarevich Alexis Petrovich
December 4, 1775	Death of Princess Tarakanova in the Peter and Paul Fortress
May 18, 1814	Birth of Bakunin
December 14, 1825	Decembrist uprising
July 13, 1826	Execution of Decembrists in the Peter and Paul Fortress
April 22, 1849	Arrest of Petrashevsky and other members of his circle
December 22, 1849	"Execution" and public degradation of Petrashevsky, Dostoyevsky and others on Semyonovsky Square.
May 17, 1851	Bakunin handed over to the Tsarist police
1853–1855	Crimean War
February 19, 1861	Proclamation by Alexander II, giving freedom to the serfs.
Summer 1862	Mysterious fires throughout Russia; appearance in St. Petersburg of *Molodaya Rossiya*.
July 7, 1862	Chernyshevsky arrested
July 15, 1862	Pisarev arrested
December 18, 1862	Pericles Argyropulo dies in prison
1863	Revolt in Poland
May 31, 1864	Chernyshevsky's public degradation in Mytny Square
April 4, 1866	Karakozov attempts to kill the Tsar
September 3, 1866	Karakozov hanged
November 21, 1869	Ivanov killed by Nechayev
July 1871	Trial of the Nechayevtsi
August 14, 1872	Nechayev arrested in Switzerland and given over to the Tsarist police

January 8, 1873	Nechayev sentenced to twenty years' hard labor in Siberia, and secretly ordered to serve his punishment in the Peter and Paul Fortress
July 1, 1876	Death of Bakunin in Switzerland
December 6, 1876	Student manifestations outside Kazan Cathedral
June 24, 1877	Birth of Ivan Kaliayev
September 1877	Trial of the 193
January 24, 1878	Vera Zasulich wounds General Trepov
March 13, 1879	Mirsky unsuccessfully attacks General Drenteln
March 31, 1878	Vera Zasulich freed by the court
August 26, 1879	Executive Committee of Narodnaya Volya condemns Alexander II to death
November 18, 1879	Unsuccessful attempt on the Tsar by Zhelyabov at Alexandrovsk
February 5, 1880	Stepan Khalturin blows up part of the Winter Palace.
February 1880	"Dictatorship" of Loris-Melikov
March 1, 1881	Assassination of Alexander II
March 1882	Khalturin kills General Strelnikov in Odessa
November 21, 1882	Death of Nechayev in the Peter and Paul Fortress
March 1, 1887	Arrest of Alexander Ulyanov
May 8, 1887	Alexander Ulyanov hanged in the courtyard of the Schlüsselburg Fortress
July 15, 1904	Yegor Sazonov assassinates Plehve
November 28, 1910	Death of Sazonov
January 1, 1905	Port Arthur falls
January 9, 1905	Father Gapon leads a deputation of workers to the Winter Palace. The workers are fired on by Cossacks
February 4, 1905	Ivan Kaliayev throws bomb and kills the Grand Duke Sergey in Moscow
May 10, 1905	Kaliayev hanged in the Schlüsselburg Fortress
December 29, 1916	Rasputin killed by Prince Yusupov and the Grand Duke Dmitry
February 26, 1917	February Revolution begins
March 2, 1917	Abdication of Nicholas II
October 26, 1917	Bolsheviks take power

INDEX

Act of Emancipation: public reading of, 163; disappointment over, 125

Act of Renunciation, 40

Adlerberg, General, in investigation of Decembrists, 49

Aesthetic Relation of Art to Reality (Chernyshevsky), 124-25

Affair of the Conspirators Sergey Nechayev, Nikolay Nicholayev, Ivan Prizhov, and Others (trial record), 181

Agent provocateur: Chernosvitov suspected as, 97; Kostamarov as, 140; Azev as, 325, 380

Akhsharumov, Dmitry: vision of the future, 71, 82-83; arrest of, 87; imprisoned in Trubetskoy Bastion, 90; effects of imprisonment on, 91; sentenced to life imprisonment, 97

Akhtirka Regiment, 45

Akimov (revolutionist), 357

Alexander I: attitude toward Pushkin's "Freedom," 65; brutality of, 39-40

Alexander II: accession to throne, 120; reliance on secret police, 120; early reactionary policies of, 134-35; reforms of, 125, 163, 246; popularity of, 147, 154; Bakunin's letter to, 120; Karakazov's attempt to assassinate, 147-48; Solovyev's attempt to assassinate, 258; pursuit of Nechayev, 203-4; reports on Nechayev sent to, 210-11; letters from Nechayev, 219-20, 229, 234-37; Trial of 193 and, 223; adoption of "dictatorship of the heart" policy, 229; revival of reactionary policies, 234; sentenced to death by Narodnaya Volya, 261; Narodnik attempts to assassinate, 227-28, 261-80; assassination of, 233, 245, 272-79, 300; tomb of, 19

Alexander III: at deathbed of Alexander II, 278-79; cowardice of, 289; reactionary policies of, 300; manifesto of Narodnaya Volya to, 283-86; Tolstoy's plea for Narodniks to, 287-88;

Ulyanov's efforts to assassinate, 309-10

Alexander Menshikov Bastion, naming of, 16

Alexandra, Grand Duchess, 371

Alexandrisky Regiment, 45

Alexandrovskaya, Varvara: in Nechayev's central organization, 180; arrest of, 188

Alexis, Tsarevich, 245; tortured and killed by Peter the Great, 15; buried in Peter and Paul Fortress, 16

Alexis Ravelin: function of, 15; cells and layout of, 21-22; conditions described, 225, 235; madness produced in, 91, 225; Pososhkov imprisoned in, 18; Trubetskoy imprisoned in, 44; Petrashevsky imprisoned in, 89; Dostoyevsky imprisoned in, 89-90; Bakunin imprisoned in, 114-19; Chernyshevsky imprisoned in, 125-26; Nechayev imprisoned in, 215-22, 226-27, 229-41; overcrowding of, 225-26; *see also* Peter and Paul Fortress

Alexopol Regiment, 45

Algashi prison: Borodulin's administration of, 346-49; Sazonov imprisoned in, 347-51; Ismailov's administration of, 350-51

Amethystov, Evlampy, 164

Amethystov, Ivan, 164

Amur Company in Irkutsk, Bakunin's employment with, 121

Ananin (revolutionist), 316

Anarchism, 107, 206; Proudhon's concept of, 107; Bakunin's concept of, 108

Andreyushkin, Pakhomy, 308; effort to assassinate Alexander III, 310; arrest of, 311; trial of, 316; execution of, 316

Ankern, Lilien, 44

Anne, Empress, cruelty of, 16-17

Annenkov, General, 134

Antisemitism, *see* Jews

429